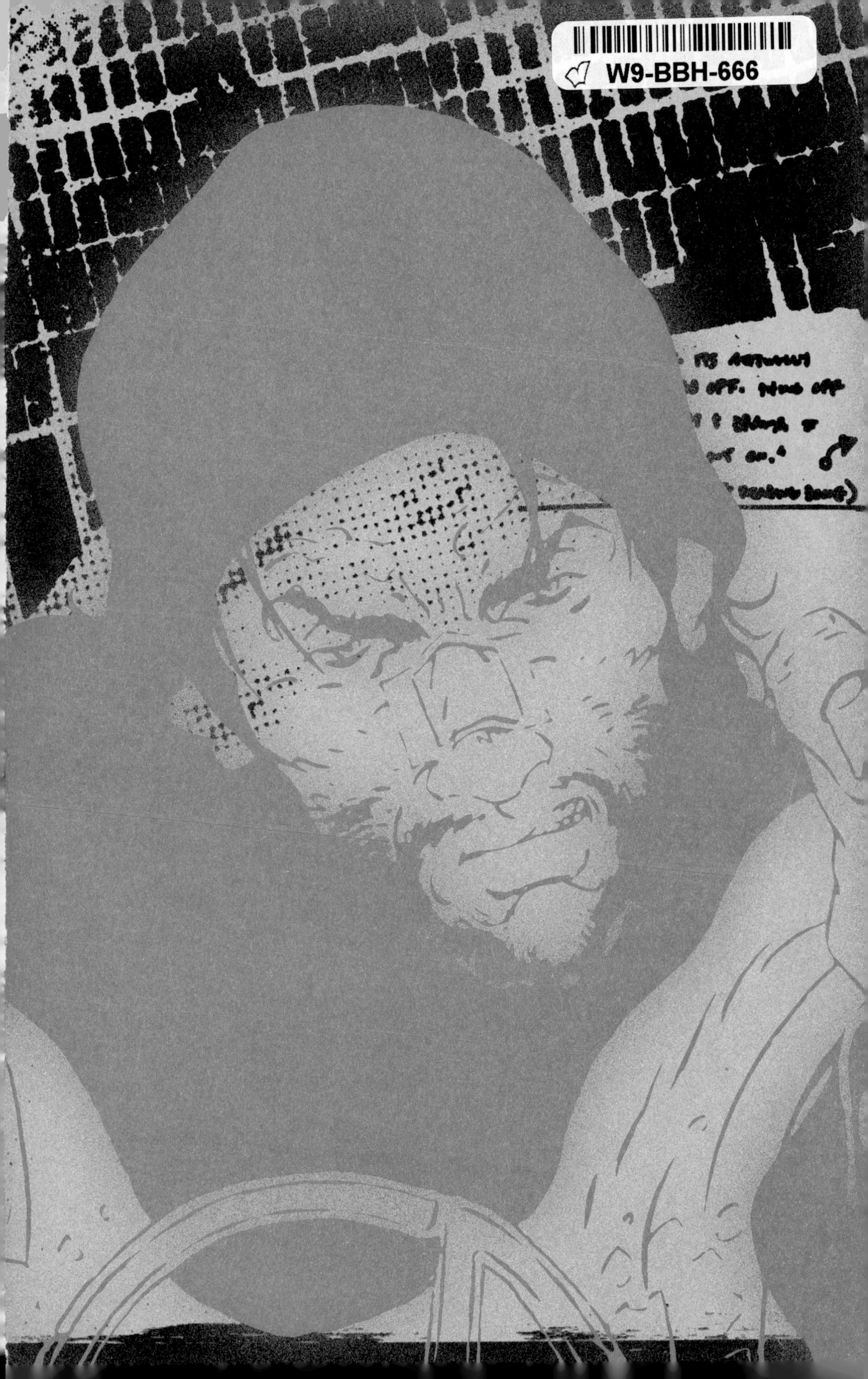

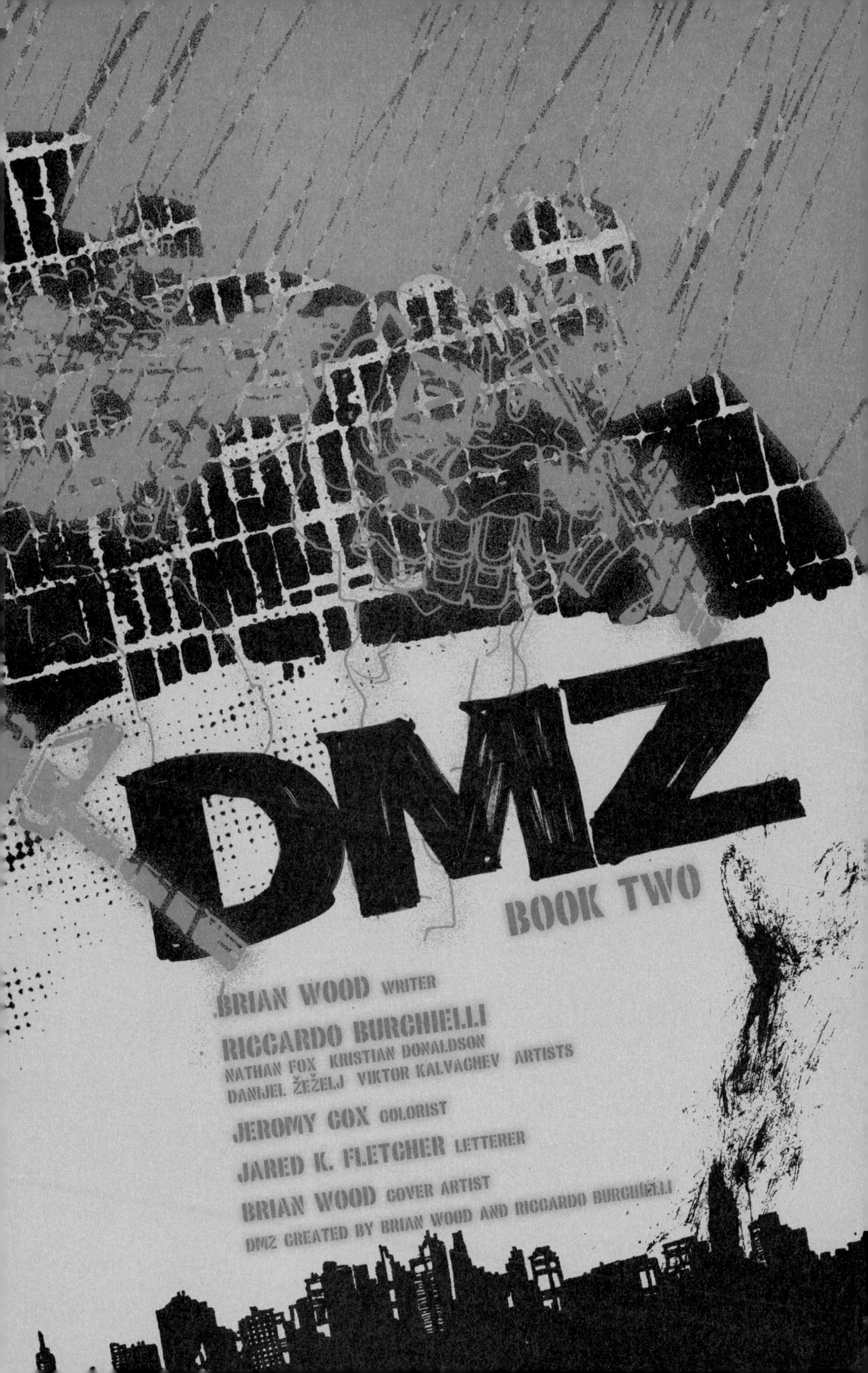

DMZ

BOOK TWO

BRIAN WOOD WRITER

RICCARDO BURCHIELLI
NATHAN FOX KRISTIAN DONALDSON
DANIJEL ŽEŽELJ VIKTOR KALVACHEV ARTISTS

JEROMY COX COLORIST

JARED K. FLETCHER LETTERER

BRIAN WOOD COVER ARTIST

DMZ CREATED BY BRIAN WOOD AND RICCARDO BURCHIELLI

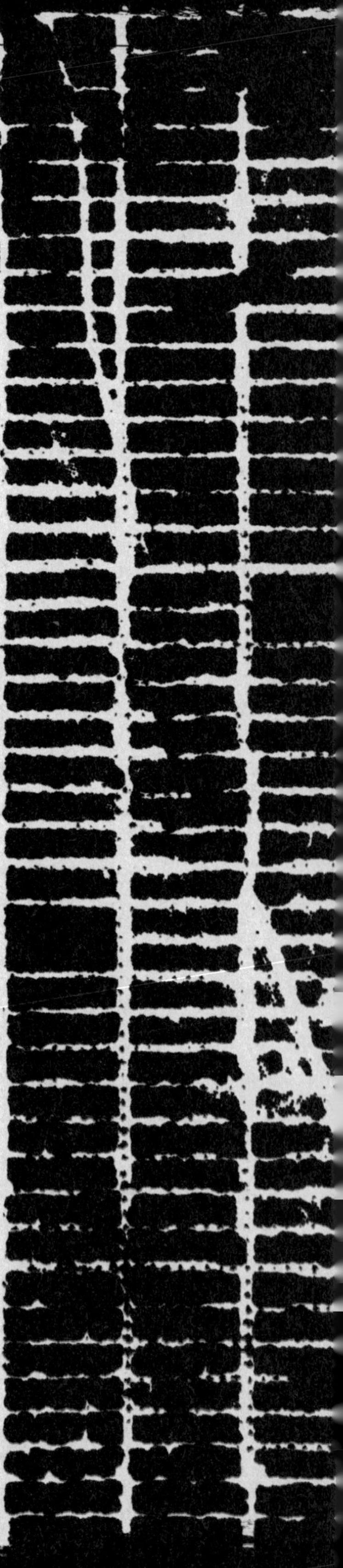

Will Dennis Editor – Original Series
Casey Seijas Assistant Editor – Original Series
Jeb Woodard Group Editor – Collected Editions
Peter Hamboussi Editor – Collected Edition
Steve Cook Design Director – Books
Louis Prandi Publication Design

Shelly Bond VP & Executive Editor – Vertigo

Diane Nelson President
Dan DiDio and Jim Lee Co-Publishers
Geoff Johns Chief Creative Officer
Amit Desai Senior VP – Marketing & Global Franchise Management
Nairi Gardiner Senior VP – Finance
Sam Ades VP – Digital Marketing
Bobbie Chase VP – Talent Development
Mark Chiarello Senior VP – Art, Design & Collected Editions
John Cunningham VP – Content Strategy
Anne DePies VP – Strategy Planning & Reporting
Don Falletti VP – Manufacturing Operations
Lawrence Ganem VP – Editorial Administration & Talent Relations
Alison Gill Senior VP – Manufacturing & Operations
Hank Kanalz Senior VP – Editorial Strategy & Administration
Jay Kogan VP – Legal Affairs
Derek Maddalena Senior VP – Sales & Business Development
Jack Mahan VP – Business Affairs
Dan Miron VP – Sales Planning & Trade Development
Nick Napolitano VP – Manufacturing Administration
Carol Roeder VP – Marketing
Eddie Scannell VP – Mass Account & Digital Sales
Courtney Simmons Senior VP – Publicity & Communications
Jim (Ski) Sokolowski VP – Comic Book Specialty & Newsstand Sales
Sandy Yi Senior VP – Global Franchise Management

DMZ logo designed by Brian Wood.

DMZ BOOK TWO
Published by DC Comics. Compilation, cover and
all new material Copyright © 2016 Brian Wood and
Riccardo Burchielli. All Rights Reserved. Originally
published in single magazine form in DMZ 13-28.
Copyright © 2007, 2008 Brian Wood and Riccardo
Burchielli. All Rights Reserved. All characters, their
distinctive likenesses and related elements featured
in this publication are trademarks of DC Comics.
VERTIGO is a trademark of DC Comics. The stories,
characters and incidents featured in this publication
are entirely fictional. DC Comics does not read or
accept unsolicited submissions of ideas, stories
or artwork.

DC Comics, 2900 West Alameda Ave., Burbank,
CA 91505
Printed in the USA. First Printing.
ISBN: 978-1-4012-6357-7

Library of Congress Cataloging-in-Publication Data

Wood, Brian, 1972- author.
 DMZ. The deluxe edition, Book two / Brian Wood ;
illustrated by Riccardo Burchielli.
   pages cm
ISBN 978-1-4012-6357-7
 1. Militia movements—United States—Comic
books, strips, etc. 2. New York (N.Y.)—Comic books,
strips, etc. 3. Graphic novels. I. Burchielli, Riccardo,
illustrator. II. Title.
 PN6727.W59D5767 2014
 741.5'973—dc23
                                     2014008612

Introduction by Cory Doctorow

There are two sides in every war: combatants and non-combatants.

Oh, I know it's not a popular belief, but it's true. There's not much ideological distance between, say, a bunch of bearded religious fanatics who want to suicide bomb skyscrapers and a bunch of suited fanatics who want to wiretap, RFID-tag, and imprison every human being on earth and deny the right to travel to anyone whose name sounds anything like the name of anyone who ever said anything nice about terrorism.

At least not when compared to the ideological distance between both of these packs of sociopathic monsters and the rest of us people who just want get onto an airplane without having our colons examined, who want to go to work, church or a mosque without having some nutjob daisy-cutter us for being in the wrong place at the wrong time.

The real "other" isn't brown people with turbans: it's people of all colors with guns, airplanes and wiretaps, no matter what side they fight on.

And tell you what, it's *mutual*. They hate and fear us like anything, those small people with small ideas, the authoritarians who know better than we do. They blame every single problem in their lives on *us*, the nebulous other who comes to their town, takes their jobs, speaks some foreign tongue (whether that's Persian or Brooklynese doesn't matter). A rape? That migrant worker looks suspicious. A theft? How about that out-of-towner with his big-city ways? Poverty, disease—even traffic jams—all the fault of some *other* who needs to be ethnically cleansed to restore us all to our pre-lapsarian glory.

Which is not to say that they're above sticking up for us if it gives them the excuse to tighten the noose. Islamic fanatics who thought of Saddam Hussein as the devil incarnate are delighted to use his toppling as the excuse to inspire another generation of jihadists. Just like the shitkickers who wouldn't have pissed on Manhattan if it was on fire are nevertheless proud to stick a yellow ribbon magnet on their Hummers and proclaim Never Forget, even as they forget that the 9/11 attacks were directed at Sodom on the Hudson, a city filled with gayers, women in bifurcated garments and brown people who smell like curry.

DMZ is a special kind of angry comic, the kind of angry war comic that tells the story of the other side in the war. Non-combatants aren't just cannon fodder or collateral damage. We've got every bit as much agency, as much control over our destinies, as the guys with the guns and the satellite photos. But you wouldn't know it from how we're depicted in the press—instead, we're the bodies blown apart on street corners, the shoeless sheep having our hemorrhoid cream confiscated at the airport.

DMZ is an inspiration to we who refuse to be dismembered and unshod. It's a wake-up call to stop letting greedy profiteers sell fresh wars to cement their authority and profitability.

If I had my way, this comic would be required reading in every civics class in America.

-30-

Cory Doctorow is an award-winning author, blogger, journalist and co-editor of the blog Boing Boing. *His novels include* Down and Out in the Magic Kingdom, Eastern Standard Tribe *and* Someone Comes to Town, Someone Leaves Town.

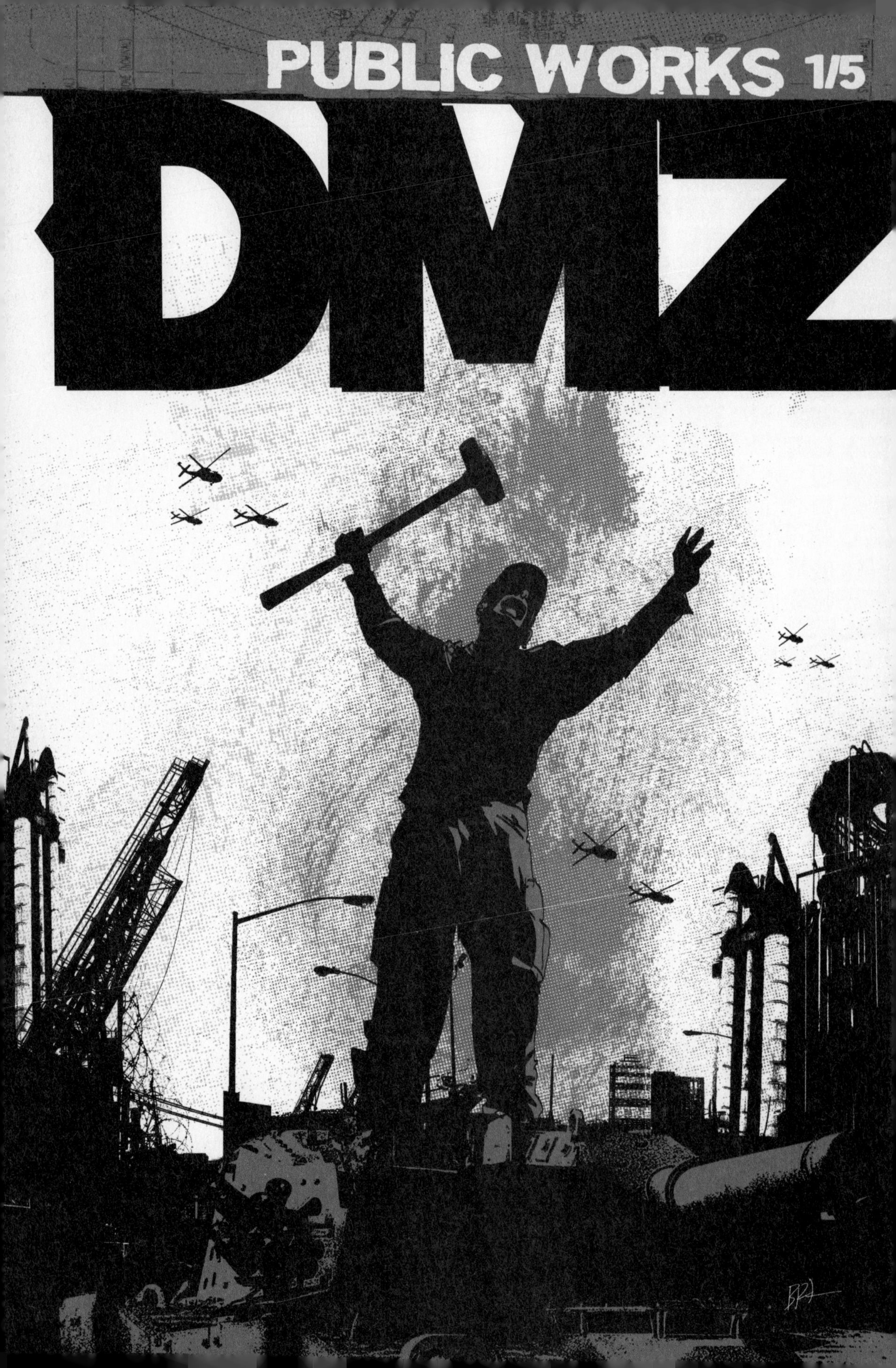
PUBLIC WORKS 1/5
DMZ

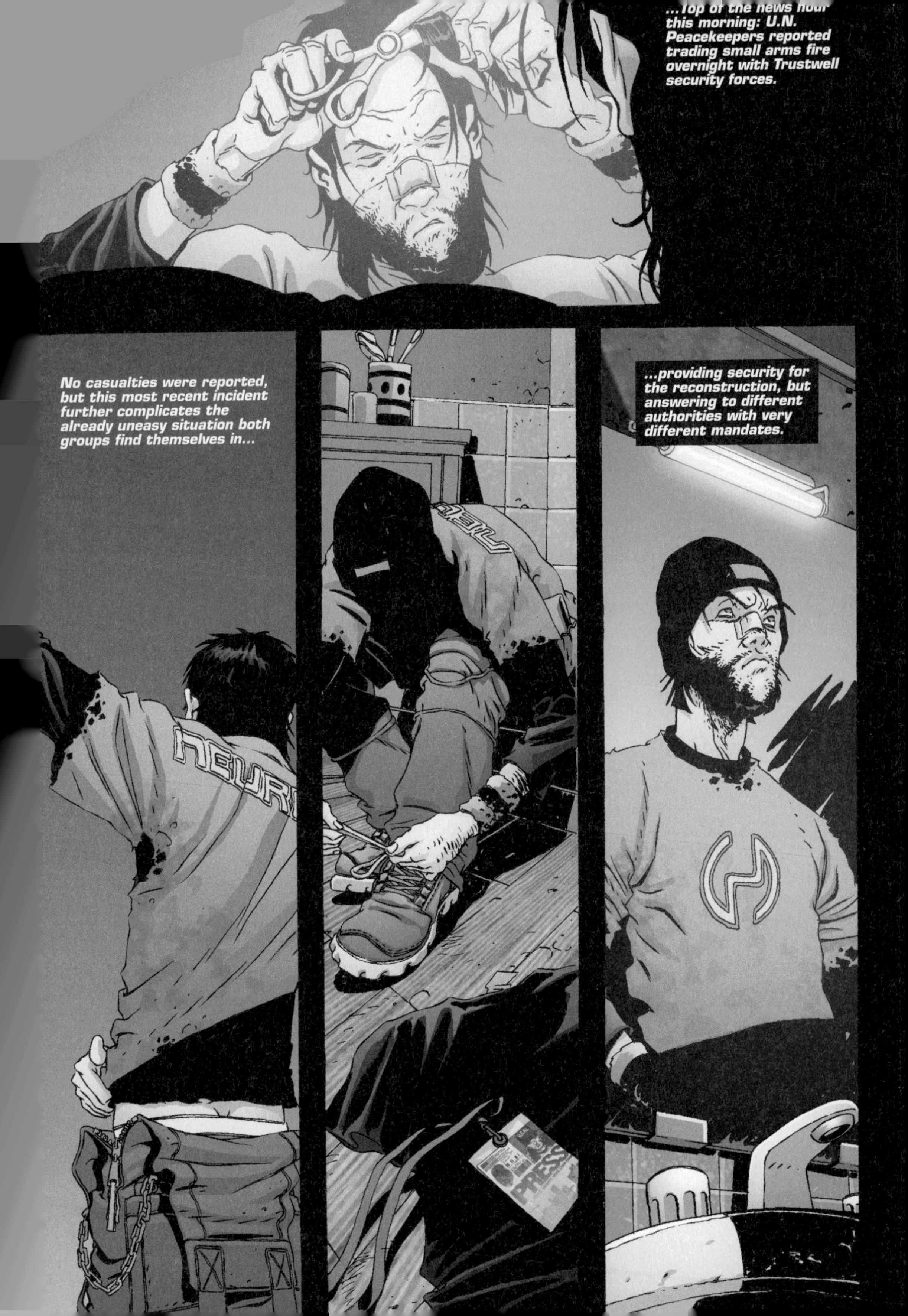
...Top of the news hour this morning: U.N. Peacekeepers reported trading small arms fire overnight with Trustwell security forces.
No casualties were reported, but this most recent incident further complicates the already uneasy situation both groups find themselves in...
...providing security for the reconstruction, but answering to different authorities with very different mandates.
NEURO
PRESS

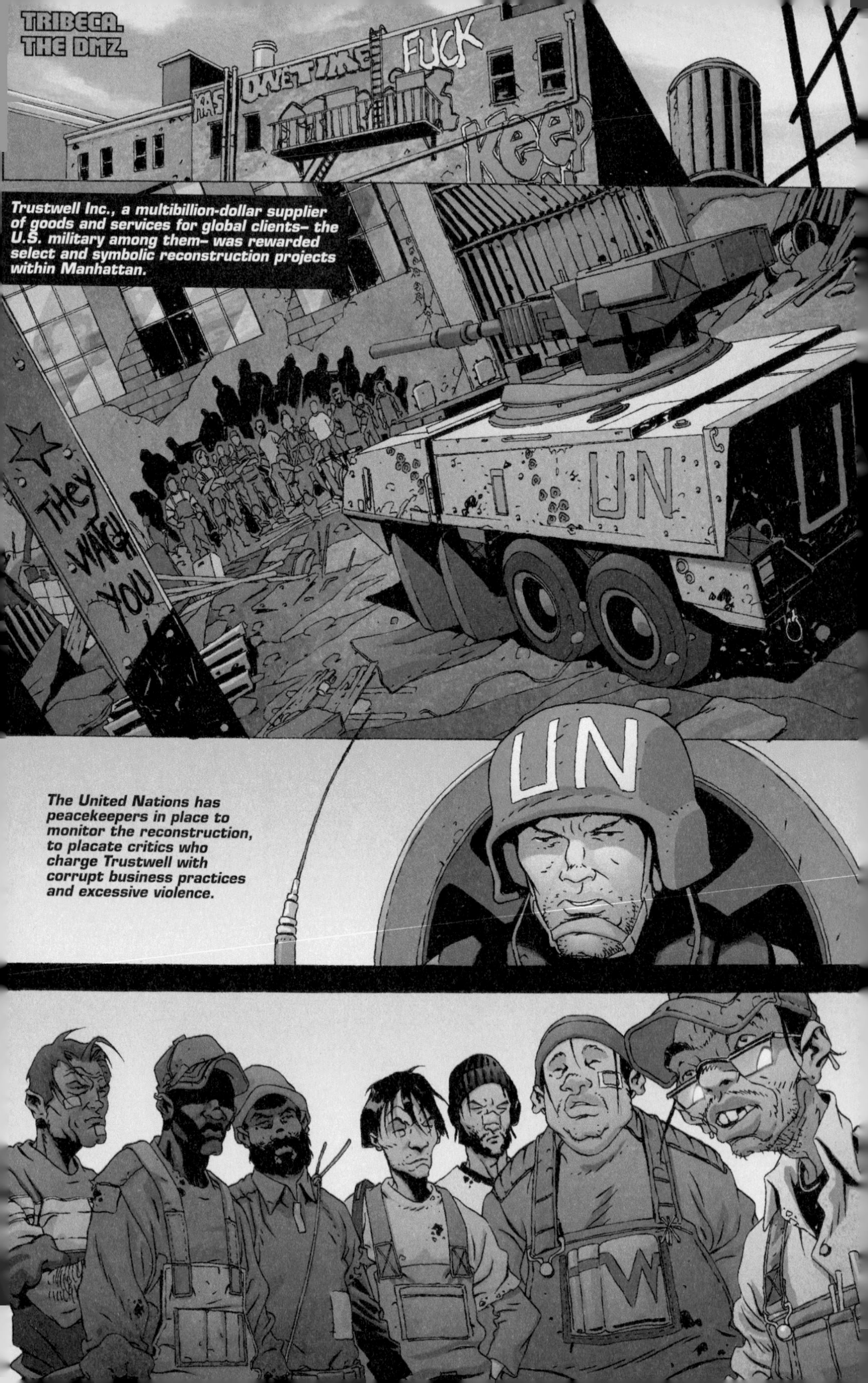
TRIBECA. THE DMZ.
Trustwell Inc., a multibillion-dollar supplier of goods and services for global clients– the U.S. military among them– was rewarded select and symbolic reconstruction projects within Manhattan.
FUCK
KEEP
THEY WATCH YOU
UN
UN
The United Nations has peacekeepers in place to monitor the reconstruction, to placate critics who charge Trustwell with corrupt business practices and excessive violence.
UN
TW

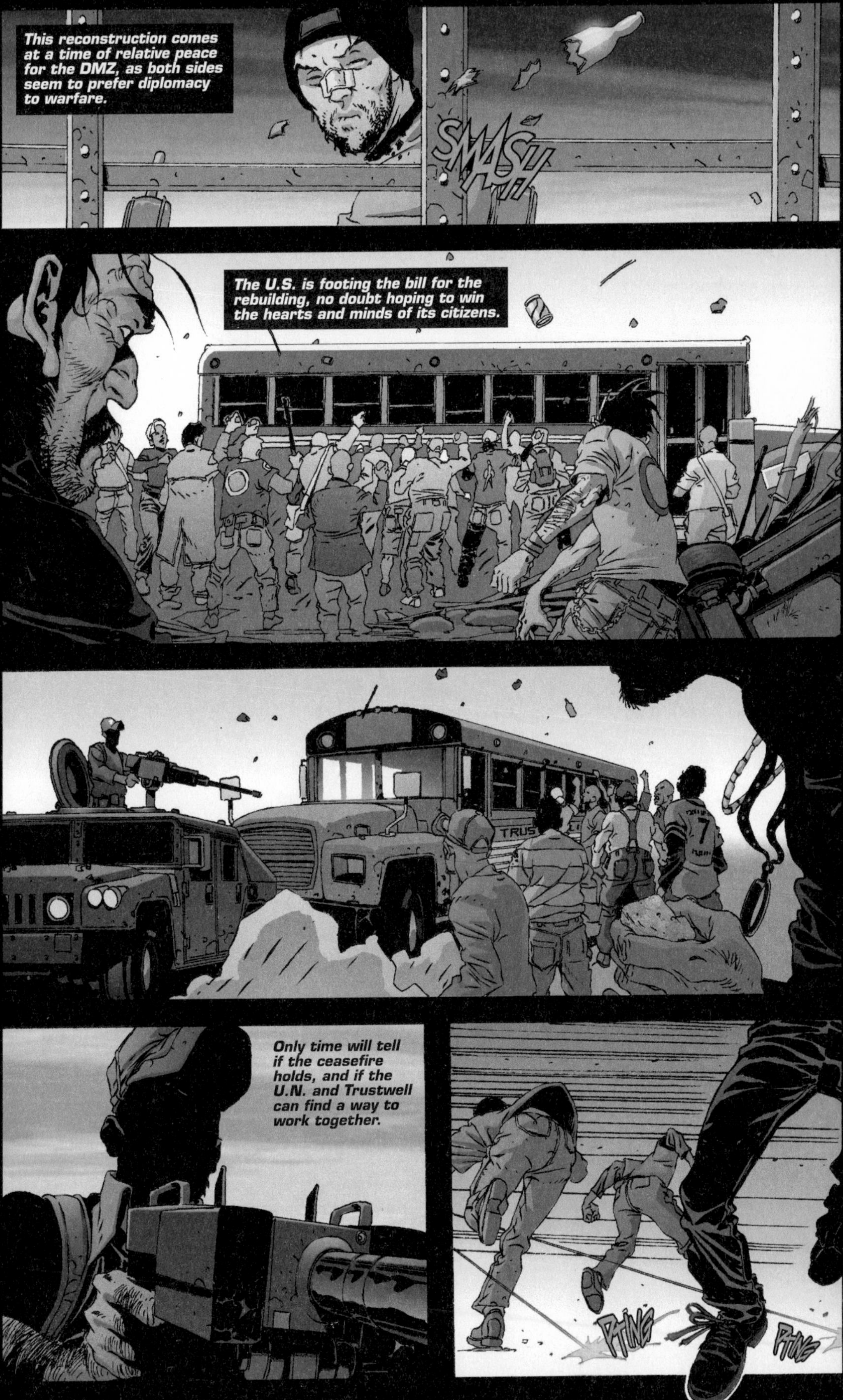
This reconstruction comes at a time of relative peace for the DMZ, as both sides seem to prefer diplomacy to warfare.
SMASH
The U.S. is footing the bill for the rebuilding, no doubt hoping to win the hearts and minds of its citizens.
TRUS
Only time will tell if the ceasefire holds, and if the U.N. and Trustwell can find a way to work together.
PTING
PTING

More news from the war, after these messages.

THIS IS IT, EVERYONE.

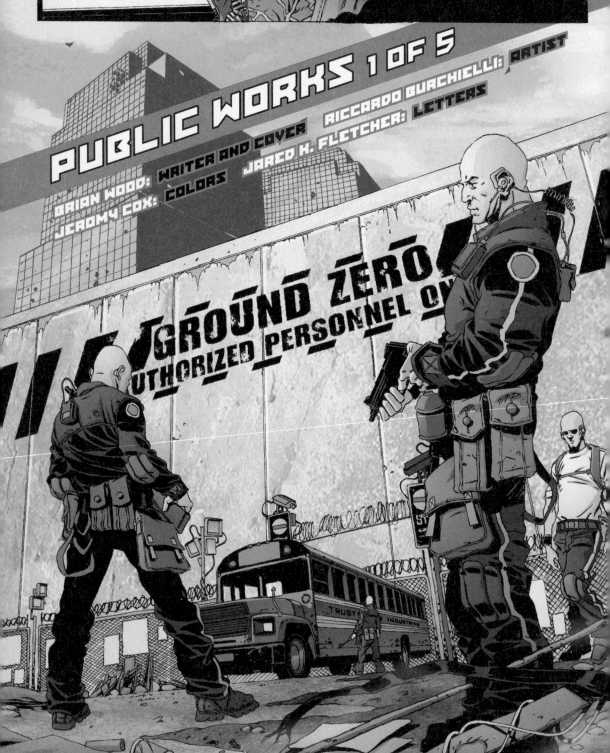

PUBLIC WORKS 1 OF 5

RICCARDO BURCHIELLI: ARTIST

BRIAN WOOD: WRITER AND COVER

JARED K. FLETCHER: LETTERS

JEROMY COX: COLORS

GROUND ZERO
UTHORIZED PERSONNEL ON

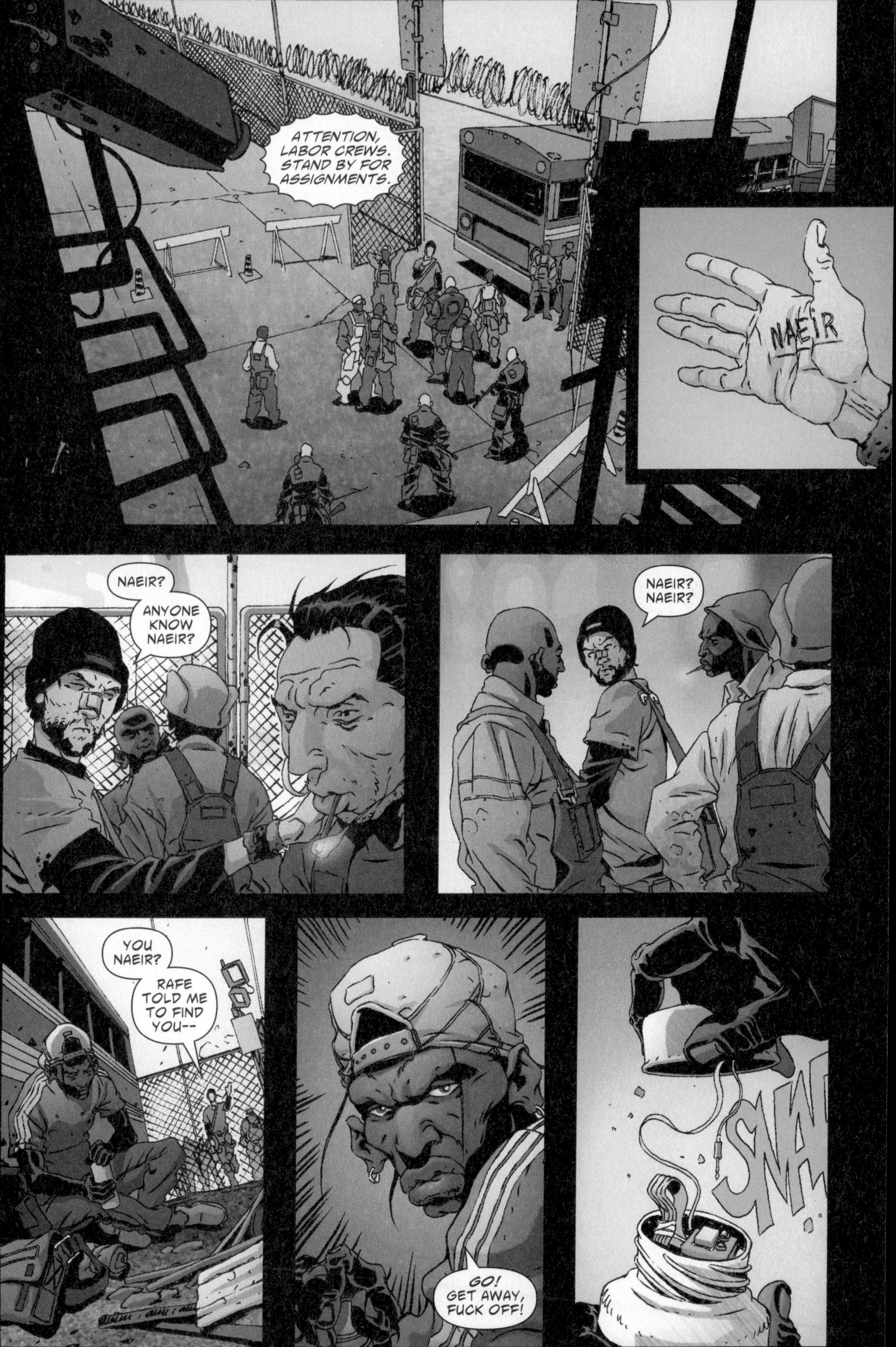
ATTENTION, LABOR CREWS. STAND BY FOR ASSIGNMENTS.
NAEIR
NAEIR?
ANYONE KNOW NAEIR?
NAEIR? NAEIR?
YOU NAEIR?
RAFE TOLD ME TO FIND YOU--
GO! GET AWAY, FUCK OFF!

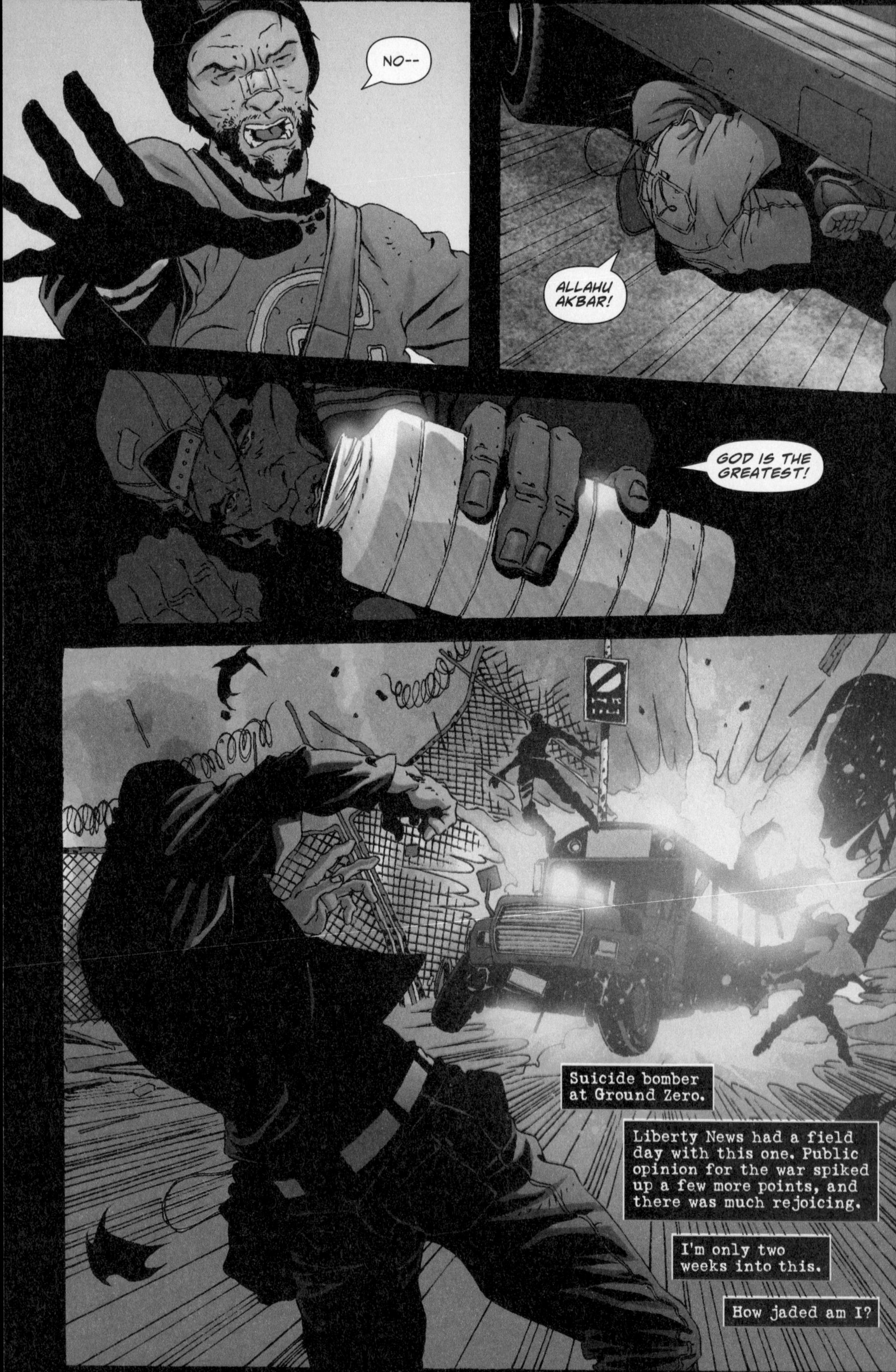
NO--
ALLAHU AKBAR!
GOD IS THE GREATEST!
Suicide bomber at Ground Zero.
Liberty News had a field day with this one. Public opinion for the war spiked up a few more points, and there was much rejoicing.
I'm only two weeks into this.
How jaded am I?

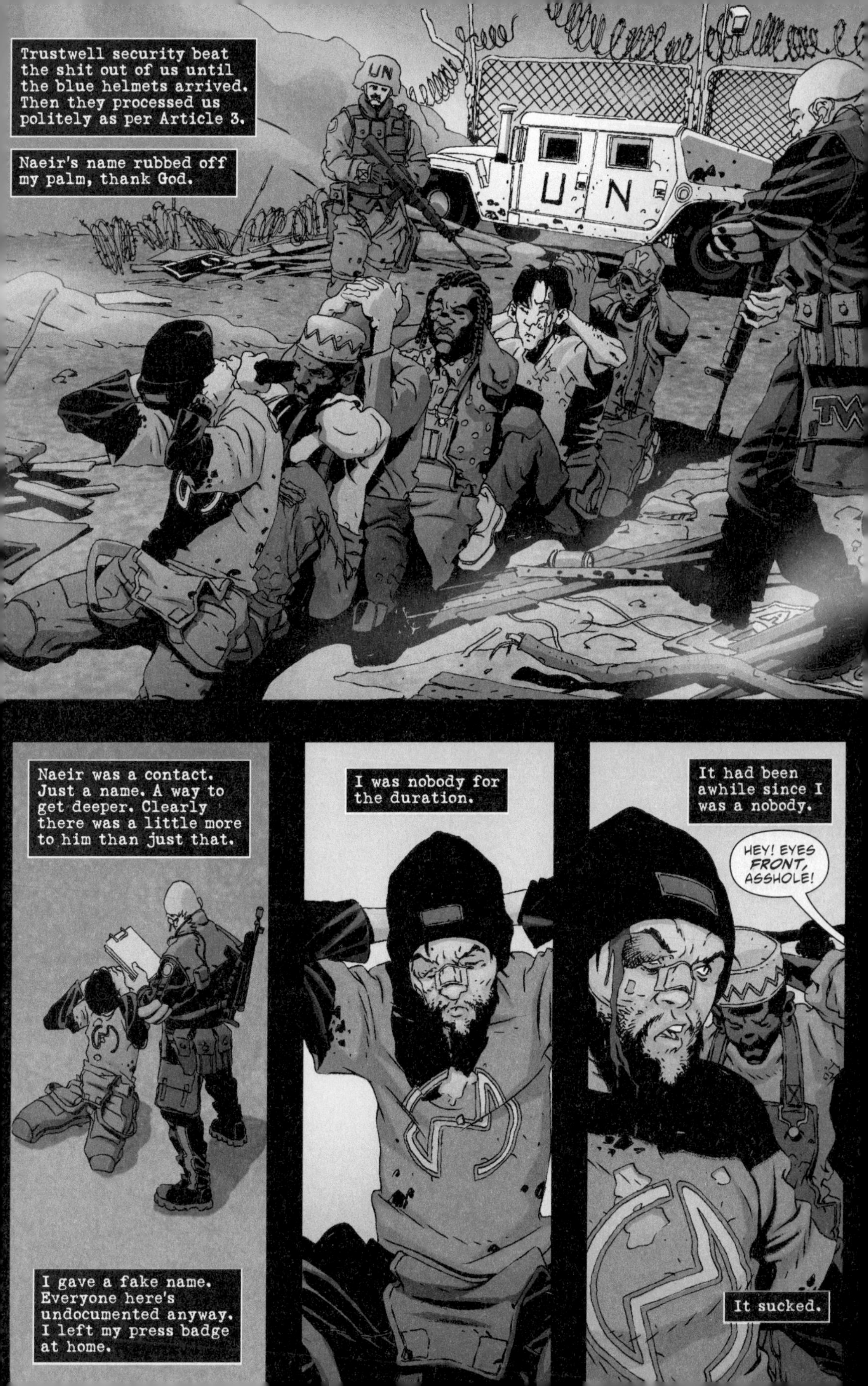
Trustwell security beat the shit out of us until the blue helmets arrived. Then they processed us politely as per Article 3.
Naeir's name rubbed off my palm, thank God.
UN
U N
Naeir was a contact. Just a name. A way to get deeper. Clearly there was a little more to him than just that.
I gave a fake name. Everyone here's undocumented anyway. I left my press badge at home.
I was nobody for the duration.
It had been awhile since I was a nobody.
HEY! EYES FRONT, ASSHOLE!
It sucked.

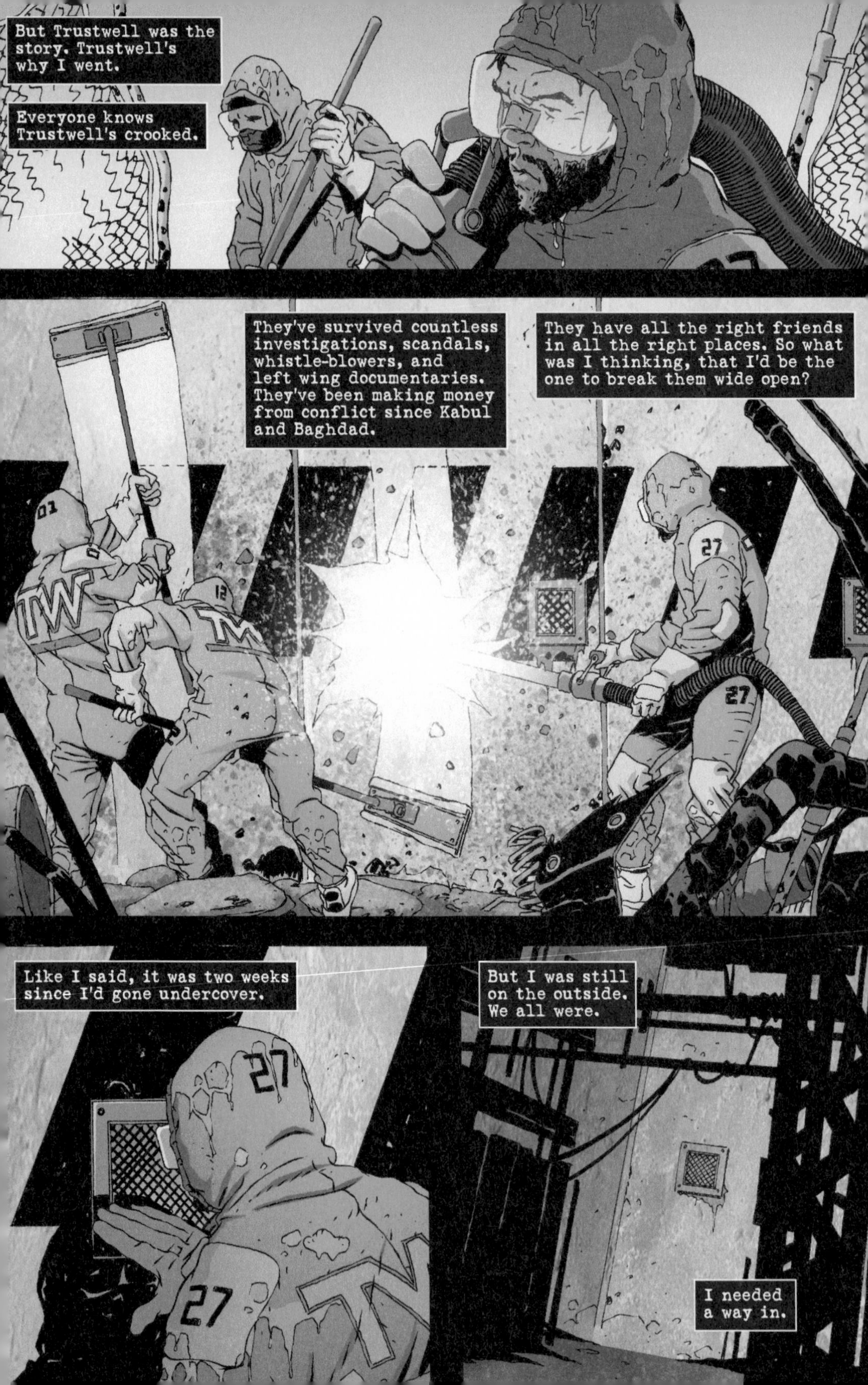
But Trustwell was the story. Trustwell's why I went.
Everyone knows Trustwell's crooked.
They've survived countless investigations, scandals, whistle-blowers, and left wing documentaries. They've been making money from conflict since Kabul and Baghdad.
They have all the right friends in all the right places. So what was I thinking, that I'd be the one to break them wide open?
Like I said, it was two weeks since I'd gone undercover.
But I was still on the outside. We all were.
I needed a way in.

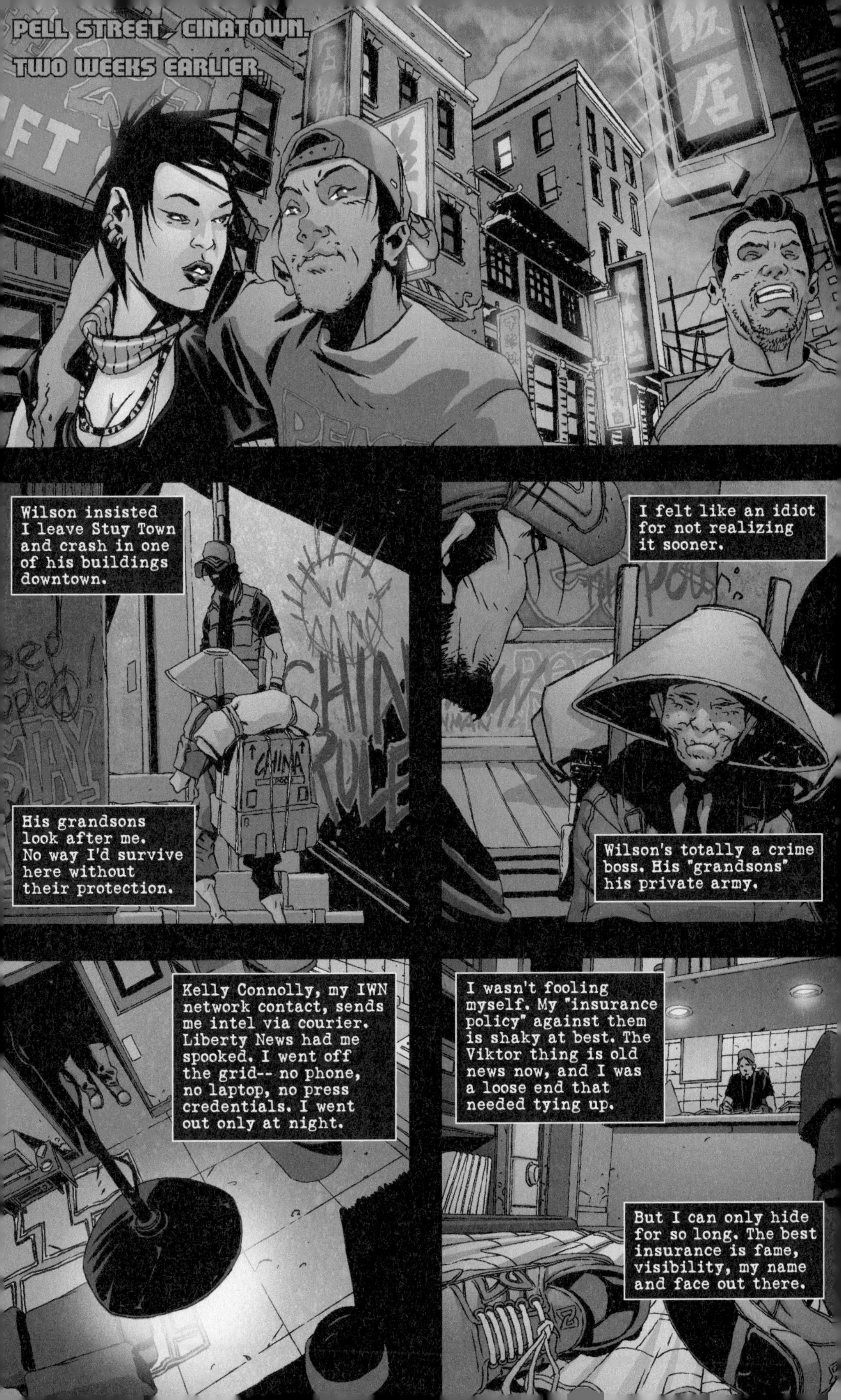
PELL STREET, CINATOWN.
TWO WEEKS EARLIER.
Wilson insisted I leave Stuy Town and crash in one of his buildings downtown.
His grandsons look after me. No way I'd survive here without their protection.
I felt like an idiot for not realizing it sooner.
Wilson's totally a crime boss. His "grandsons" his private army.
Kelly Connolly, my IWN network contact, sends me intel via courier. Liberty News had me spooked. I went off the grid-- no phone, no laptop, no press credentials. I went out only at night.
I wasn't fooling myself. My "insurance policy" against them is shaky at best. The Viktor thing is old news now, and I was a loose end that needed tying up.
But I can only hide for so long. The best insurance is fame, visibility, my name and face out there.

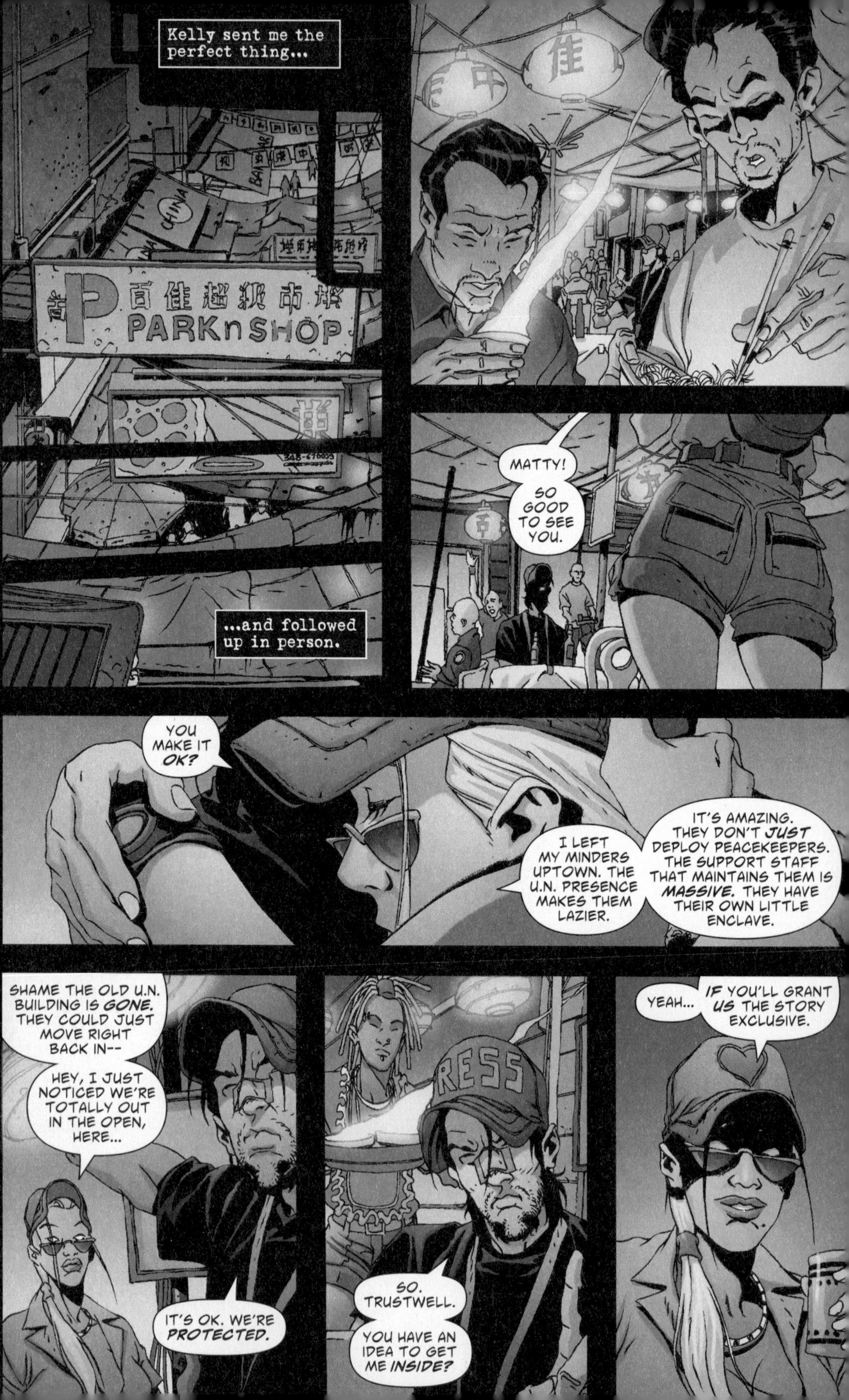

Kelly sent me the perfect thing...
PARKnSHOP
...and followed up in person.
MATTY!
SO GOOD TO SEE YOU.
YOU MAKE IT OK?
I LEFT MY MINDERS UPTOWN. THE U.N. PRESENCE MAKES THEM LAZIER.
IT'S AMAZING. THEY DON'T JUST DEPLOY PEACEKEEPERS. THE SUPPORT STAFF THAT MAINTAINS THEM IS MASSIVE. THEY HAVE THEIR OWN LITTLE ENCLAVE.
SHAME THE OLD U.N. BUILDING IS GONE. THEY COULD JUST MOVE RIGHT BACK IN--
HEY, I JUST NOTICED WE'RE TOTALLY OUT IN THE OPEN, HERE...
IT'S OK. WE'RE PROTECTED.
RESS
SO. TRUSTWELL.
YOU HAVE AN IDEA TO GET ME INSIDE?
YEAH... IF YOU'LL GRANT US THE STORY EXCLUSIVE.

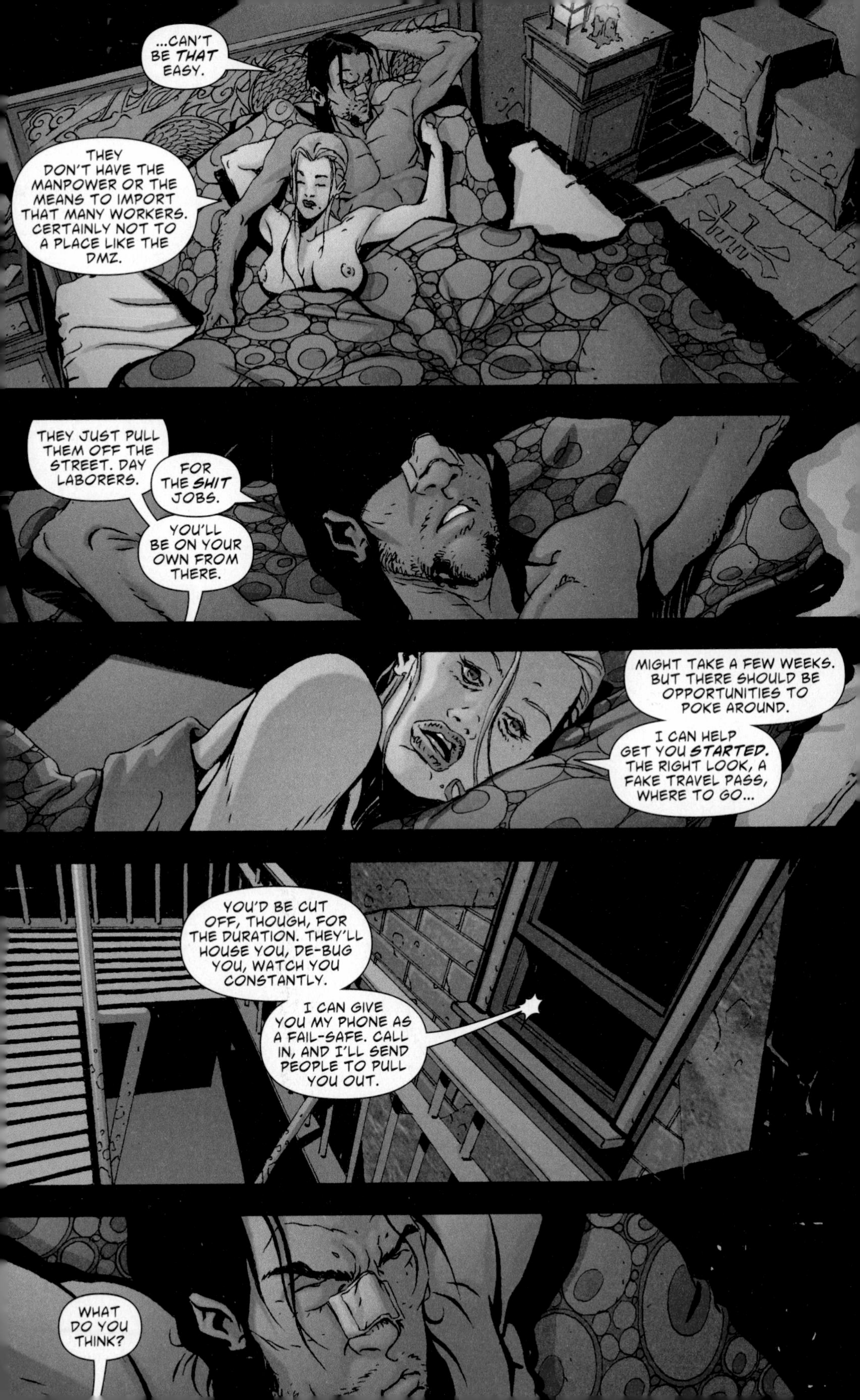
...CAN'T BE THAT EASY.
THEY DON'T HAVE THE MANPOWER OR THE MEANS TO IMPORT THAT MANY WORKERS. CERTAINLY NOT TO A PLACE LIKE THE DMZ.
THEY JUST PULL THEM OFF THE STREET. DAY LABORERS.
FOR THE SHIT JOBS.
YOU'LL BE ON YOUR OWN FROM THERE.
MIGHT TAKE A FEW WEEKS. BUT THERE SHOULD BE OPPORTUNITIES TO POKE AROUND.
I CAN HELP GET YOU STARTED. THE RIGHT LOOK, A FAKE TRAVEL PASS, WHERE TO GO...
YOU'D BE CUT OFF, THOUGH, FOR THE DURATION. THEY'LL HOUSE YOU, DE-BUG YOU, WATCH YOU CONSTANTLY.
I CAN GIVE YOU MY PHONE AS A FAIL-SAFE. CALL IN, AND I'LL SEND PEOPLE TO PULL YOU OUT.
WHAT DO YOU THINK?

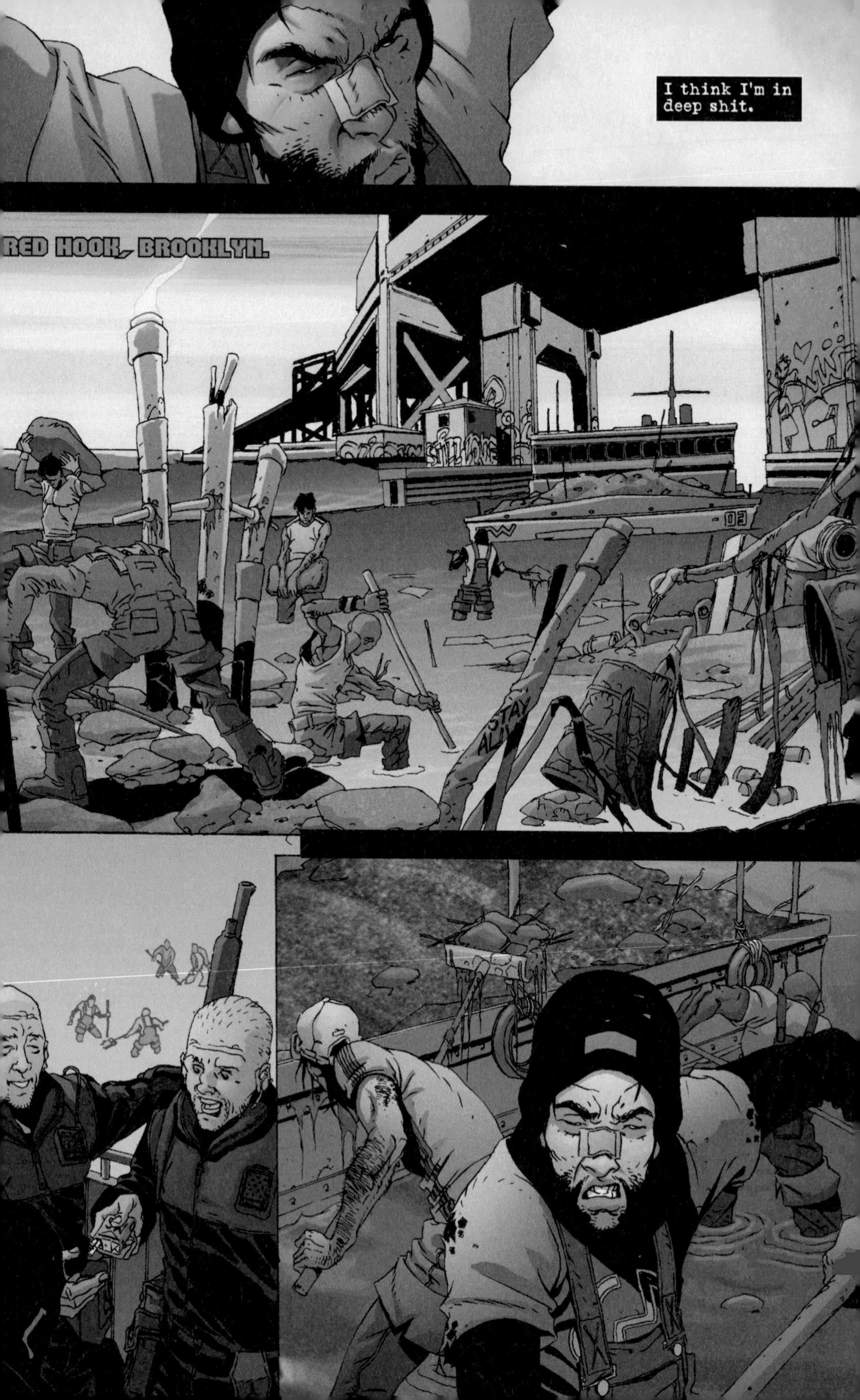
I think I'm in deep shit.
RED HOOK, BROOKLYN.
STAY ALIVE
STAY

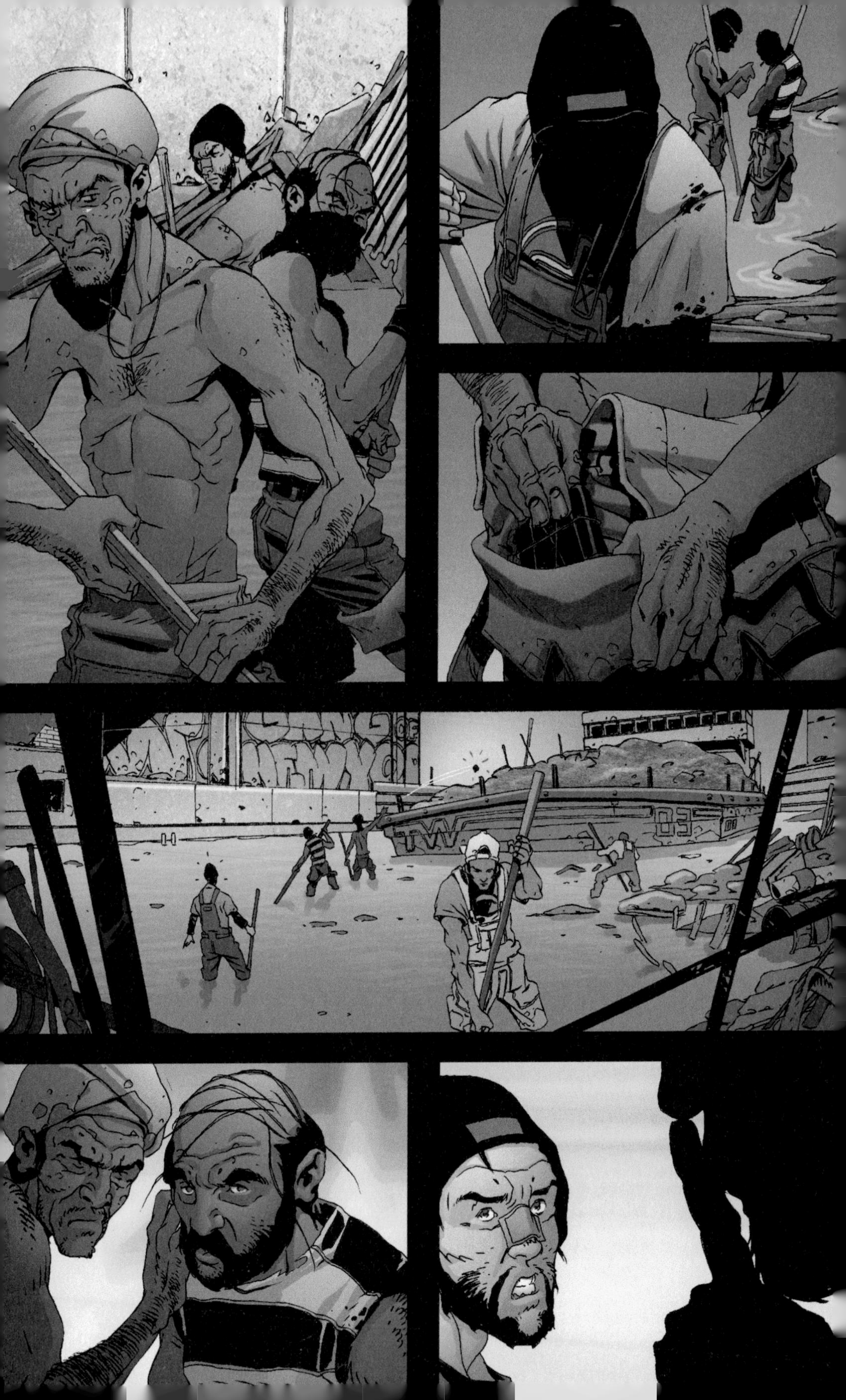

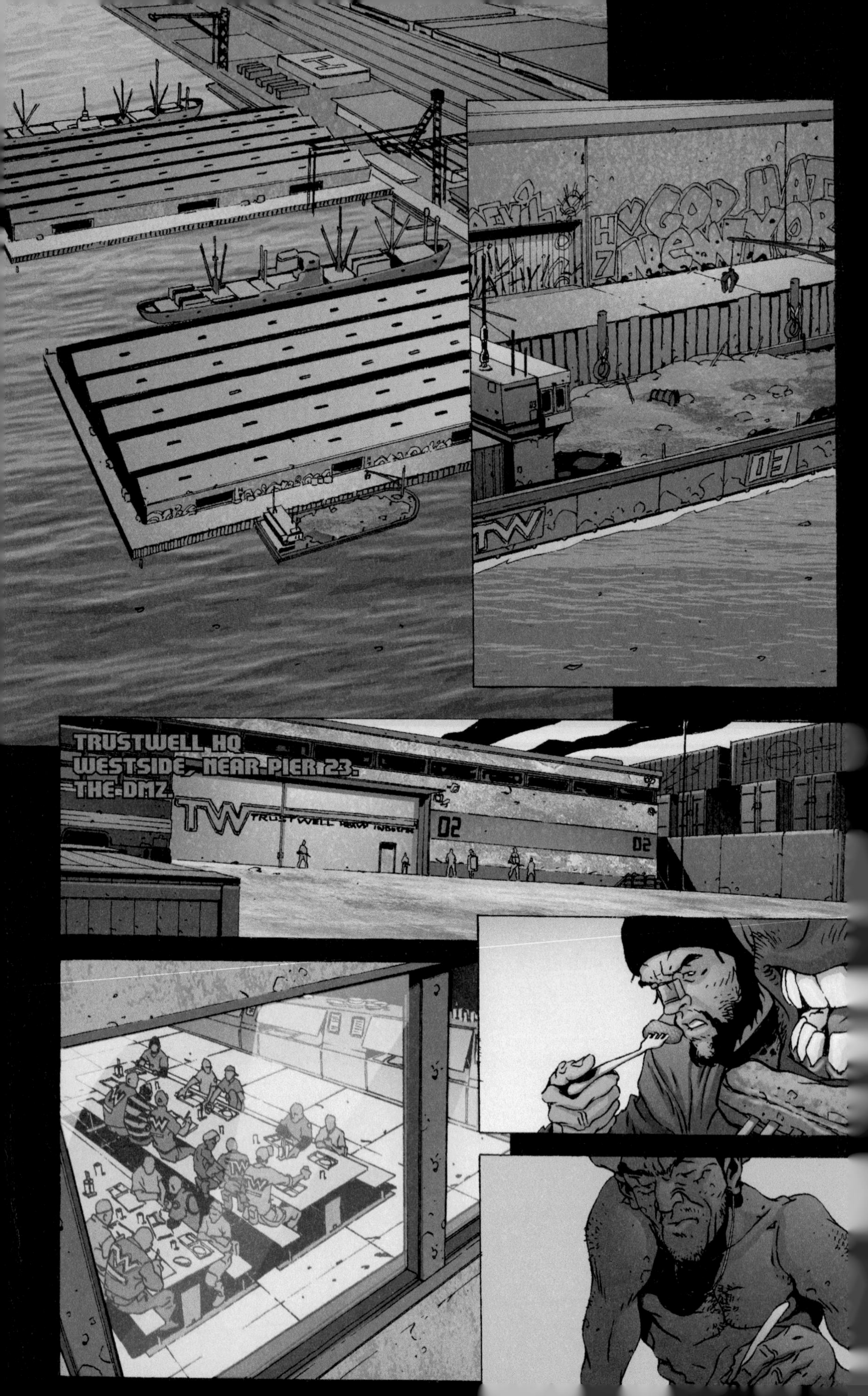
TRUSTWELL HQ
WESTSIDE, NEAR PIER 23.
THE DMZ.
TW
03
TW TRUSTWELL
02
02

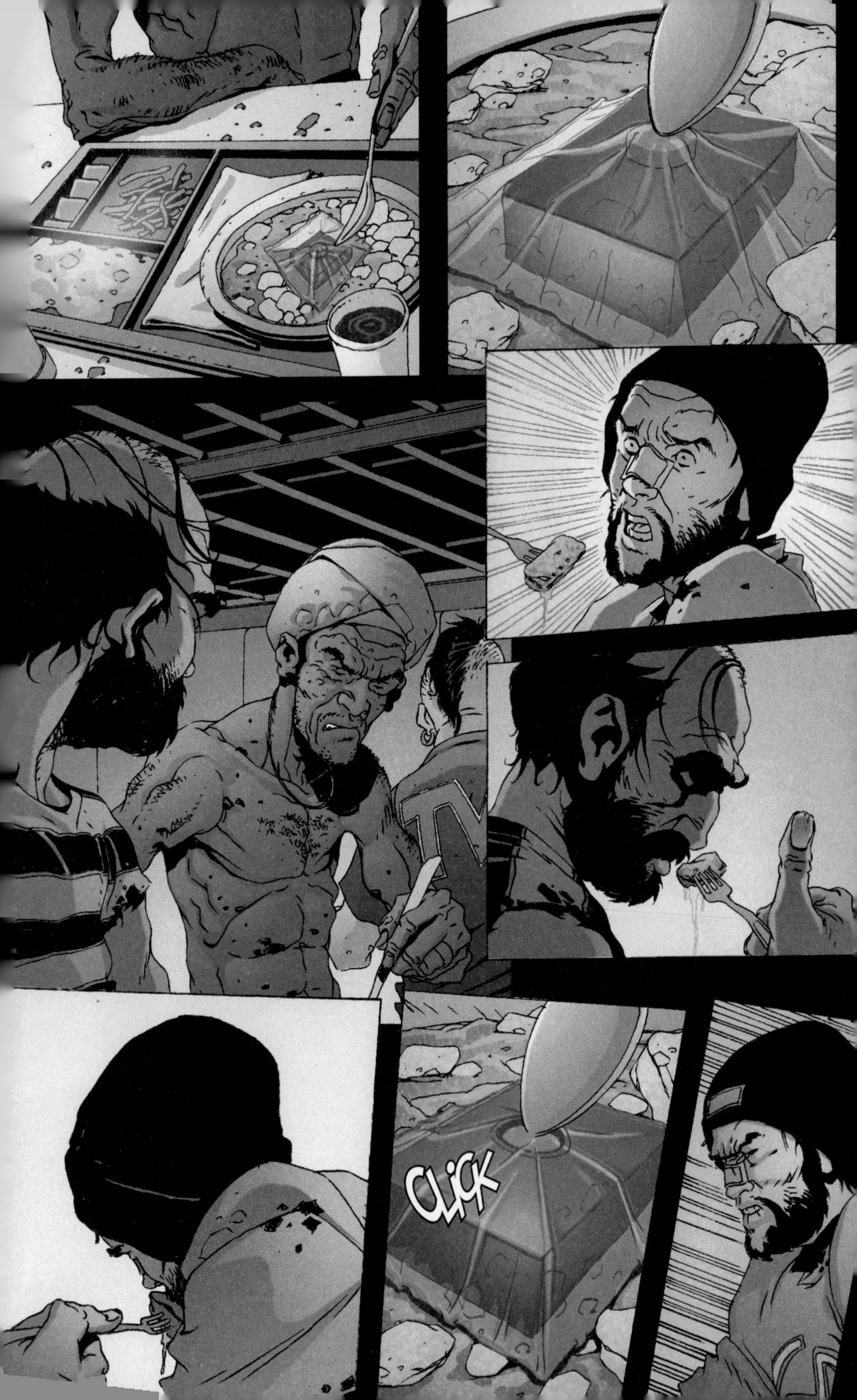
CLICK

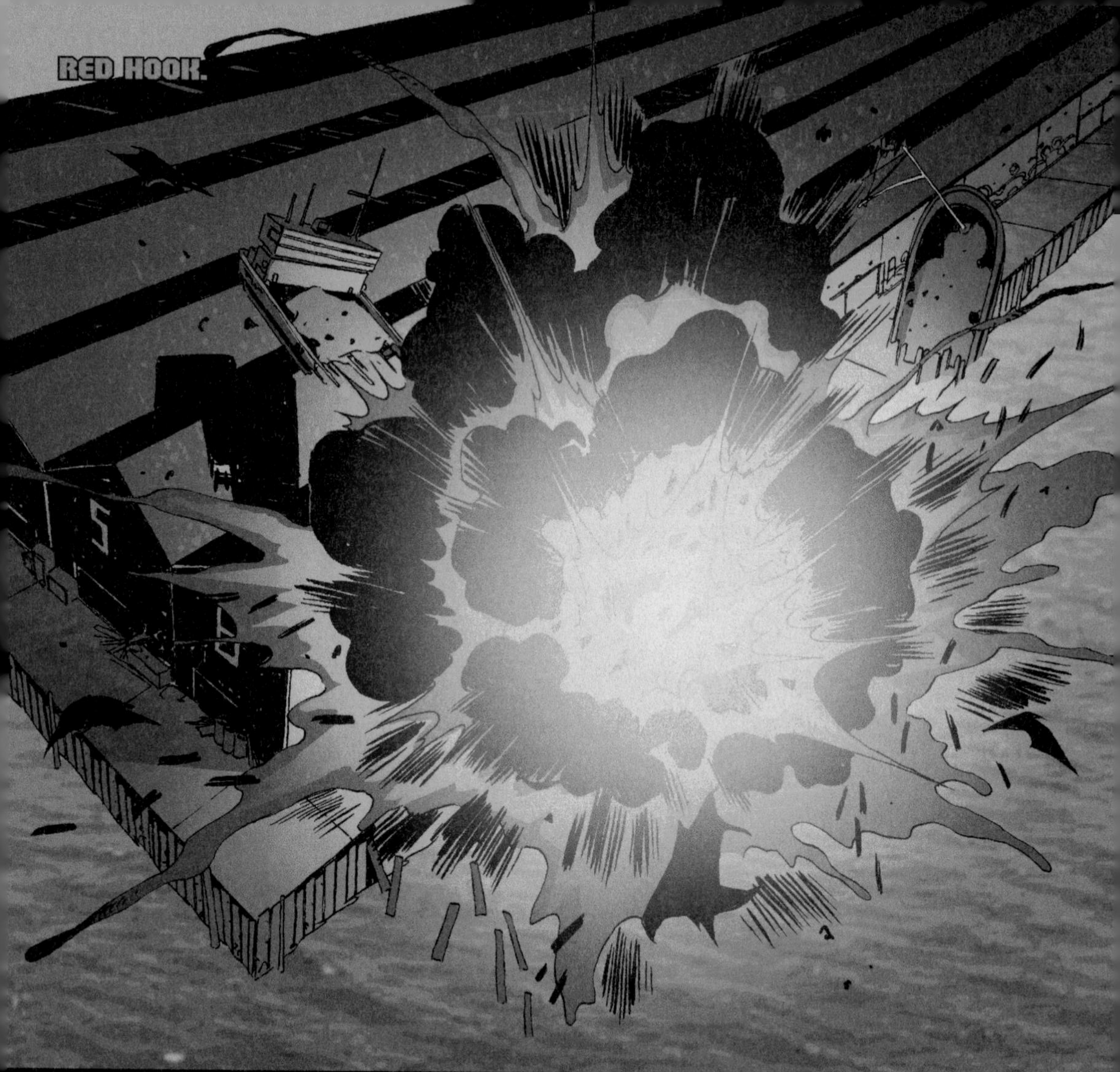
RED HOOK.

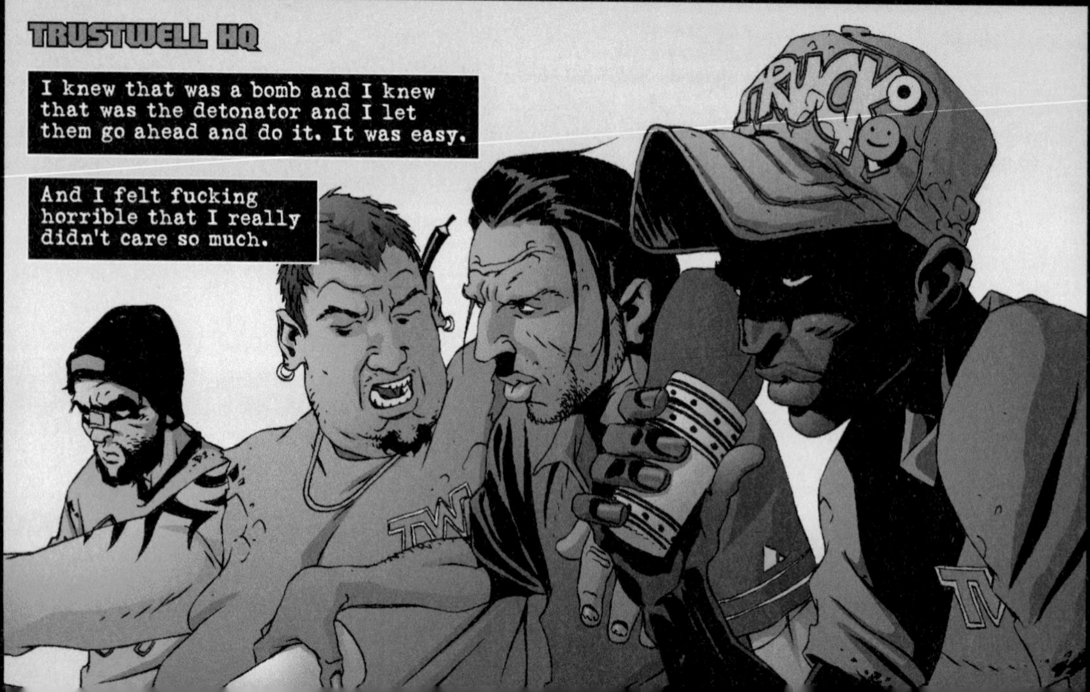
TRUSTWELL HQ
I knew that was a bomb and I knew that was the detonator and I let them go ahead and do it. It was easy.
And I felt fucking horrible that I really didn't care so much.
TRUCKO

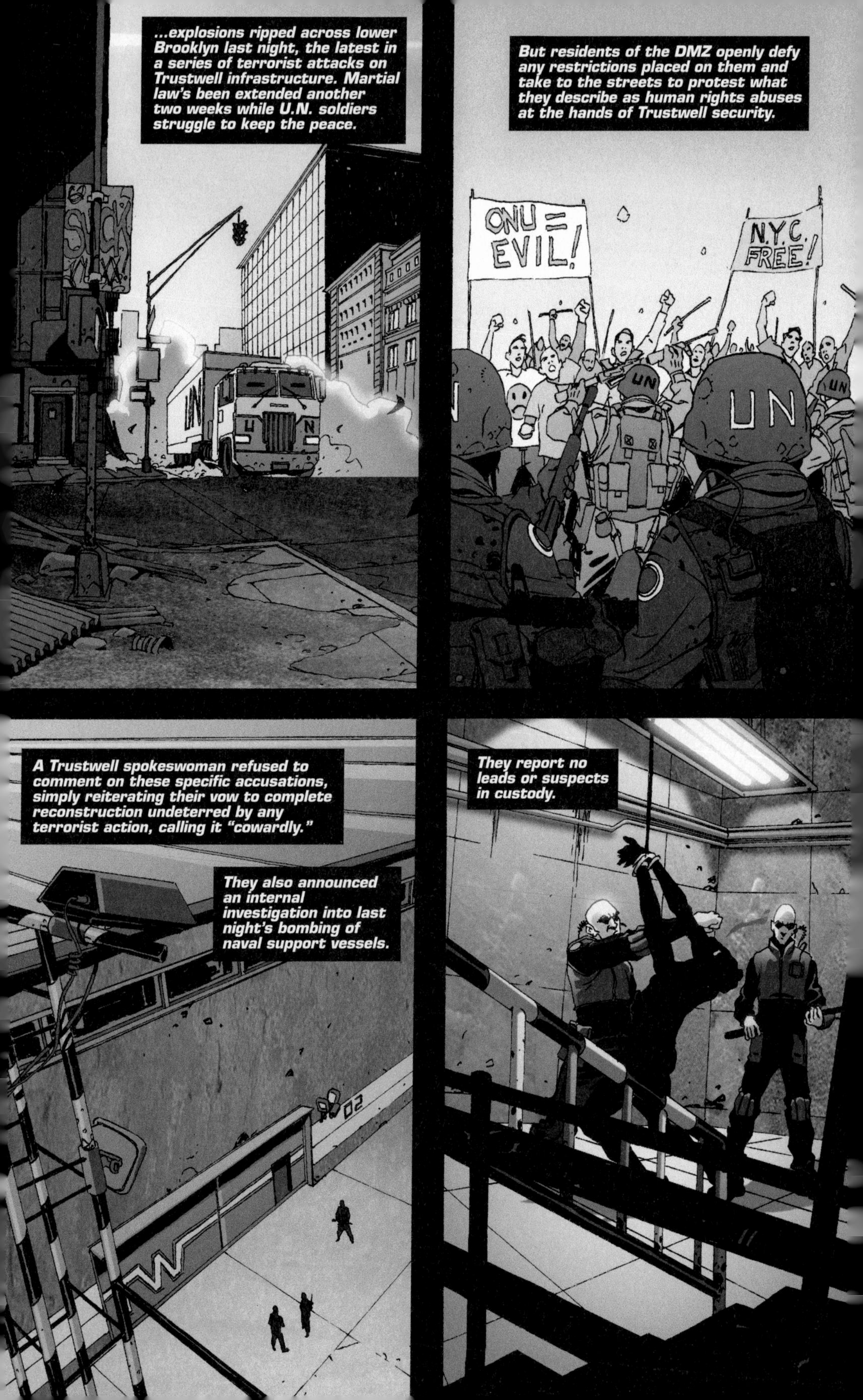
...explosions ripped across lower Brooklyn last night, the latest in a series of terrorist attacks on Trustwell infrastructure. Martial law's been extended another two weeks while U.N. soldiers struggle to keep the peace.
UN
U N
But residents of the DMZ openly defy any restrictions placed on them and take to the streets to protest what they describe as human rights abuses at the hands of Trustwell security.
ONU = EVIL!
N.Y.C. FREE!
UN
A Trustwell spokeswoman refused to comment on these specific accusations, simply reiterating their vow to complete reconstruction undeterred by any terrorist action, calling it "cowardly."
They also announced an internal investigation into last night's bombing of naval support vessels.
They report no leads or suspects in custody.

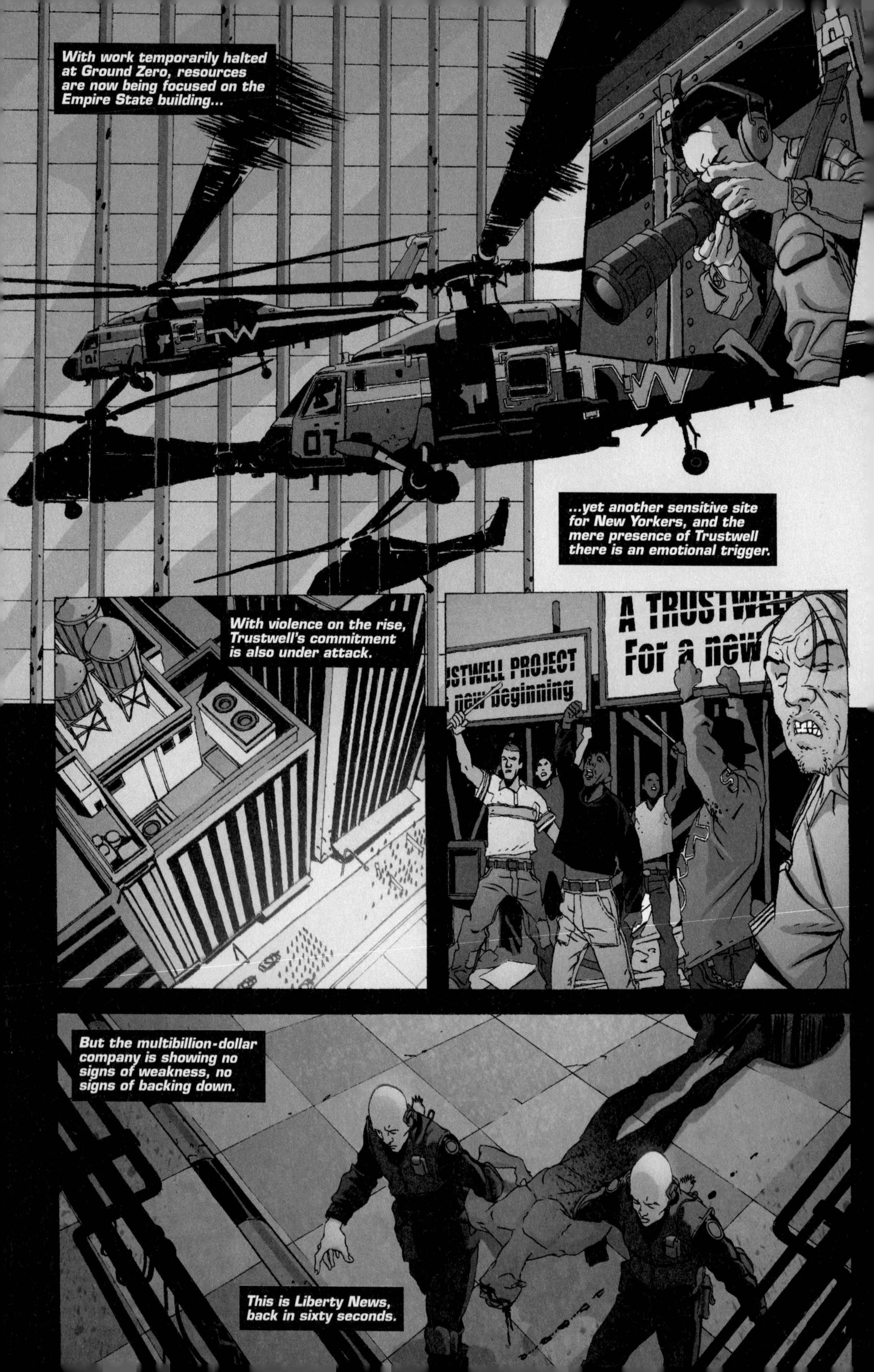
With work temporarily halted at Ground Zero, resources are now being focused on the Empire State building...
TW
01
TW
...yet another sensitive site for New Yorkers, and the mere presence of Trustwell there is an emotional trigger.
With violence on the rise, Trustwell's commitment is also under attack.
A TRUSTWEL
For a new
USTWELL PROJECT
new beginning
But the multibillion-dollar company is showing no signs of weakness, no signs of backing down.
This is Liberty News, back in sixty seconds.

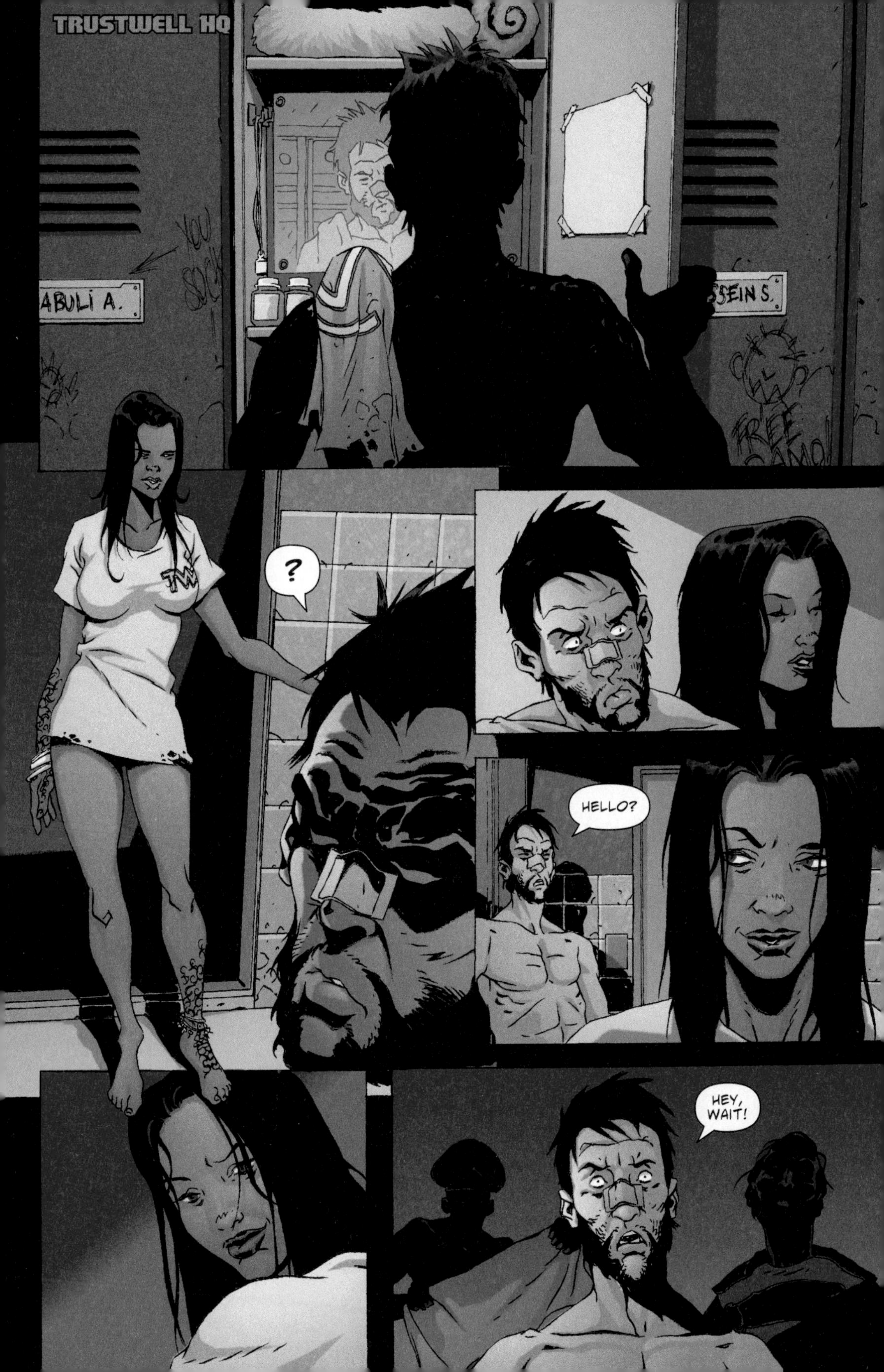

TRUSTWELL HQ
YOU SUCK
ABULI A.
SSEIN S.
FREE
?
HELLO?
HEY, WAIT!

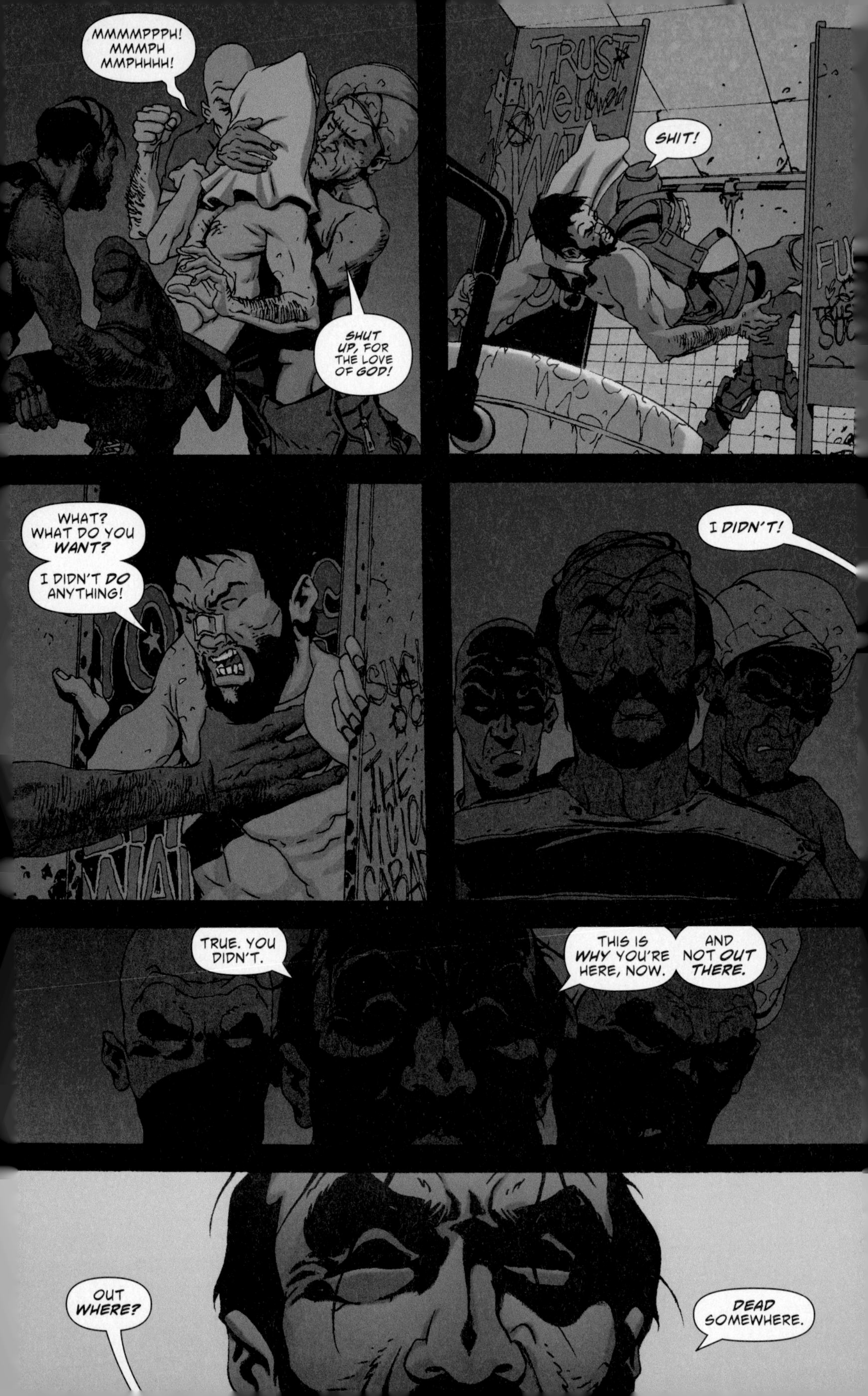
MMMMPPPH! MMMPH MMPHHHH!
SHUT UP, FOR THE LOVE OF GOD!
TRUST
SHIT!
WHAT? WHAT DO YOU WANT?
I DIDN'T DO ANYTHING!
I DIDN'T!
TRUE. YOU DIDN'T.
THIS IS WHY YOU'RE HERE, NOW.
AND NOT OUT THERE.
OUT WHERE?
DEAD SOMEWHERE.

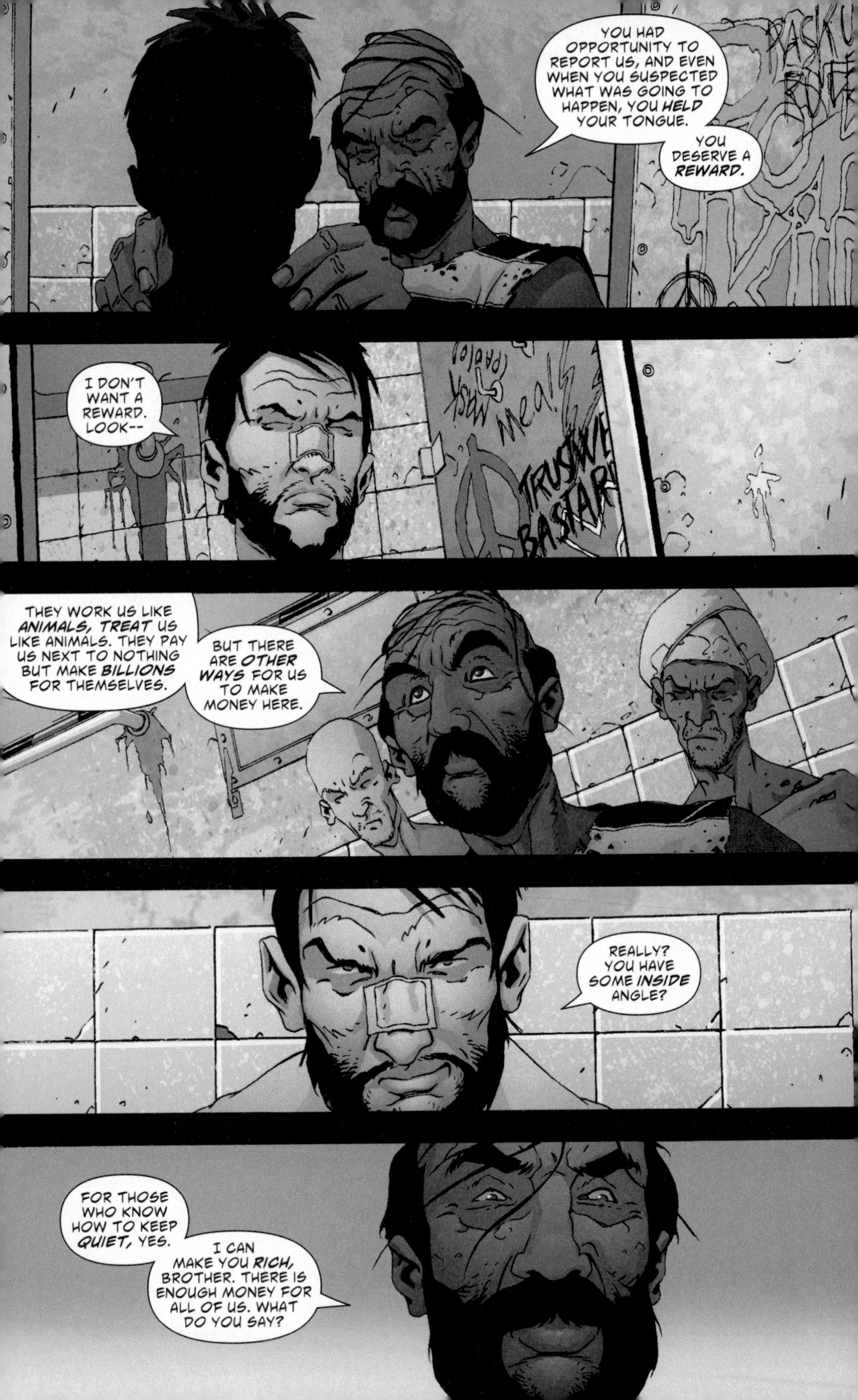
YOU HAD OPPORTUNITY TO REPORT US, AND EVEN WHEN YOU SUSPECTED WHAT WAS GOING TO HAPPEN, YOU HELD YOUR TONGUE.
YOU DESERVE A REWARD.
I DON'T WANT A REWARD. LOOK--
THEY WORK US LIKE ANIMALS, TREAT US LIKE ANIMALS. THEY PAY US NEXT TO NOTHING BUT MAKE BILLIONS FOR THEMSELVES.
BUT THERE ARE OTHER WAYS FOR US TO MAKE MONEY HERE.
REALLY? YOU HAVE SOME INSIDE ANGLE?
FOR THOSE WHO KNOW HOW TO KEEP QUIET, YES.
I CAN MAKE YOU RICH, BROTHER. THERE IS ENOUGH MONEY FOR ALL OF US. WHAT DO YOU SAY?

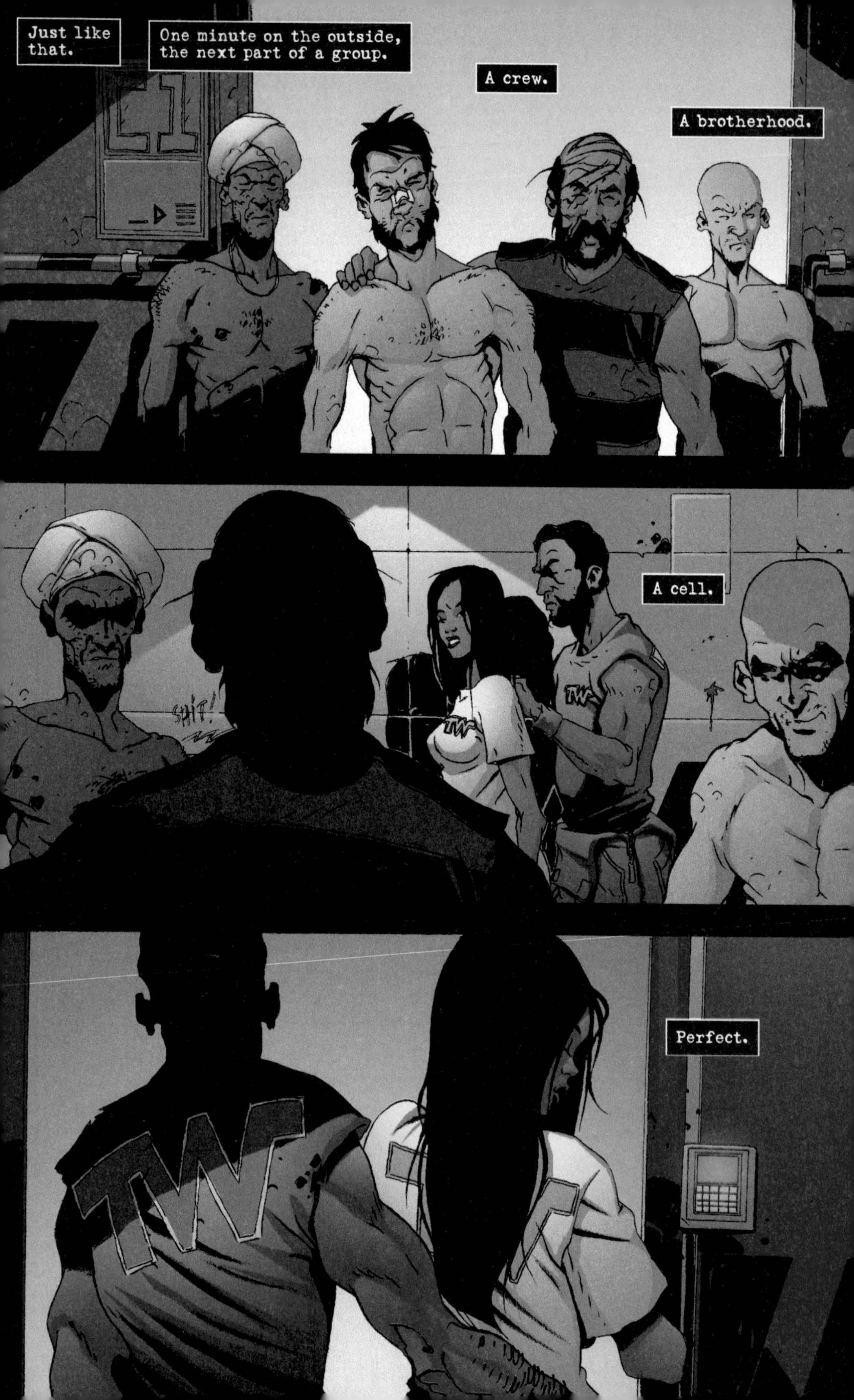
Just like that.
One minute on the outside, the next part of a group.
A crew.
A brotherhood.
A cell.
SHIT!
Perfect.

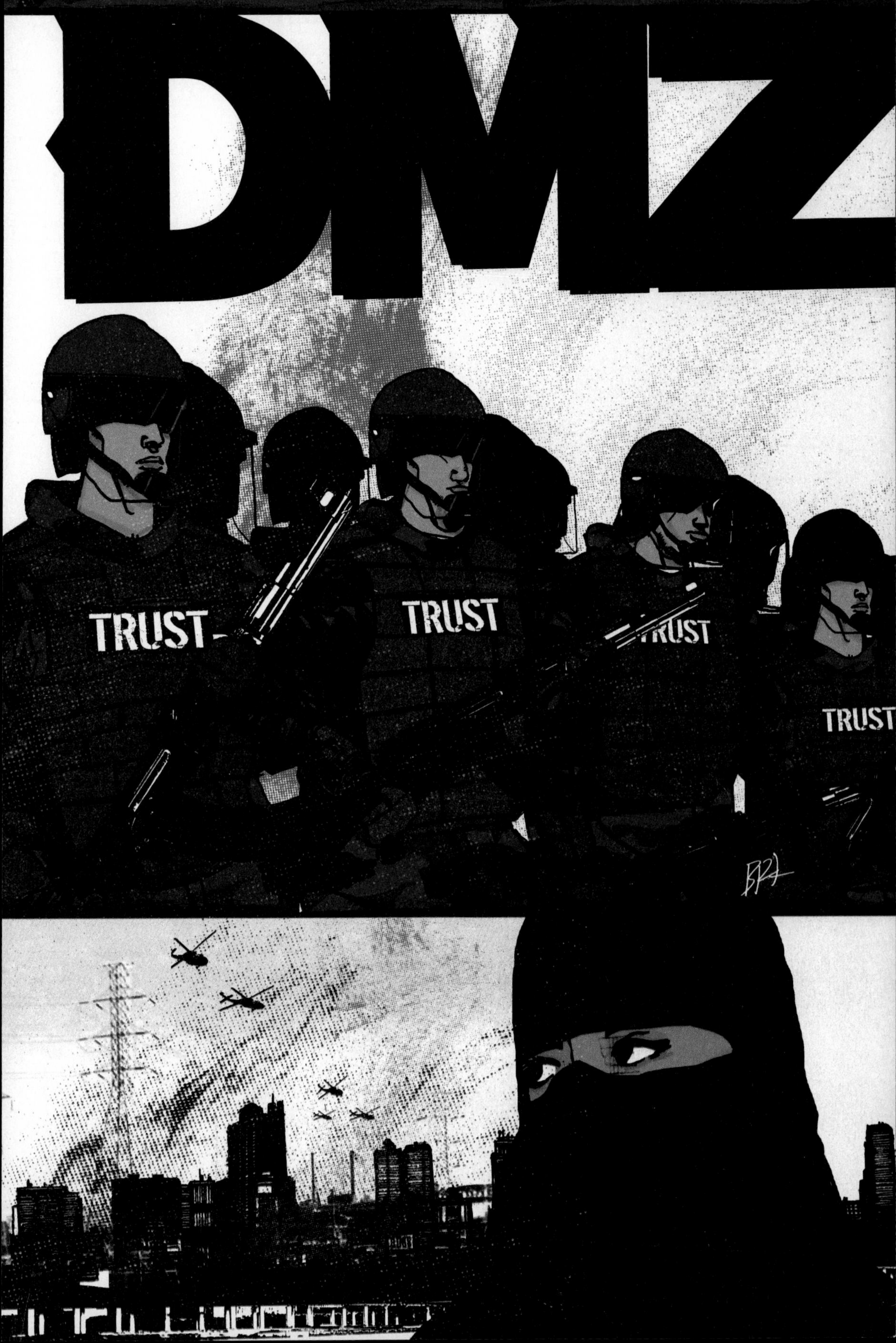
DMZ
TRUST
TRUST
TRUST
TRUST

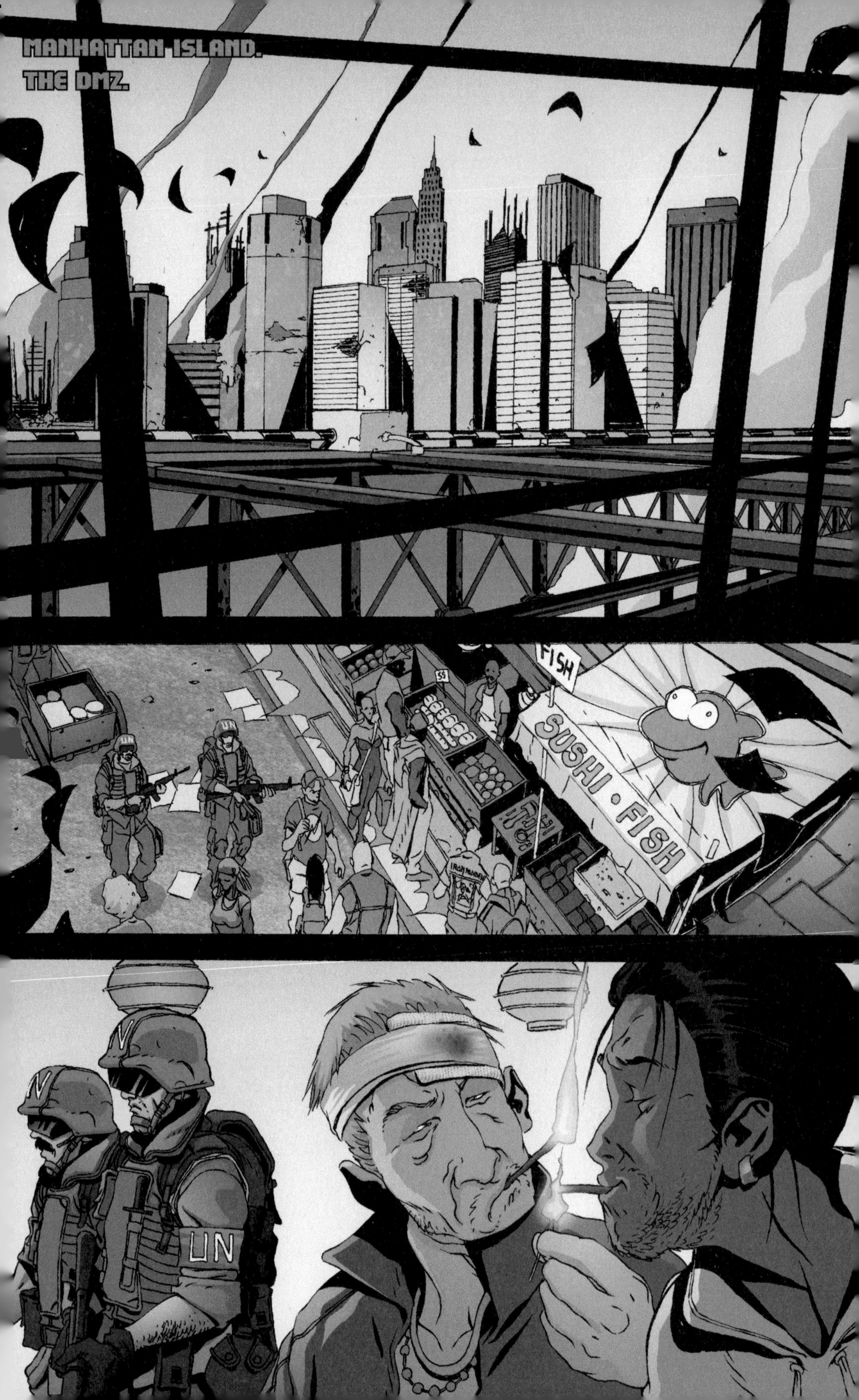
MANHATTAN ISLAND.
THE DMZ.
FISH
SUSHI • FISH
UN

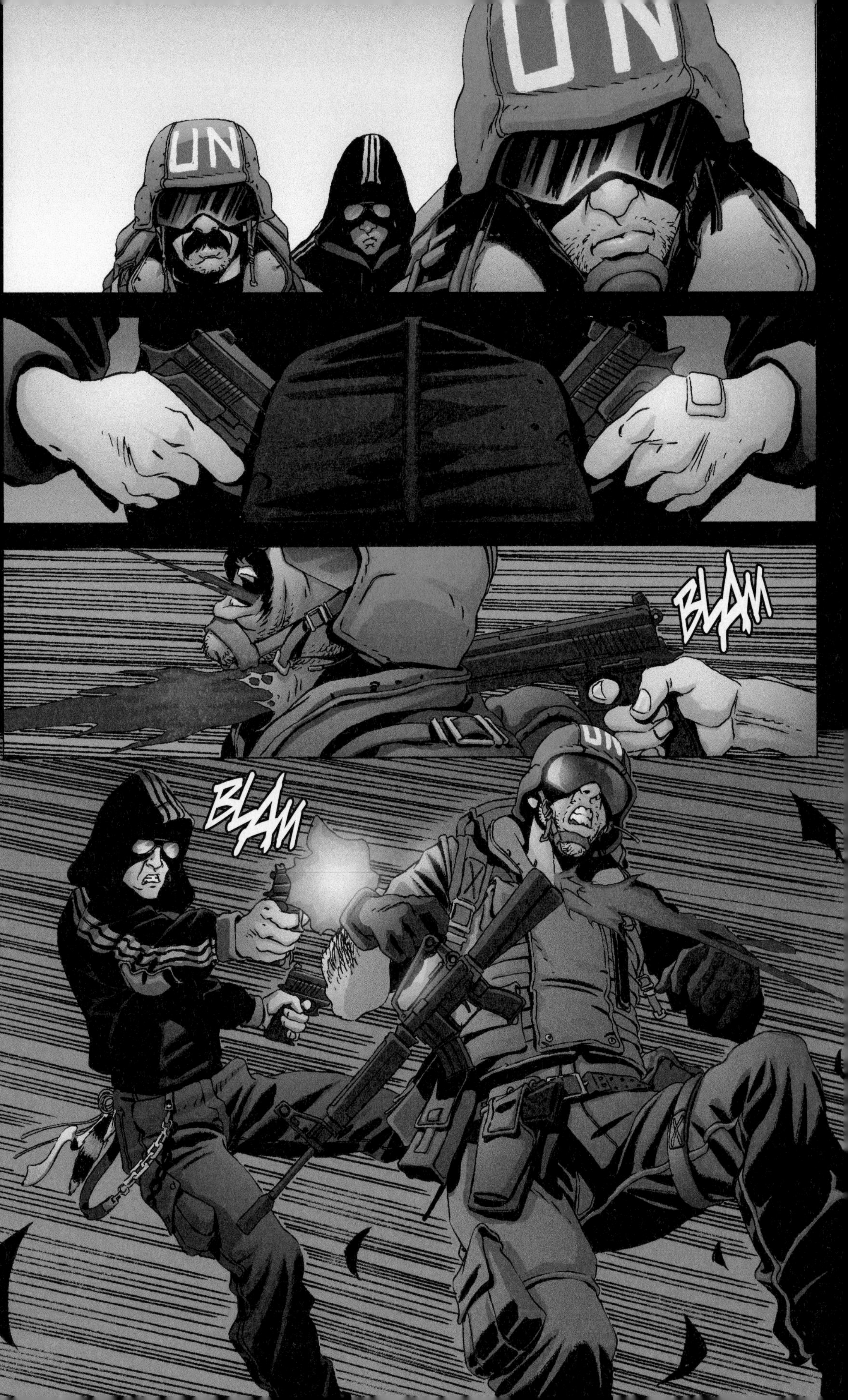
BLAM
BLAM

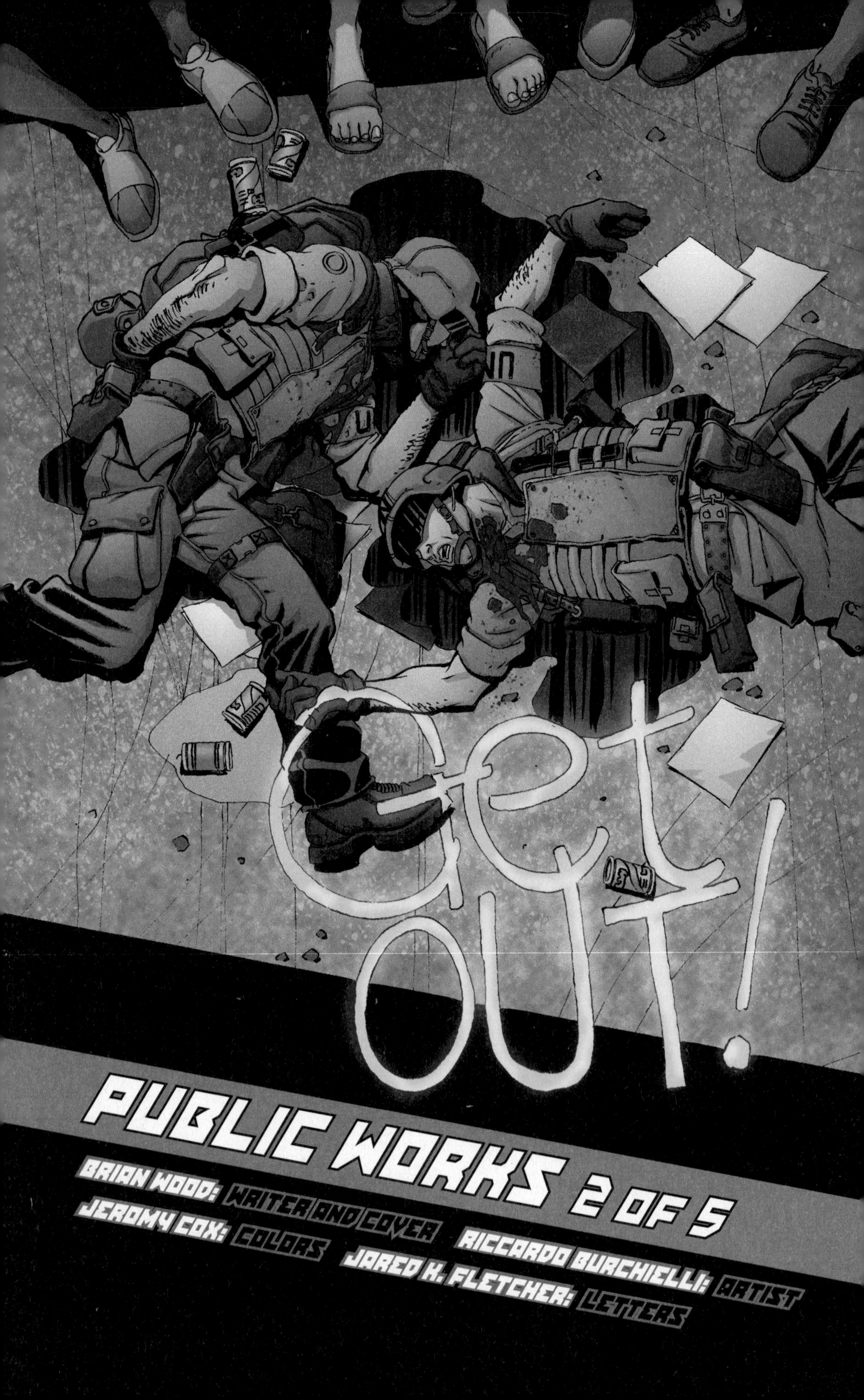
get out!
PUBLIC WORKS 2 OF 5
BRIAN WOOD: WRITER AND COVER
RICCARDO BURCHIELLI: ARTIST
JEROMY COX: COLORS
JARED K. FLETCHER: LETTERS

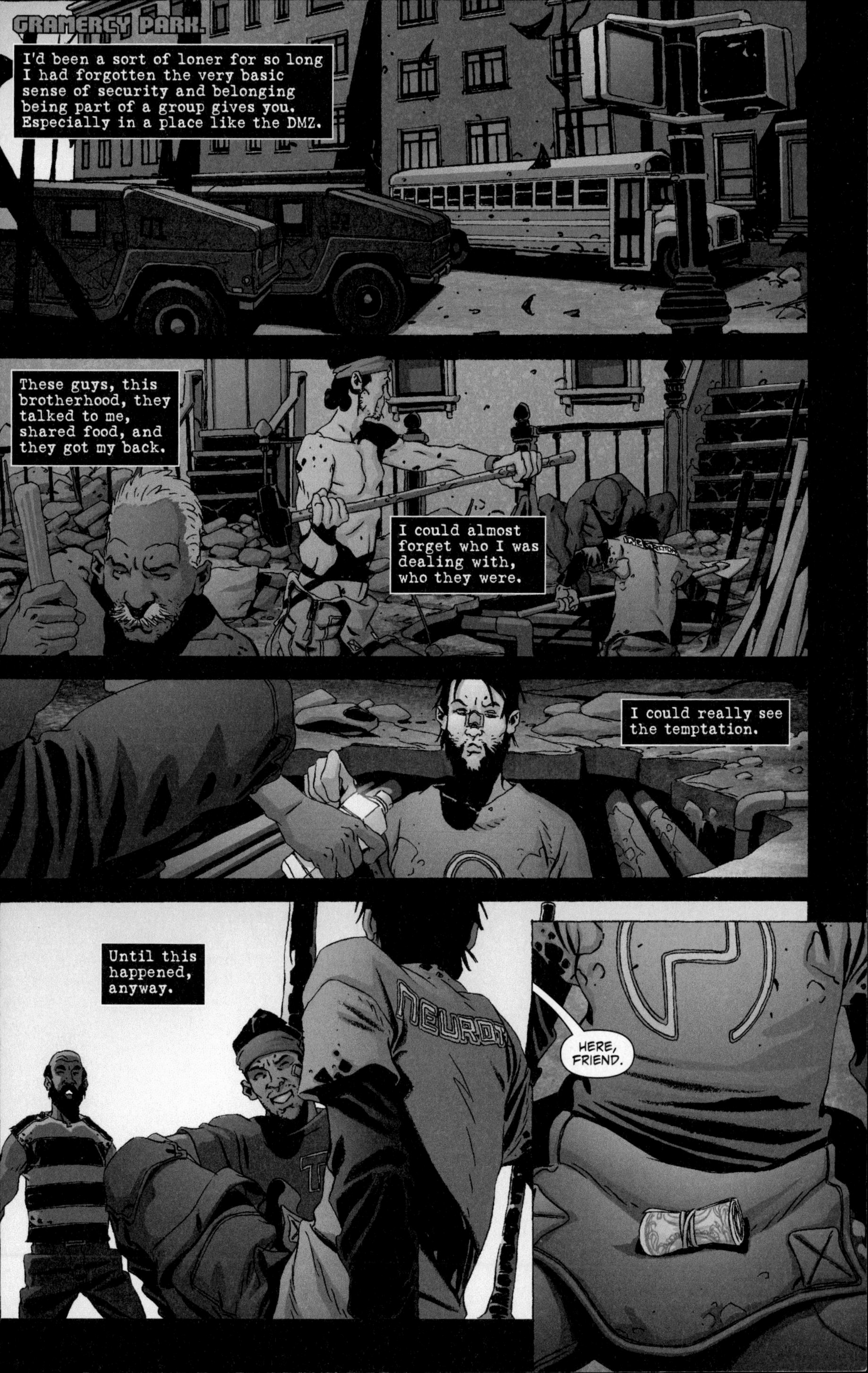
GRAMERCY PARK.
I'd been a sort of loner for so long I had forgotten the very basic sense of security and belonging being part of a group gives you. Especially in a place like the DMZ.
These guys, this brotherhood, they talked to me, shared food, and they got my back.
I could almost forget who I was dealing with, who they were.
I could really see the temptation.
Until this happened, anyway.
HERE, FRIEND.

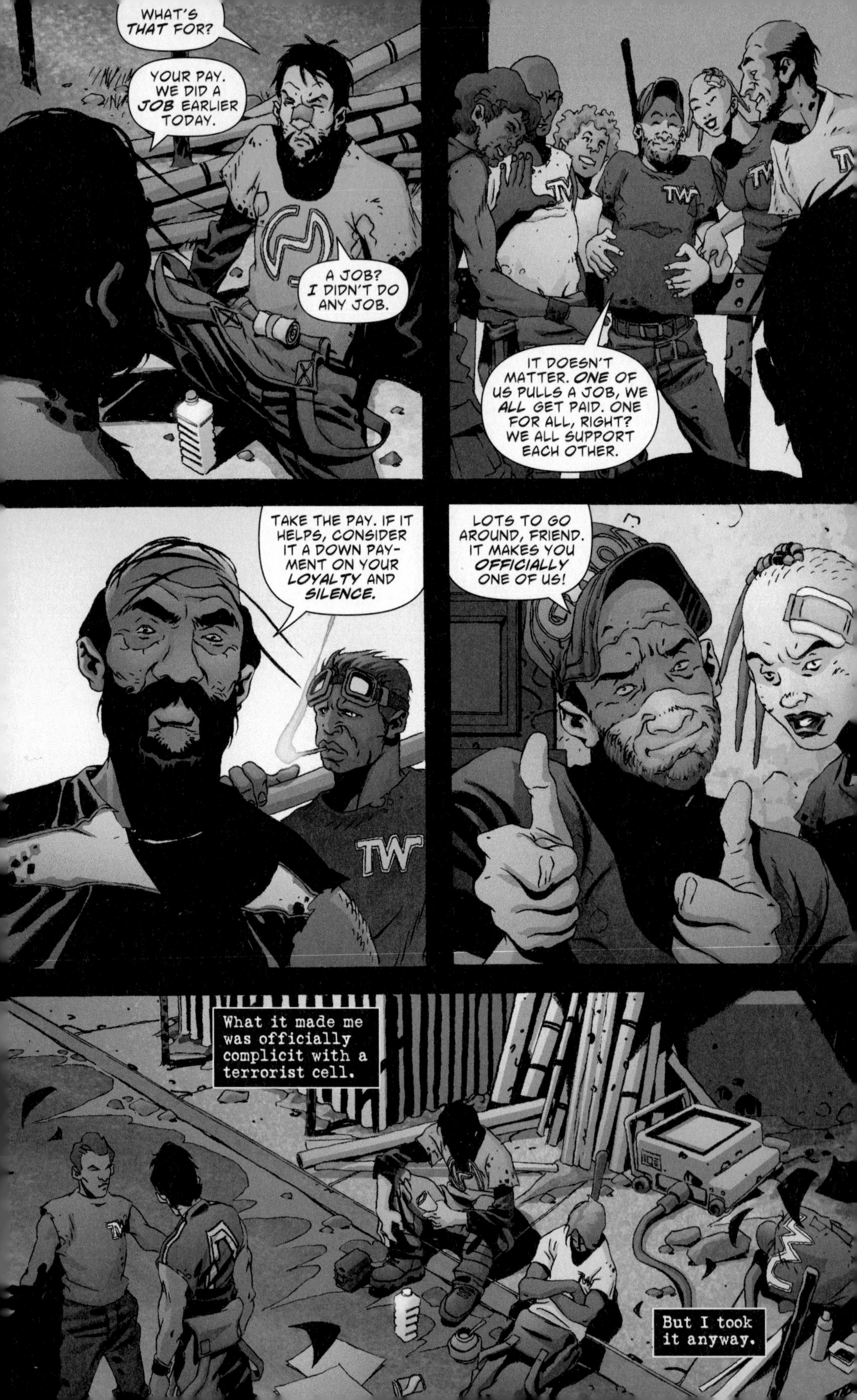
WHAT'S THAT FOR?
YOUR PAY. WE DID A JOB EARLIER TODAY.
A JOB? I DIDN'T DO ANY JOB.
IT DOESN'T MATTER. ONE OF US PULLS A JOB, WE ALL GET PAID. ONE FOR ALL, RIGHT? WE ALL SUPPORT EACH OTHER.
TAKE THE PAY. IF IT HELPS, CONSIDER IT A DOWN PAY-MENT ON YOUR LOYALTY AND SILENCE.
LOTS TO GO AROUND, FRIEND. IT MAKES YOU OFFICIALLY ONE OF US!
What it made me was officially complicit with a terrorist cell.
But I took it anyway.

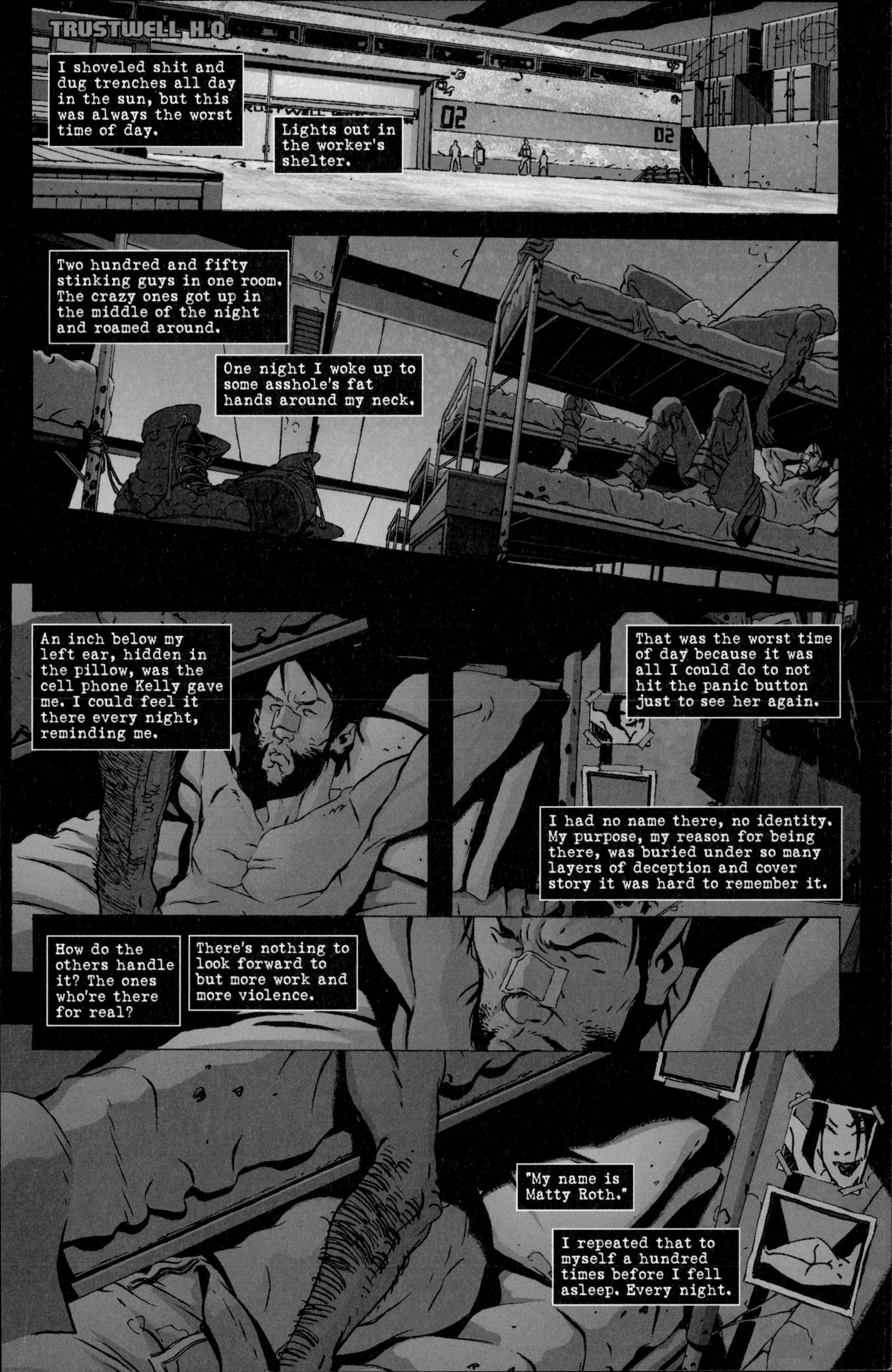
TRUSTWELL H.Q.
I shoveled shit and dug trenches all day in the sun, but this was always the worst time of day.
Lights out in the worker's shelter.
02
02
Two hundred and fifty stinking guys in one room. The crazy ones got up in the middle of the night and roamed around.
One night I woke up to some asshole's fat hands around my neck.
An inch below my left ear, hidden in the pillow, was the cell phone Kelly gave me. I could feel it there every night, reminding me.
That was the worst time of day because it was all I could do to not hit the panic button just to see her again.
I had no name there, no identity. My purpose, my reason for being there, was buried under so many layers of deception and cover story it was hard to remember it.
How do the others handle it? The ones who're there for real?
There's nothing to look forward to but more work and more violence.
"My name is Matty Roth."
I repeated that to myself a hundred times before I fell asleep. Every night.

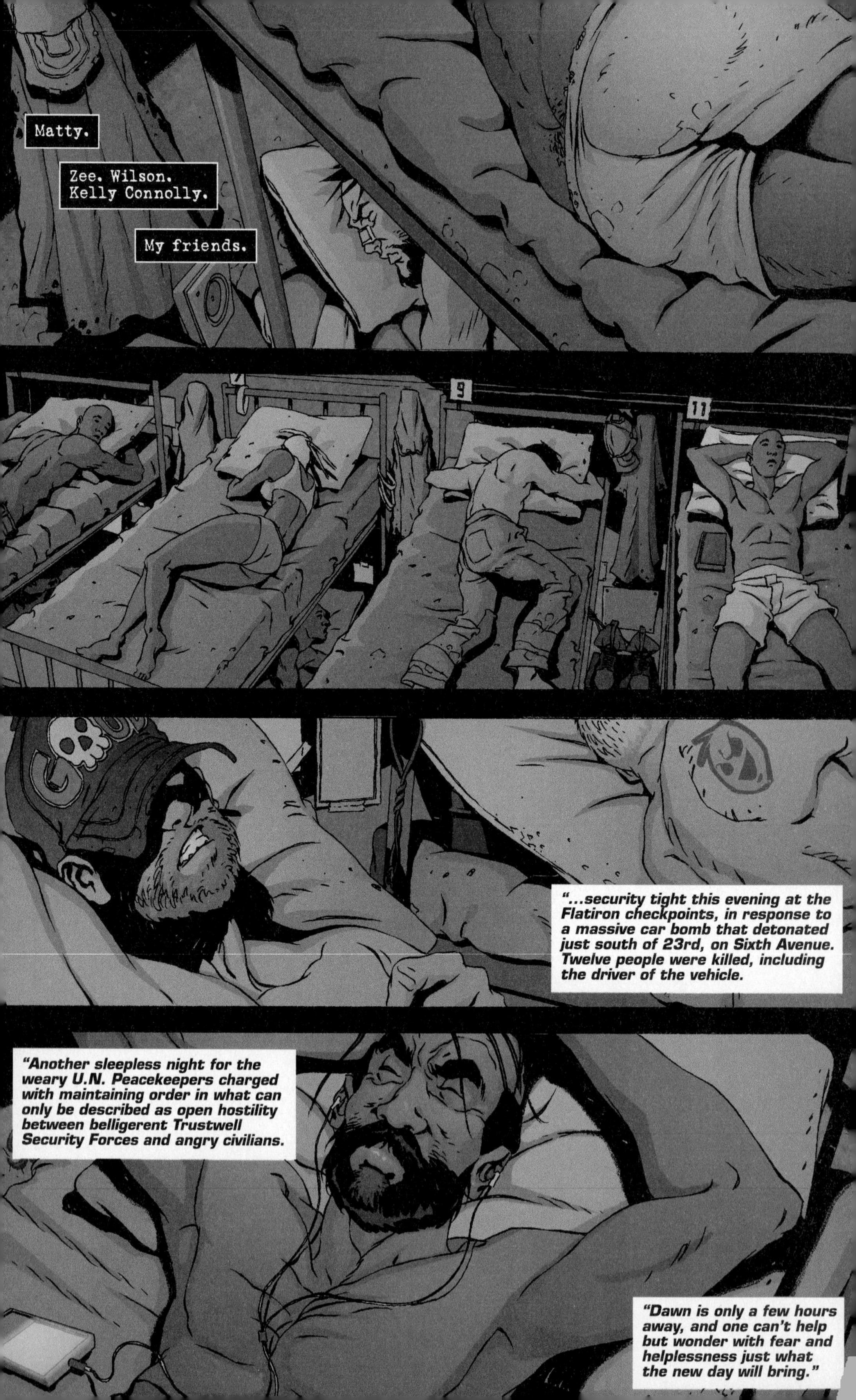
Matty.
Zee. Wilson. Kelly Connolly.
My friends.
9
11
"...security tight this evening at the Flatiron checkpoints, in response to a massive car bomb that detonated just south of 23rd, on Sixth Avenue. Twelve people were killed, including the driver of the vehicle.
"Another sleepless night for the weary U.N. Peacekeepers charged with maintaining order in what can only be described as open hostility between belligerent Trustwell Security Forces and angry civilians.
"Dawn is only a few hours away, and one can't help but wonder with fear and helplessness just what the new day will bring."

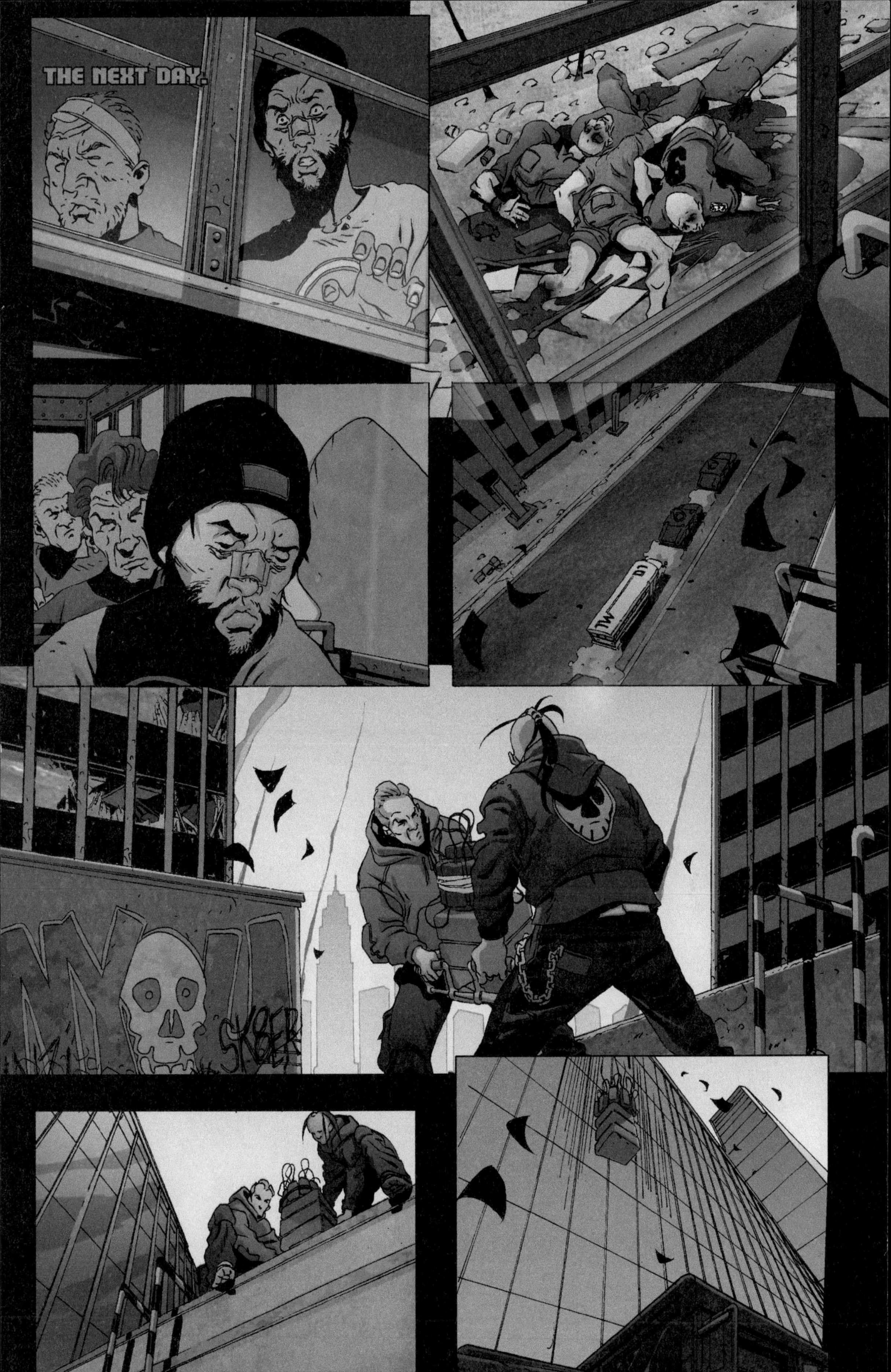
THE NEXT DAY.
SKBER

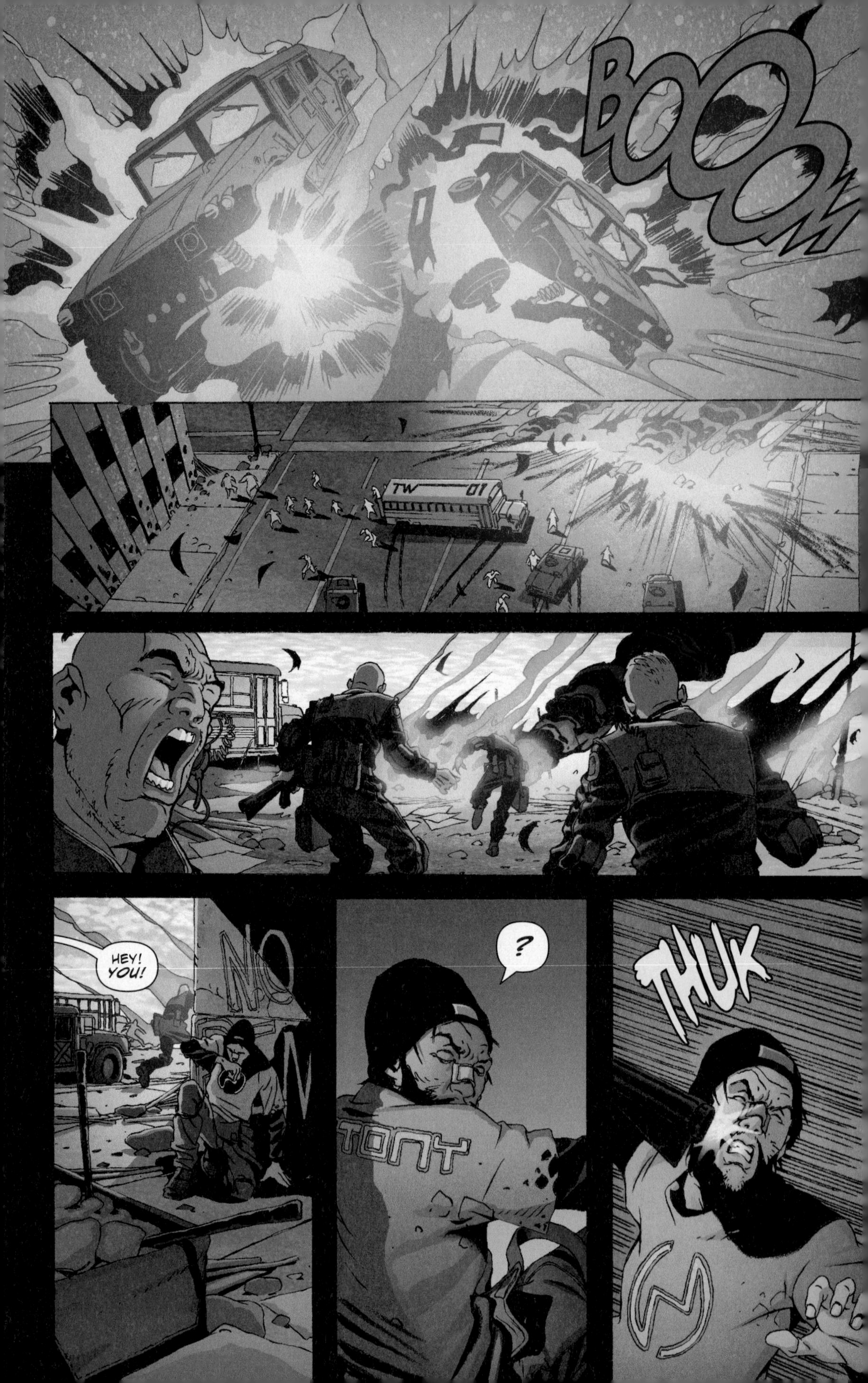
BOOOOM
TW 01
HEY! YOU!
NO
?
TONY
THUK

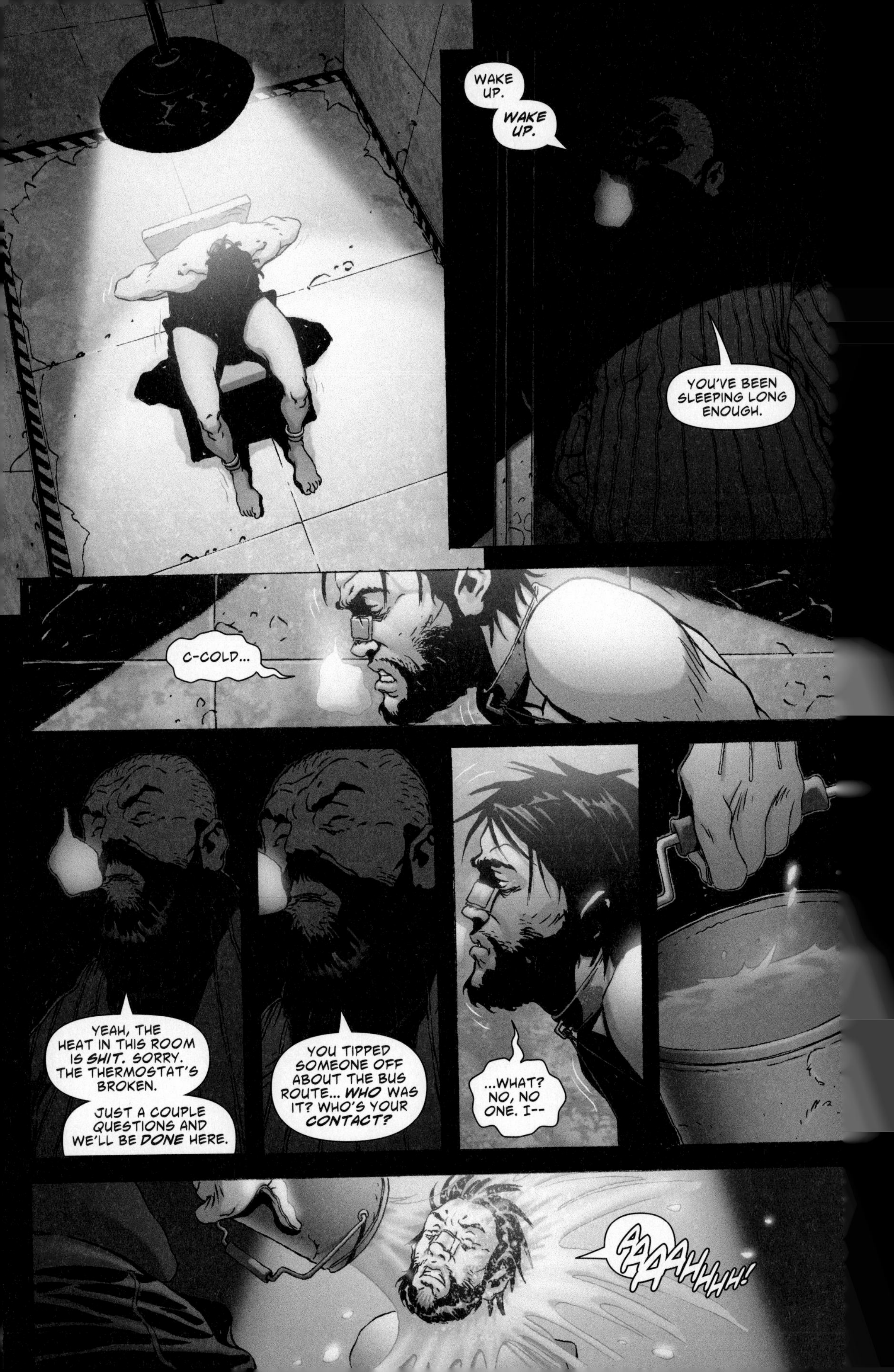
WAKE UP.
WAKE UP.
YOU'VE BEEN SLEEPING LONG ENOUGH.
C-COLD...
YEAH, THE HEAT IN THIS ROOM IS SHIT. SORRY. THE THERMOSTAT'S BROKEN.
JUST A COUPLE QUESTIONS AND WE'LL BE DONE HERE.
YOU TIPPED SOMEONE OFF ABOUT THE BUS ROUTE... WHO WAS IT? WHO'S YOUR CONTACT?
...WHAT? NO, NO ONE. I--
AAAAHHHH!

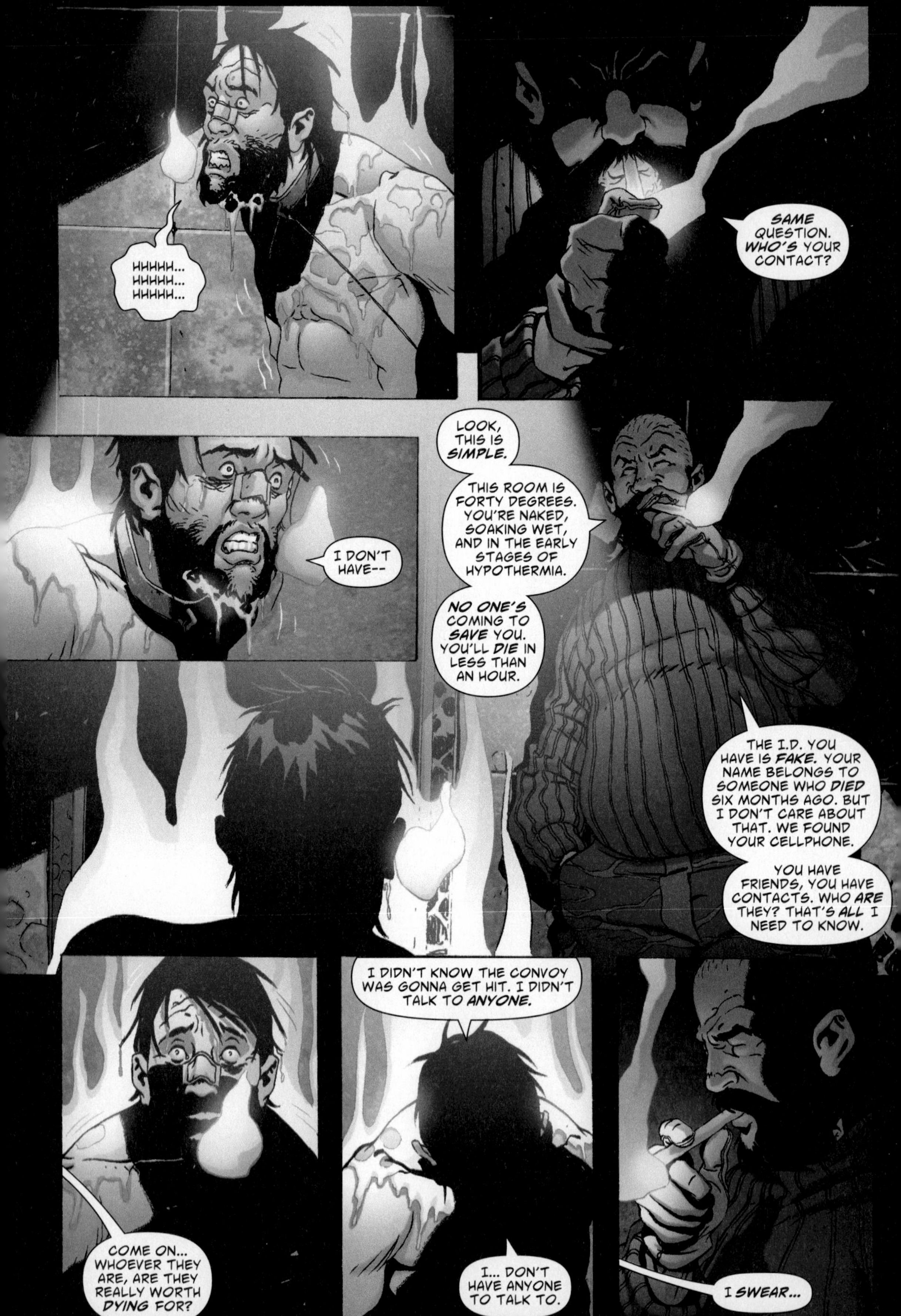
HHHHH... HHHHH... HHHHH...
SAME QUESTION. WHO'S YOUR CONTACT?
I DON'T HAVE--
LOOK, THIS IS SIMPLE.
THIS ROOM IS FORTY DEGREES. YOU'RE NAKED, SOAKING WET, AND IN THE EARLY STAGES OF HYPOTHERMIA.
NO ONE'S COMING TO SAVE YOU. YOU'LL DIE IN LESS THAN AN HOUR.
THE I.D. YOU HAVE IS FAKE. YOUR NAME BELONGS TO SOMEONE WHO DIED SIX MONTHS AGO. BUT I DON'T CARE ABOUT THAT. WE FOUND YOUR CELLPHONE.
YOU HAVE FRIENDS, YOU HAVE CONTACTS. WHO ARE THEY? THAT'S ALL I NEED TO KNOW.
COME ON... WHOEVER THEY ARE, ARE THEY REALLY WORTH DYING FOR?
I DIDN'T KNOW THE CONVOY WAS GONNA GET HIT. I DIDN'T TALK TO ANYONE.
I... DON'T HAVE ANYONE TO TALK TO.
I SWEAR...

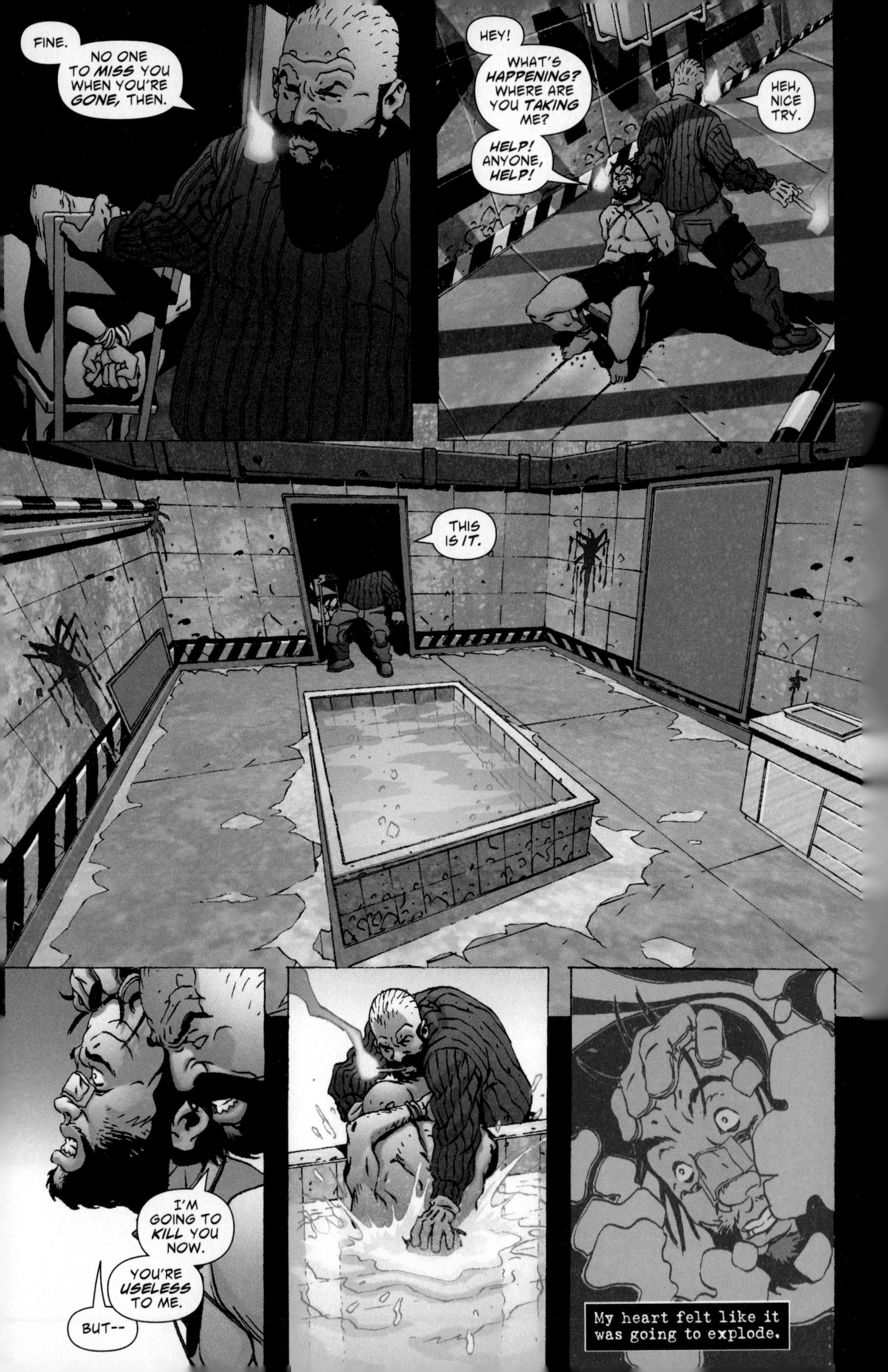
FINE.
NO ONE TO MISS YOU WHEN YOU'RE GONE, THEN.
HEY!
WHAT'S HAPPENING? WHERE ARE YOU TAKING ME?
HELP! ANYONE, HELP!
HEH, NICE TRY.
THIS IS IT.
I'M GOING TO KILL YOU NOW.
YOU'RE USELESS TO ME.
BUT--
My heart felt like it was going to explode.

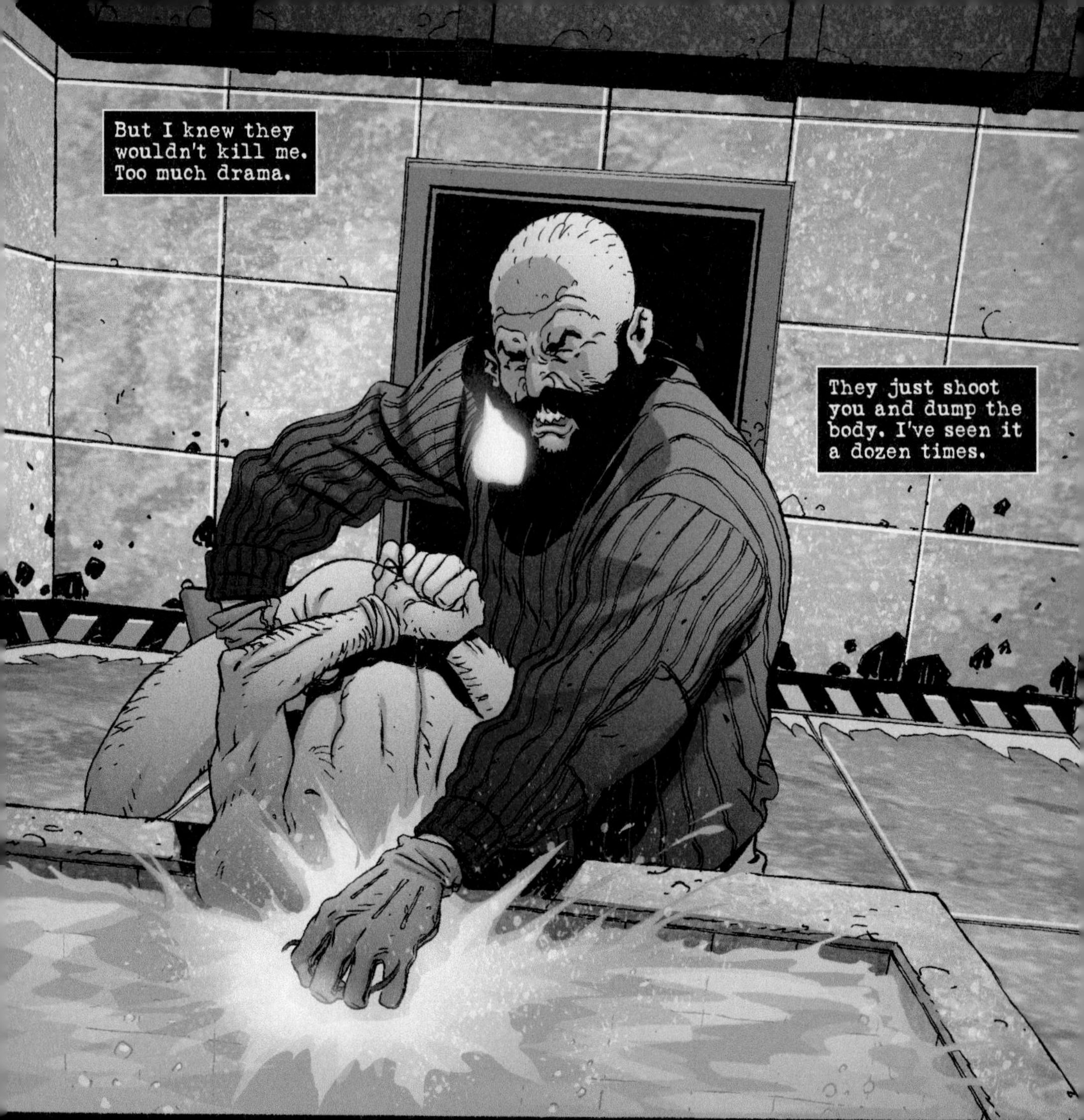
But I knew they wouldn't kill me. Too much drama.
They just shoot you and dump the body. I've seen it a dozen times.

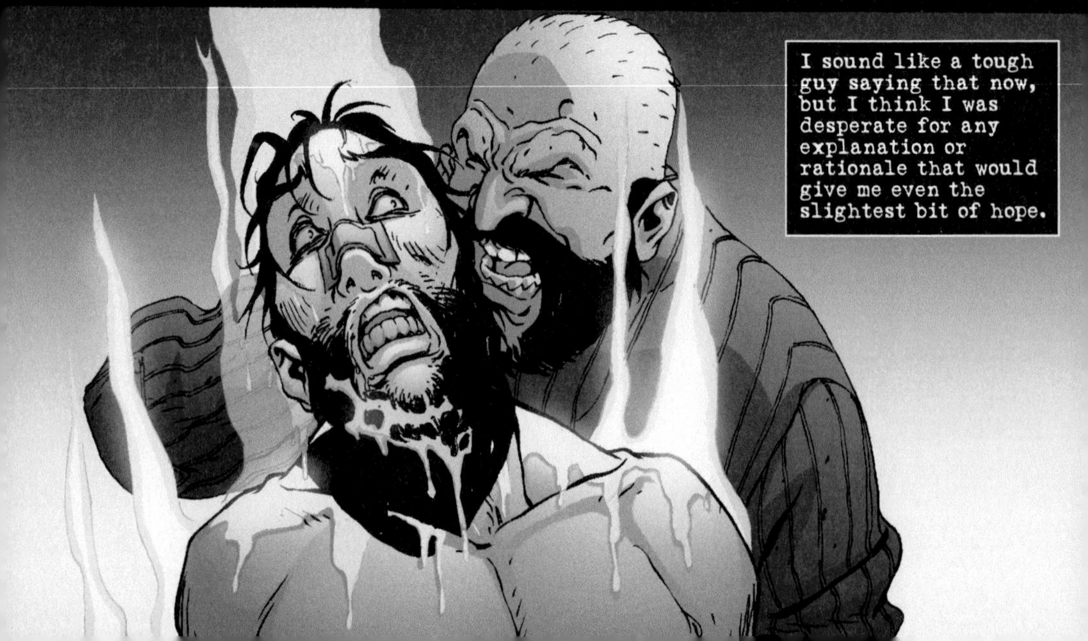
I sound like a tough guy saying that now, but I think I was desperate for any explanation or rationale that would give me even the slightest bit of hope.

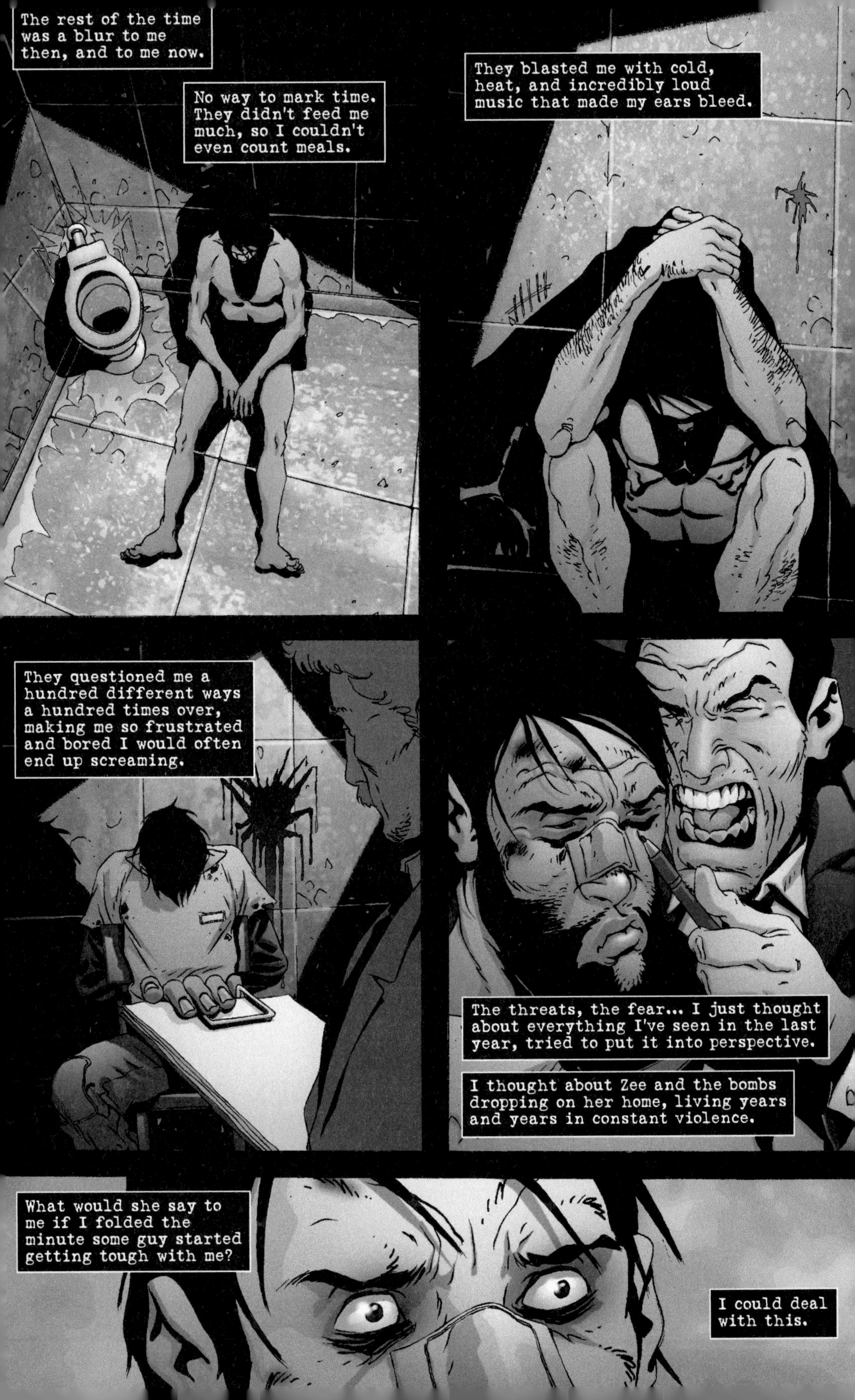
The rest of the time was a blur to me then, and to me now.
No way to mark time. They didn't feed me much, so I couldn't even count meals.
They blasted me with cold, heat, and incredibly loud music that made my ears bleed.
They questioned me a hundred different ways a hundred times over, making me so frustrated and bored I would often end up screaming.
The threats, the fear... I just thought about everything I've seen in the last year, tried to put it into perspective.
I thought about Zee and the bombs dropping on her home, living years and years in constant violence.
What would she say to me if I folded the minute some guy started getting tough with me?
I could deal with this.

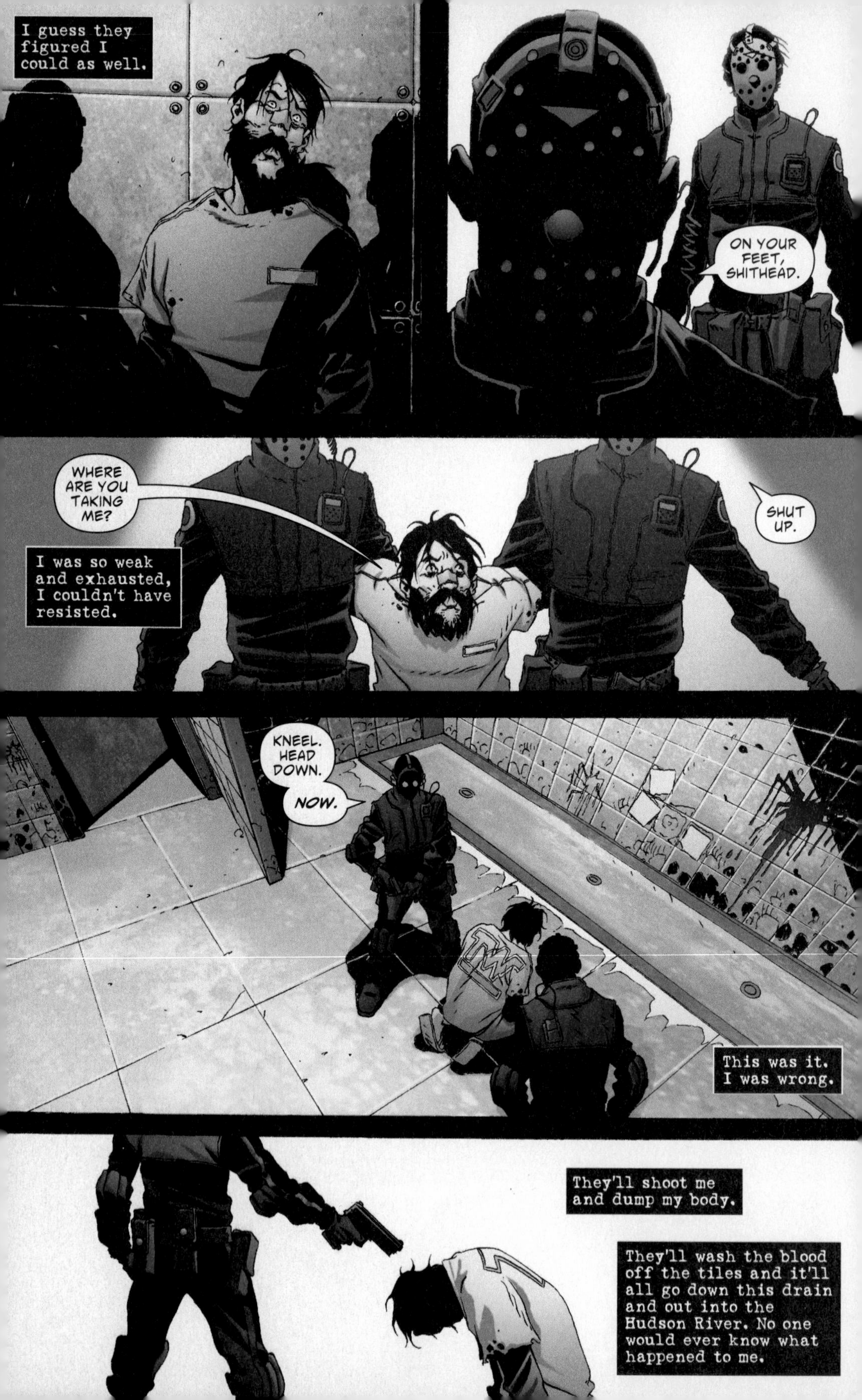
I guess they figured I could as well.
ON YOUR FEET, SHITHEAD.
WHERE ARE YOU TAKING ME?
I was so weak and exhausted, I couldn't have resisted.
SHUT UP.
KNEEL. HEAD DOWN.
NOW.
This was it. I was wrong.
They'll shoot me and dump my body.
They'll wash the blood off the tiles and it'll all go down this drain and out into the Hudson River. No one would ever know what happened to me.

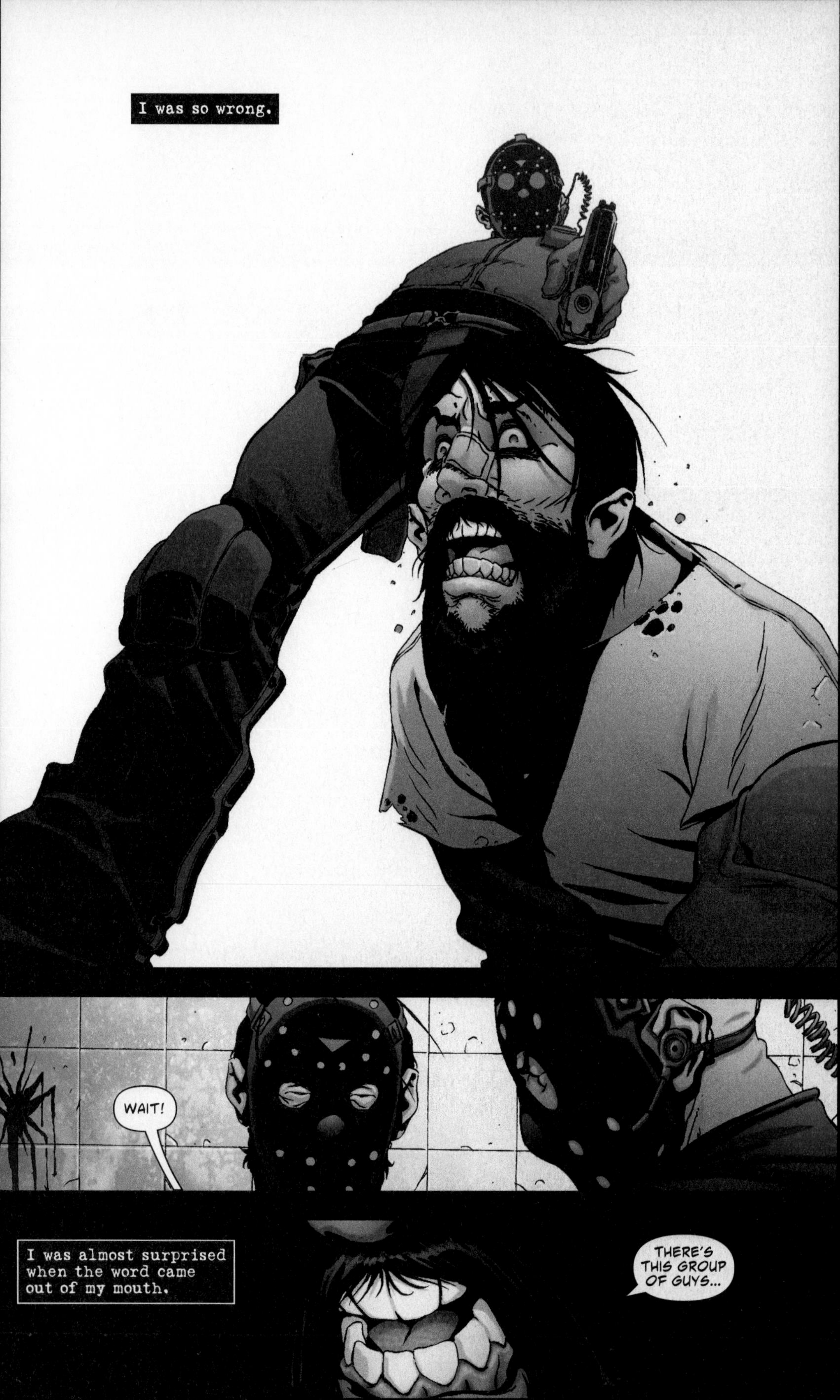
I was so wrong.
WAIT!
I was almost surprised when the word came out of my mouth.
THERE'S THIS GROUP OF GUYS...

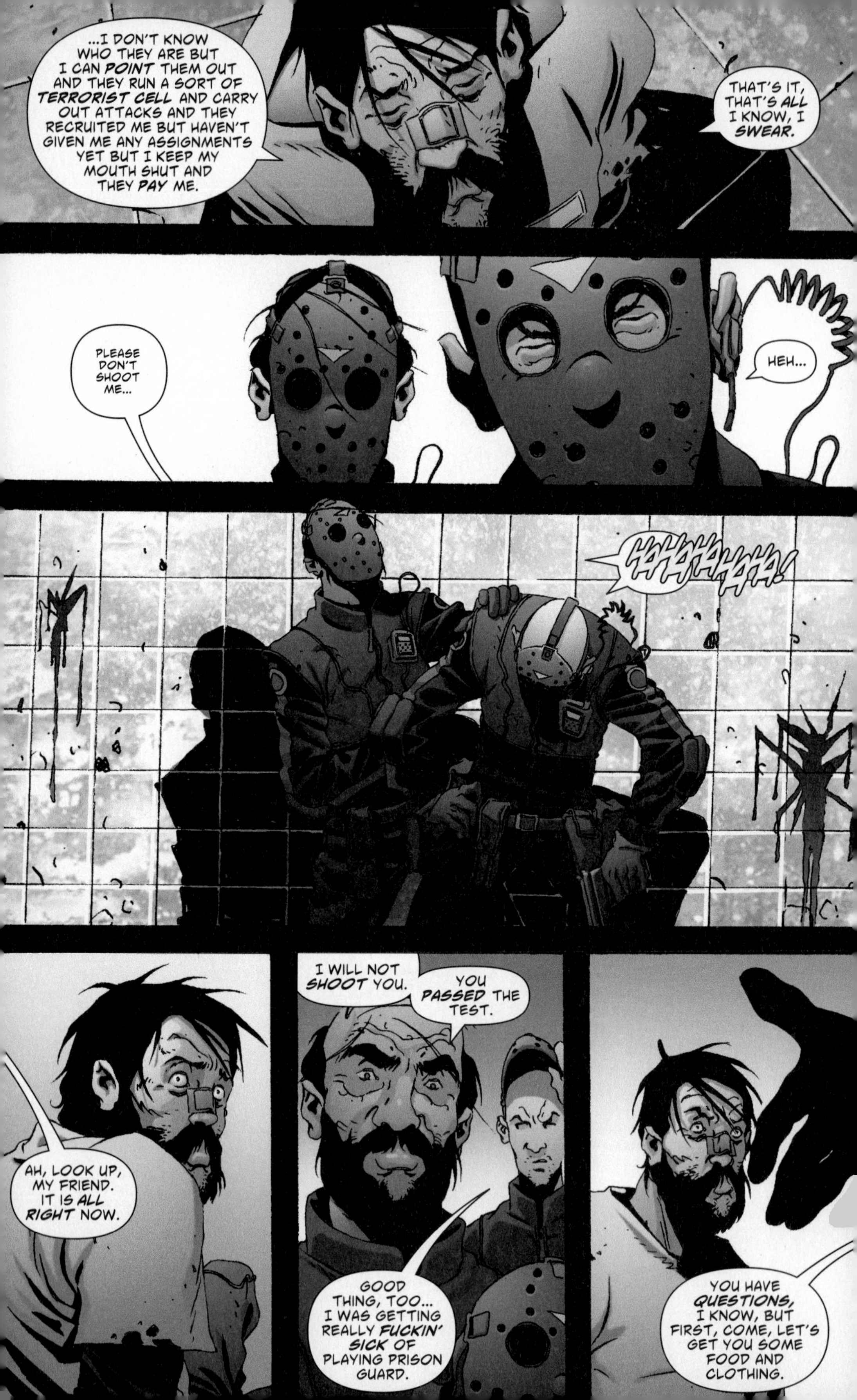
...I DON'T KNOW WHO THEY ARE BUT I CAN POINT THEM OUT AND THEY RUN A SORT OF TERRORIST CELL AND CARRY OUT ATTACKS AND THEY RECRUITED ME BUT HAVEN'T GIVEN ME ANY ASSIGNMENTS YET BUT I KEEP MY MOUTH SHUT AND THEY PAY ME.
THAT'S IT, THAT'S ALL I KNOW, I SWEAR.
PLEASE DON'T SHOOT ME...
HEH...
HAHAHAHAHA!
I WILL NOT SHOOT YOU.
YOU PASSED THE TEST.
AH, LOOK UP, MY FRIEND. IT IS ALL RIGHT NOW.
GOOD THING, TOO... I WAS GETTING REALLY FUCKIN' SICK OF PLAYING PRISON GUARD.
YOU HAVE QUESTIONS, I KNOW, BUT FIRST, COME, LET'S GET YOU SOME FOOD AND CLOTHING.

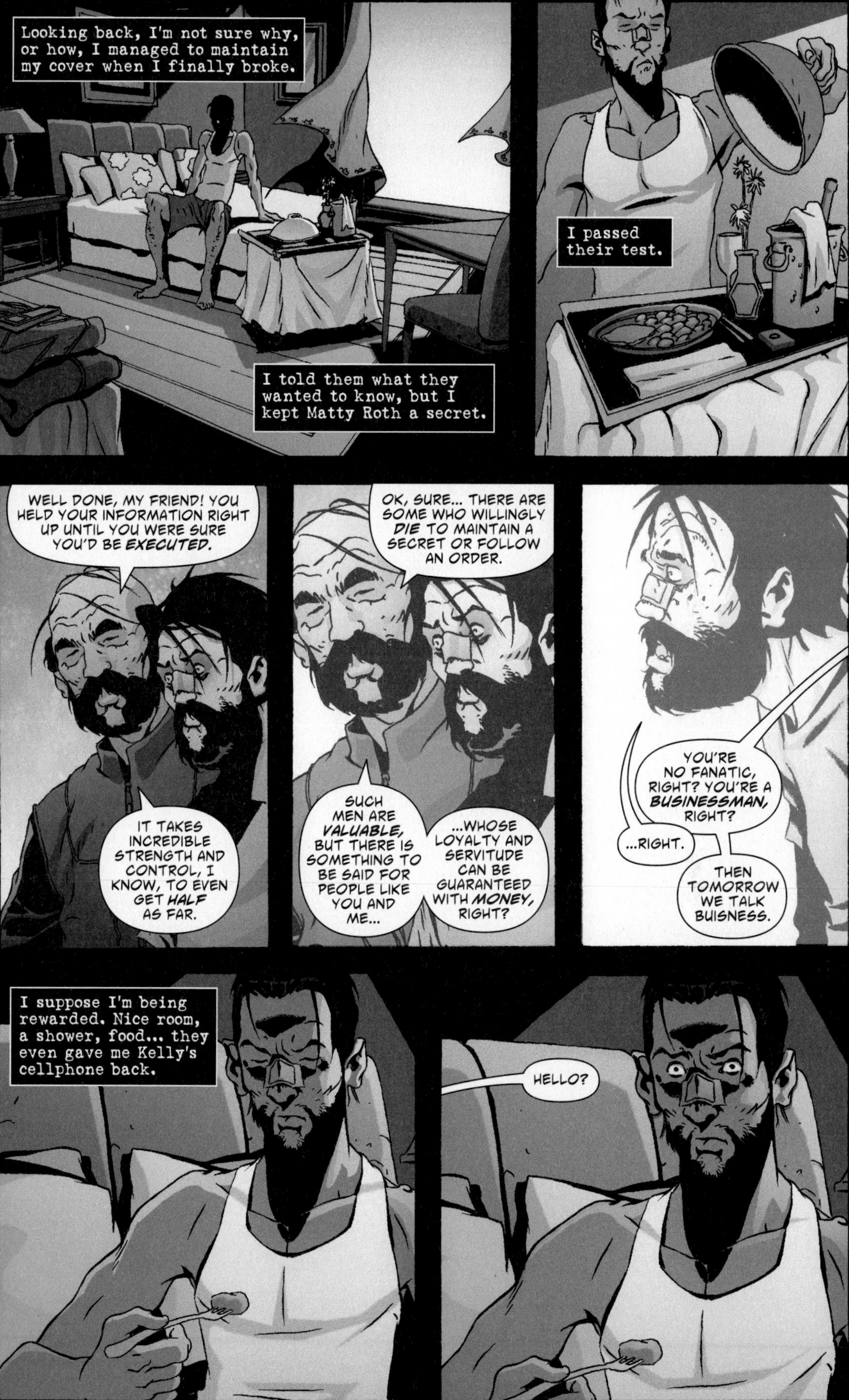
Looking back, I'm not sure why, or how, I managed to maintain my cover when I finally broke.
I told them what they wanted to know, but I kept Matty Roth a secret.
I passed their test.
WELL DONE, MY FRIEND! YOU HELD YOUR INFORMATION RIGHT UP UNTIL YOU WERE SURE YOU'D BE EXECUTED.
IT TAKES INCREDIBLE STRENGTH AND CONTROL, I KNOW, TO EVEN GET HALF AS FAR.
OK, SURE... THERE ARE SOME WHO WILLINGLY DIE TO MAINTAIN A SECRET OR FOLLOW AN ORDER.
SUCH MEN ARE VALUABLE, BUT THERE IS SOMETHING TO BE SAID FOR PEOPLE LIKE YOU AND ME...
...WHOSE LOYALTY AND SERVITUDE CAN BE GUARANTEED WITH MONEY, RIGHT?
YOU'RE NO FANATIC, RIGHT? YOU'RE A BUSINESSMAN, RIGHT?
...RIGHT.
THEN TOMORROW WE TALK BUISNESS.
I suppose I'm being rewarded. Nice room, a shower, food... they even gave me Kelly's cellphone back.
HELLO?

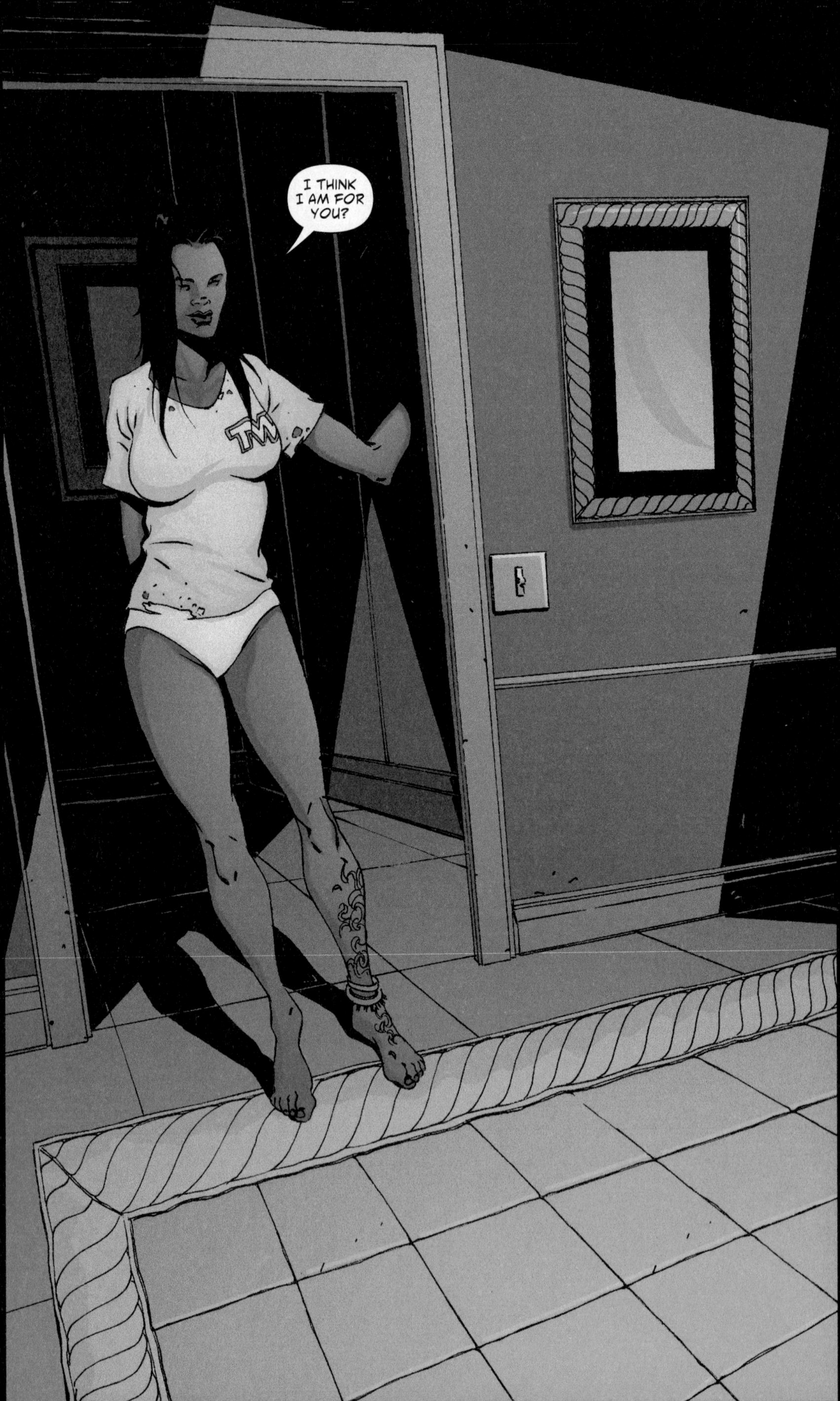
I THINK I AM FOR YOU?

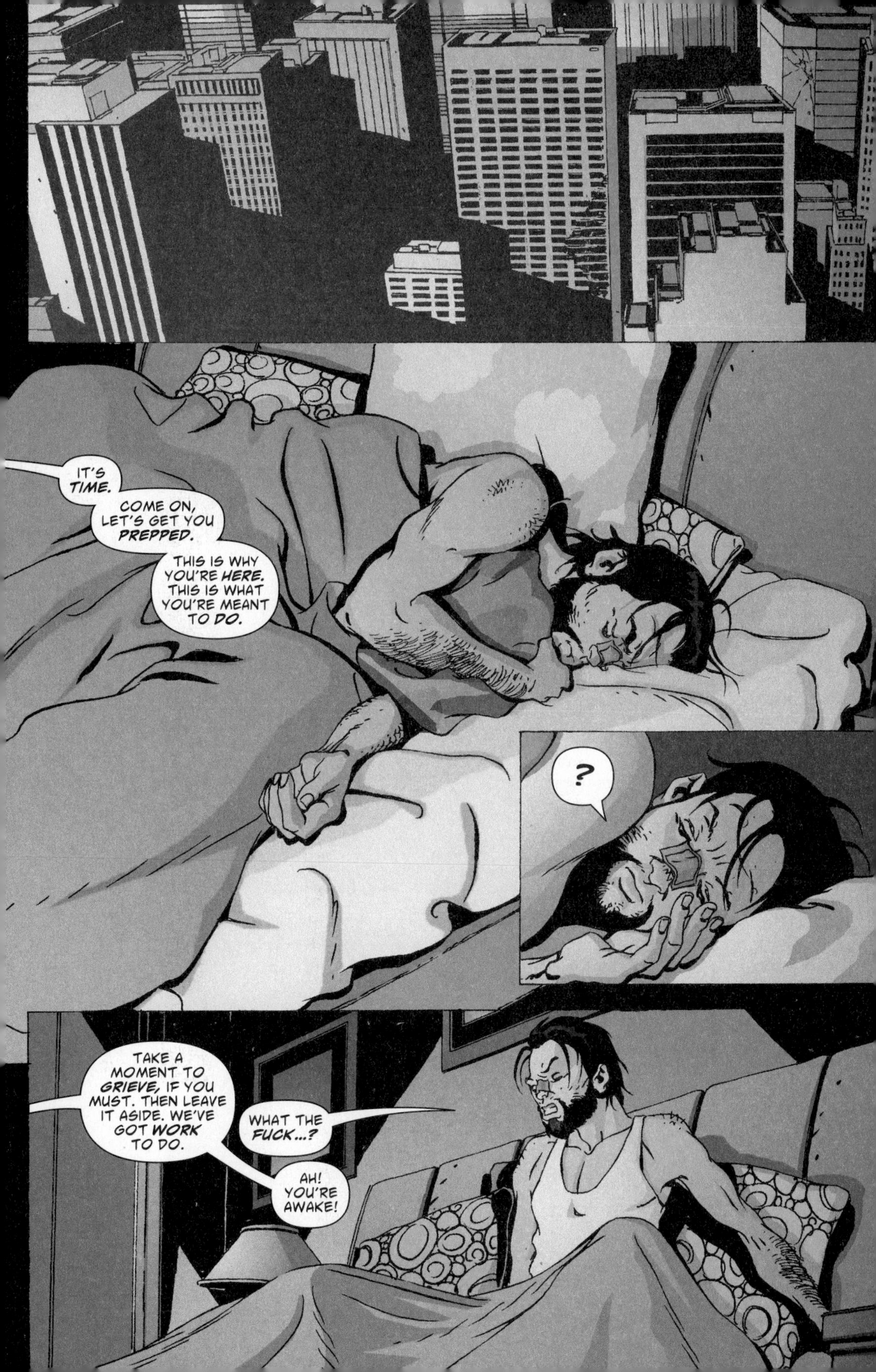
IT'S TIME.
COME ON, LET'S GET YOU PREPPED.
THIS IS WHY YOU'RE HERE. THIS IS WHAT YOU'RE MEANT TO DO.
?
TAKE A MOMENT TO GRIEVE, IF YOU MUST. THEN LEAVE IT ASIDE. WE'VE GOT WORK TO DO.
WHAT THE FUCK...?
AH! YOU'RE AWAKE!

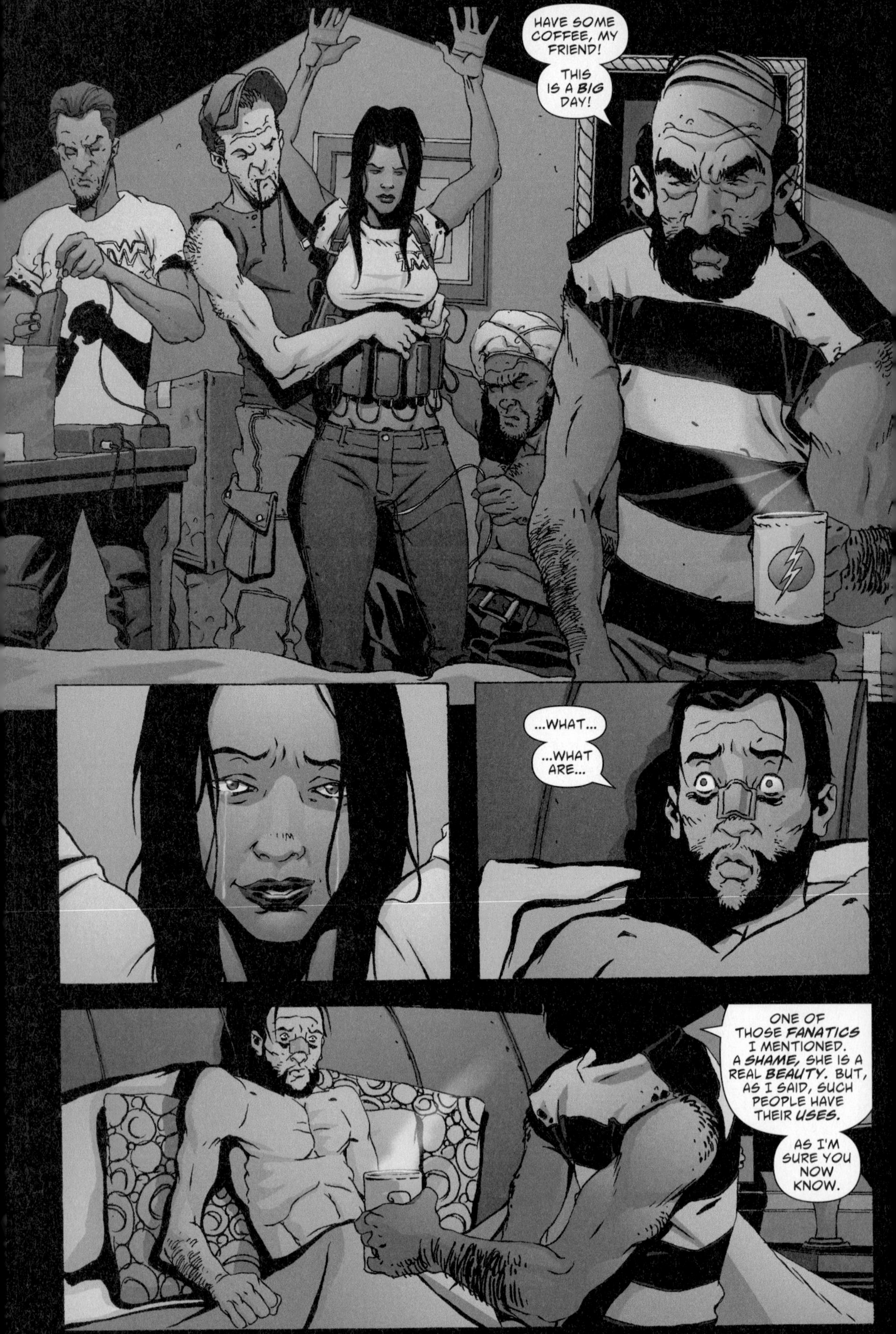
HAVE SOME COFFEE, MY FRIEND!
THIS IS A BIG DAY!
...WHAT...
...WHAT ARE...
ONE OF THOSE FANATICS I MENTIONED. A SHAME, SHE IS A REAL BEAUTY. BUT, AS I SAID, SUCH PEOPLE HAVE THEIR USES.
AS I'M SURE YOU NOW KNOW.

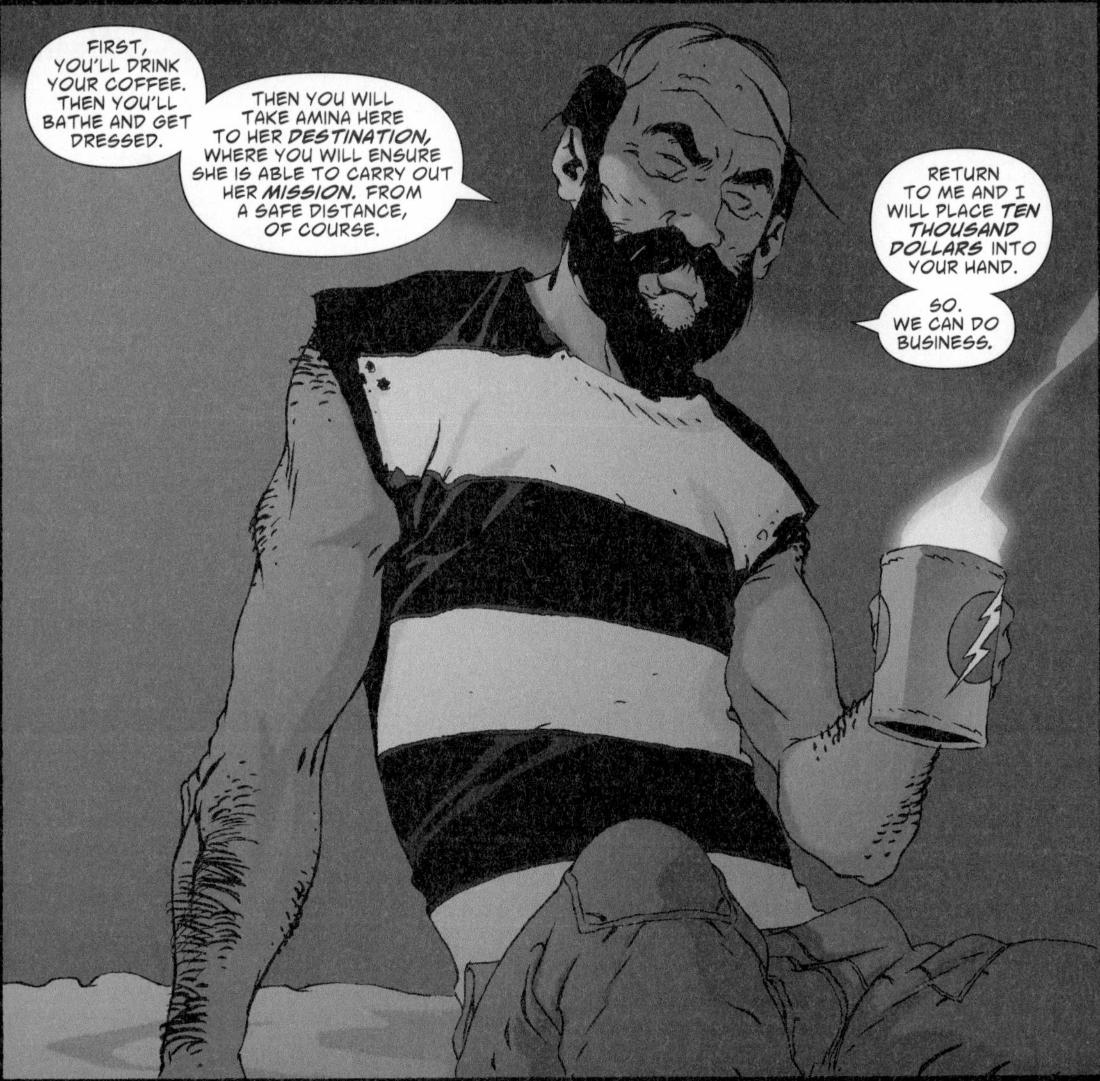
FIRST, YOU'LL DRINK YOUR COFFEE. THEN YOU'LL BATHE AND GET DRESSED.
THEN YOU WILL TAKE AMINA HERE TO HER DESTINATION, WHERE YOU WILL ENSURE SHE IS ABLE TO CARRY OUT HER MISSION. FROM A SAFE DISTANCE, OF COURSE.
RETURN TO ME AND I WILL PLACE TEN THOUSAND DOLLARS INTO YOUR HAND.
SO. WE CAN DO BUSINESS.

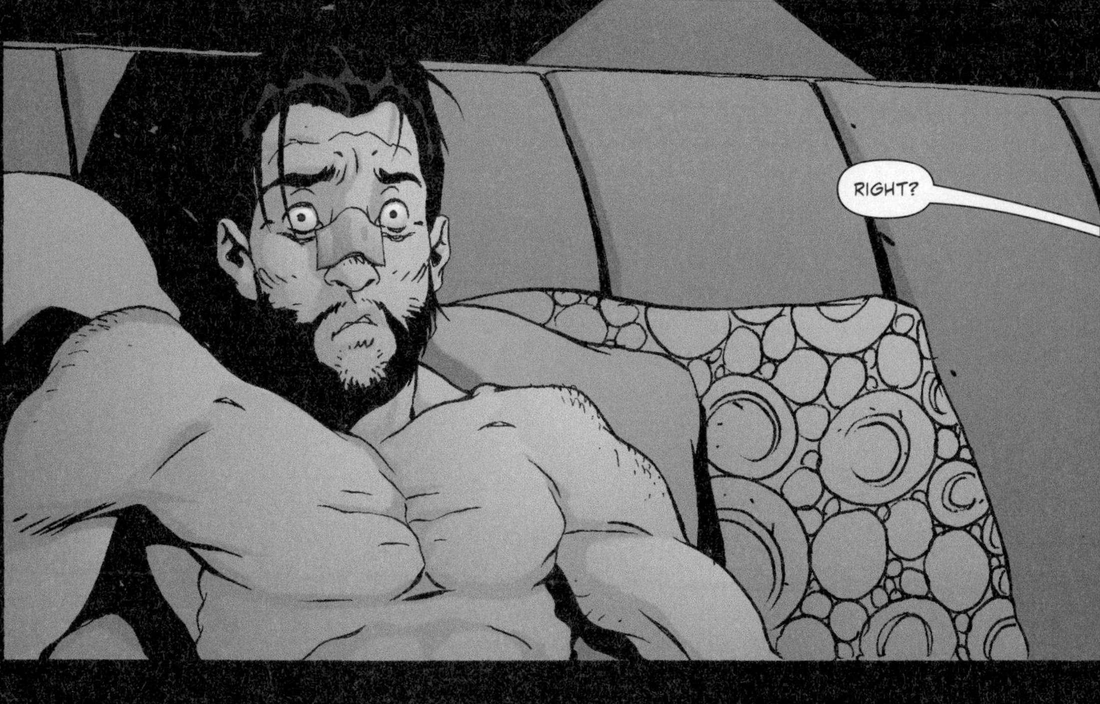
RIGHT?

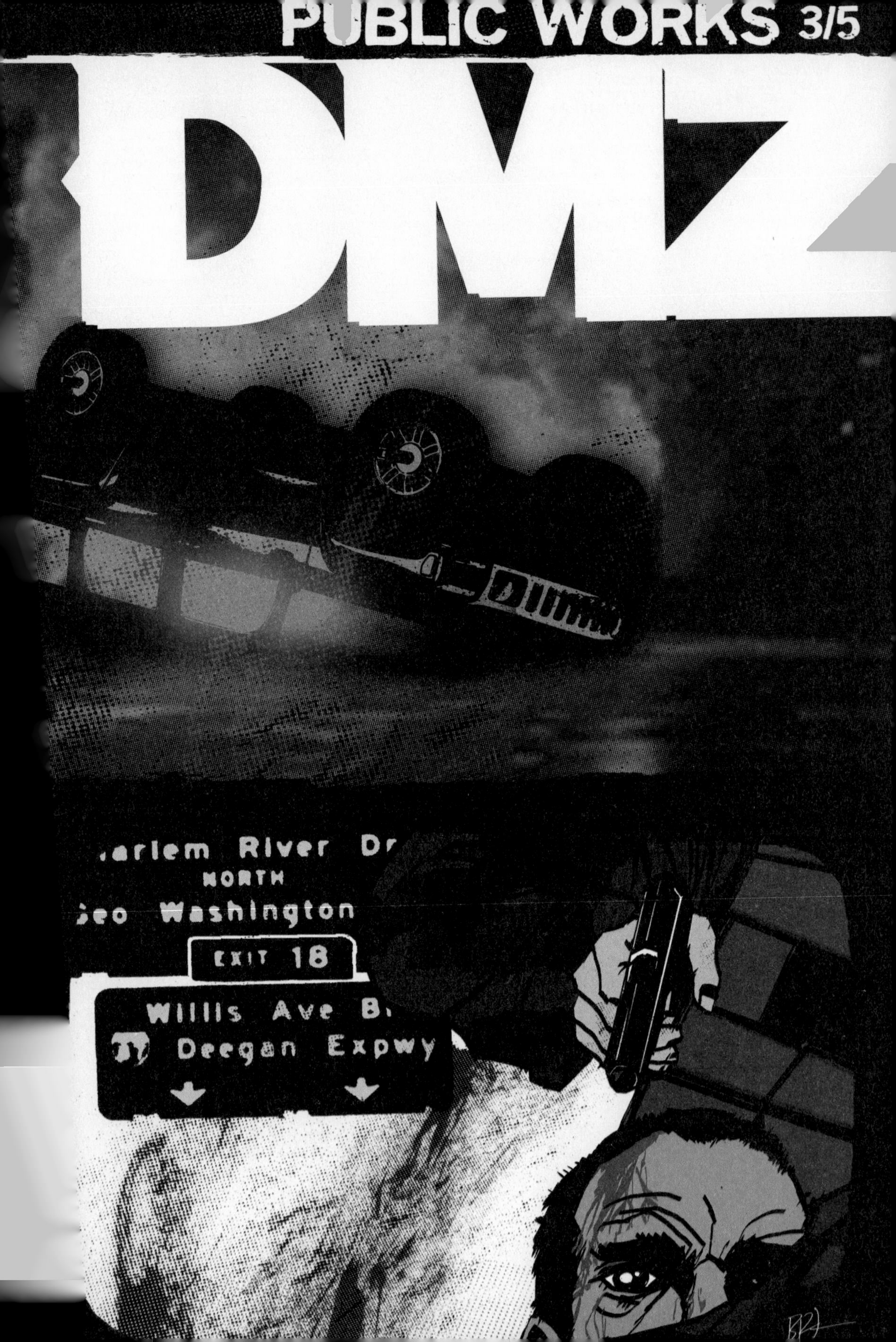
PUBLIC WORKS 3/5
DMZ
arlem River Dr
NORTH
eo Washington
EXIT 18
Willis Ave B
Deegan Expwy

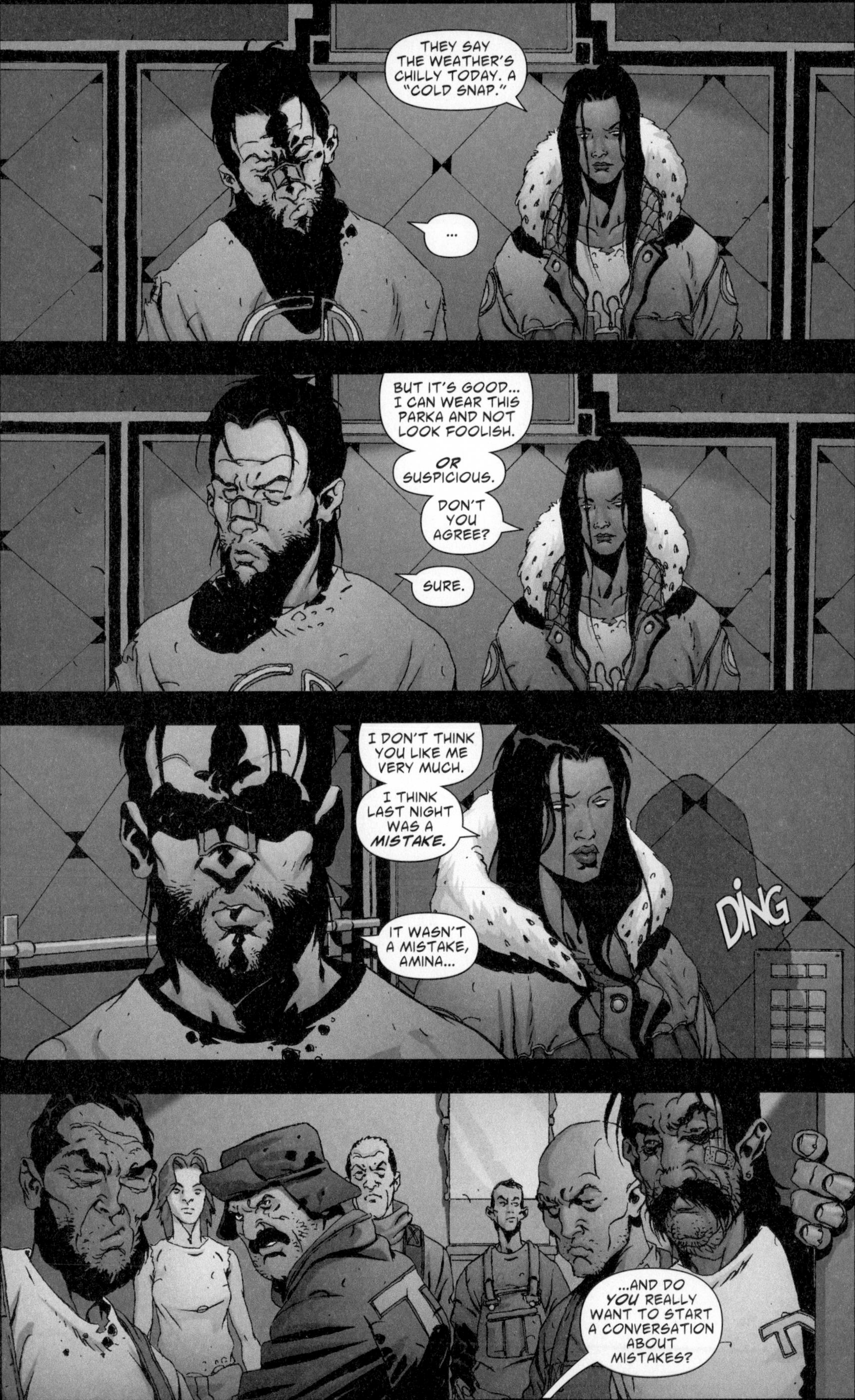
THEY SAY THE WEATHER'S CHILLY TODAY. A "COLD SNAP."
...
BUT IT'S GOOD... I CAN WEAR THIS PARKA AND NOT LOOK FOOLISH.
OR SUSPICIOUS.
DON'T YOU AGREE?
SURE.
I DON'T THINK YOU LIKE ME VERY MUCH.
I THINK LAST NIGHT WAS A MISTAKE.
IT WASN'T A MISTAKE, AMINA...
DING
...AND DO YOU REALLY WANT TO START A CONVERSATION ABOUT MISTAKES?

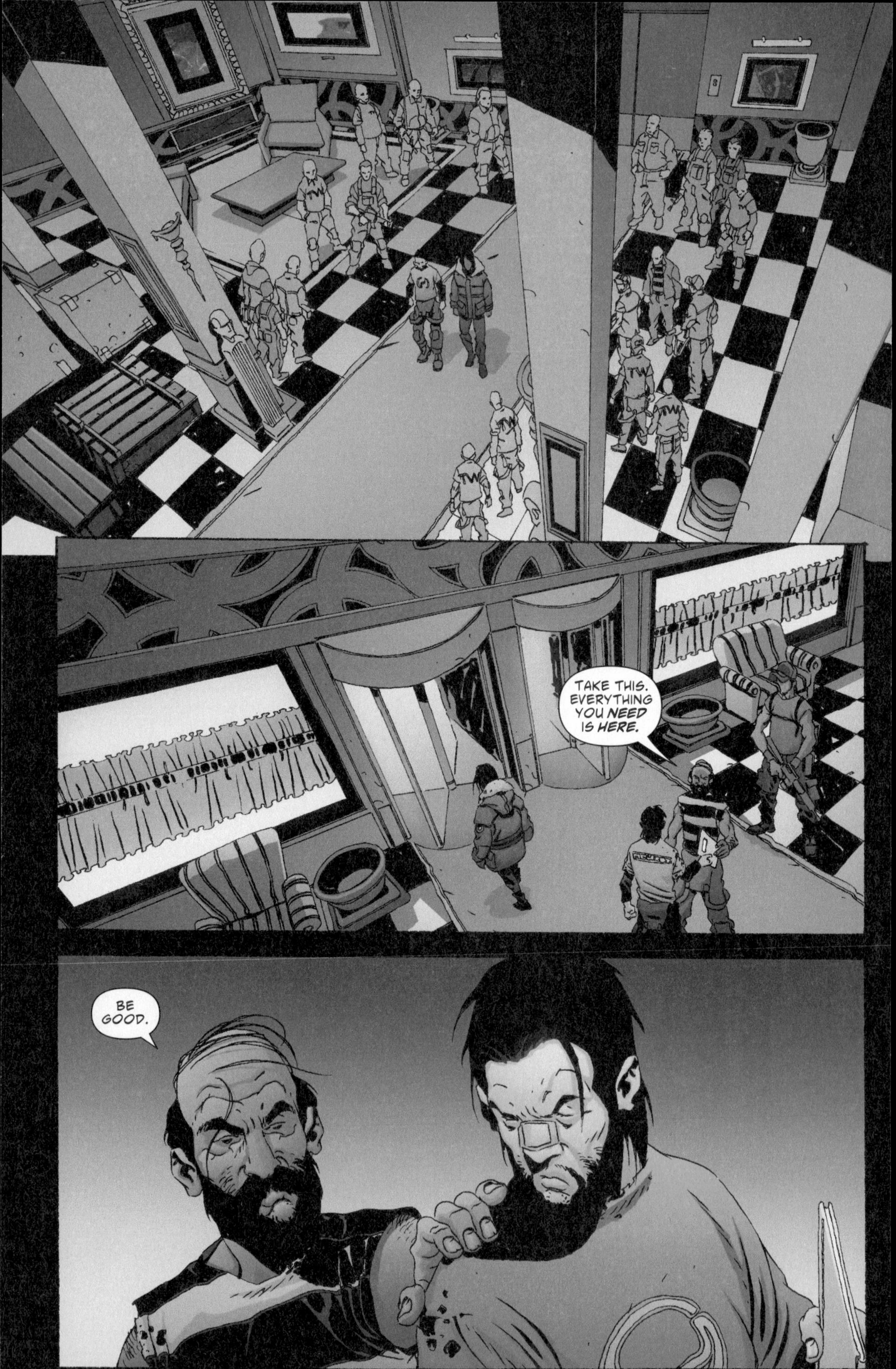
TAKE THIS. EVERYTHING YOU NEED IS HERE.
BE GOOD.

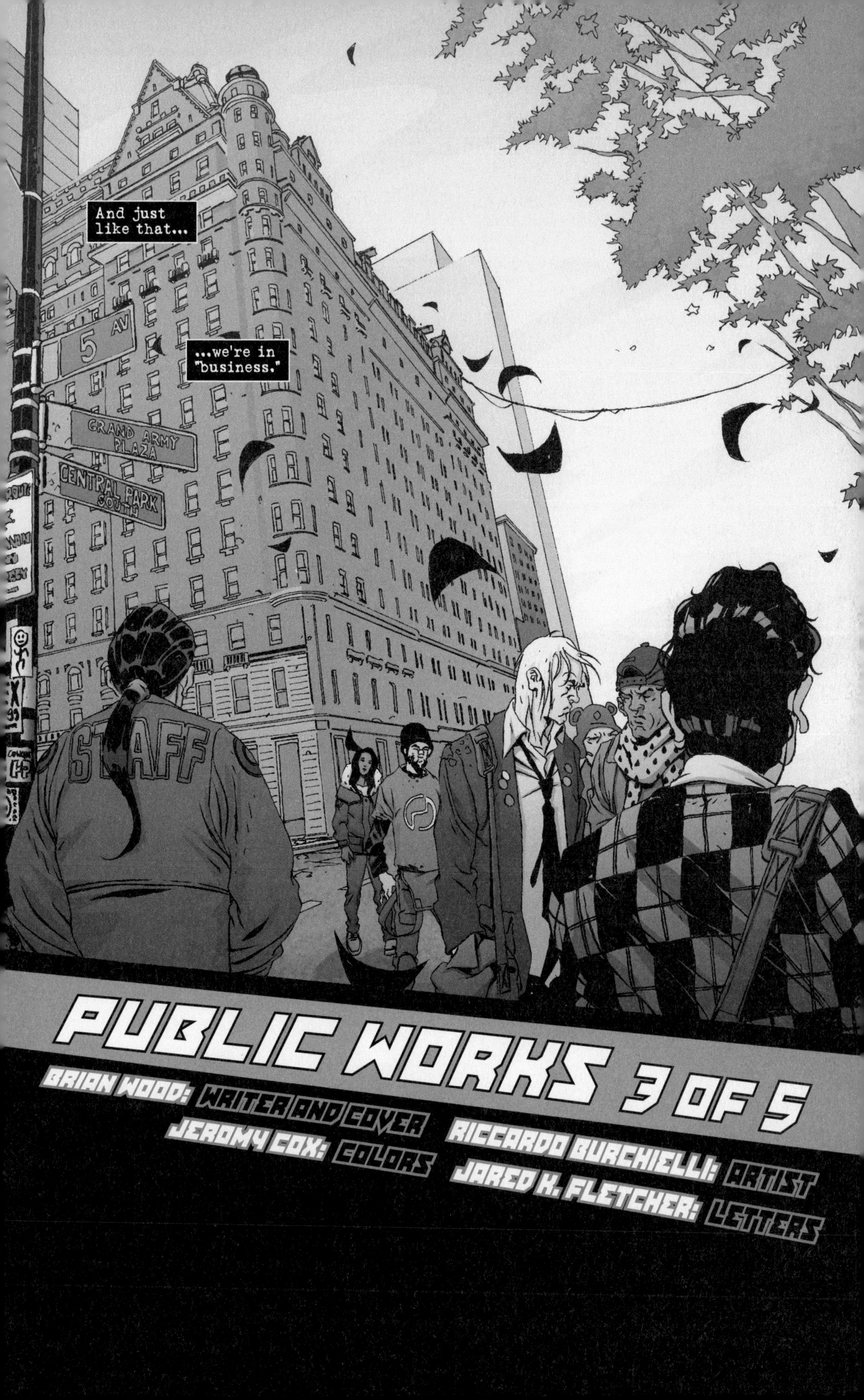
And just like that...
...we're in "business."
5 AV
GRAND ARMY PLAZA
CENTRAL PARK SOUTH
STAFF
PUBLIC WORKS 3 OF 5
BRIAN WOOD: WRITER AND COVER
RICCARDO BURCHIELLI: ARTIST
JEROMY COX: COLORS
JARED K. FLETCHER: LETTERS

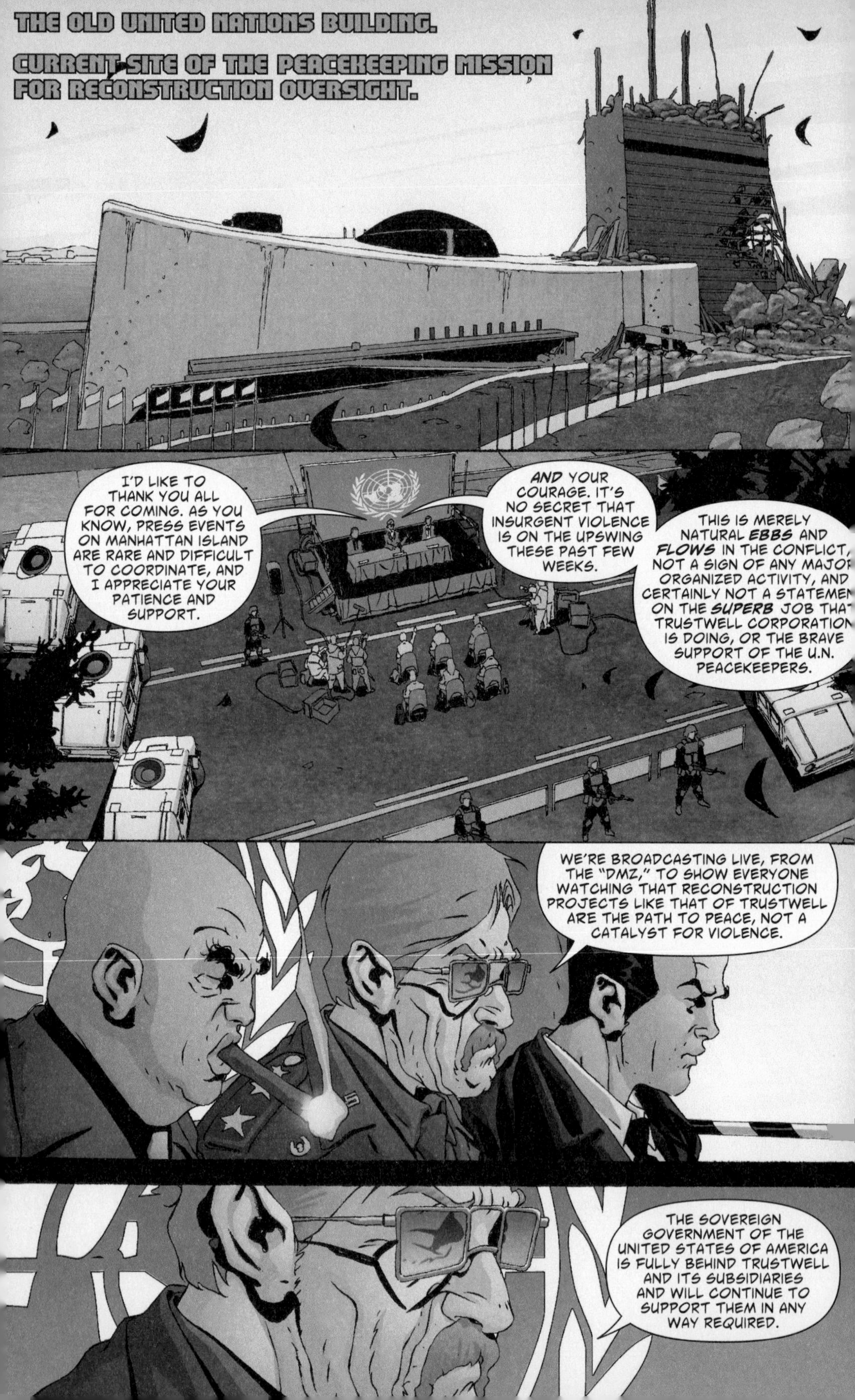
THE OLD UNITED NATIONS BUILDING.
CURRENT SITE OF THE PEACEKEEPING MISSION FOR RECONSTRUCTION OVERSIGHT.
I'D LIKE TO THANK YOU ALL FOR COMING. AS YOU KNOW, PRESS EVENTS ON MANHATTAN ISLAND ARE RARE AND DIFFICULT TO COORDINATE, AND I APPRECIATE YOUR PATIENCE AND SUPPORT.
AND YOUR COURAGE. IT'S NO SECRET THAT INSURGENT VIOLENCE IS ON THE UPSWING THESE PAST FEW WEEKS.
THIS IS MERELY NATURAL EBBS AND FLOWS IN THE CONFLICT, NOT A SIGN OF ANY MAJOR ORGANIZED ACTIVITY, AND CERTAINLY NOT A STATEMENT ON THE SUPERB JOB THAT TRUSTWELL CORPORATION IS DOING, OR THE BRAVE SUPPORT OF THE U.N. PEACEKEEPERS.
WE'RE BROADCASTING LIVE, FROM THE "DMZ," TO SHOW EVERYONE WATCHING THAT RECONSTRUCTION PROJECTS LIKE THAT OF TRUSTWELL ARE THE PATH TO PEACE, NOT A CATALYST FOR VIOLENCE.
THE SOVEREIGN GOVERNMENT OF THE UNITED STATES OF AMERICA IS FULLY BEHIND TRUSTWELL AND ITS SUBSIDIARIES AND WILL CONTINUE TO SUPPORT THEM IN ANY WAY REQUIRED.

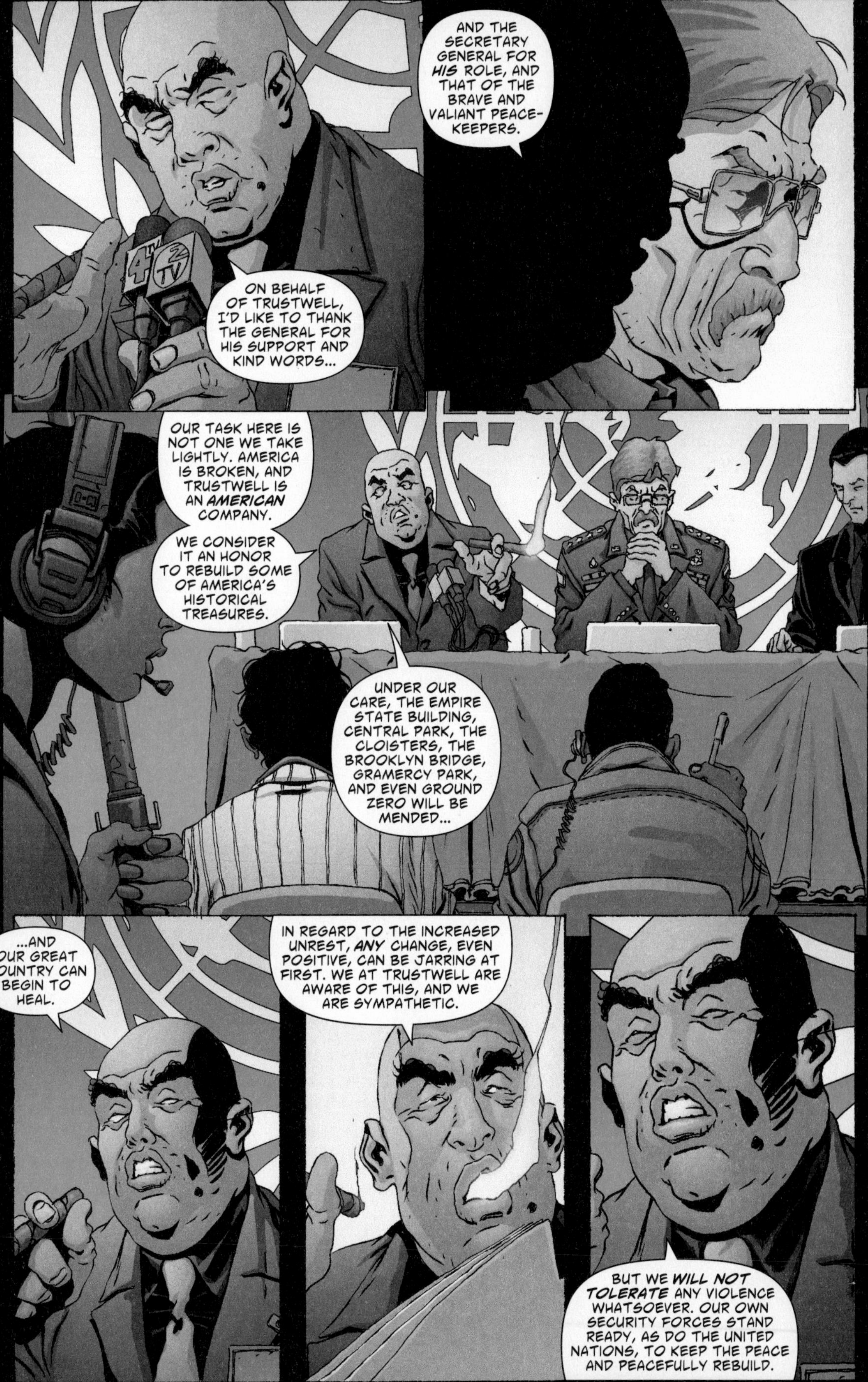
ON BEHALF OF TRUSTWELL, I'D LIKE TO THANK THE GENERAL FOR HIS SUPPORT AND KIND WORDS...
AND THE SECRETARY GENERAL FOR *HIS* ROLE, AND THAT OF THE BRAVE AND VALIANT PEACE-KEEPERS.
4
2 TV
OUR TASK HERE IS NOT ONE WE TAKE LIGHTLY. AMERICA IS BROKEN, AND TRUSTWELL IS AN *AMERICAN* COMPANY.
WE CONSIDER IT AN HONOR TO REBUILD SOME OF AMERICA'S HISTORICAL TREASURES.
UNDER OUR CARE, THE EMPIRE STATE BUILDING, CENTRAL PARK, THE CLOISTERS, THE BROOKLYN BRIDGE, GRAMERCY PARK, AND EVEN GROUND ZERO WILL BE MENDED...
...AND OUR GREAT COUNTRY CAN BEGIN TO HEAL.
IN REGARD TO THE INCREASED UNREST, *ANY* CHANGE, EVEN POSITIVE, CAN BE JARRING AT FIRST. WE AT TRUSTWELL ARE AWARE OF THIS, AND WE ARE SYMPATHETIC.
BUT WE ***WILL NOT TOLERATE*** ANY VIOLENCE WHATSOEVER. OUR OWN SECURITY FORCES STAND READY, AS DO THE UNITED NATIONS, TO KEEP THE PEACE AND PEACEFULLY REBUILD.

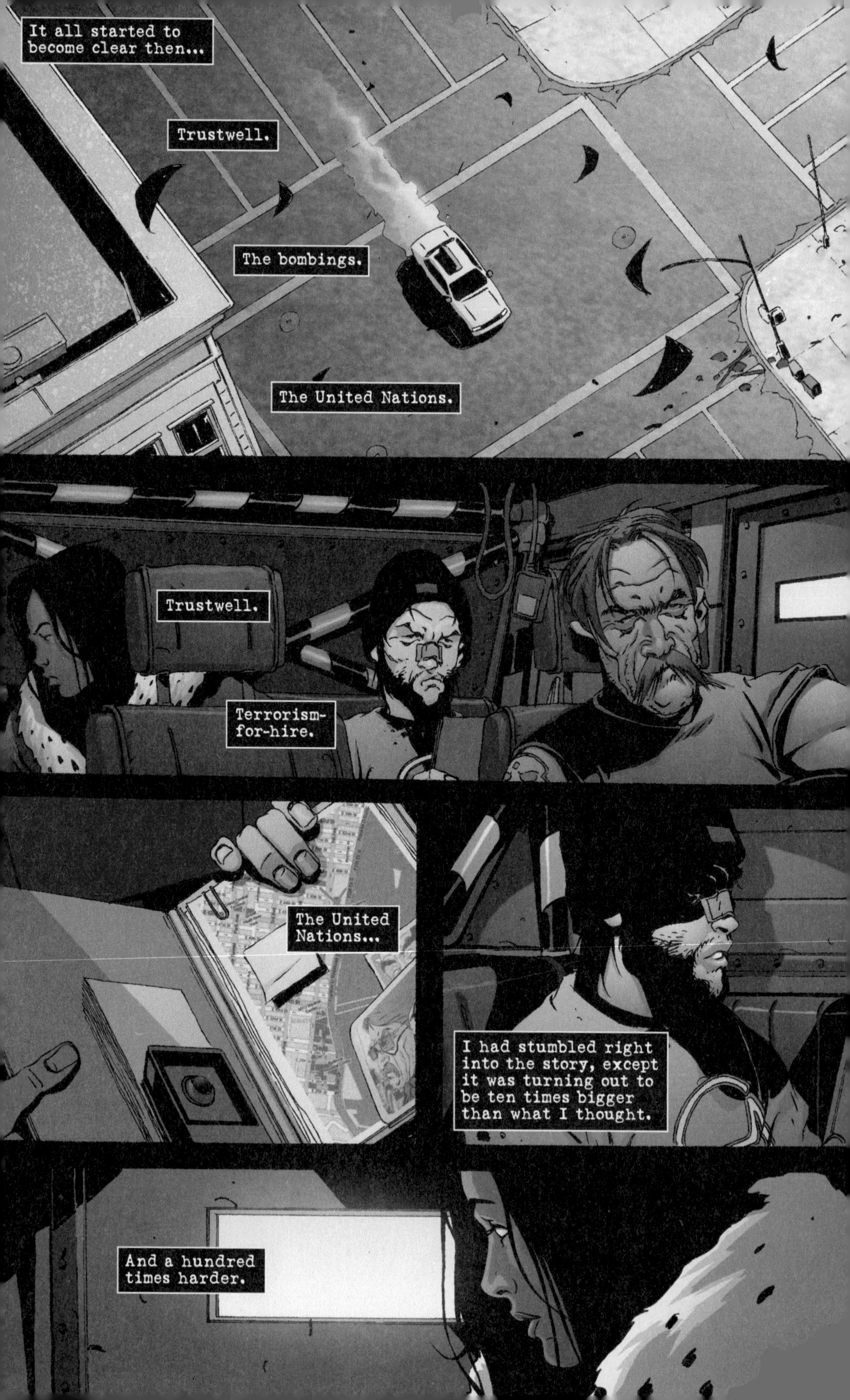
It all started to become clear then...
Trustwell.
The bombings.
The United Nations.
Trustwell.
Terrorism-for-hire.
The United Nations...
I had stumbled right into the story, except it was turning out to be ten times bigger than what I thought.
And a hundred times harder.

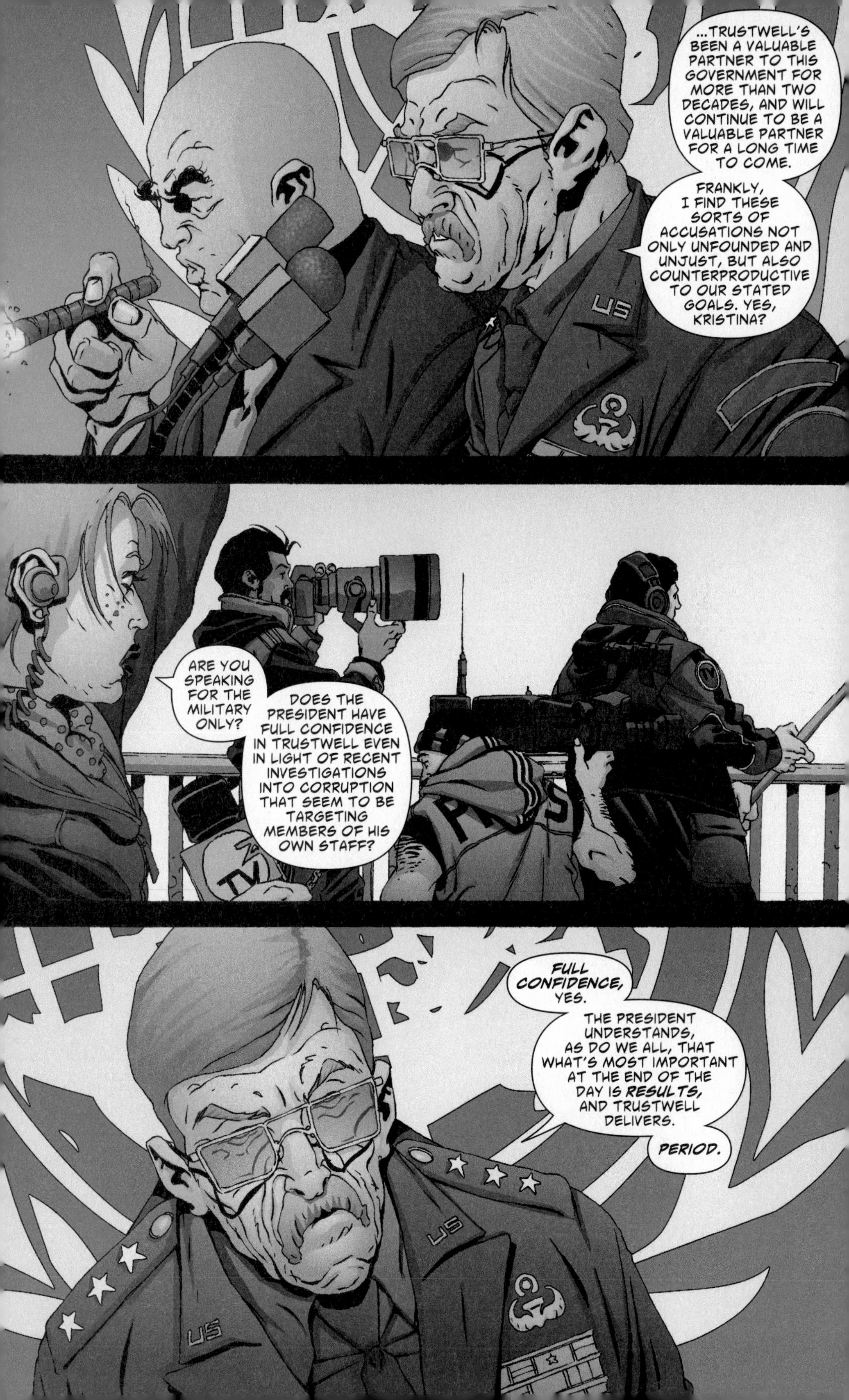
...TRUSTWELL'S BEEN A VALUABLE PARTNER TO THIS GOVERNMENT FOR MORE THAN TWO DECADES, AND WILL CONTINUE TO BE A VALUABLE PARTNER FOR A LONG TIME TO COME.
FRANKLY, I FIND THESE SORTS OF ACCUSATIONS NOT ONLY UNFOUNDED AND UNJUST, BUT ALSO COUNTERPRODUCTIVE TO OUR STATED GOALS. YES, KRISTINA?
ARE YOU SPEAKING FOR THE MILITARY ONLY?
DOES THE PRESIDENT HAVE FULL CONFIDENCE IN TRUSTWELL EVEN IN LIGHT OF RECENT INVESTIGATIONS INTO CORRUPTION THAT SEEM TO BE TARGETING MEMBERS OF HIS OWN STAFF?
FULL CONFIDENCE, YES.
THE PRESIDENT UNDERSTANDS, AS DO WE ALL, THAT WHAT'S MOST IMPORTANT AT THE END OF THE DAY IS *RESULTS*, AND TRUSTWELL DELIVERS.
PERIOD.

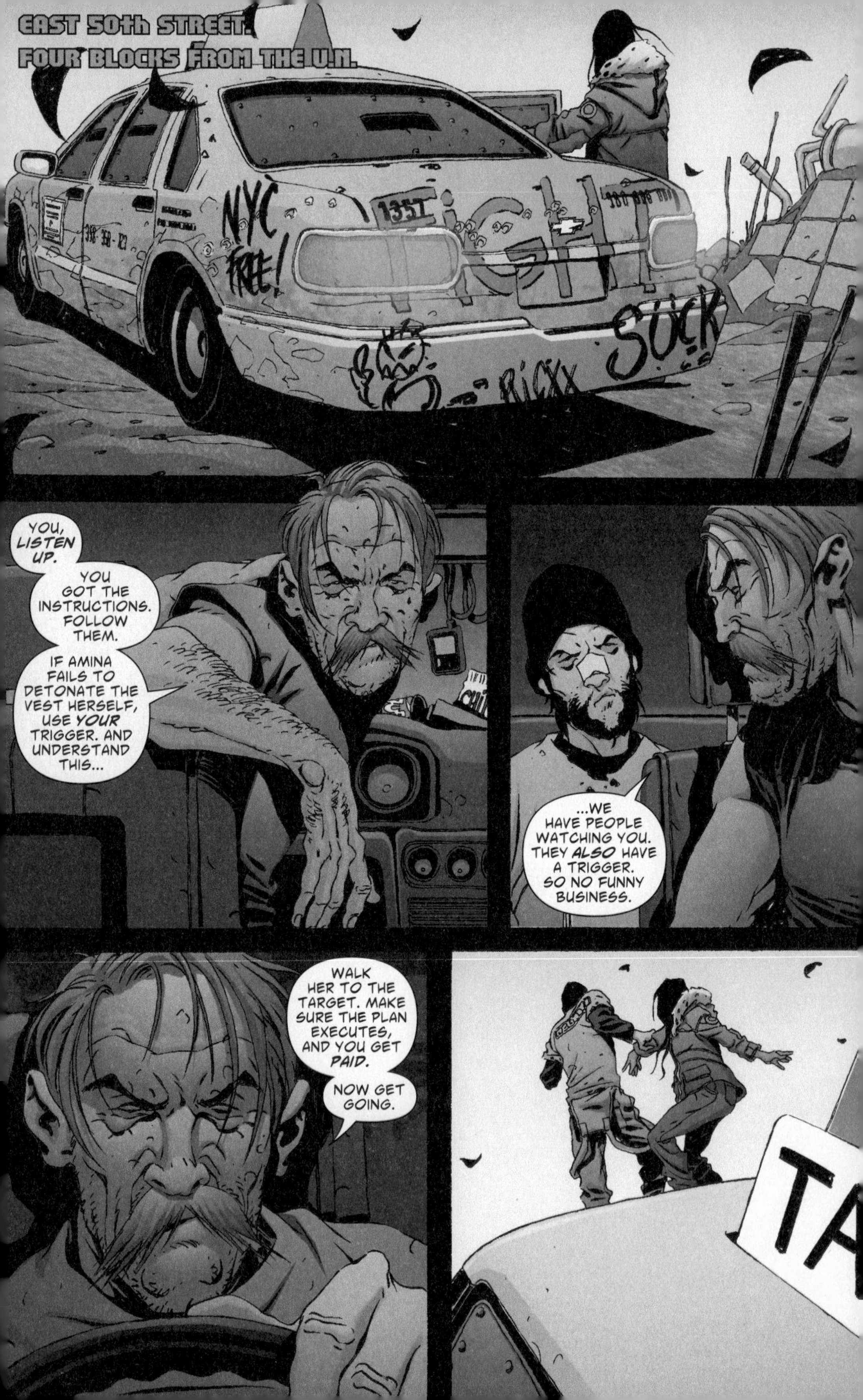
EAST 50th STREET:
FOUR BLOCKS FROM THE U.N.
NYC FREE!
SUCK
YOU, LISTEN UP.
YOU GOT THE INSTRUCTIONS. FOLLOW THEM.
IF AMINA FAILS TO DETONATE THE VEST HERSELF, USE YOUR TRIGGER. AND UNDERSTAND THIS...
...WE HAVE PEOPLE WATCHING YOU. THEY ALSO HAVE A TRIGGER. SO NO FUNNY BUSINESS.
WALK HER TO THE TARGET. MAKE SURE THE PLAN EXECUTES, AND YOU GET PAID.
NOW GET GOING.

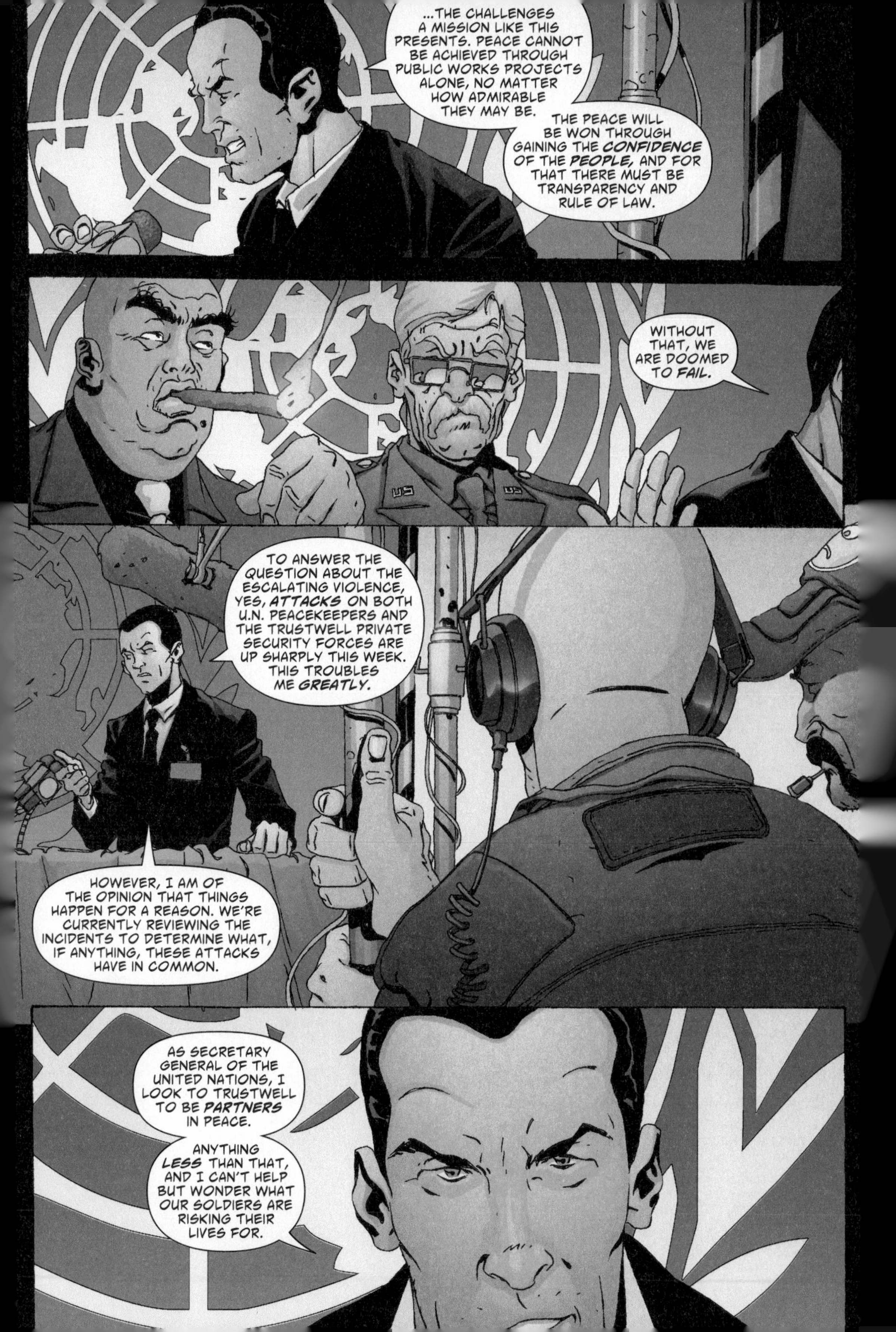
...THE CHALLENGES A MISSION LIKE THIS PRESENTS. PEACE CANNOT BE ACHIEVED THROUGH PUBLIC WORKS PROJECTS ALONE, NO MATTER HOW ADMIRABLE THEY MAY BE.
THE PEACE WILL BE WON THROUGH GAINING THE CONFIDENCE OF THE PEOPLE, AND FOR THAT THERE MUST BE TRANSPARENCY AND RULE OF LAW.
WITHOUT THAT, WE ARE DOOMED TO FAIL.
TO ANSWER THE QUESTION ABOUT THE ESCALATING VIOLENCE, YES, ATTACKS ON BOTH U.N. PEACEKEEPERS AND THE TRUSTWELL PRIVATE SECURITY FORCES ARE UP SHARPLY THIS WEEK. THIS TROUBLES ME GREATLY.
HOWEVER, I AM OF THE OPINION THAT THINGS HAPPEN FOR A REASON. WE'RE CURRENTLY REVIEWING THE INCIDENTS TO DETERMINE WHAT, IF ANYTHING, THESE ATTACKS HAVE IN COMMON.
AS SECRETARY GENERAL OF THE UNITED NATIONS, I LOOK TO TRUSTWELL TO BE PARTNERS IN PEACE.
ANYTHING LESS THAN THAT, AND I CAN'T HELP BUT WONDER WHAT OUR SOLDIERS ARE RISKING THEIR LIVES FOR.

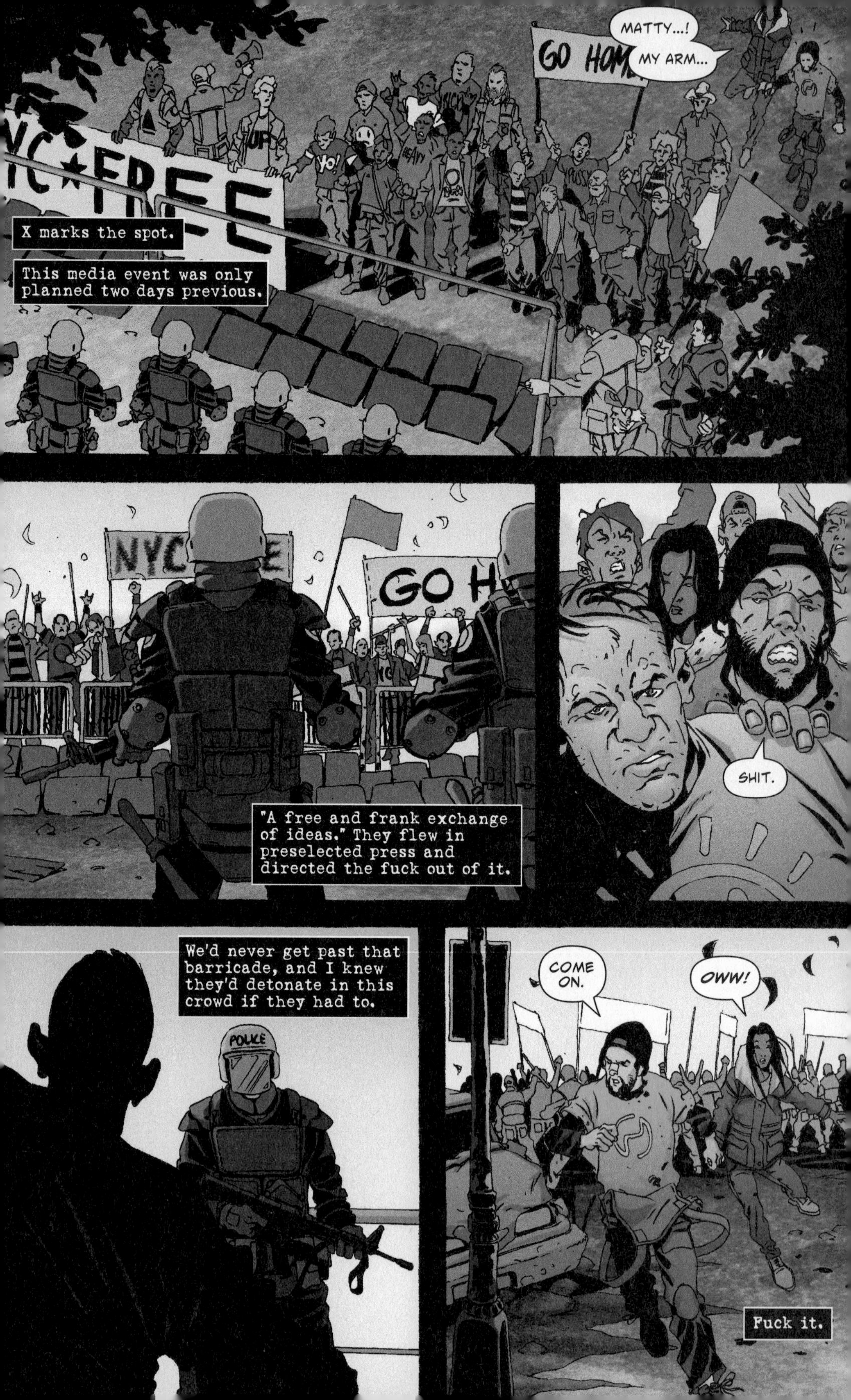
MATTY...!
MY ARM...
GO HOM
NYC★FREE
X marks the spot.
This media event was only planned two days previous.
NYC
GO H
"A free and frank exchange of ideas." They flew in preselected press and directed the fuck out of it.
SHIT.
We'd never get past that barricade, and I knew they'd detonate in this crowd if they had to.
POLICE
COME ON.
OWW!
Fuck it.

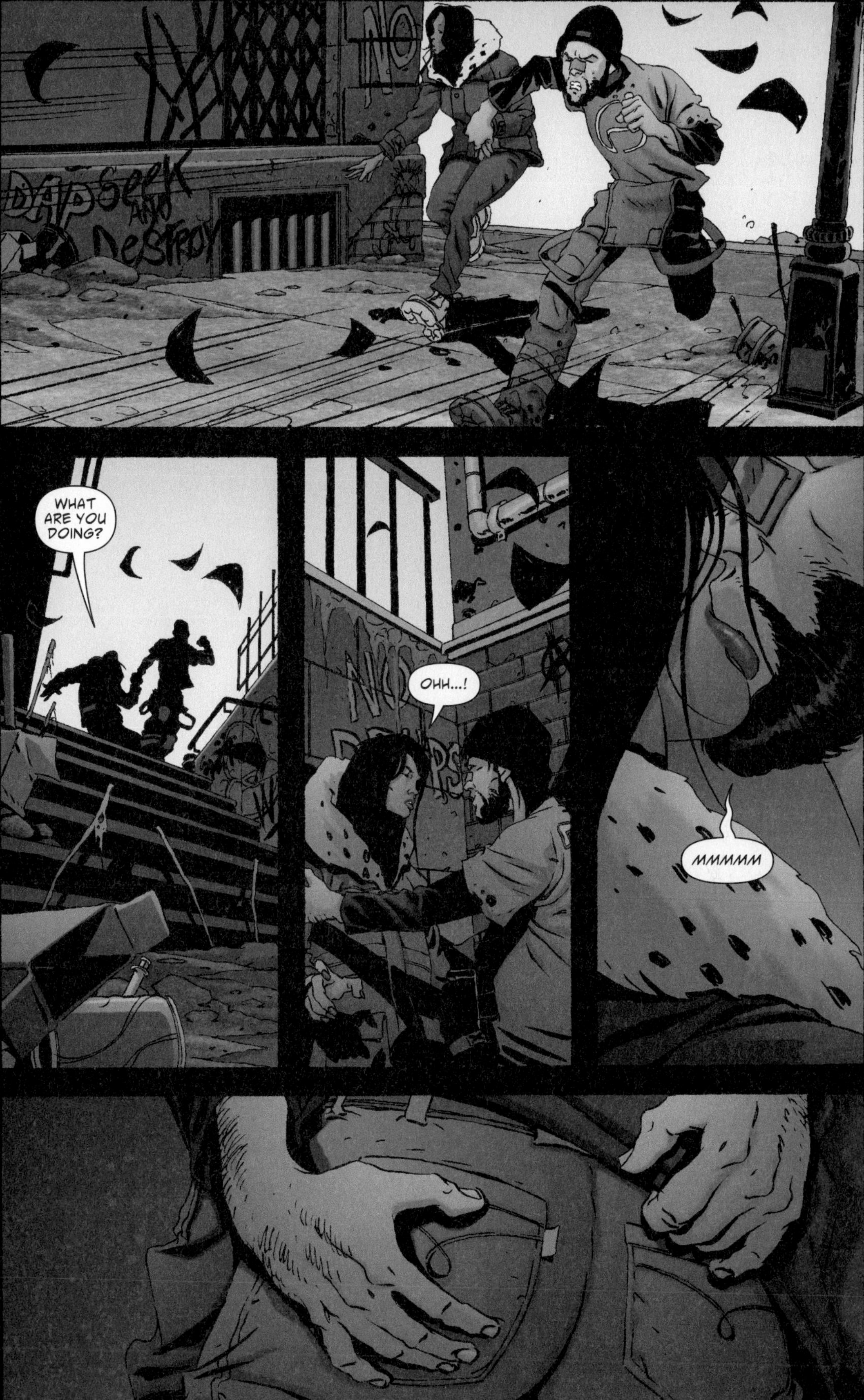
NO
SEEK AND DESTROY
WHAT ARE YOU DOING?
OHH...!
MMMMM

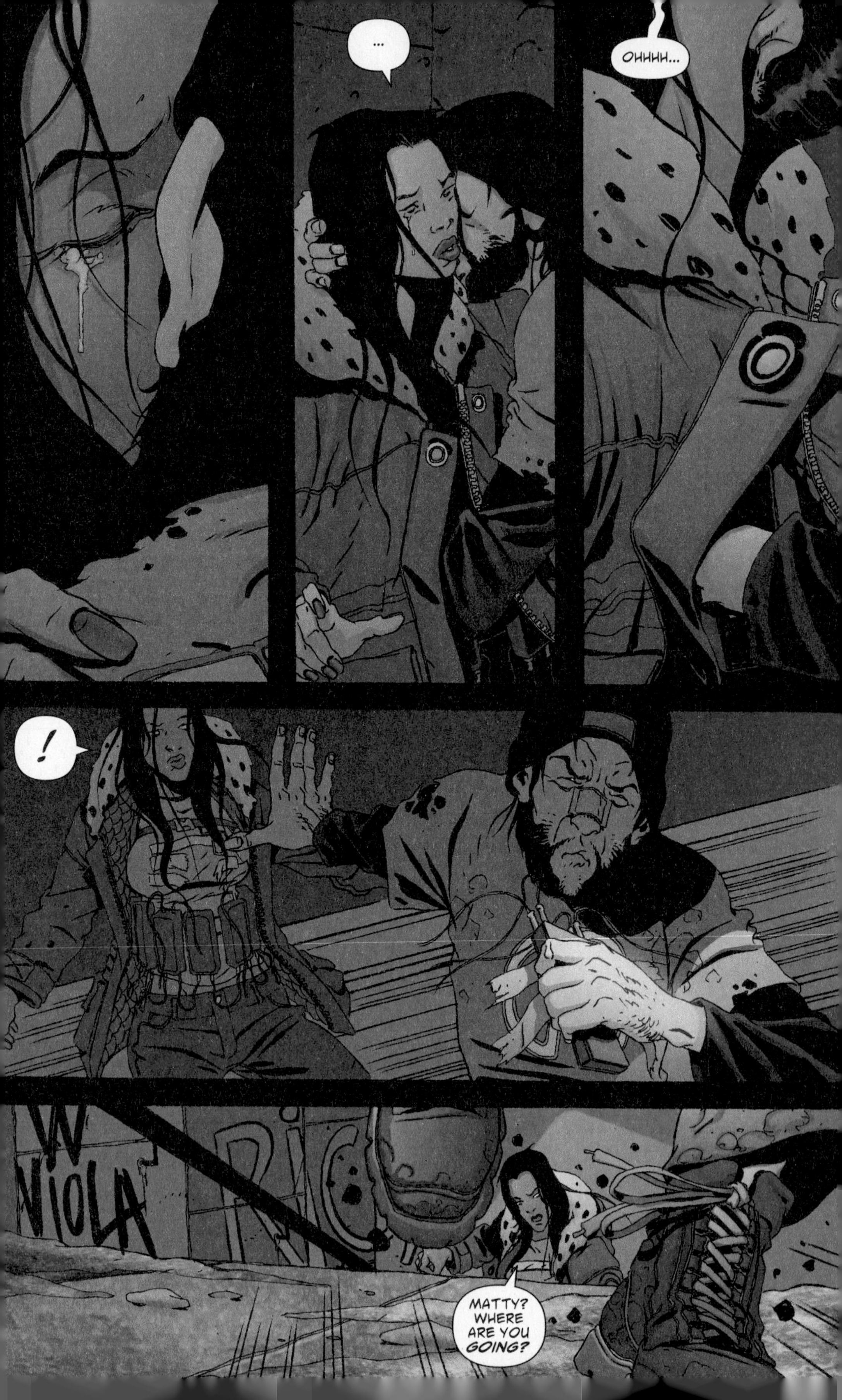
...
OHHHH...
!
NIOLA
MATTY? WHERE ARE YOU *GOING?*

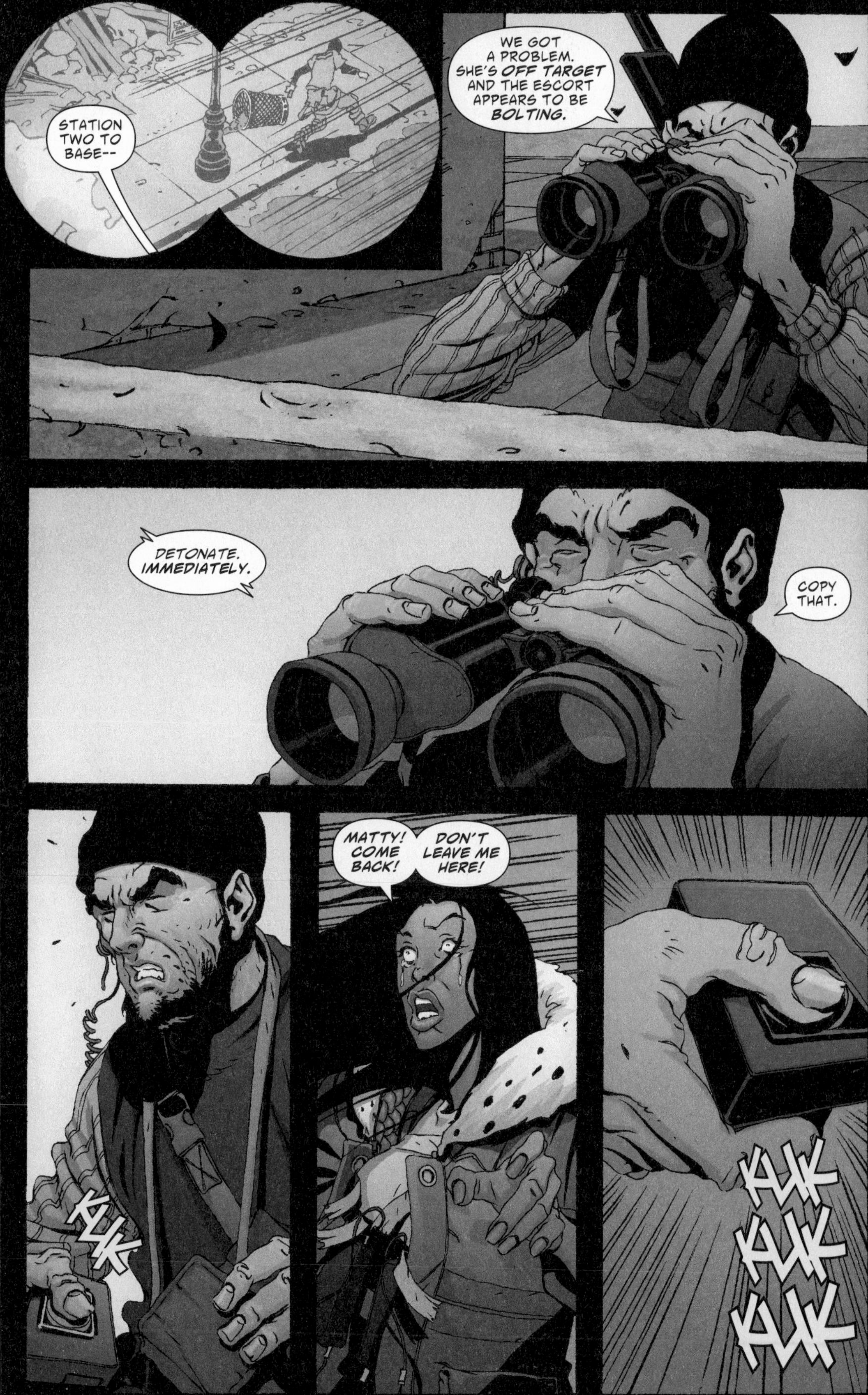
STATION TWO TO BASE--
WE GOT A PROBLEM. SHE'S OFF TARGET AND THE ESCORT APPEARS TO BE BOLTING.
DETONATE. IMMEDIATELY.
COPY THAT.
KLIK
MATTY! COME BACK!
DON'T LEAVE ME HERE!
KLIK
KLIK
KLIK

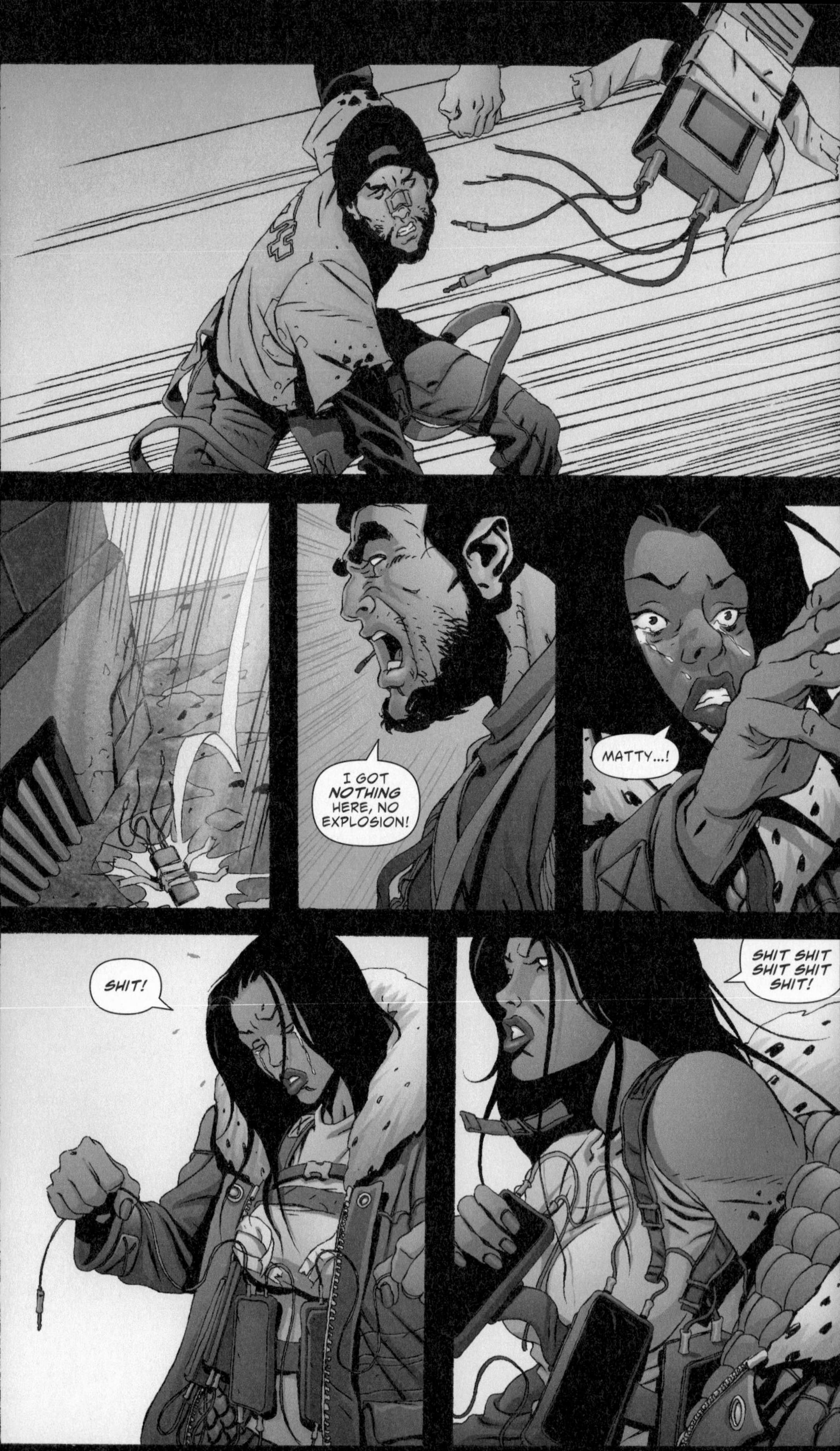
I GOT NOTHING HERE, NO EXPLOSION!
MATTY...!
SHIT!
SHIT SHIT SHIT SHIT SHIT!

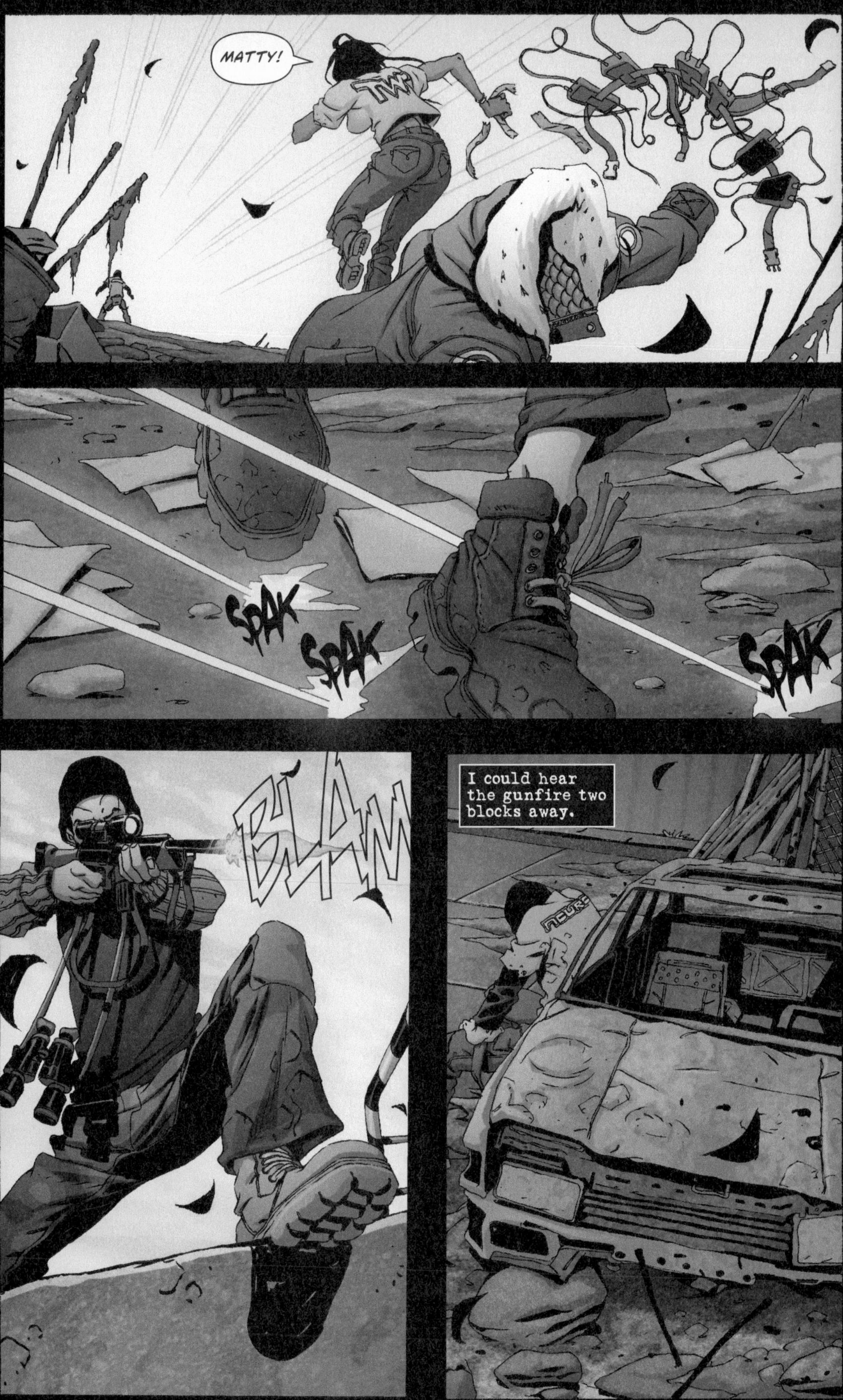
MATTY!
SPAK
SPAK
SPAK
BLAM
I could hear the gunfire two blocks away.

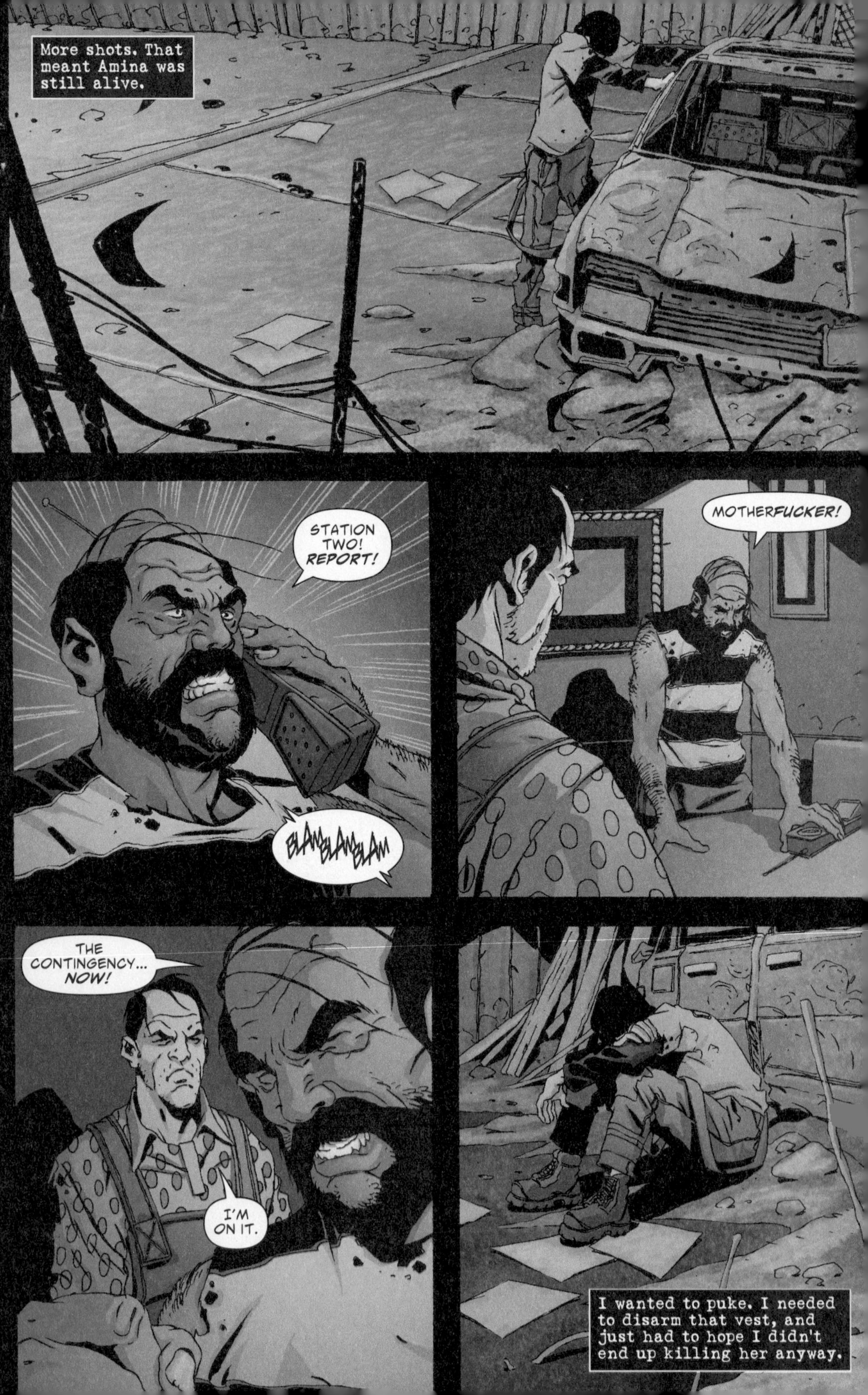
More shots. That meant Amina was still alive.
STATION TWO! REPORT!
BLAMBLAMBLAM
MOTHERFUCKER!
THE CONTINGENCY... NOW!
I'M ON IT.
I wanted to puke. I needed to disarm that vest, and just had to hope I didn't end up killing her anyway.

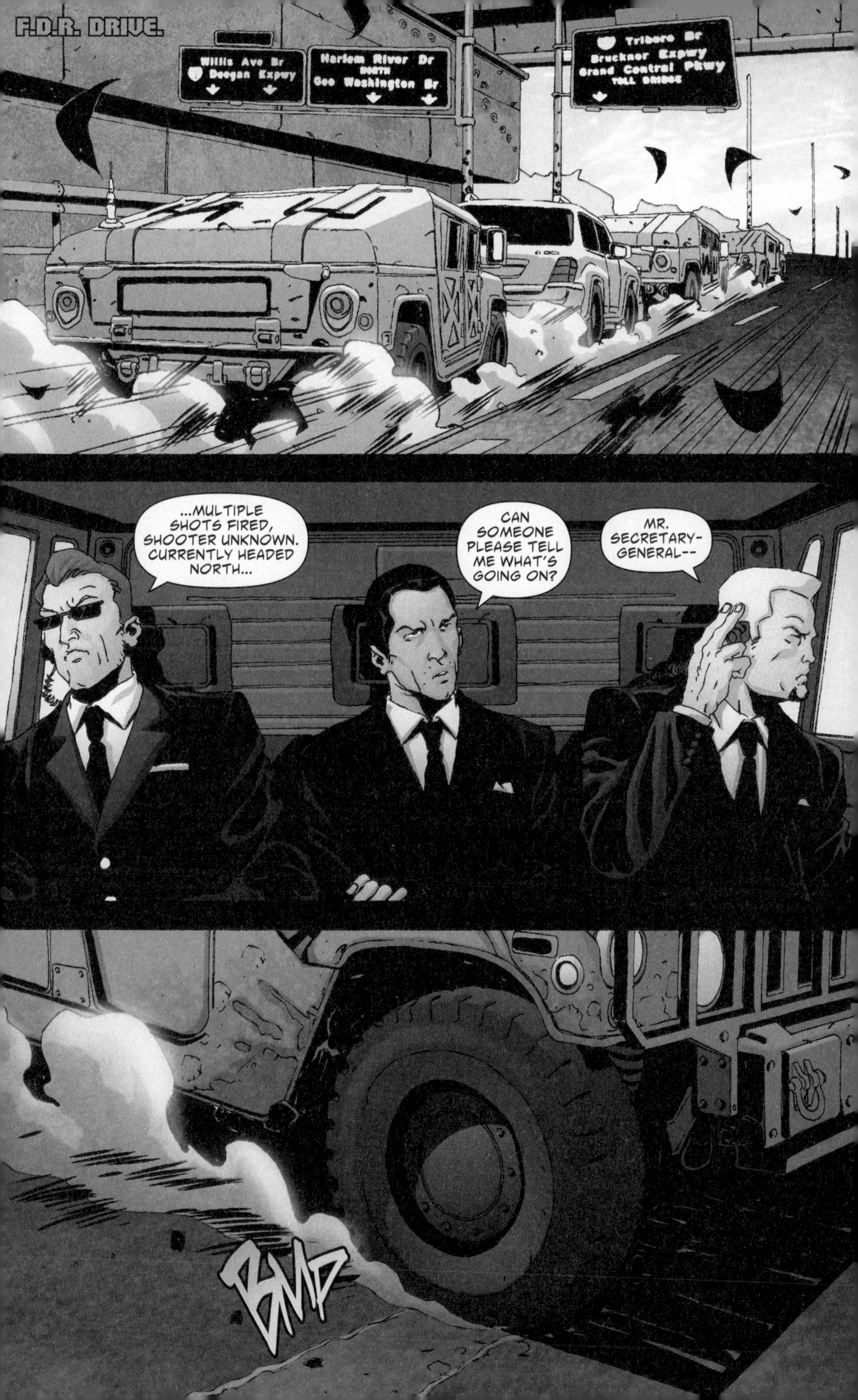
F.D.R. DRIVE.
Willis Ave Br
Deegan Expwy
Harlem River Dr
NORTH
Geo Washington Br
Triboro Br
Bruckner Expwy
Grand Central Pkwy
TOLL BRIDGE
...MULTIPLE SHOTS FIRED, SHOOTER UNKNOWN. CURRENTLY HEADED NORTH...
CAN SOMEONE PLEASE TELL ME WHAT'S GOING ON?
MR. SECRETARY-GENERAL--
BMP

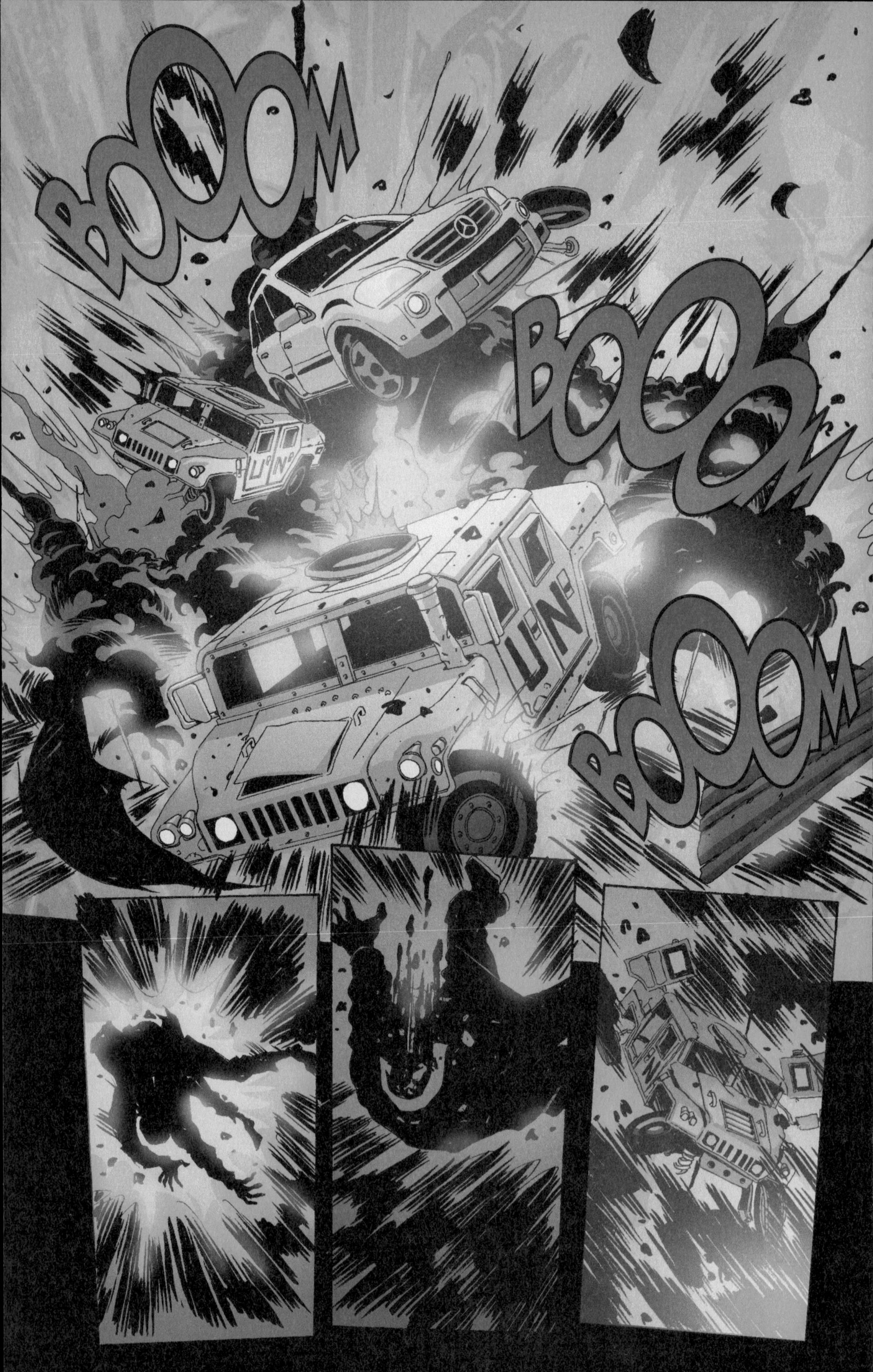
BOOOOM
BOOOOM
BOOOOM

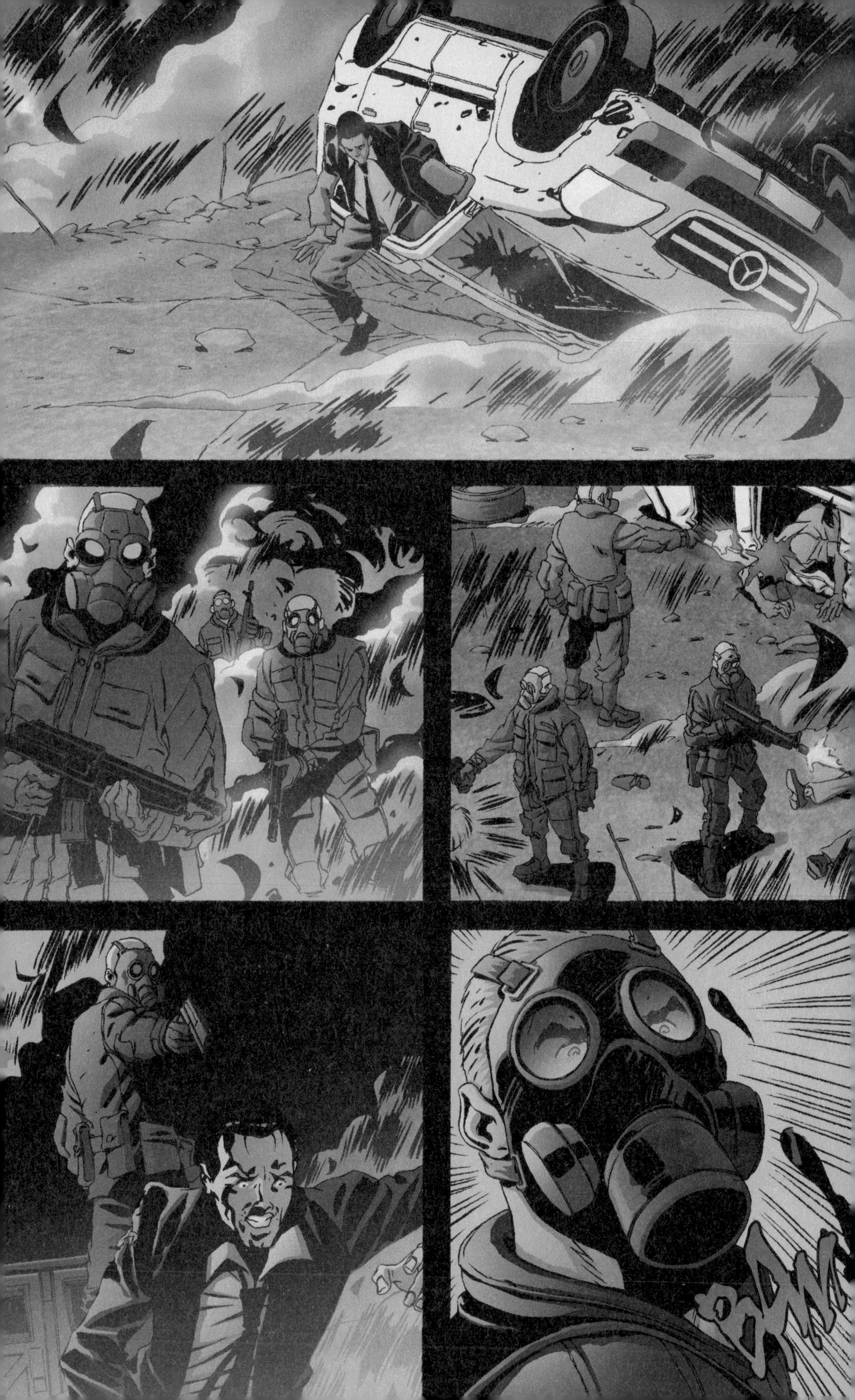

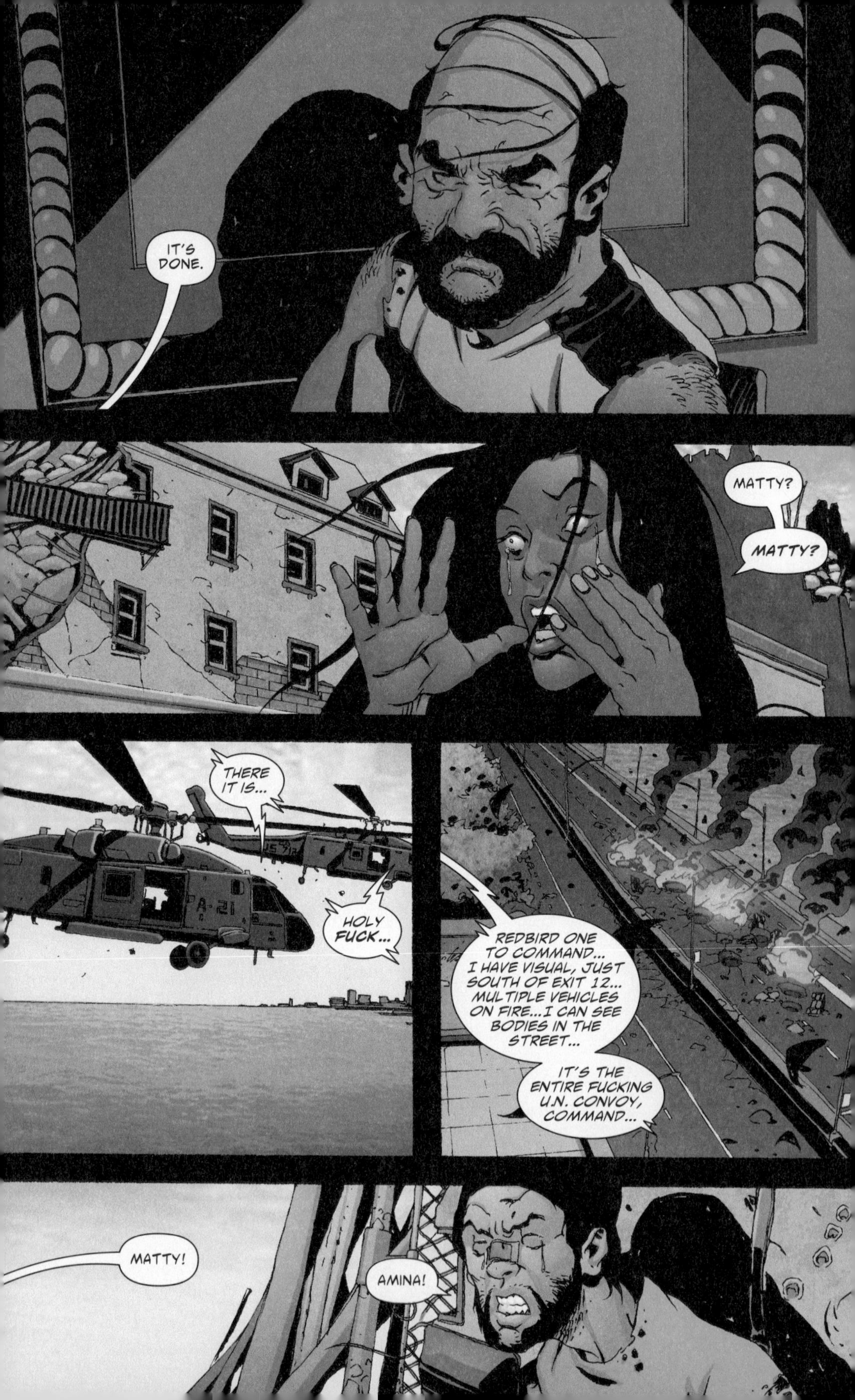
IT'S DONE.
MATTY?
MATTY?
THERE IT IS...
HOLY FUCK...
REDBIRD ONE TO COMMAND... I HAVE VISUAL, JUST SOUTH OF EXIT 12... MULTIPLE VEHICLES ON FIRE...I CAN SEE BODIES IN THE STREET...
IT'S THE ENTIRE FUCKING U.N. CONVOY, COMMAND...
MATTY!
AMINA!

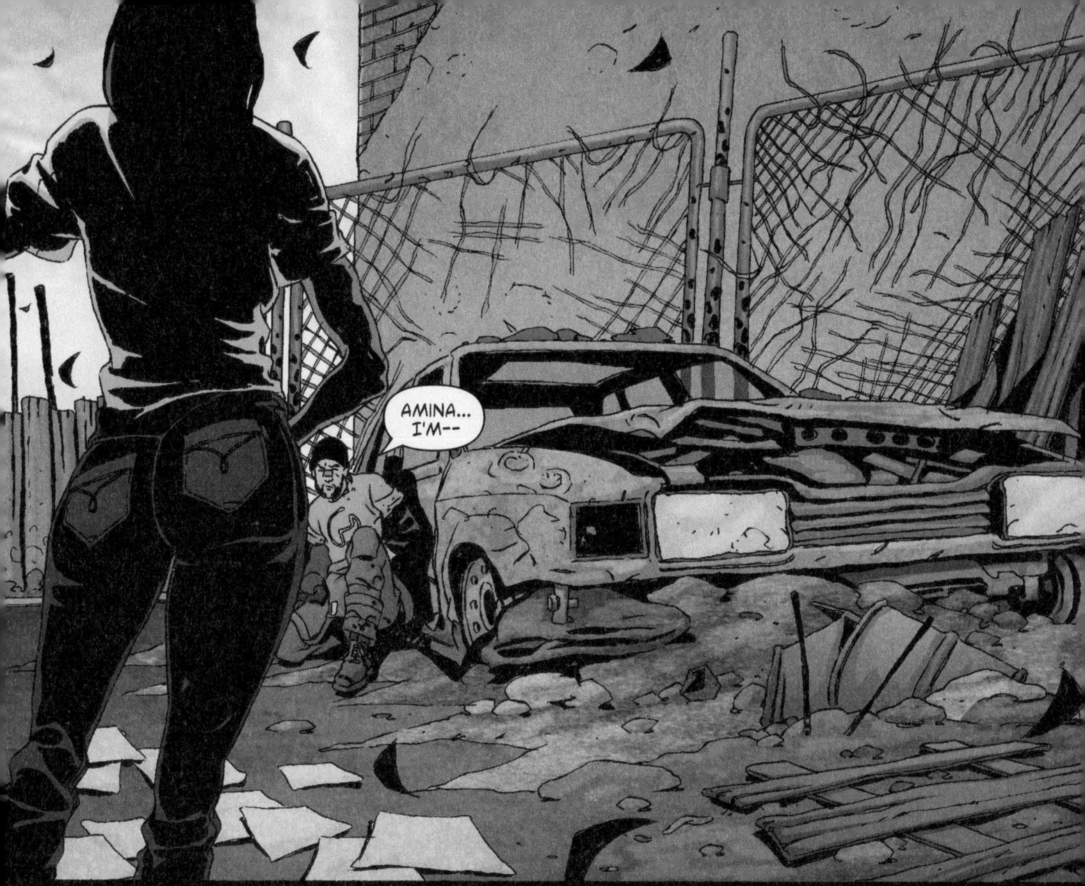
AMINA... I'M--

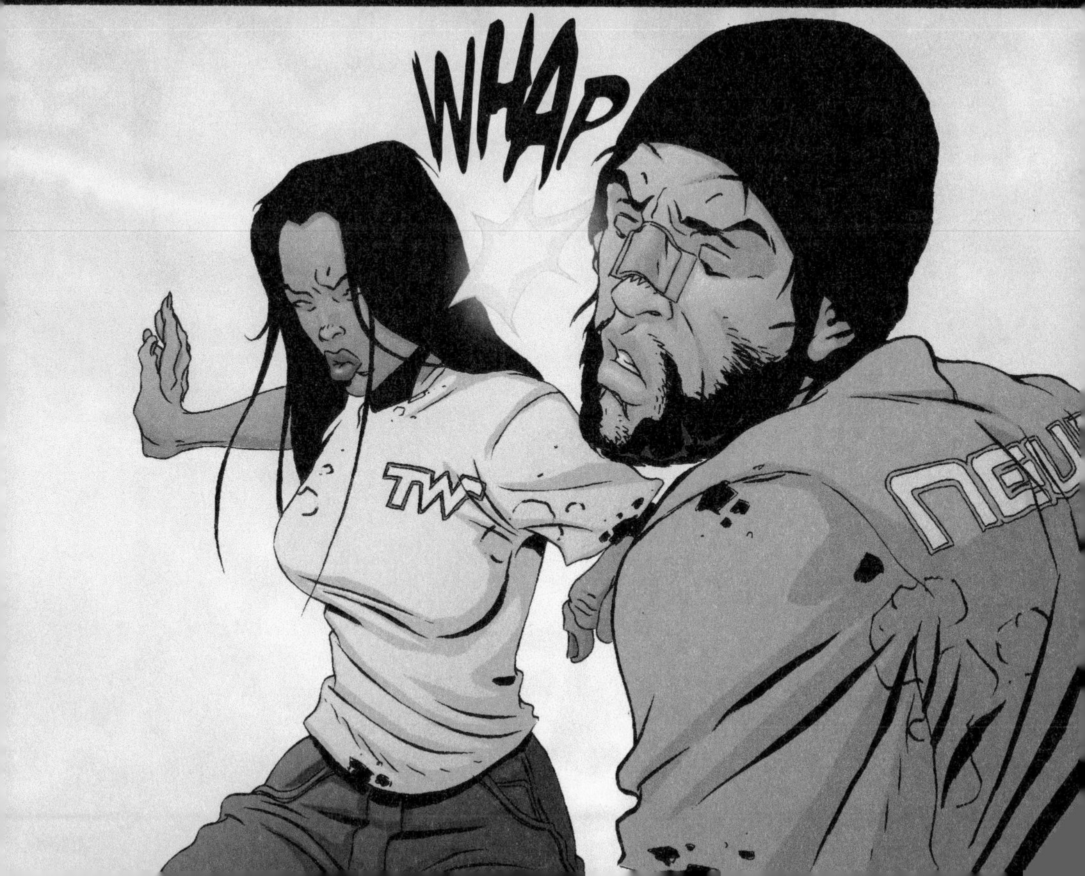
WHAP

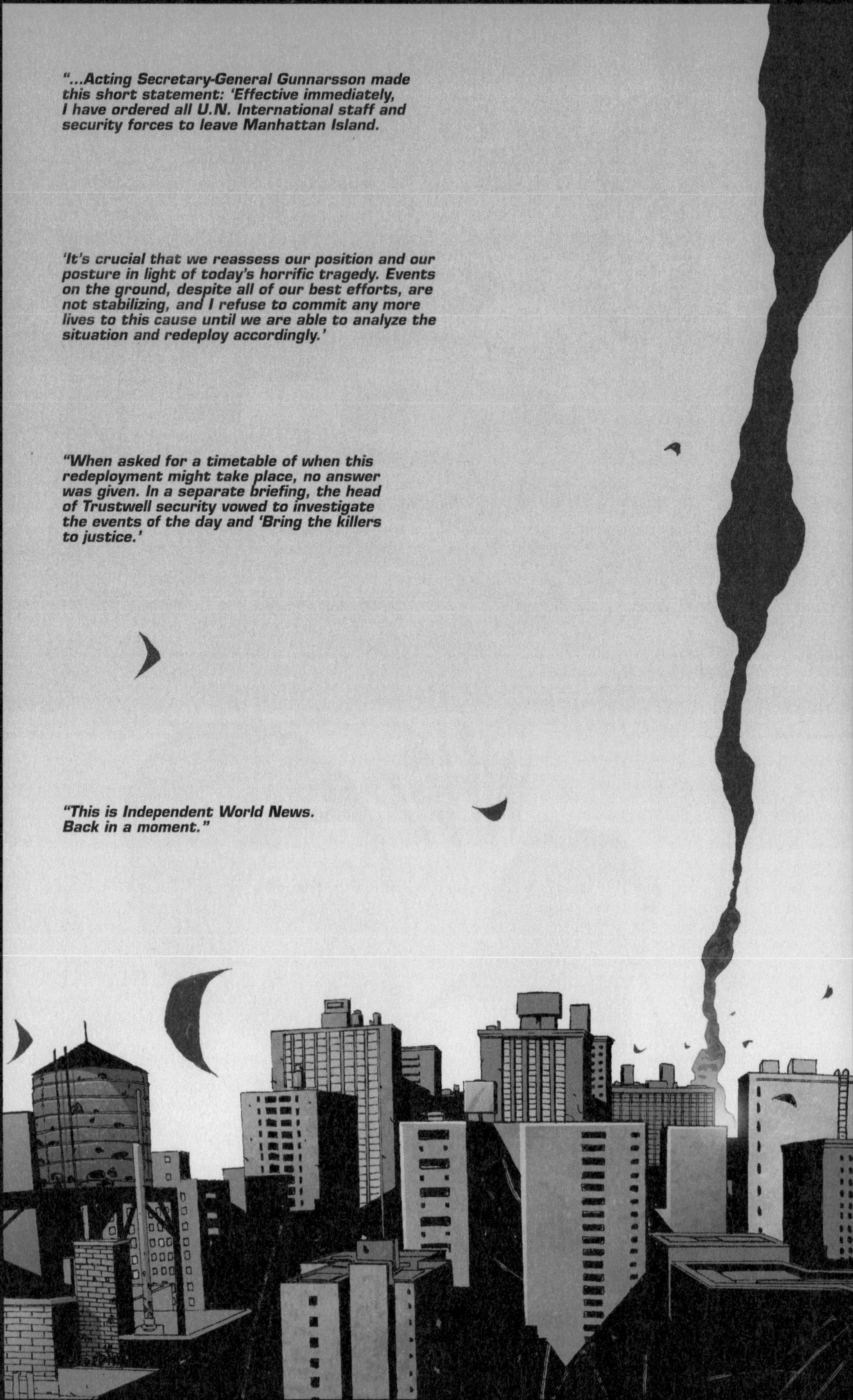
"...Acting Secretary-General Gunnarsson made this short statement: 'Effective immediately, I have ordered all U.N. International staff and security forces to leave Manhattan Island.
'It's crucial that we reassess our position and our posture in light of today's horrific tragedy. Events on the ground, despite all of our best efforts, are not stabilizing, and I refuse to commit any more lives to this cause until we are able to analyze the situation and redeploy accordingly.'
"When asked for a timetable of when this redeployment might take place, no answer was given. In a separate briefing, the head of Trustwell security vowed to investigate the events of the day and 'Bring the killers to justice.'
"This is Independent World News. Back in a moment."

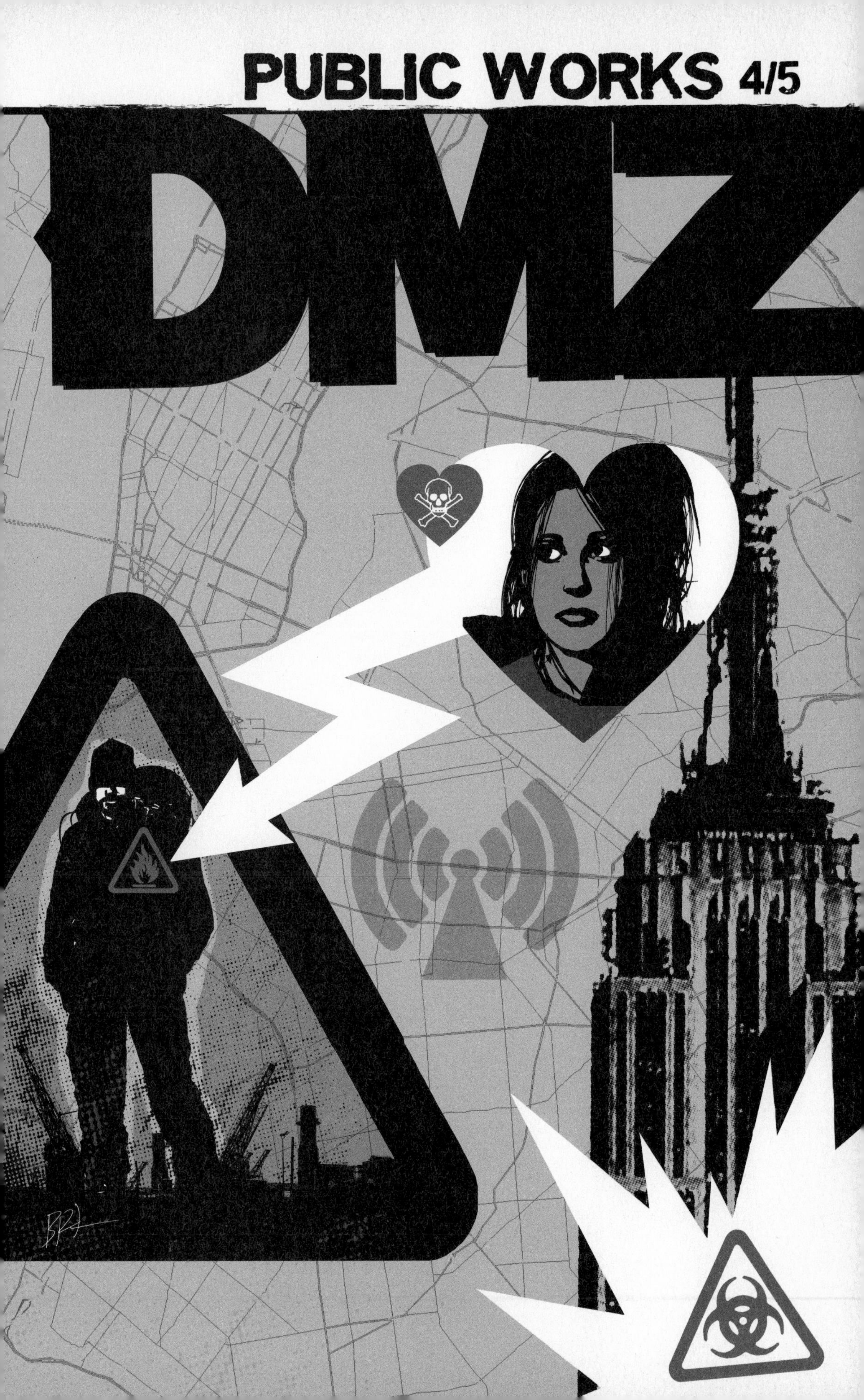
PUBLIC WORKS 4/5
DMZ

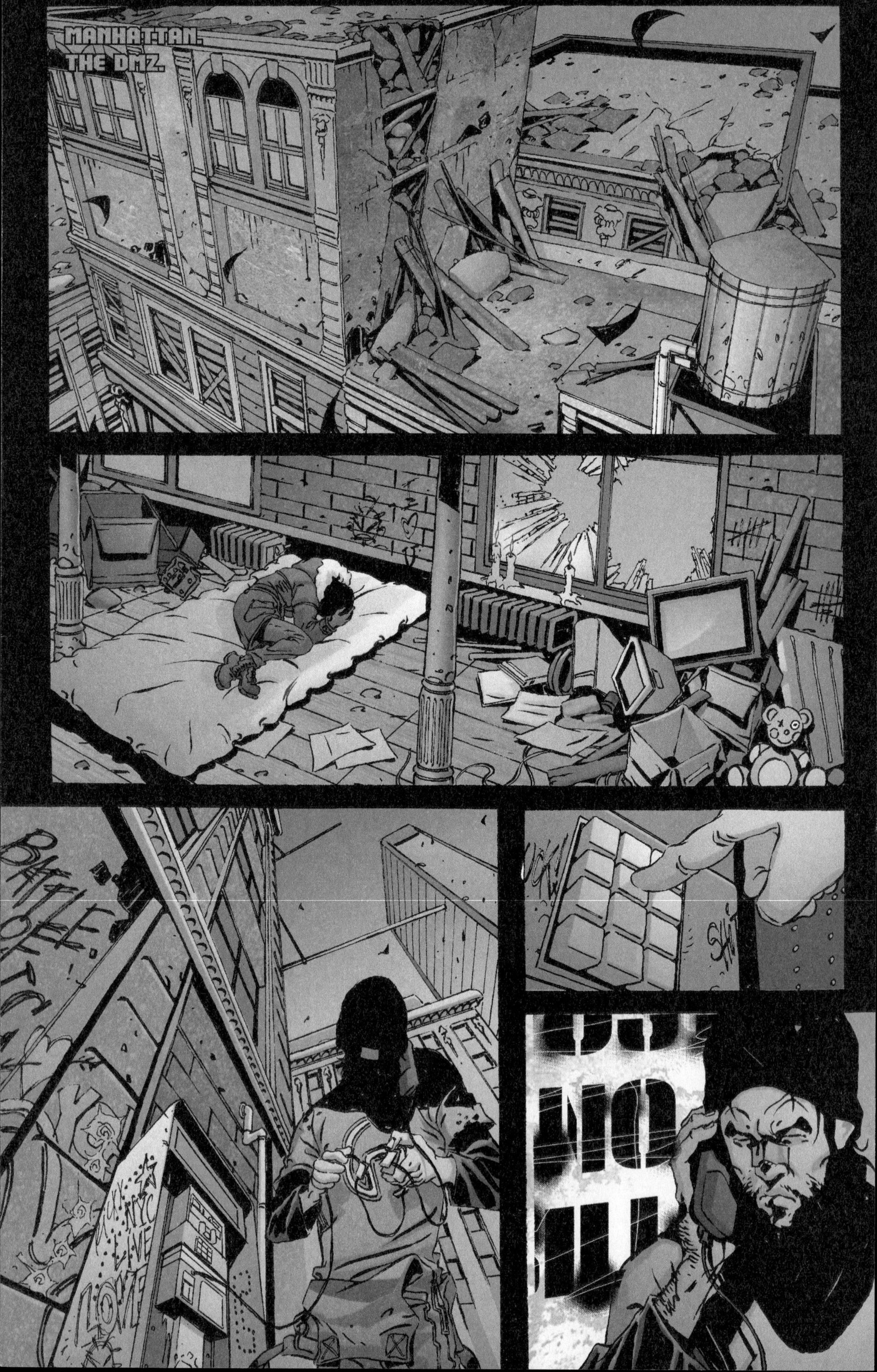
MANHATTAN.
THE DMZ.

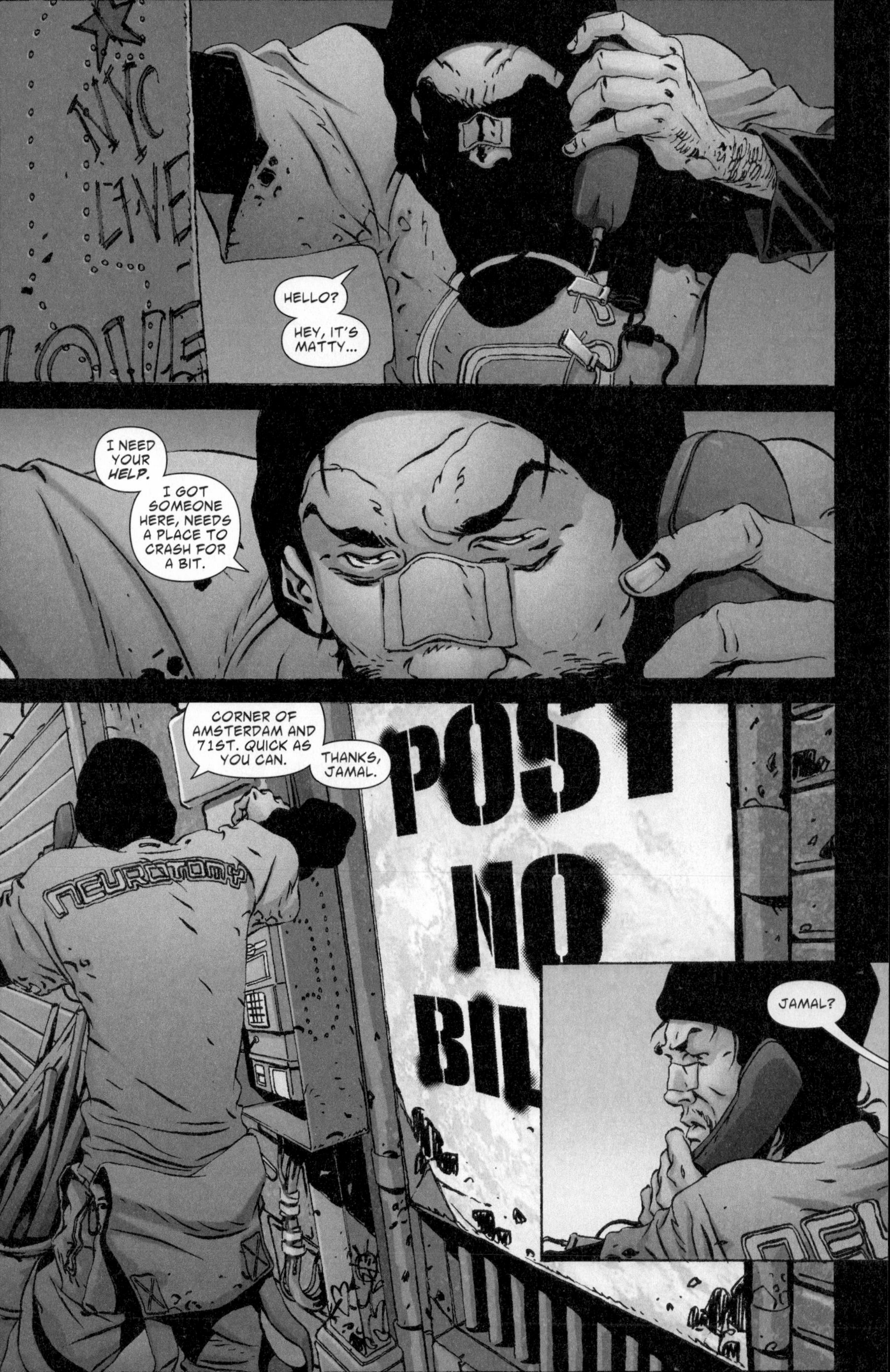
NYC
LIVE
LOVE
HELLO?
HEY, IT'S MATTY...
I NEED YOUR *HELP*.
I GOT SOMEONE HERE, NEEDS A PLACE TO CRASH FOR A BIT.
CORNER OF AMSTERDAM AND 71ST. QUICK AS YOU CAN.
THANKS, JAMAL.
POST NO BIL
NEUROTOMY
JAMAL?

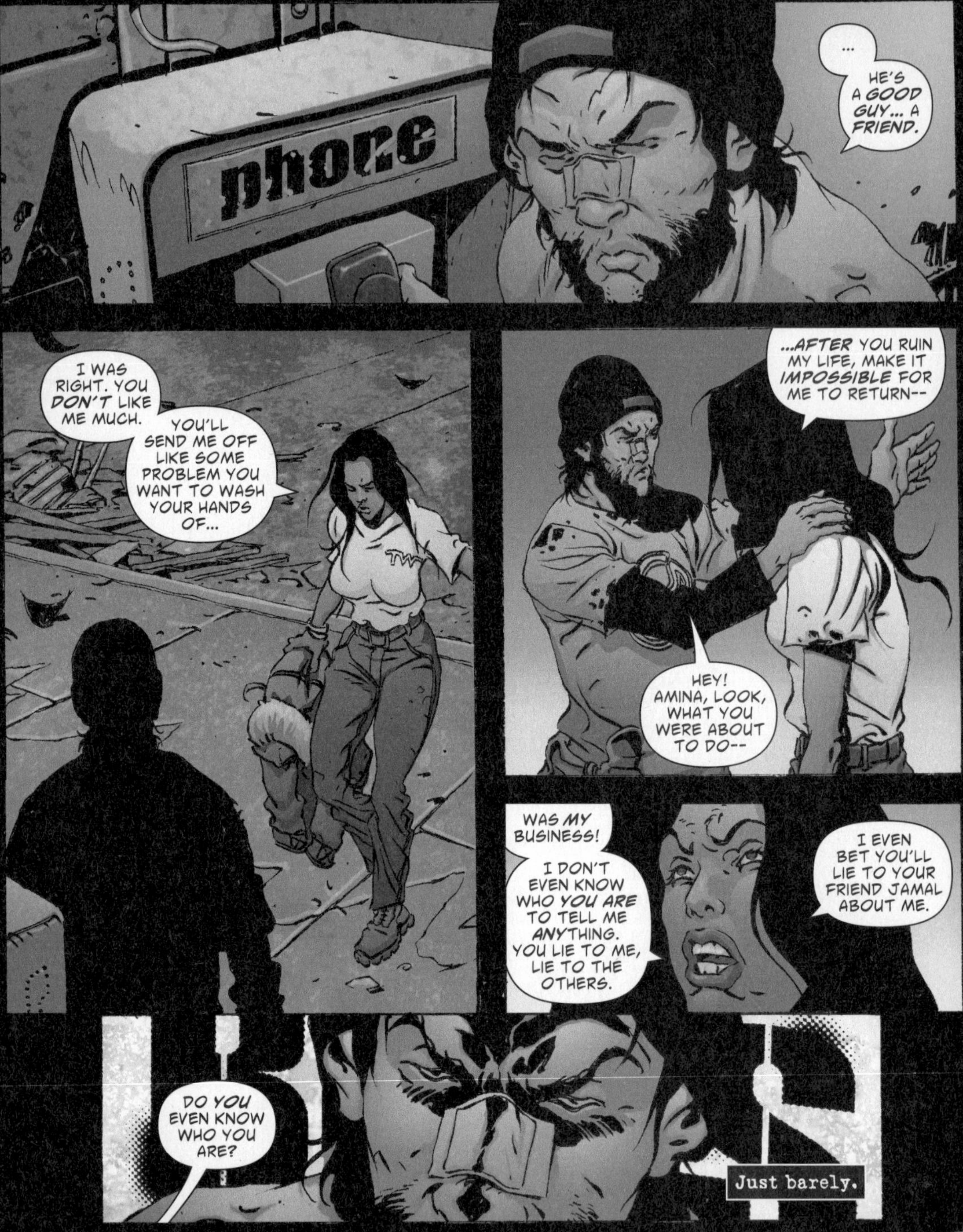
phone
...
HE'S A GOOD GUY... A FRIEND.
I WAS RIGHT. YOU DON'T LIKE ME MUCH.
YOU'LL SEND ME OFF LIKE SOME PROBLEM YOU WANT TO WASH YOUR HANDS OF...
...AFTER YOU RUIN MY LIFE, MAKE IT IMPOSSIBLE FOR ME TO RETURN--
HEY! AMINA, LOOK, WHAT YOU WERE ABOUT TO DO--
WAS MY BUSINESS!
I DON'T EVEN KNOW WHO YOU ARE TO TELL ME ANYTHING. YOU LIE TO ME, LIE TO THE OTHERS.
I EVEN BET YOU'LL LIE TO YOUR FRIEND JAMAL ABOUT ME.
DO YOU EVEN KNOW WHO YOU ARE?
Just barely.

PUBLIC WORKS 4 OF 5

BRIAN WOOD: WRITER AND COVER RICCARDO BURCHIELLI: ARTIST
JEROMY COX: COLORS JARED K. FLETCHER: LETTERS

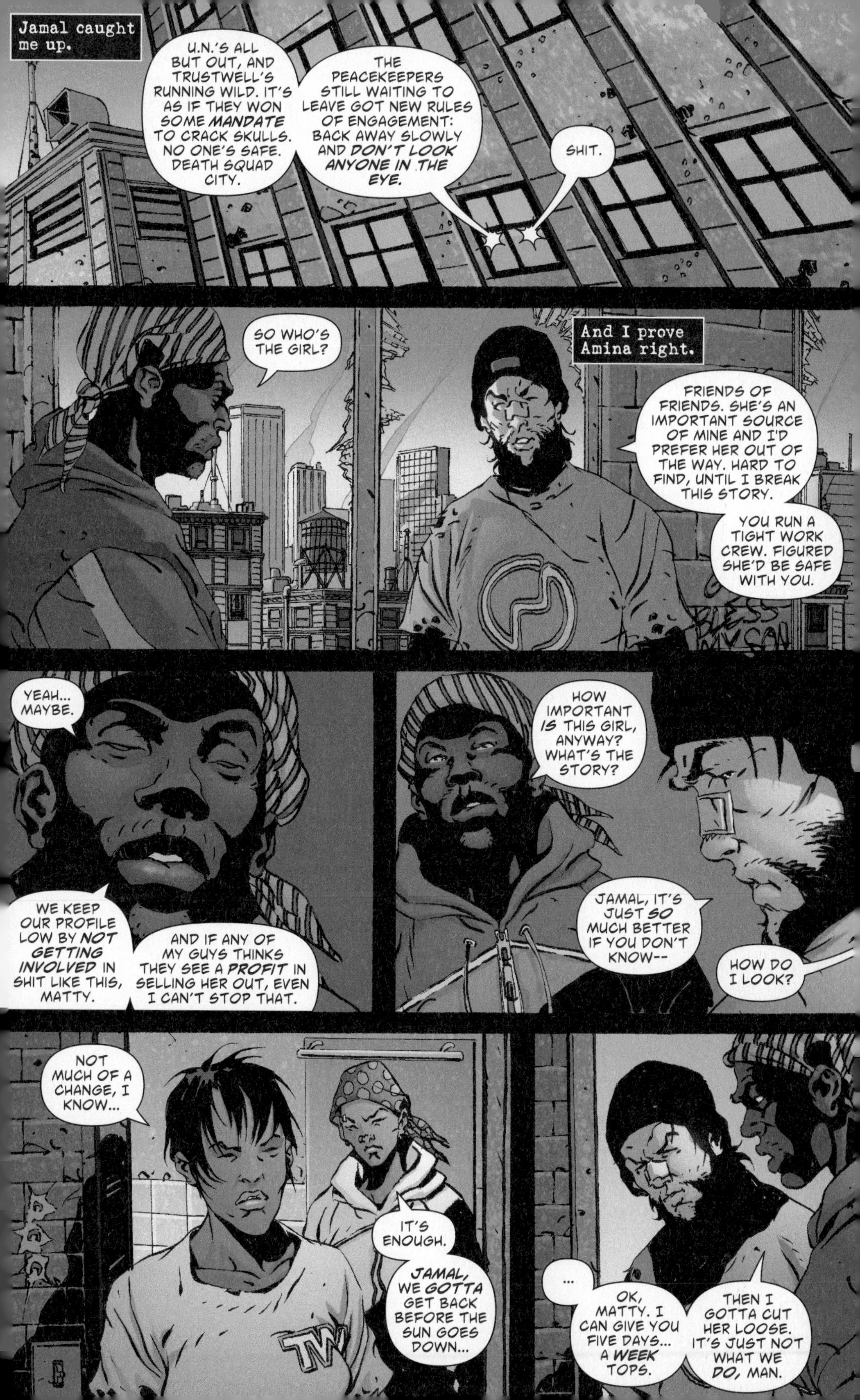
Jamal caught me up.
U.N.'S ALL BUT OUT, AND TRUSTWELL'S RUNNING WILD. IT'S AS IF THEY WON SOME MANDATE TO CRACK SKULLS. NO ONE'S SAFE. DEATH SQUAD CITY.
THE PEACEKEEPERS STILL WAITING TO LEAVE GOT NEW RULES OF ENGAGEMENT: BACK AWAY SLOWLY AND DON'T LOOK ANYONE IN THE EYE.
SHIT.
SO WHO'S THE GIRL?
And I prove Amina right.
FRIENDS OF FRIENDS. SHE'S AN IMPORTANT SOURCE OF MINE AND I'D PREFER HER OUT OF THE WAY. HARD TO FIND, UNTIL I BREAK THIS STORY.
YOU RUN A TIGHT WORK CREW. FIGURED SHE'D BE SAFE WITH YOU.
YEAH... MAYBE.
WE KEEP OUR PROFILE LOW BY NOT GETTING INVOLVED IN SHIT LIKE THIS, MATTY.
AND IF ANY OF MY GUYS THINKS THEY SEE A PROFIT IN SELLING HER OUT, EVEN I CAN'T STOP THAT.
HOW IMPORTANT IS THIS GIRL, ANYWAY? WHAT'S THE STORY?
JAMAL, IT'S JUST SO MUCH BETTER IF YOU DON'T KNOW--
HOW DO I LOOK?
NOT MUCH OF A CHANGE, I KNOW...
IT'S ENOUGH.
JAMAL, WE GOTTA GET BACK BEFORE THE SUN GOES DOWN...
...
OK, MATTY. I CAN GIVE YOU FIVE DAYS... A WEEK TOPS.
THEN I GOTTA CUT HER LOOSE. IT'S JUST NOT WHAT WE DO, MAN.

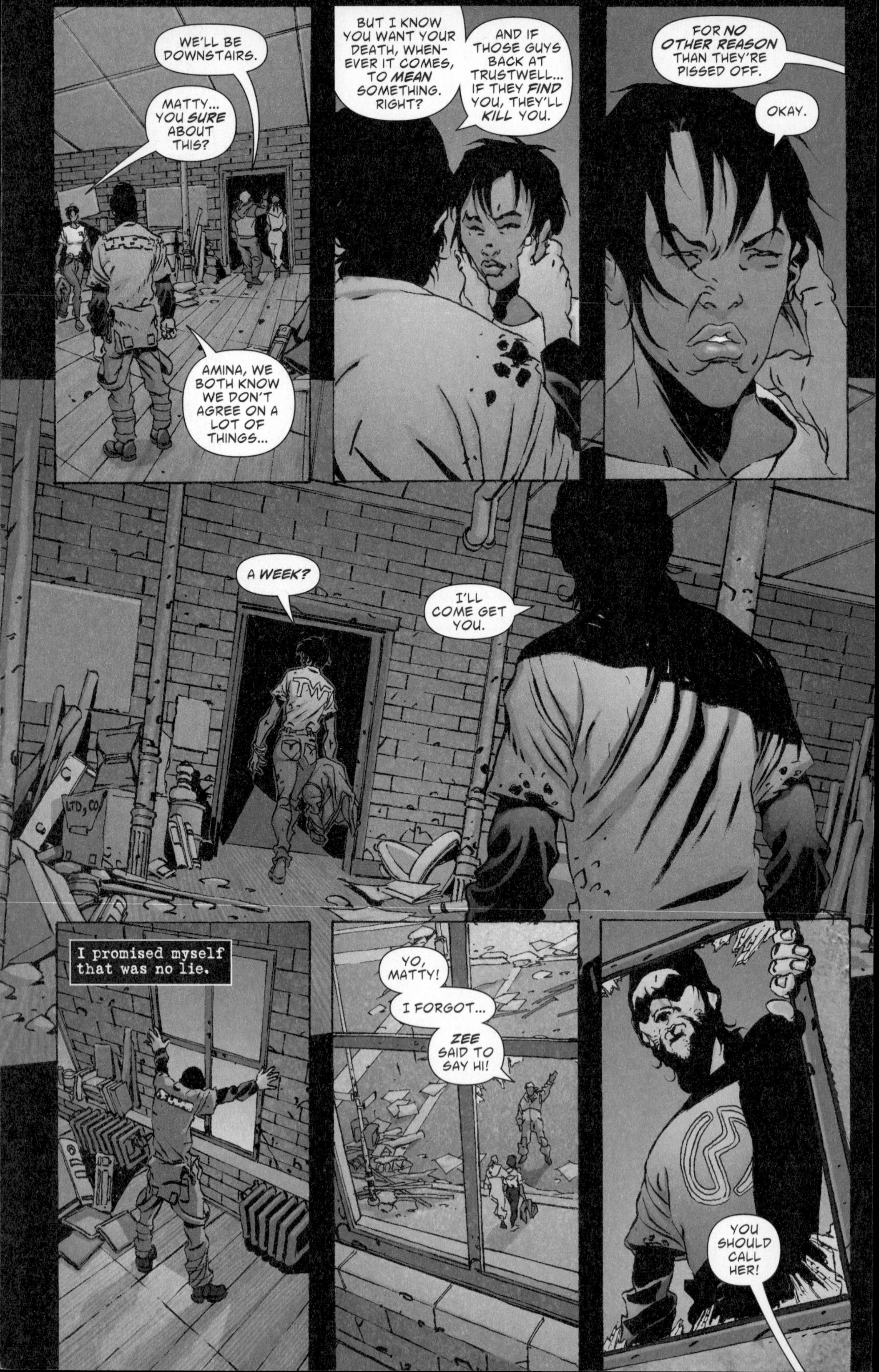
WE'LL BE DOWNSTAIRS.
MATTY... YOU SURE ABOUT THIS?
AMINA, WE BOTH KNOW WE DON'T AGREE ON A LOT OF THINGS...
BUT I KNOW YOU WANT YOUR DEATH, WHENEVER IT COMES, TO MEAN SOMETHING. RIGHT?
AND IF THOSE GUYS BACK AT TRUSTWELL... IF THEY FIND YOU, THEY'LL KILL YOU.
FOR NO OTHER REASON THAN THEY'RE PISSED OFF.
OKAY.
A WEEK?
I'LL COME GET YOU.
I promised myself that was no lie.
YO, MATTY!
I FORGOT...
ZEE SAID TO SAY HI!
YOU SHOULD CALL HER!

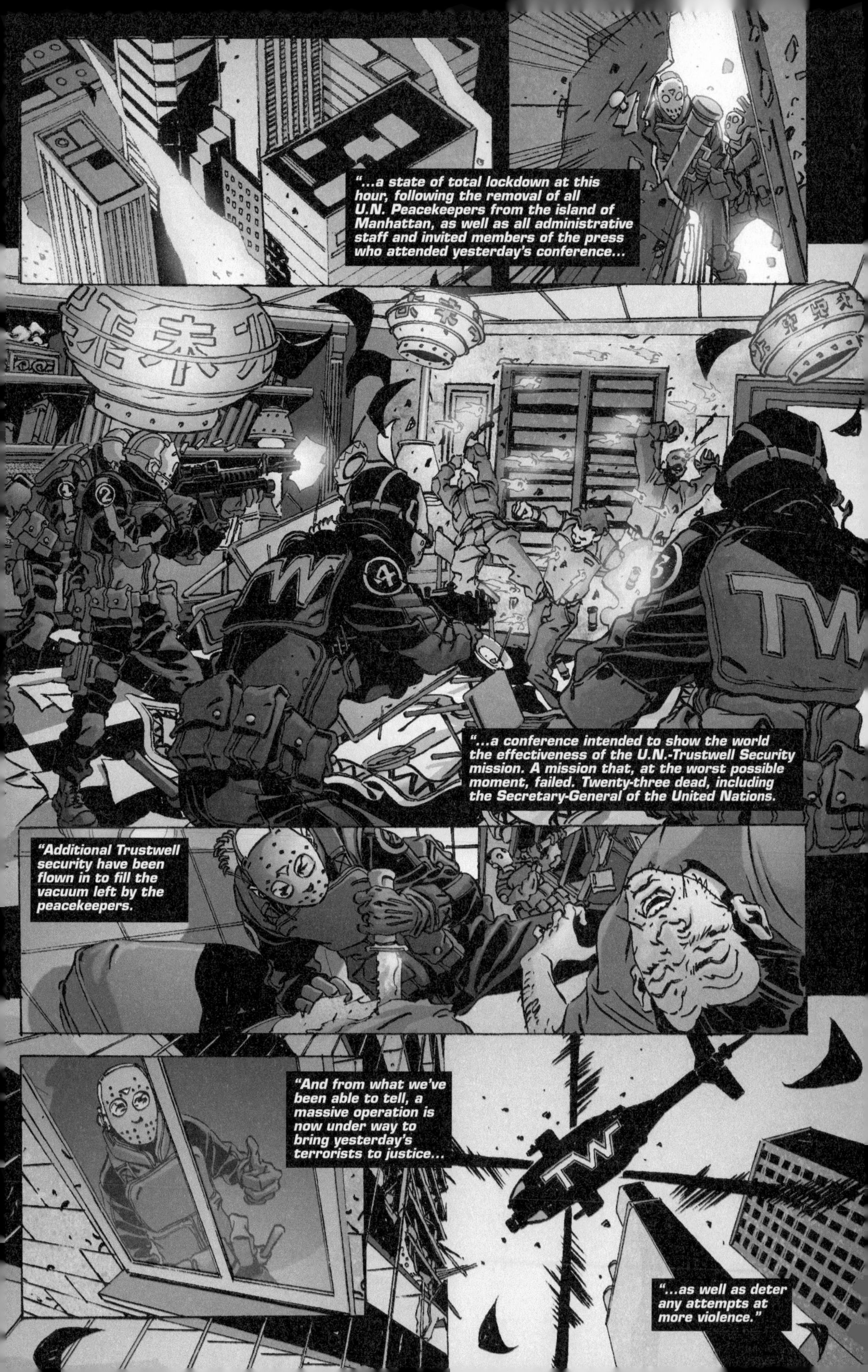
"...a state of total lockdown at this hour, following the removal of all U.N. Peacekeepers from the island of Manhattan, as well as all administrative staff and invited members of the press who attended yesterday's conference...
"...a conference intended to show the world the effectiveness of the U.N.-Trustwell Security mission. A mission that, at the worst possible moment, failed. Twenty-three dead, including the Secretary-General of the United Nations.
"Additional Trustwell security have been flown in to fill the vacuum left by the peacekeepers.
"And from what we've been able to tell, a massive operation is now under way to bring yesterday's terrorists to justice...
"...as well as deter any attempts at more violence."

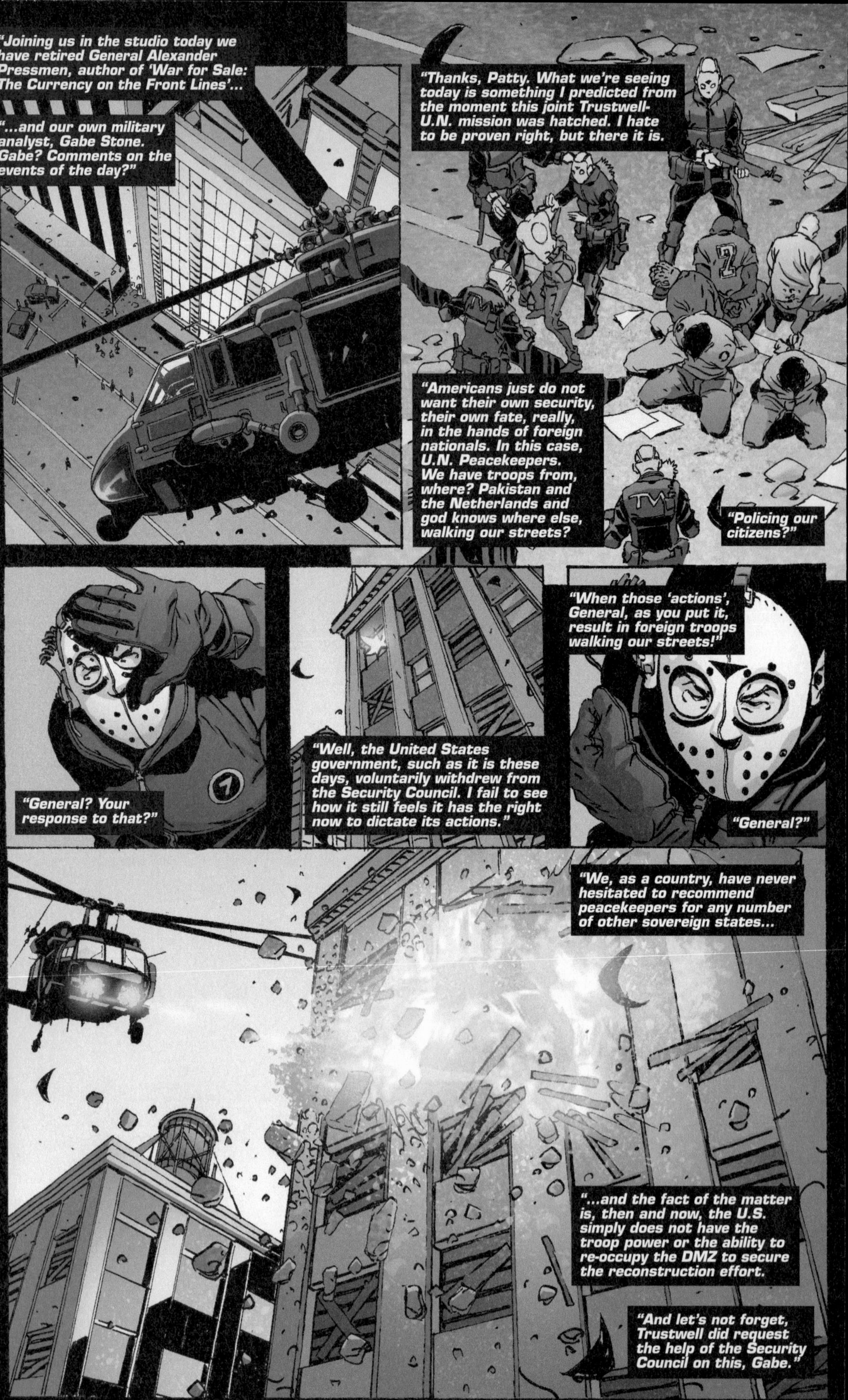
"Joining us in the studio today we have retired General Alexander Pressmen, author of 'War for Sale: The Currency on the Front Lines'...
"...and our own military analyst, Gabe Stone. Gabe? Comments on the events of the day?"
"Thanks, Patty. What we're seeing today is something I predicted from the moment this joint Trustwell-U.N. mission was hatched. I hate to be proven right, but there it is.
"Americans just do not want their own security, their own fate, really, in the hands of foreign nationals. In this case, U.N. Peacekeepers. We have troops from, where? Pakistan and the Netherlands and god knows where else, walking our streets?
"Policing our citizens?"
"General? Your response to that?"
"Well, the United States government, such as it is these days, voluntarily withdrew from the Security Council. I fail to see how it still feels it has the right now to dictate its actions."
"When those 'actions', General, as you put it, result in foreign troops walking our streets!"
"General?"
"We, as a country, have never hesitated to recommend peacekeepers for any number of other sovereign states...
"...and the fact of the matter is, then and now, the U.S. simply does not have the troop power or the ability to re-occupy the DMZ to secure the reconstruction effort.
"And let's not forget, Trustwell did request the help of the Security Council on this, Gabe."

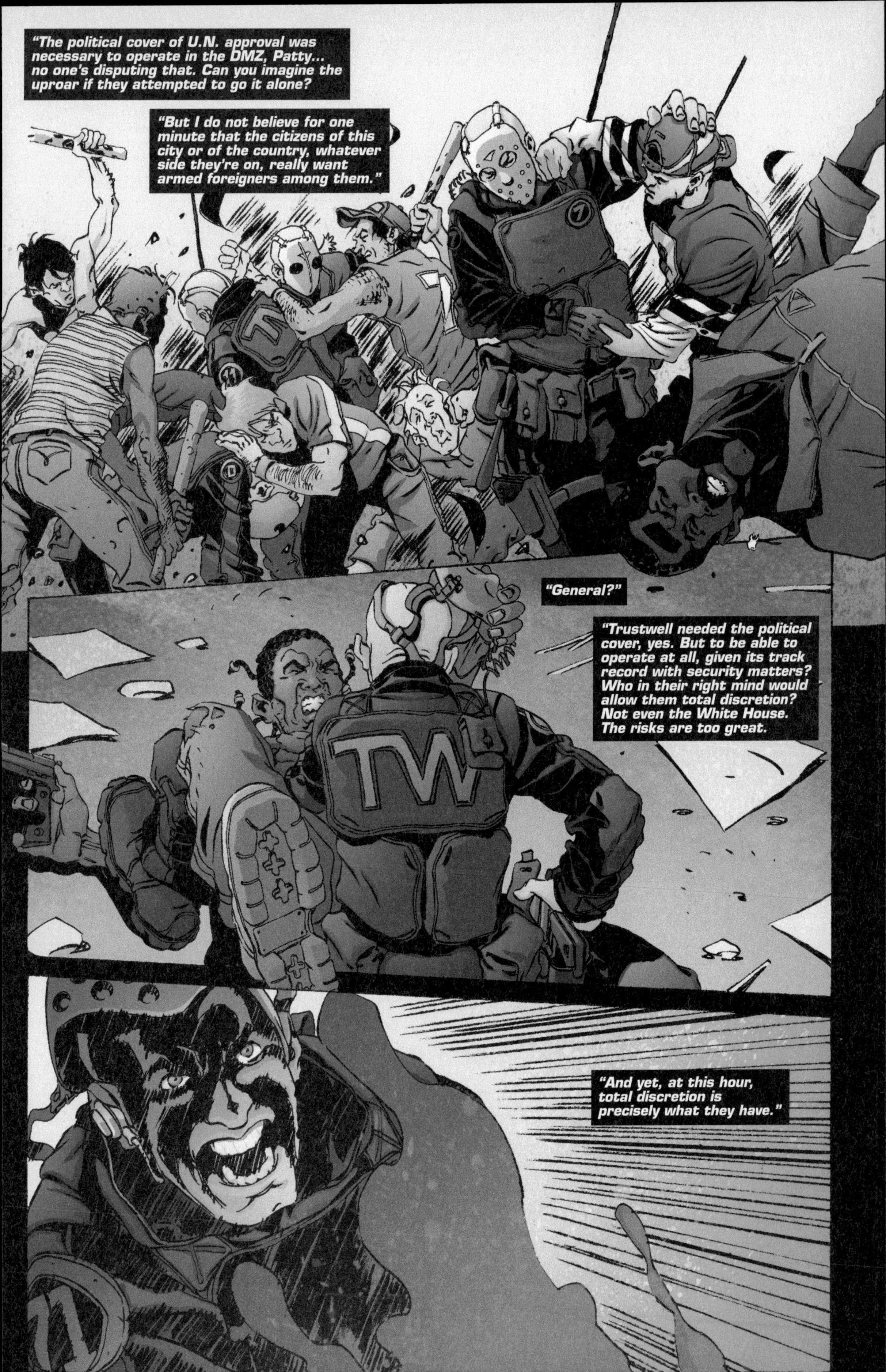
"The political cover of U.N. approval was necessary to operate in the DMZ, Patty... no one's disputing that. Can you imagine the uproar if they attempted to go it alone?
"But I do not believe for one minute that the citizens of this city or of the country, whatever side they're on, really want armed foreigners among them."
"General?"
"Trustwell needed the political cover, yes. But to be able to operate at all, given its track record with security matters? Who in their right mind would allow them total discretion? Not even the White House. The risks are too great.
TW
"And yet, at this hour, total discretion is precisely what they have."

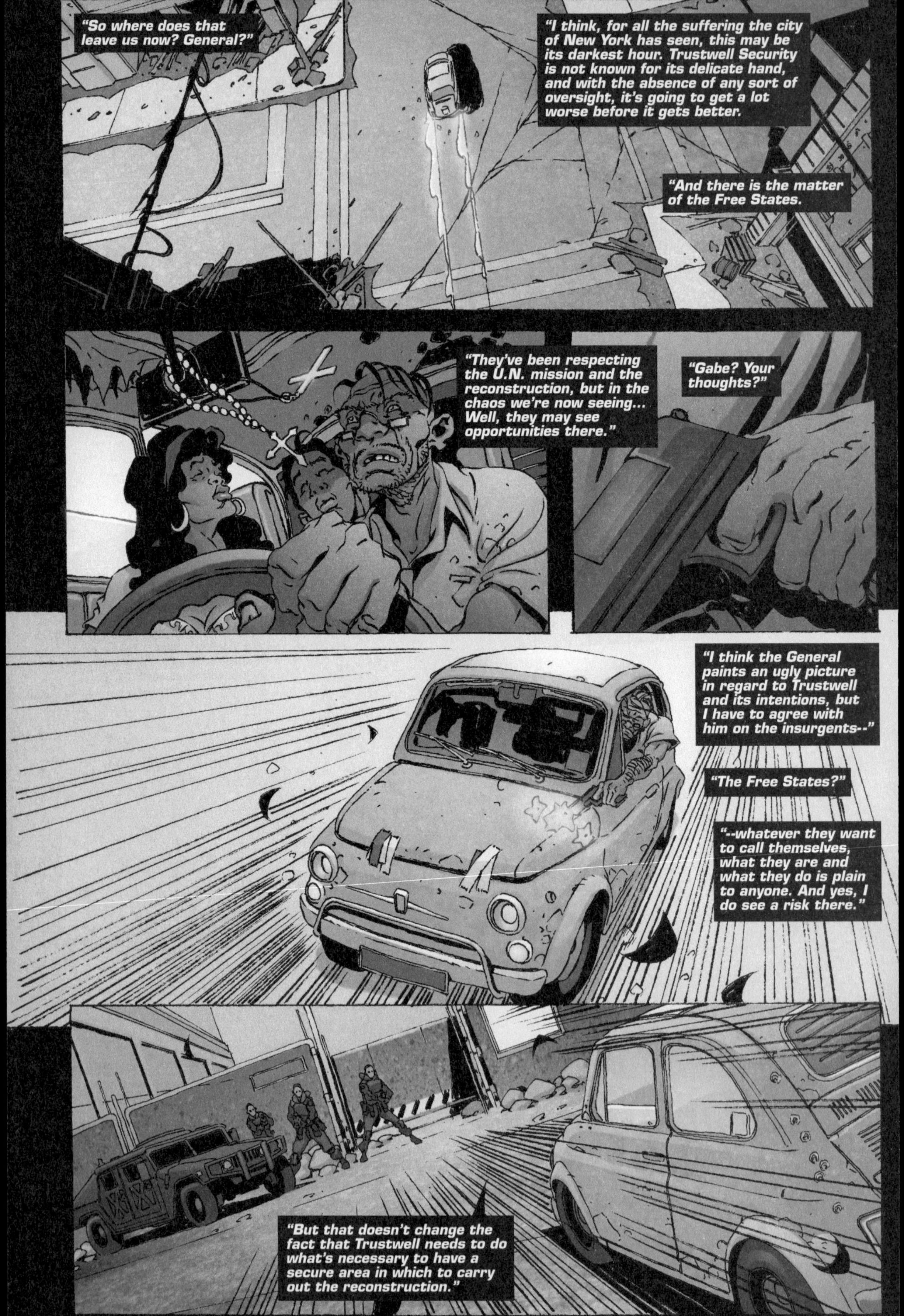

"So where does that leave us now? General?"
"I think, for all the suffering the city of New York has seen, this may be its darkest hour. Trustwell Security is not known for its delicate hand, and with the absence of any sort of oversight, it's going to get a lot worse before it gets better.
"And there is the matter of the Free States.
"They've been respecting the U.N. mission and the reconstruction, but in the chaos we're now seeing... Well, they may see opportunities there."
"Gabe? Your thoughts?"
"I think the General paints an ugly picture in regard to Trustwell and its intentions, but I have to agree with him on the insurgents--"
"The Free States?"
"--whatever they want to call themselves, what they are and what they do is plain to anyone. And yes, I do see a risk there."
"But that doesn't change the fact that Trustwell needs to do what's necessary to have a secure area in which to carry out the reconstruction."

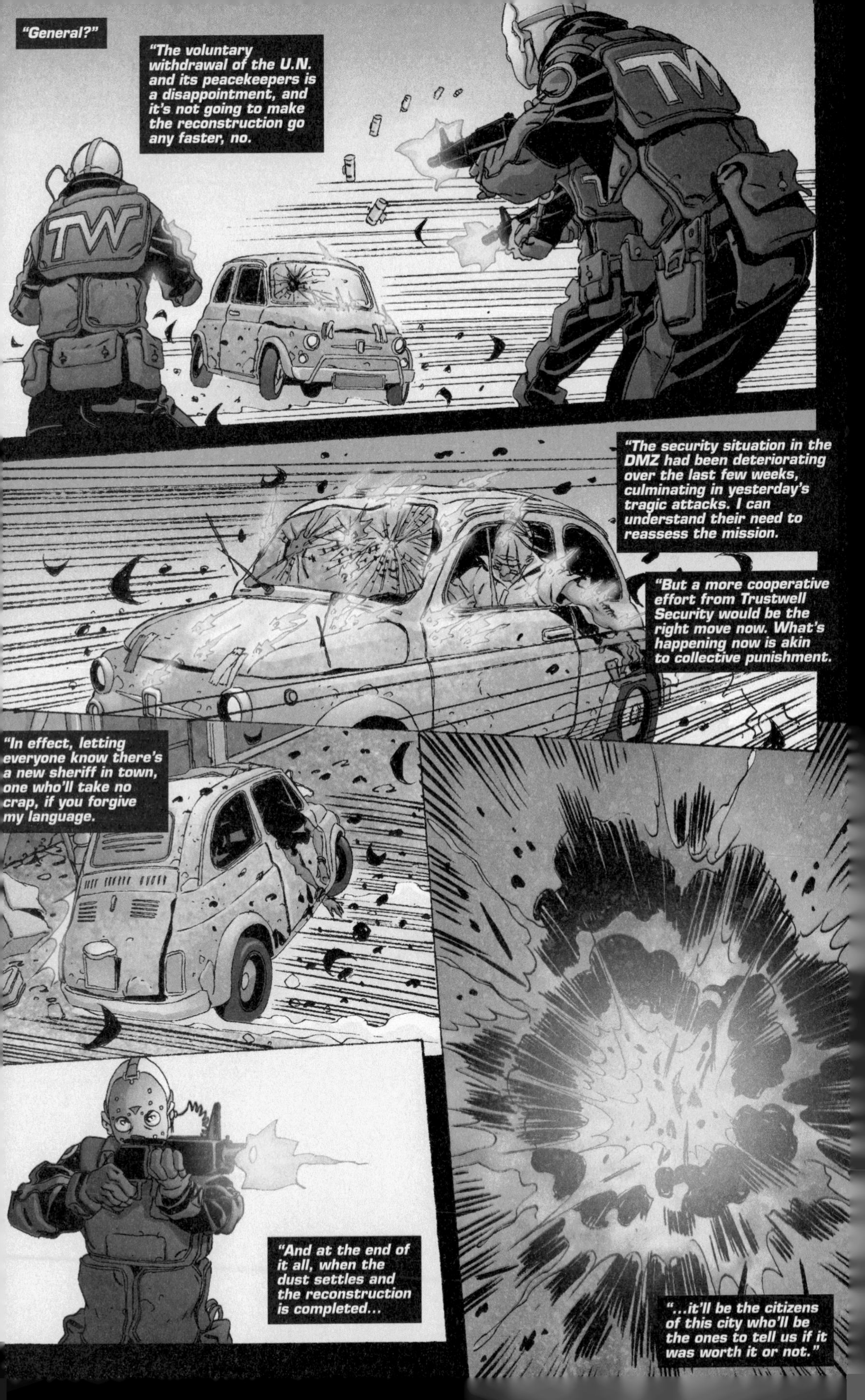
"General?"
"The voluntary withdrawal of the U.N. and its peacekeepers is a disappointment, and it's not going to make the reconstruction go any faster, no.
"The security situation in the DMZ had been deteriorating over the last few weeks, culminating in yesterday's tragic attacks. I can understand their need to reassess the mission.
"But a more cooperative effort from Trustwell Security would be the right move now. What's happening now is akin to collective punishment.
"In effect, letting everyone know there's a new sheriff in town, one who'll take no crap, if you forgive my language.
"And at the end of it all, when the dust settles and the reconstruction is completed...
"...it'll be the citizens of this city who'll be the ones to tell us if it was worth it or not."
TW
TW

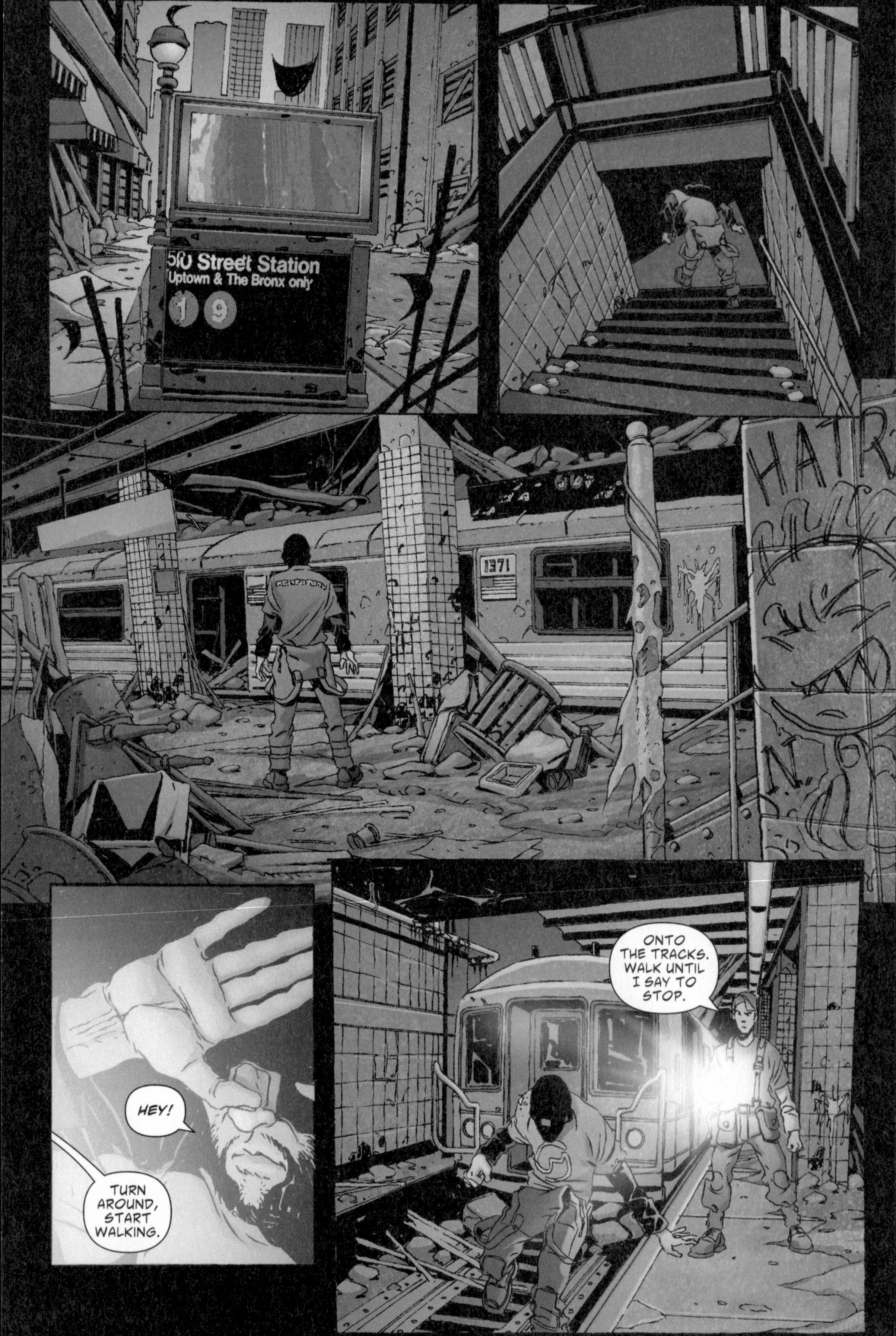
Street Station
Uptown & The Bronx only
1
9
1371
HEY!
TURN AROUND, START WALKING.
ONTO THE TRACKS. WALK UNTIL I SAY TO STOP.

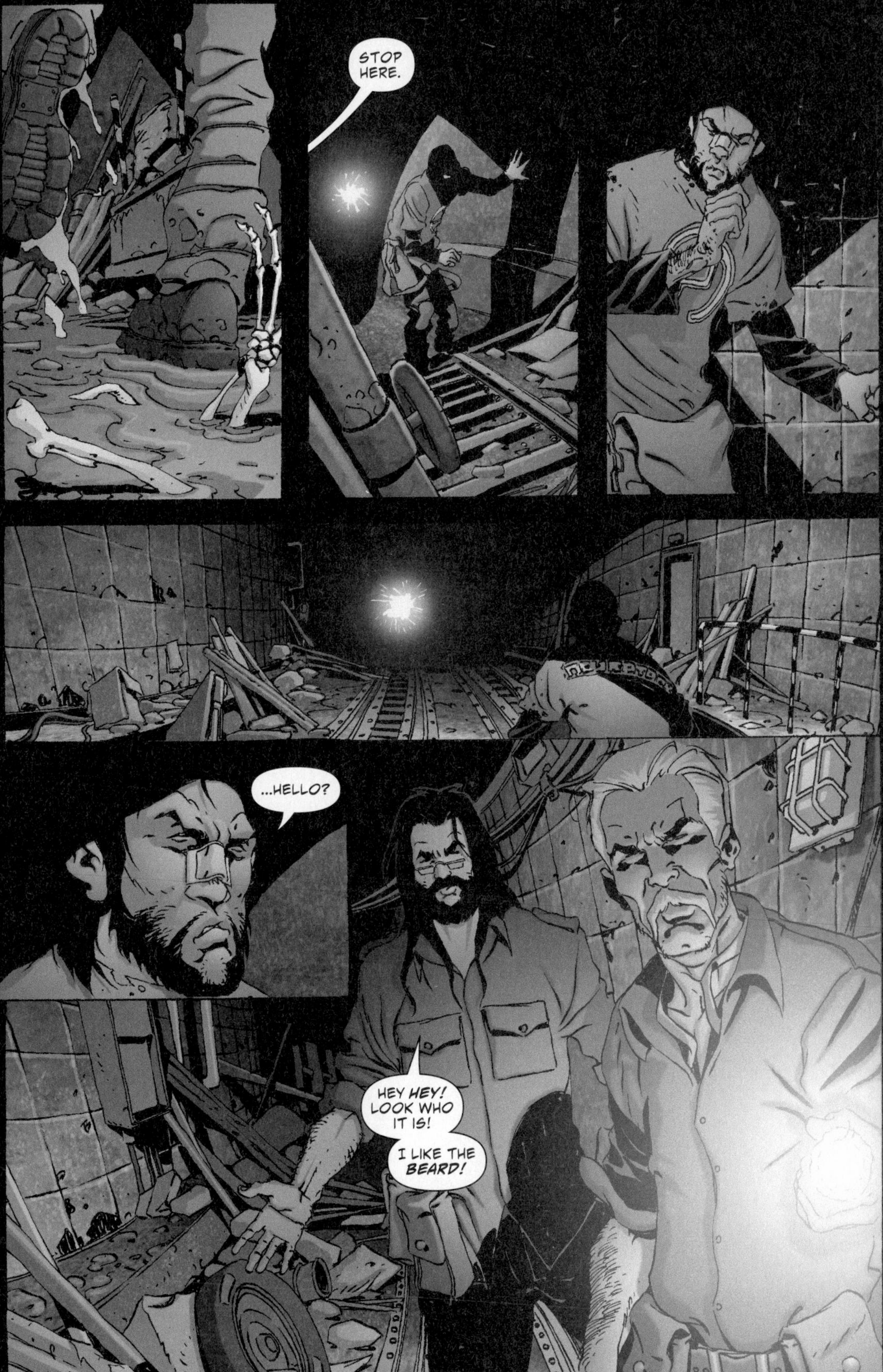
STOP HERE.
...HELLO?
HEY HEY! LOOK WHO IT IS!
I LIKE THE BEARD!

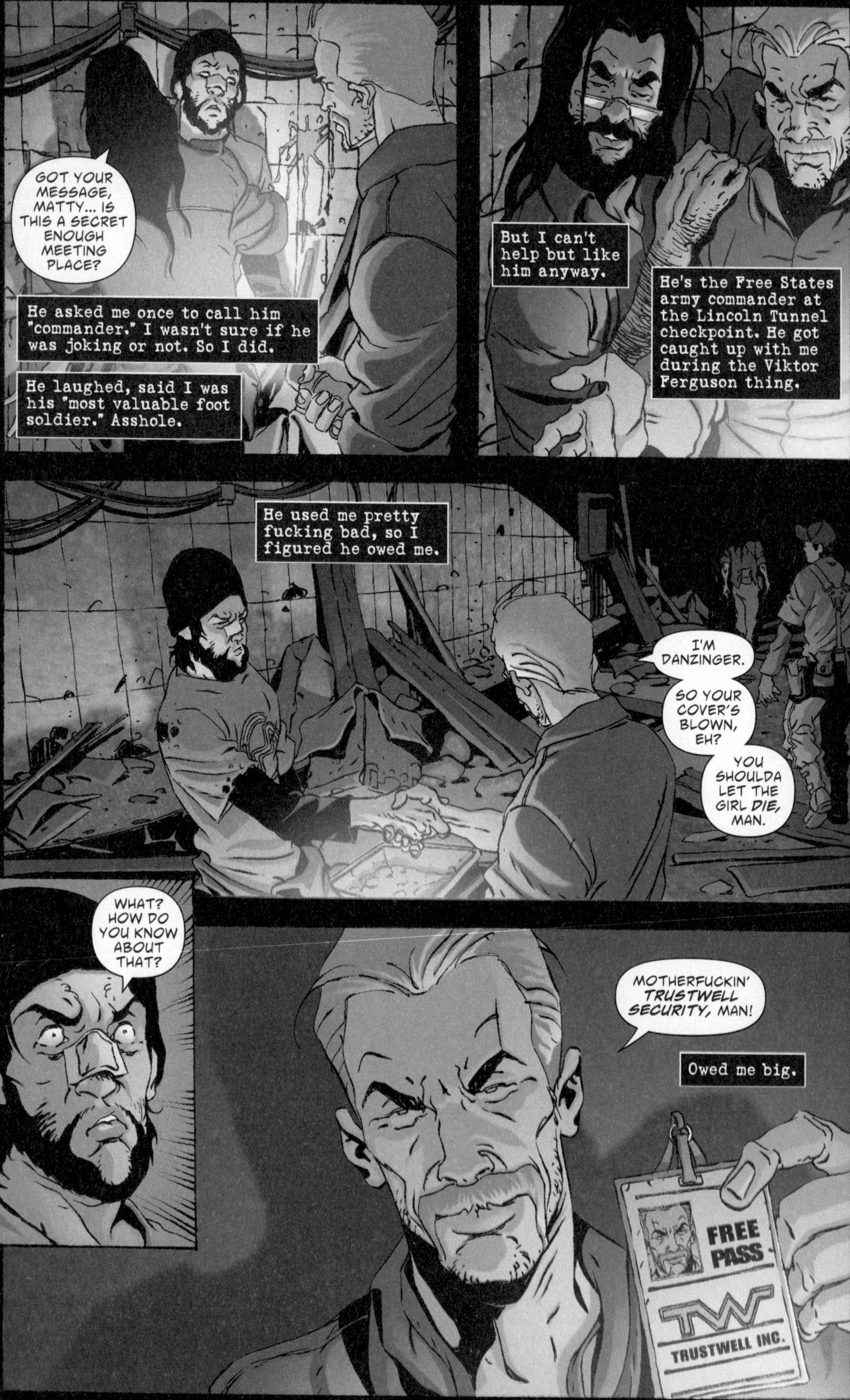
GOT YOUR MESSAGE, MATTY... IS THIS A SECRET ENOUGH MEETING PLACE?
He asked me once to call him "commander." I wasn't sure if he was joking or not. So I did.
He laughed, said I was his "most valuable foot soldier." Asshole.
But I can't help but like him anyway.
He's the Free States army commander at the Lincoln Tunnel checkpoint. He got caught up with me during the Viktor Ferguson thing.
He used me pretty fucking bad, so I figured he owed me.
I'M DANZINGER.
SO YOUR COVER'S BLOWN, EH?
YOU SHOULDA LET THE GIRL DIE, MAN.
WHAT? HOW DO YOU KNOW ABOUT THAT?
MOTHERFUCKIN' TRUSTWELL SECURITY, MAN!
Owed me big.
FREE PASS
TW
TRUSTWELL INC.

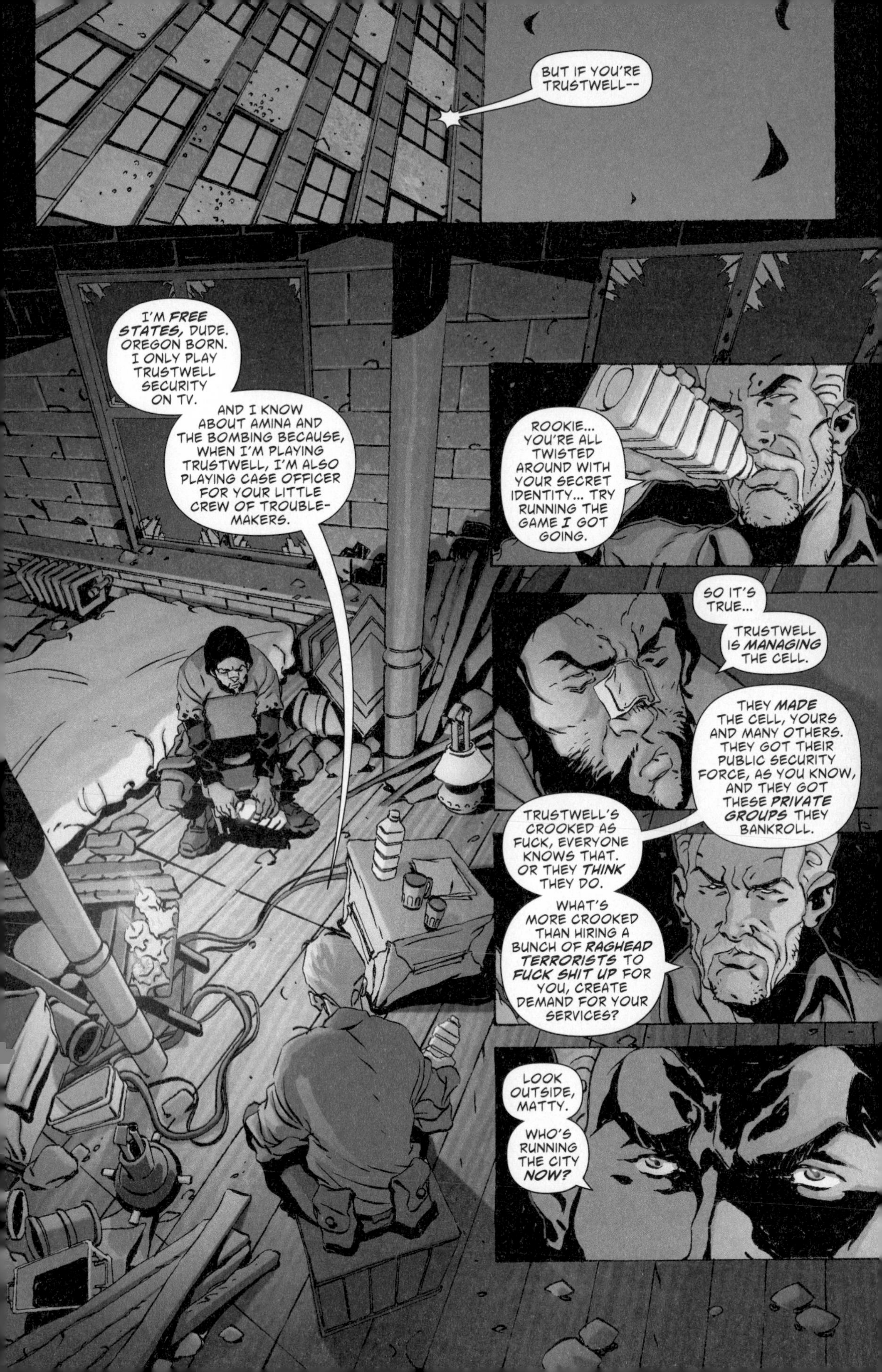
BUT IF YOU'RE TRUSTWELL--
I'M FREE STATES, DUDE. OREGON BORN. I ONLY PLAY TRUSTWELL SECURITY ON TV.
AND I KNOW ABOUT AMINA AND THE BOMBING BECAUSE, WHEN I'M PLAYING TRUSTWELL, I'M ALSO PLAYING CASE OFFICER FOR YOUR LITTLE CREW OF TROUBLE-MAKERS.
ROOKIE... YOU'RE ALL TWISTED AROUND WITH YOUR SECRET IDENTITY... TRY RUNNING THE GAME I GOT GOING.
SO IT'S TRUE...
TRUSTWELL IS MANAGING THE CELL.
THEY MADE THE CELL, YOURS AND MANY OTHERS. THEY GOT THEIR PUBLIC SECURITY FORCE, AS YOU KNOW, AND THEY GOT THESE PRIVATE GROUPS THEY BANKROLL.
TRUSTWELL'S CROOKED AS FUCK, EVERYONE KNOWS THAT. OR THEY THINK THEY DO.
WHAT'S MORE CROOKED THAN HIRING A BUNCH OF RAGHEAD TERRORISTS TO FUCK SHIT UP FOR YOU, CREATE DEMAND FOR YOUR SERVICES?
LOOK OUTSIDE, MATTY.
WHO'S RUNNING THE CITY NOW?

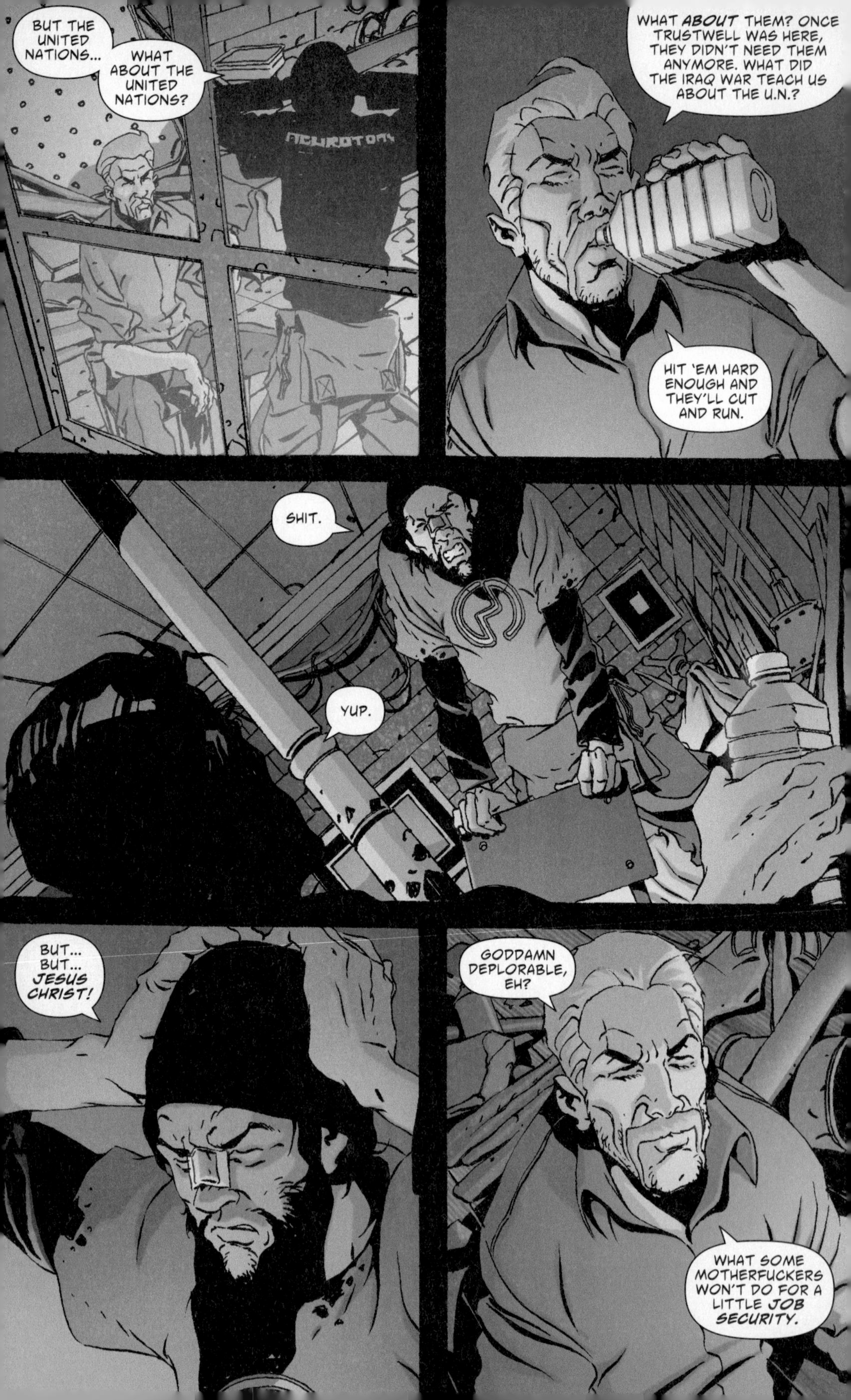
BUT THE UNITED NATIONS...
WHAT ABOUT THE UNITED NATIONS?
WHAT *ABOUT* THEM? ONCE TRUSTWELL WAS HERE, THEY DIDN'T NEED THEM ANYMORE. WHAT DID THE IRAQ WAR TEACH US ABOUT THE U.N.?
HIT 'EM HARD ENOUGH AND THEY'LL CUT AND RUN.
SHIT.
YUP.
BUT... BUT... *JESUS CHRIST!*
GODDAMN DEPLORABLE, EH?
WHAT SOME MOTHERFUCKERS WON'T DO FOR A LITTLE *JOB SECURITY.*

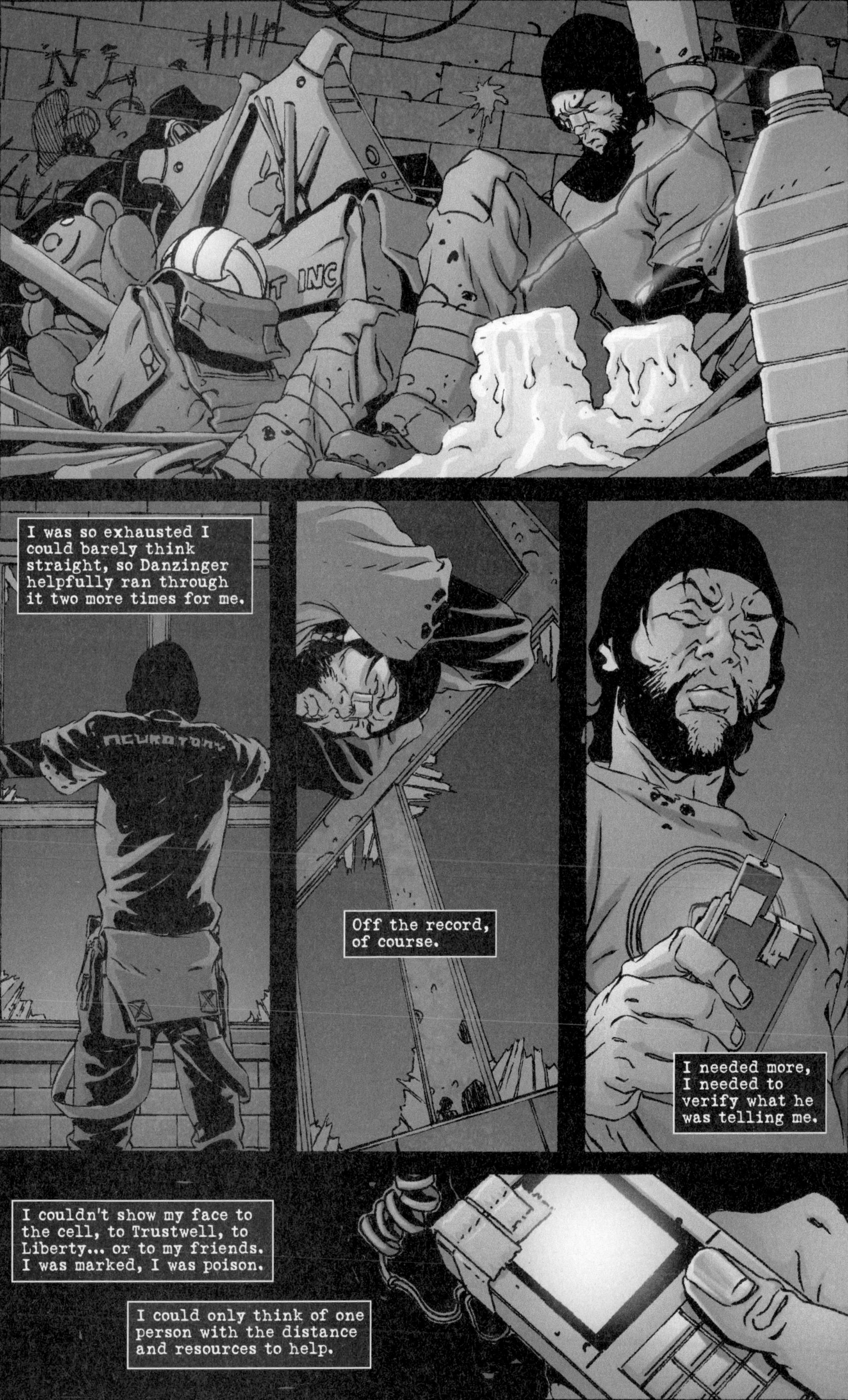
I was so exhausted I could barely think straight, so Danzinger helpfully ran through it two more times for me.
Off the record, of course.
I needed more, I needed to verify what he was telling me.
I couldn't show my face to the cell, to Trustwell, to Liberty... or to my friends. I was marked, I was poison.
I could only think of one person with the distance and resources to help.

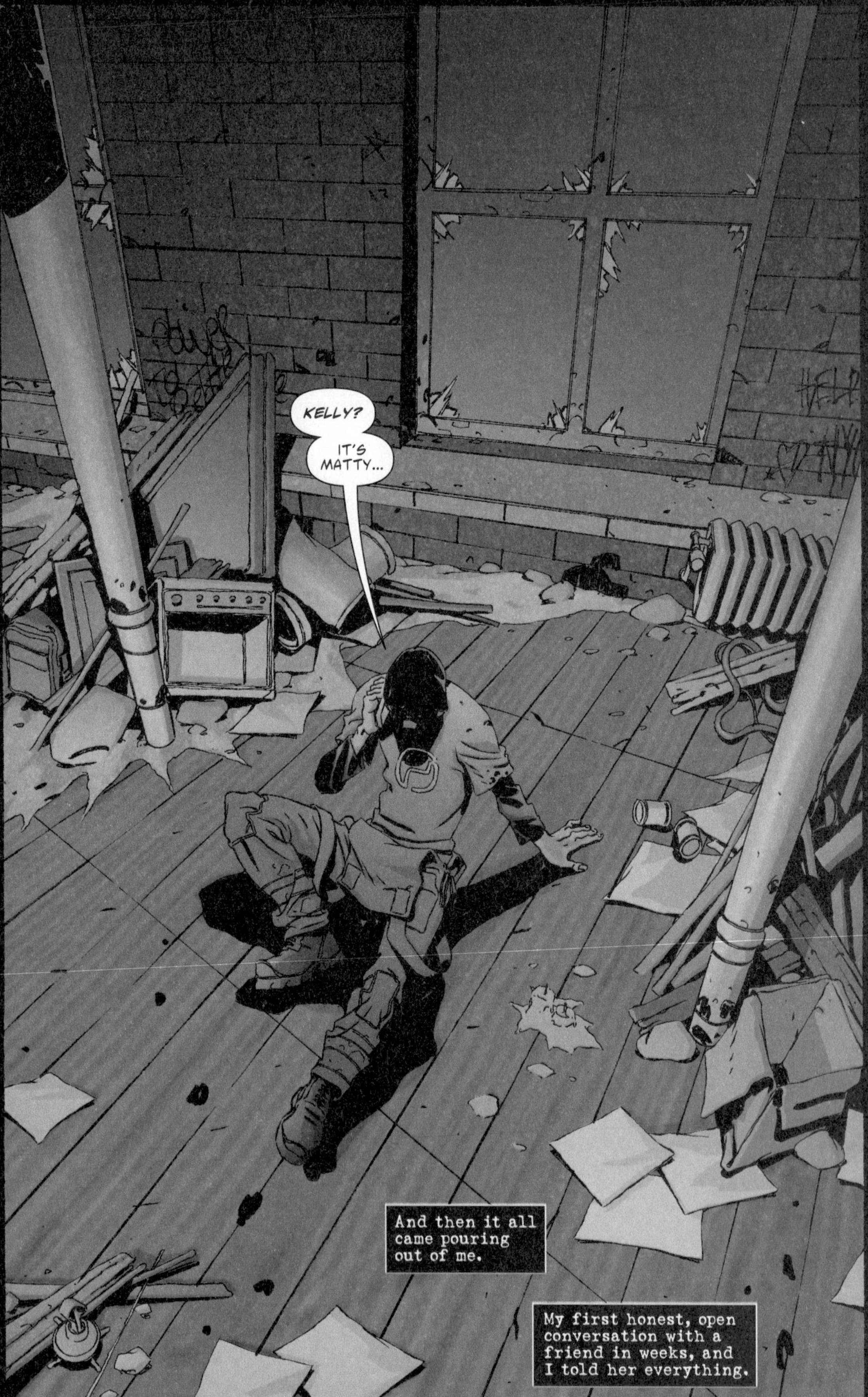
KELLY?
IT'S MATTY...
And then it all came pouring out of me.
My first honest, open conversation with a friend in weeks, and I told her everything.

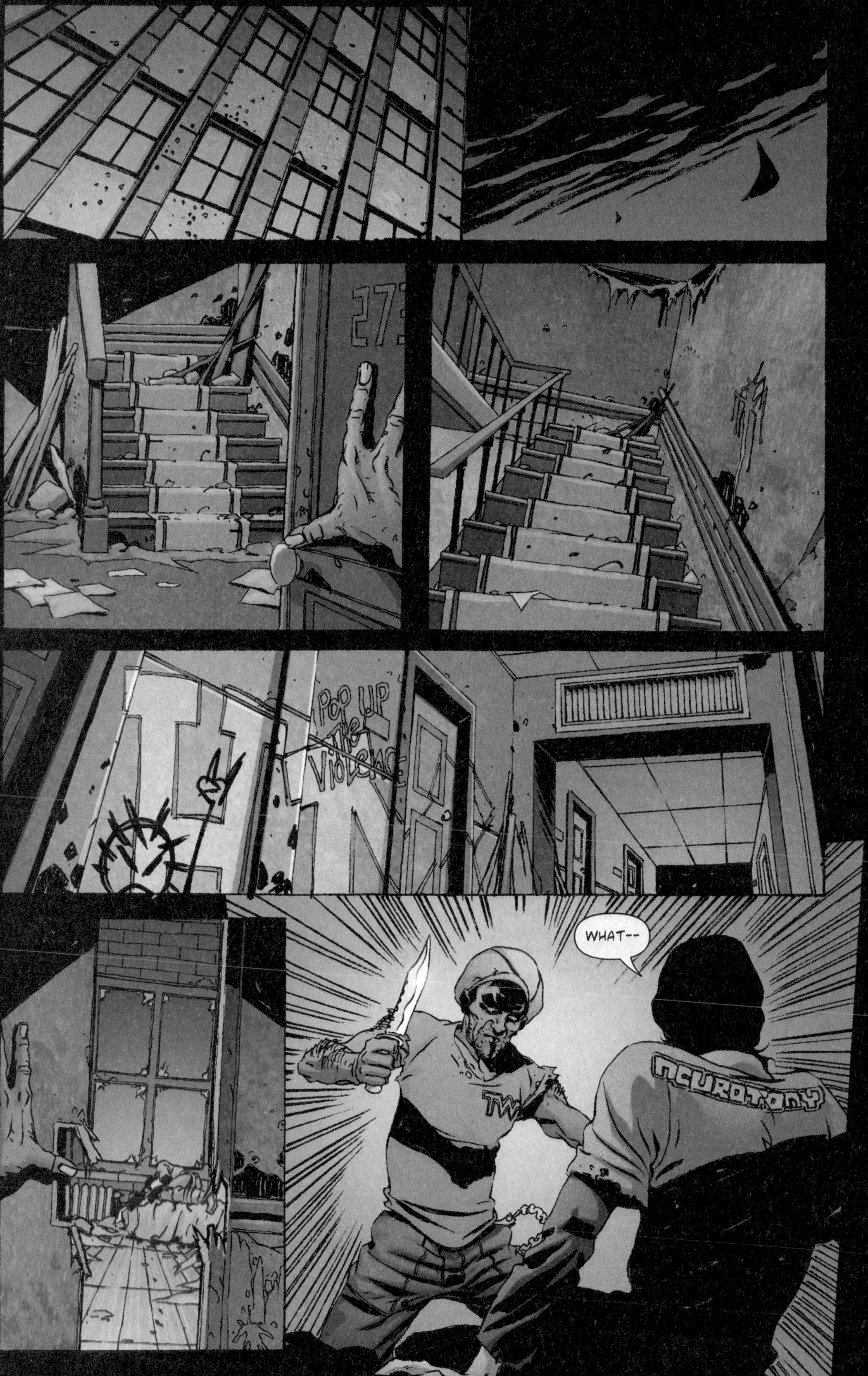
273
POP UP THE VIOLENCE
WHAT--
TW
NEUROTONY

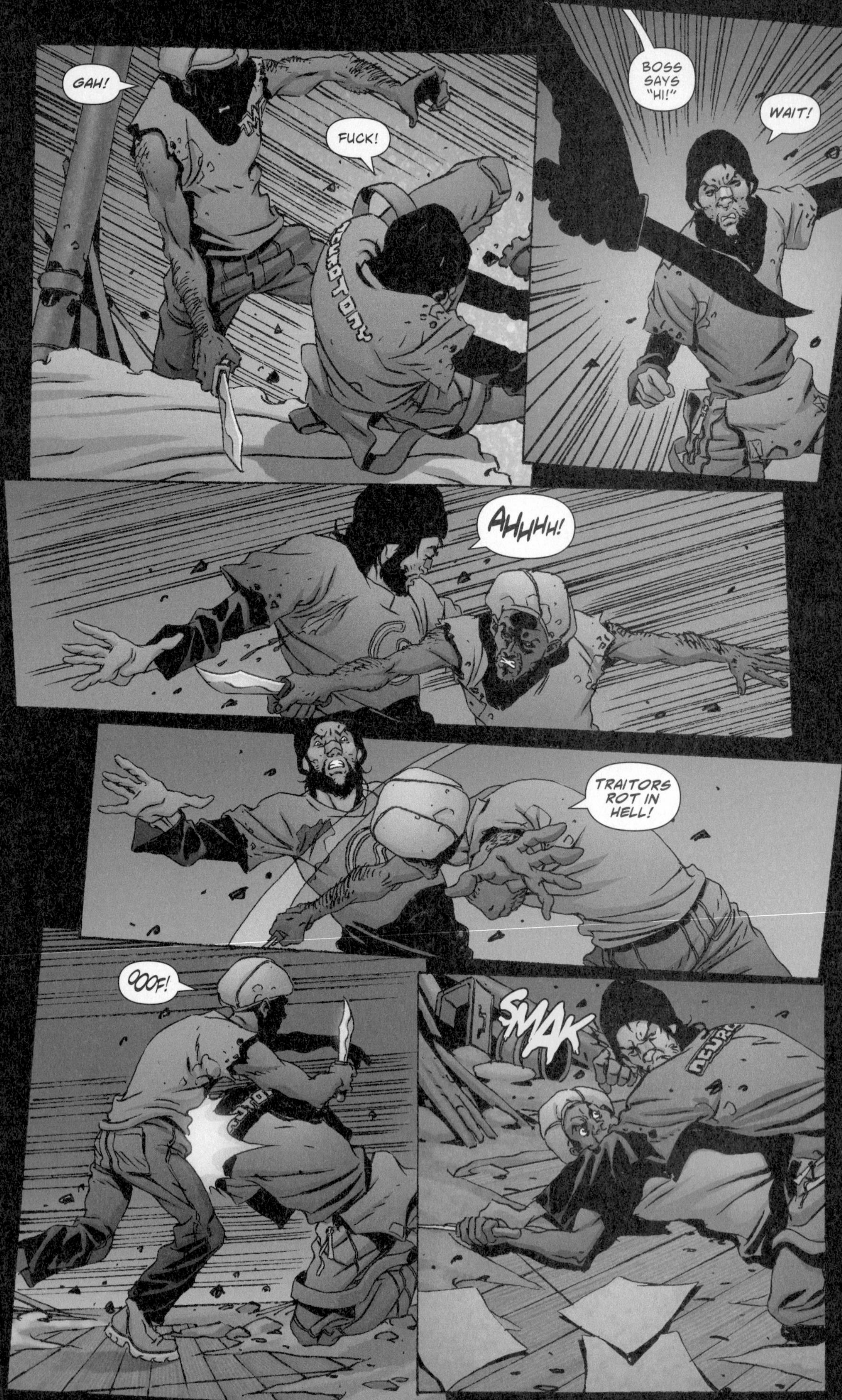
GAH!
FUCK!
BOSS SAYS "HI!"
WAIT!
AHHHH!
TRAITORS ROT IN HELL!
OOOF!
SMAK

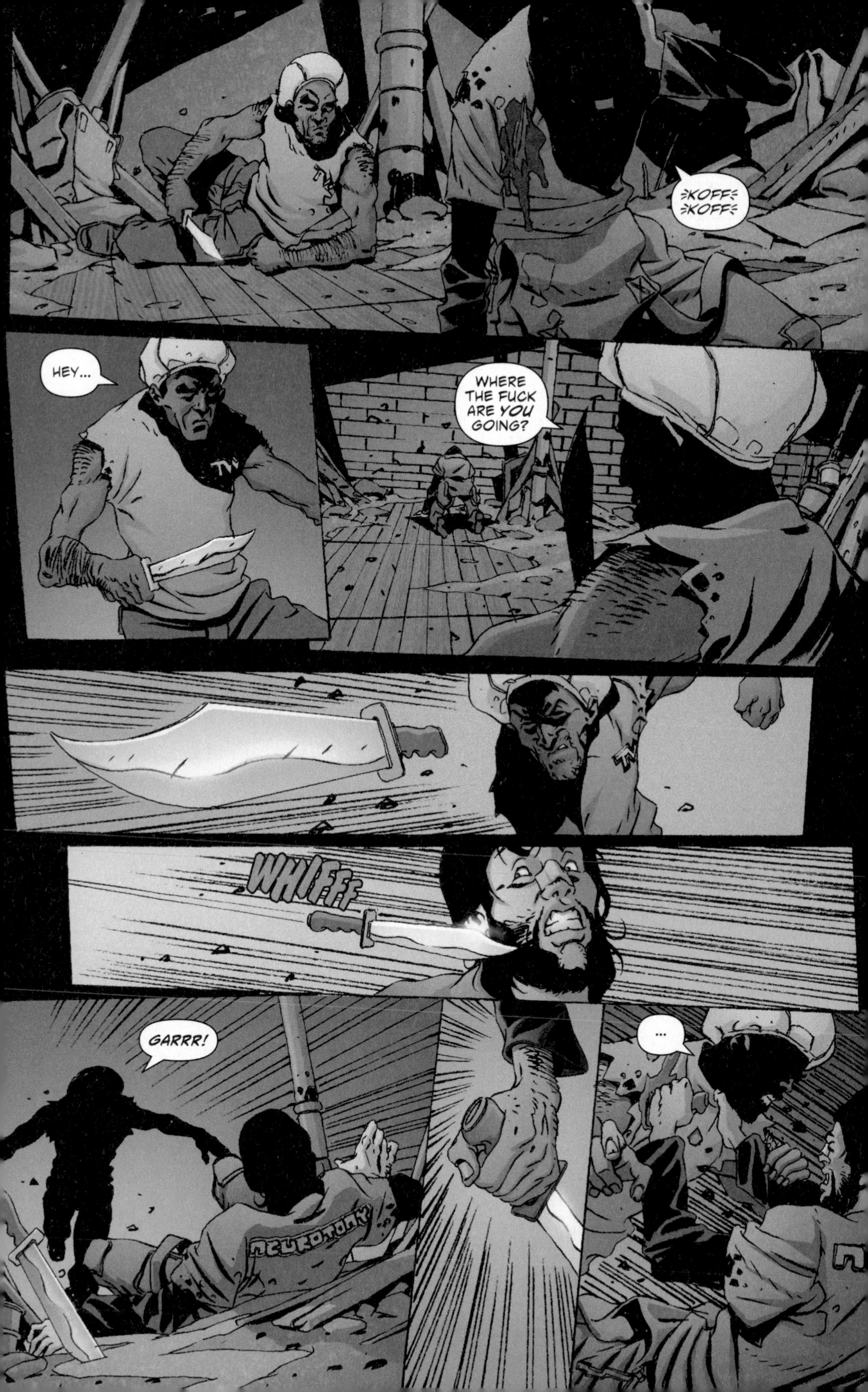
KOFF KOFF
HEY...
WHERE THE FUCK ARE YOU GOING?
WHIFFF
GARRR!
...

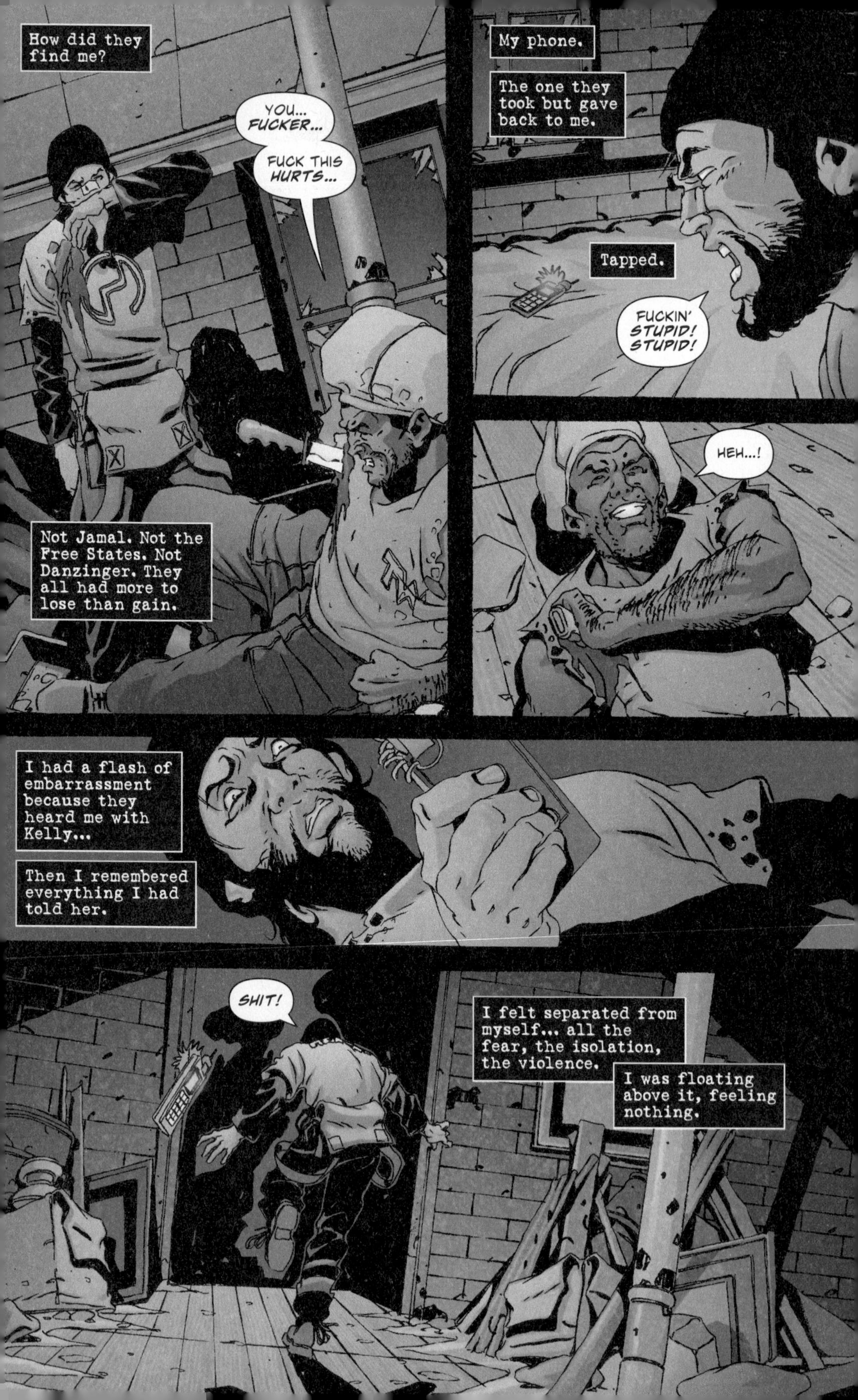
How did they find me?
YOU... FUCKER...
FUCK THIS HURTS...
Not Jamal. Not the Free States. Not Danzinger. They all had more to lose than gain.
My phone.
The one they took but gave back to me.
Tapped.
FUCKIN' STUPID! STUPID!
HEH...!
I had a flash of embarrassment because they heard me with Kelly...
Then I remembered everything I had told her.
SHIT!
I felt separated from myself... all the fear, the isolation, the violence.
I was floating above it, feeling nothing.

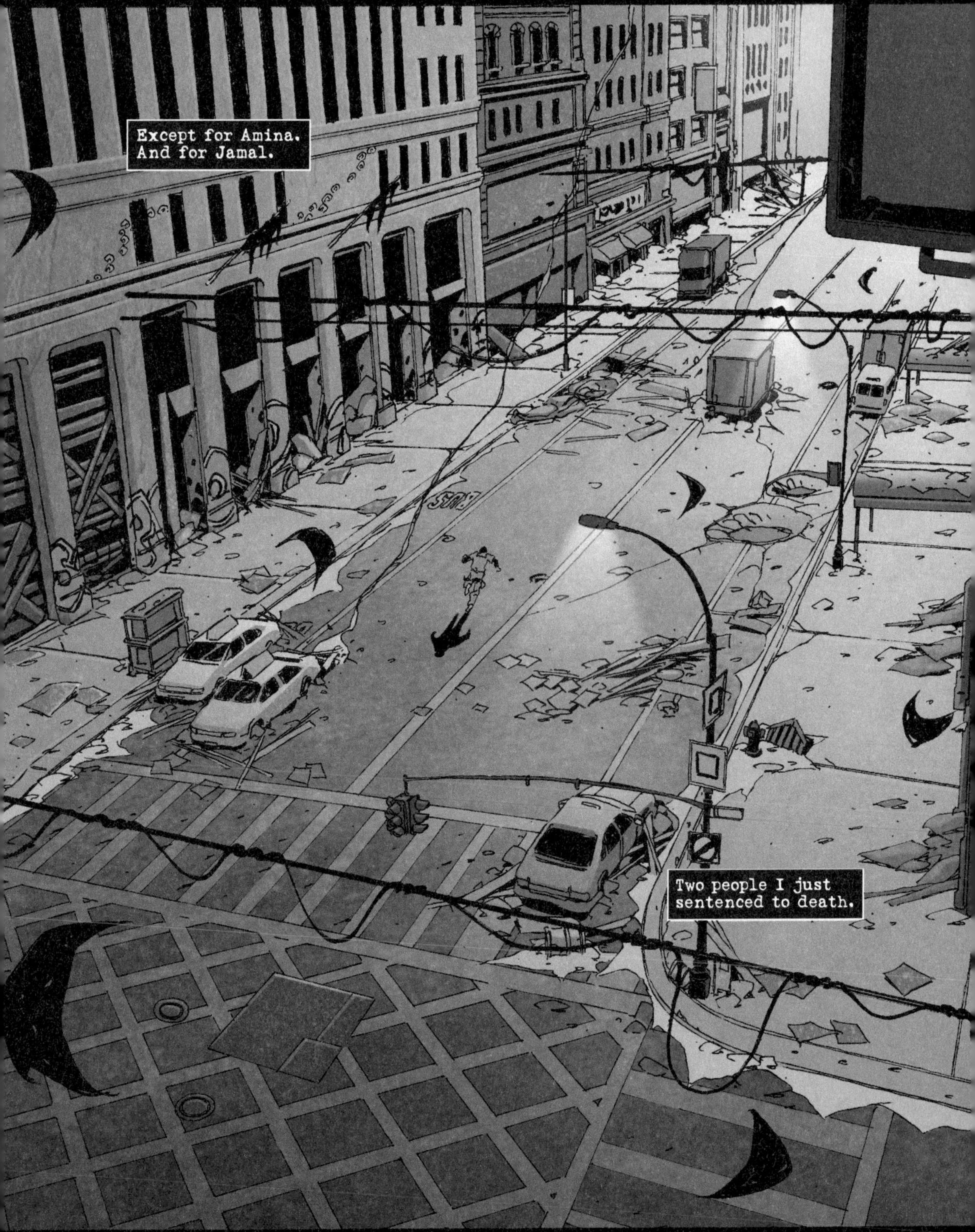
Except for Amina.
And for Jamal.
Two people I just
sentenced to death.

PUBLIC WORKS 5/5

DMZ

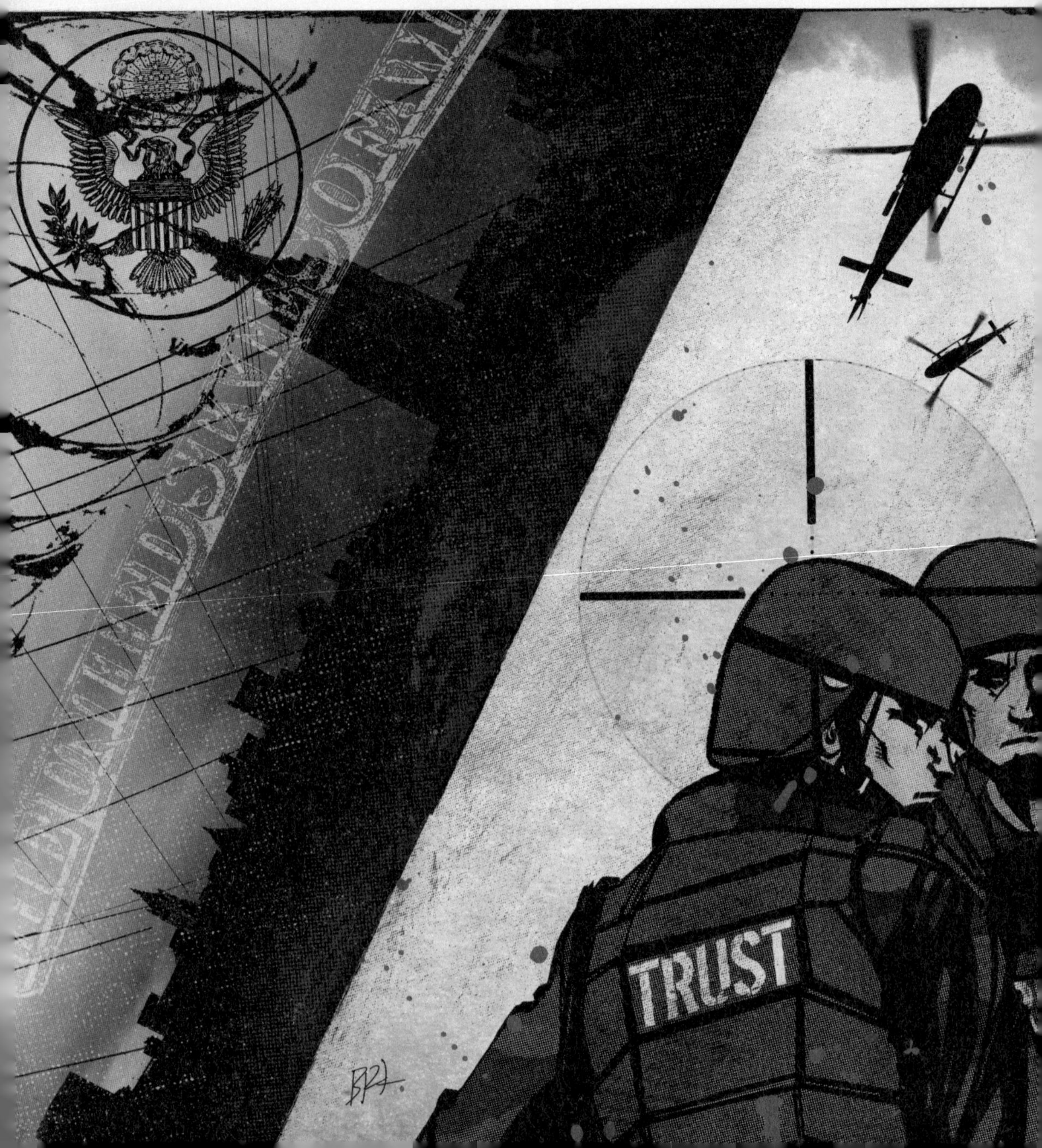
TRUST

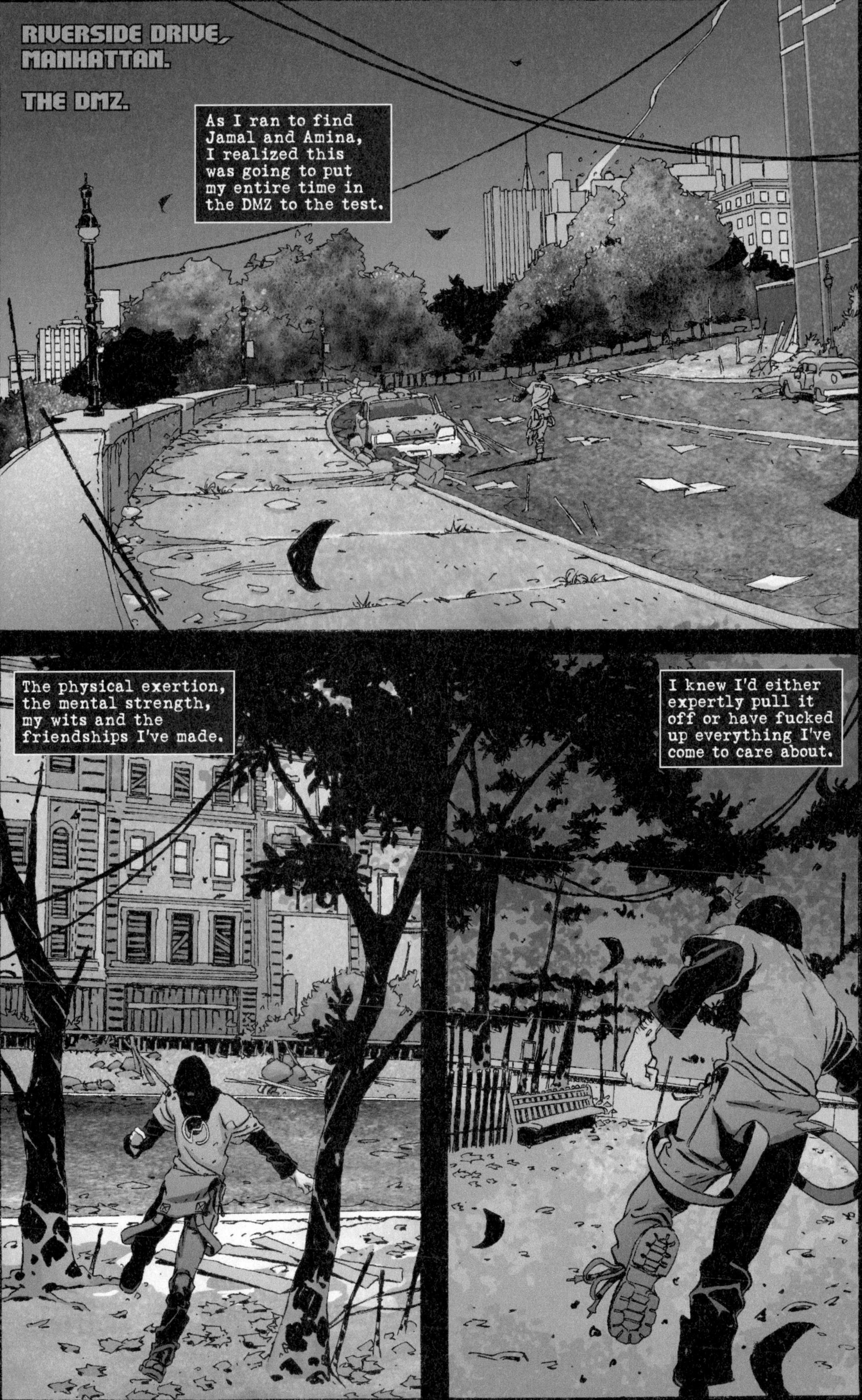
RIVERSIDE DRIVE, MANHATTAN.
THE DMZ.
As I ran to find Jamal and Amina, I realized this was going to put my entire time in the DMZ to the test.
The physical exertion, the mental strength, my wits and the friendships I've made.
I knew I'd either expertly pull it off or have fucked up everything I've come to care about.

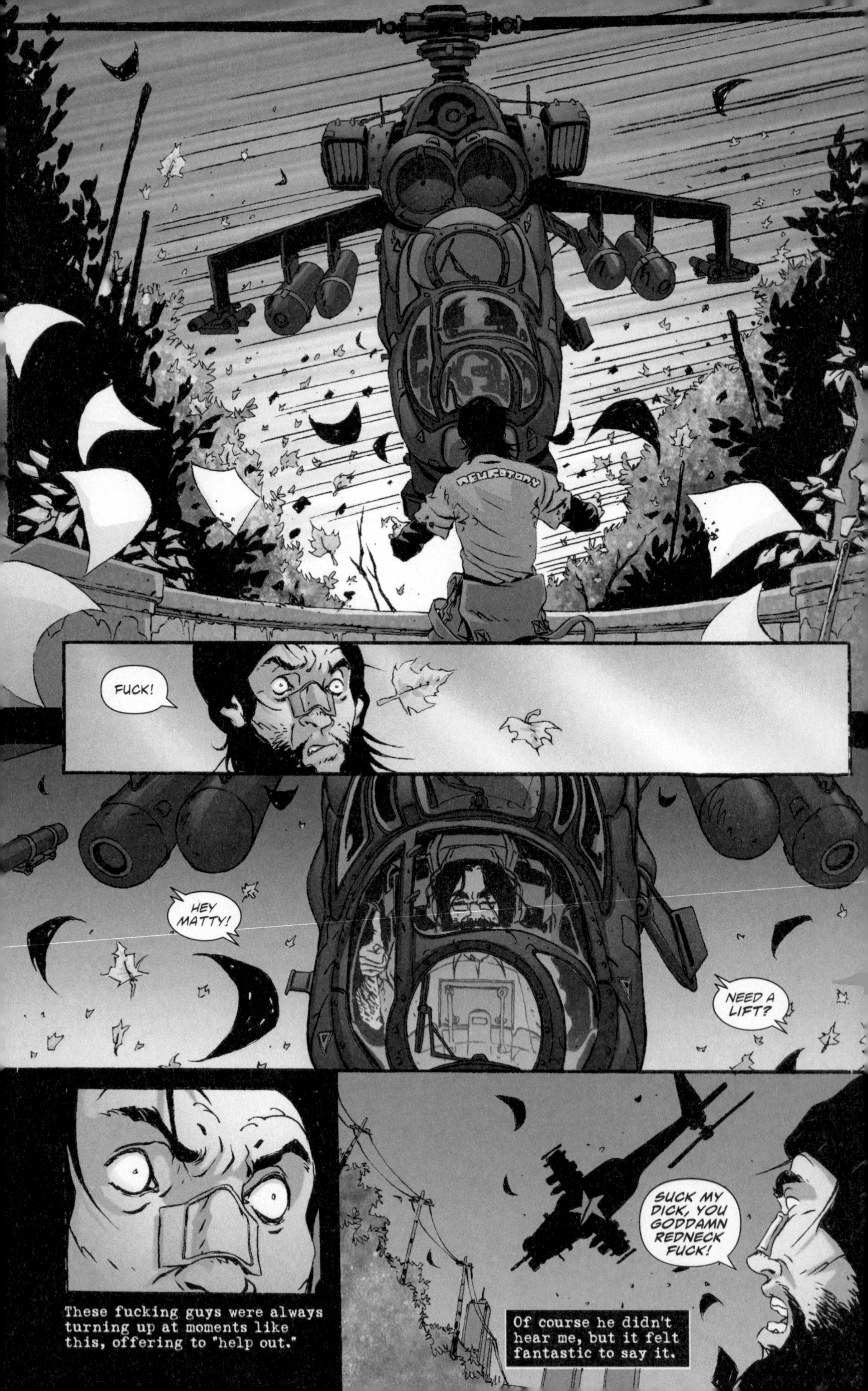
FUCK!
HEY MATTY!
NEED A LIFT?
These fucking guys were always turning up at moments like this, offering to "help out."
SUCK MY DICK, YOU GODDAMN REDNECK FUCK!
Of course he didn't hear me, but it felt fantastic to say it.

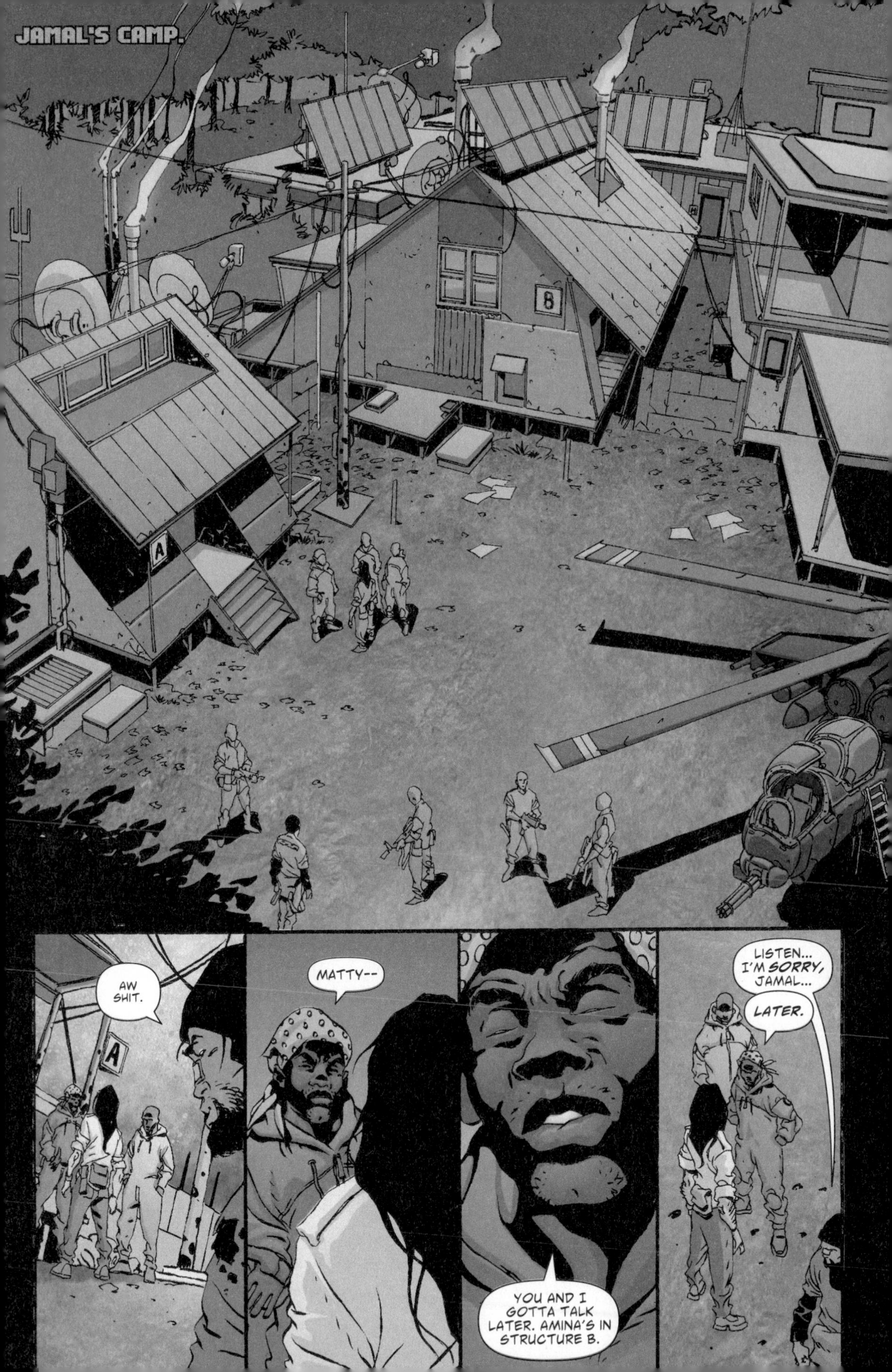
JAMAL'S CAMP.
A
B
AW SHIT.
A
MATTY--
YOU AND I GOTTA TALK LATER. AMINA'S IN STRUCTURE B.
LISTEN... I'M SORRY, JAMAL...
LATER.

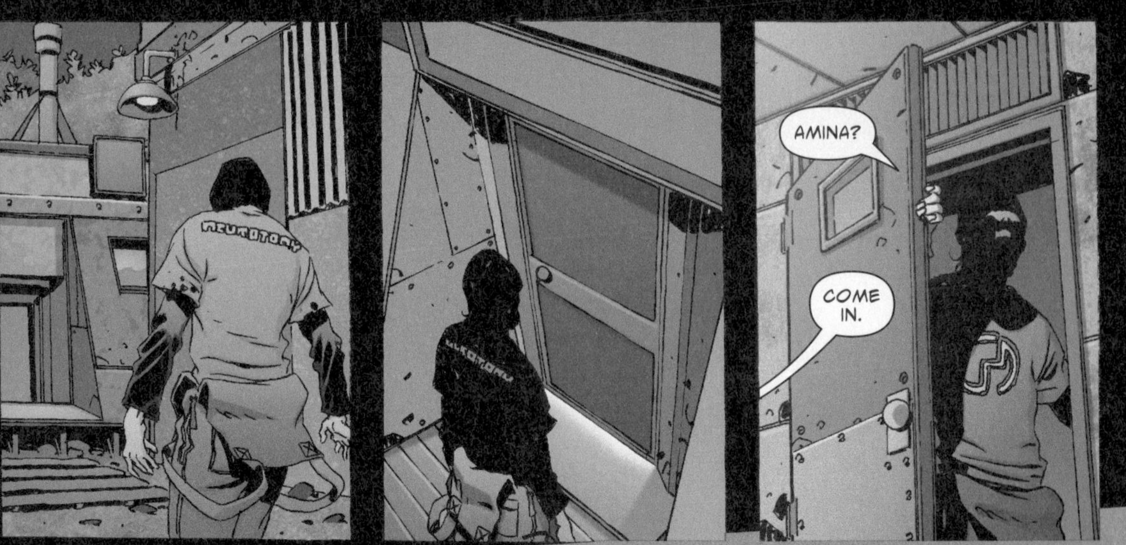
AMINA?
COME IN.

PUBLIC WORKS 5 OF 5

BRIAN WOOD: WRITER AND COVER
RICCARDO BURCHIELLI: ARTIST
JEROMY COX: COLORS
JARED K. FLETCHER: LETTERS

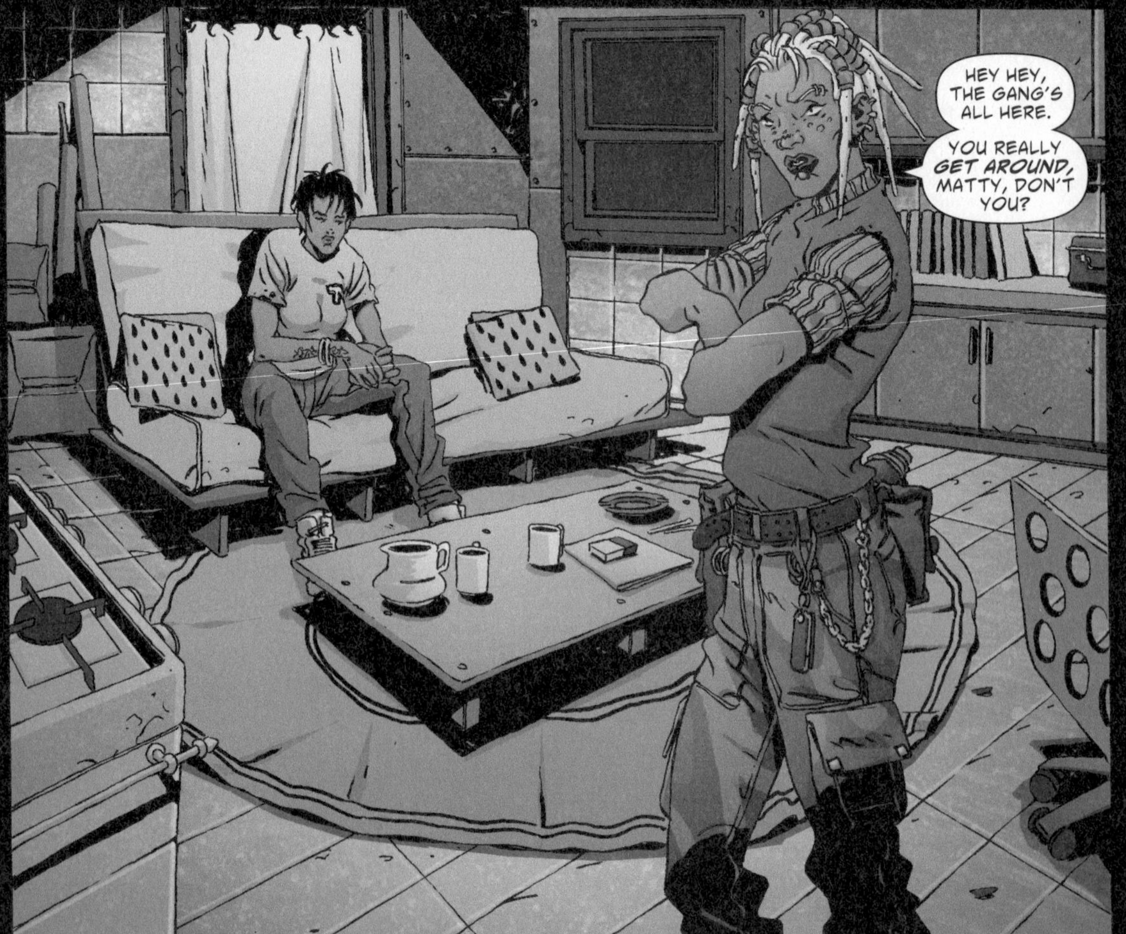
HEY HEY, THE GANG'S ALL HERE.
YOU REALLY *GET AROUND*, MATTY, DON'T YOU?

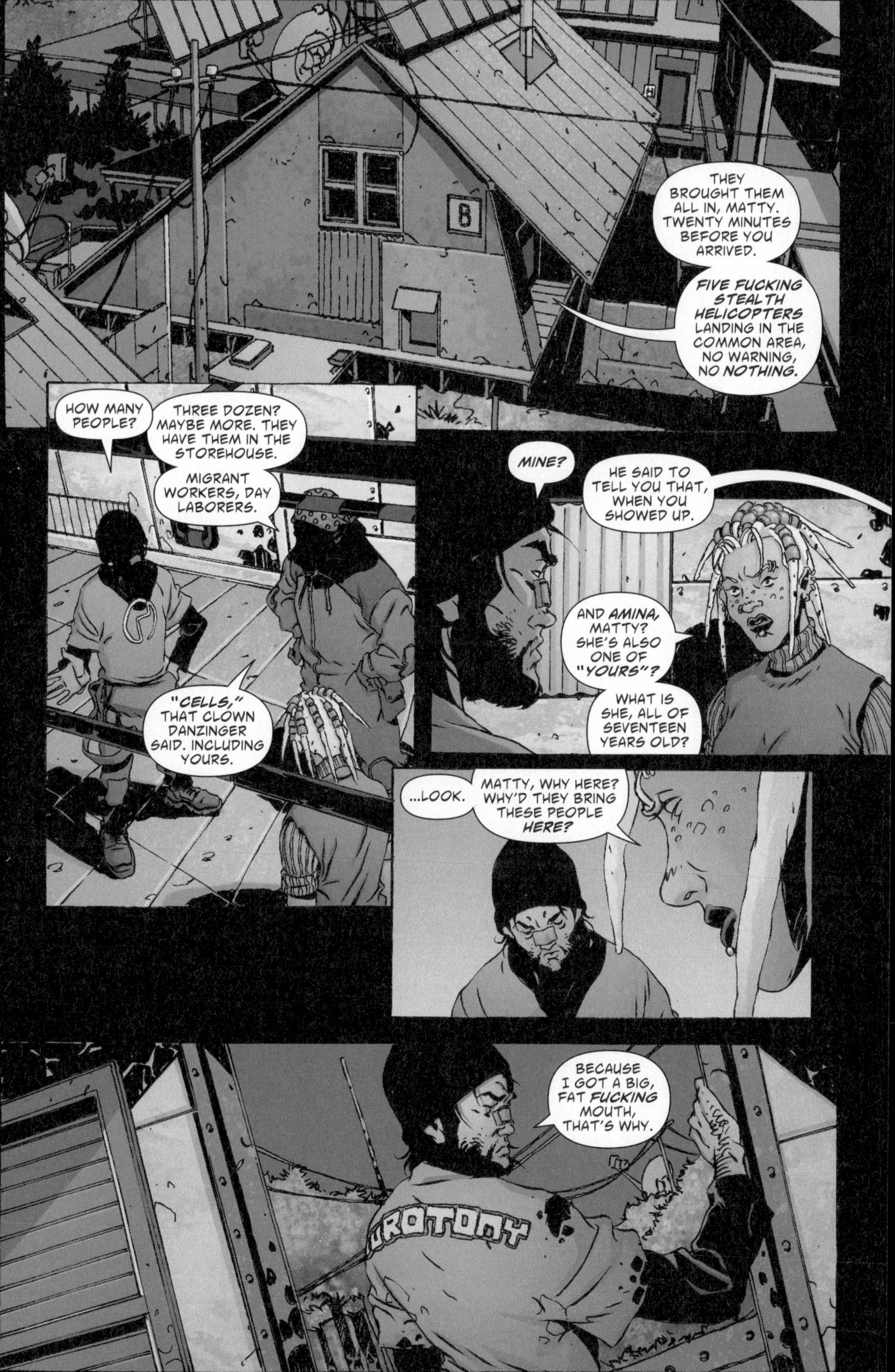
THEY BROUGHT THEM ALL IN, MATTY. TWENTY MINUTES BEFORE YOU ARRIVED.
FIVE FUCKING STEALTH HELICOPTERS LANDING IN THE COMMON AREA, NO WARNING, NO NOTHING.
HOW MANY PEOPLE?
THREE DOZEN? MAYBE MORE. THEY HAVE THEM IN THE STOREHOUSE.
MIGRANT WORKERS, DAY LABORERS.
"CELLS," THAT CLOWN DANZINGER SAID. INCLUDING YOURS.
MINE?
HE SAID TO TELL YOU THAT, WHEN YOU SHOWED UP.
AND AMINA, MATTY? SHE'S ALSO ONE OF "YOURS"?
WHAT IS SHE, ALL OF SEVENTEEN YEARS OLD?
...LOOK.
MATTY, WHY HERE? WHY'D THEY BRING THESE PEOPLE HERE?
BECAUSE I GOT A BIG, FAT FUCKING MOUTH, THAT'S WHY.
UROTOMY

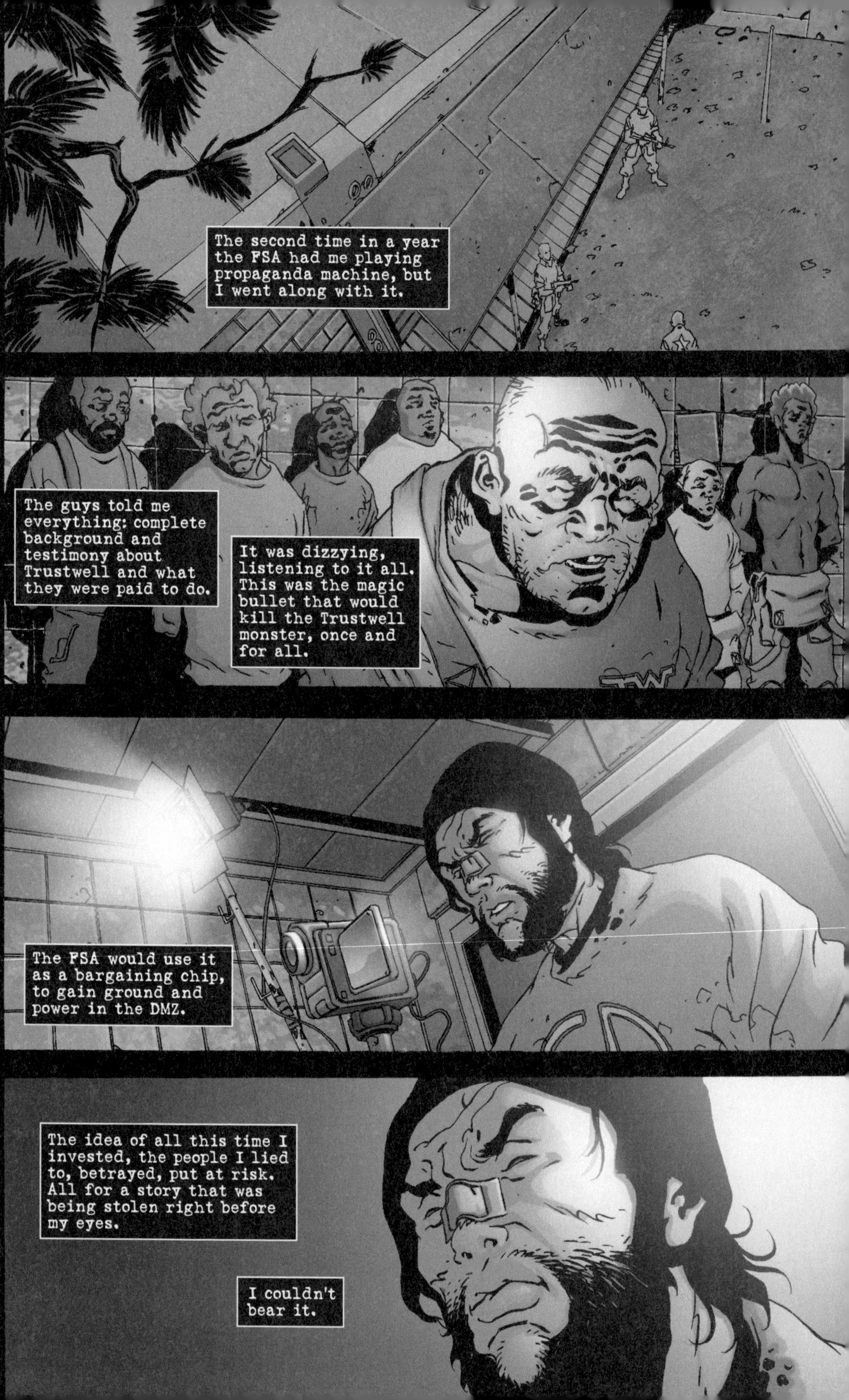
The second time in a year the FSA had me playing propaganda machine, but I went along with it.
The guys told me everything: complete background and testimony about Trustwell and what they were paid to do.
It was dizzying, listening to it all. This was the magic bullet that would kill the Trustwell monster, once and for all.
The FSA would use it as a bargaining chip, to gain ground and power in the DMZ.
The idea of all this time I invested, the people I lied to, betrayed, put at risk. All for a story that was being stolen right before my eyes.
I couldn't bear it.

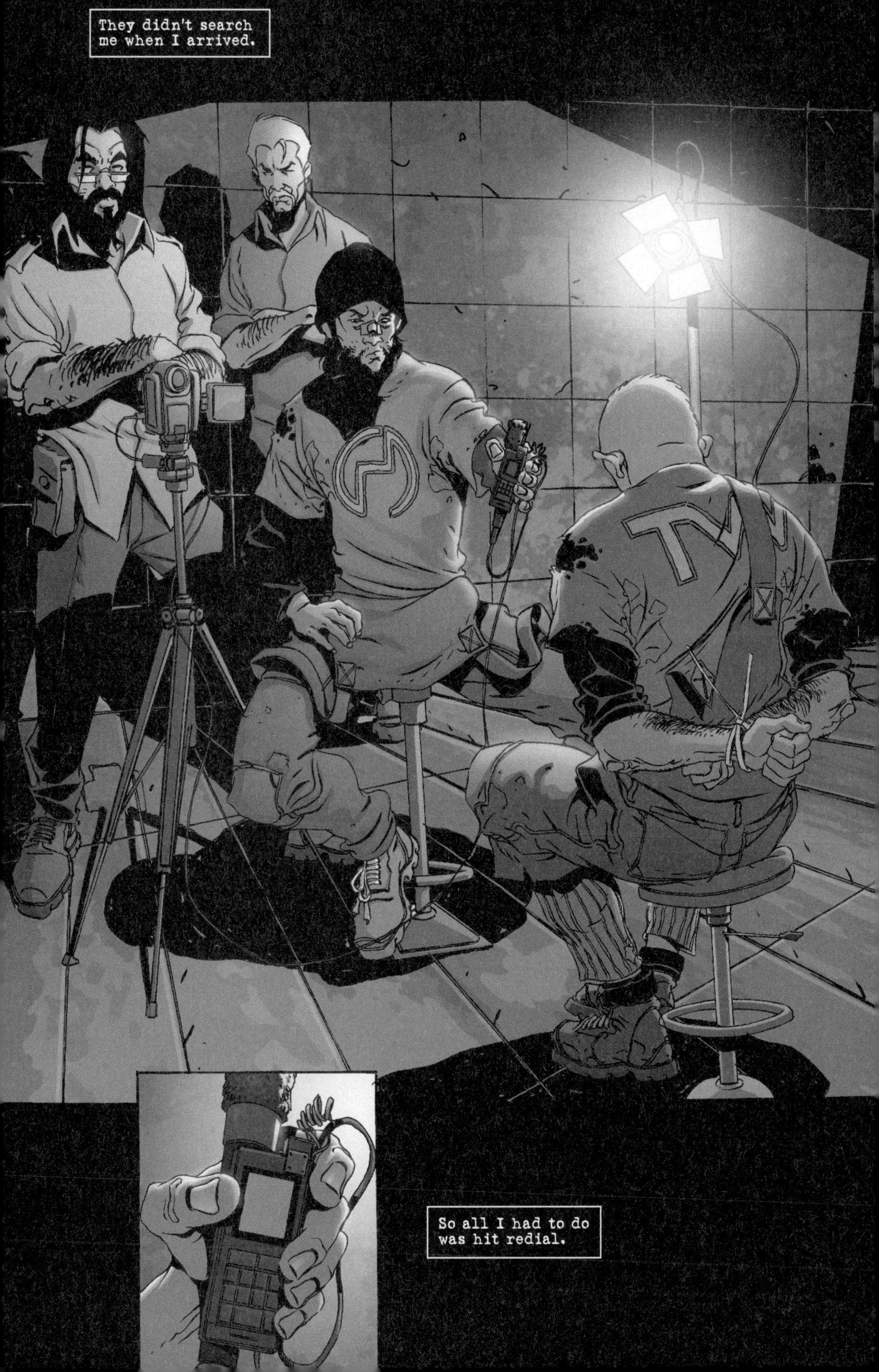
They didn't search me when I arrived.
So all I had to do was hit redial.

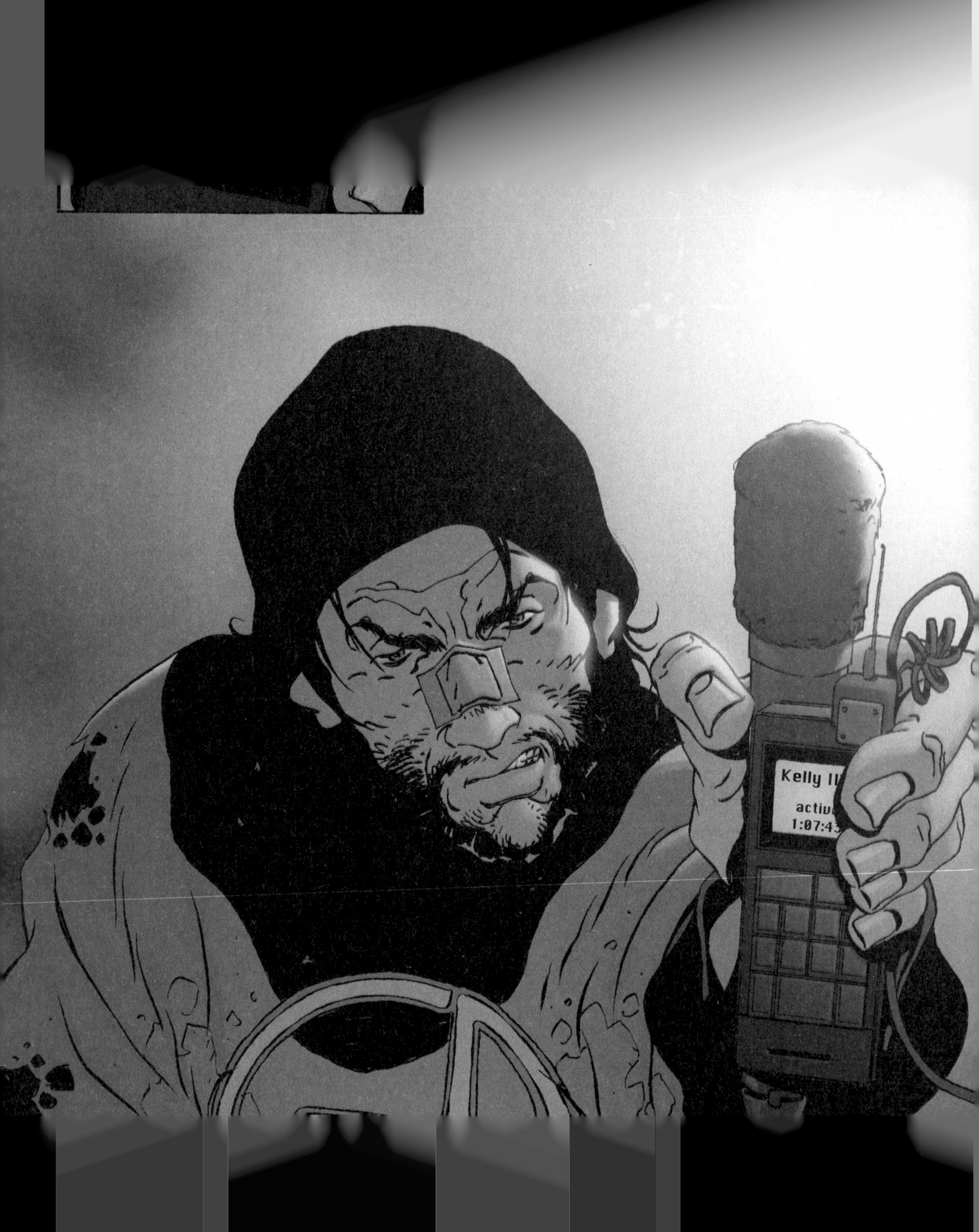
Kelly II
activ
1:07:4

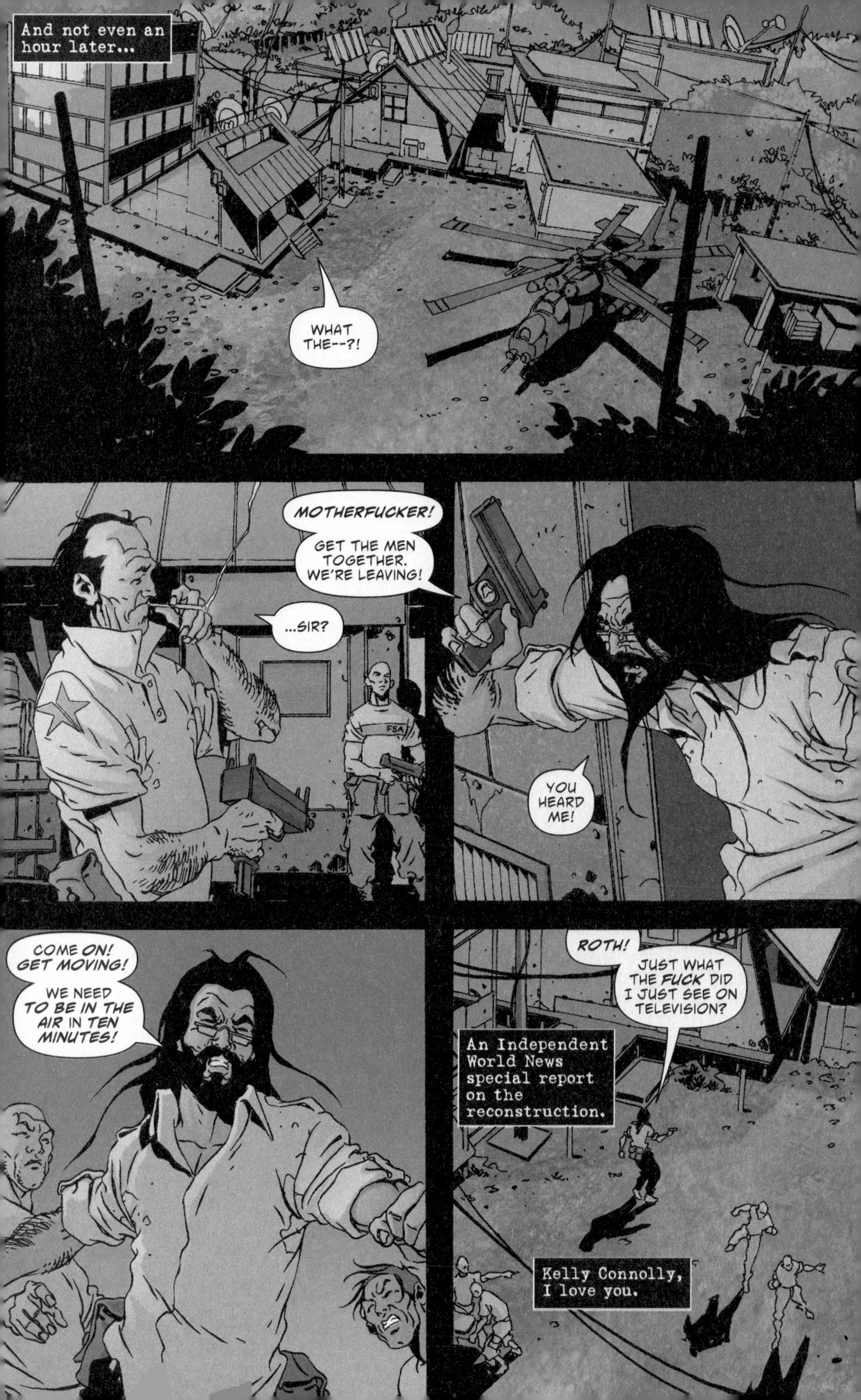

And not even an hour later...
WHAT THE--?!
MOTHERFUCKER!
GET THE MEN TOGETHER. WE'RE LEAVING!
...SIR?
YOU HEARD ME!
COME ON! GET MOVING!
WE NEED TO BE IN THE AIR IN TEN MINUTES!
ROTH!
JUST WHAT THE FUCK DID I JUST SEE ON TELEVISION?
An Independent World News special report on the reconstruction.
Kelly Connolly, I love you.

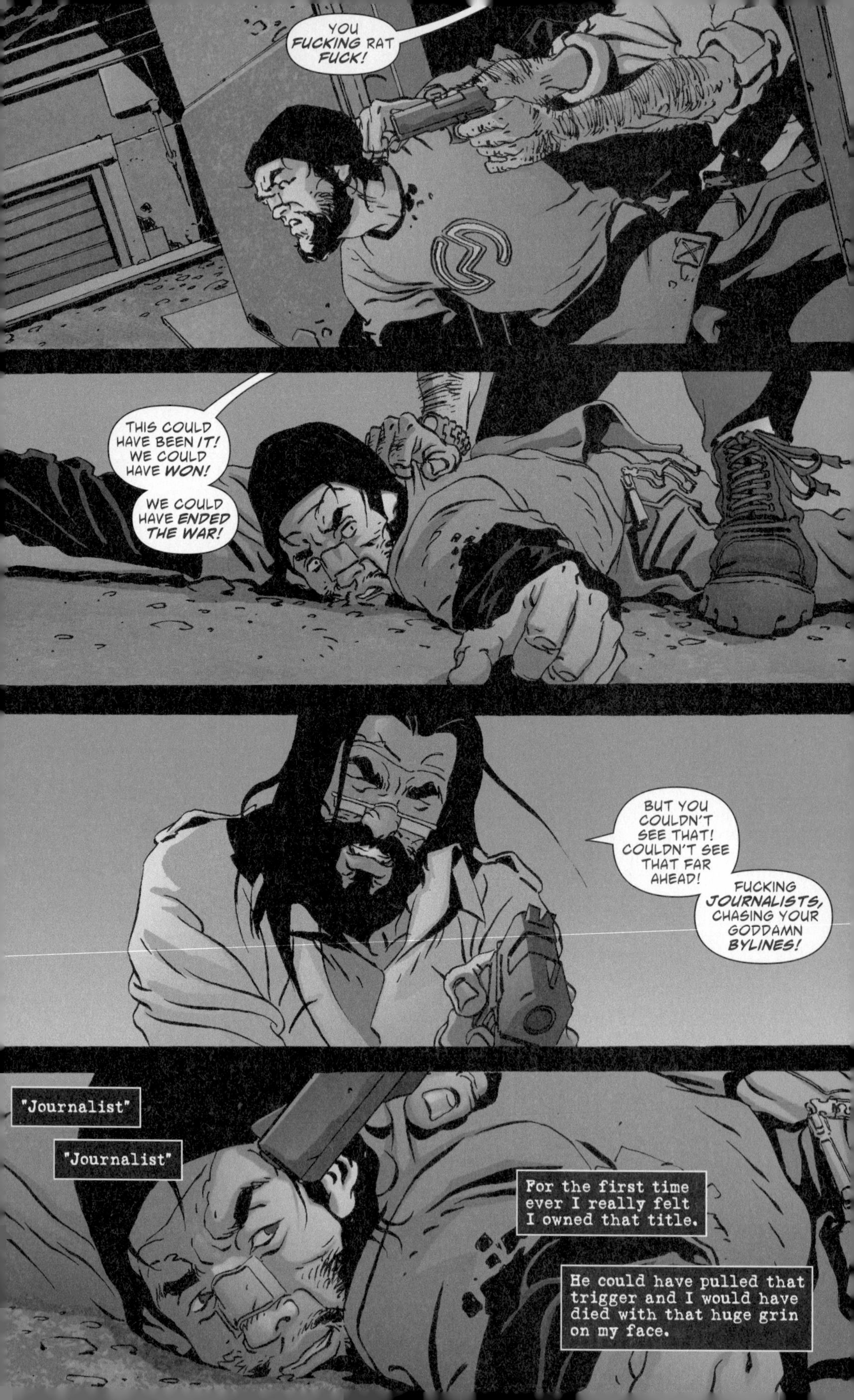
YOU FUCKING RAT FUCK!
THIS COULD HAVE BEEN IT! WE COULD HAVE WON!
WE COULD HAVE ENDED THE WAR!
BUT YOU COULDN'T SEE THAT! COULDN'T SEE THAT FAR AHEAD!
FUCKING JOURNALISTS, CHASING YOUR GODDAMN BYLINES!
"Journalist"
"Journalist"
For the first time ever I really felt I owned that title.
He could have pulled that trigger and I would have died with that huge grin on my face.

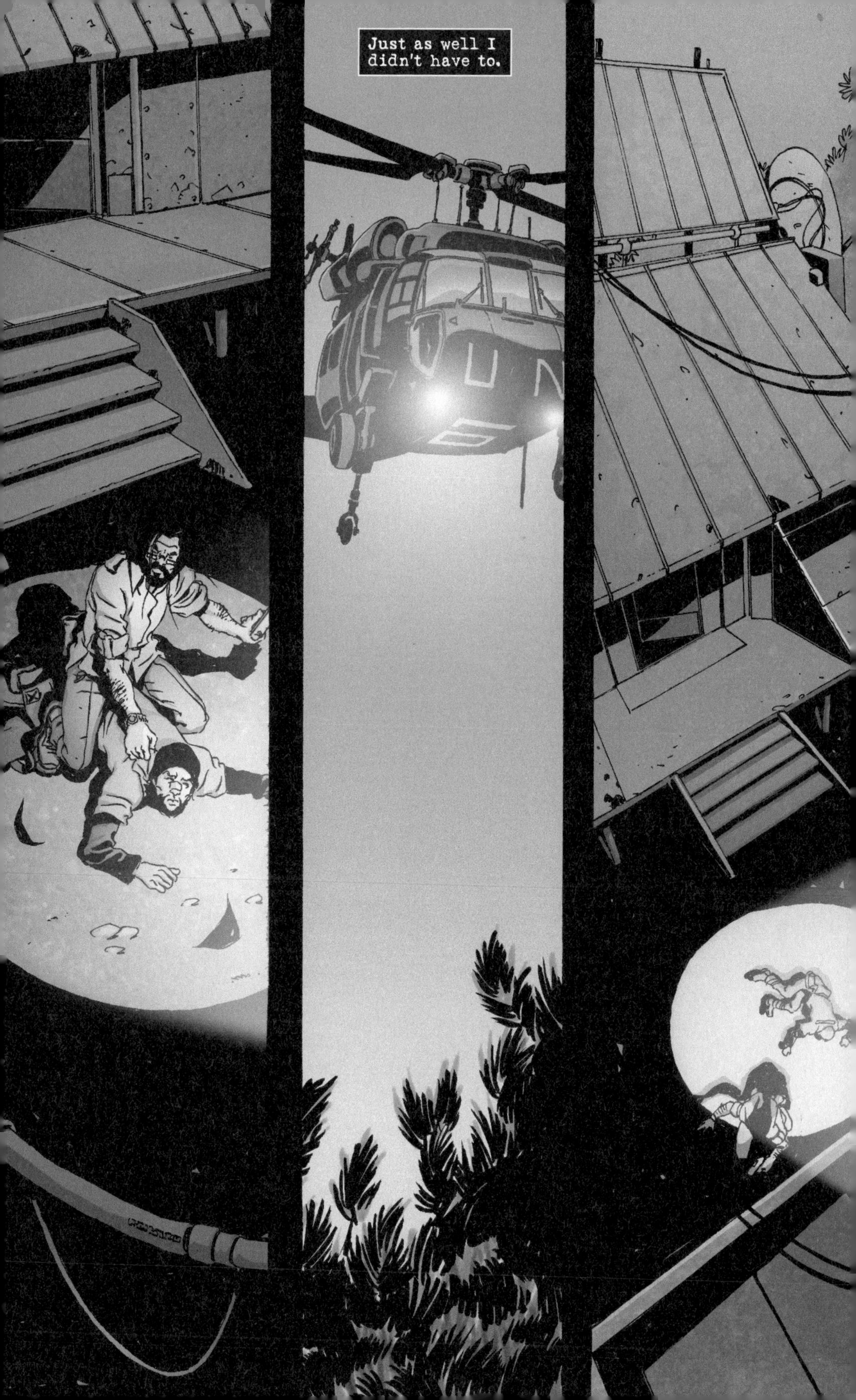
Just as well I didn't have to.

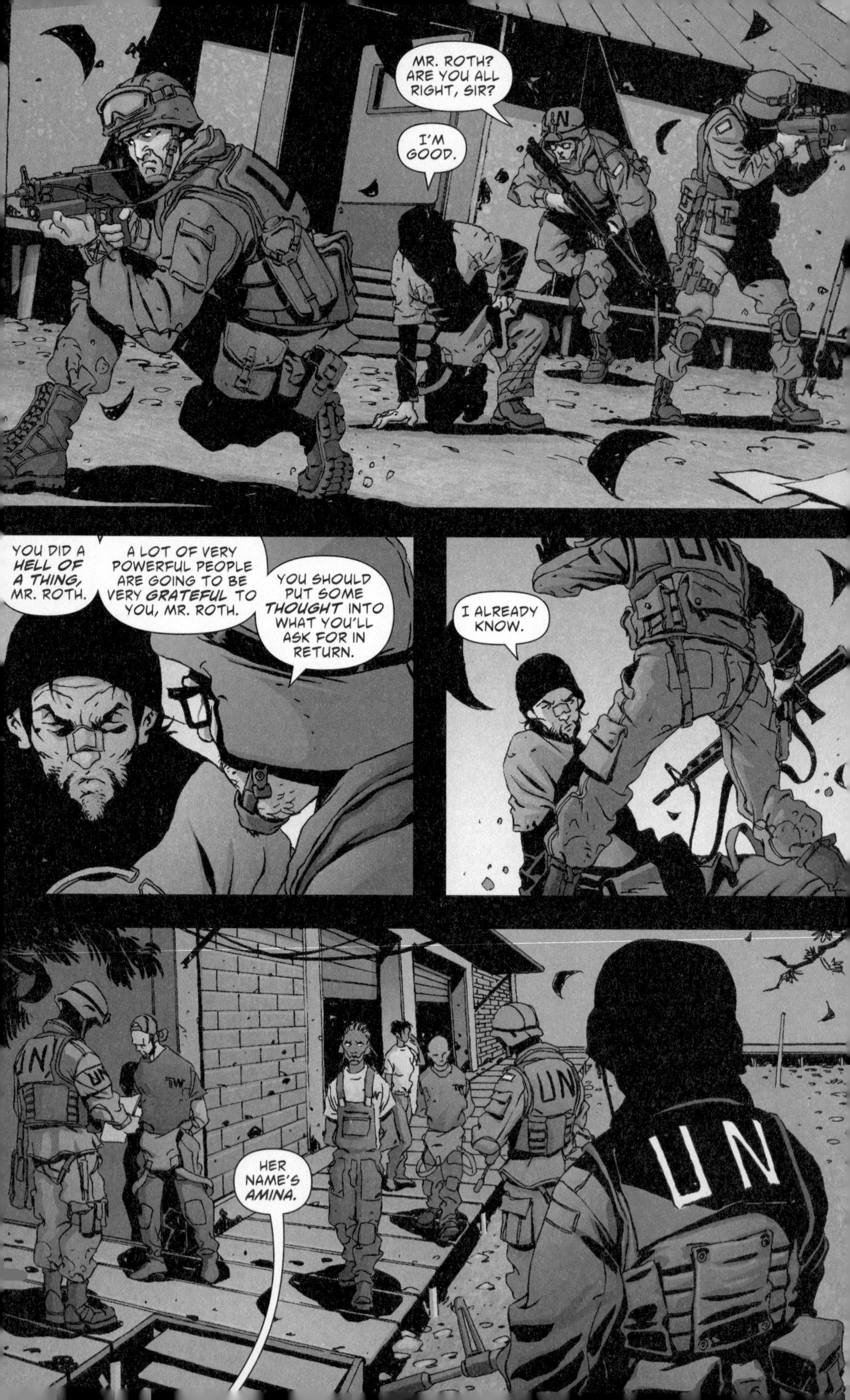
MR. ROTH? ARE YOU ALL RIGHT, SIR?
I'M GOOD.
YOU DID A HELL OF A THING, MR. ROTH.
A LOT OF VERY POWERFUL PEOPLE ARE GOING TO BE VERY GRATEFUL TO YOU, MR. ROTH.
YOU SHOULD PUT SOME THOUGHT INTO WHAT YOU'LL ASK FOR IN RETURN.
I ALREADY KNOW.
UN
TW
HER NAME'S AMINA.

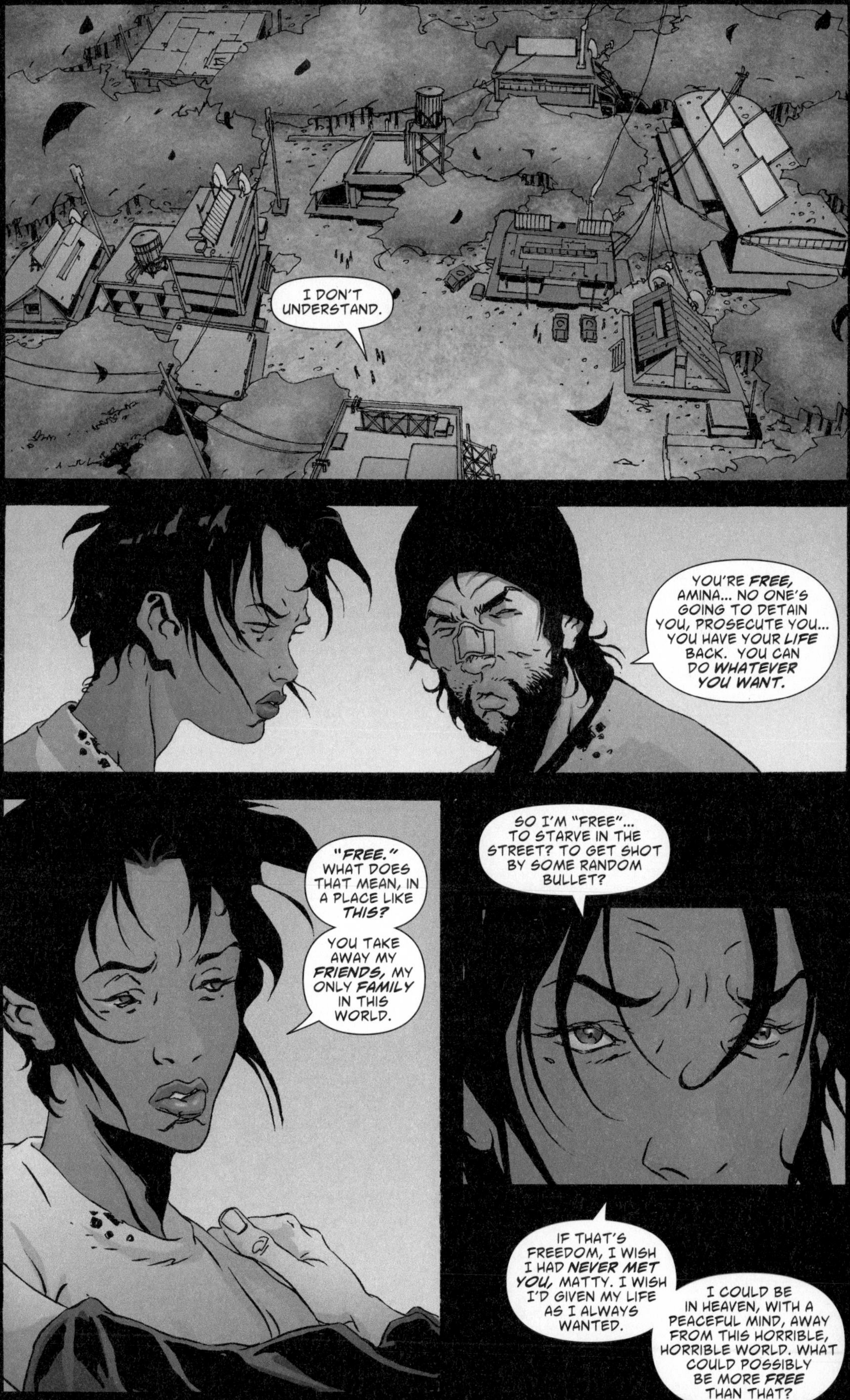

I DON'T UNDERSTAND.
YOU'RE ***FREE,*** AMINA... NO ONE'S GOING TO DETAIN YOU, PROSECUTE YOU... YOU HAVE YOUR ***LIFE*** BACK. YOU CAN DO ***WHATEVER YOU WANT.***
"FREE." WHAT DOES THAT MEAN, IN A PLACE LIKE ***THIS?***
YOU TAKE AWAY MY ***FRIENDS,*** MY ONLY ***FAMILY*** IN THIS WORLD.
SO I'M "FREE"... TO STARVE IN THE STREET? TO GET SHOT BY SOME RANDOM BULLET?
IF THAT'S FREEDOM, I WISH I HAD ***NEVER MET YOU,*** MATTY. I WISH I'D GIVEN MY LIFE AS I ALWAYS WANTED.
I COULD BE IN HEAVEN, WITH A PEACEFUL MIND, AWAY FROM THIS HORRIBLE, HORRIBLE WORLD. WHAT COULD POSSIBLY BE MORE ***FREE*** THAN THAT?

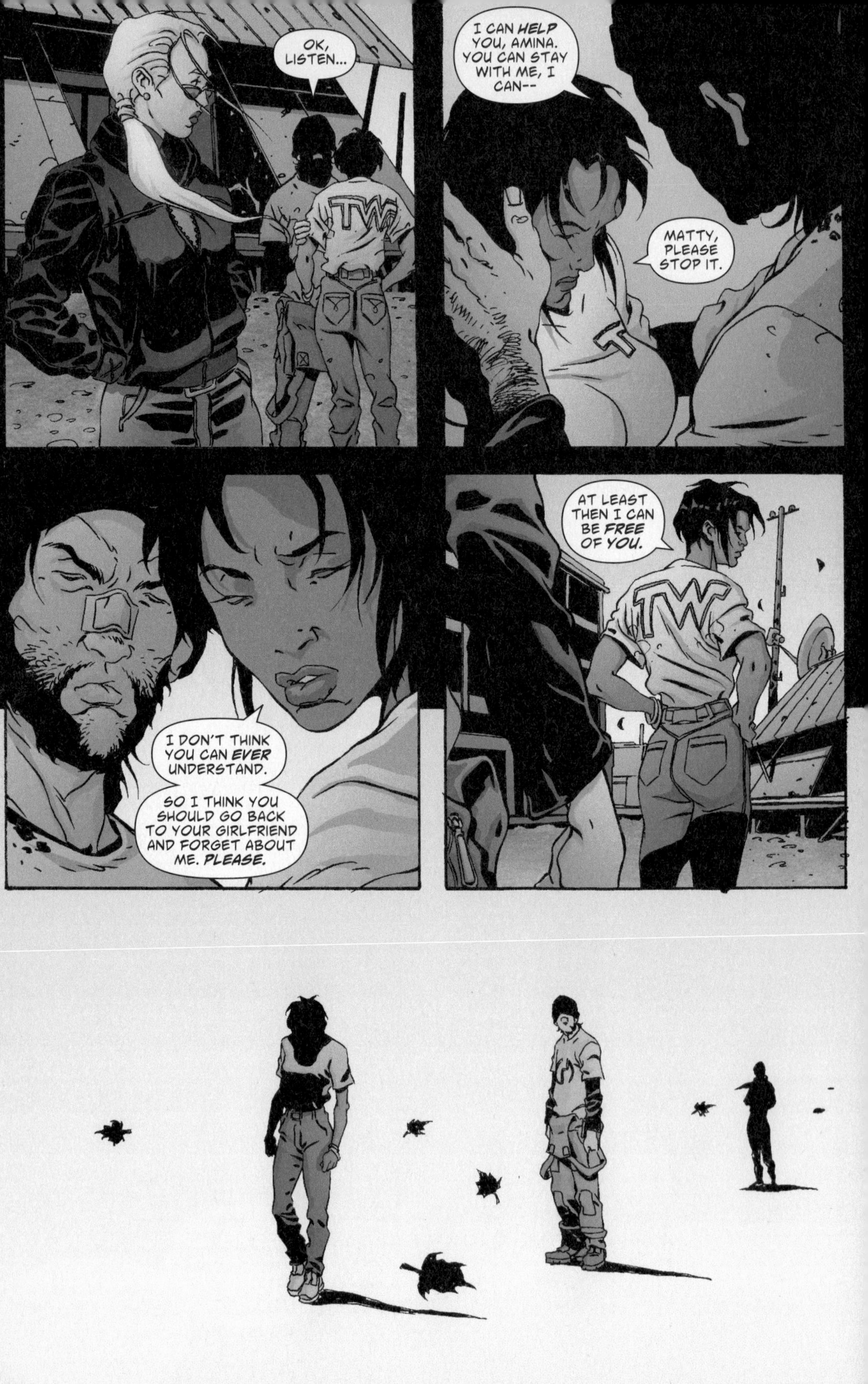
OK, LISTEN...
I CAN HELP YOU, AMINA. YOU CAN STAY WITH ME, I CAN--
MATTY, PLEASE STOP IT.
I DON'T THINK YOU CAN EVER UNDERSTAND.
SO I THINK YOU SHOULD GO BACK TO YOUR GIRLFRIEND AND FORGET ABOUT ME. PLEASE.
AT LEAST THEN I CAN BE FREE OF YOU.

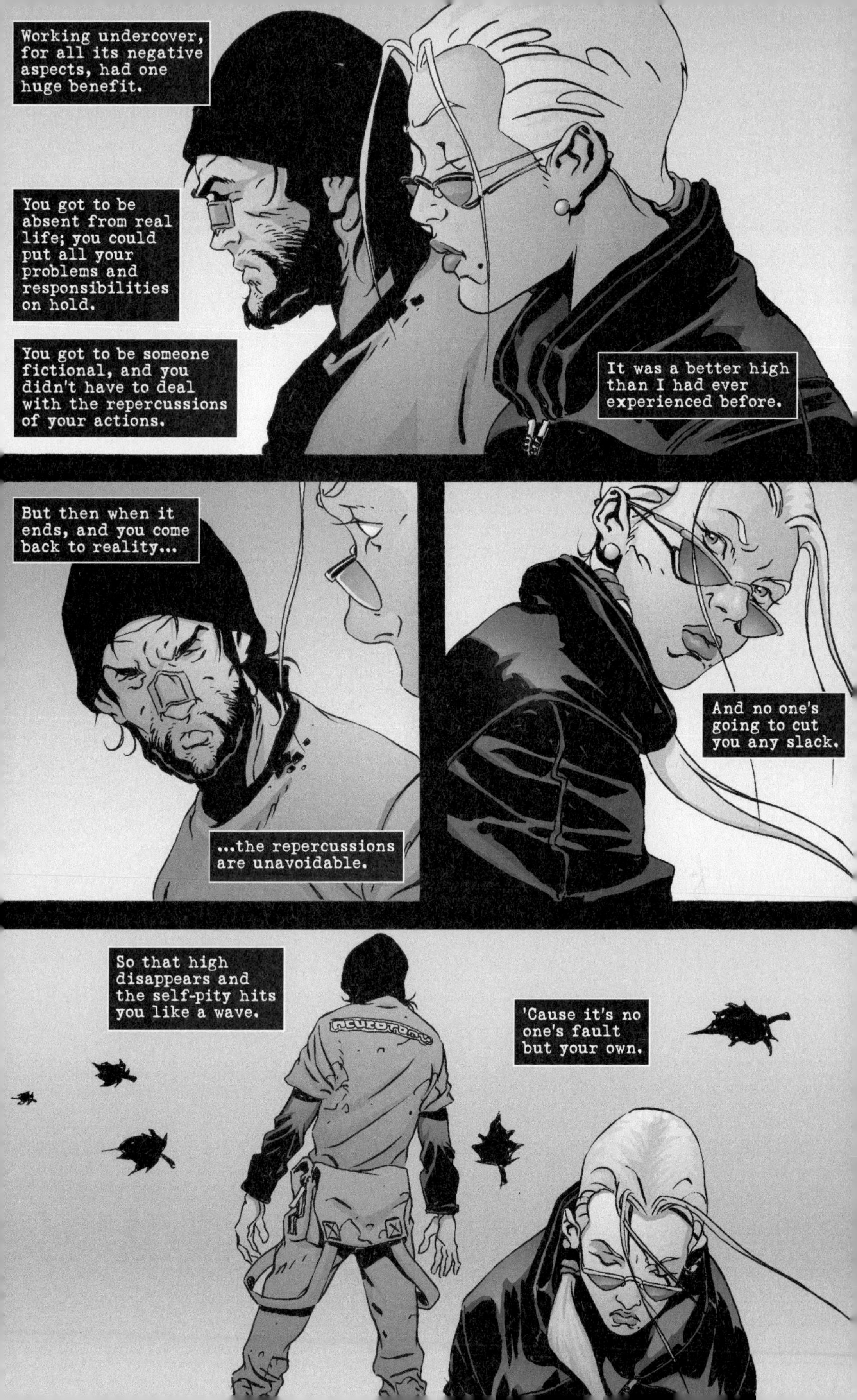
Working undercover, for all its negative aspects, had one huge benefit.
You got to be absent from real life; you could put all your problems and responsibilities on hold.
You got to be someone fictional, and you didn't have to deal with the repercussions of your actions.
It was a better high than I had ever experienced before.
But then when it ends, and you come back to reality...
...the repercussions are unavoidable.
And no one's going to cut you any slack.
So that high disappears and the self-pity hits you like a wave.
'Cause it's no one's fault but your own.

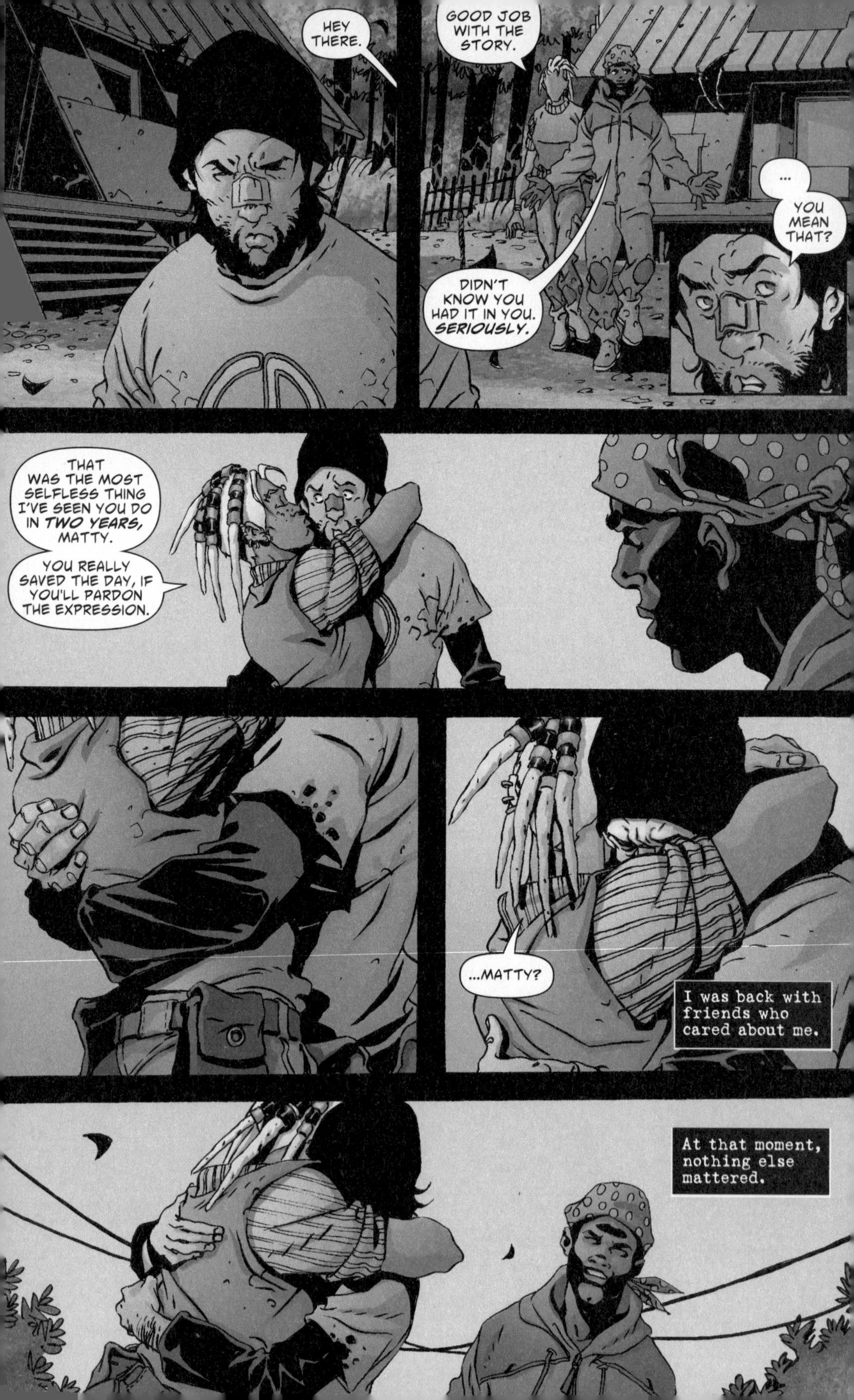
HEY THERE.
GOOD JOB WITH THE STORY.
DIDN'T KNOW YOU HAD IT IN YOU. SERIOUSLY.
...
YOU MEAN THAT?
THAT WAS THE MOST SELFLESS THING I'VE SEEN YOU DO IN TWO YEARS, MATTY.
YOU REALLY SAVED THE DAY, IF YOU'LL PARDON THE EXPRESSION.
...MATTY?
I was back with friends who cared about me.
At that moment, nothing else mattered.

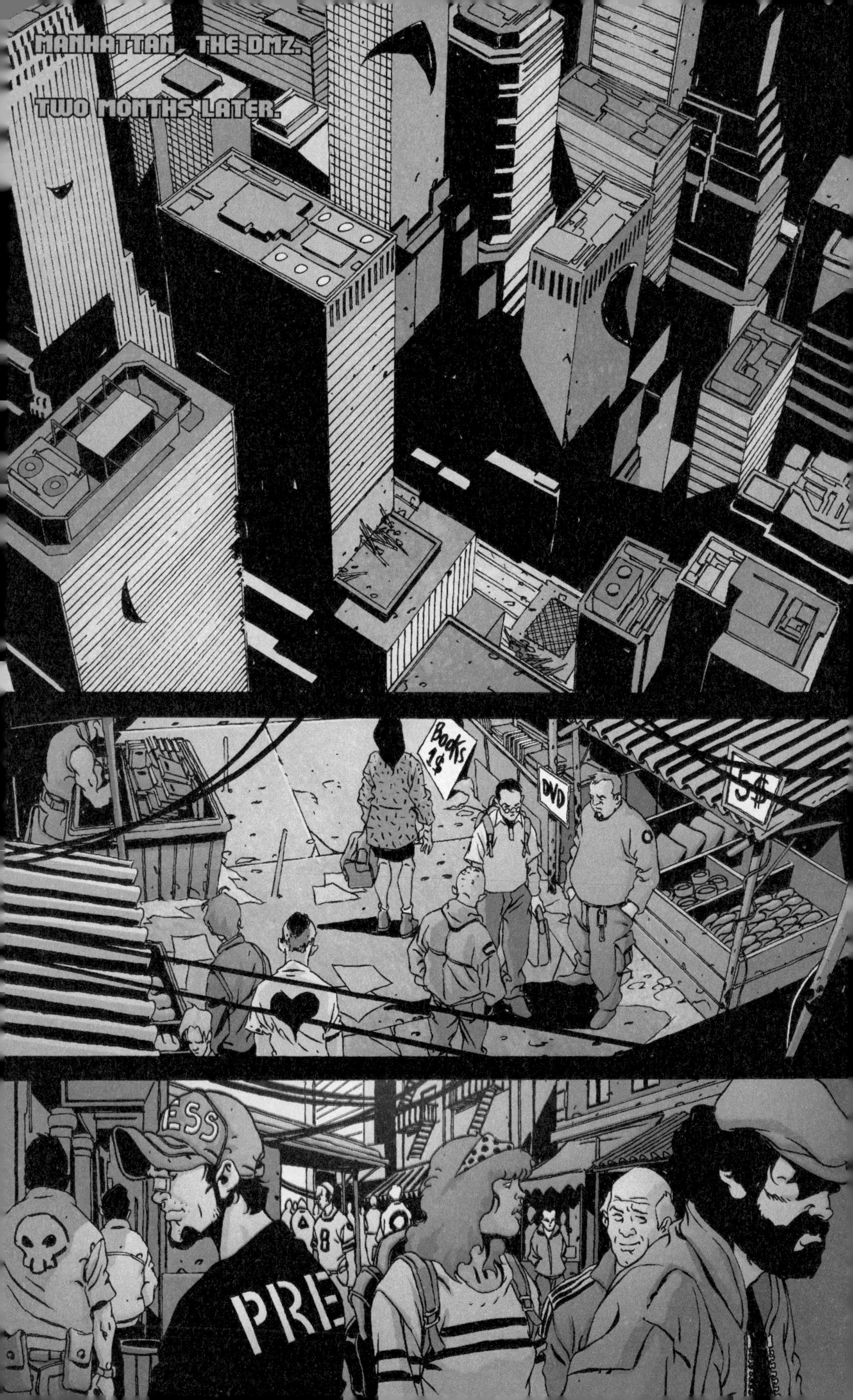

MANHATTAN. THE DMZ.
TWO MONTHS LATER.
Books 1$
DVD
5$
ESS
PRE

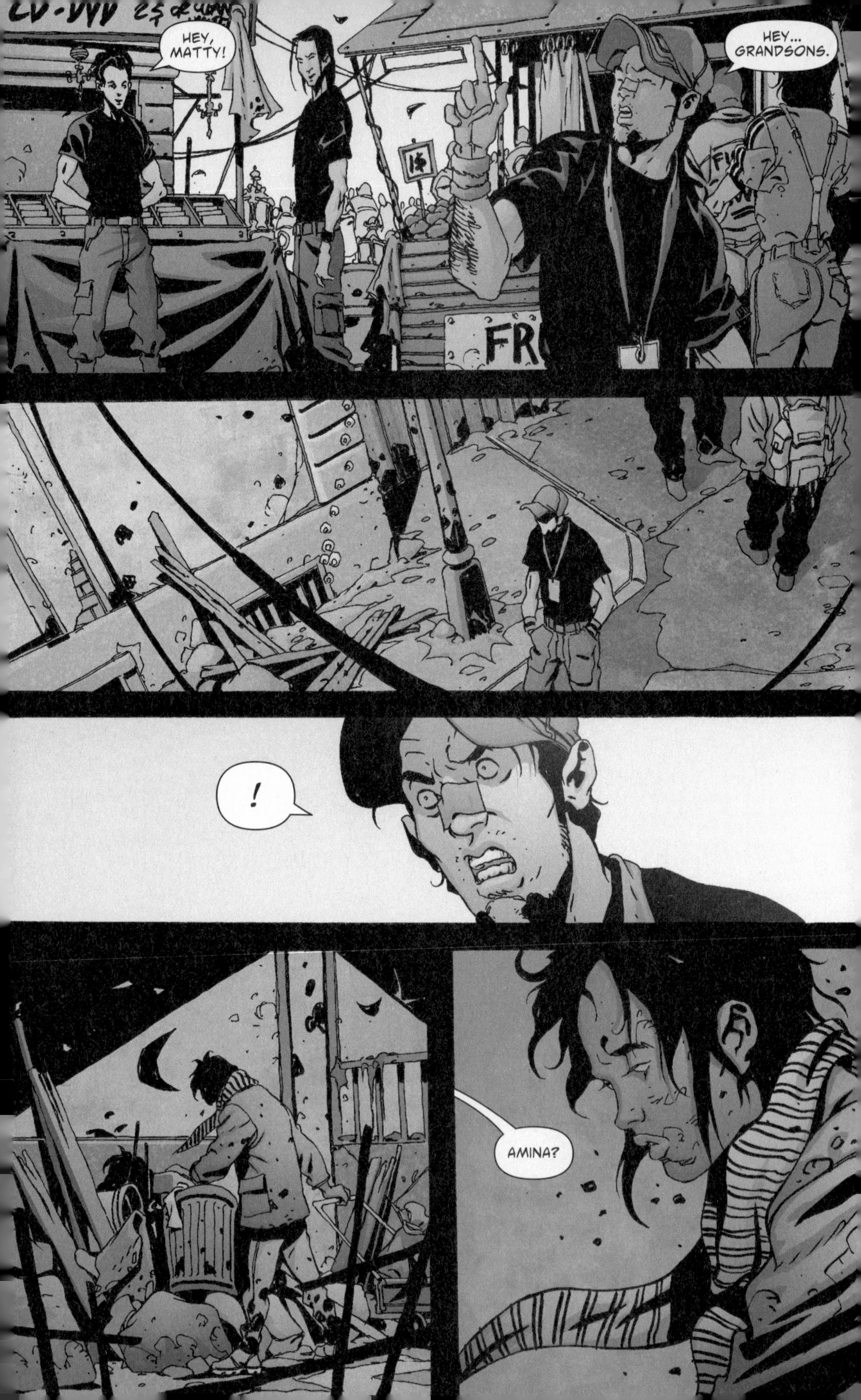
HEY, MATTY!
HEY... GRANDSONS.
FR
!
AMINA?

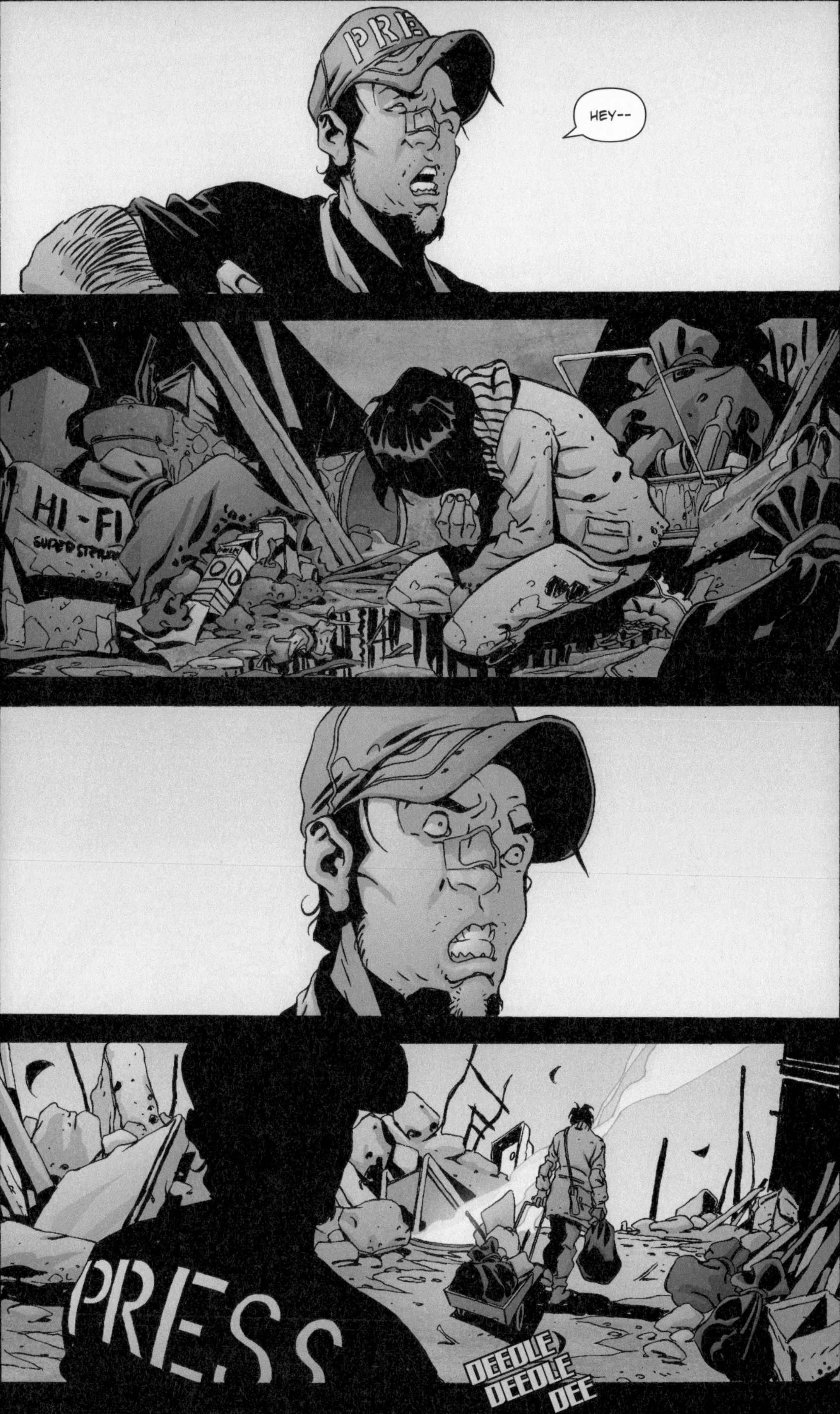
HEY--
HI-FI
PRESS
DEEDLE DEEDLE DEE

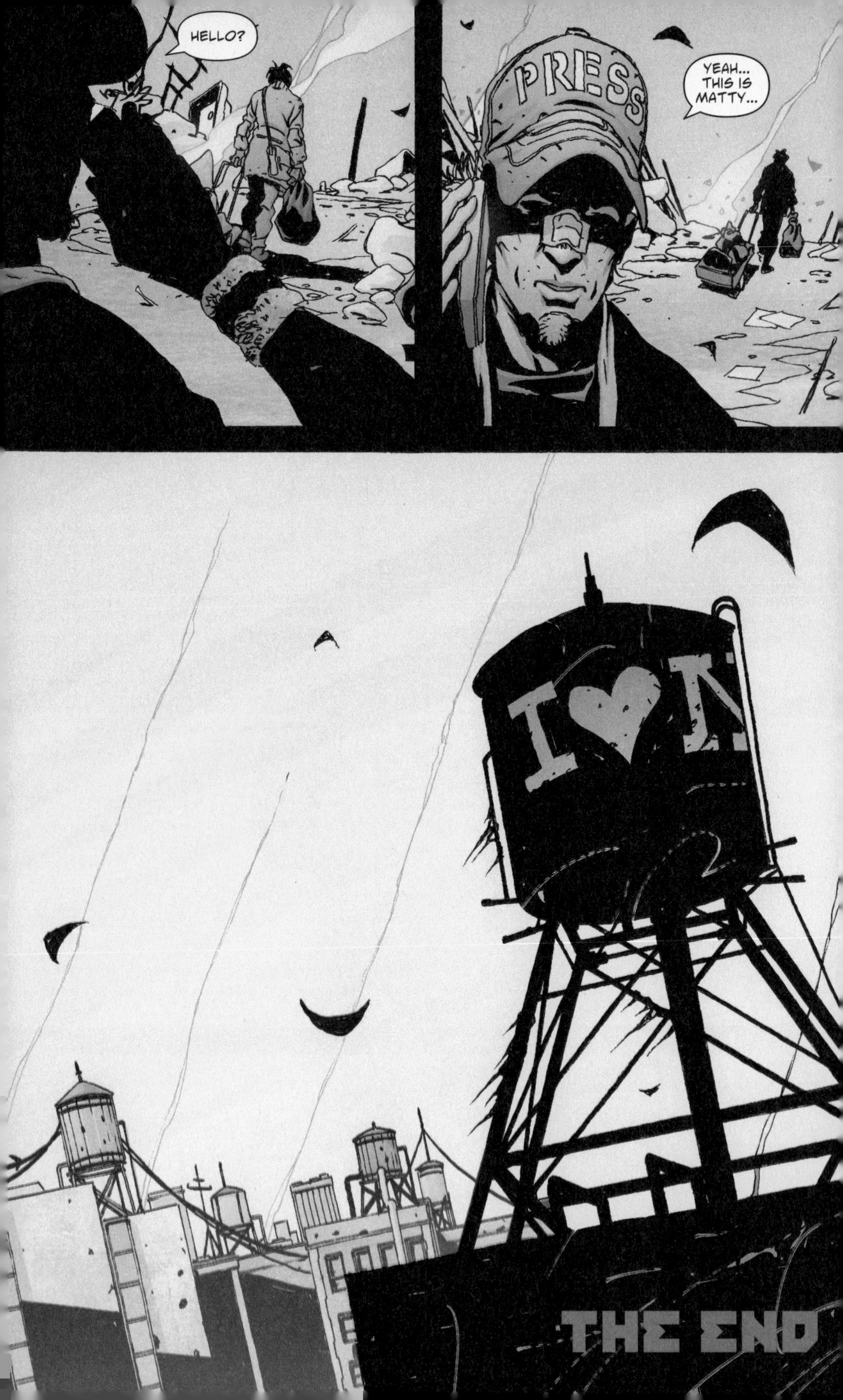
HELLO?
PRESS
YEAH... THIS IS MATTY...
THE END

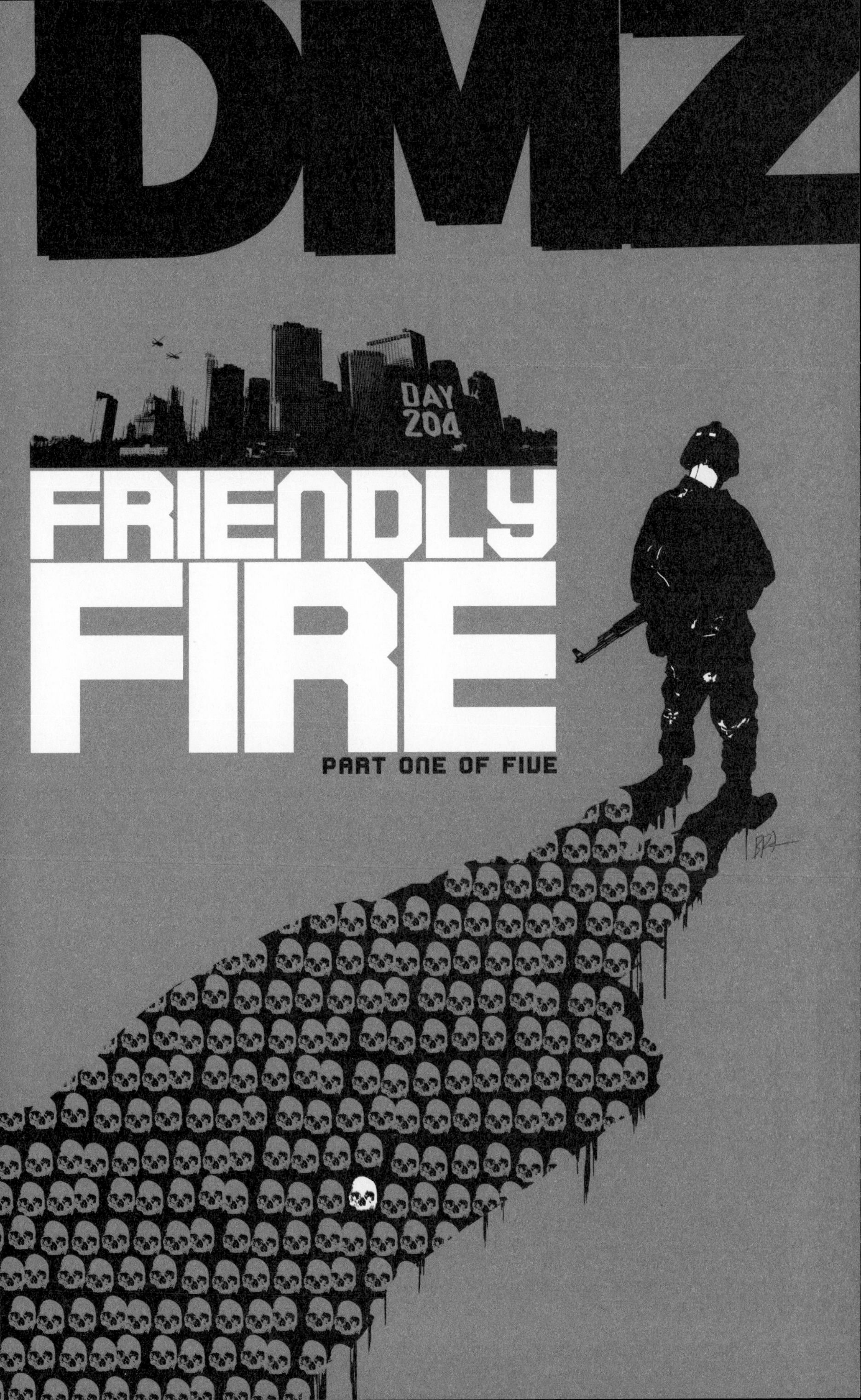
DMZ
DAY 204
FRIENDLY FIRE
PART ONE OF FIVE

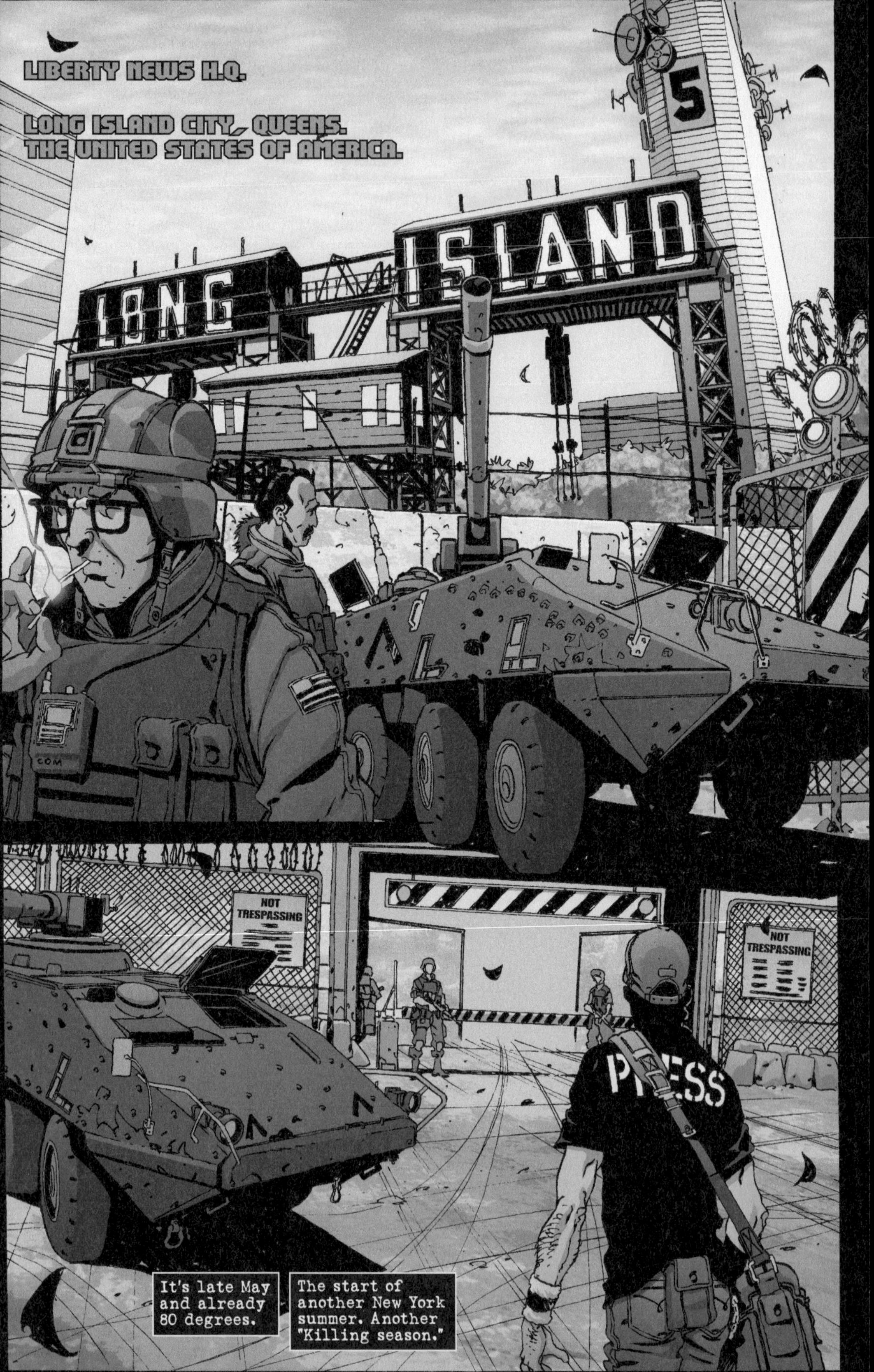
LIBERTY NEWS H.Q.
LONG ISLAND CITY, QUEENS.
THE UNITED STATES OF AMERICA.
5
LONG ISLAND
COM
NOT TRESPASSING
NOT TRESPASSING
PRESS
It's late May and already 80 degrees.
The start of another New York summer. Another "Killing season."

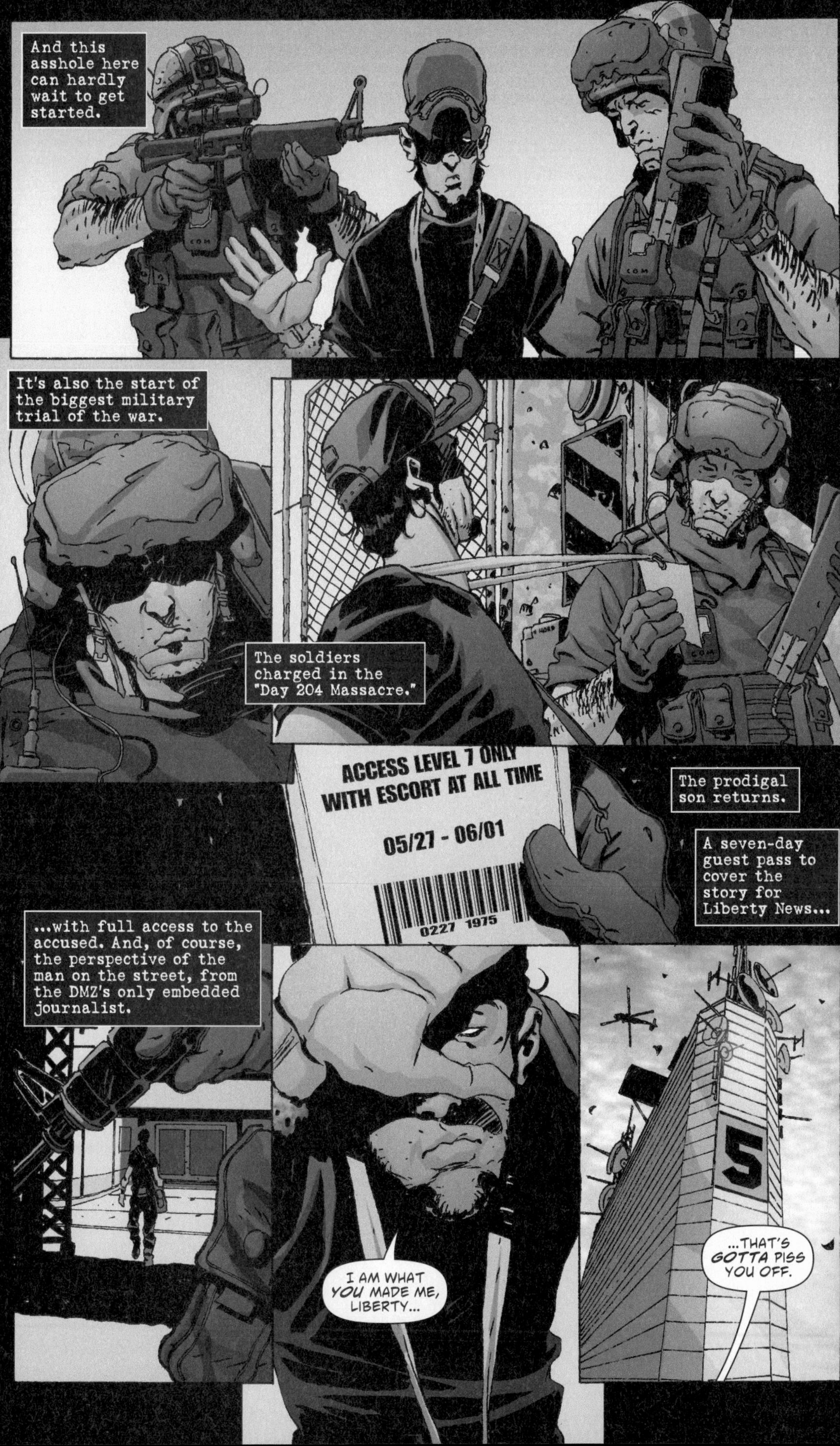

And this asshole here can hardly wait to get started.
It's also the start of the biggest military trial of the war.
The soldiers charged in the "Day 204 Massacre."
ACCESS LEVEL 7 ONLY WITH ESCORT AT ALL TIME
05/27 - 06/01
0227 1975
The prodigal son returns.
A seven-day guest pass to cover the story for Liberty News...
...with full access to the accused. And, of course, the perspective of the man on the street, from the DMZ's only embedded journalist.
I AM WHAT *YOU* MADE ME, LIBERTY...
...THAT'S *GOTTA* PISS YOU OFF.

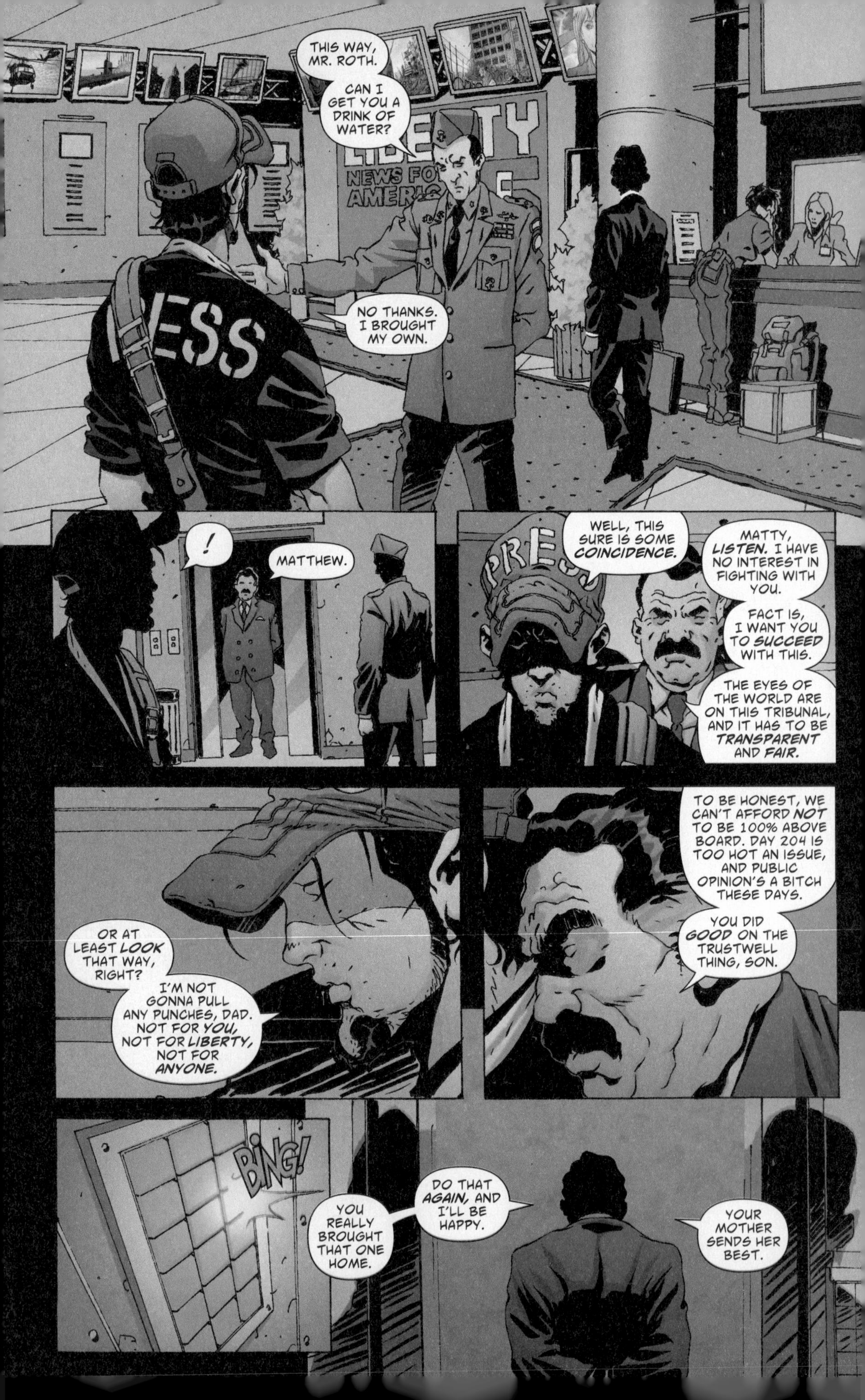
LIBERTY NEWS FOR AMERICA
THIS WAY, MR. ROTH.
CAN I GET YOU A DRINK OF WATER?
ESS
NO THANKS. I BROUGHT MY OWN.
!
MATTHEW.
PRES
WELL, THIS SURE IS SOME COINCIDENCE.
MATTY, LISTEN. I HAVE NO INTEREST IN FIGHTING WITH YOU.
FACT IS, I WANT YOU TO SUCCEED WITH THIS.
THE EYES OF THE WORLD ARE ON THIS TRIBUNAL, AND IT HAS TO BE TRANSPARENT AND FAIR.
OR AT LEAST LOOK THAT WAY, RIGHT?
I'M NOT GONNA PULL ANY PUNCHES, DAD. NOT FOR YOU, NOT FOR LIBERTY, NOT FOR ANYONE.
TO BE HONEST, WE CAN'T AFFORD NOT TO BE 100% ABOVE BOARD. DAY 204 IS TOO HOT AN ISSUE, AND PUBLIC OPINION'S A BITCH THESE DAYS.
YOU DID GOOD ON THE TRUSTWELL THING, SON.
BING!
YOUR MOTHER SENDS HER BEST.
YOU REALLY BROUGHT THAT ONE HOME.
DO THAT AGAIN, AND I'LL BE HAPPY.

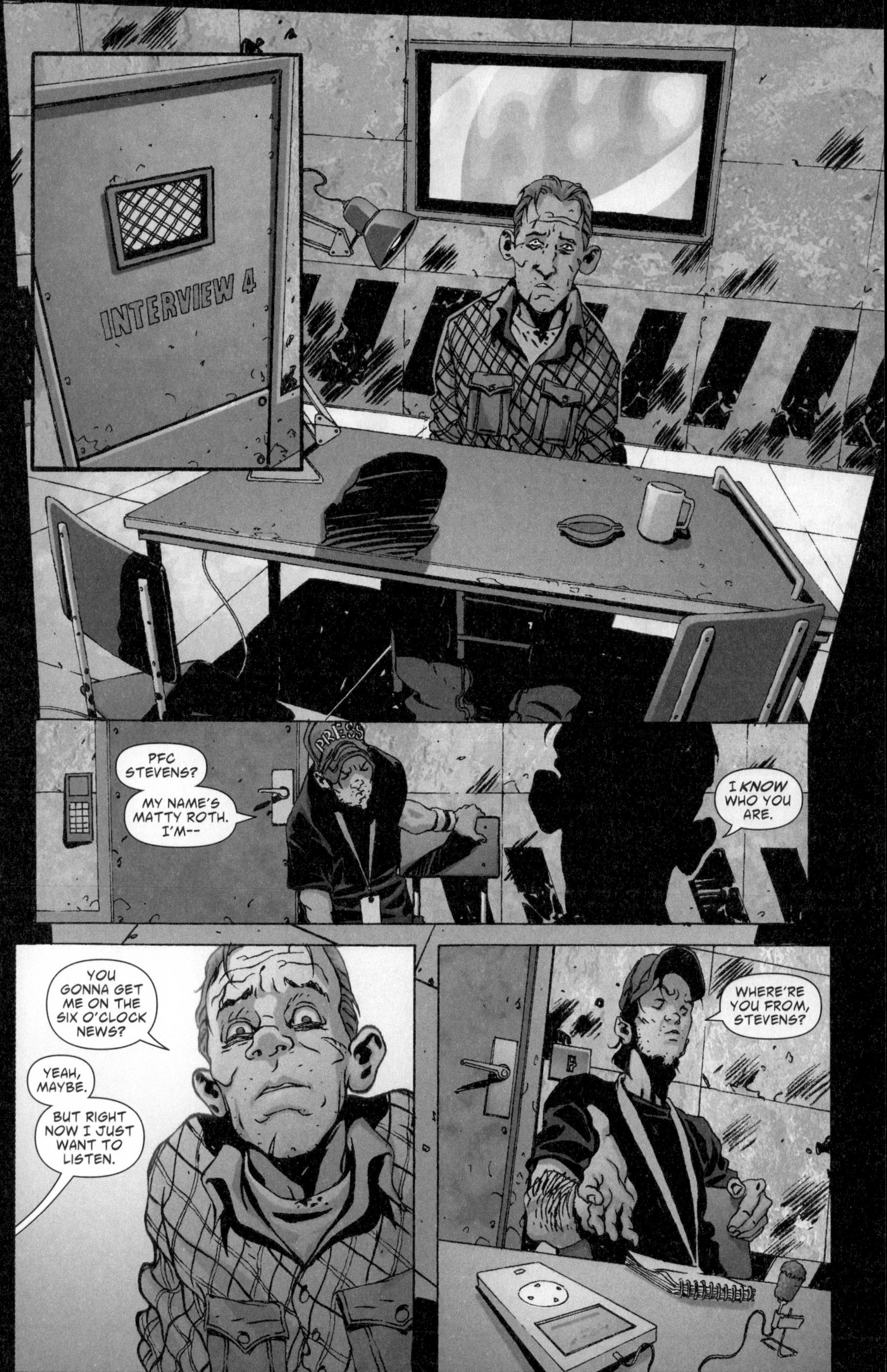
INTERVIEW 4
PRESS
PFC STEVENS?
MY NAME'S MATTY ROTH. I'M--
I KNOW WHO YOU ARE.
YOU GONNA GET ME ON THE SIX O'CLOCK NEWS?
YEAH, MAYBE.
BUT RIGHT NOW I JUST WANT TO LISTEN.
WHERE'RE YOU FROM, STEVENS?

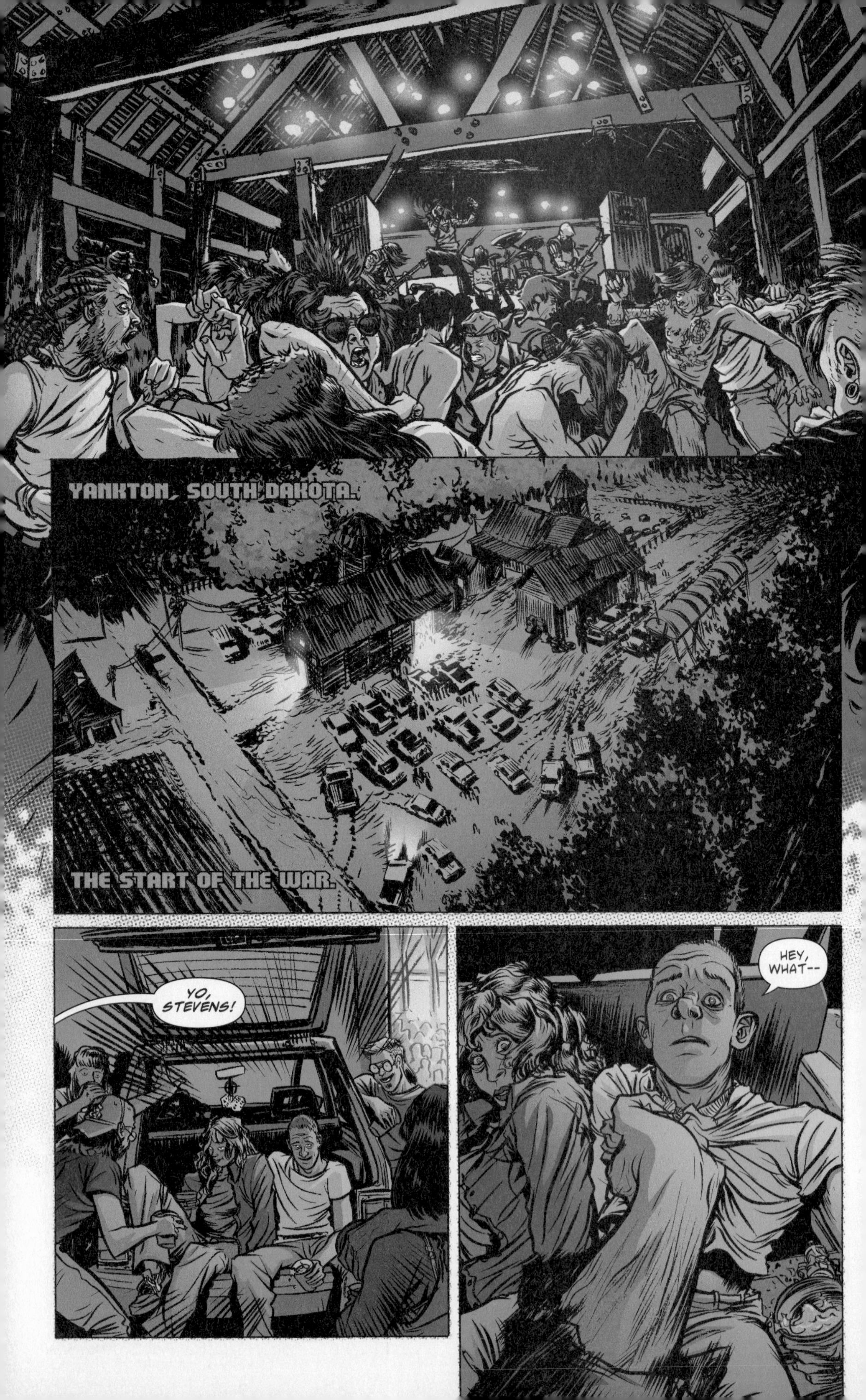
YANKTON, SOUTH DAKOTA.
THE START OF THE WAR.
YO, STEVENS!
HEY, WHAT--

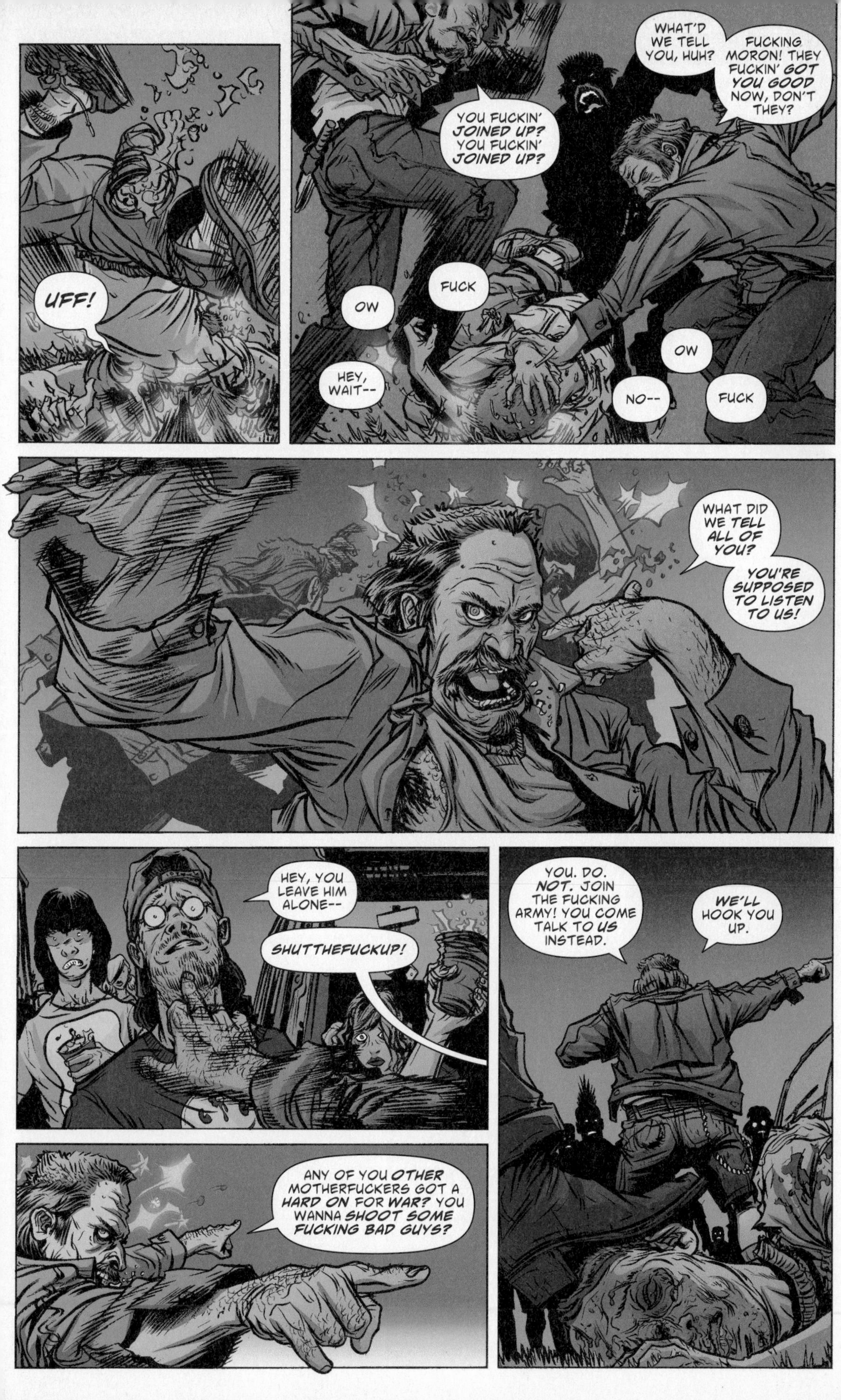
UFF!
YOU FUCKIN' JOINED UP? YOU FUCKIN' JOINED UP?
WHAT'D WE TELL YOU, HUH?
FUCKING MORON! THEY FUCKIN' GOT YOU GOOD NOW, DON'T THEY?
FUCK
OW
HEY, WAIT--
OW
NO--
FUCK
WHAT DID WE TELL ALL OF YOU?
YOU'RE SUPPOSED TO LISTEN TO US!
HEY, YOU LEAVE HIM ALONE--
SHUTTHEFUCKUP!
ANY OF YOU OTHER MOTHERFUCKERS GOT A HARD ON FOR WAR? YOU WANNA SHOOT SOME FUCKING BAD GUYS?
YOU. DO. NOT. JOIN THE FUCKING ARMY! YOU COME TALK TO US INSTEAD.
WE'LL HOOK YOU UP.

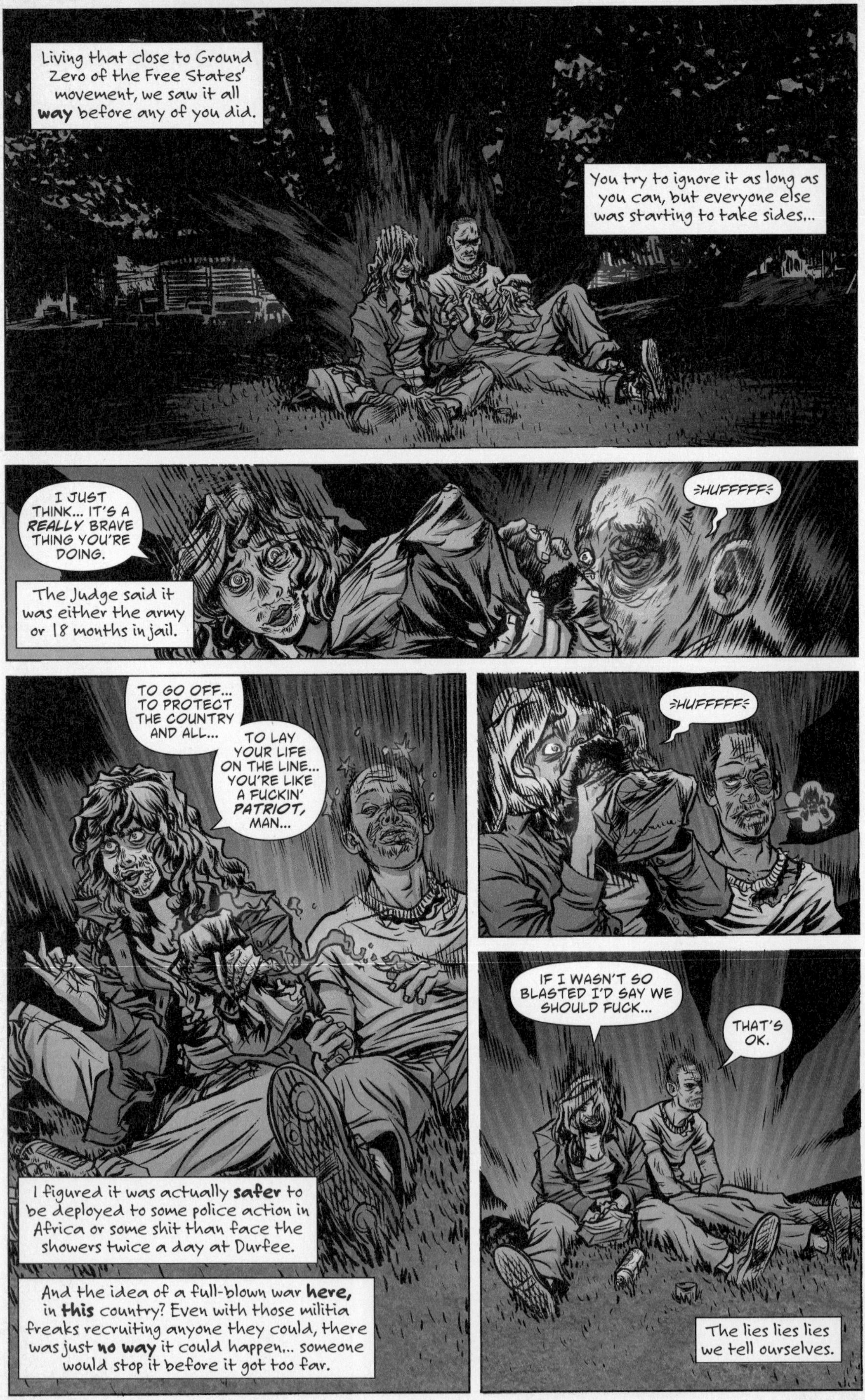
Living that close to Ground Zero of the Free States' movement, we saw it all **way** before any of you did.
You try to ignore it as long as you can, but everyone else was starting to take sides...
I JUST THINK... IT'S A *REALLY* BRAVE THING YOU'RE DOING.
The Judge said it was either the army or 18 months in jail.
HUFFFFF
TO GO OFF... TO PROTECT THE COUNTRY AND ALL...
TO LAY YOUR LIFE ON THE LINE... YOU'RE LIKE A FUCKIN' *PATRIOT,* MAN...
I figured it was actually **safer** to be deployed to some police action in Africa or some shit than face the showers twice a day at Durfee.
And the idea of a full-blown war **here,** in **this** country? Even with those militia freaks recruiting anyone they could, there was just **no way** it could happen... someone would stop it before it got too far.
HUFFFFF
IF I WASN'T SO BLASTED I'D SAY WE SHOULD FUCK...
THAT'S OK.
The lies lies lies we tell ourselves.

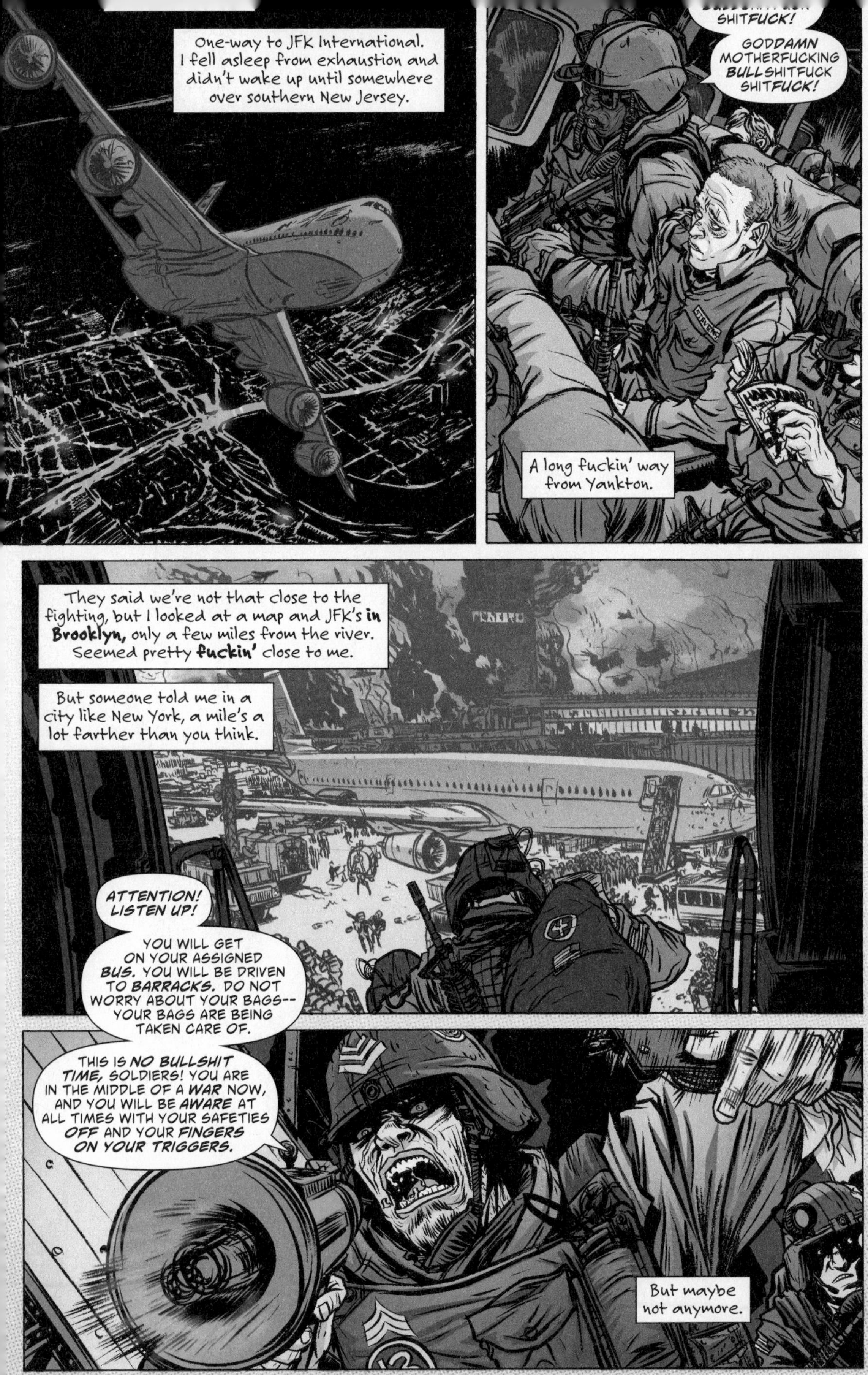

One-way to JFK International. I fell asleep from exhaustion and didn't wake up until somewhere over southern New Jersey.
SHITFUCK!
GODDAMN MOTHERFUCKING BULLSHITFUCK SHITFUCK!
A long fuckin' way from Yankton.
They said we're not that close to the fighting, but I looked at a map and JFK's in Brooklyn, only a few miles from the river. Seemed pretty fuckin' close to me.
But someone told me in a city like New York, a mile's a lot farther than you think.
ATTENTION! LISTEN UP!
YOU WILL GET ON YOUR ASSIGNED BUS. YOU WILL BE DRIVEN TO BARRACKS. DO NOT WORRY ABOUT YOUR BAGS-- YOUR BAGS ARE BEING TAKEN CARE OF.
THIS IS NO BULLSHIT TIME, SOLDIERS! YOU ARE IN THE MIDDLE OF A WAR NOW, AND YOU WILL BE AWARE AT ALL TIMES WITH YOUR SAFETIES OFF AND YOUR FINGERS ON YOUR TRIGGERS.
But maybe not anymore.

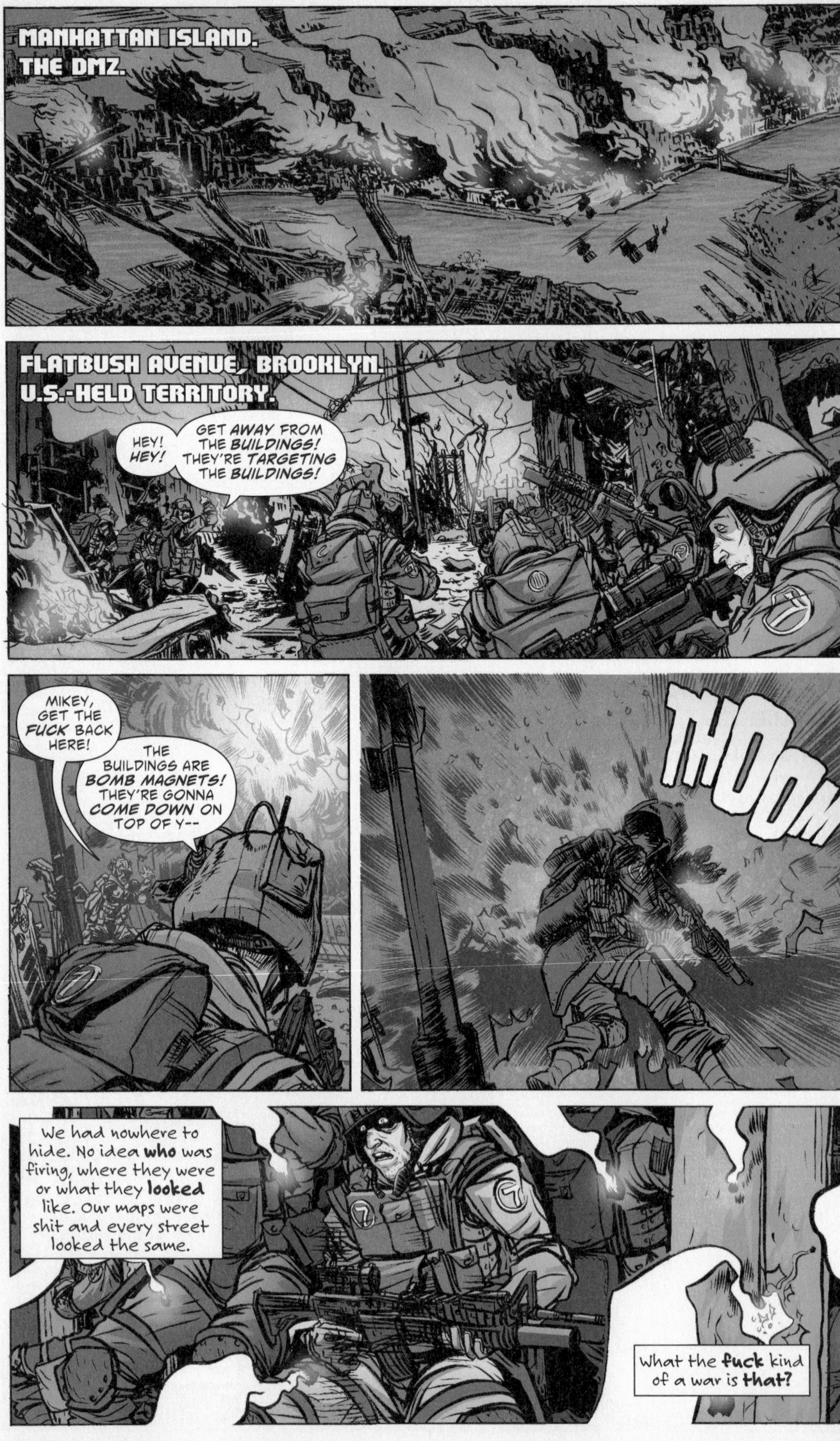
MANHATTAN ISLAND.
THE DMZ.
FLATBUSH AVENUE, BROOKLYN.
U.S.-HELD TERRITORY.
HEY! HEY!
GET AWAY FROM THE BUILDINGS! THEY'RE TARGETING THE BUILDINGS!
MIKEY, GET THE FUCK BACK HERE!
THE BUILDINGS ARE BOMB MAGNETS! THEY'RE GONNA COME DOWN ON TOP OF Y--
THOOM
We had nowhere to hide. No idea who was firing, where they were or what they looked like. Our maps were shit and every street looked the same.
What the fuck kind of a war is that?

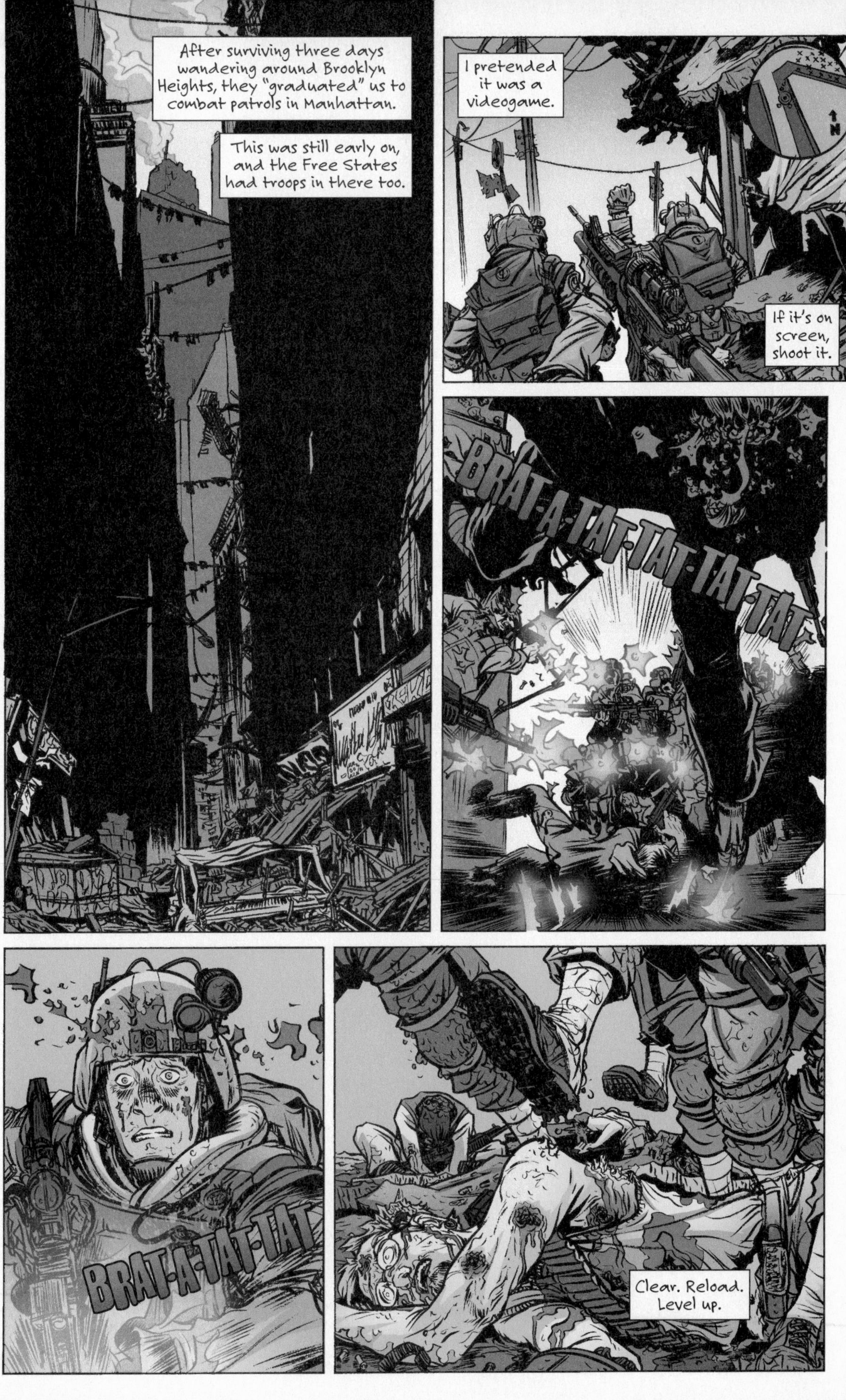
After surviving three days wandering around Brooklyn Heights, they "graduated" us to combat patrols in Manhattan.
This was still early on, and the Free States had troops in there too.
I pretended it was a videogame.
If it's on screen, shoot it.
BRAT-A-TAT-TAT-TAT-TAT-TAT
BRAT-A-TAT-TAT
Clear. Reload. Level up.

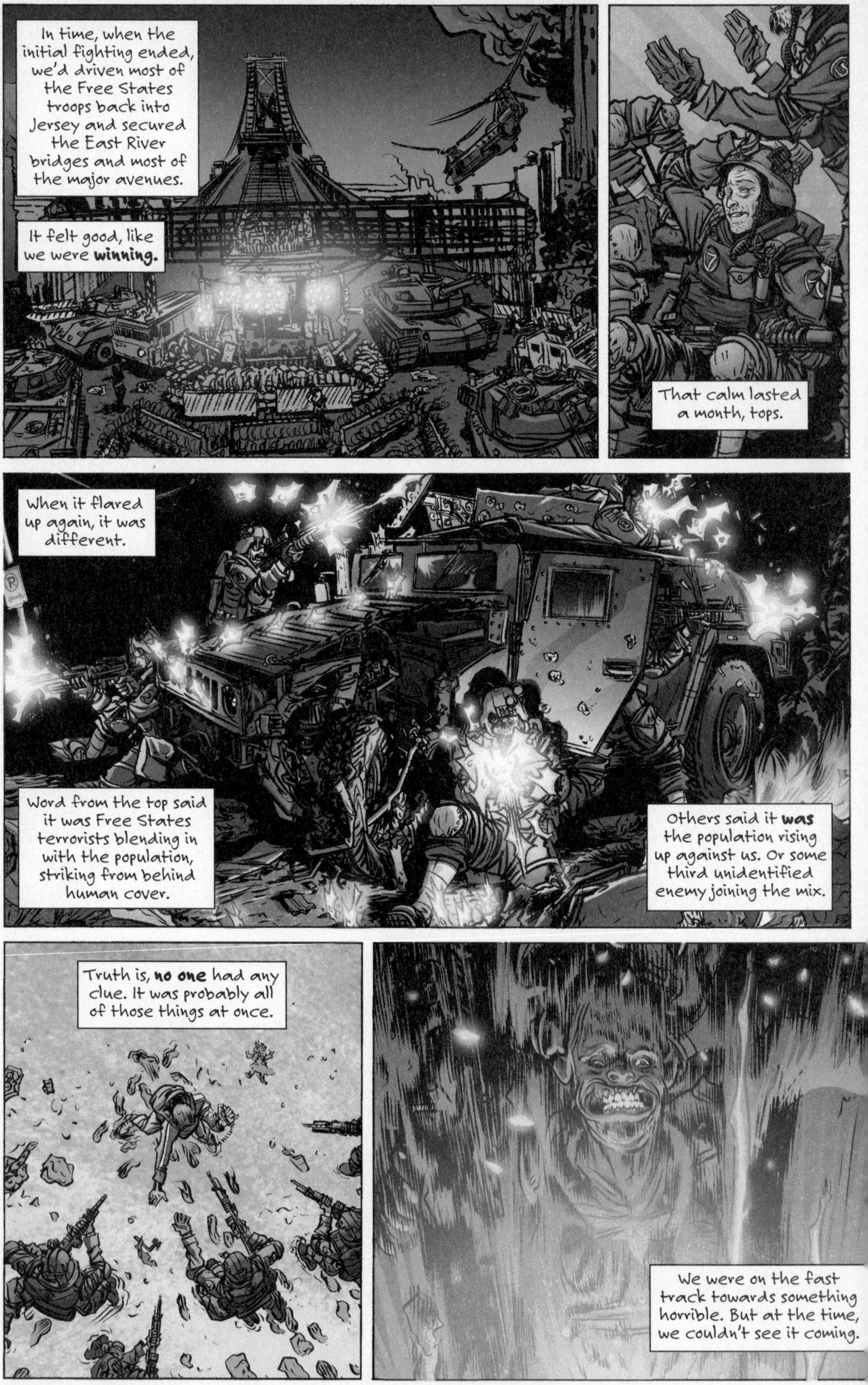
In time, when the initial fighting ended, we'd driven most of the Free States troops back into Jersey and secured the East River bridges and most of the major avenues.
It felt good, like we were **winning.**
That calm lasted a month, tops.
When it flared up again, it was different.
Word from the top said it was Free States terrorists blending in with the population, striking from behind human cover.
Others said it **was** the population rising up against us. Or some third unidentified enemy joining the mix.
Truth is, **no one** had any clue. It was probably all of those things at once.
We were on the fast track towards something horrible. But at the time, we couldn't see it coming.

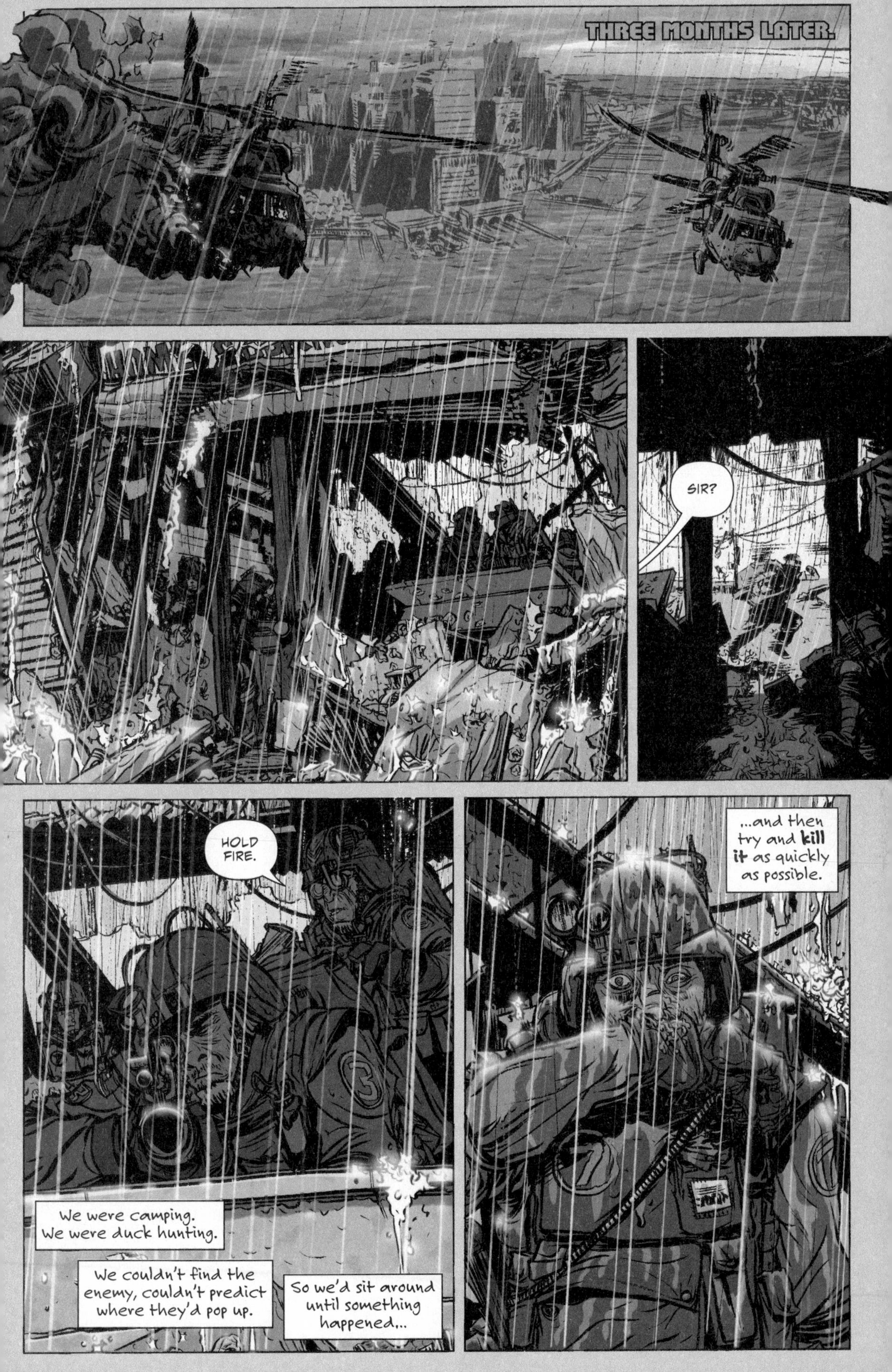
THREE MONTHS LATER.
SIR?
HOLD FIRE.
We were camping. We were duck hunting.
We couldn't find the enemy, couldn't predict where they'd pop up.
So we'd sit around until something happened...
...and then try and **kill it** as quickly as possible.

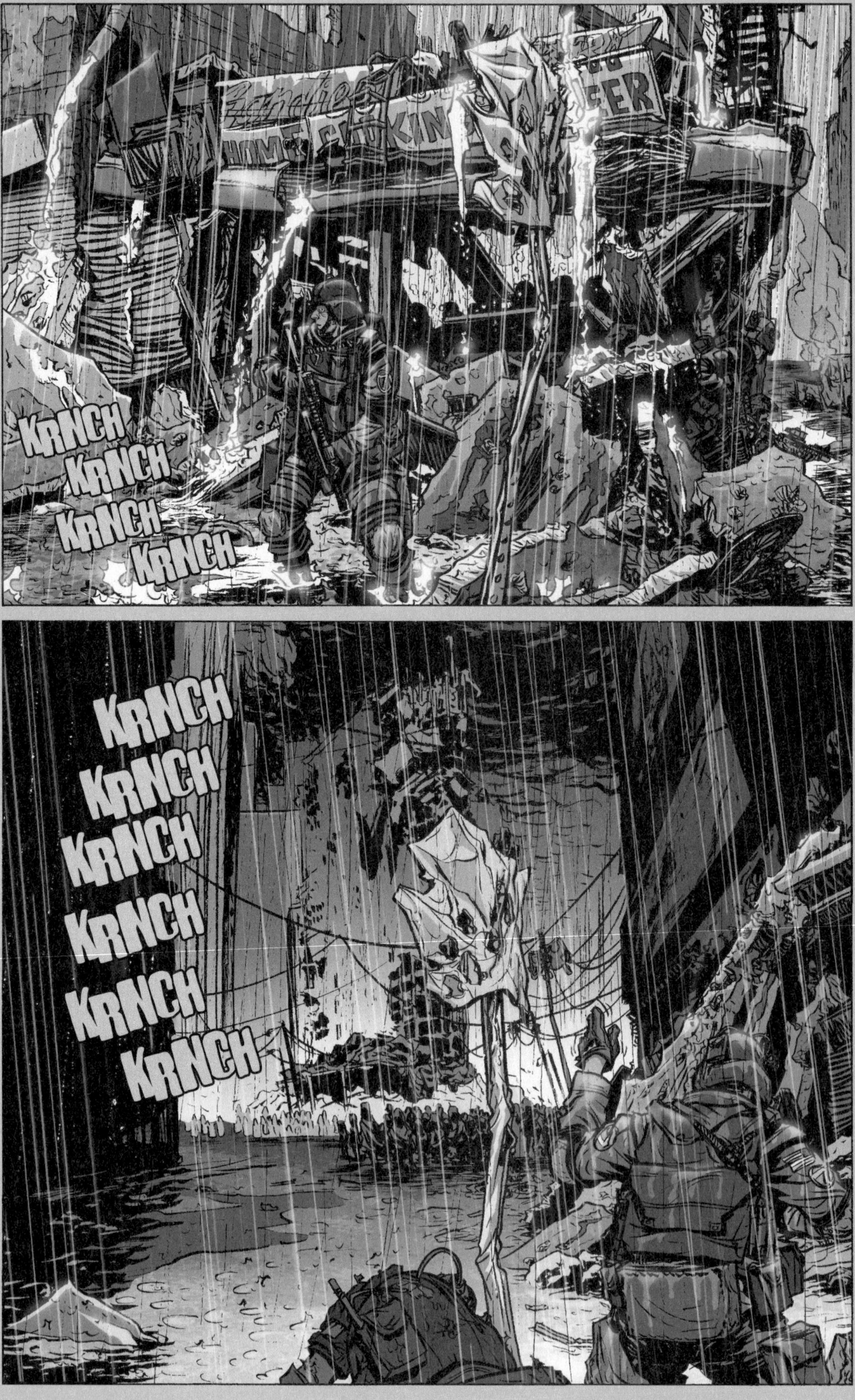

KRNCH
KRNCH
KRNCH
KRNCH
KRNCH
KRNCH
KRNCH
KRNCH
KRNCH
KRNCH

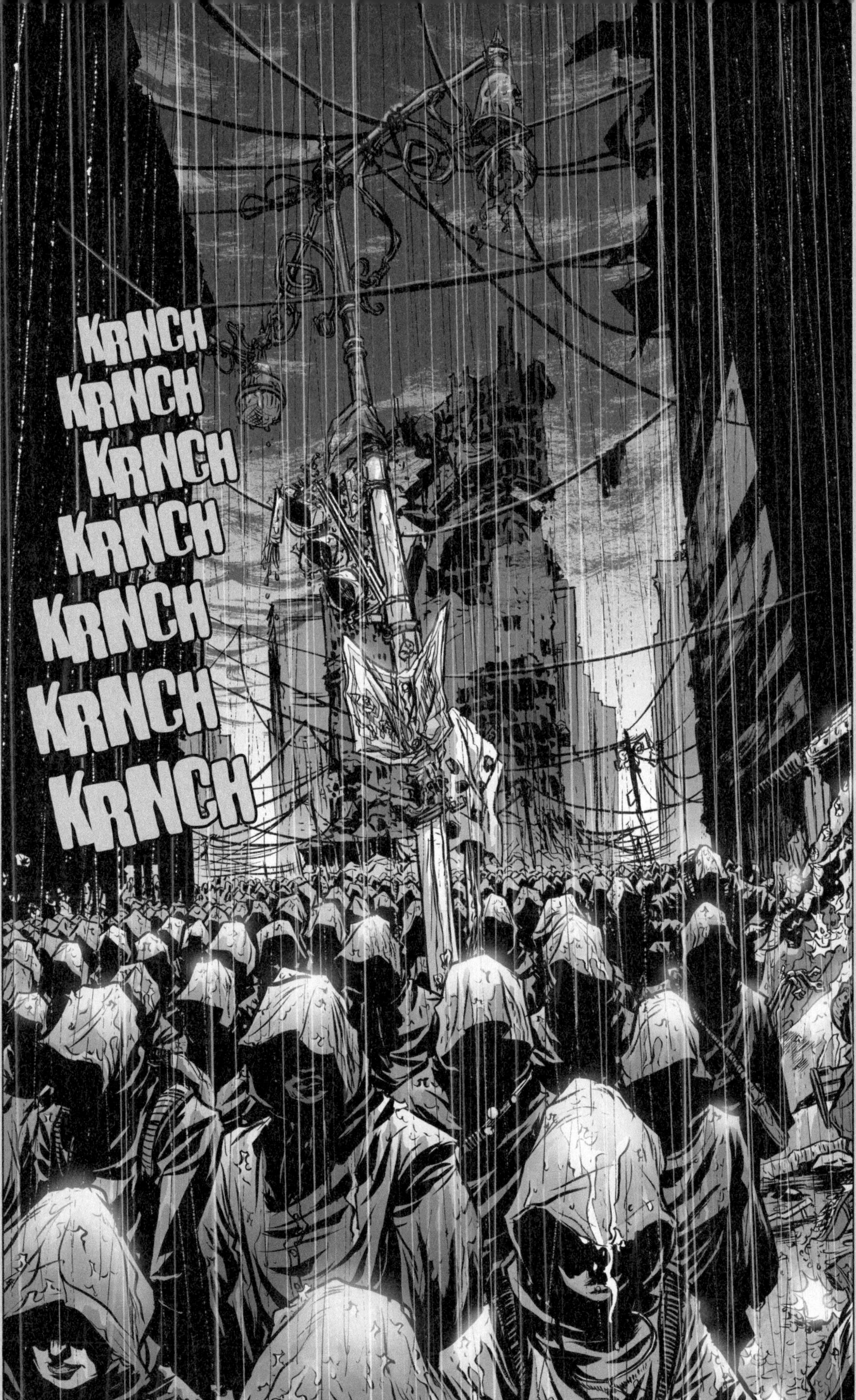
KRNCH
KRNCH
KRNCH
KRNCH
KRNCH
KRNCH
KRNCH

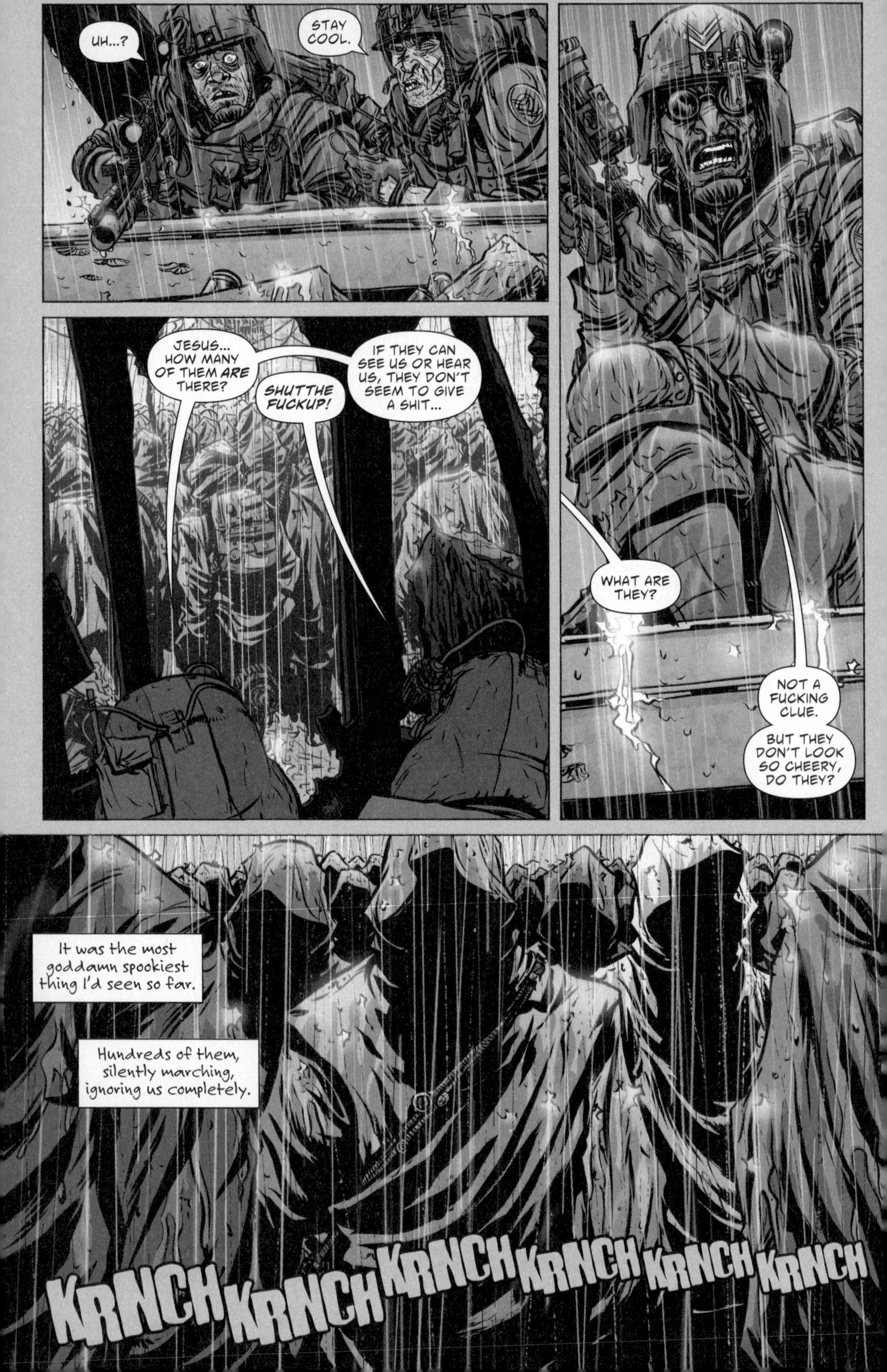
UH...?
STAY COOL.
JESUS... HOW MANY OF THEM ARE THERE?
SHUT THE FUCKUP!
IF THEY CAN SEE US OR HEAR US, THEY DON'T SEEM TO GIVE A SHIT...
WHAT ARE THEY?
NOT A FUCKING CLUE.
BUT THEY DON'T LOOK SO CHEERY, DO THEY?
It was the most goddamn spookiest thing I'd seen so far.
Hundreds of them, silently marching, ignoring us completely.
KRNCH KRNCH KRNCH KRNCH KRNCH KRNCH

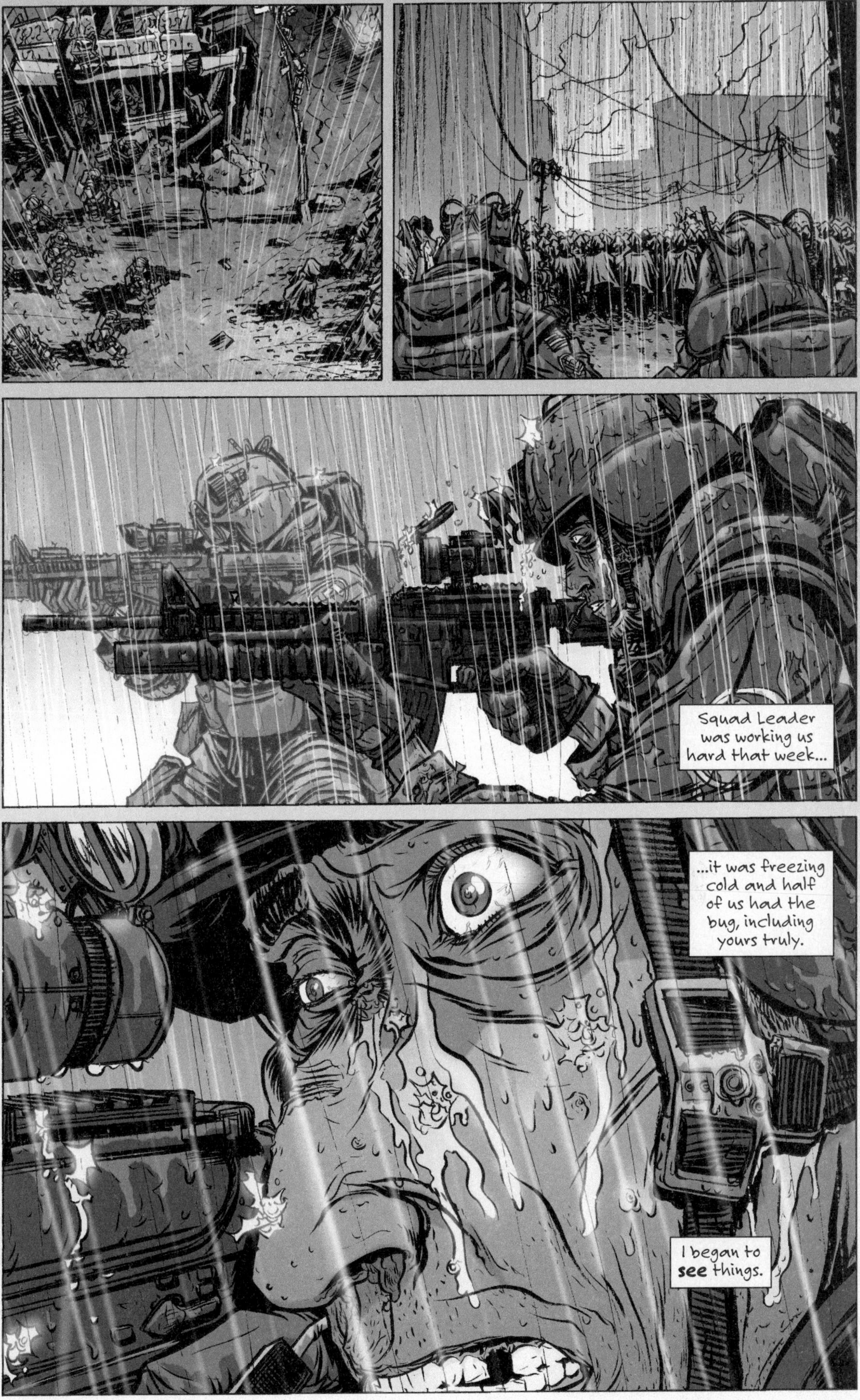
Squad Leader was working us hard that week...
...it was freezing cold and half of us had the bug, including yours truly.
I began to **see** things.

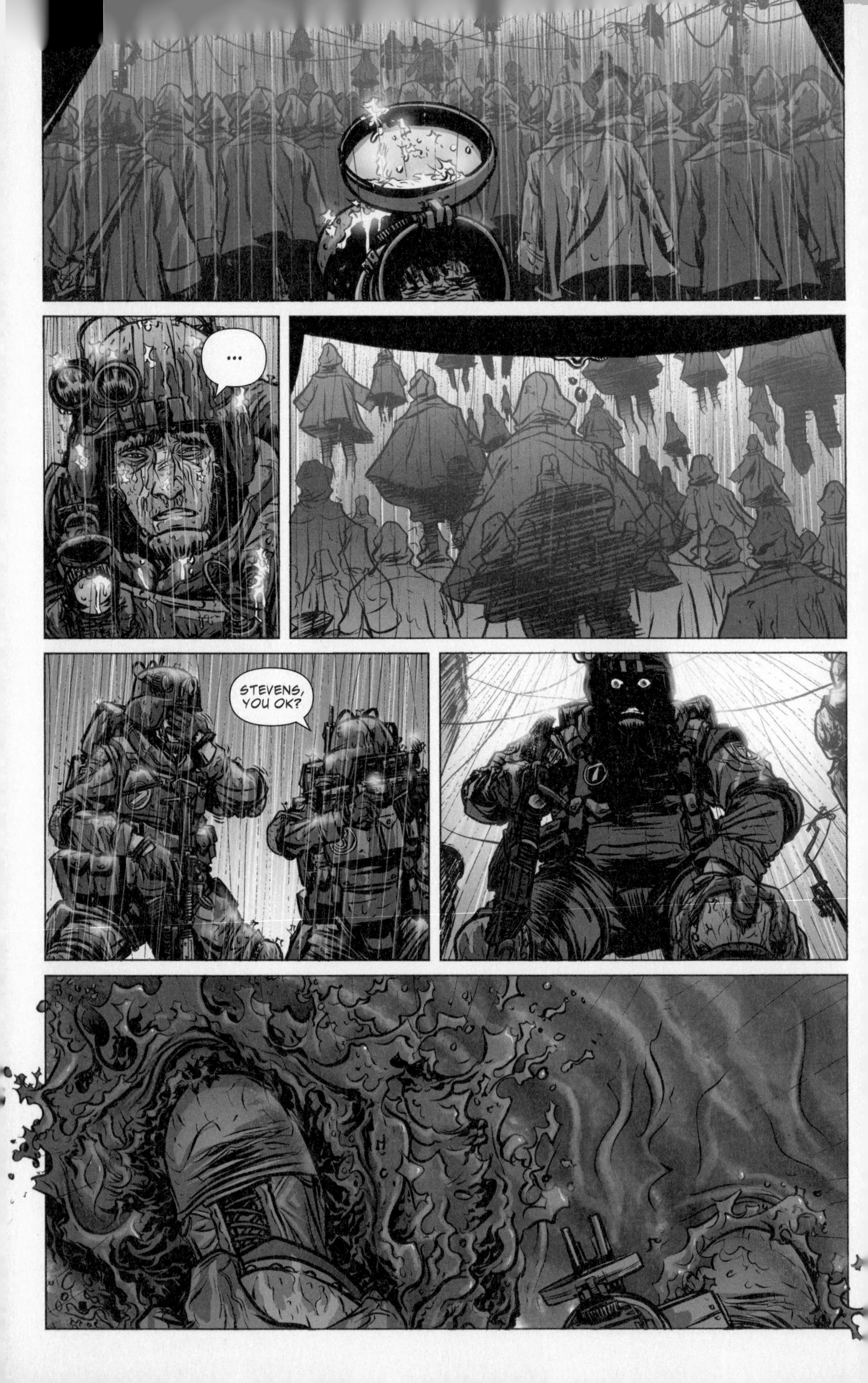
...
STEVENS, YOU OK?

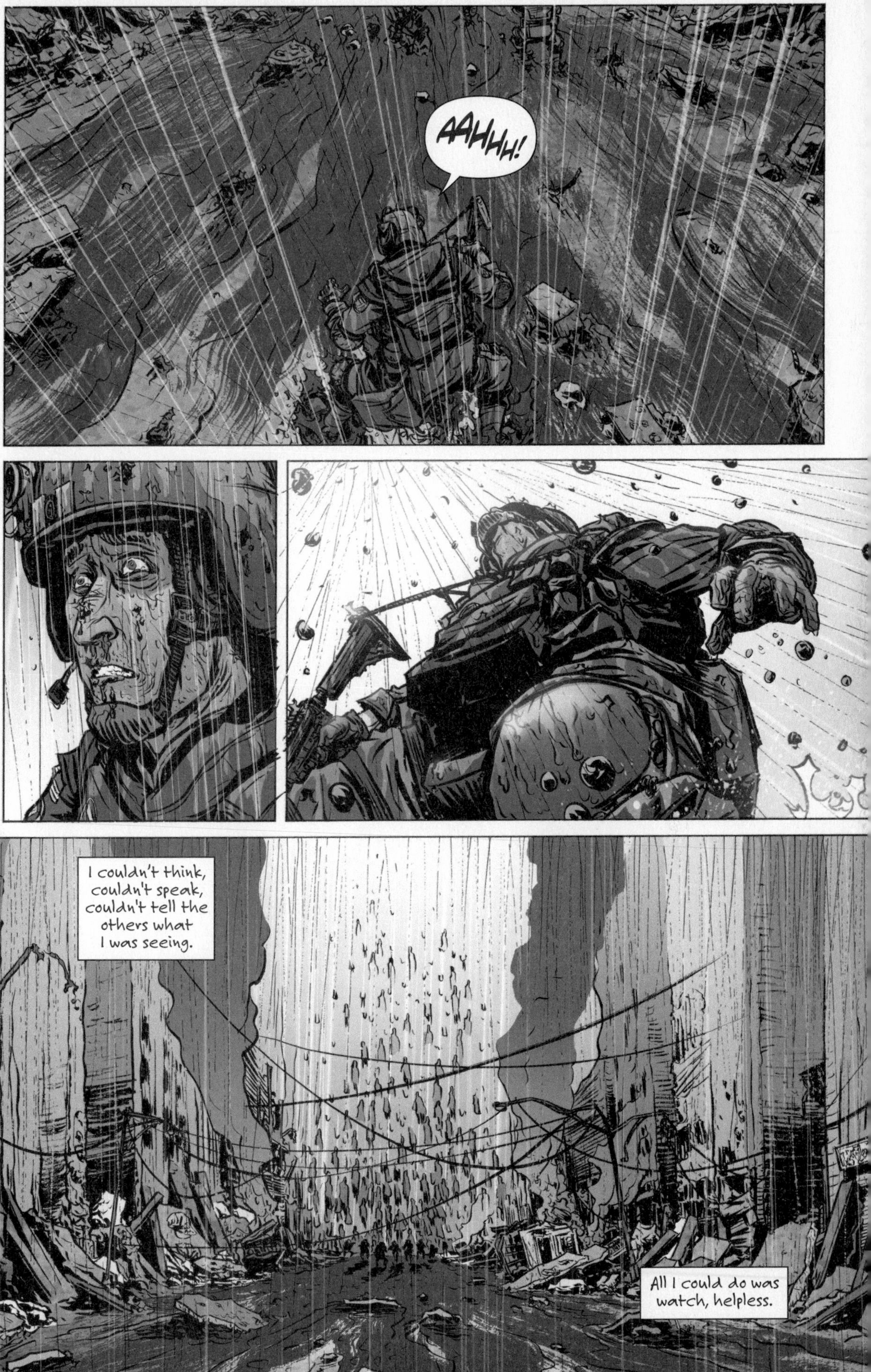
AAHHHH!
I couldn't think, couldn't speak, couldn't tell the others what I was seeing.
All I could do was watch, helpless.

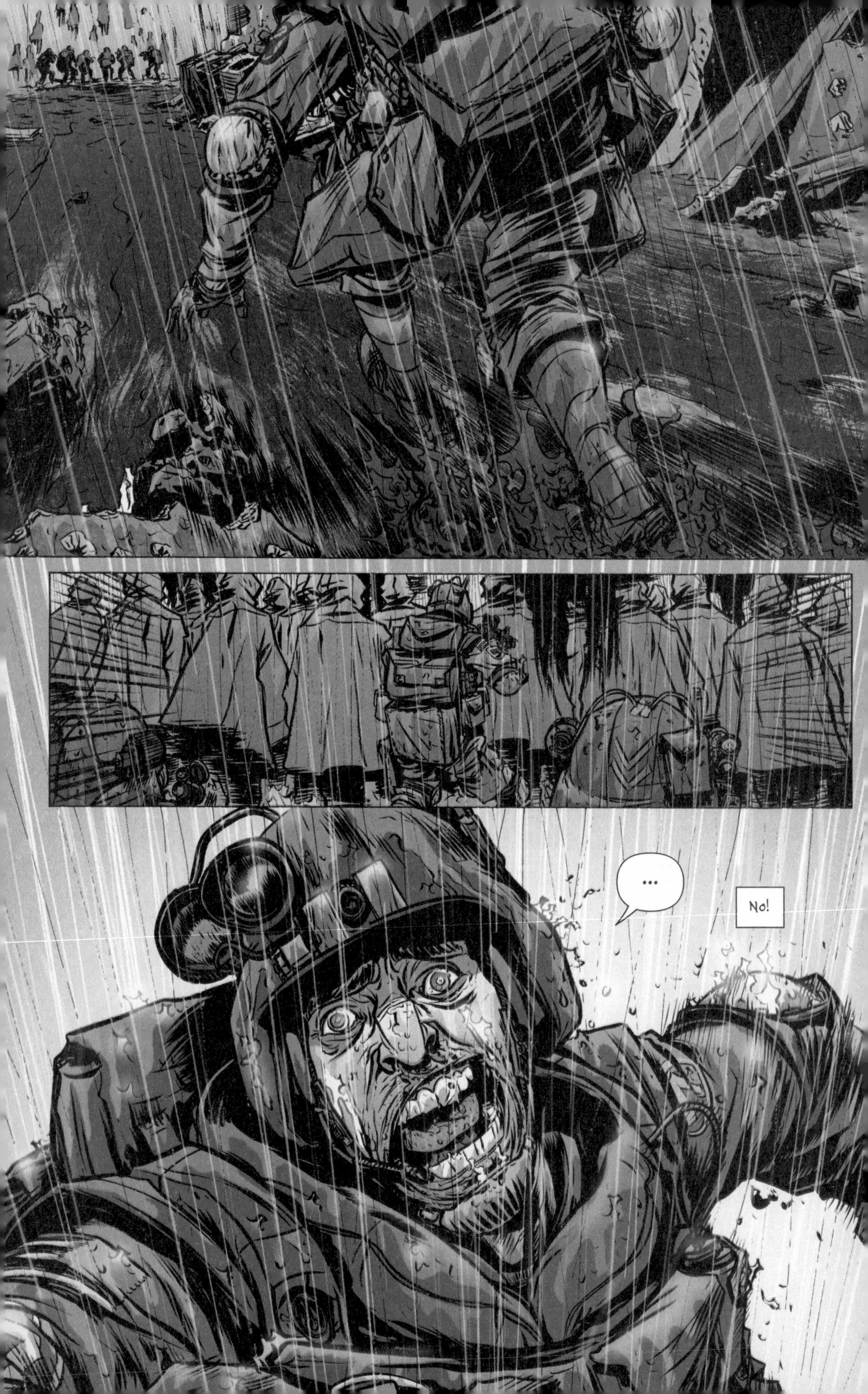
...
No!

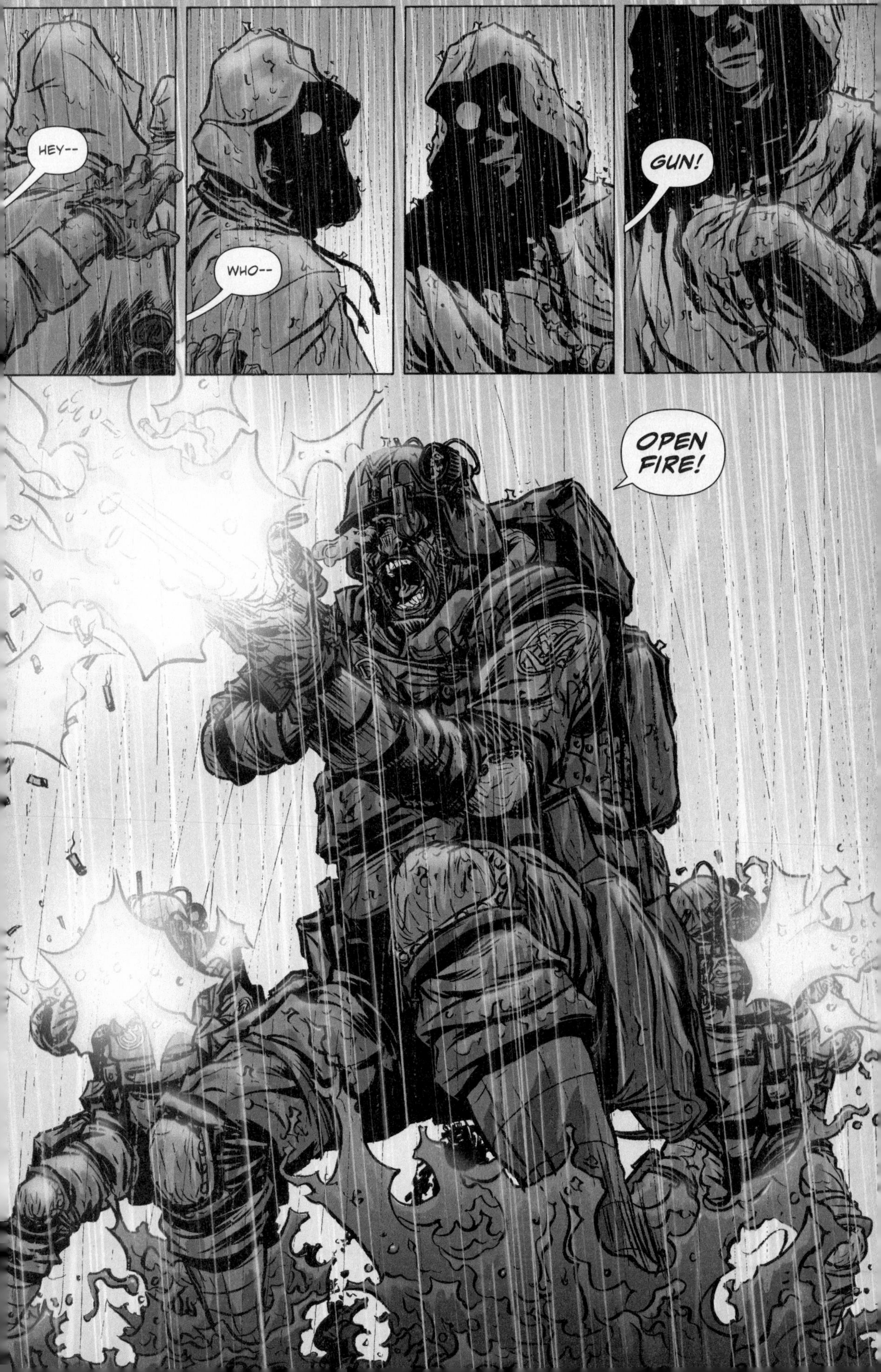
HEY--
WHO--
GUN!
OPEN FIRE!

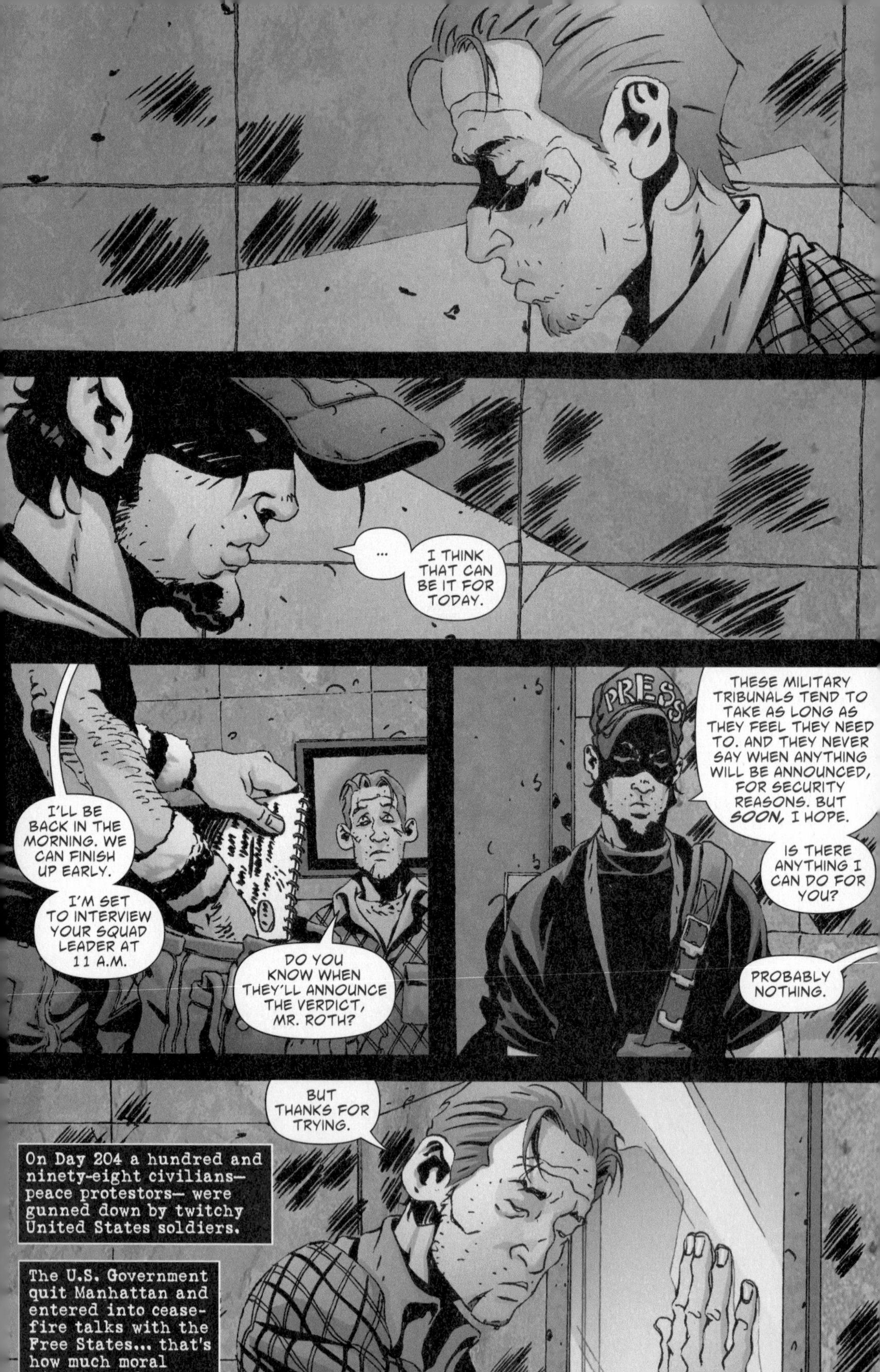
...
I THINK THAT CAN BE IT FOR TODAY.
I'LL BE BACK IN THE MORNING. WE CAN FINISH UP EARLY.
I'M SET TO INTERVIEW YOUR SQUAD LEADER AT 11 A.M.
DO YOU KNOW WHEN THEY'LL ANNOUNCE THE VERDICT, MR. ROTH?
PRESS
THESE MILITARY TRIBUNALS TEND TO TAKE AS LONG AS THEY FEEL THEY NEED TO. AND THEY NEVER SAY WHEN ANYTHING WILL BE ANNOUNCED, FOR SECURITY REASONS. BUT SOON, I HOPE.
IS THERE ANYTHING I CAN DO FOR YOU?
PROBABLY NOTHING.
BUT THANKS FOR TRYING.
On Day 204 a hundred and ninety-eight civilians— peace protestors— were gunned down by twitchy United States soldiers.
The U.S. Government quit Manhattan and entered into cease-fire talks with the Free States... that's how much moral high ground was lost that day.

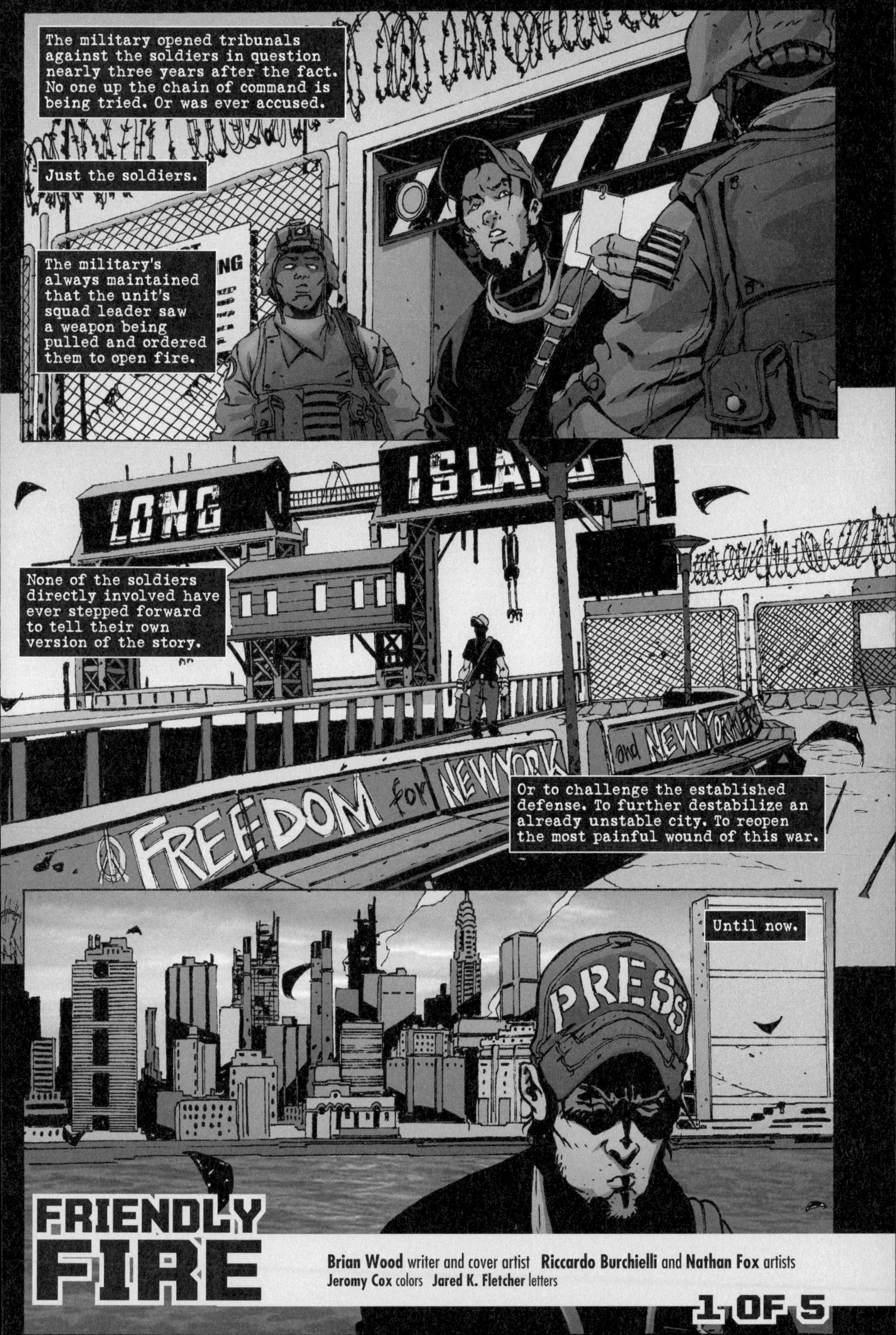
The military opened tribunals against the soldiers in question nearly three years after the fact. No one up the chain of command is being tried. Or was ever accused.
Just the soldiers.
The military's always maintained that the unit's squad leader saw a weapon being pulled and ordered them to open fire.
LONG
ISLAND
None of the soldiers directly involved have ever stepped forward to tell their own version of the story.
FREEDOM for NEW YORK
and NEW YORKERS
Or to challenge the established defense. To further destabilize an already unstable city. To reopen the most painful wound of this war.
Until now.
PRESS
FRIENDLY FIRE
Brian Wood writer and cover artist Riccardo Burchielli and Nathan Fox artists
Jeromy Cox colors Jared K. Fletcher letters
1 OF 5

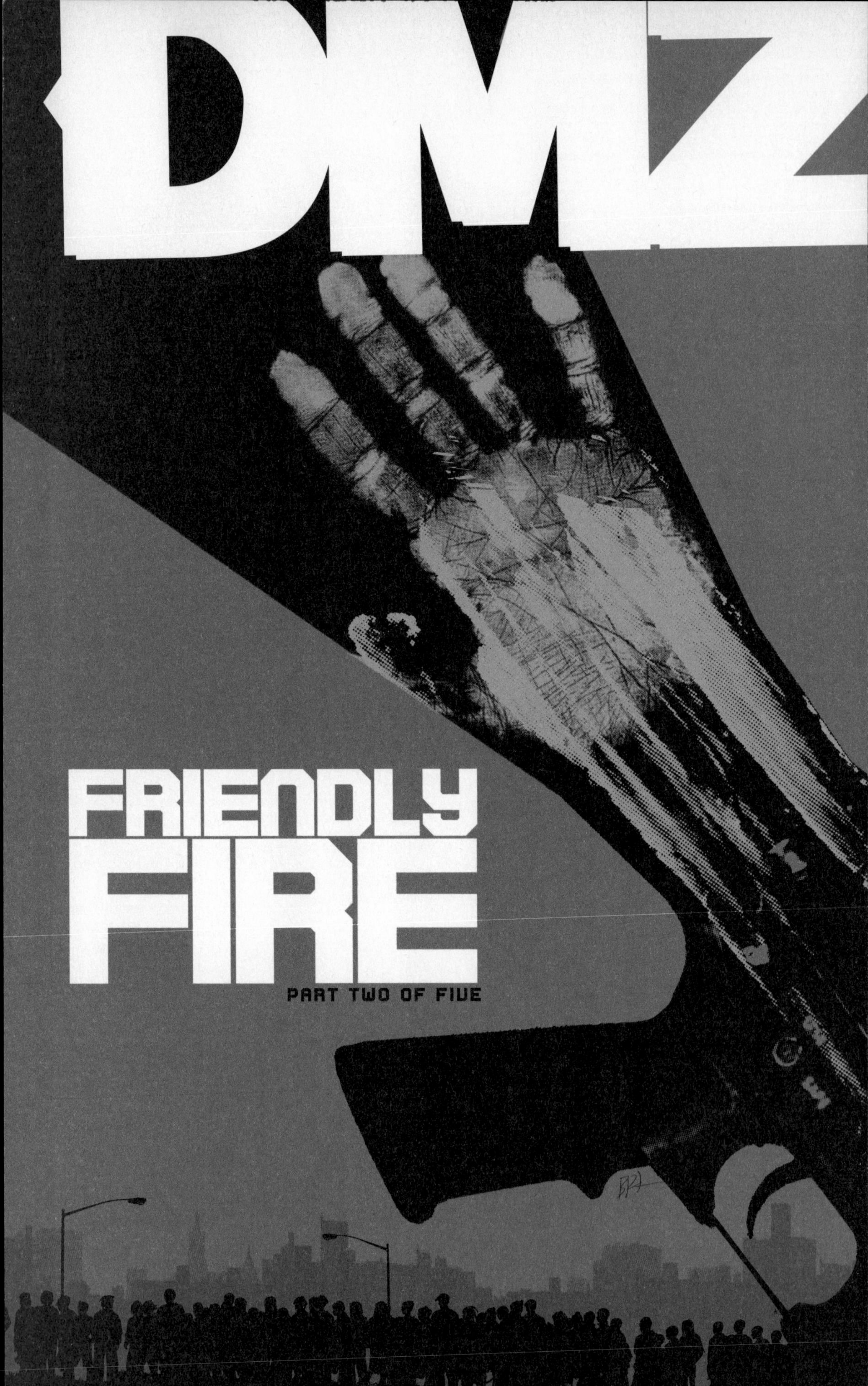
DMZ
FRIENDLY
FIRE
PART TWO OF FIVE

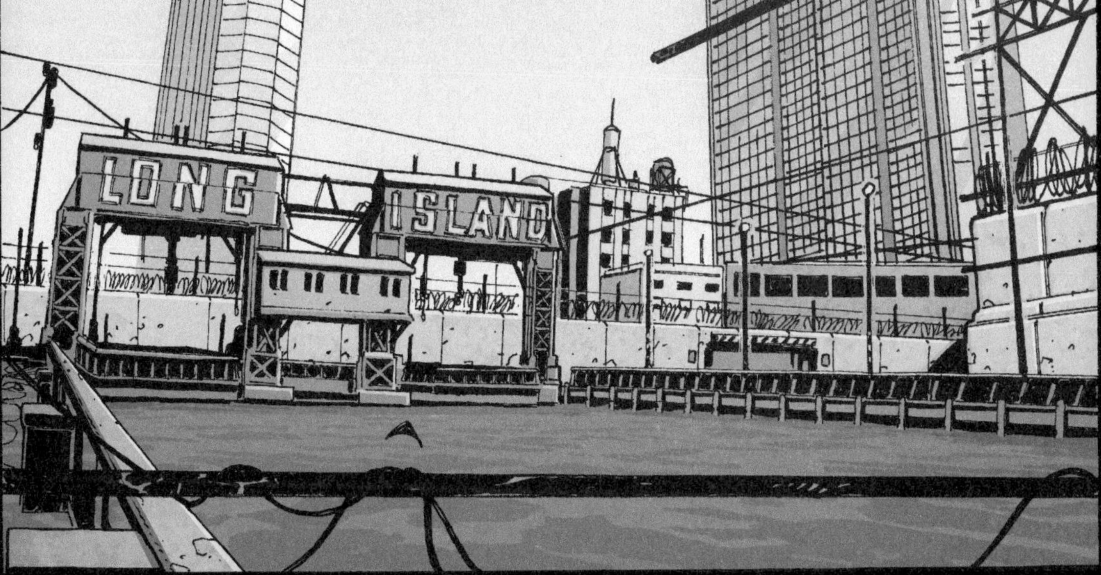
LONG
ISLAND

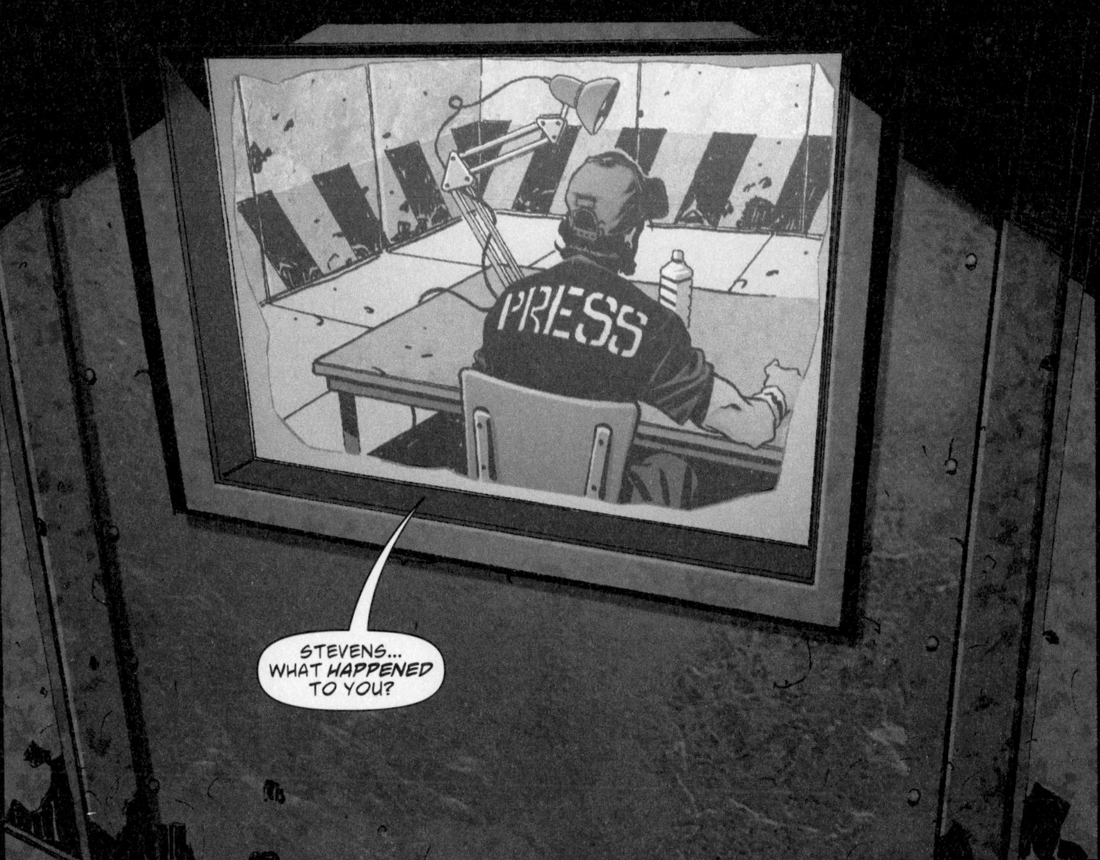
PRESS
STEVENS... WHAT HAPPENED TO YOU?

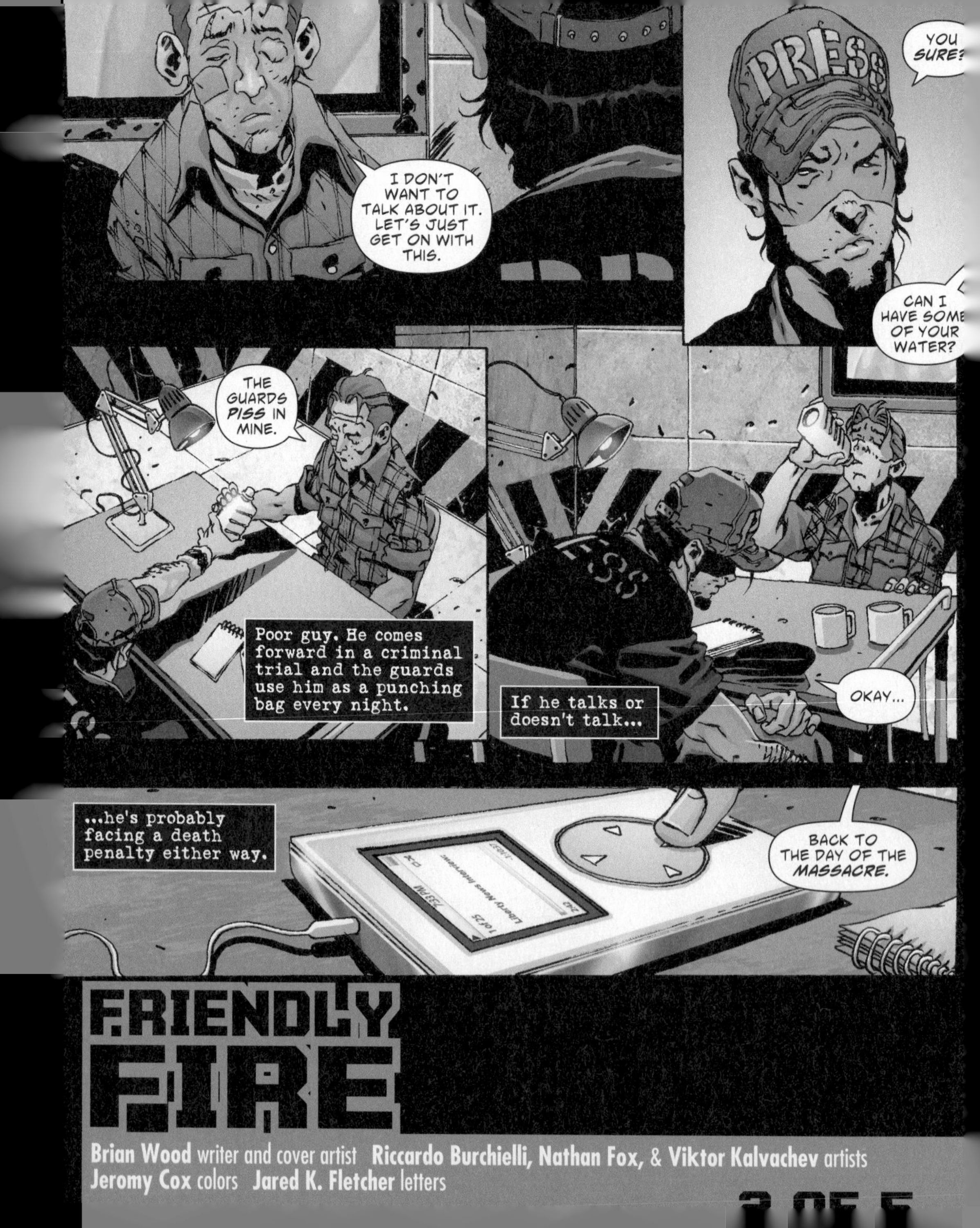
I DON'T WANT TO TALK ABOUT IT. LET'S JUST GET ON WITH THIS.
PRESS
YOU SURE?
CAN I HAVE SOME OF YOUR WATER?
THE GUARDS PISS IN MINE.
Poor guy. He comes forward in a criminal trial and the guards use him as a punching bag every night.
If he talks or doesn't talk...
OKAY...
...he's probably facing a death penalty either way.
BACK TO THE DAY OF THE MASSACRE.

FRIENDLY FIRE

Brian Wood writer and cover artist **Riccardo Burchielli, Nathan Fox, & Viktor Kalvachev** artists
Jeromy Cox colors **Jared K. Fletcher** letters

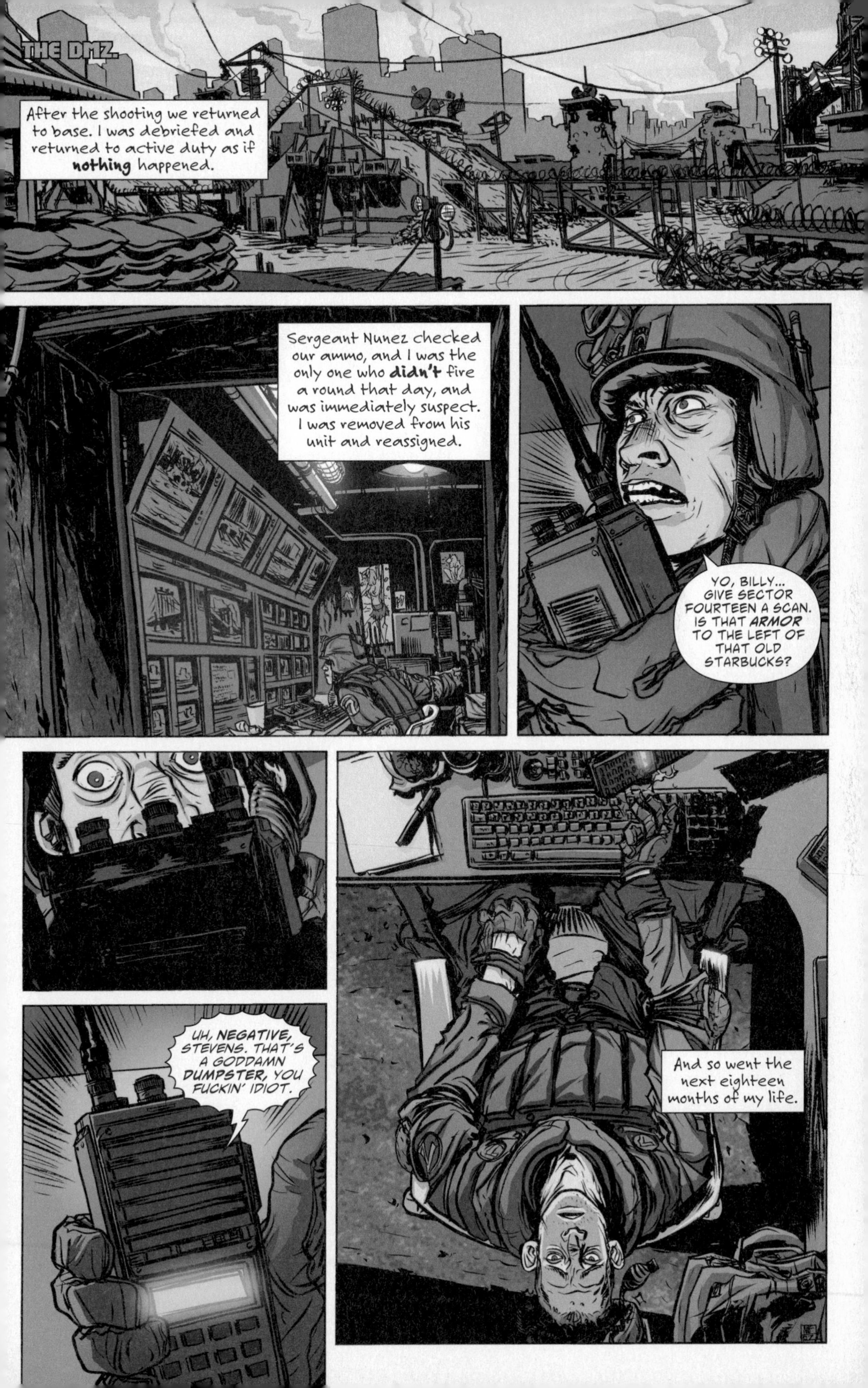
THE DMZ.
After the shooting we returned to base. I was debriefed and returned to active duty as if **nothing** happened.
Sergeant Nunez checked our ammo, and I was the only one who **didn't** fire a round that day, and was immediately suspect. I was removed from his unit and reassigned.
YO, BILLY... GIVE SECTOR FOURTEEN A SCAN. IS THAT *ARMOR* TO THE LEFT OF THAT OLD STARBUCKS?
UH, **NEGATIVE**, STEVENS. THAT'S A GODDAMN **DUMPSTER**, YOU FUCKIN' IDIOT.
And so went the next eighteen months of my life.

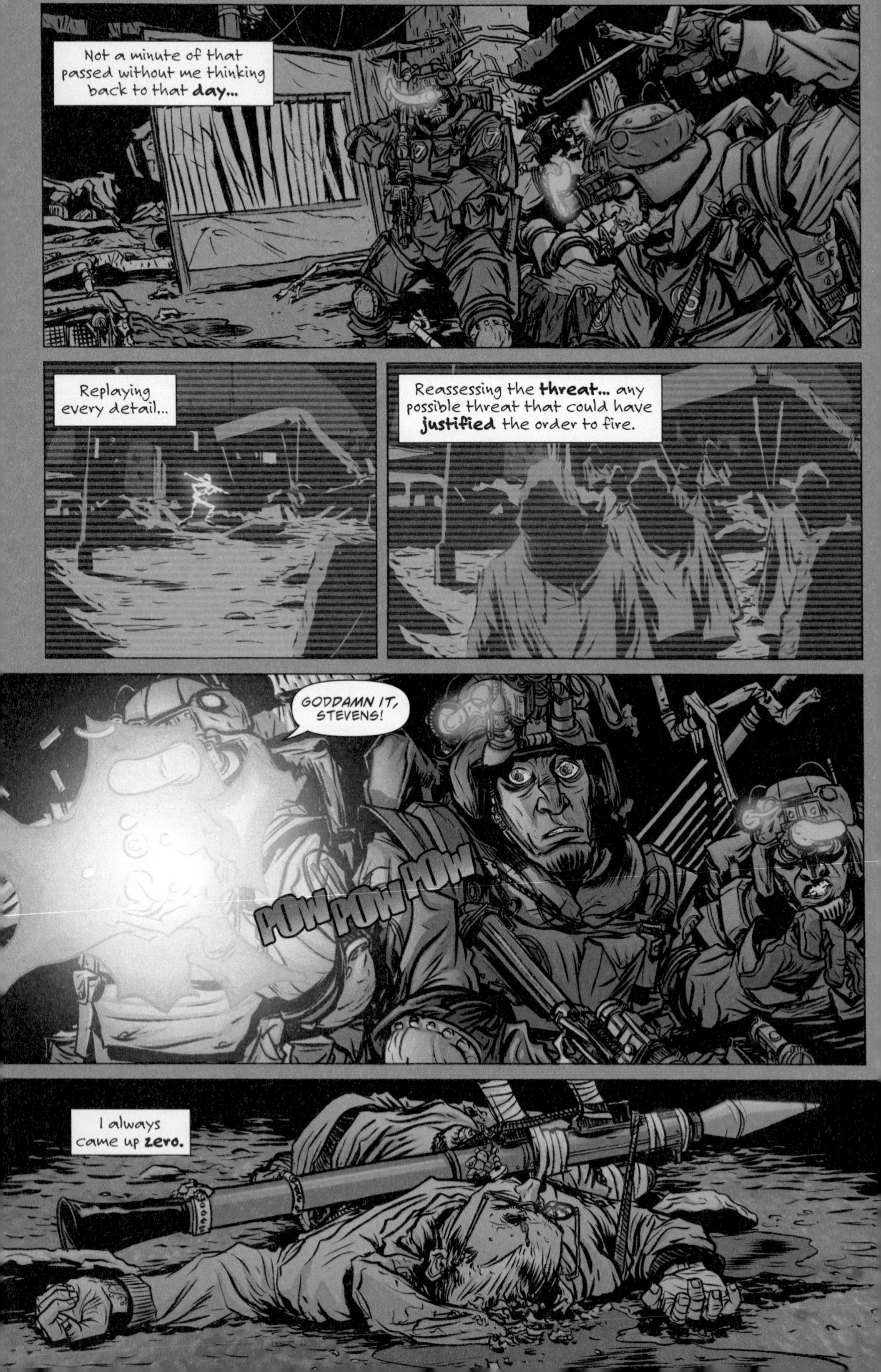
Not a minute of that passed without me thinking back to that **day...**
Replaying every detail...
Reassessing the **threat...** any possible threat that could have **justified** the order to fire.
GODDAMN IT, STEVENS!
POW POW POW
I always came up **zero.**

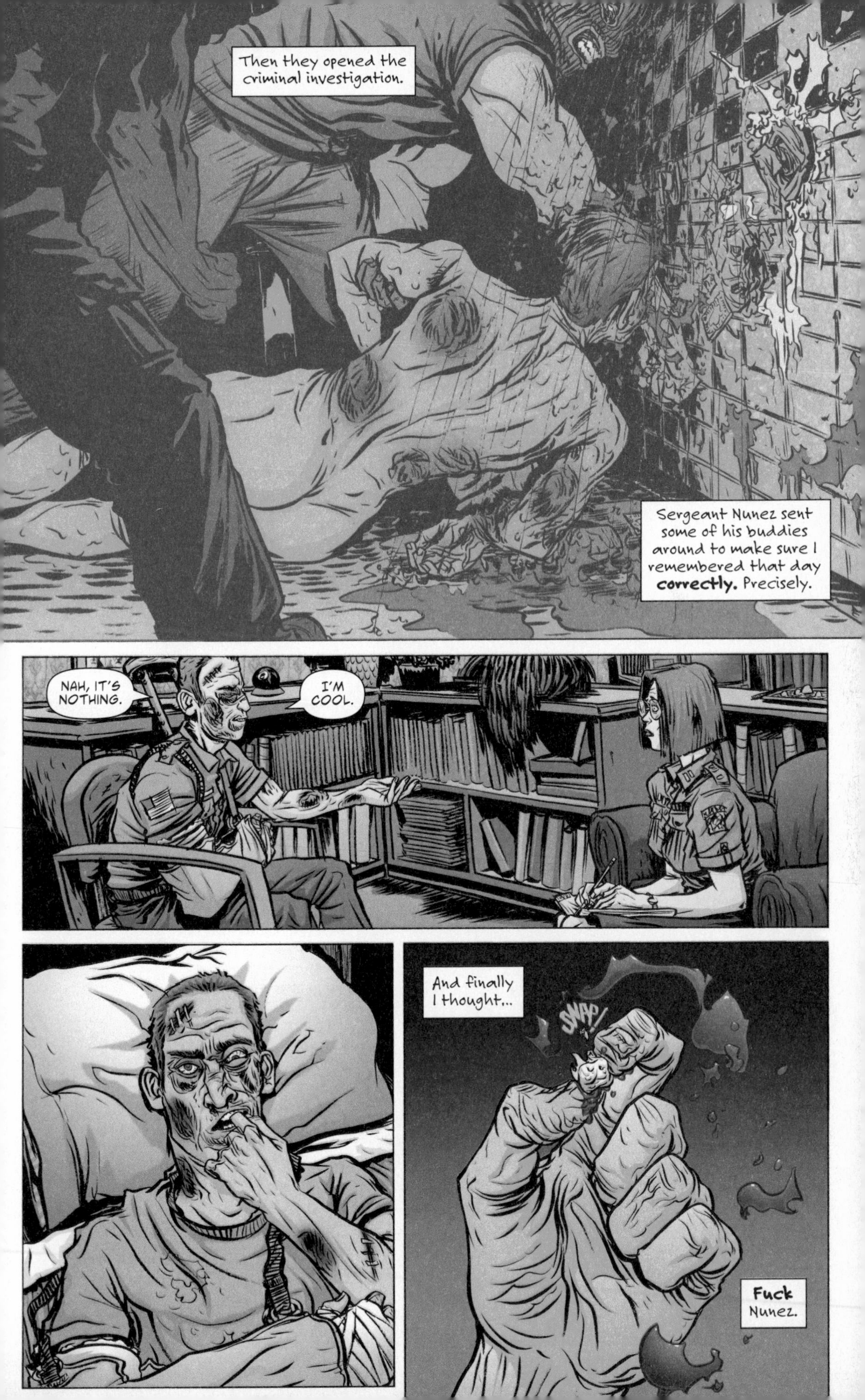
Then they opened the criminal investigation.
Sergeant Nunez sent some of his buddies around to make sure I remembered that day **correctly.** Precisely.
NAH, IT'S NOTHING.
I'M COOL.
And finally I thought...
SNAP!
Fuck Nunez.

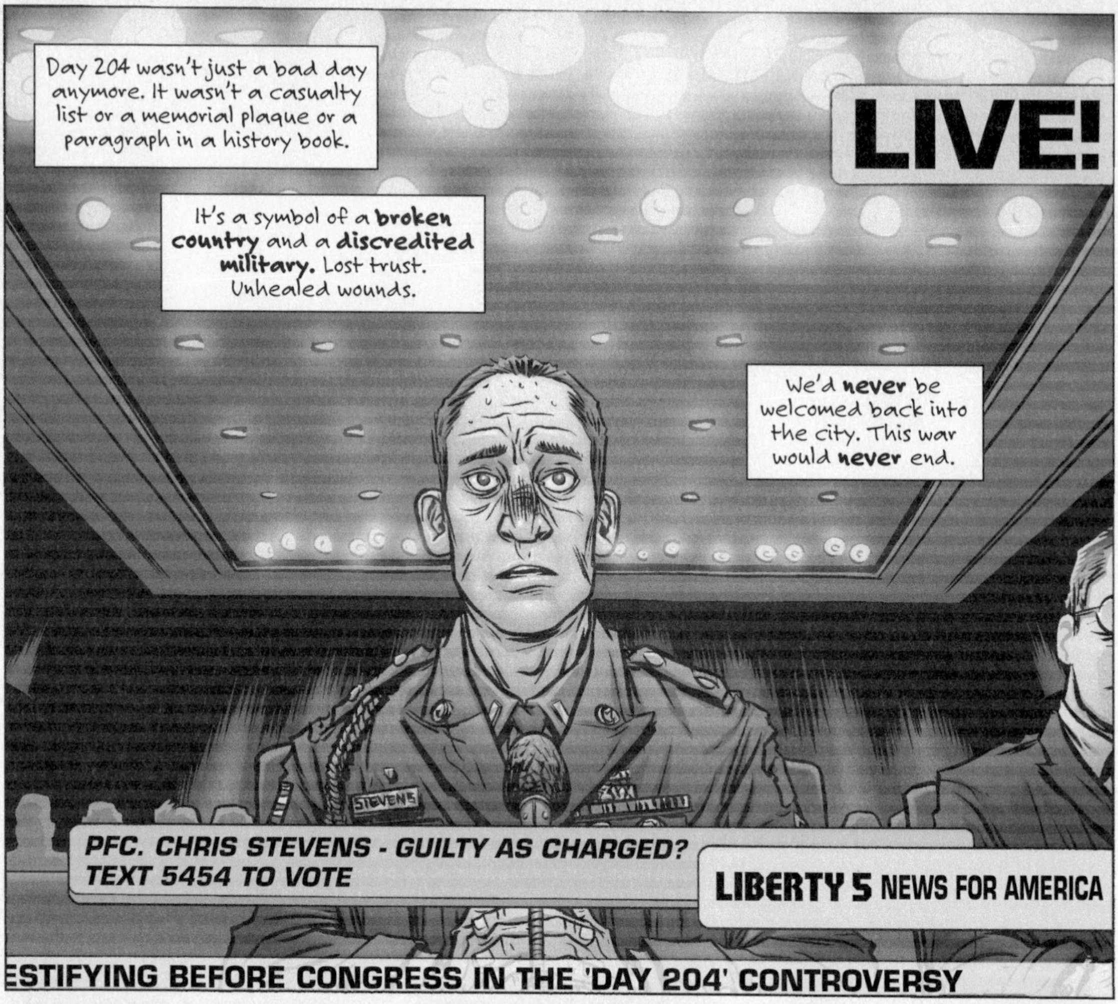
Day 204 wasn't just a bad day anymore. It wasn't a casualty list or a memorial plaque or a paragraph in a history book.
LIVE!
It's a symbol of a **broken country** and a **discredited military.** Lost trust. Unhealed wounds.
We'd **never** be welcomed back into the city. This war would **never** end.
STEVENS
PFC. CHRIS STEVENS - GUILTY AS CHARGED?
TEXT 5454 TO VOTE
LIBERTY 5 NEWS FOR AMERICA
ESTIFYING BEFORE CONGRESS IN THE 'DAY 204' CONTROVERSY

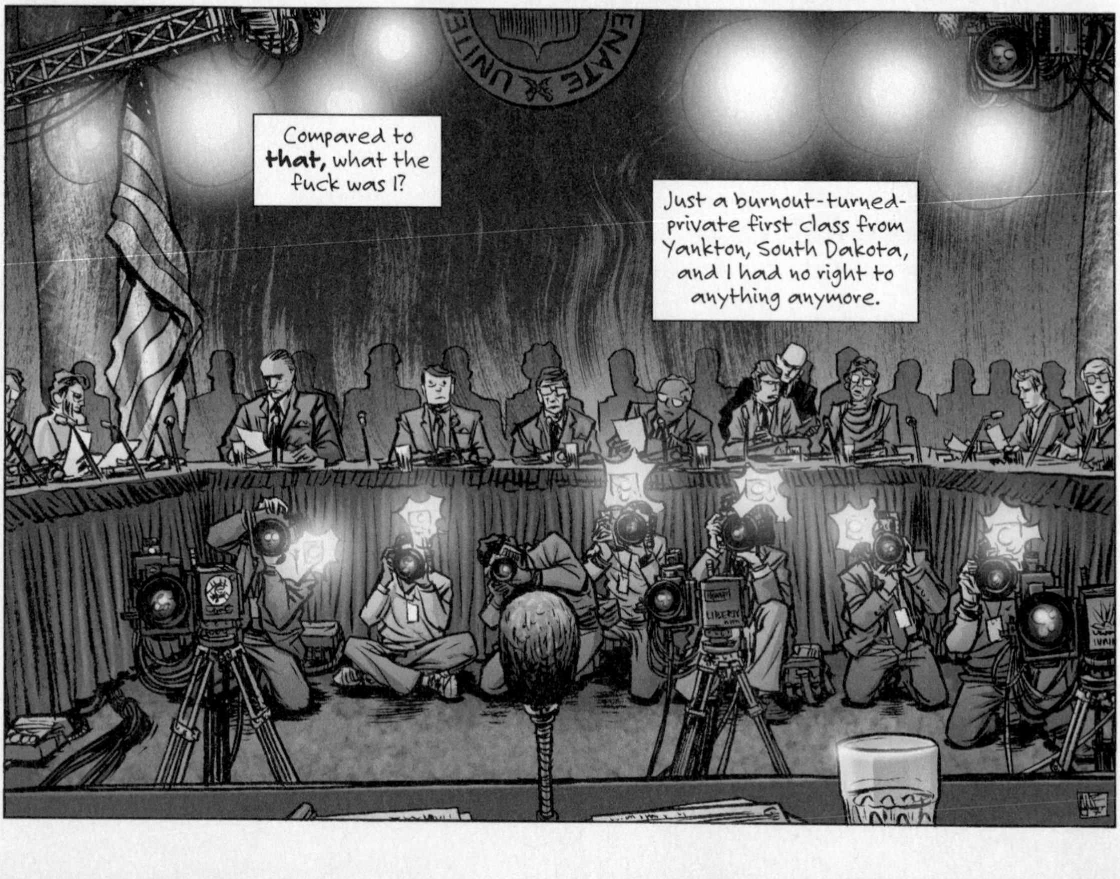
Compared to **that,** what the fuck was I?
Just a burnout-turned-private first class from Yankton, South Dakota, and I had no right to anything anymore.

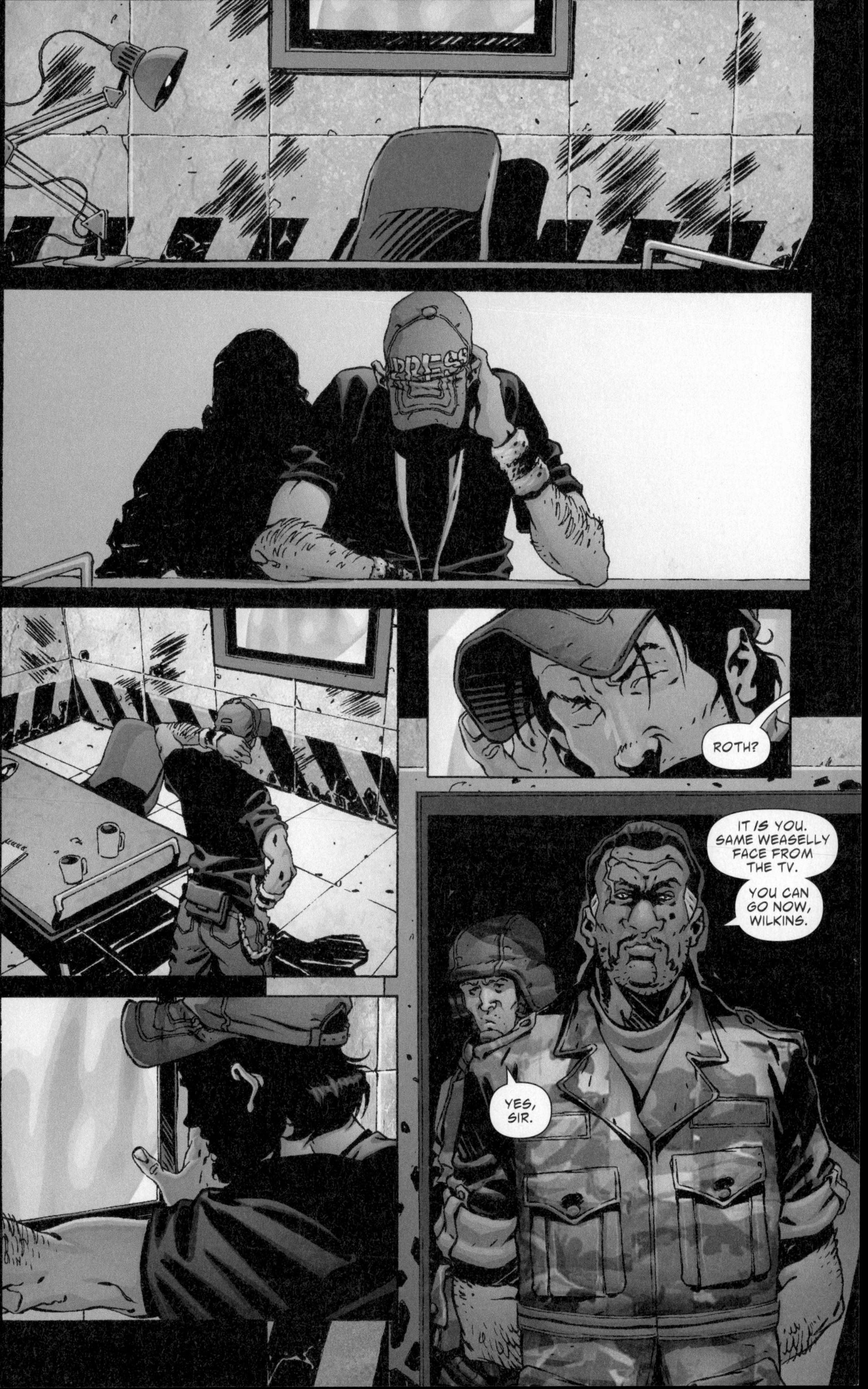
ROTH?
IT IS YOU. SAME WEASELLY FACE FROM THE TV.
YOU CAN GO NOW, WILKINS.
YES, SIR.

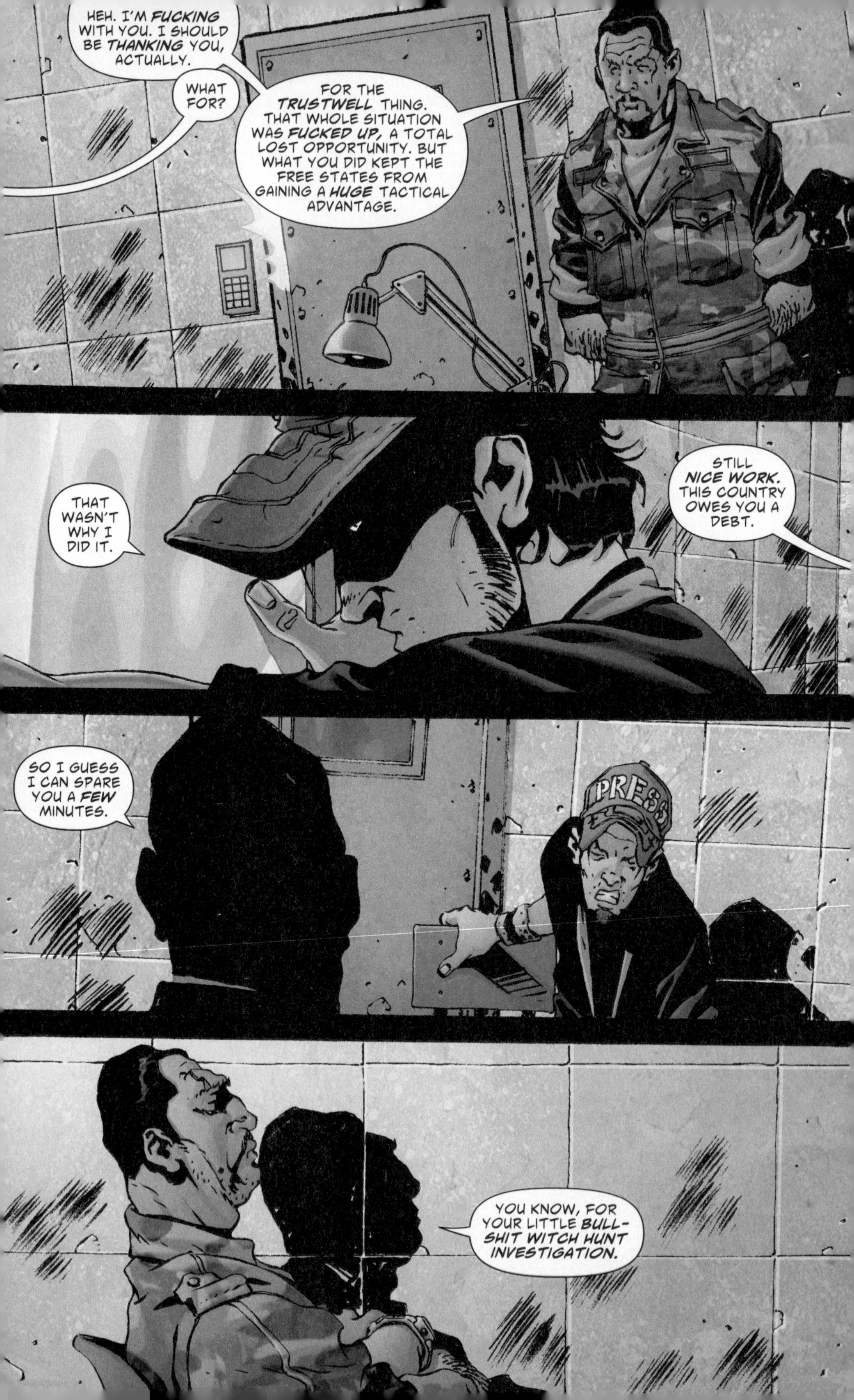
HEH. I'M FUCKING WITH YOU. I SHOULD BE THANKING YOU, ACTUALLY.
WHAT FOR?
FOR THE TRUSTWELL THING. THAT WHOLE SITUATION WAS FUCKED UP, A TOTAL LOST OPPORTUNITY. BUT WHAT YOU DID KEPT THE FREE STATES FROM GAINING A HUGE TACTICAL ADVANTAGE.
THAT WASN'T WHY I DID IT.
STILL NICE WORK. THIS COUNTRY OWES YOU A DEBT.
SO I GUESS I CAN SPARE YOU A FEW MINUTES.
PRESS
YOU KNOW, FOR YOUR LITTLE BULL-SHIT WITCH HUNT INVESTIGATION.

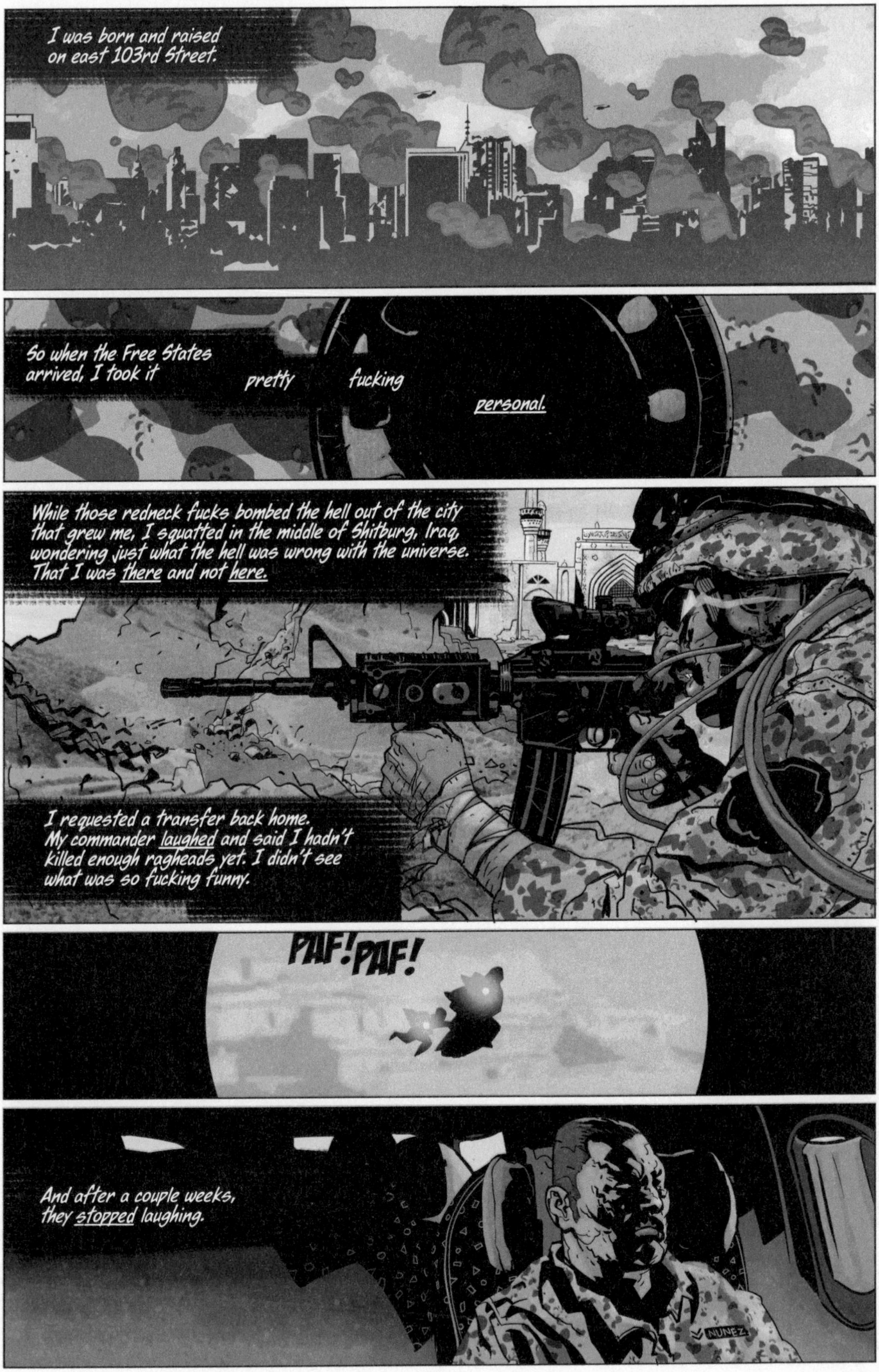
I was born and raised on east 103rd Street.
So when the Free States arrived, I took it
pretty
fucking
personal.
While those redneck fucks bombed the hell out of the city that grew me, I squatted in the middle of Shitburg, Iraq, wondering just what the hell was wrong with the universe. That I was there and not here.
I requested a transfer back home. My commander laughed and said I hadn't killed enough ragheads yet. I didn't see what was so fucking funny.
PAF! PAF!
And after a couple weeks, they stopped laughing.
NUNEZ

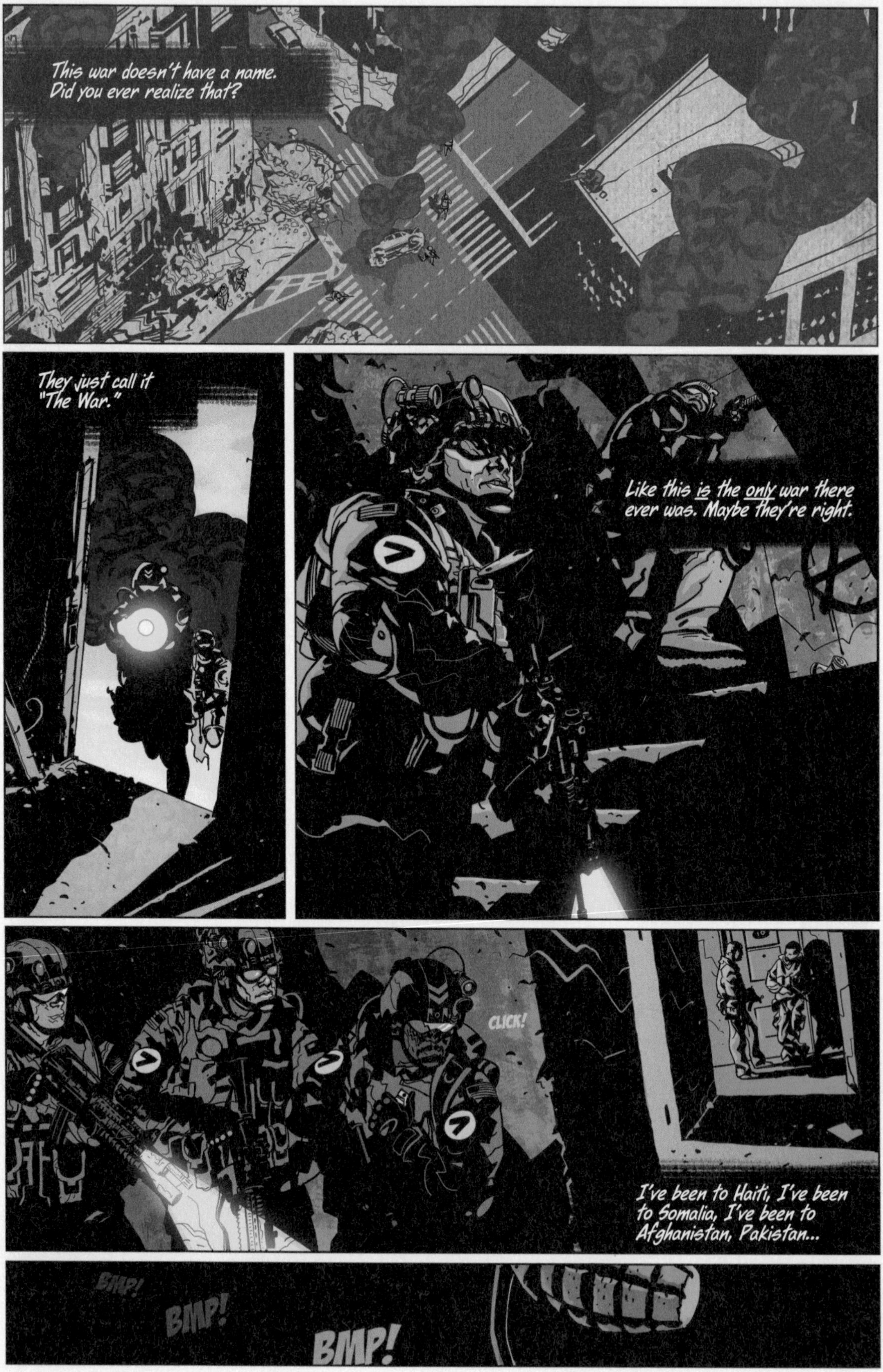
This war doesn't have a name. Did you ever realize that?
They just call it "The War."
Like this is the only war there ever was. Maybe they're right.
CLICK!
I've been to Haiti, I've been to Somalia, I've been to Afghanistan, Pakistan...
BMP!
BMP!
BMP!

...and three tours in Iraq.

But this is *my* war.
I was *born* for this shit.

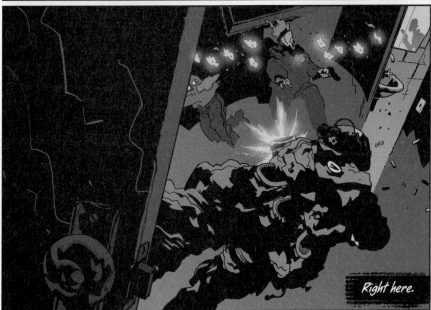

Right here.

You'd have to *kill* me to
get me away from it.

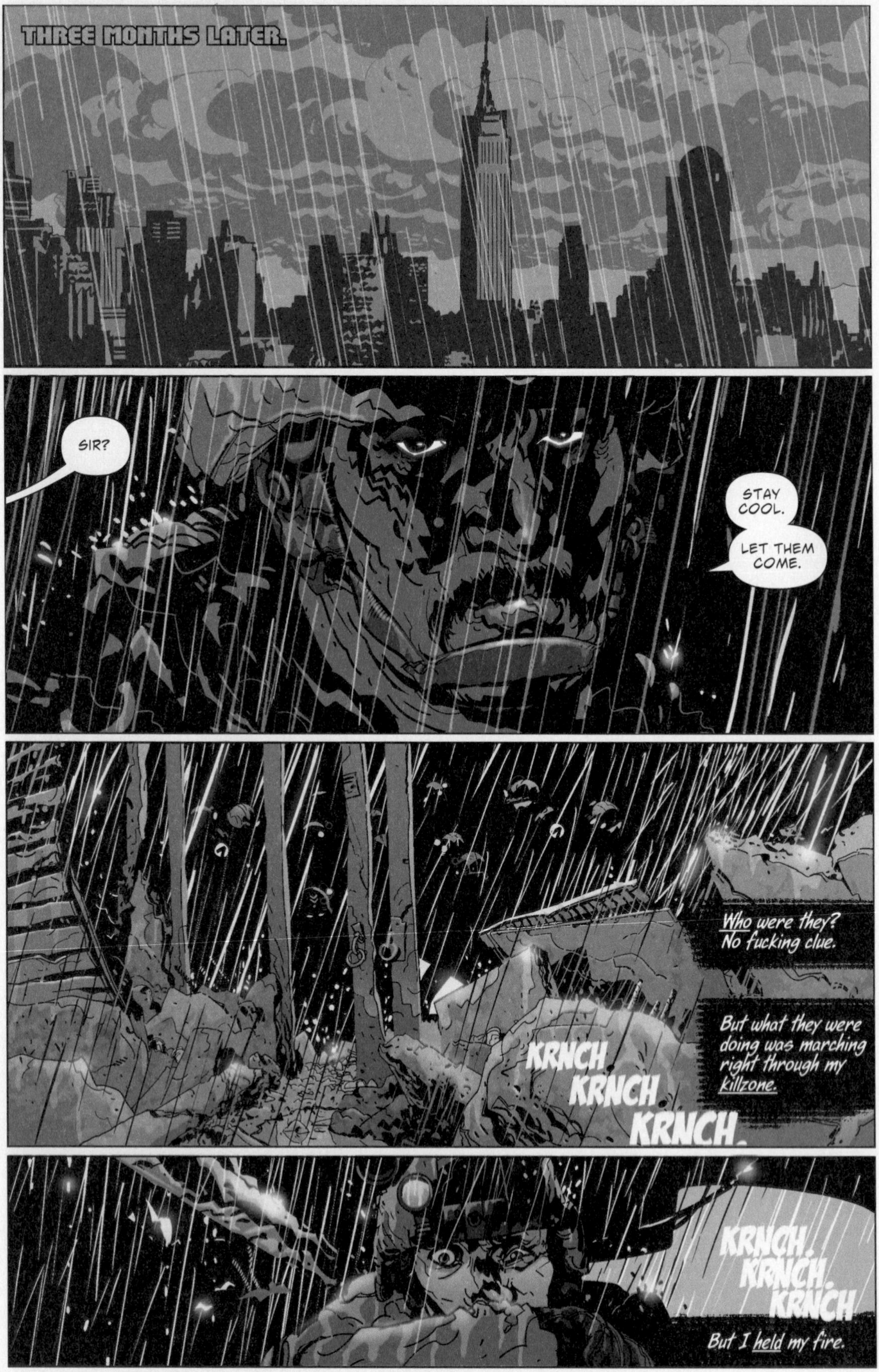
THREE MONTHS LATER.
SIR?
STAY COOL.
LET THEM COME.
Who were they? No fucking clue.
But what they were doing was marching right through my killzone.
KRNCH KRNCH KRNCH
KRNCH. KRNCH. KRNCH
But I held my fire.

KRNCH.

KRNCH.

KRNCH.

KRNCH.

KRNCH.

KRNCH.

KRNCH.

KRNCH.

KRNCH.

KRNCH.

KRNCH.

KRNCH.

I don't give a fuck what we know now. That's for the people, like you, Roth, sitting in judgment way *after* the fact.

When you're in the war with a loaded weapon and an army of whatever-the-fucks marching towards you, all that matters is *what's going on right then*.

SIR?

MOVE OUT. FOLLOW THEM.

The rules of engagement were broad back then.

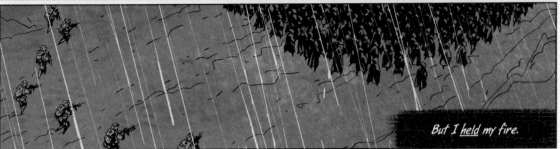

But I *held* my fire.

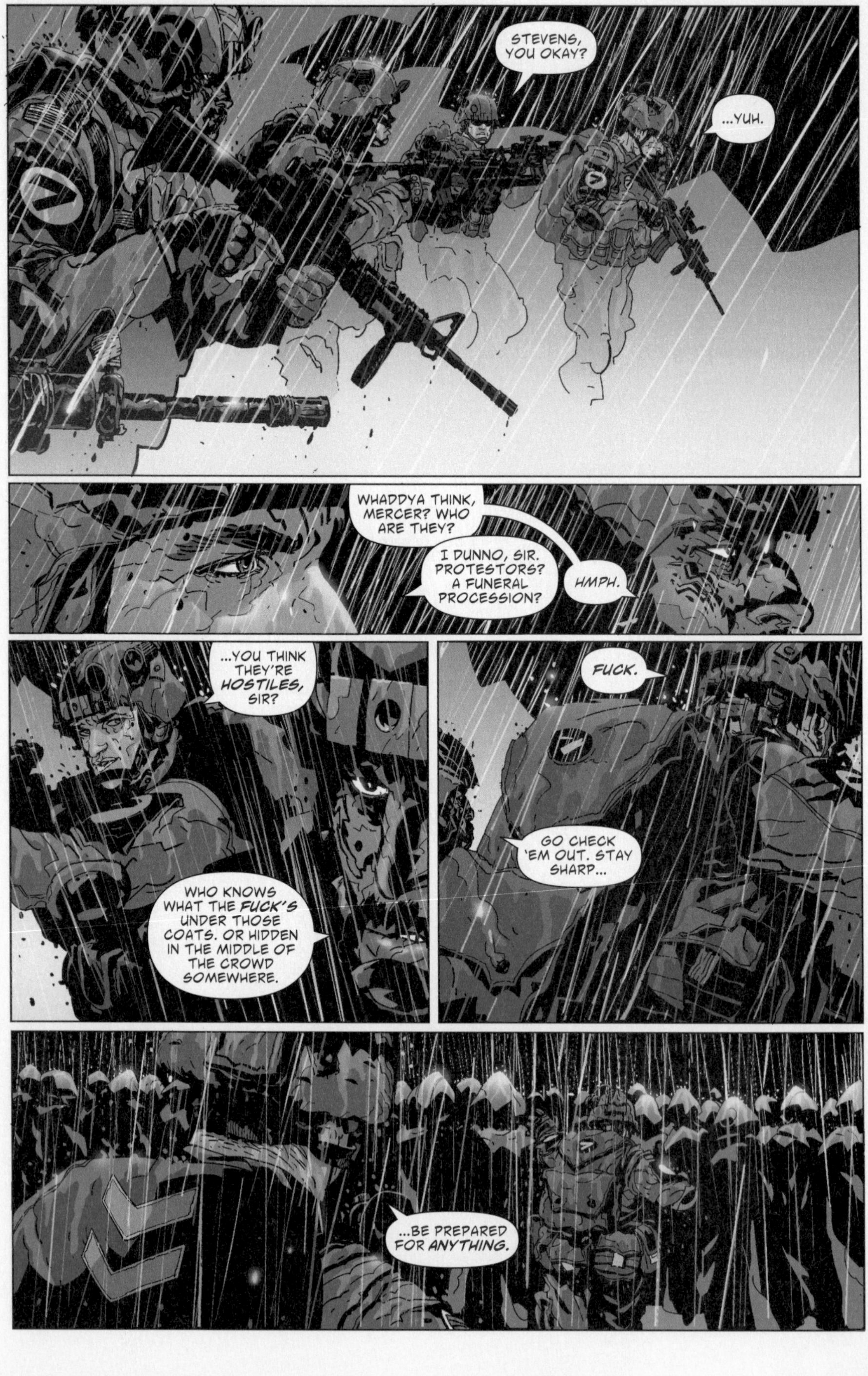
STEVENS, YOU OKAY?
...YUH.
WHADDYA THINK, MERCER? WHO ARE THEY?
I DUNNO, SIR. PROTESTORS? A FUNERAL PROCESSION?
HMPH.
...YOU THINK THEY'RE HOSTILES, SIR?
WHO KNOWS WHAT THE FUCK'S UNDER THOSE COATS. OR HIDDEN IN THE MIDDLE OF THE CROWD SOMEWHERE.
FUCK.
GO CHECK 'EM OUT. STAY SHARP...
...BE PREPARED FOR ANYTHING.

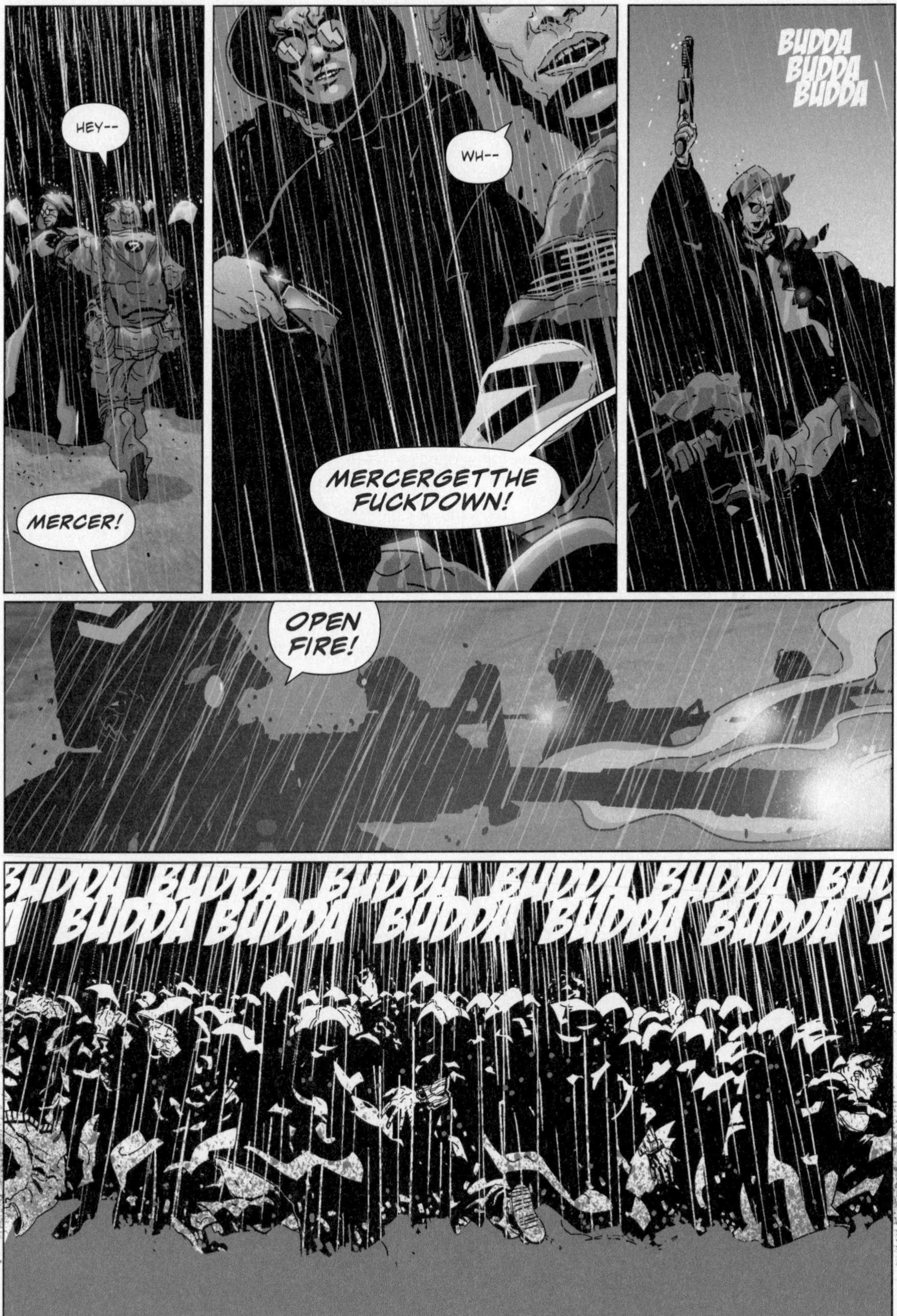
HEY--
MERCER!
WH--
MERCERGETTHE FUCKDOWN!
BUDDA BUDDA BUDDA
OPEN FIRE!
BUDDA BUDDA BUDDA BUDDA BUDDA BUDDA BUDDA BUDDA BUDDA BUDDA

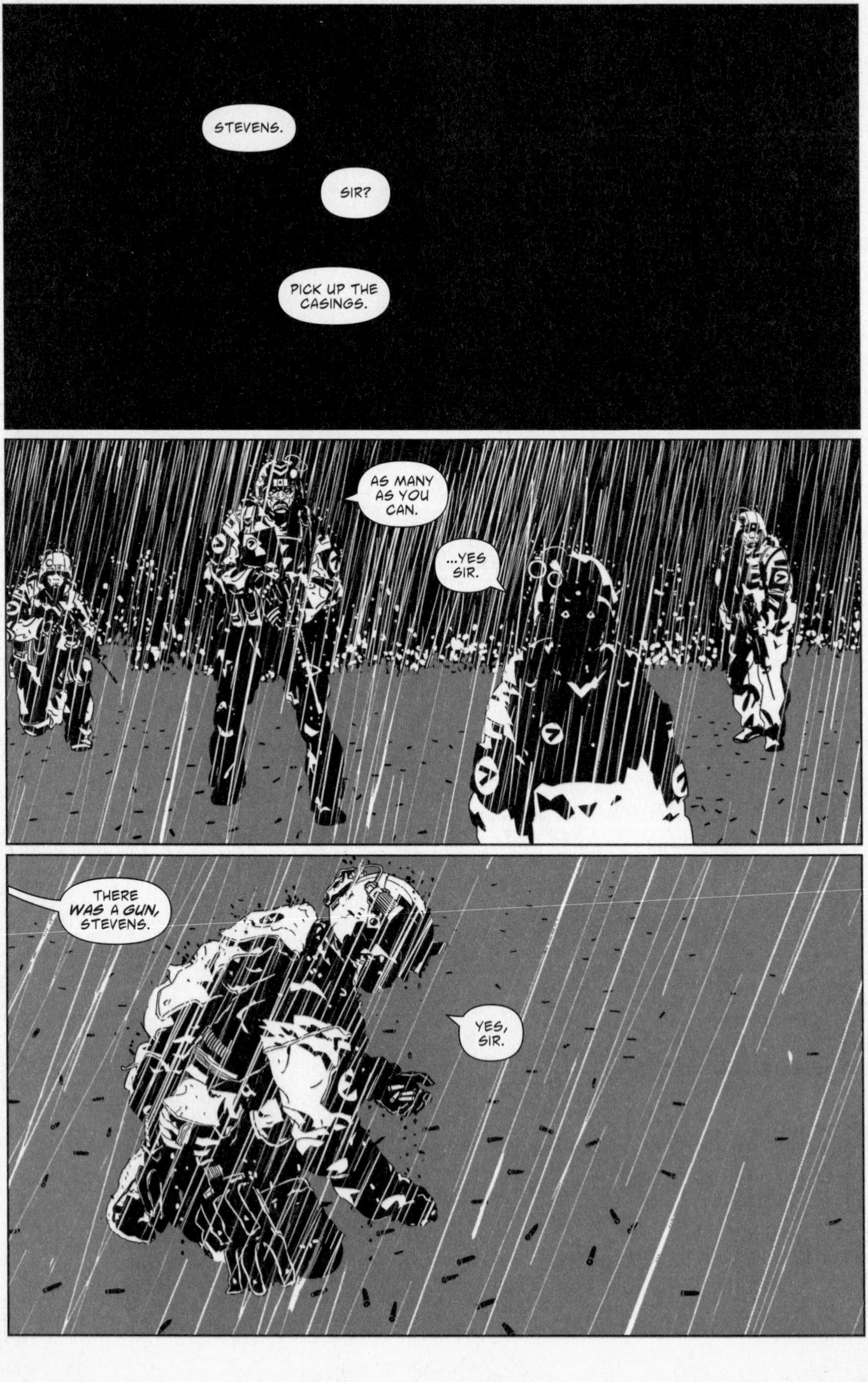
STEVENS.
SIR?
PICK UP THE CASINGS.
AS MANY AS YOU CAN.
...YES SIR.
THERE WAS A GUN, STEVENS.
YES, SIR.

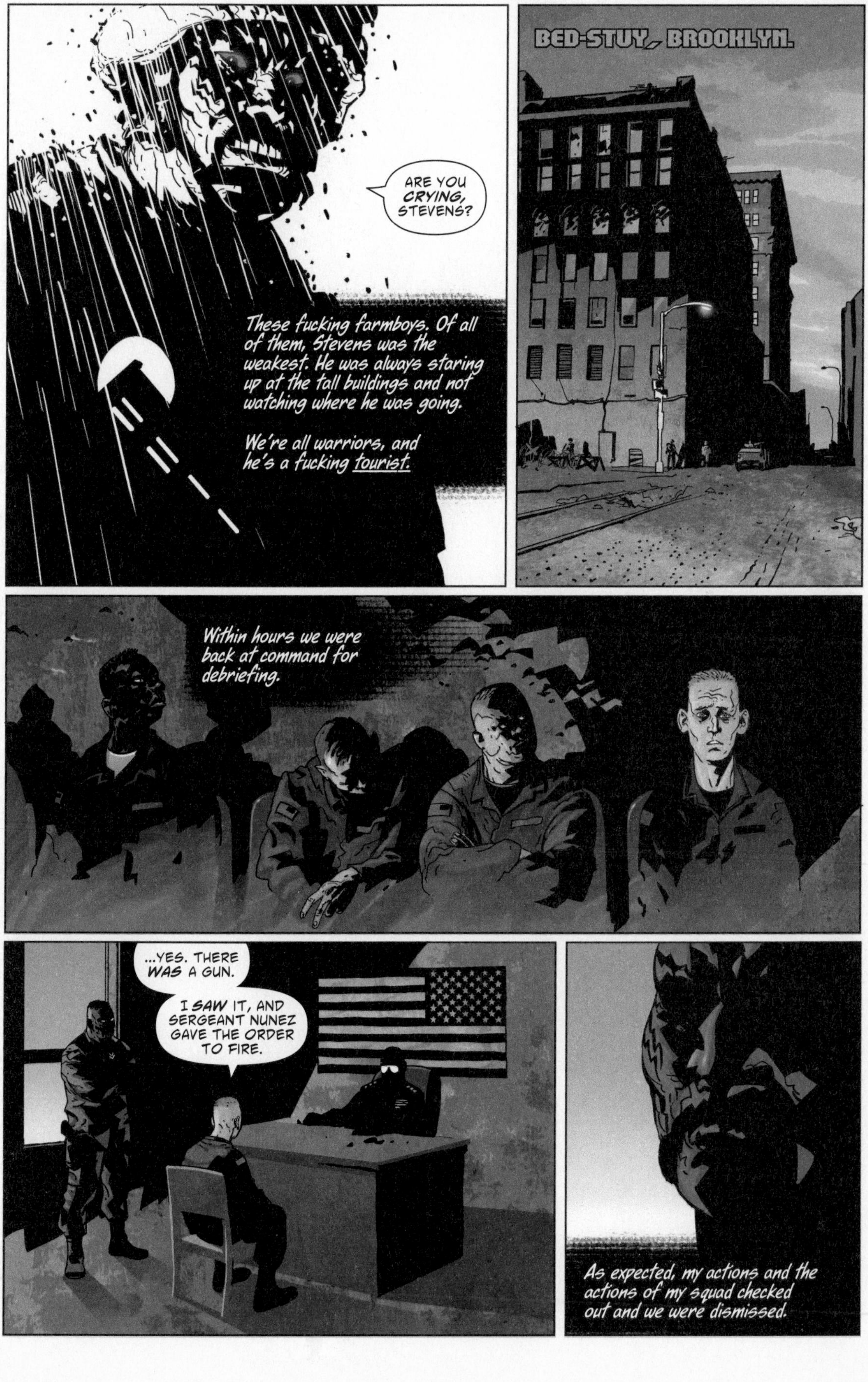
ARE YOU CRYING, STEVENS?
These fucking farmboys. Of all of them, Stevens was the weakest. He was always staring up at the tall buildings and not watching where he was going.
We're all warriors, and he's a fucking tourist.
BED-STUY, BROOKLYN.
Within hours we were back at command for debriefing.
...YES. THERE WAS A GUN.
I SAW IT, AND SERGEANT NUNEZ GAVE THE ORDER TO FIRE.
As expected, my actions and the actions of my squad checked out and we were dismissed.

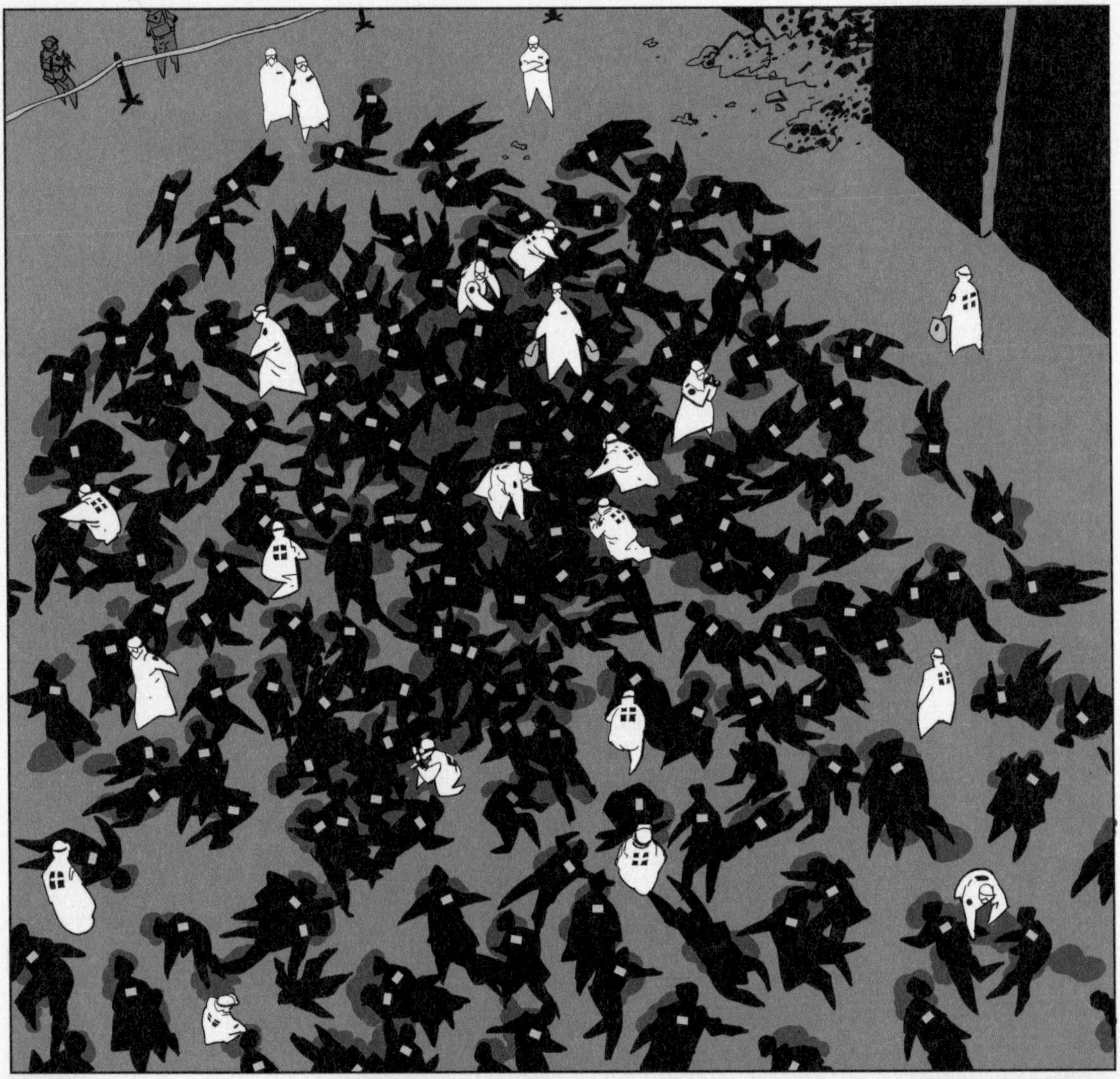

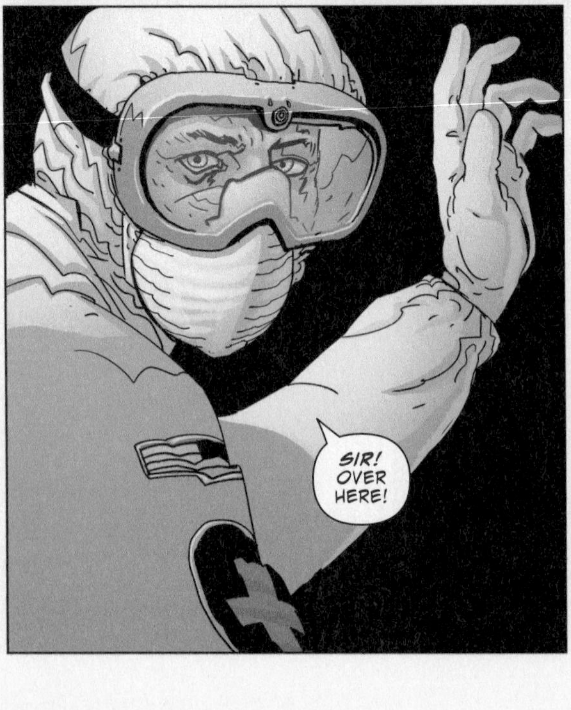
SIR! OVER HERE!

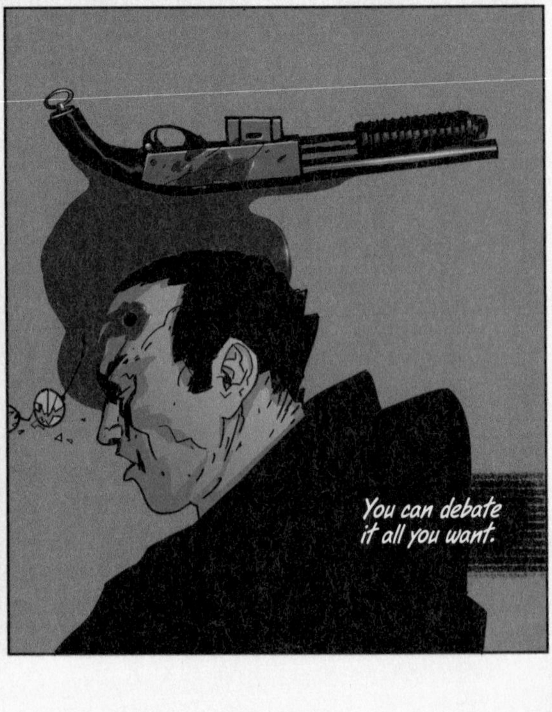
You can debate it all you want.

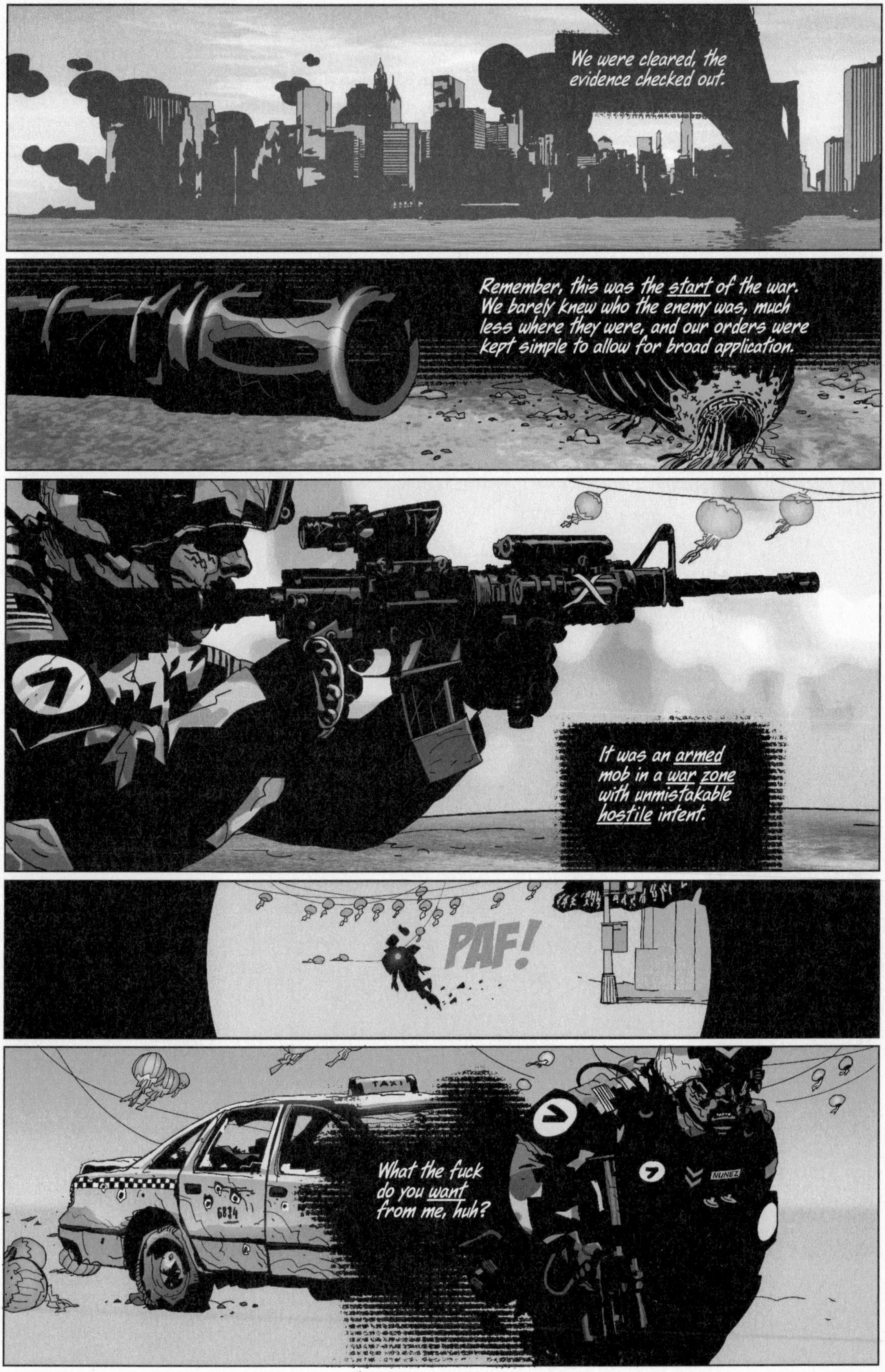
We were cleared, the evidence checked out.
Remember, this was the start of the war. We barely knew who the enemy was, much less where they were, and our orders were kept simple to allow for broad application.
It was an armed mob in a war zone with unmistakable hostile intent.
PAF!
TAXI
6834
What the fuck do you want from me, huh?
NUNEZ

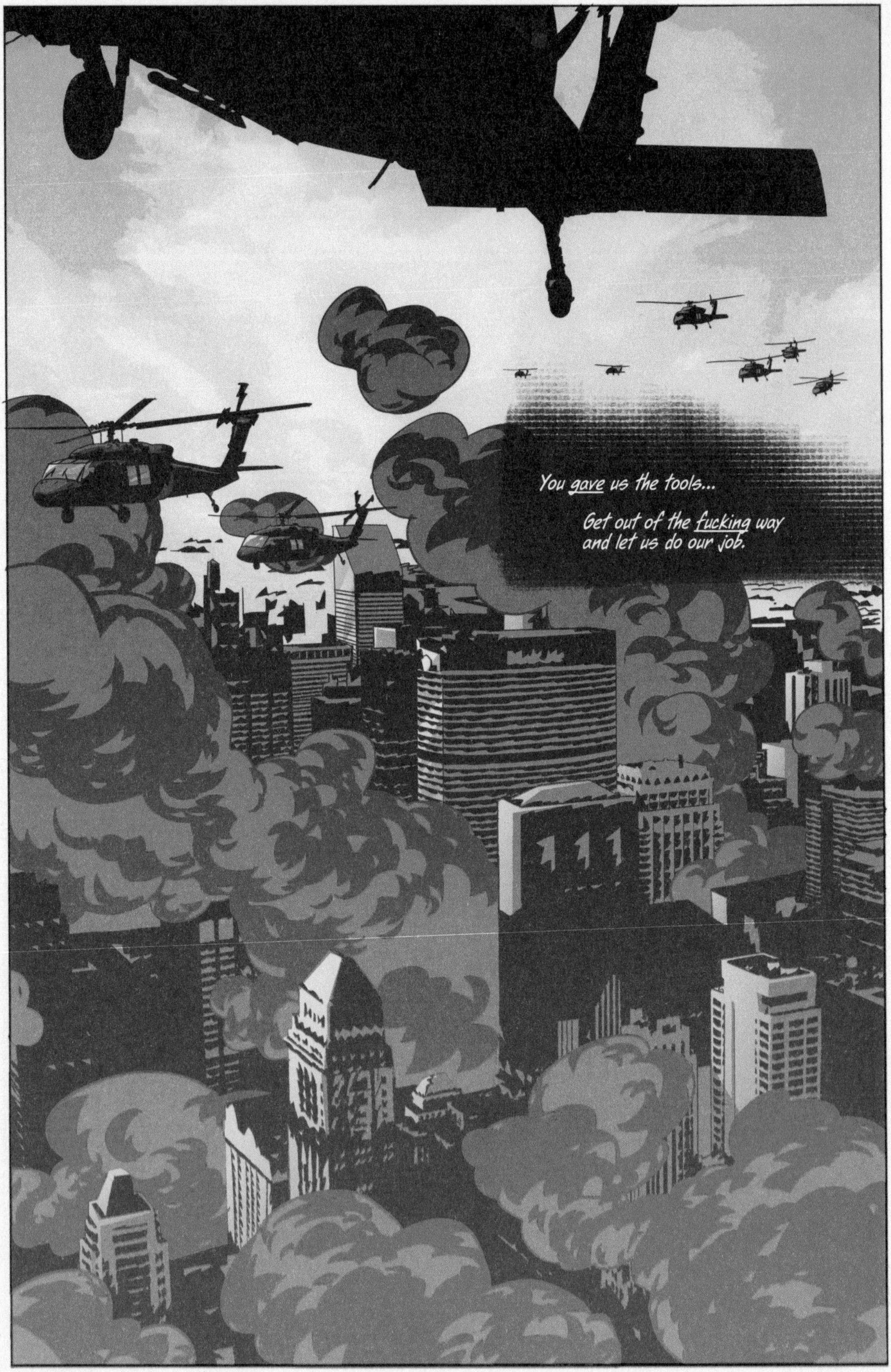
You gave us the tools...
Get out of the fucking way and let us do our job.

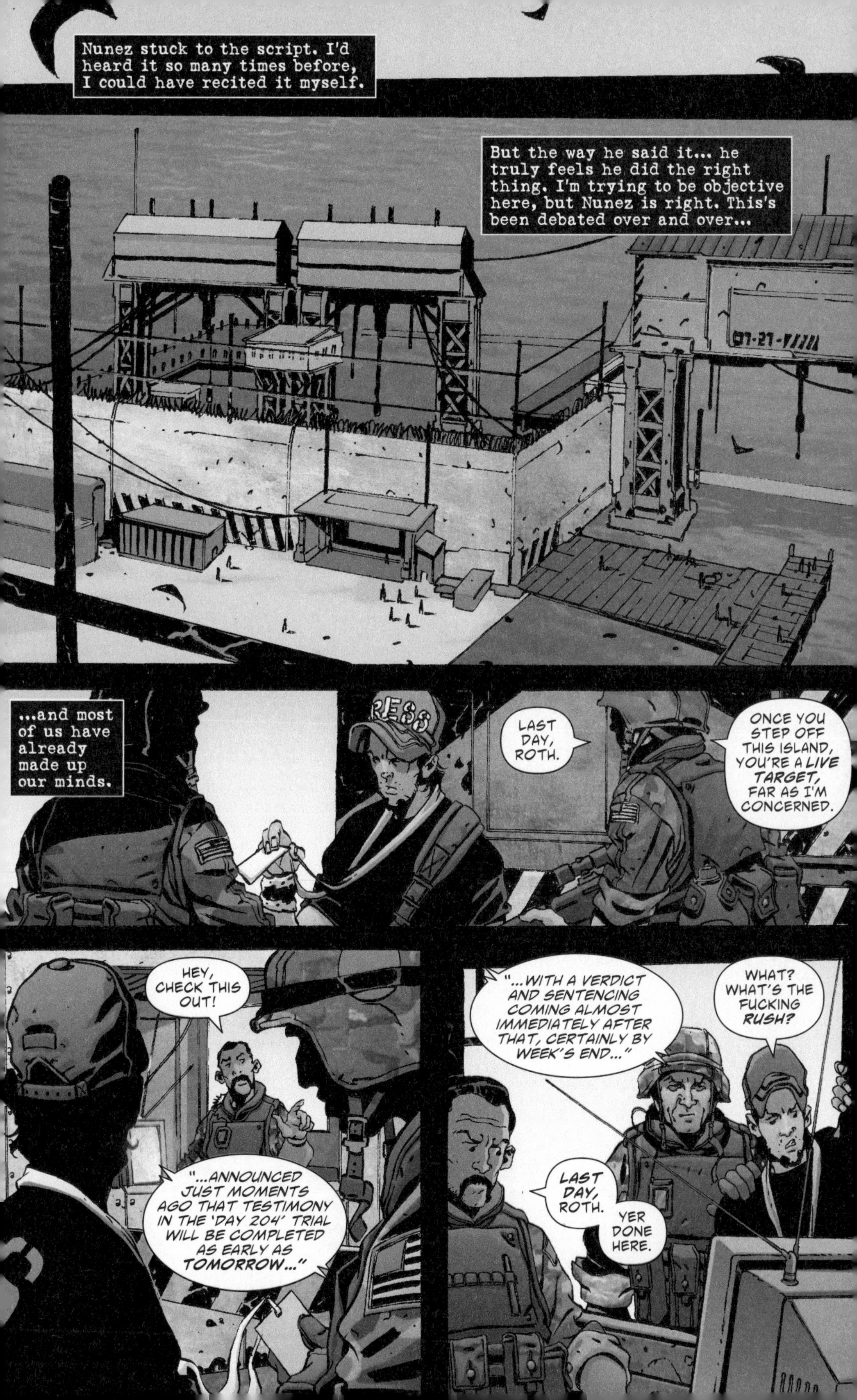
Nunez stuck to the script. I'd heard it so many times before, I could have recited it myself.
But the way he said it... he truly feels he did the right thing. I'm trying to be objective here, but Nunez is right. This's been debated over and over...
...and most of us have already made up our minds.
LAST DAY, ROTH.
ONCE YOU STEP OFF THIS ISLAND, YOU'RE A LIVE TARGET, FAR AS I'M CONCERNED.
HEY, CHECK THIS OUT!
"...ANNOUNCED JUST MOMENTS AGO THAT TESTIMONY IN THE 'DAY 204' TRIAL WILL BE COMPLETED AS EARLY AS TOMORROW..."
"...WITH A VERDICT AND SENTENCING COMING ALMOST IMMEDIATELY AFTER THAT, CERTAINLY BY WEEK'S END..."
WHAT? WHAT'S THE FUCKING RUSH?
LAST DAY, ROTH.
YER DONE HERE.

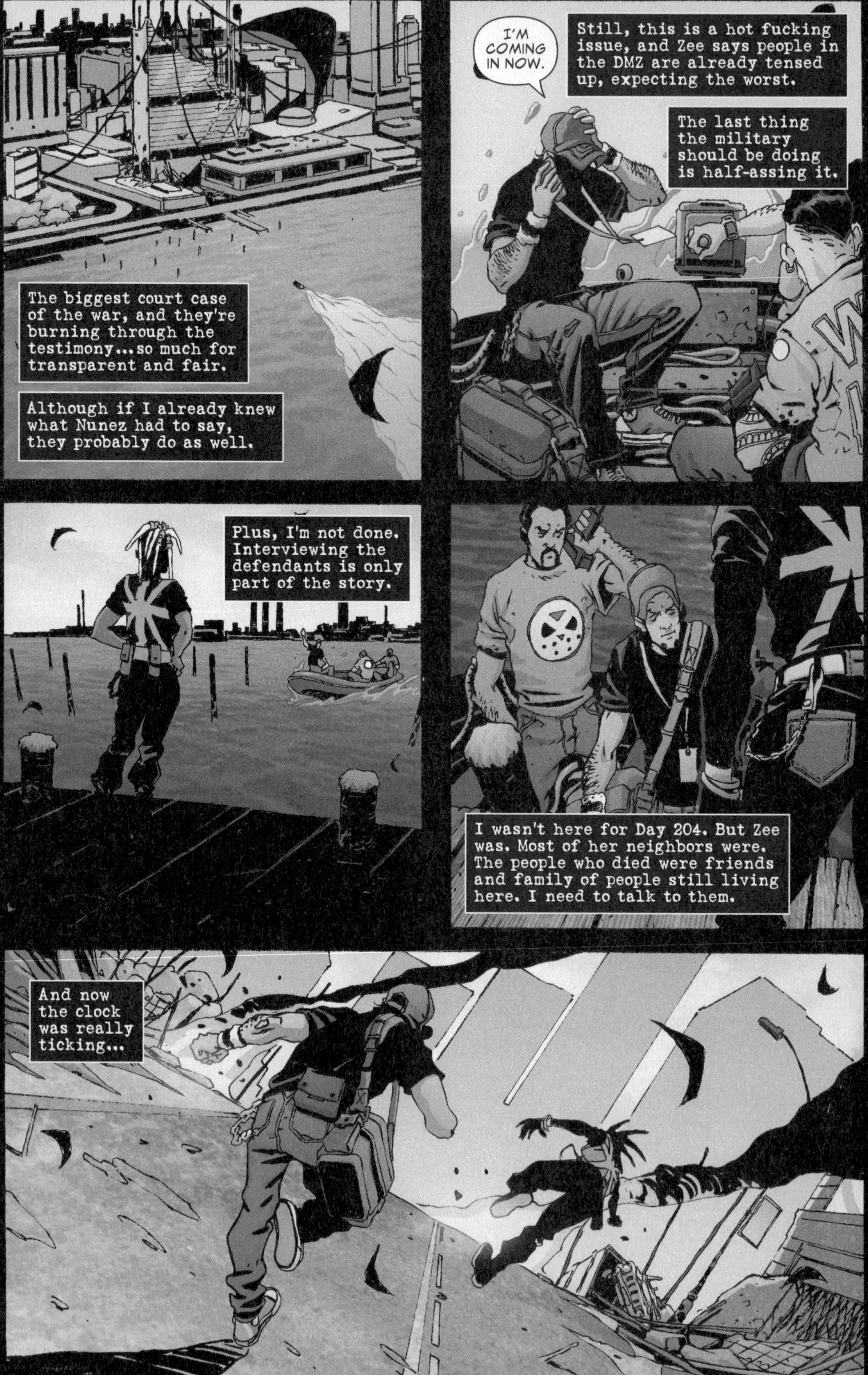
The biggest court case of the war, and they're burning through the testimony...so much for transparent and fair.
Although if I already knew what Nunez had to say, they probably do as well.
I'M COMING IN NOW.
Still, this is a hot fucking issue, and Zee says people in the DMZ are already tensed up, expecting the worst.
The last thing the military should be doing is half-assing it.
Plus, I'm not done. Interviewing the defendants is only part of the story.
I wasn't here for Day 204. But Zee was. Most of her neighbors were. The people who died were friends and family of people still living here. I need to talk to them.
And now the clock was really ticking...

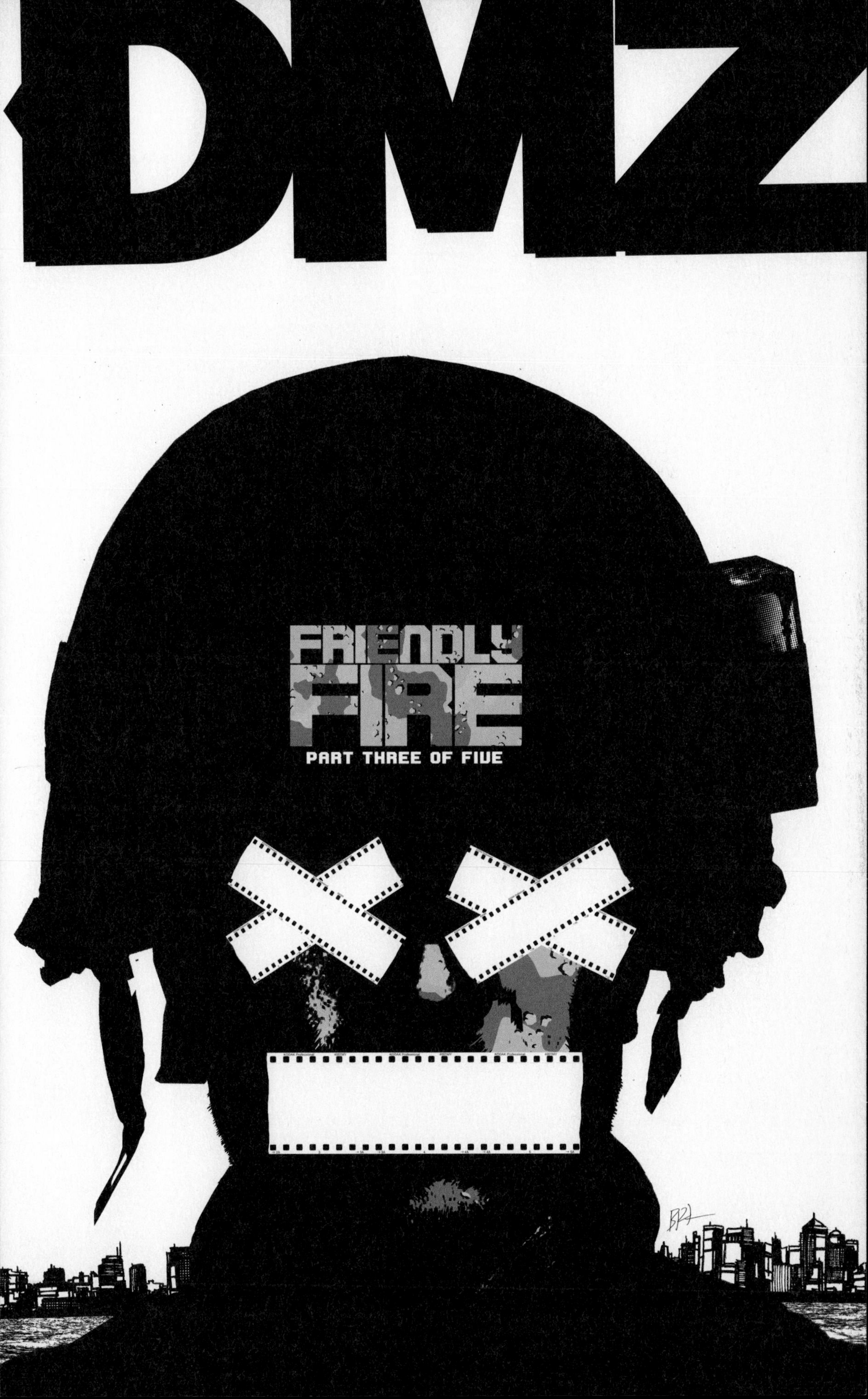
DMZ
FRIENDLY FIRE
PART THREE OF FIVE

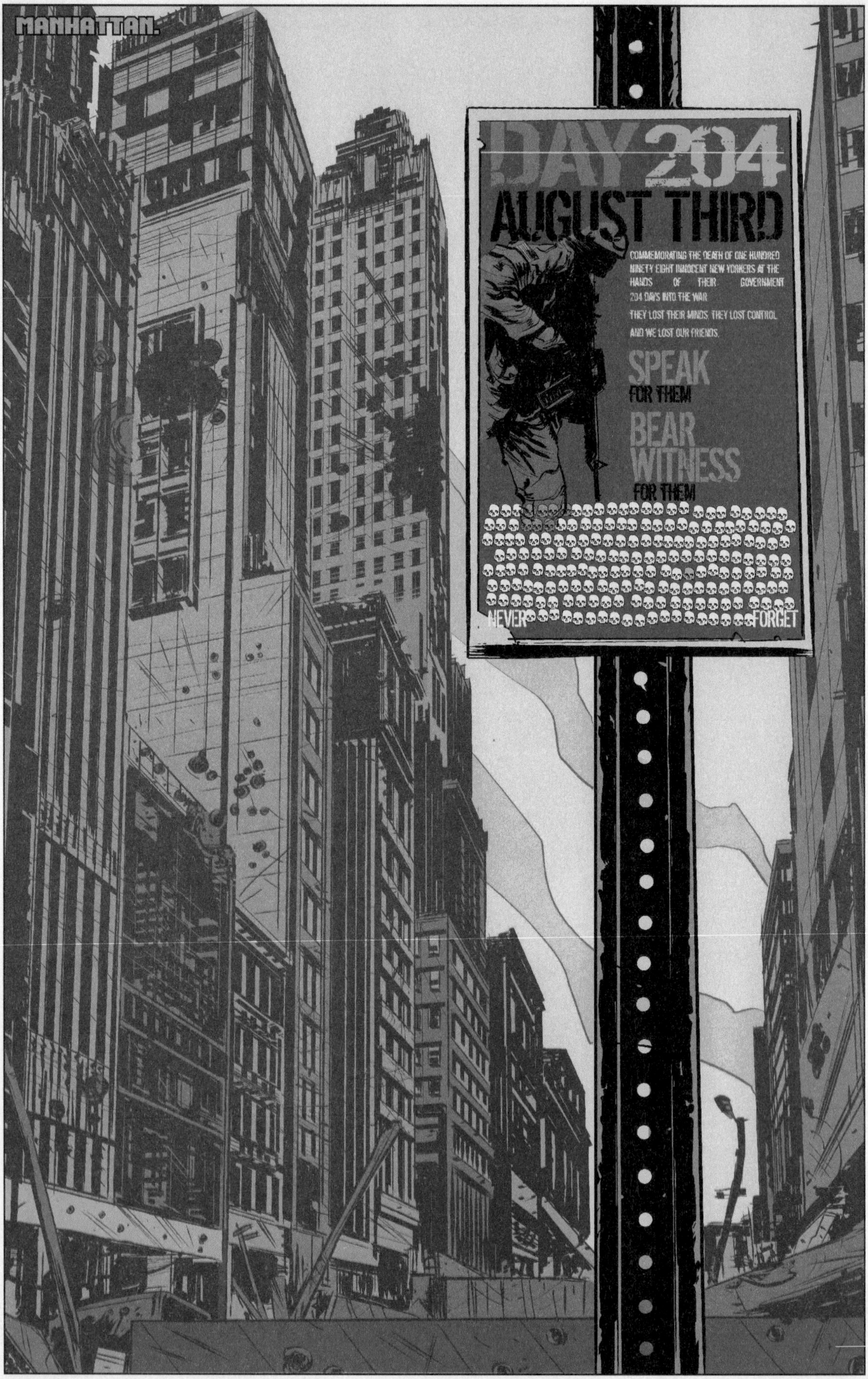
MANHATTAN.
DAY 204
AUGUST THIRD
COMMEMORATING THE DEATH OF ONE HUNDRED NINETY EIGHT INNOCENT NEW YORKERS AT THE HANDS OF THEIR GOVERNMENT 204 DAYS INTO THE WAR
THEY LOST THEIR MINDS. THEY LOST CONTROL
AND WE LOST OUR FRIENDS.
SPEAK
FOR THEM
BEAR WITNESS
FOR THEM
NEVER
FORGET

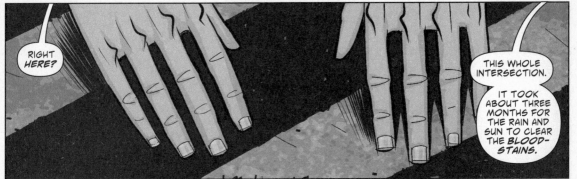

RIGHT *HERE?*

THIS WHOLE INTERSECTION.

IT TOOK ABOUT THREE MONTHS FOR THE RAIN AND SUN TO CLEAR THE *BLOOD-STAINS.*

I'VE *WALKED* BY HERE BEFORE.

THERE'S NO MARKER?

METALWORKERS MADE A PLAQUE, BUT SOLDIERS STOLE IT FIRST CHANCE THEY GOT.

WE DON'T NEED A MARKER ANYWAY. *EVERYONE* KNOWS IT HAPPENED HERE.

EXCEPT *ME.*

WELL, IT'S NOT IN ANY *GUIDEBOOKS.*

DON'T GIVE ME THAT *LOOK.* THIS IS A PAINFUL THING, MATTY.

WE ONLY TEND TO TALK ABOUT IT WHEN WE HAVE TO, AND EDUCATING NEWBIES ISN'T HIGH ON ANYONE'S PRIORITY LIST.

I'VE BEEN HERE A *YEAR* AND A HALF, ZEE.

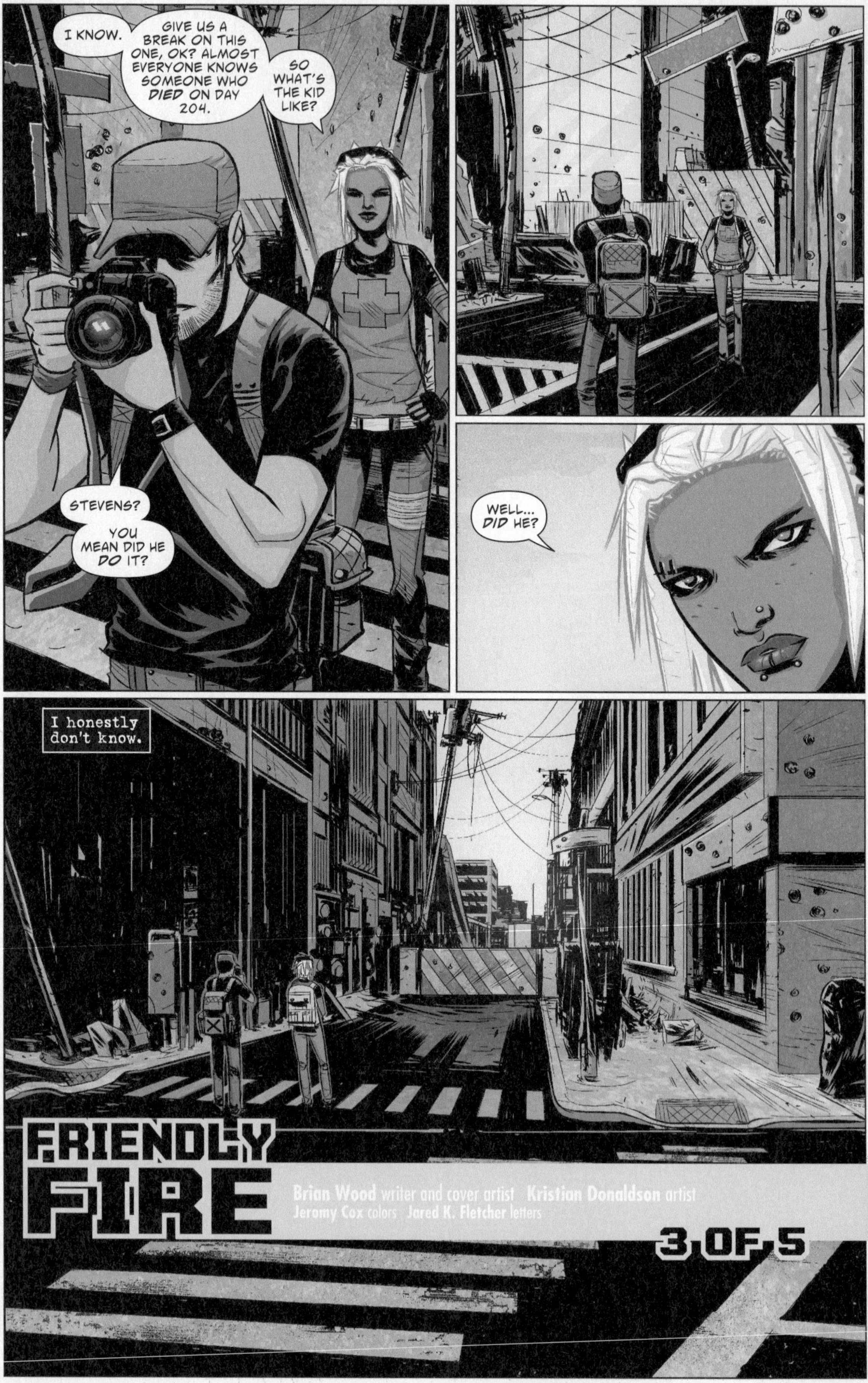
I KNOW.
GIVE US A BREAK ON THIS ONE, OK? ALMOST EVERYONE KNOWS SOMEONE WHO DIED ON DAY 204.
SO WHAT'S THE KID LIKE?
STEVENS?
YOU MEAN DID HE DO IT?
WELL... DID HE?
I honestly don't know.
FRIENDLY FIRE
Brian Wood writer and cover artist Kristian Donaldson artist
Jeromy Cox colors Jared K. Fletcher letters
3 OF 5

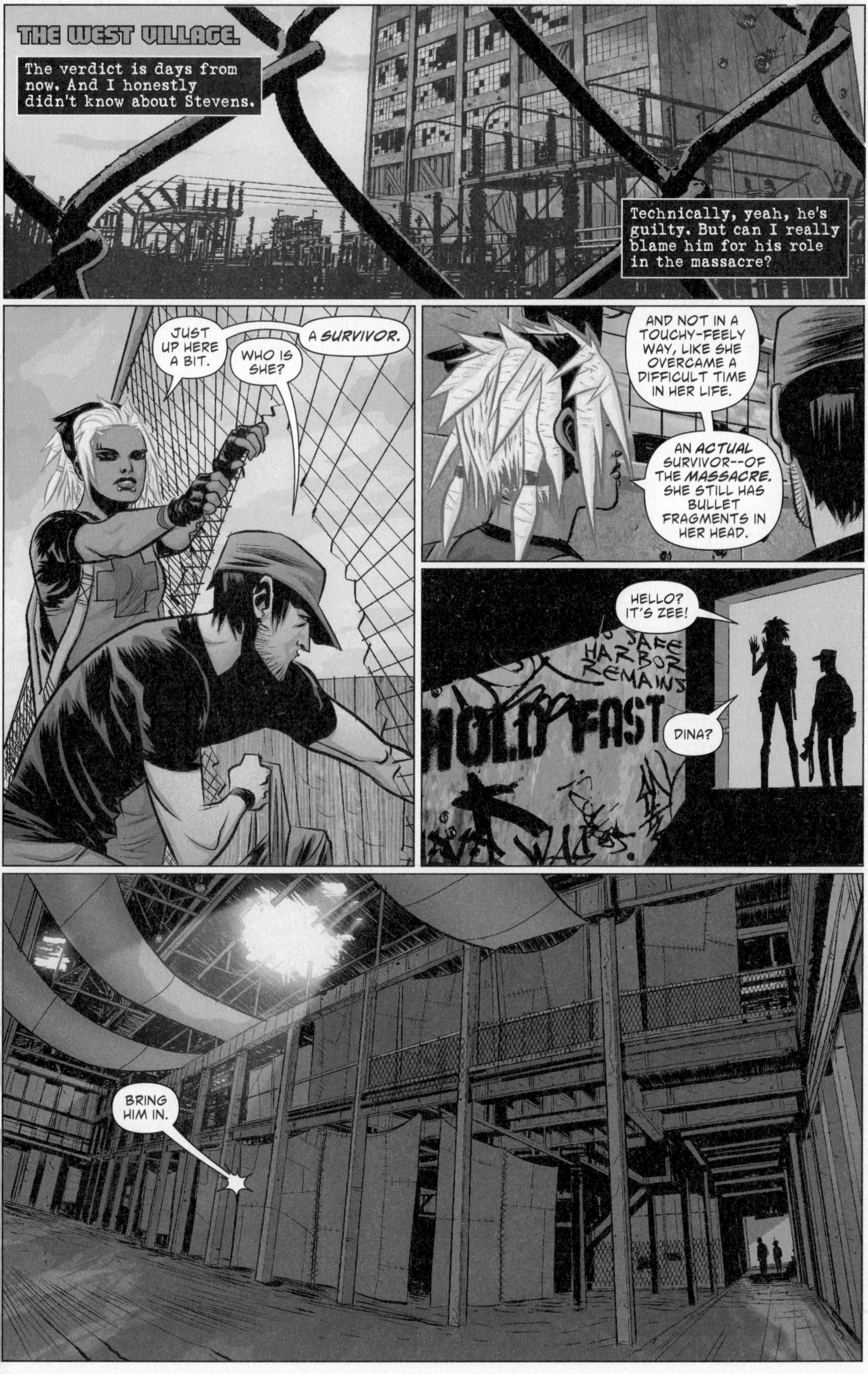
THE WEST VILLAGE.
The verdict is days from now. And I honestly didn't know about Stevens.
Technically, yeah, he's guilty. But can I really blame him for his role in the massacre?
JUST UP HERE A BIT.
WHO IS SHE?
A SURVIVOR.
AND NOT IN A TOUCHY-FEELY WAY, LIKE SHE OVERCAME A DIFFICULT TIME IN HER LIFE.
AN ACTUAL SURVIVOR--OF THE MASSACRE. SHE STILL HAS BULLET FRAGMENTS IN HER HEAD.
SAFE HARBOR REMAINS
HOLD FAST
HELLO? IT'S ZEE!
DINA?
BRING HIM IN.

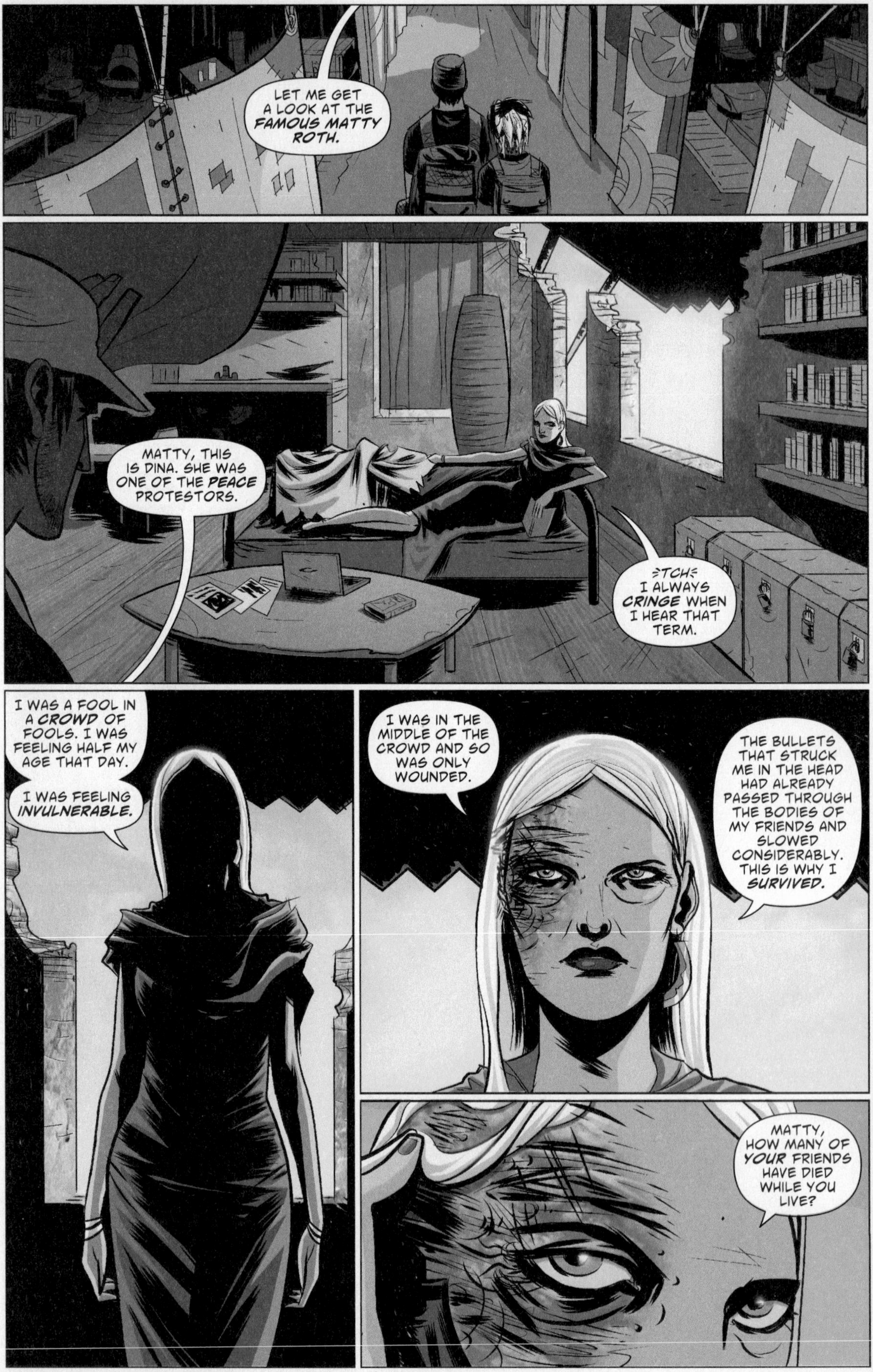
LET ME GET A LOOK AT THE FAMOUS MATTY ROTH.
MATTY, THIS IS DINA. SHE WAS ONE OF THE PEACE PROTESTORS.
TCH I ALWAYS CRINGE WHEN I HEAR THAT TERM.
I WAS A FOOL IN A CROWD OF FOOLS. I WAS FEELING HALF MY AGE THAT DAY.
I WAS FEELING INVULNERABLE.
I WAS IN THE MIDDLE OF THE CROWD AND SO WAS ONLY WOUNDED.
THE BULLETS THAT STRUCK ME IN THE HEAD HAD ALREADY PASSED THROUGH THE BODIES OF MY FRIENDS AND SLOWED CONSIDERABLY. THIS IS WHY I SURVIVED.
MATTY, HOW MANY OF YOUR FRIENDS HAVE DIED WHILE YOU LIVE?

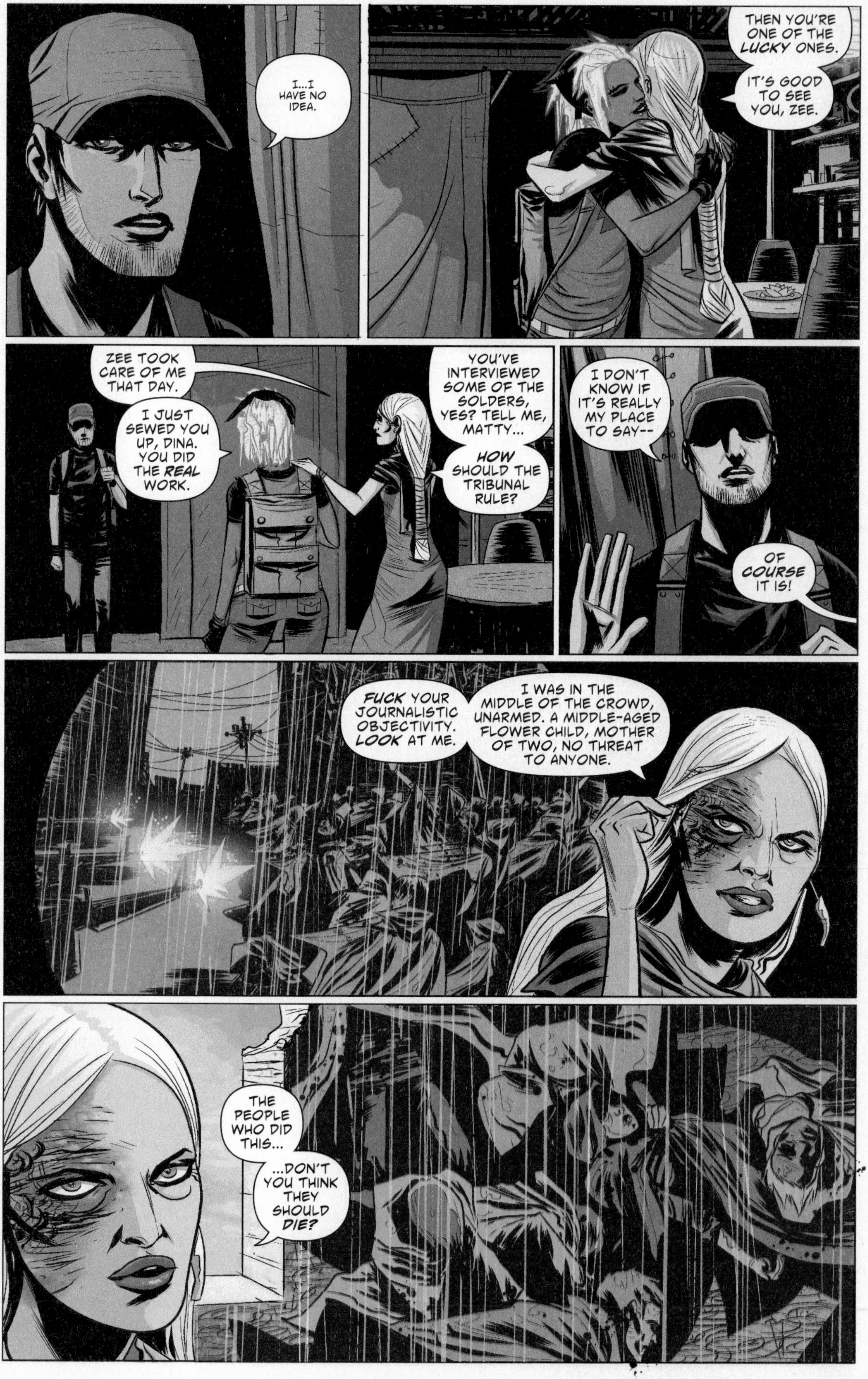

I...I HAVE NO IDEA.
THEN YOU'RE ONE OF THE *LUCKY* ONES.
IT'S GOOD TO SEE YOU, ZEE.
ZEE TOOK CARE OF ME THAT DAY.
I JUST SEWED YOU UP, DINA. YOU DID THE *REAL* WORK.
YOU'VE INTERVIEWED SOME OF THE SOLDERS, YES? TELL ME, MATTY...
HOW SHOULD THE TRIBUNAL RULE?
I DON'T KNOW IF IT'S REALLY MY PLACE TO SAY--
OF *COURSE* IT IS!
FUCK YOUR JOURNALISTIC OBJECTIVITY. *LOOK* AT ME.
I WAS IN THE MIDDLE OF THE CROWD, UNARMED. A MIDDLE-AGED FLOWER CHILD, MOTHER OF TWO, NO THREAT TO ANYONE.
THE PEOPLE WHO DID THIS...
...DON'T YOU THINK THEY SHOULD *DIE?*

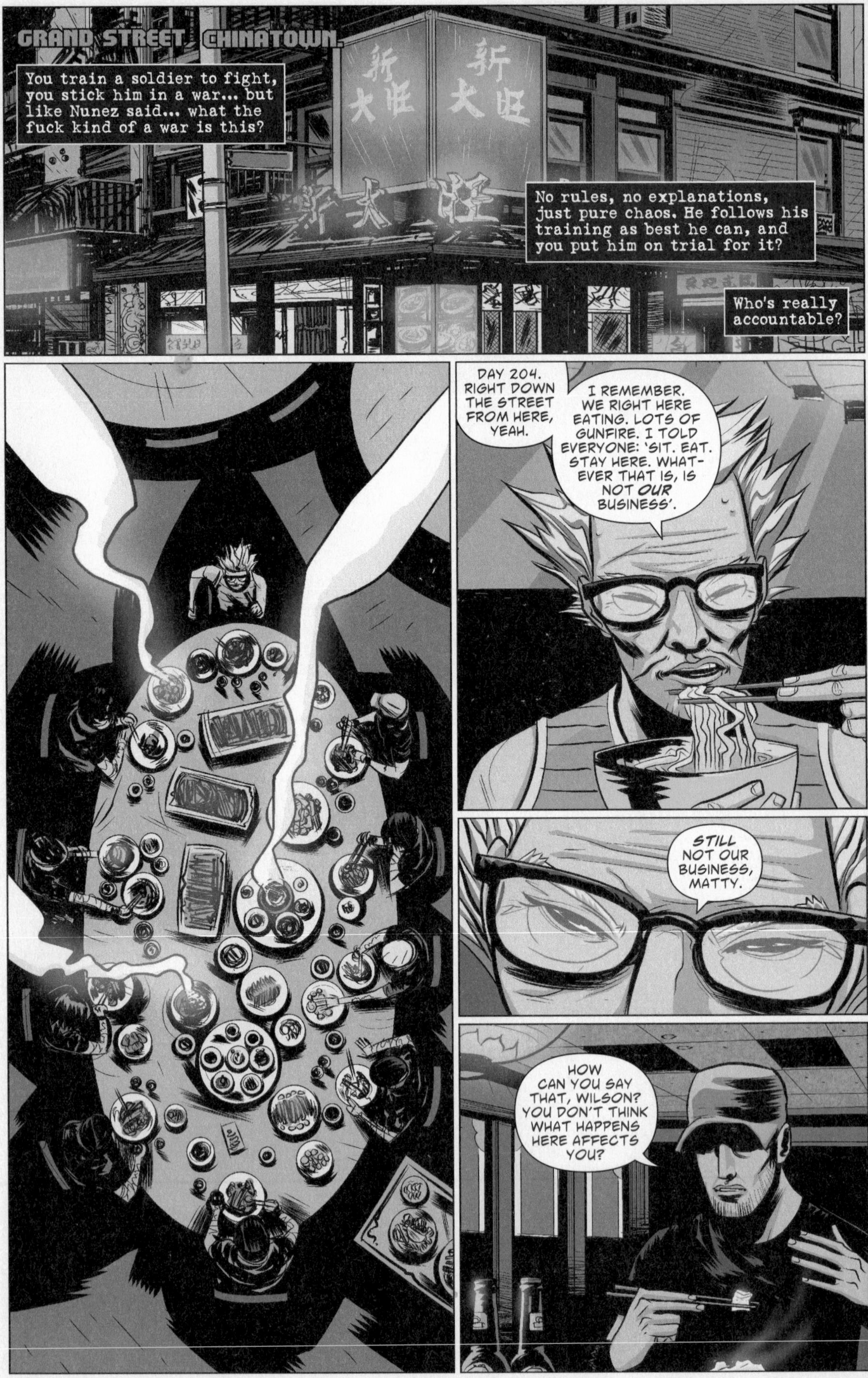
GRAND STREET, CHINATOWN.
You train a soldier to fight, you stick him in a war... but like Nunez said... what the fuck kind of a war is this?
新大旺
No rules, no explanations, just pure chaos. He follows his training as best he can, and you put him on trial for it?
Who's really accountable?
DAY 204. RIGHT DOWN THE STREET FROM HERE, YEAH.
I REMEMBER. WE RIGHT HERE EATING. LOTS OF GUNFIRE. I TOLD EVERYONE: 'SIT. EAT. STAY HERE. WHAT-EVER THAT IS, IS NOT *OUR* BUSINESS'.
STILL NOT OUR BUSINESS, MATTY.
HOW CAN YOU SAY THAT, WILSON? YOU DON'T THINK WHAT HAPPENS HERE AFFECTS YOU?

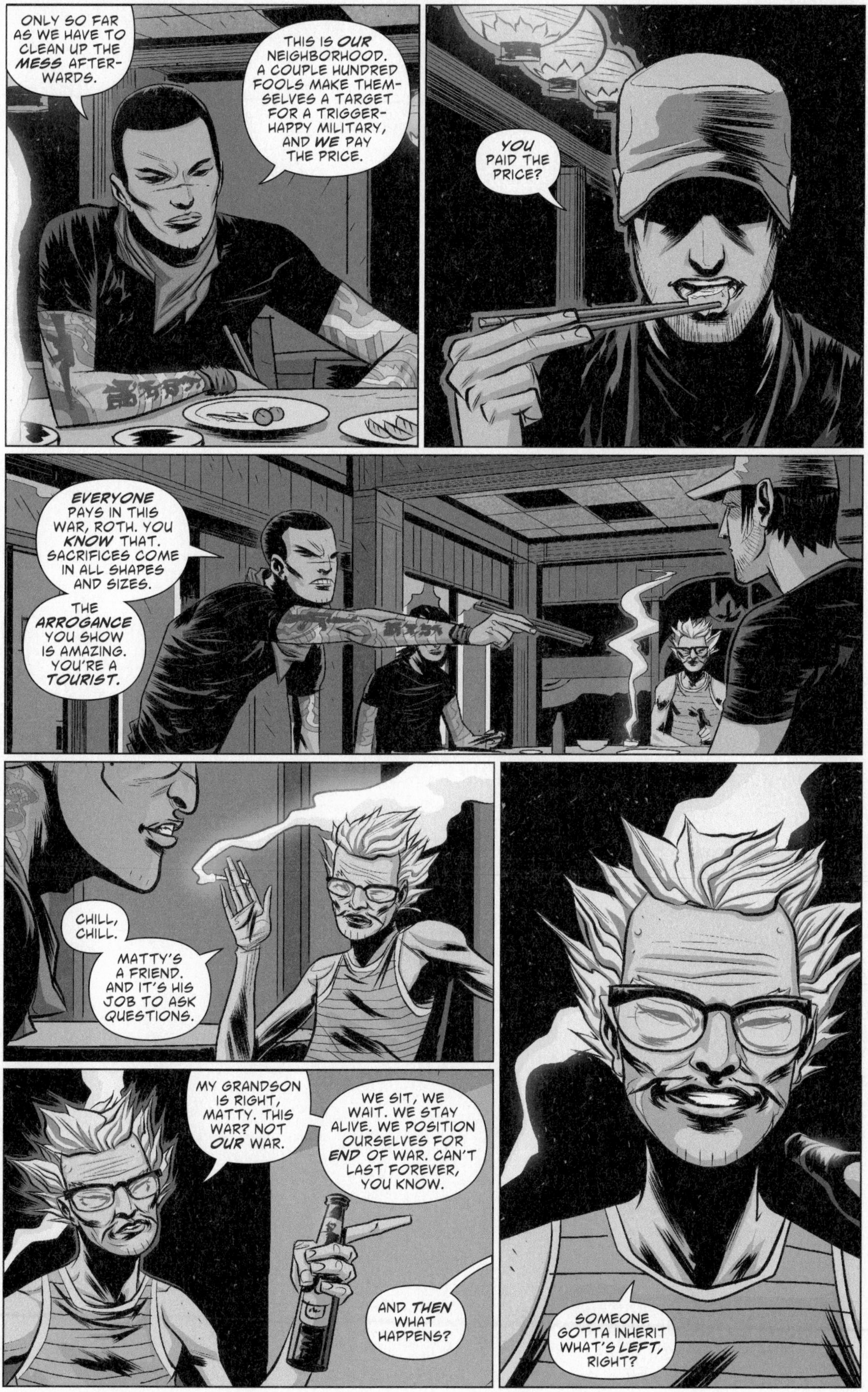
ONLY SO FAR AS WE HAVE TO CLEAN UP THE MESS AFTER-WARDS.
THIS IS OUR NEIGHBORHOOD. A COUPLE HUNDRED FOOLS MAKE THEM-SELVES A TARGET FOR A TRIGGER-HAPPY MILITARY, AND WE PAY THE PRICE.
YOU PAID THE PRICE?
EVERYONE PAYS IN THIS WAR, ROTH. YOU KNOW THAT. SACRIFICES COME IN ALL SHAPES AND SIZES.
THE ARROGANCE YOU SHOW IS AMAZING. YOU'RE A TOURIST.
CHILL, CHILL.
MATTY'S A FRIEND. AND IT'S HIS JOB TO ASK QUESTIONS.
MY GRANDSON IS RIGHT, MATTY. THIS WAR? NOT OUR WAR.
WE SIT, WE WAIT. WE STAY ALIVE. WE POSITION OURSELVES FOR END OF WAR. CAN'T LAST FOREVER, YOU KNOW.
AND THEN WHAT HAPPENS?
SOMEONE GOTTA INHERIT WHAT'S LEFT, RIGHT?

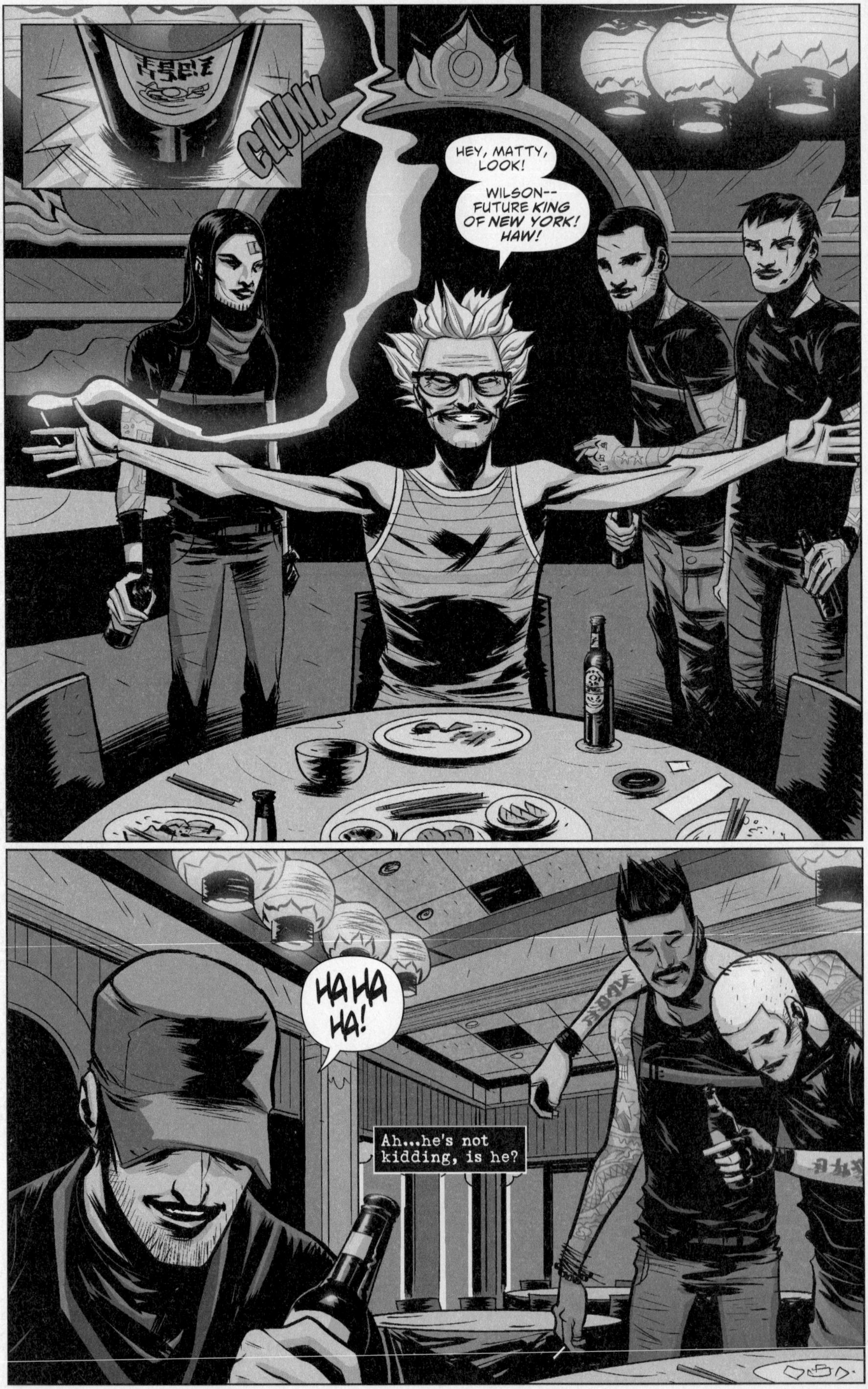
CLUNK
HEY, MATTY, LOOK!
WILSON-- FUTURE KING OF NEW YORK! HAW!
HA HA HA!
Ah...he's not kidding, is he?

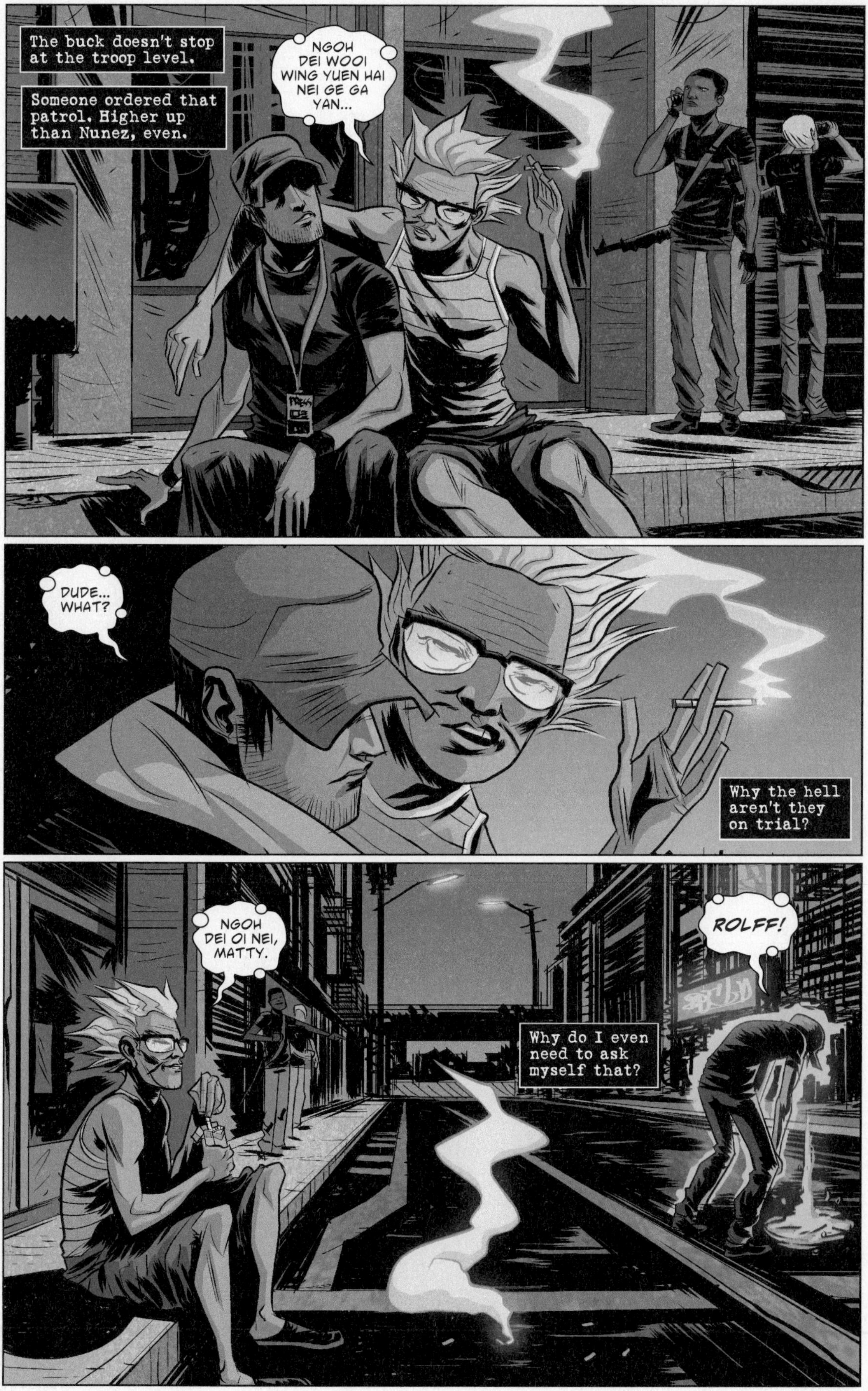
The buck doesn't stop at the troop level.
Someone ordered that patrol. Higher up than Nunez, even.
NGOH DEI WOOI WING YUEN HAI NEI GE GA YAN...
DUDE... WHAT?
Why the hell aren't they on trial?
NGOH DEI OI NEI, MATTY.
Why do I even need to ask myself that?
ROLFF!

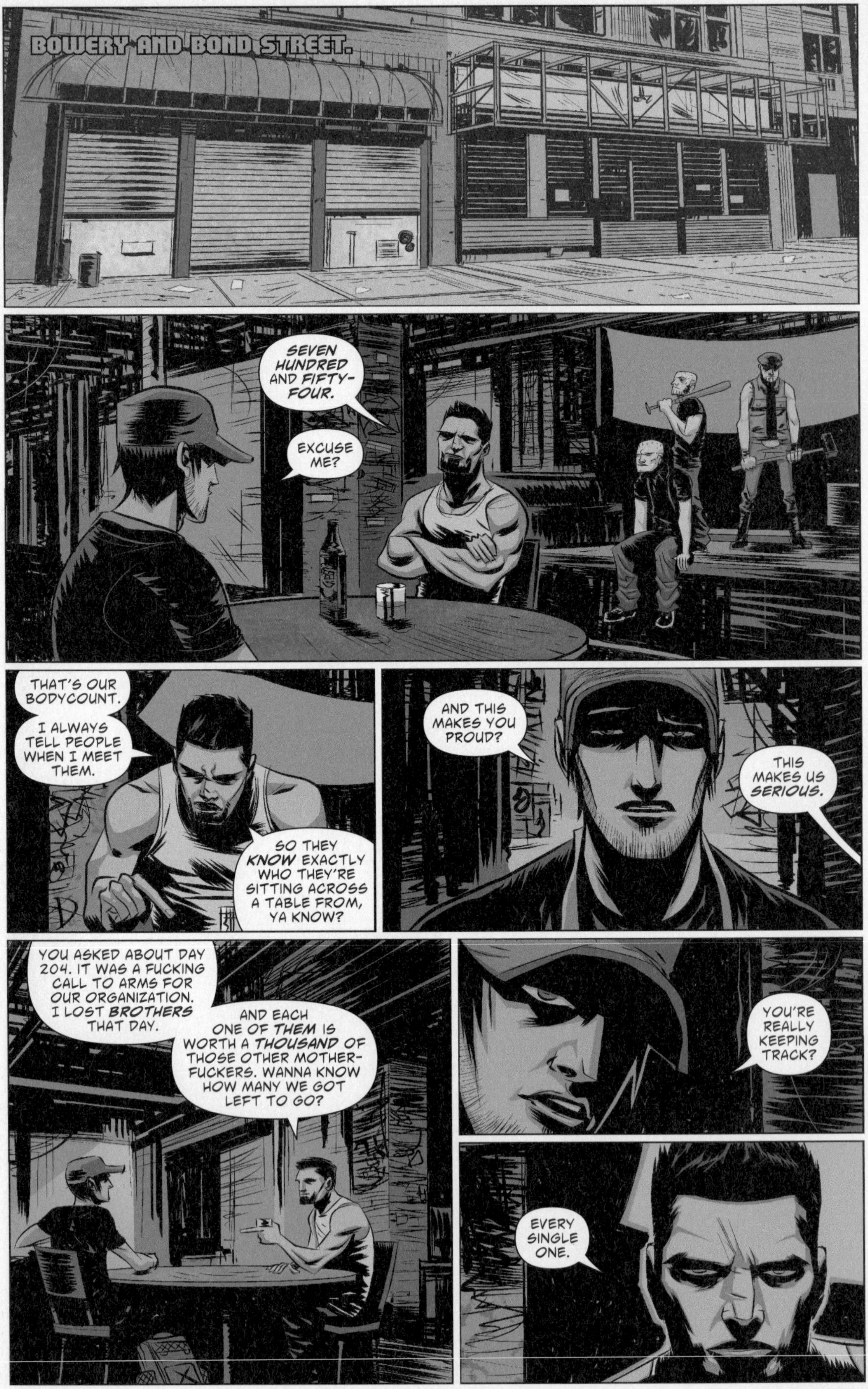
BOWERY AND BOND STREET.
SEVEN HUNDRED AND FIFTY-FOUR.
EXCUSE ME?
THAT'S OUR BODYCOUNT.
I ALWAYS TELL PEOPLE WHEN I MEET THEM.
SO THEY KNOW EXACTLY WHO THEY'RE SITTING ACROSS A TABLE FROM, YA KNOW?
AND THIS MAKES YOU PROUD?
THIS MAKES US SERIOUS.
YOU ASKED ABOUT DAY 204. IT WAS A FUCKING CALL TO ARMS FOR OUR ORGANIZATION. I LOST BROTHERS THAT DAY.
AND EACH ONE OF THEM IS WORTH A THOUSAND OF THOSE OTHER MOTHER-FUCKERS. WANNA KNOW HOW MANY WE GOT LEFT TO GO?
YOU'RE REALLY KEEPING TRACK?
EVERY SINGLE ONE.

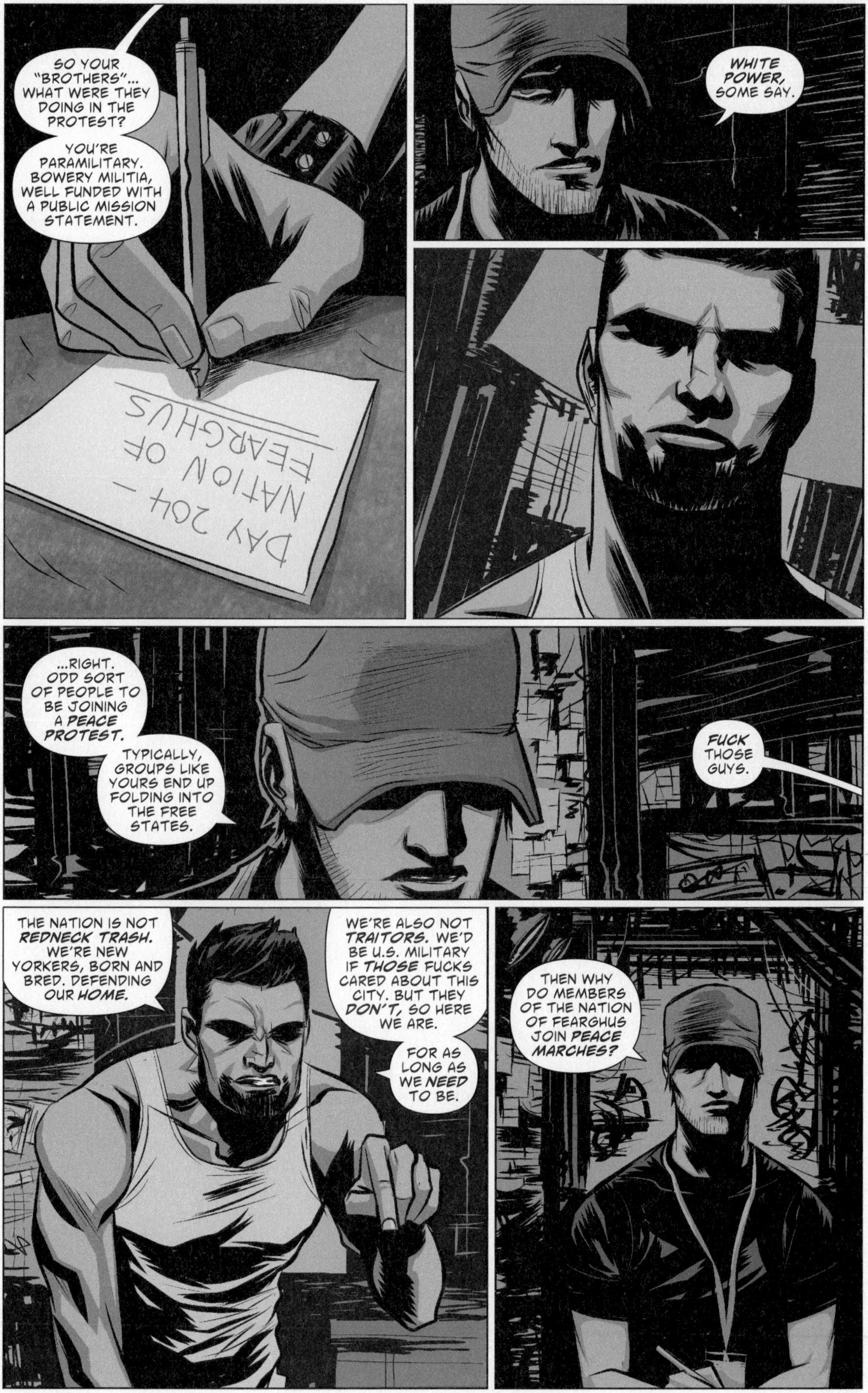

SO YOUR "BROTHERS"... WHAT WERE THEY DOING IN THE PROTEST?
YOU'RE PARAMILITARY. BOWERY MILITIA, WELL FUNDED WITH A PUBLIC MISSION STATEMENT.
DAY 204 — NATION OF FEARGHUS
WHITE POWER, SOME SAY.
...RIGHT. ODD SORT OF PEOPLE TO BE JOINING A PEACE PROTEST.
TYPICALLY, GROUPS LIKE YOURS END UP FOLDING INTO THE FREE STATES.
FUCK THOSE GUYS.
THE NATION IS NOT REDNECK TRASH. WE'RE NEW YORKERS, BORN AND BRED. DEFENDING OUR HOME.
WE'RE ALSO NOT TRAITORS. WE'D BE U.S. MILITARY IF THOSE FUCKS CARED ABOUT THIS CITY. BUT THEY DON'T, SO HERE WE ARE.
FOR AS LONG AS WE NEED TO BE.
THEN WHY DO MEMBERS OF THE NATION OF FEARGHUS JOIN PEACE MARCHES?

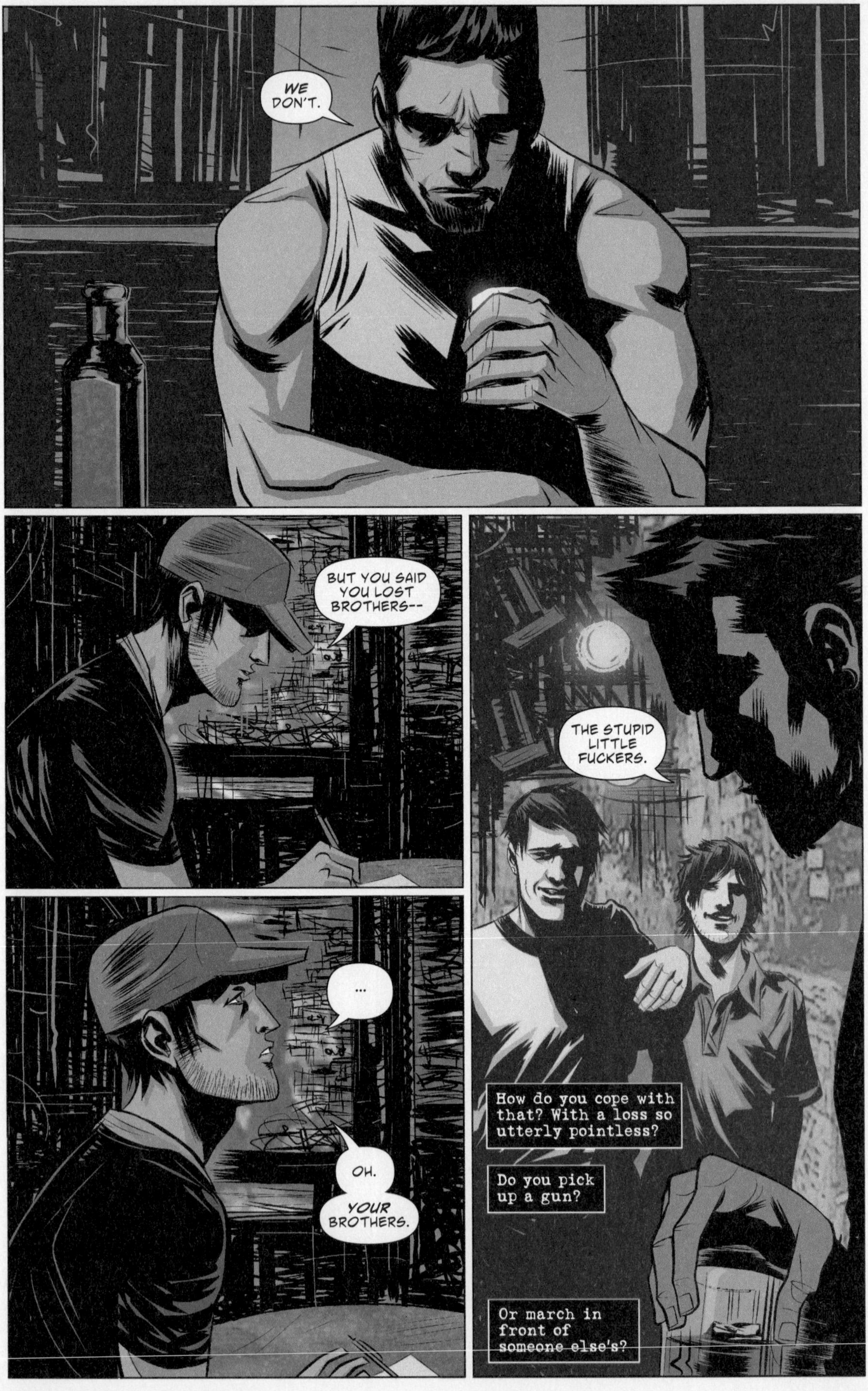
WE DON'T.
BUT YOU SAID YOU LOST BROTHERS--
...
OH.
YOUR BROTHERS.
THE STUPID LITTLE FUCKERS.
How do you cope with that? With a loss so utterly pointless?
Do you pick up a gun?
Or march in front of someone else's?

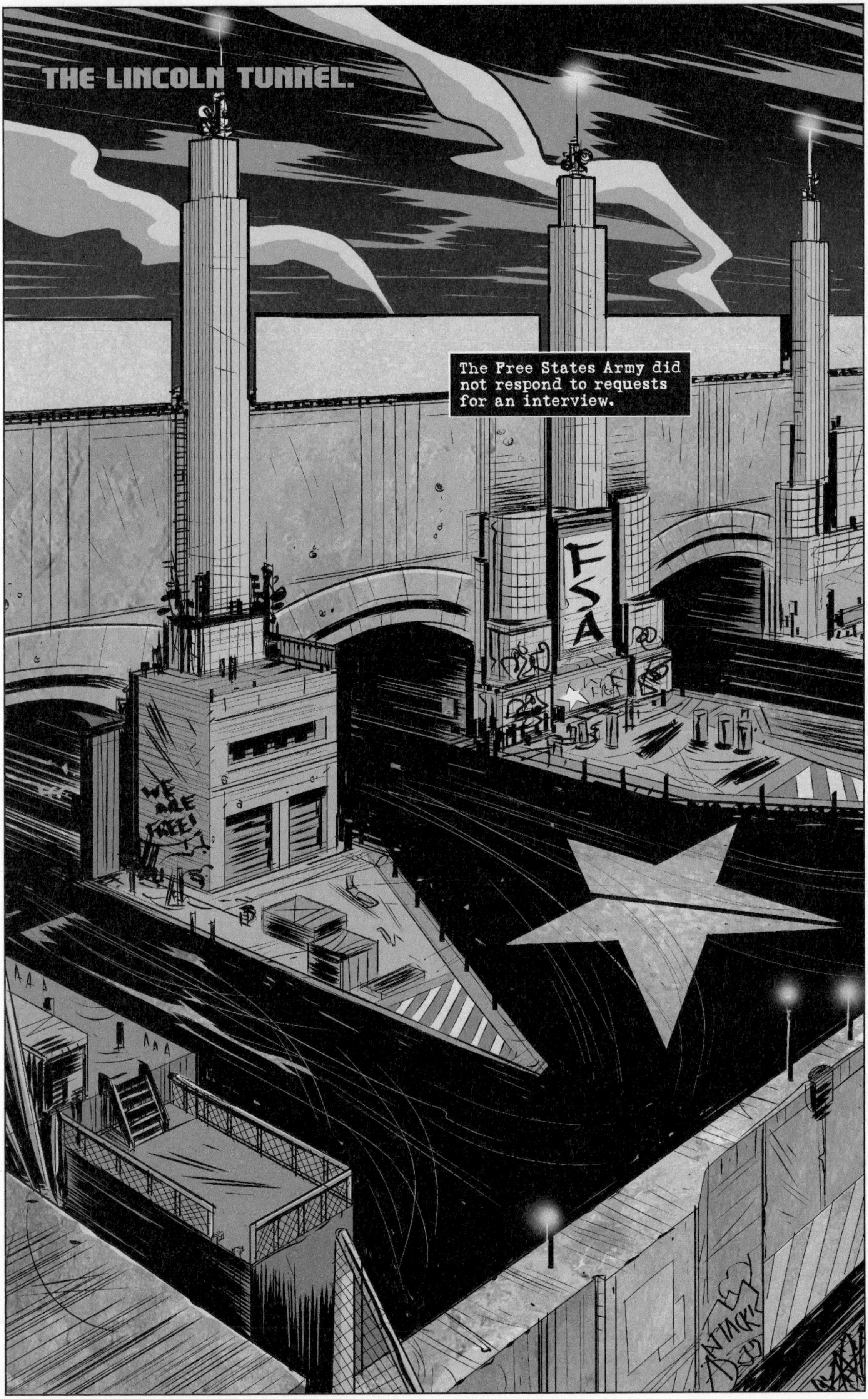
THE LINCOLN TUNNEL.
The Free States Army did not respond to requests for an interview.
FSA
WE ARE FREE!

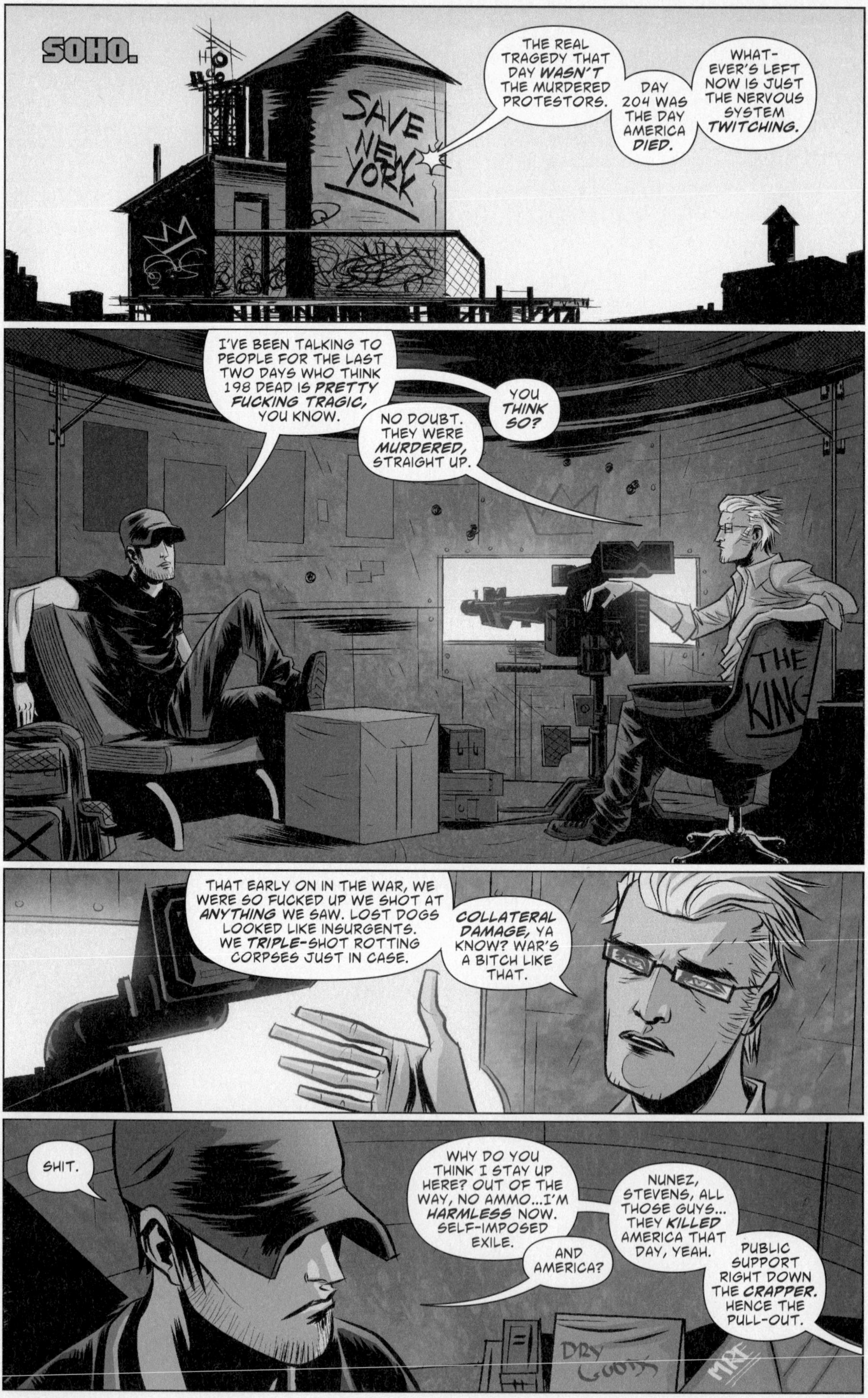
SOHO.
SAVE NEW YORK
THE REAL TRAGEDY THAT DAY WASN'T THE MURDERED PROTESTORS.
DAY 204 WAS THE DAY AMERICA DIED.
WHAT-EVER'S LEFT NOW IS JUST THE NERVOUS SYSTEM TWITCHING.
I'VE BEEN TALKING TO PEOPLE FOR THE LAST TWO DAYS WHO THINK 198 DEAD IS PRETTY FUCKING TRAGIC, YOU KNOW.
YOU THINK SO?
NO DOUBT. THEY WERE MURDERED, STRAIGHT UP.
THE KING
THAT EARLY ON IN THE WAR, WE WERE SO FUCKED UP WE SHOT AT ANYTHING WE SAW. LOST DOGS LOOKED LIKE INSURGENTS. WE TRIPLE-SHOT ROTTING CORPSES JUST IN CASE.
COLLATERAL DAMAGE, YA KNOW? WAR'S A BITCH LIKE THAT.
SHIT.
WHY DO YOU THINK I STAY UP HERE? OUT OF THE WAY, NO AMMO...I'M HARMLESS NOW. SELF-IMPOSED EXILE.
AND AMERICA?
NUNEZ, STEVENS, ALL THOSE GUYS... THEY KILLED AMERICA THAT DAY, YEAH.
PUBLIC SUPPORT RIGHT DOWN THE CRAPPER. HENCE THE PULL-OUT.
DRY GOODS

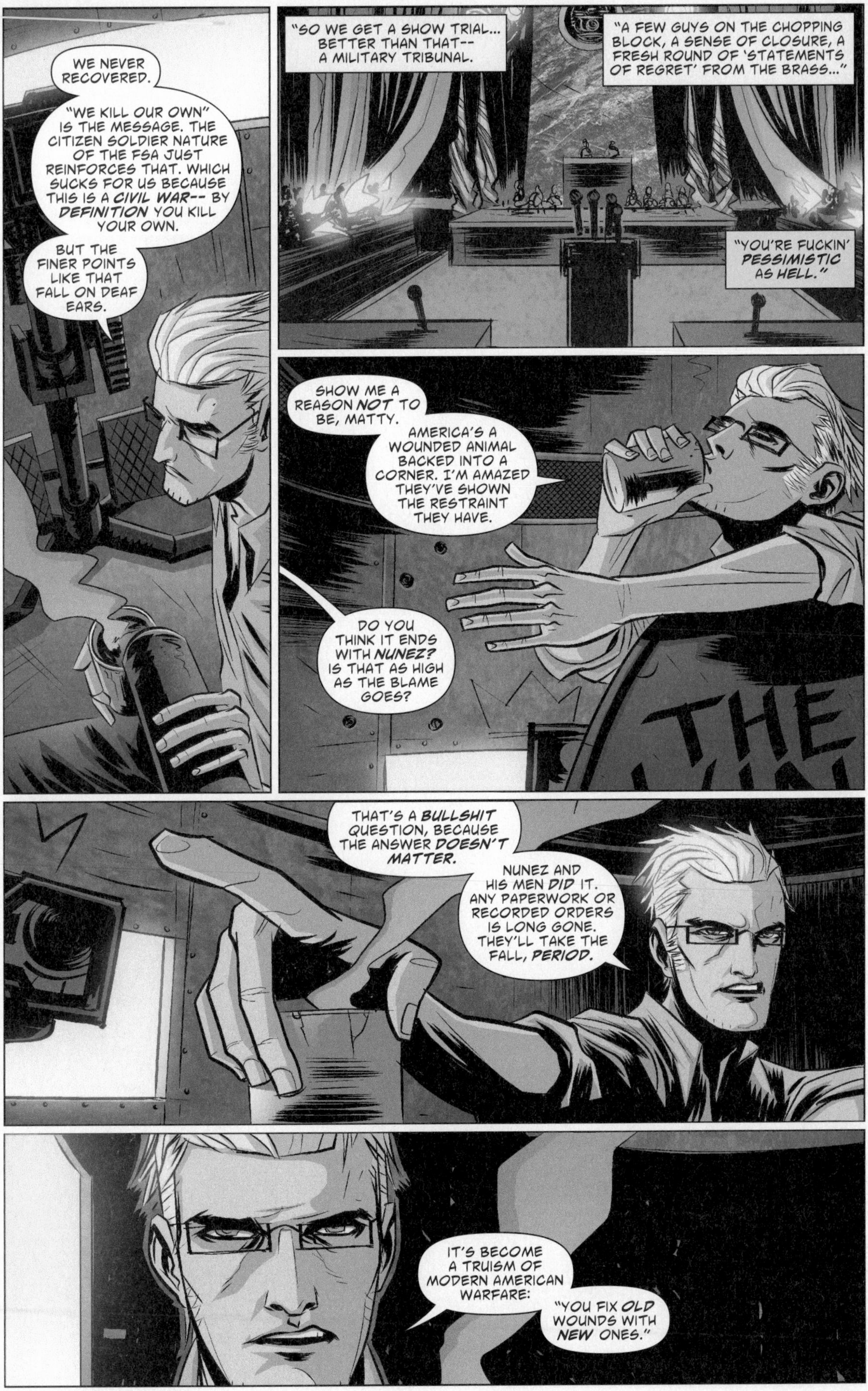
WE NEVER RECOVERED.
"WE KILL OUR OWN" IS THE MESSAGE. THE CITIZEN SOLDIER NATURE OF THE FSA JUST REINFORCES THAT. WHICH SUCKS FOR US BECAUSE THIS IS A *CIVIL WAR--* BY *DEFINITION* YOU KILL YOUR OWN.
BUT THE FINER POINTS LIKE THAT FALL ON DEAF EARS.
"SO WE GET A SHOW TRIAL... BETTER THAN THAT-- A MILITARY TRIBUNAL.
"A FEW GUYS ON THE CHOPPING BLOCK, A SENSE OF CLOSURE, A FRESH ROUND OF 'STATEMENTS OF REGRET' FROM THE BRASS..."
"YOU'RE FUCKIN' *PESSIMISTIC* AS *HELL*."
SHOW ME A REASON *NOT* TO BE, MATTY.
AMERICA'S A WOUNDED ANIMAL BACKED INTO A CORNER. I'M AMAZED THEY'VE SHOWN THE RESTRAINT THEY HAVE.
DO YOU THINK IT ENDS WITH *NUNEZ?* IS THAT AS HIGH AS THE BLAME GOES?
THE
THAT'S A *BULLSHIT* QUESTION, BECAUSE THE ANSWER *DOESN'T MATTER.*
NUNEZ AND HIS MEN *DID* IT. ANY PAPERWORK OR RECORDED ORDERS IS LONG GONE. THEY'LL TAKE THE FALL, *PERIOD.*
IT'S BECOME A TRUISM OF MODERN AMERICAN WARFARE:
"YOU FIX *OLD* WOUNDS WITH *NEW* ONES."

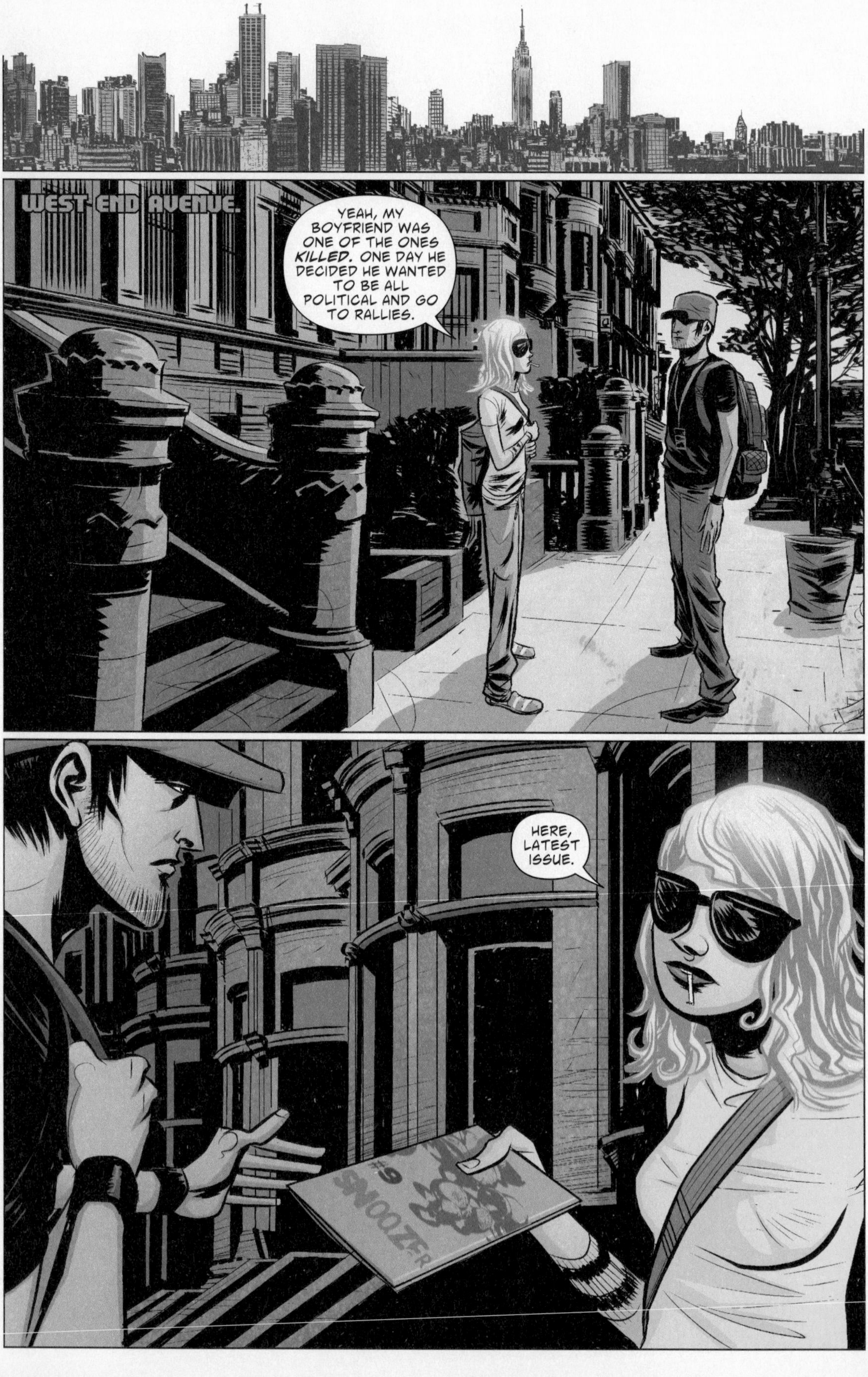
WEST END AVENUE.
YEAH, MY BOYFRIEND WAS ONE OF THE ONES KILLED. ONE DAY HE DECIDED HE WANTED TO BE ALL POLITICAL AND GO TO RALLIES.
HERE, LATEST ISSUE.
#9 SNOOZER

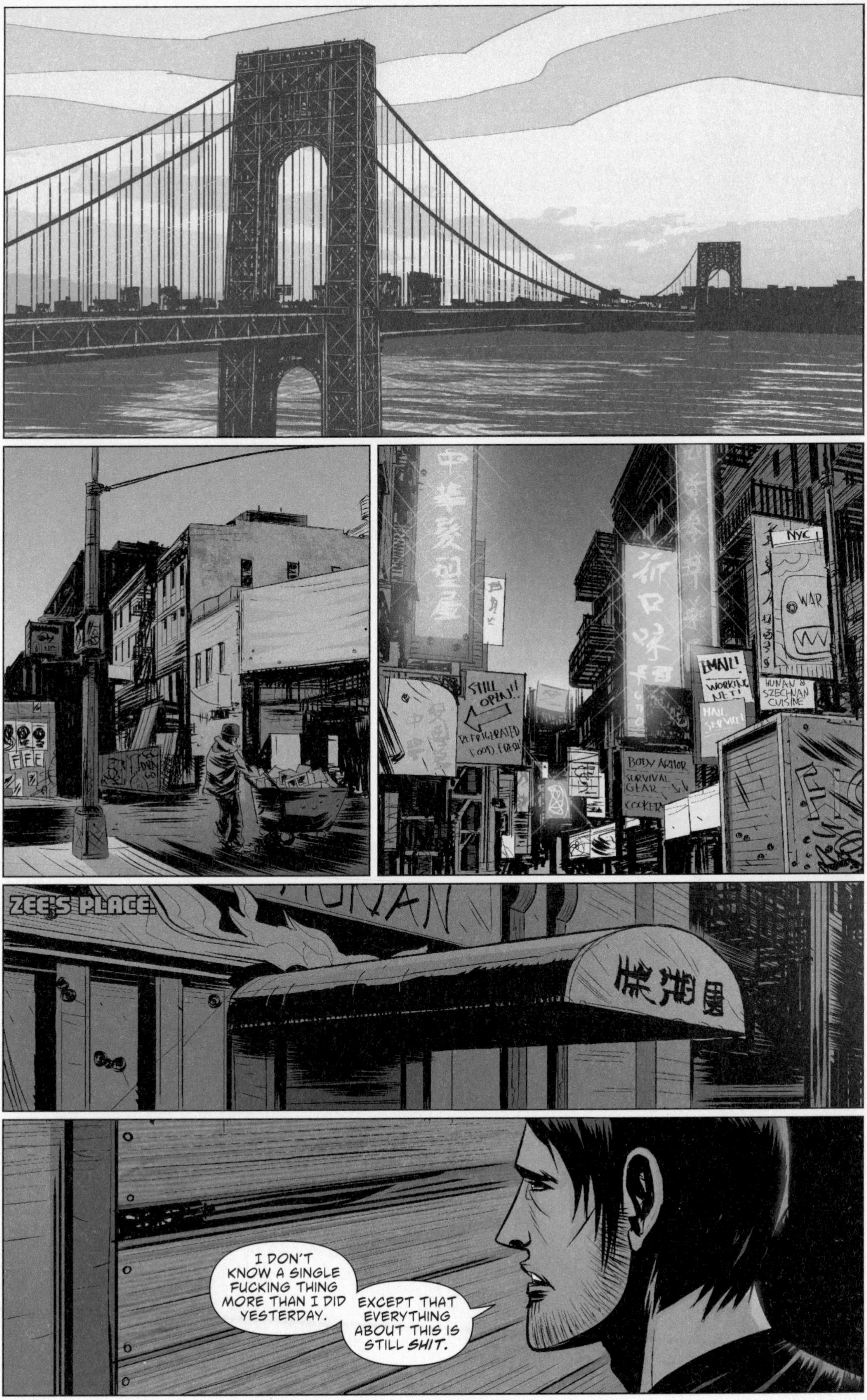
STILL OPEN!!
REFRIGERATED FOOD FRESH
NYC
WAR
EMAIL! WORKING NET!
HUNAN & SZECHUAN CUISINE
BODY ARMOR
SURVIVAL GEAR
ZEE'S PLACE.
I DON'T KNOW A SINGLE FUCKING THING MORE THAN I DID YESTERDAY.
EXCEPT THAT EVERYTHING ABOUT THIS IS STILL *SHIT*.

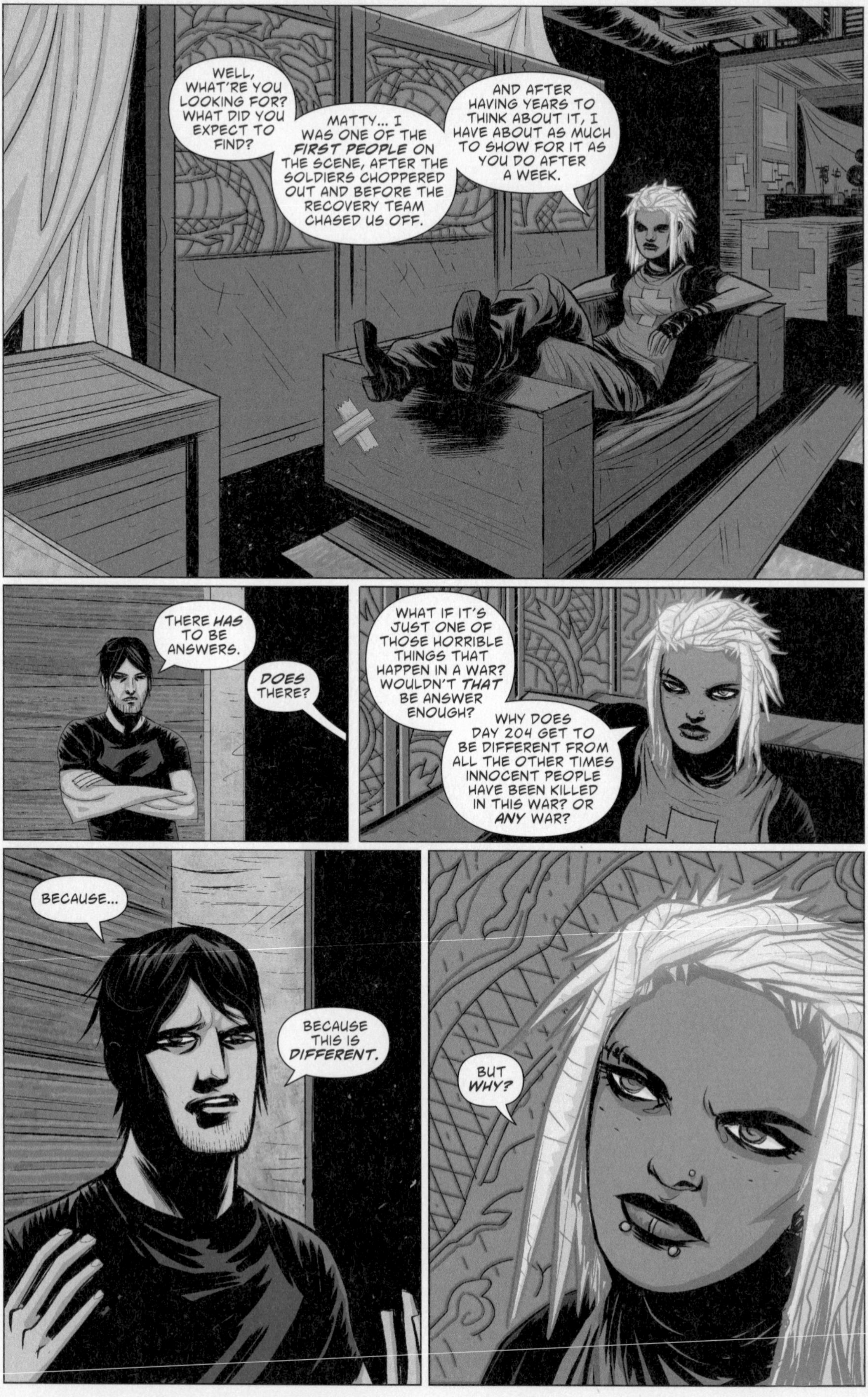
WELL, WHAT'RE YOU LOOKING FOR? WHAT DID YOU EXPECT TO FIND?
MATTY... I WAS ONE OF THE *FIRST PEOPLE* ON THE SCENE, AFTER THE SOLDIERS CHOPPERED OUT AND BEFORE THE RECOVERY TEAM CHASED US OFF.
AND AFTER HAVING YEARS TO THINK ABOUT IT, I HAVE ABOUT AS MUCH TO SHOW FOR IT AS YOU DO AFTER A WEEK.
THERE *HAS* TO BE ANSWERS.
DOES THERE?
WHAT IF IT'S JUST ONE OF THOSE HORRIBLE THINGS THAT HAPPEN IN A WAR? WOULDN'T *THAT* BE ANSWER ENOUGH?
WHY DOES DAY 204 GET TO BE DIFFERENT FROM ALL THE OTHER TIMES INNOCENT PEOPLE HAVE BEEN KILLED IN THIS WAR? OR *ANY* WAR?
BECAUSE...
BECAUSE THIS IS *DIFFERENT.*
BUT *WHY?*

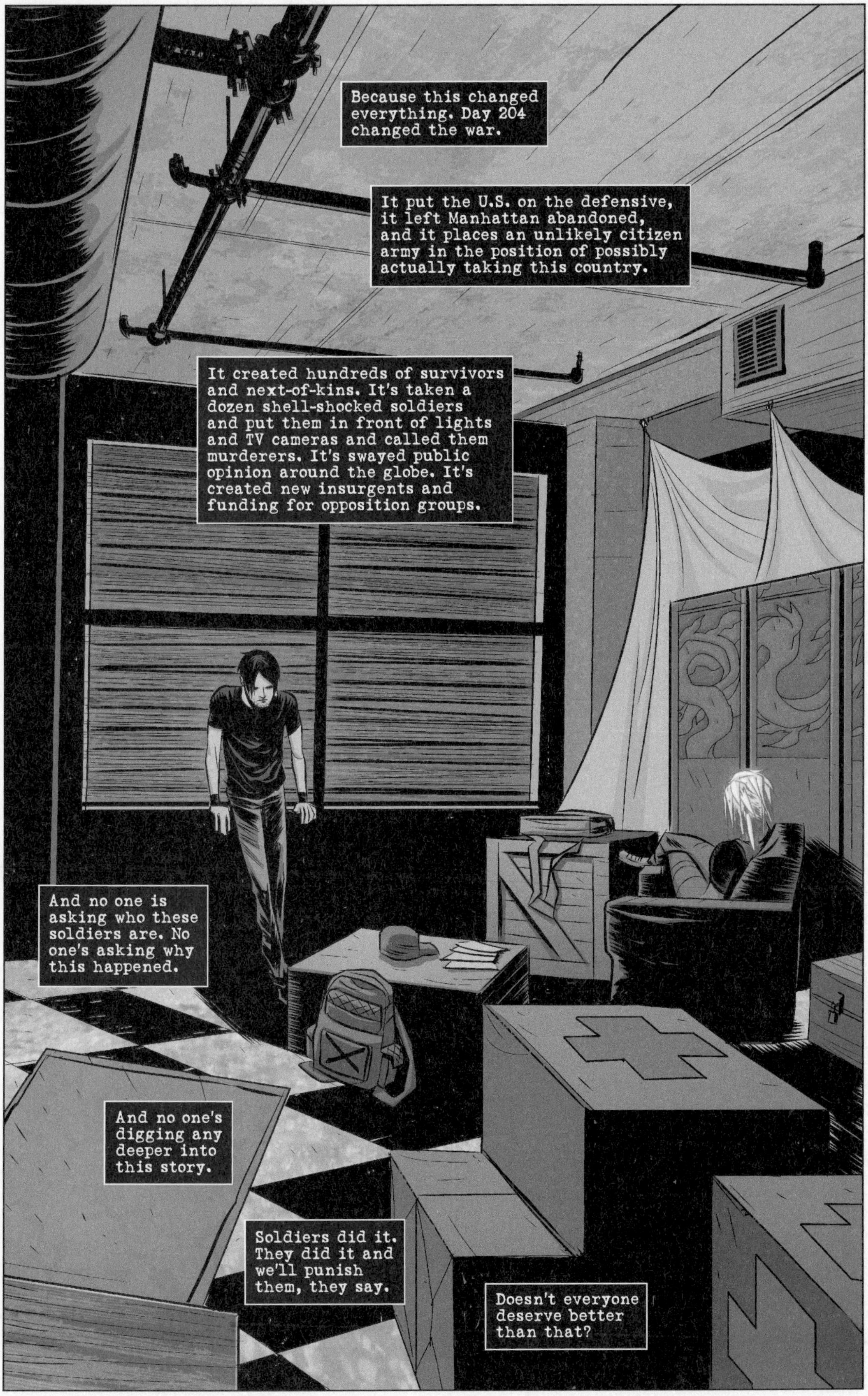

Because this changed everything. Day 204 changed the war.
It put the U.S. on the defensive, it left Manhattan abandoned, and it places an unlikely citizen army in the position of possibly actually taking this country.
It created hundreds of survivors and next-of-kins. It's taken a dozen shell-shocked soldiers and put them in front of lights and TV cameras and called them murderers. It's swayed public opinion around the globe. It's created new insurgents and funding for opposition groups.
And no one is asking who these soldiers are. No one's asking why this happened.
And no one's digging any deeper into this story.
Soldiers did it. They did it and we'll punish them, they say.
Doesn't everyone deserve better than that?

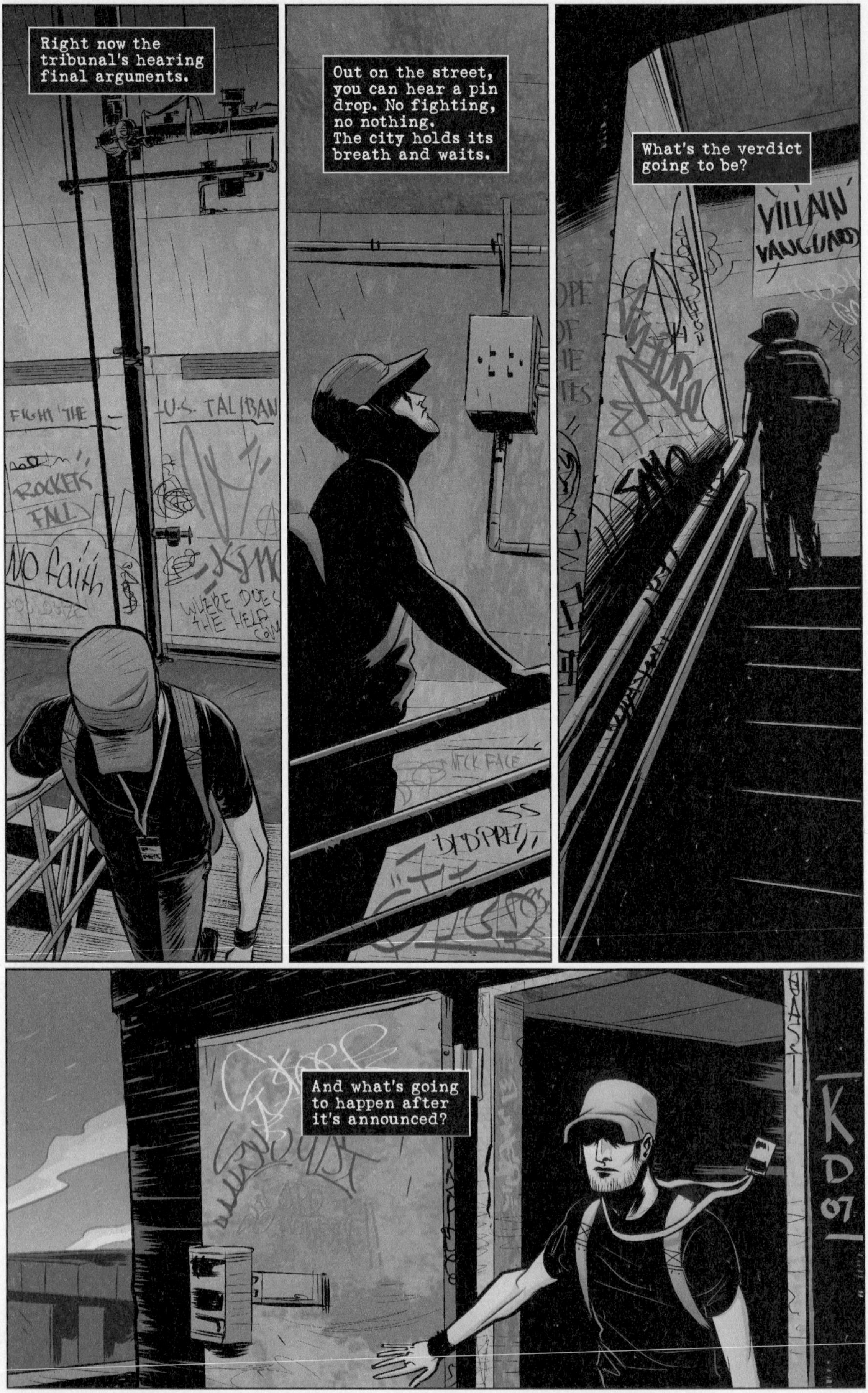
Right now the tribunal's hearing final arguments.
FIGHT THE
U.S. TALIBAN
ROCKETS FALL
NO faith
Out on the street, you can hear a pin drop. No fighting, no nothing.
The city holds its breath and waits.
NECK FACE
What's the verdict going to be?
VILLAIN VANGUARD
And what's going to happen after it's announced?

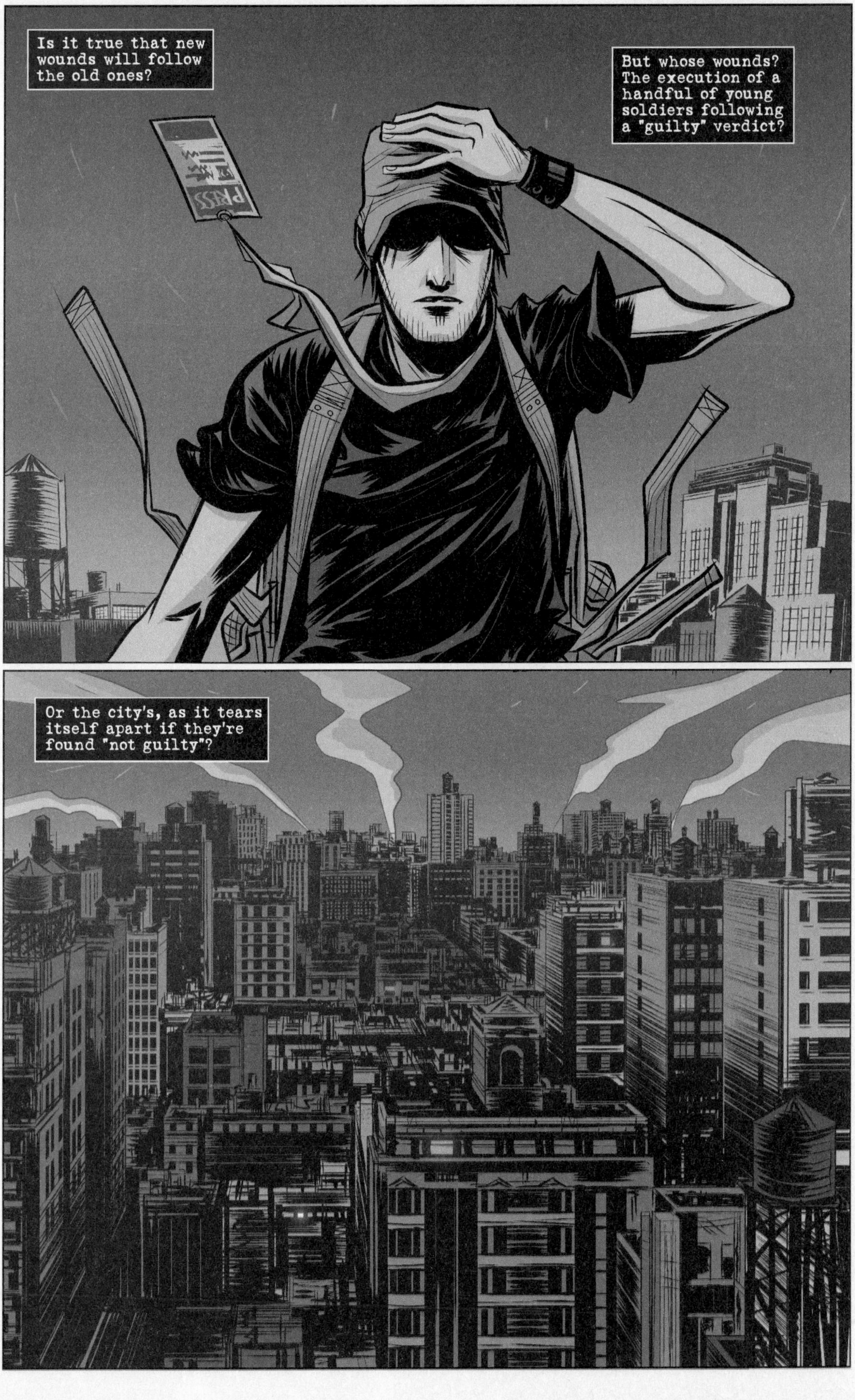
Is it true that new wounds will follow the old ones?
But whose wounds? The execution of a handful of young soldiers following a "guilty" verdict?
Or the city's, as it tears itself apart if they're found "not guilty"?

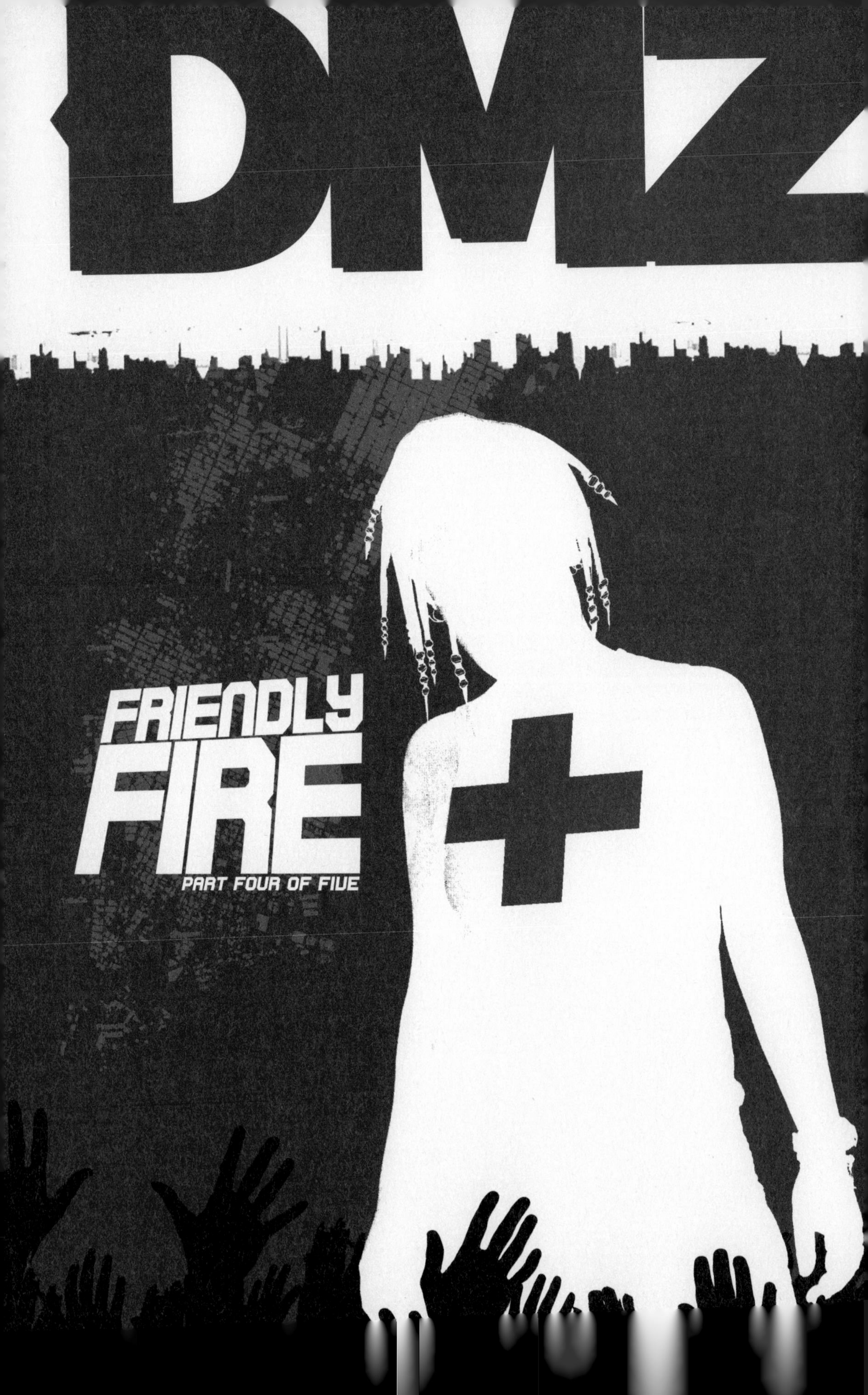
DMZ
FRIENDLY
FIRE
PART FOUR OF FIVE

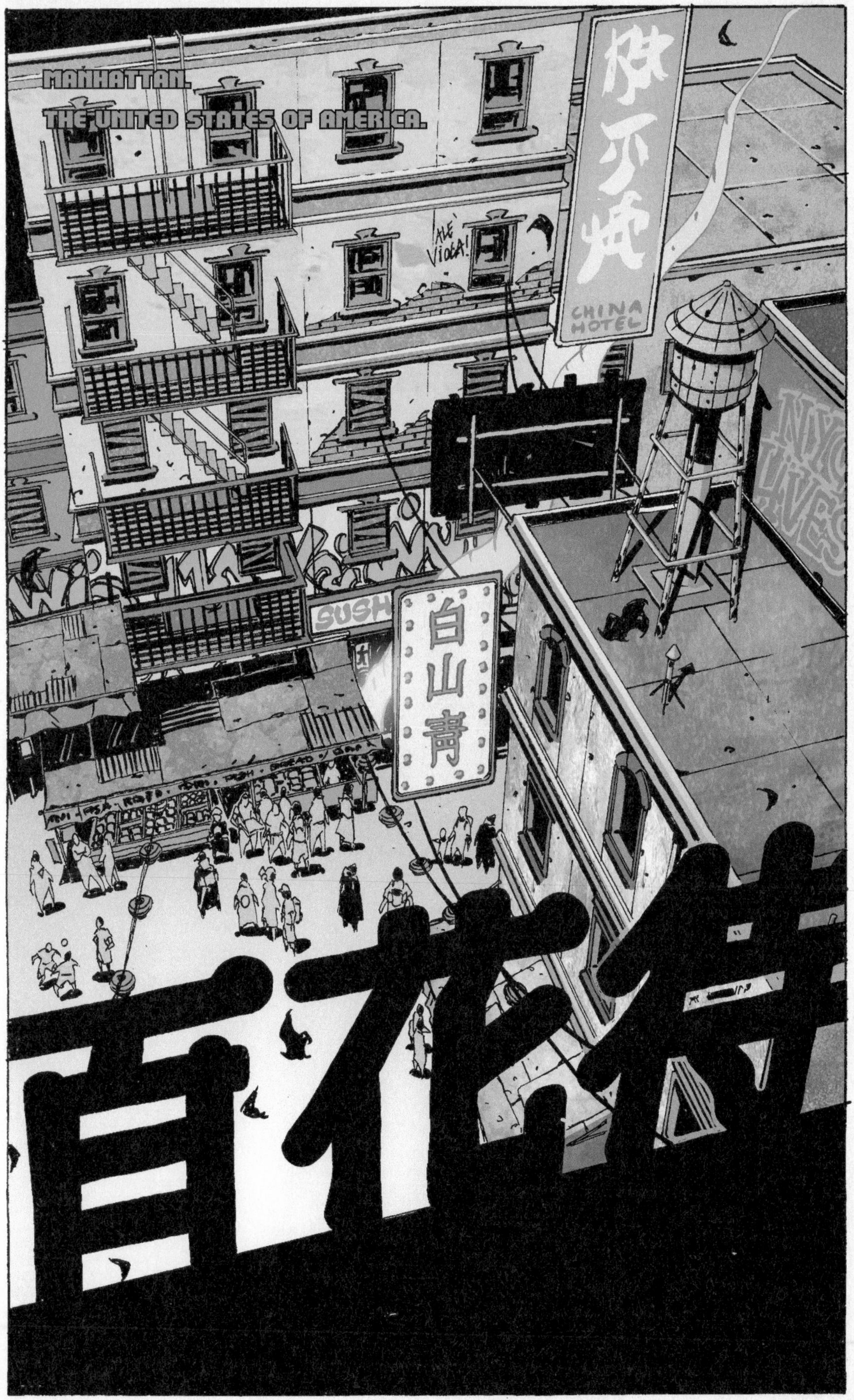
MANHATTAN.
THE UNITED STATES OF AMERICA.
CHINA HOTEL

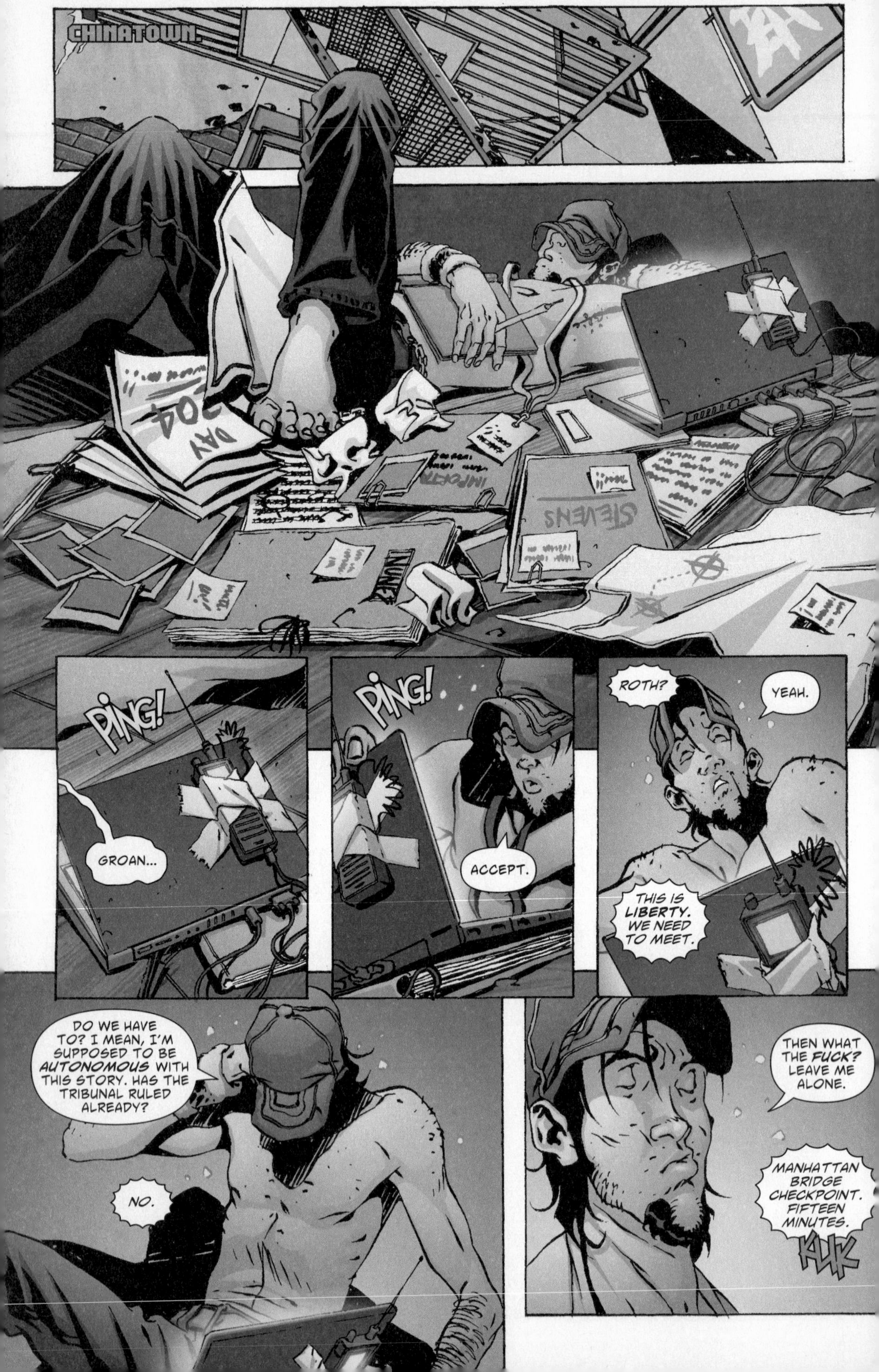
CHINATOWN.
DAY 204
IMPORTA
STEVENS
PING!
GROAN...
PING!
ACCEPT.
ROTH?
YEAH.
THIS IS LIBERTY. WE NEED TO MEET.
DO WE HAVE TO? I MEAN, I'M SUPPOSED TO BE AUTONOMOUS WITH THIS STORY. HAS THE TRIBUNAL RULED ALREADY?
NO.
THEN WHAT THE FUCK? LEAVE ME ALONE.
MANHATTAN BRIDGE CHECKPOINT. FIFTEEN MINUTES.
KLIK

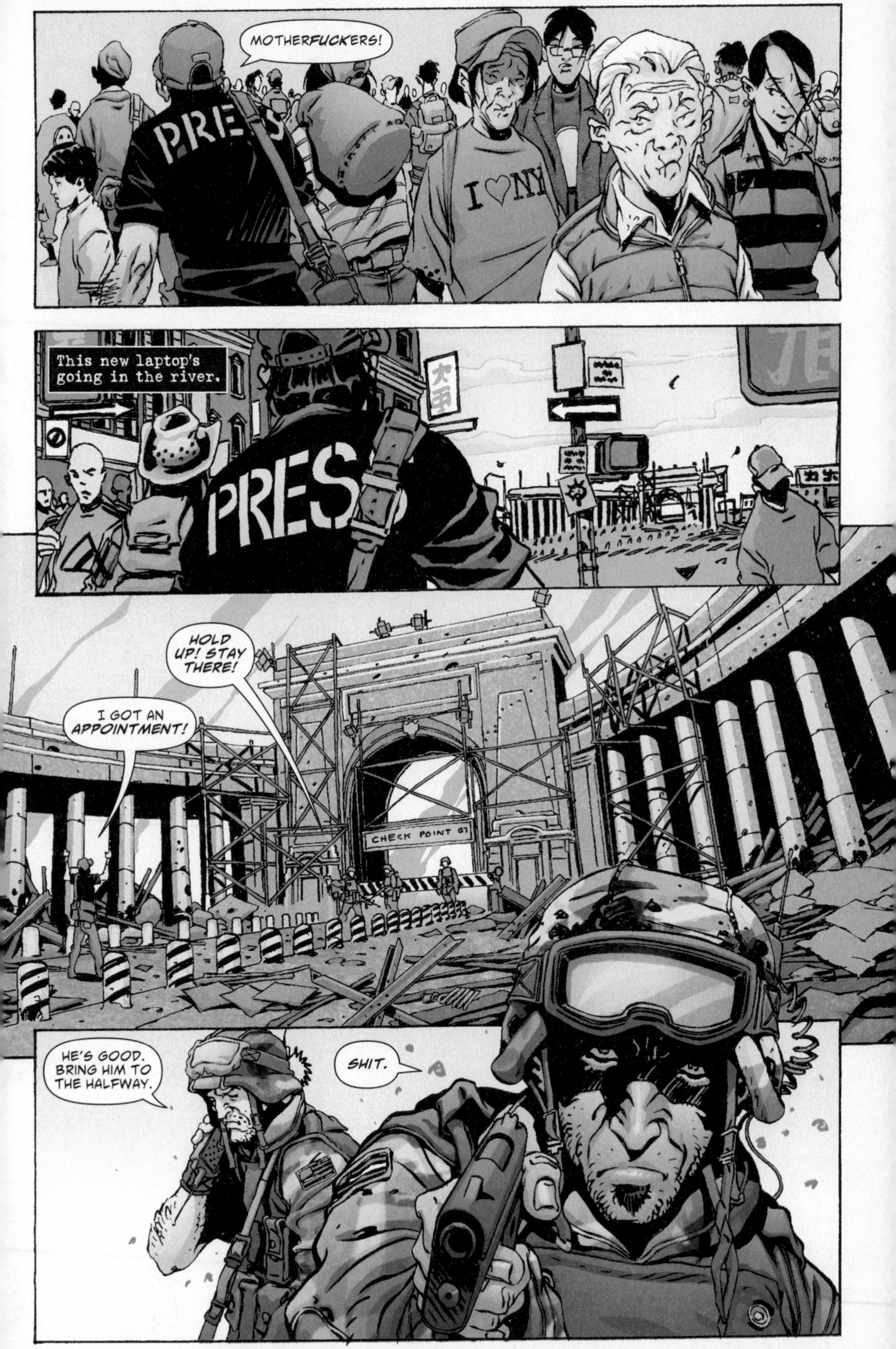
MOTHERFUCKERS!
This new laptop's going in the river.
I GOT AN APPOINTMENT!
HOLD UP! STAY THERE!
CHECK POINT 07
HE'S GOOD. BRING HIM TO THE HALFWAY.
SHIT.

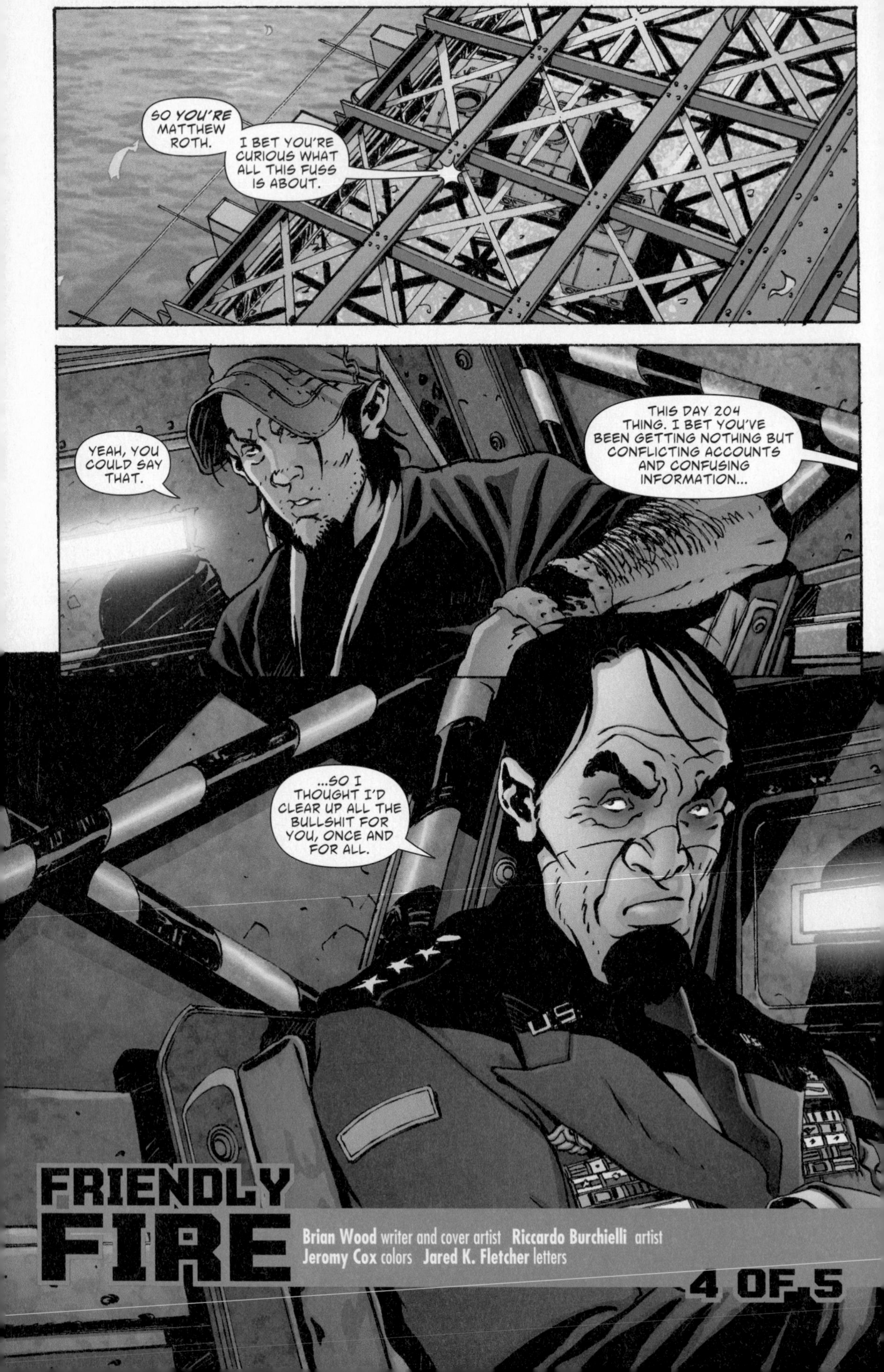
SO YOU'RE MATTHEW ROTH.
I BET YOU'RE CURIOUS WHAT ALL THIS FUSS IS ABOUT.
YEAH, YOU COULD SAY THAT.
THIS DAY 204 THING. I BET YOU'VE BEEN GETTING NOTHING BUT CONFLICTING ACCOUNTS AND CONFUSING INFORMATION...
...SO I THOUGHT I'D CLEAR UP ALL THE BULLSHIT FOR YOU, ONCE AND FOR ALL.
FRIENDLY FIRE
Brian Wood writer and cover artist Riccardo Burchielli artist
Jeromy Cox colors Jared K. Fletcher letters
4 OF 5

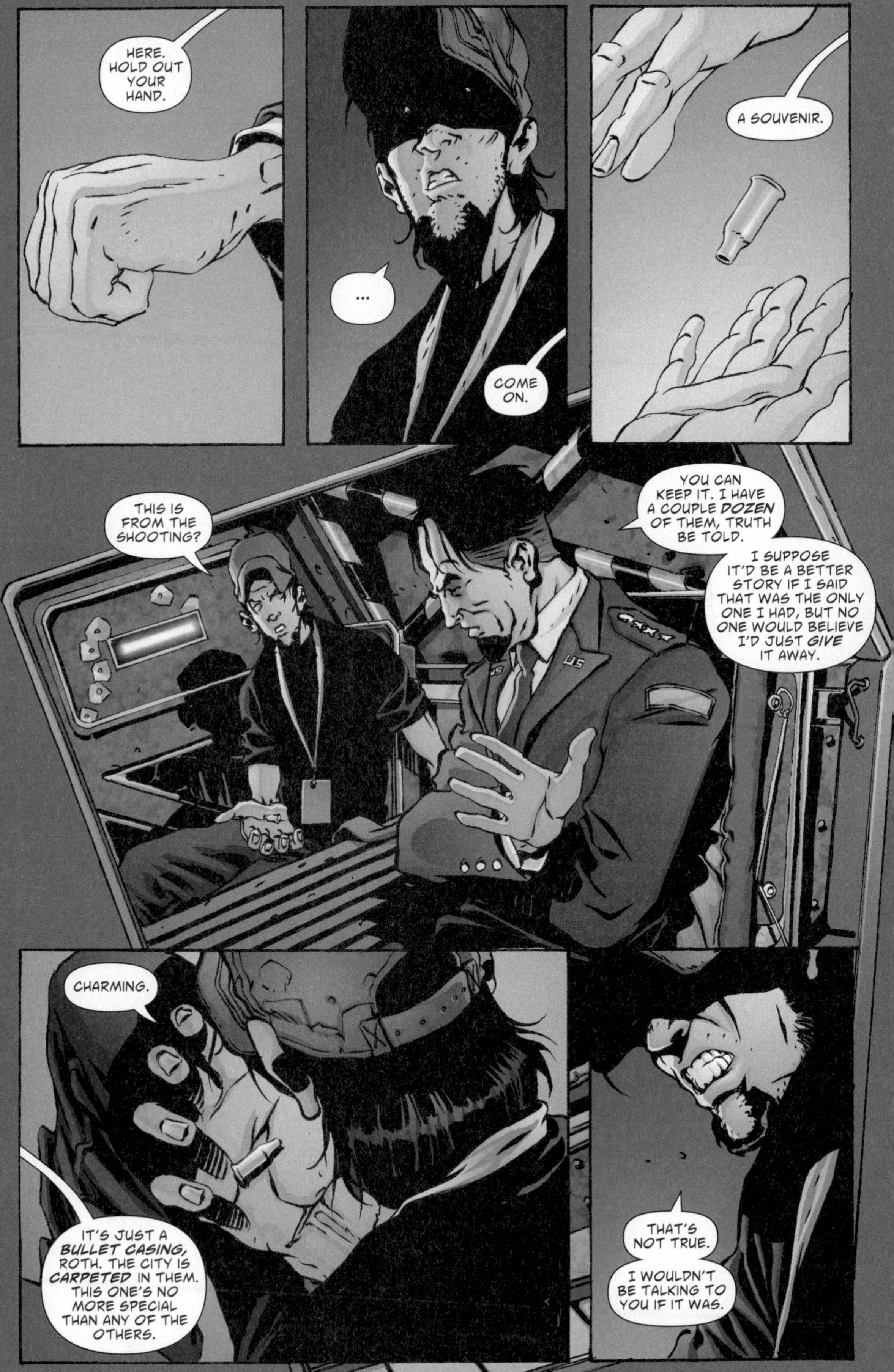
HERE. HOLD OUT YOUR HAND.
...
COME ON.
A SOUVENIR.
THIS IS FROM THE SHOOTING?
YOU CAN KEEP IT. I HAVE A COUPLE DOZEN OF THEM, TRUTH BE TOLD.
I SUPPOSE IT'D BE A BETTER STORY IF I SAID THAT WAS THE ONLY ONE I HAD, BUT NO ONE WOULD BELIEVE I'D JUST GIVE IT AWAY.
CHARMING.
IT'S JUST A BULLET CASING, ROTH. THE CITY IS CARPETED IN THEM. THIS ONE'S NO MORE SPECIAL THAN ANY OF THE OTHERS.
THAT'S NOT TRUE.
I WOULDN'T BE TALKING TO YOU IF IT WAS.

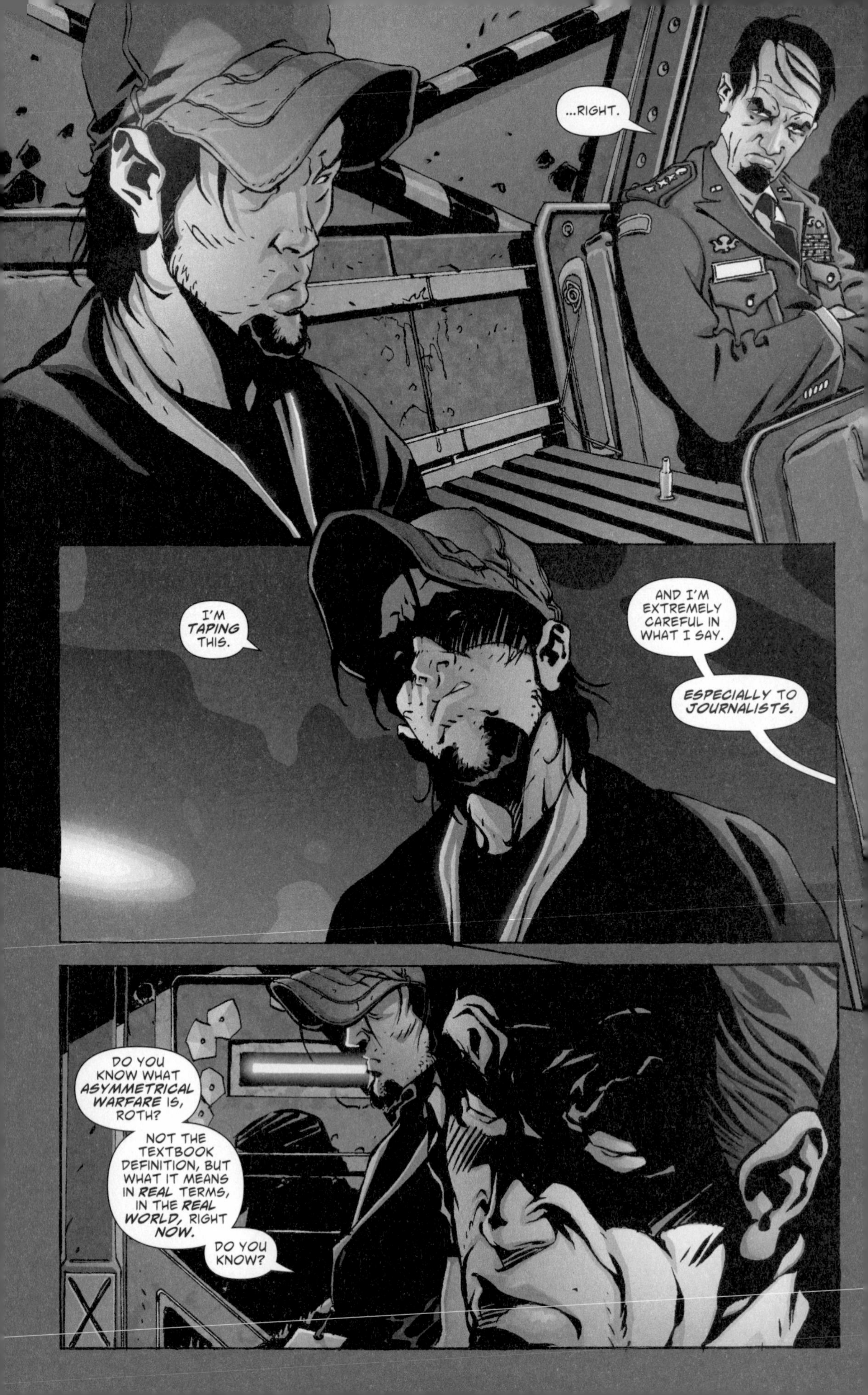
...RIGHT.
I'M TAPING THIS.
AND I'M EXTREMELY CAREFUL IN WHAT I SAY.
ESPECIALLY TO JOURNALISTS.
DO YOU KNOW WHAT ASYMMETRICAL WARFARE IS, ROTH?
NOT THE TEXTBOOK DEFINITION, BUT WHAT IT MEANS IN REAL TERMS, IN THE REAL WORLD, RIGHT NOW.
DO YOU KNOW?

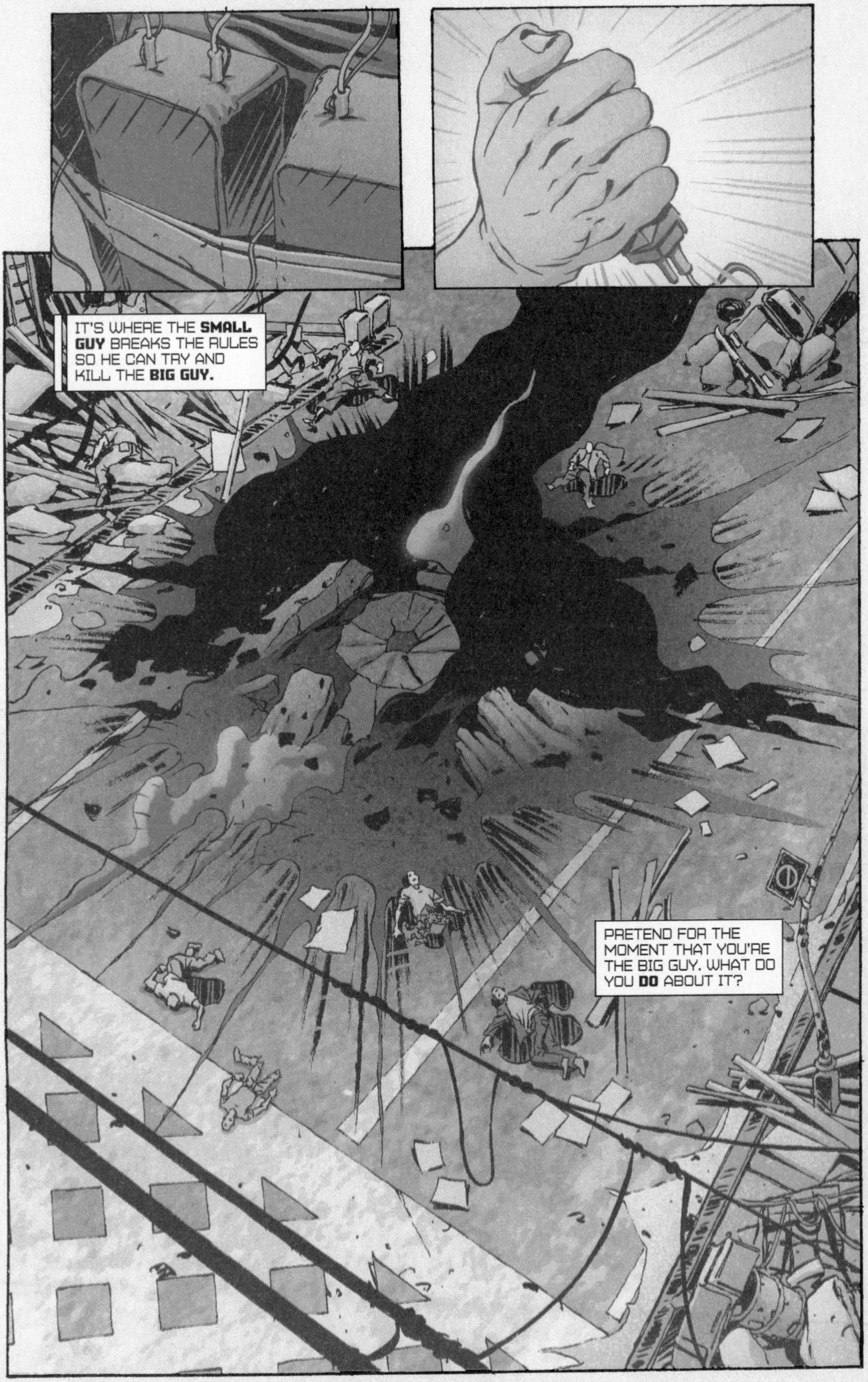
IT'S WHERE THE SMALL GUY BREAKS THE RULES SO HE CAN TRY AND KILL THE BIG GUY.
PRETEND FOR THE MOMENT THAT YOU'RE THE BIG GUY. WHAT DO YOU DO ABOUT IT?

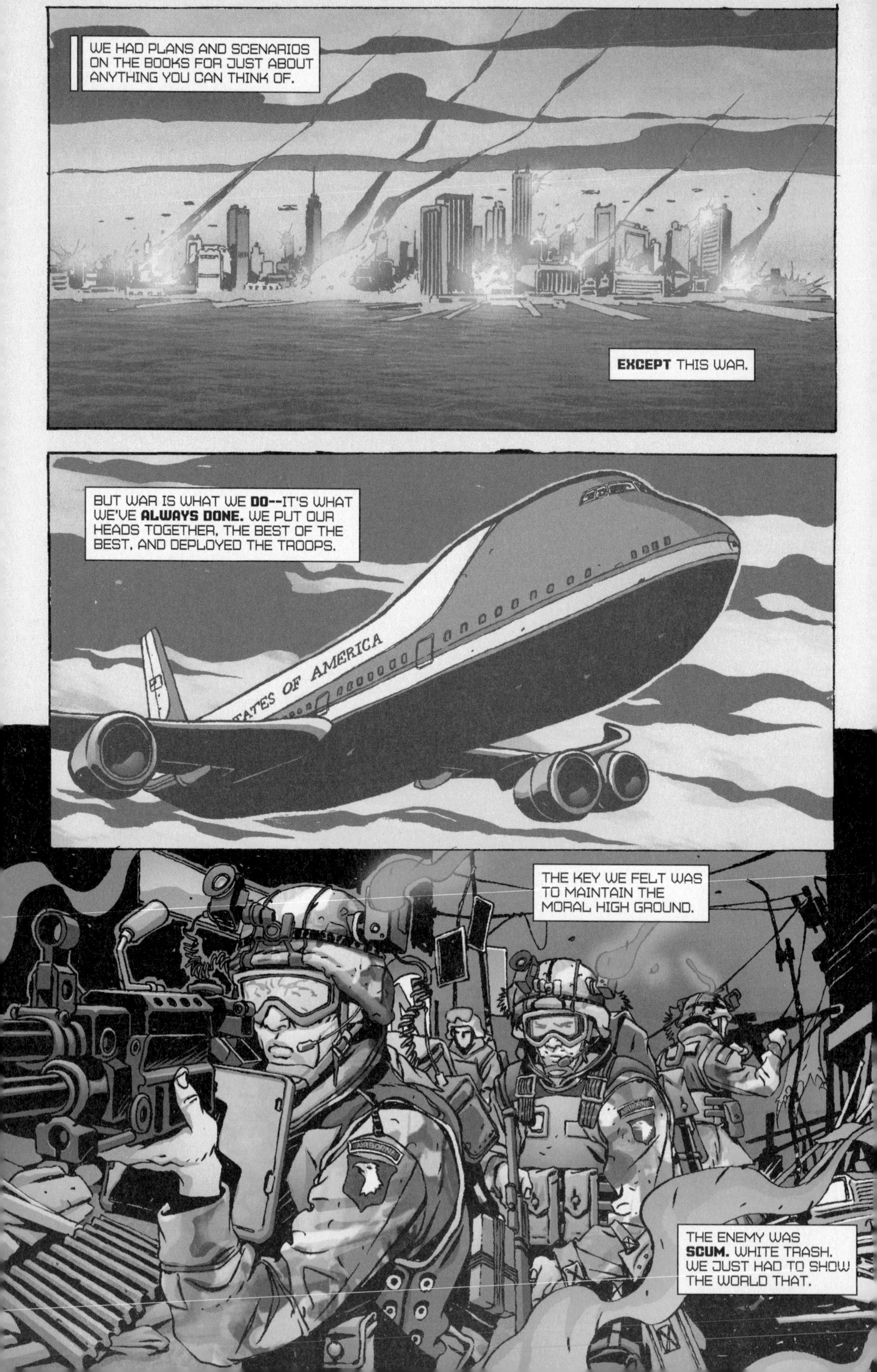
WE HAD PLANS AND SCENARIOS ON THE BOOKS FOR JUST ABOUT ANYTHING YOU CAN THINK OF.
EXCEPT THIS WAR.
BUT WAR IS WHAT WE DO--IT'S WHAT WE'VE ALWAYS DONE. WE PUT OUR HEADS TOGETHER, THE BEST OF THE BEST, AND DEPLOYED THE TROOPS.
THE KEY WE FELT WAS TO MAINTAIN THE MORAL HIGH GROUND.
THE ENEMY WAS SCUM. WHITE TRASH. WE JUST HAD TO SHOW THE WORLD THAT.

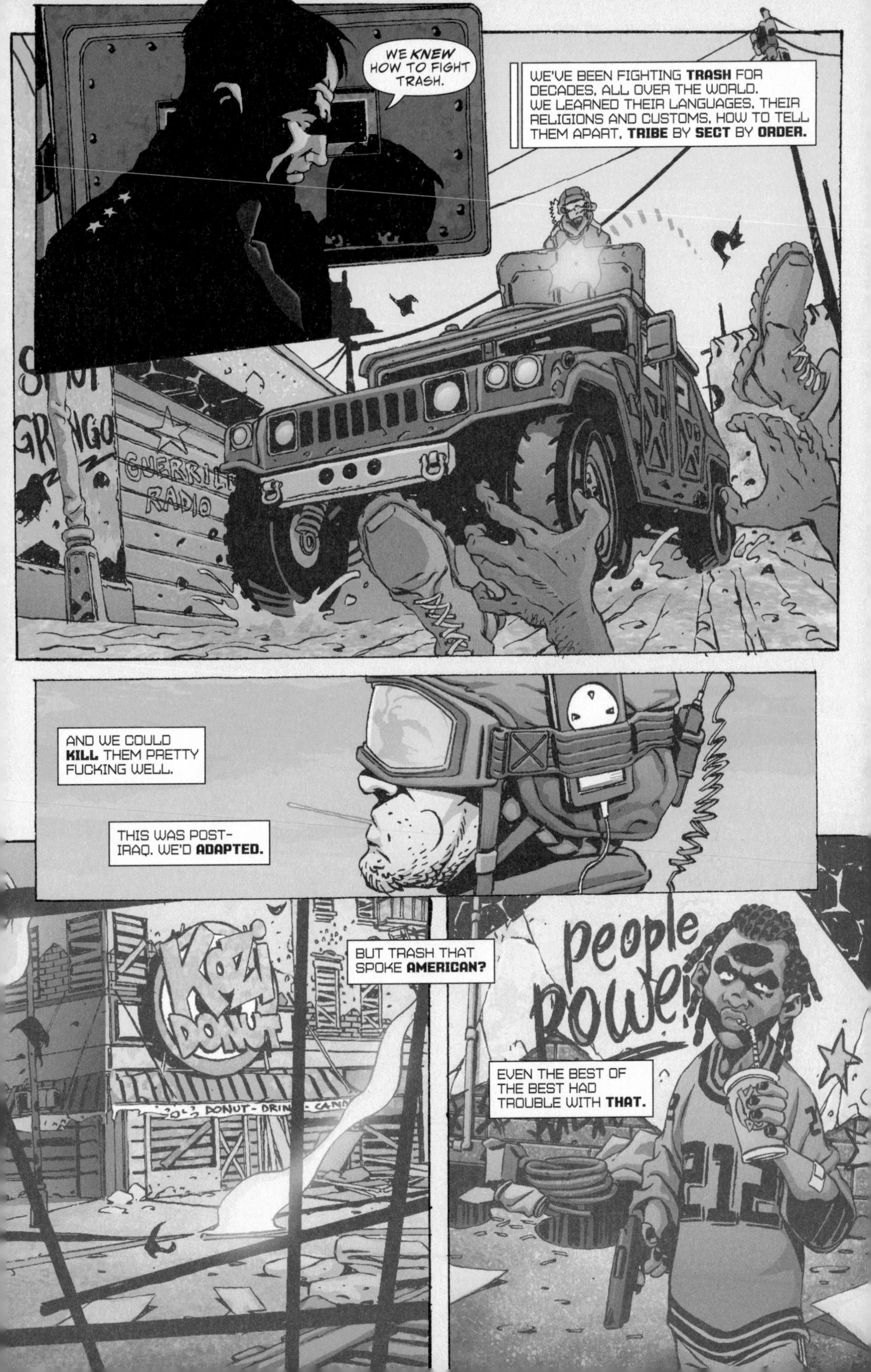

WE KNEW HOW TO FIGHT TRASH.
WE'VE BEEN FIGHTING TRASH FOR DECADES, ALL OVER THE WORLD. WE LEARNED THEIR LANGUAGES, THEIR RELIGIONS AND CUSTOMS, HOW TO TELL THEM APART, TRIBE BY SECT BY ORDER.
GRINGO
RADIO
AND WE COULD KILL THEM PRETTY FUCKING WELL.
THIS WAS POST-IRAQ. WE'D ADAPTED.
DONUT
BUT TRASH THAT SPOKE AMERICAN?
people
EVEN THE BEST OF THE BEST HAD TROUBLE WITH THAT.

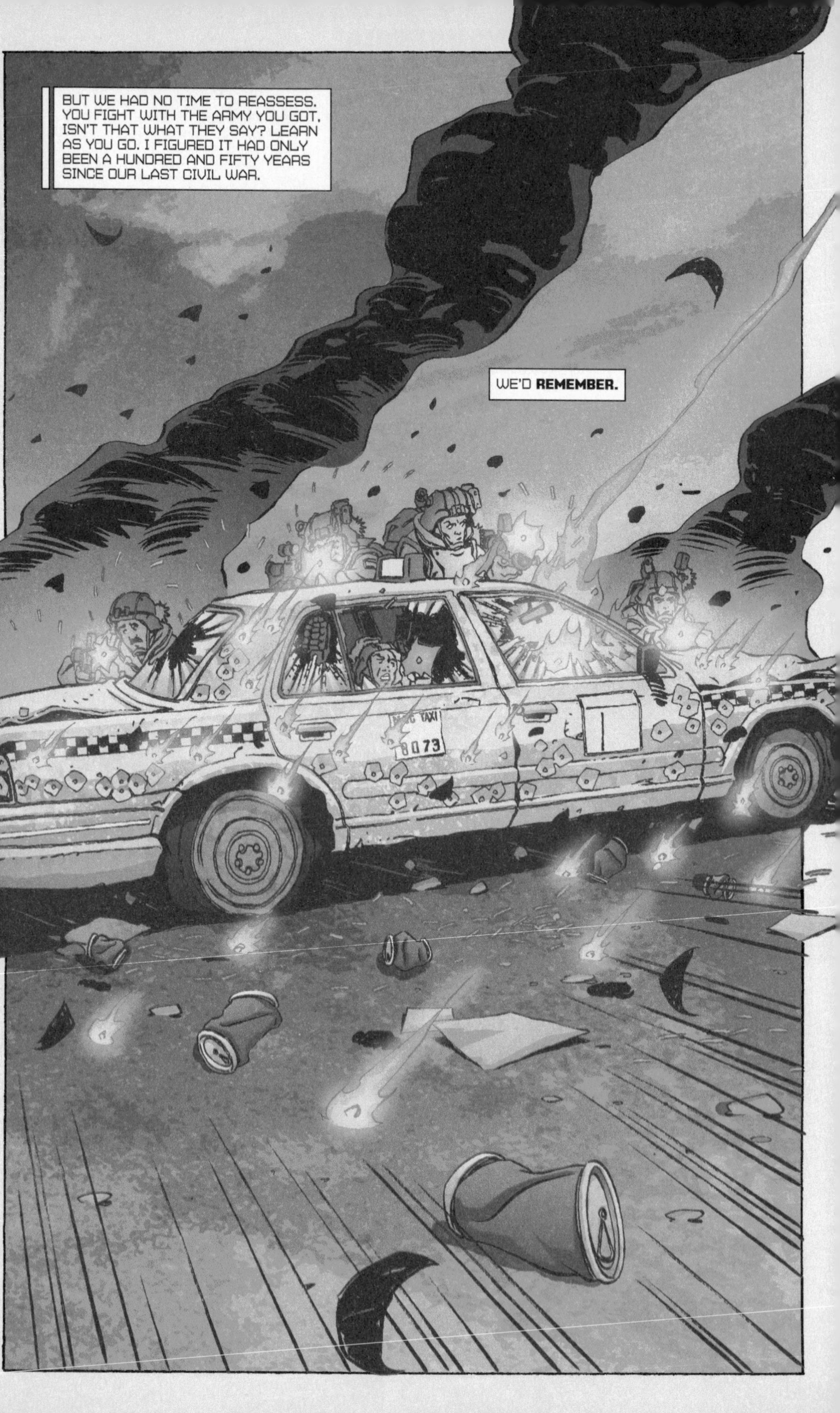
BUT WE HAD NO TIME TO REASSESS. YOU FIGHT WITH THE ARMY YOU GOT, ISN'T THAT WHAT THEY SAY? LEARN AS YOU GO. I FIGURED IT HAD ONLY BEEN A HUNDRED AND FIFTY YEARS SINCE OUR LAST CIVIL WAR.
WE'D **REMEMBER.**

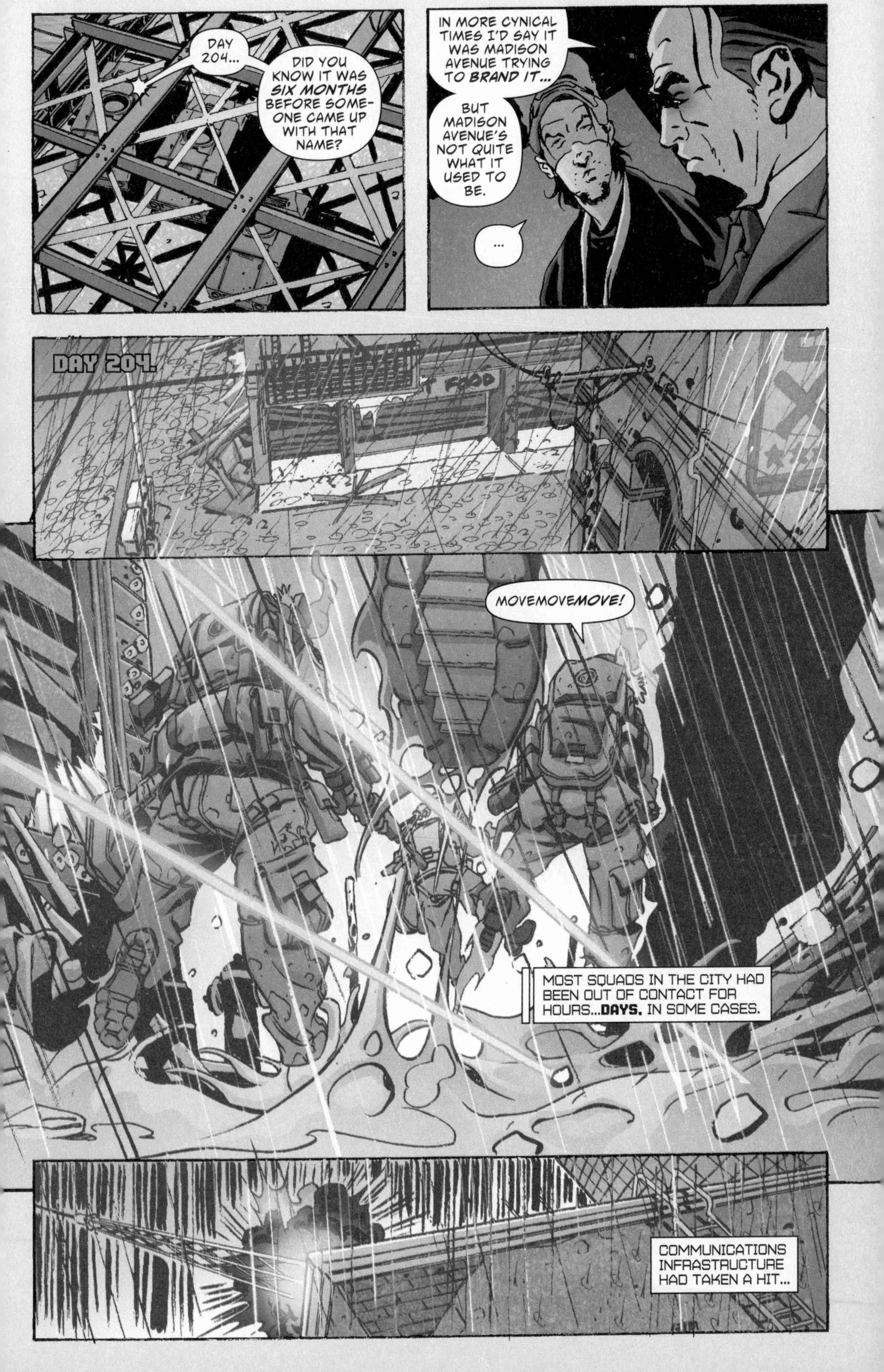
DAY 204...
DID YOU KNOW IT WAS SIX MONTHS BEFORE SOME-ONE CAME UP WITH THAT NAME?
IN MORE CYNICAL TIMES I'D SAY IT WAS MADISON AVENUE TRYING TO BRAND IT...
BUT MADISON AVENUE'S NOT QUITE WHAT IT USED TO BE.
...
DAY 204.
MOVEMOVEMOVE!
MOST SQUADS IN THE CITY HAD BEEN OUT OF CONTACT FOR HOURS...DAYS. IN SOME CASES.
COMMUNICATIONS INFRASTRUCTURE HAD TAKEN A HIT...

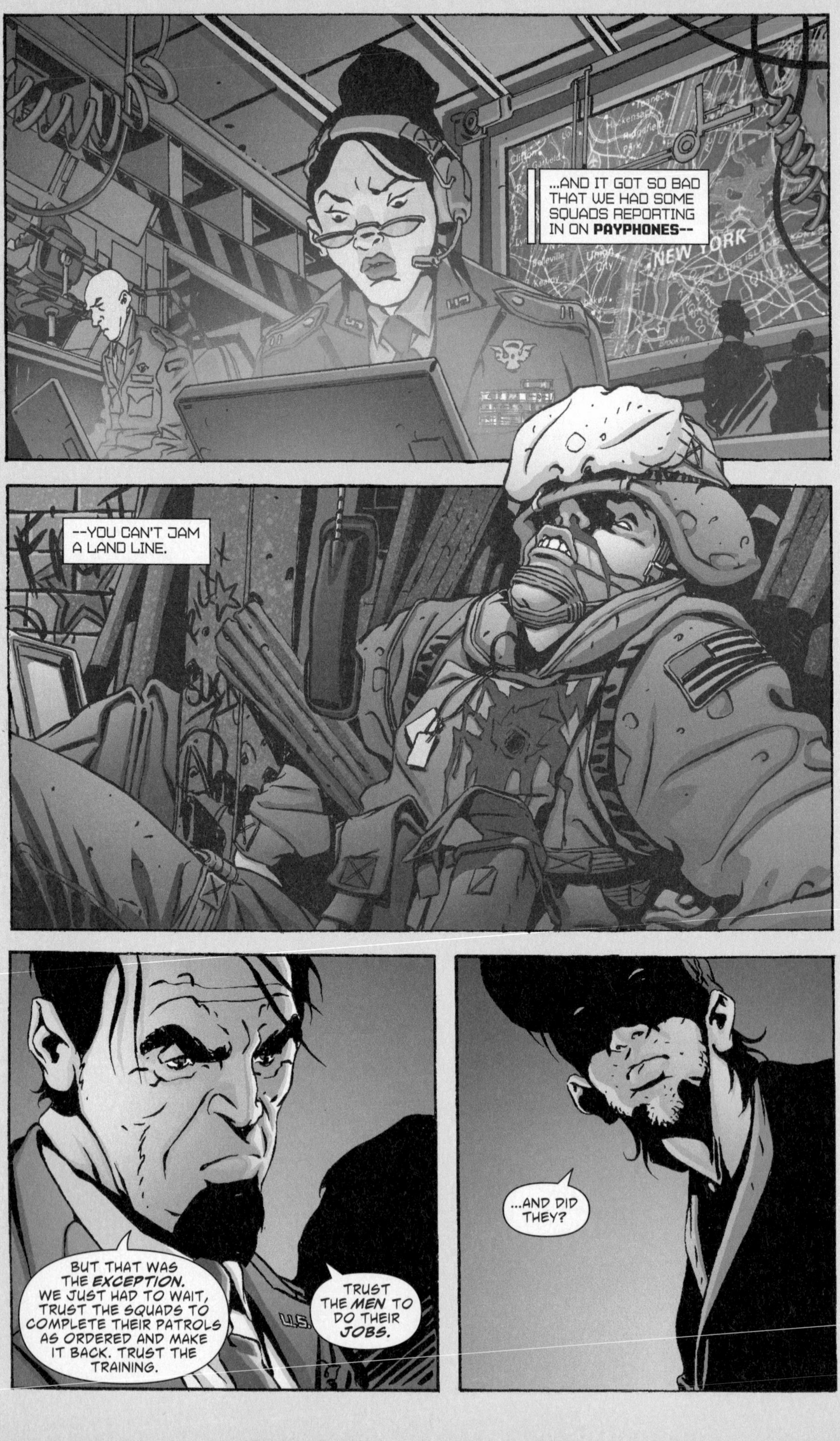

...AND IT GOT SO BAD THAT WE HAD SOME SQUADS REPORTING IN ON **PAYPHONES**--
NEW YORK
--YOU CAN'T JAM A LAND LINE.
BUT THAT WAS THE *EXCEPTION.* WE JUST HAD TO WAIT, TRUST THE SQUADS TO COMPLETE THEIR PATROLS AS ORDERED AND MAKE IT BACK. TRUST THE TRAINING.
TRUST THE *MEN* TO DO THEIR *JOBS.*
U.S.
...AND DID THEY?

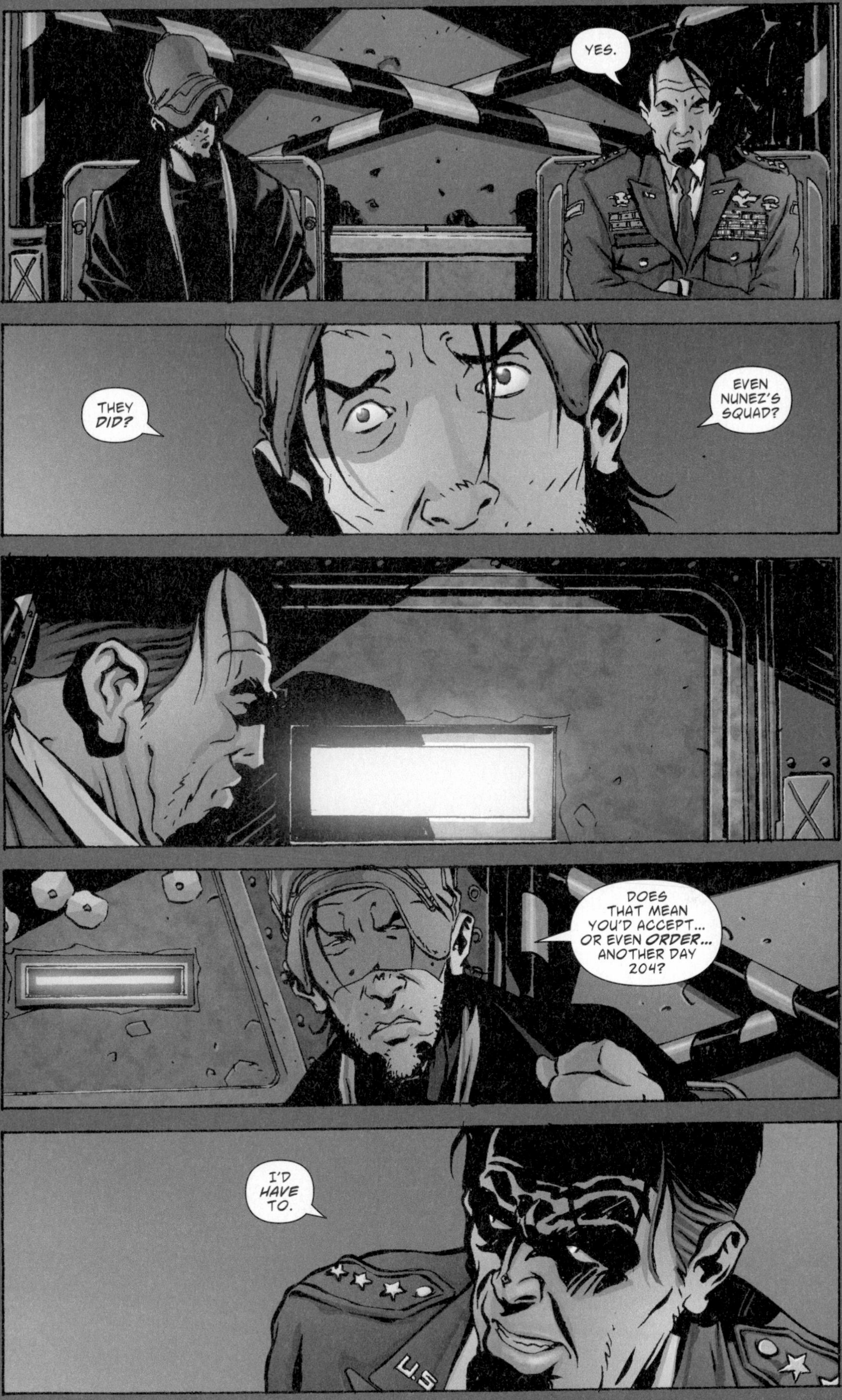
YES.
THEY DID?
EVEN NUNEZ'S SQUAD?
DOES THAT MEAN YOU'D ACCEPT... OR EVEN ORDER... ANOTHER DAY 204?
I'D HAVE TO.
U.S

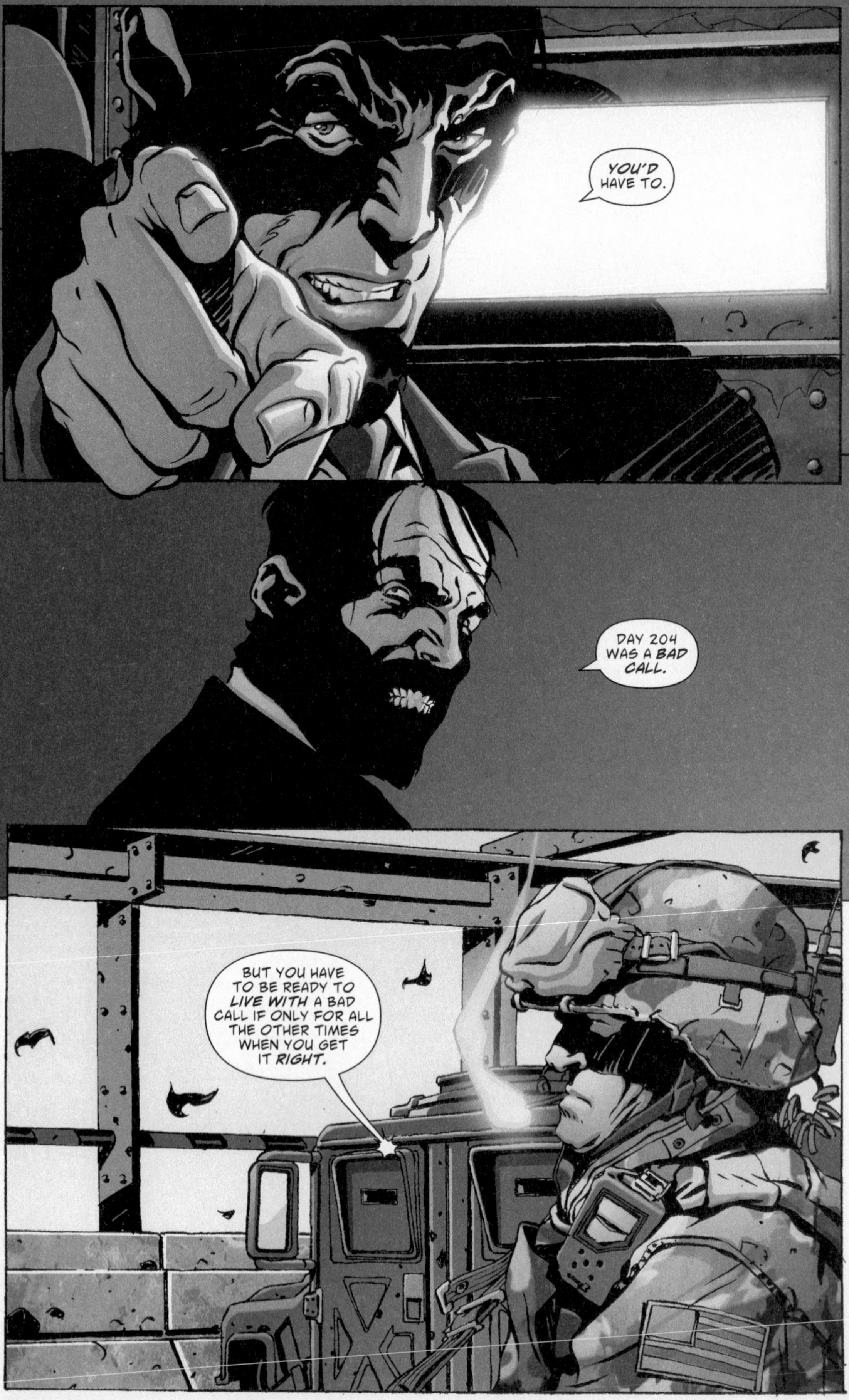
YOU'D HAVE TO.
DAY 204 WAS A BAD CALL.
BUT YOU HAVE TO BE READY TO LIVE WITH A BAD CALL IF ONLY FOR ALL THE OTHER TIMES WHEN YOU GET IT RIGHT.

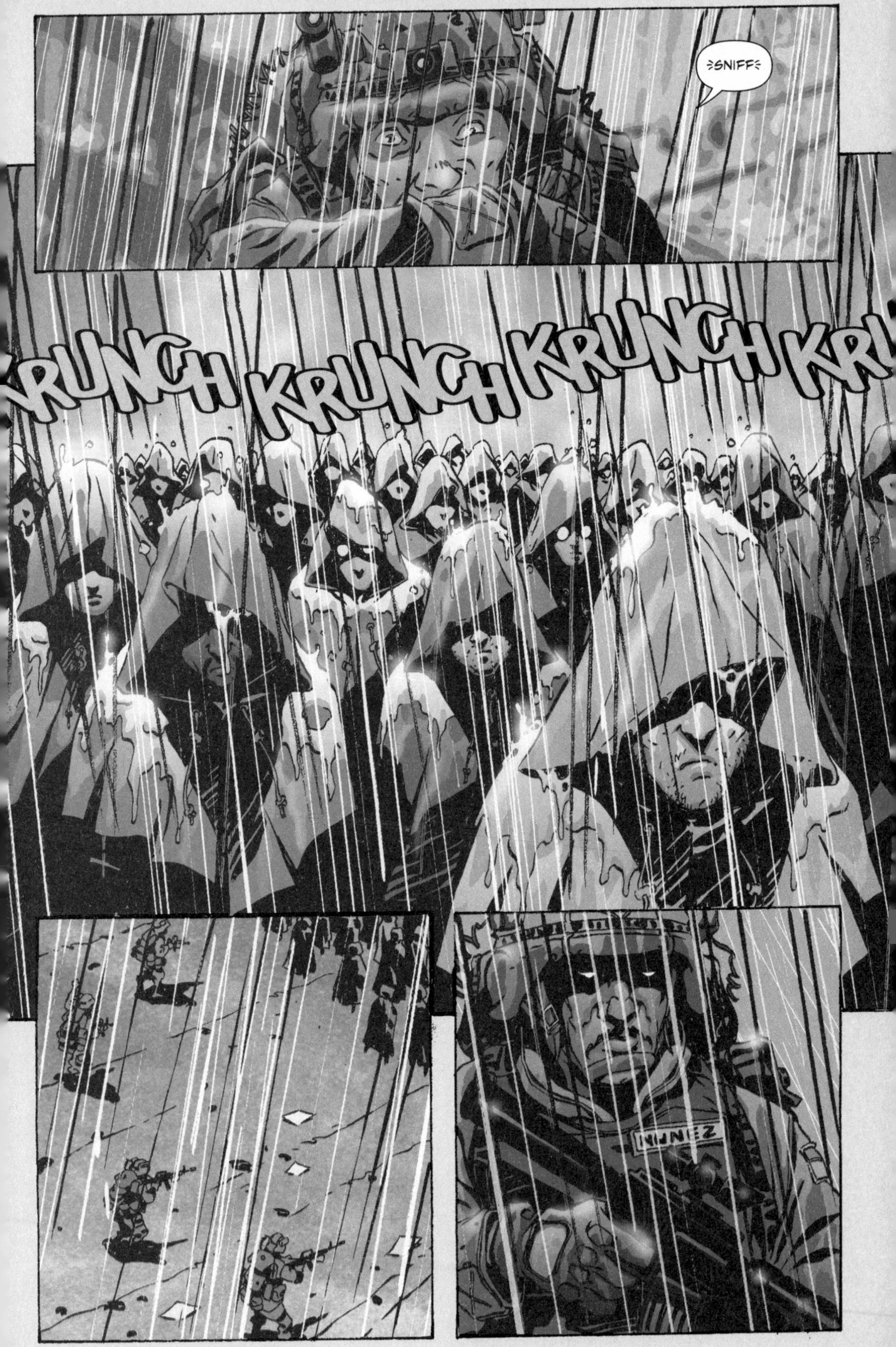
SNIFF
KRUNCH KRUNCH KRUNCH KR
NUNEZ

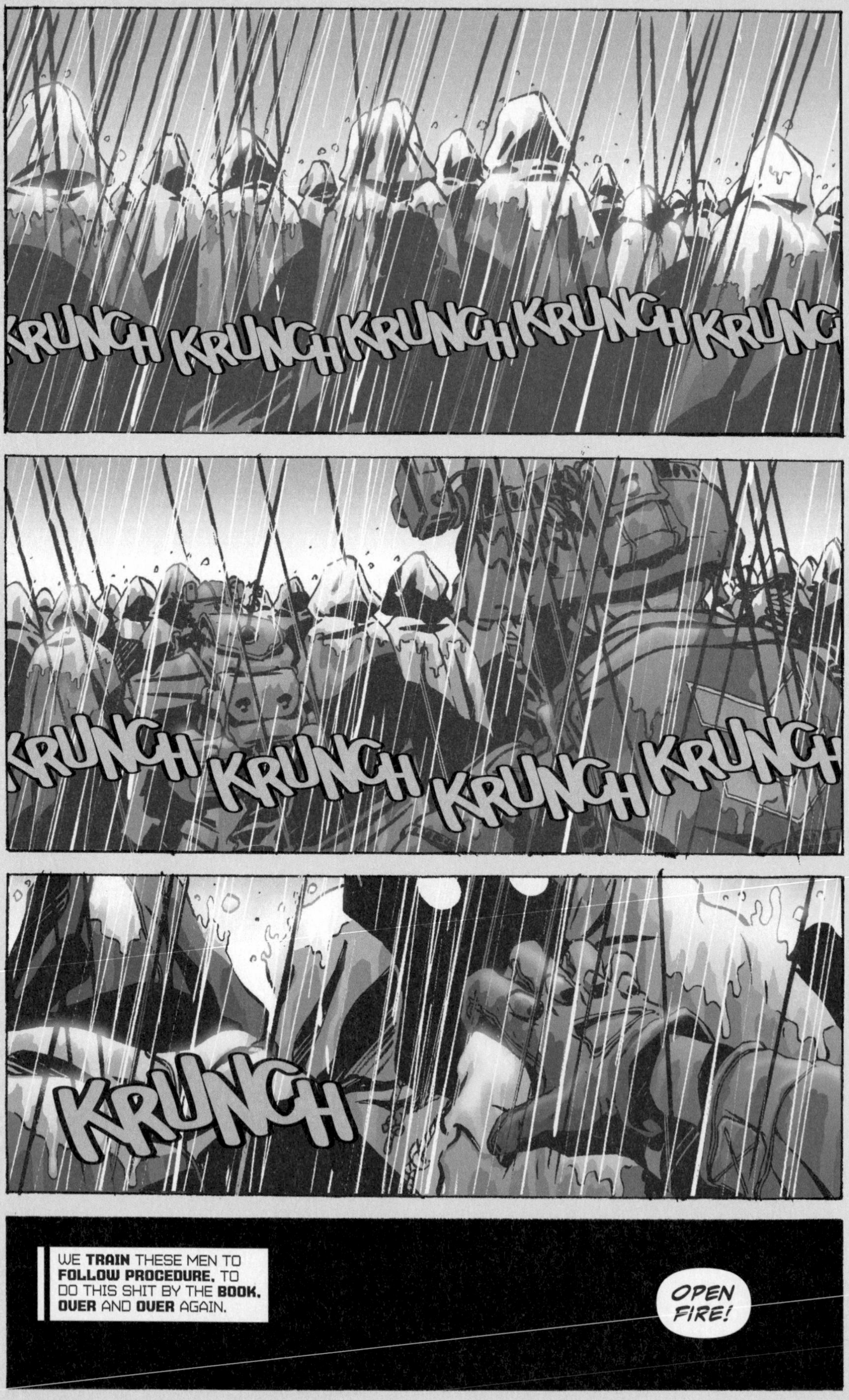
KRUNCH KRUNCH KRUNCH KRUNCH KRUNC
KRUNCH KRUNCH KRUNCH KRUNCH
KRUNCH
WE TRAIN THESE MEN TO FOLLOW PROCEDURE. TO DO THIS SHIT BY THE BOOK. OVER AND OVER AGAIN.
OPEN FIRE!

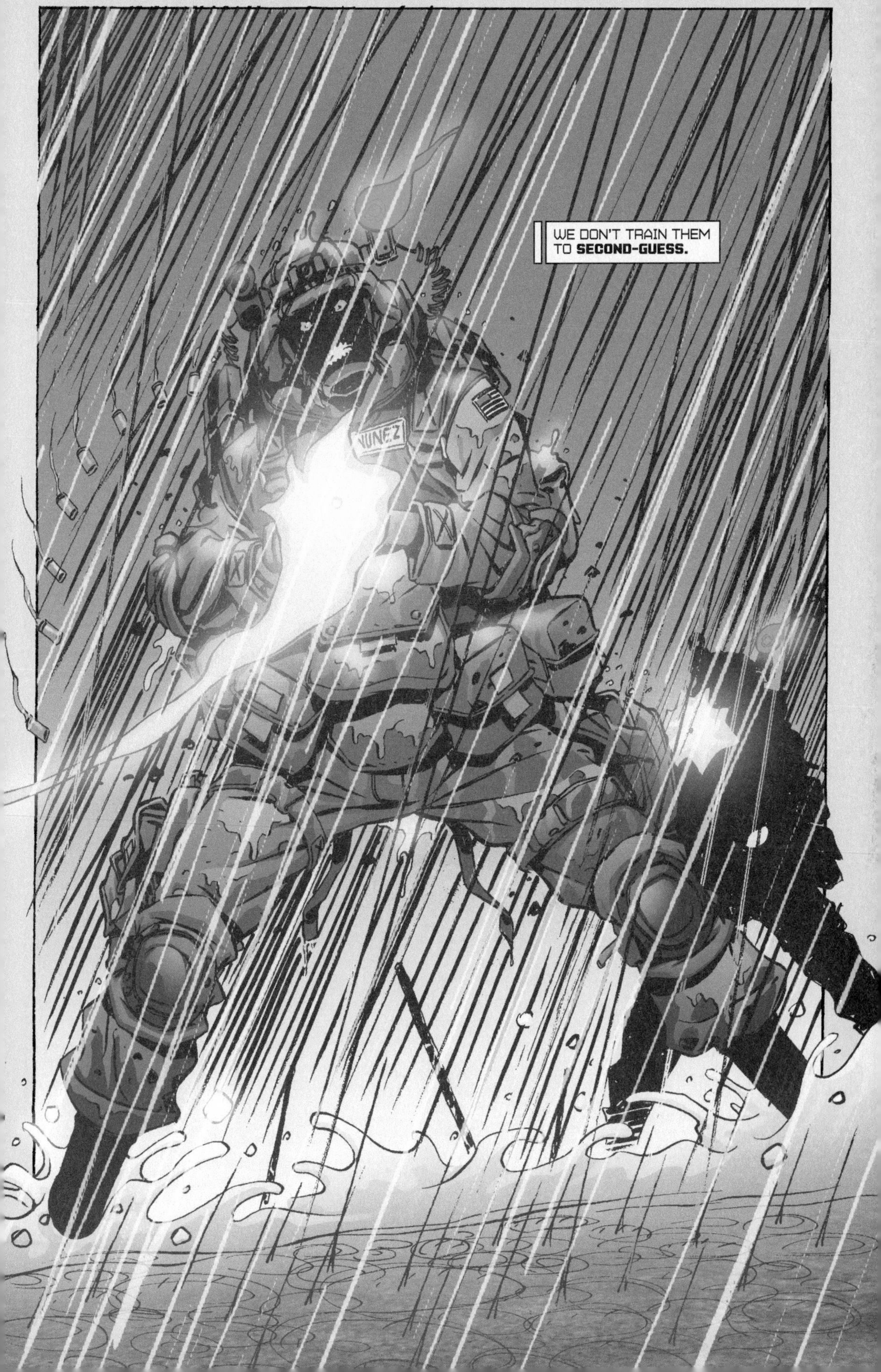
WE DON'T TRAIN THEM TO **SECOND-GUESS.**
NUNEZ

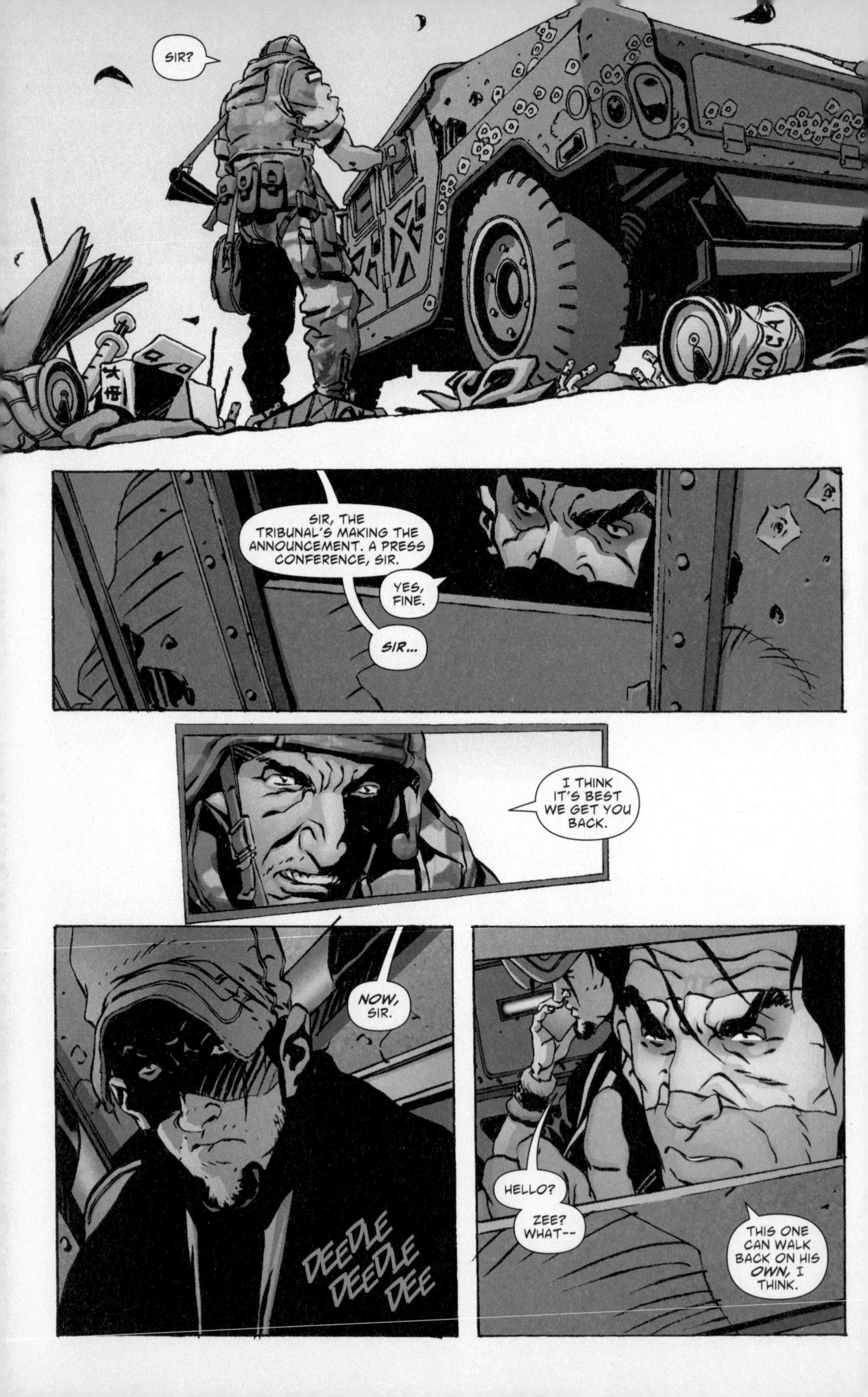
SIR?
SIR, THE TRIBUNAL'S MAKING THE ANNOUNCEMENT. A PRESS CONFERENCE, SIR.
YES, FINE.
SIR...
I THINK IT'S BEST WE GET YOU BACK.
NOW, SIR.
DEEDLE DEEDLE DEE
HELLO?
ZEE? WHAT--
THIS ONE CAN WALK BACK ON HIS OWN, I THINK.

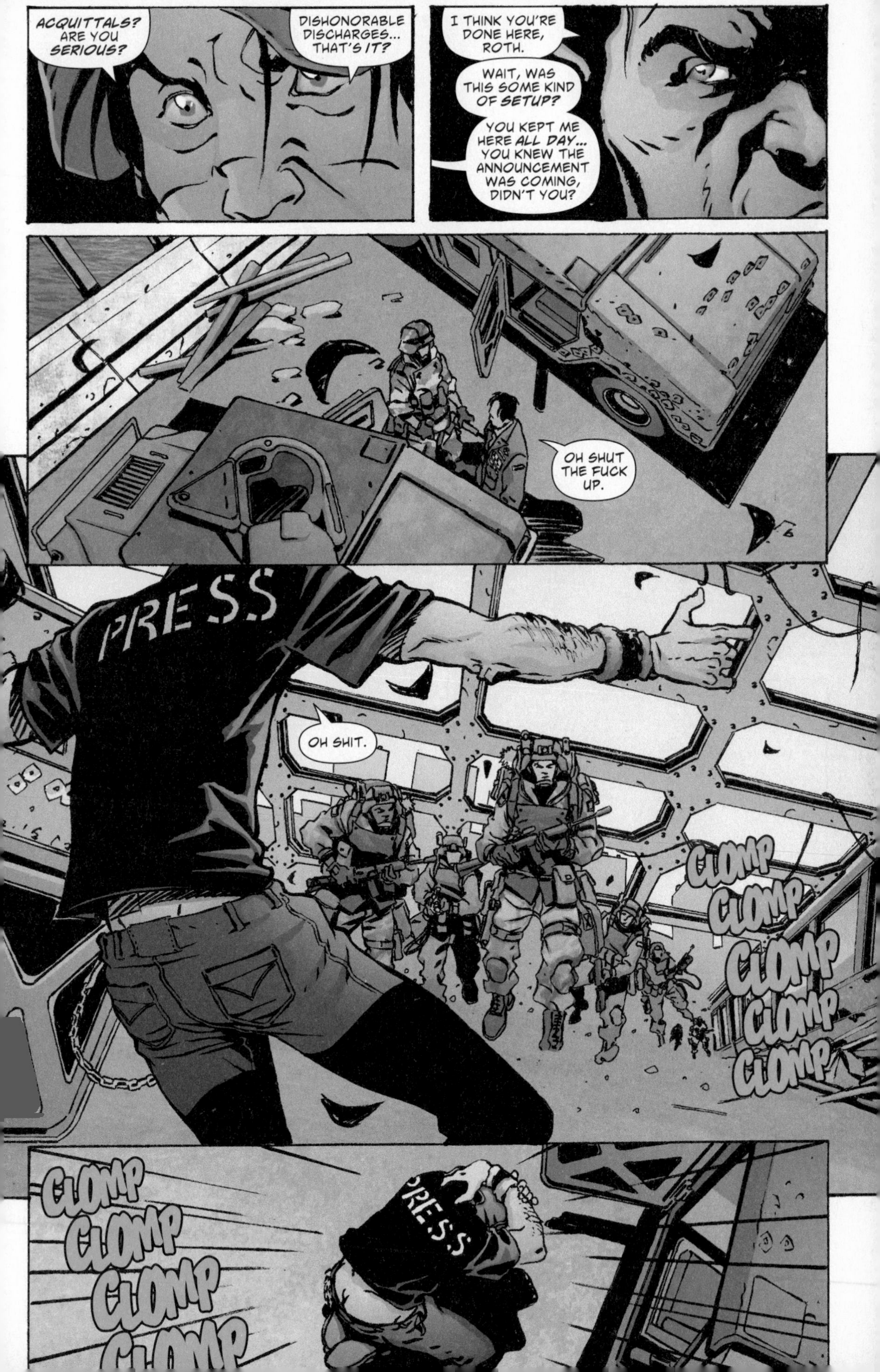
ACQUITTALS? ARE YOU SERIOUS?
DISHONORABLE DISCHARGES... THAT'S IT?
I THINK YOU'RE DONE HERE, ROTH.
WAIT, WAS THIS SOME KIND OF SETUP?
YOU KEPT ME HERE ALL DAY... YOU KNEW THE ANNOUNCEMENT WAS COMING, DIDN'T YOU?
OH SHUT THE FUCK UP.
PRESS
OH SHIT.
CLOMP CLOMP CLOMP CLOMP CLOMP
CLOMP CLOMP CLOMP
PRESS

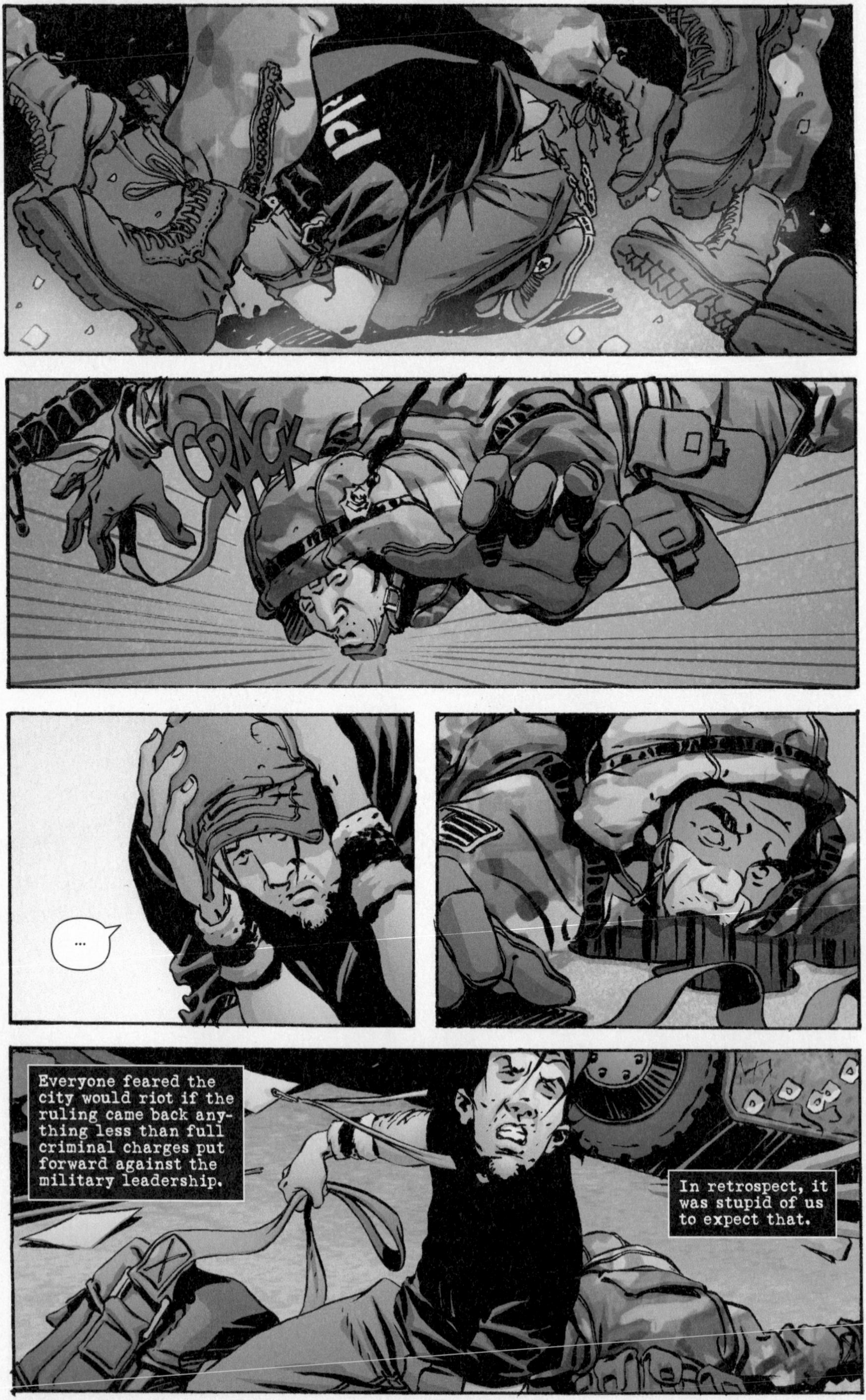
CRACK
...
Everyone feared the city would riot if the ruling came back anything less than full criminal charges put forward against the military leadership.
In retrospect, it was stupid of us to expect that.

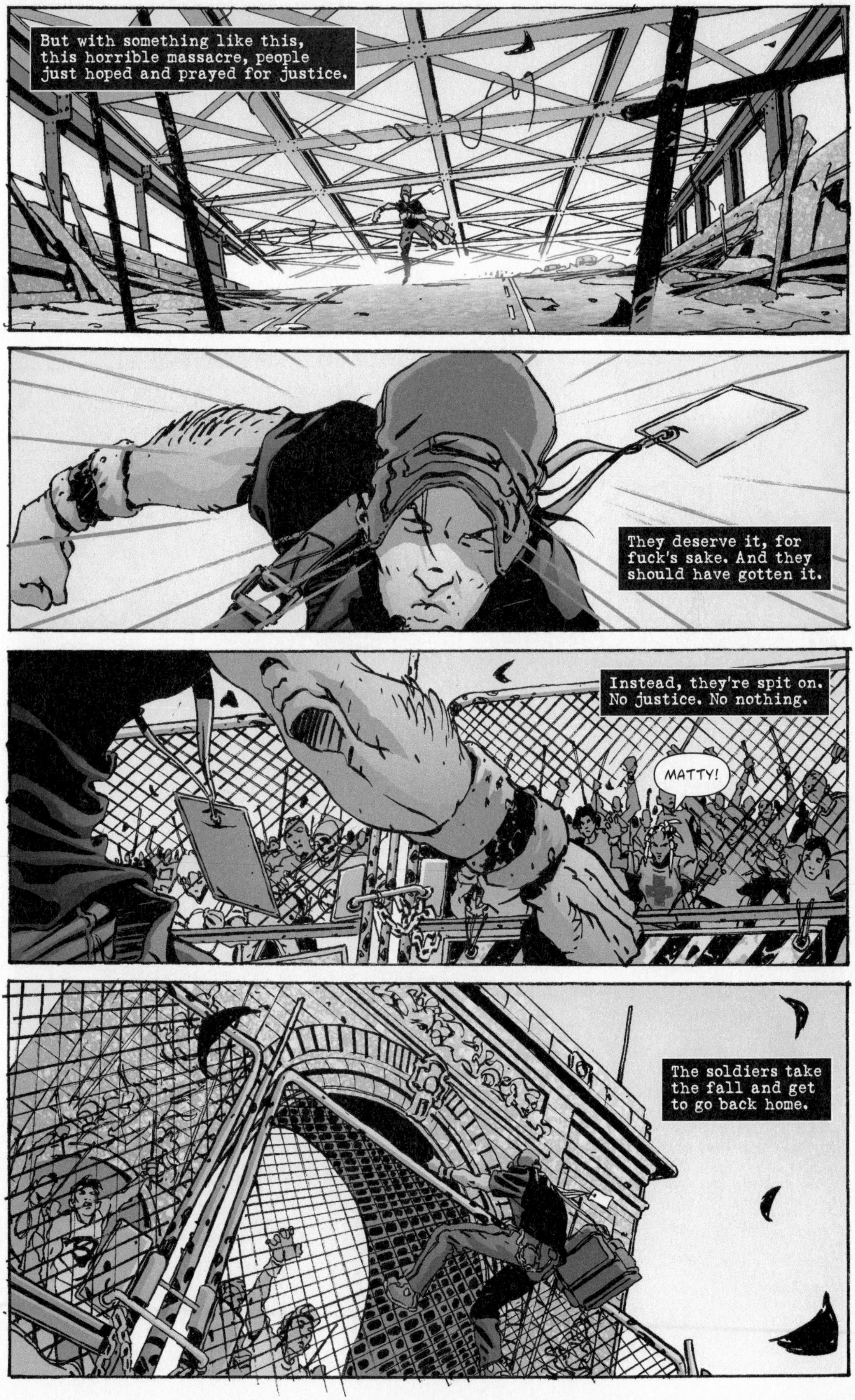
But with something like this, this horrible massacre, people just hoped and prayed for justice.
They deserve it, for fuck's sake. And they should have gotten it.
Instead, they're spit on. No justice. No nothing.
MATTY!
The soldiers take the fall and get to go back home.

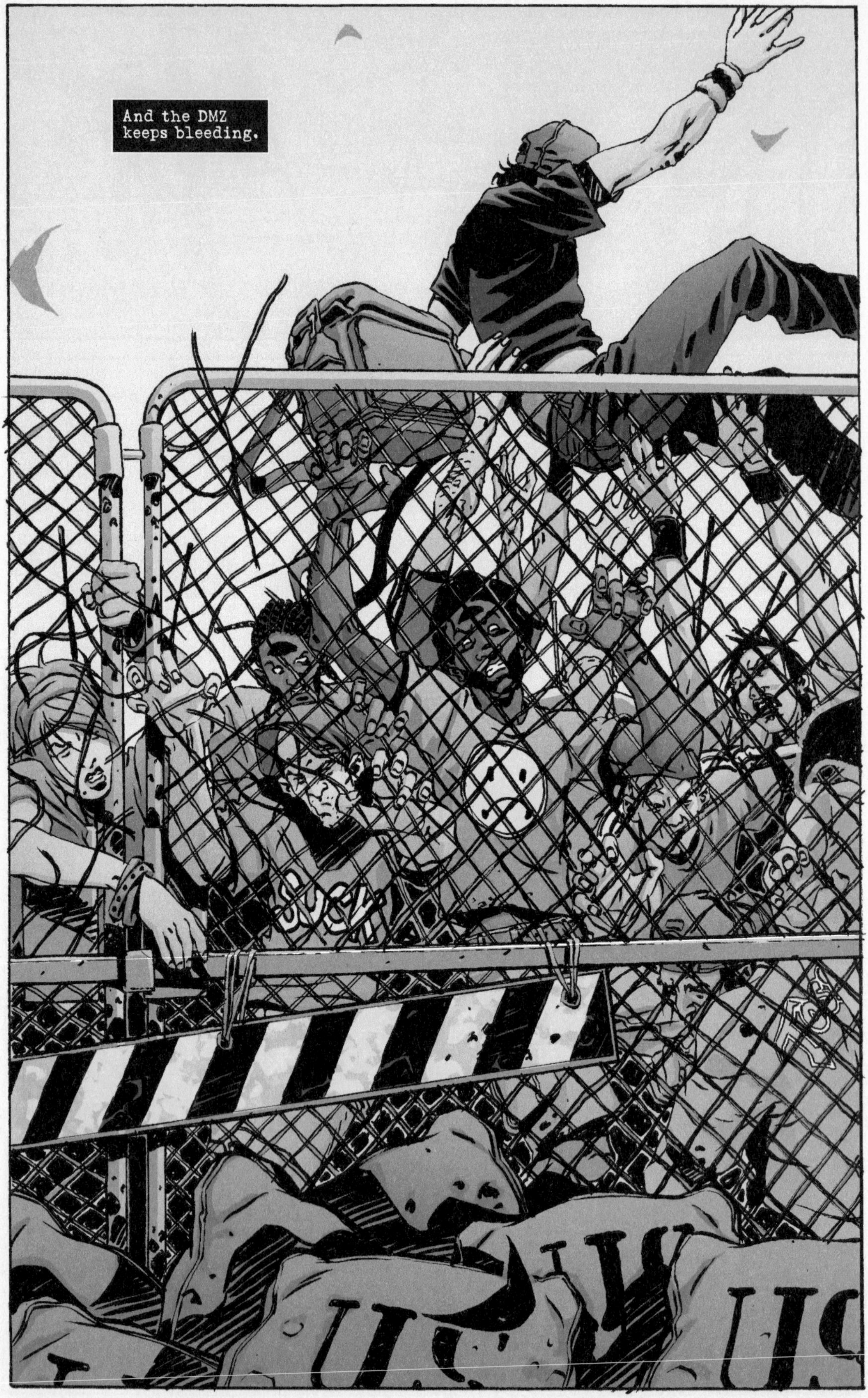
And the DMZ keeps bleeding.

DM Z

FRIENDLY FIRE

PART FIVE OF FIVE

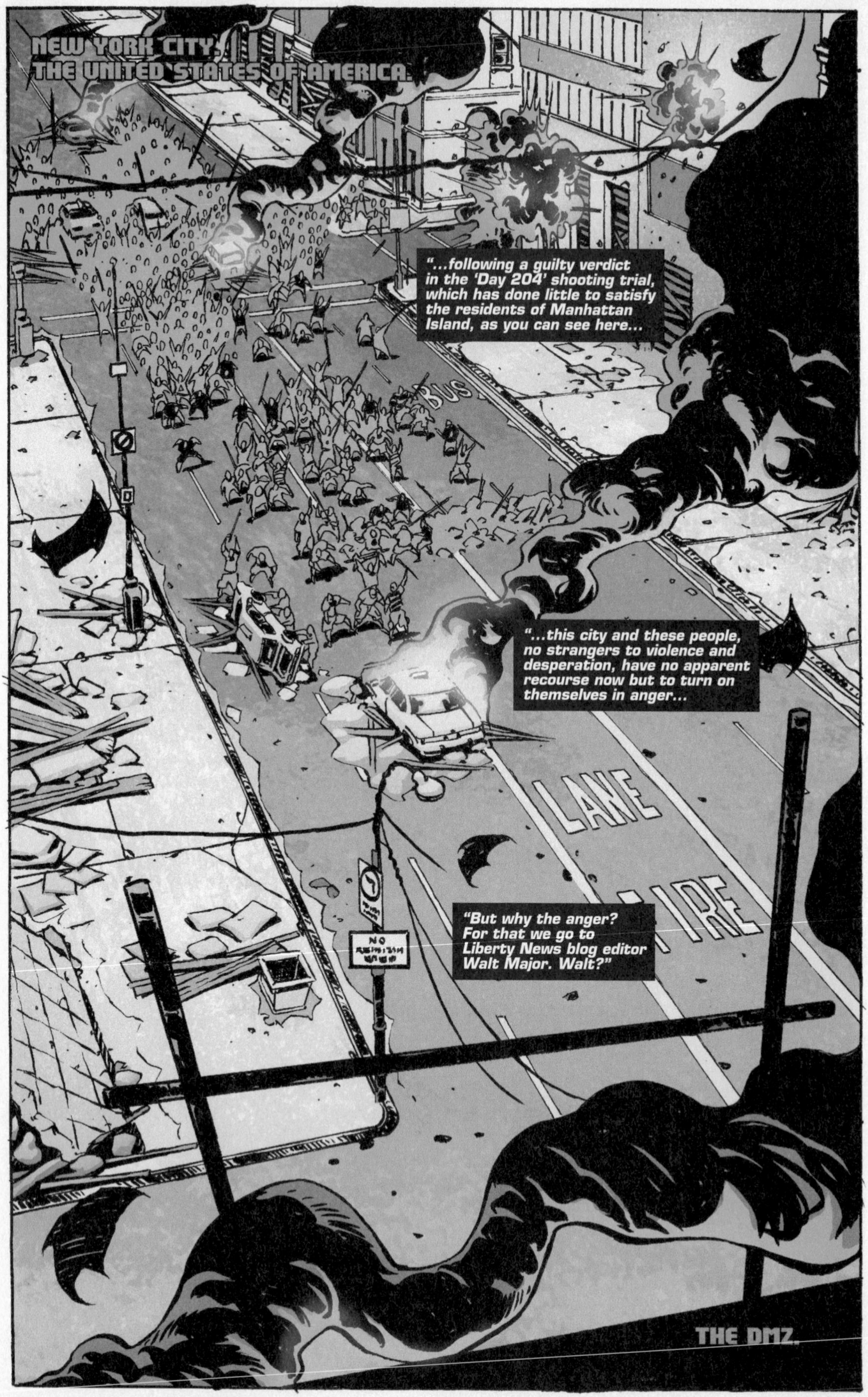
NEW YORK CITY.
THE UNITED STATES OF AMERICA.
"...following a guilty verdict in the 'Day 204' shooting trial, which has done little to satisfy the residents of Manhattan Island, as you can see here...
"...this city and these people, no strangers to violence and desperation, have no apparent recourse now but to turn on themselves in anger...
"But why the anger? For that we go to Liberty News blog editor Walt Major. Walt?"
BUS
LANE
THE DMZ.

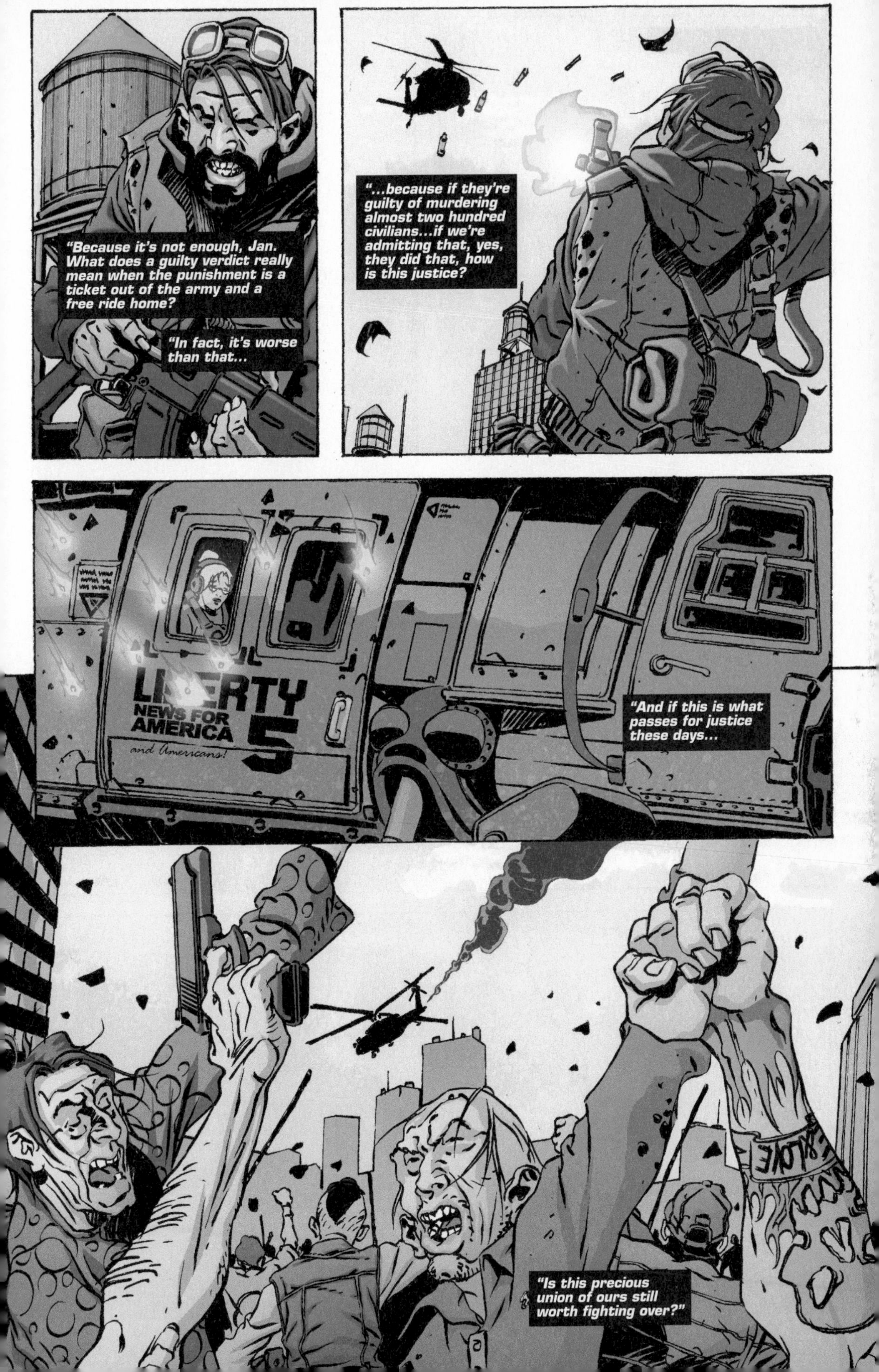
"Because it's not enough, Jan. What does a guilty verdict really mean when the punishment is a ticket out of the army and a free ride home?
"In fact, it's worse than that...
"...because if they're guilty of murdering almost two hundred civilians...if we're admitting that, yes, they did that, how is this justice?
LIBERTY NEWS FOR AMERICA 5
and Americans!
"And if this is what passes for justice these days...
"Is this precious union of ours still worth fighting over?"

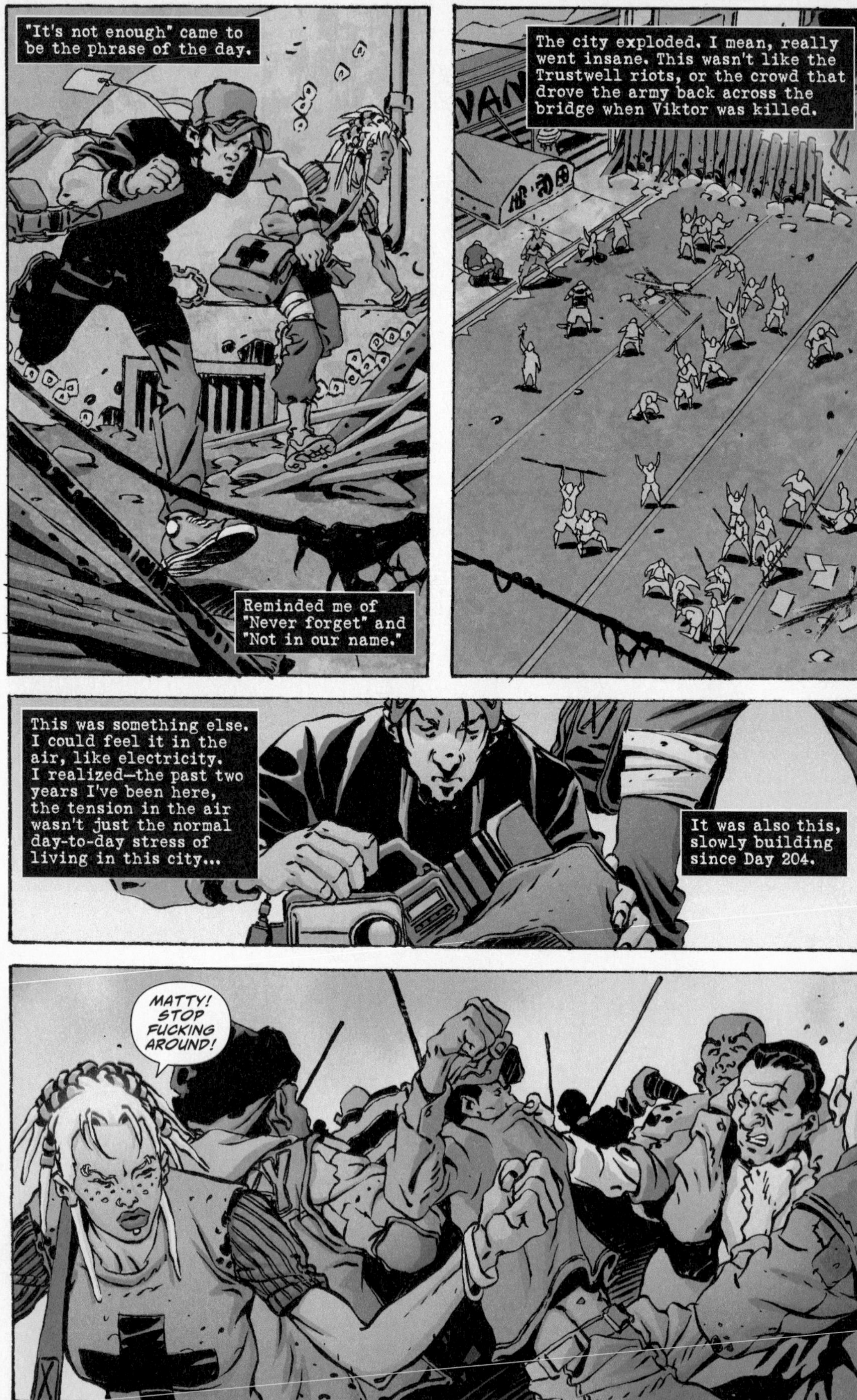
"It's not enough" came to be the phrase of the day.
Reminded me of "Never forget" and "Not in our name."
The city exploded. I mean, really went insane. This wasn't like the Trustwell riots, or the crowd that drove the army back across the bridge when Viktor was killed.
This was something else. I could feel it in the air, like electricity. I realized—the past two years I've been here, the tension in the air wasn't just the normal day-to-day stress of living in this city...
It was also this, slowly building since Day 204.
MATTY! STOP FUCKING AROUND!

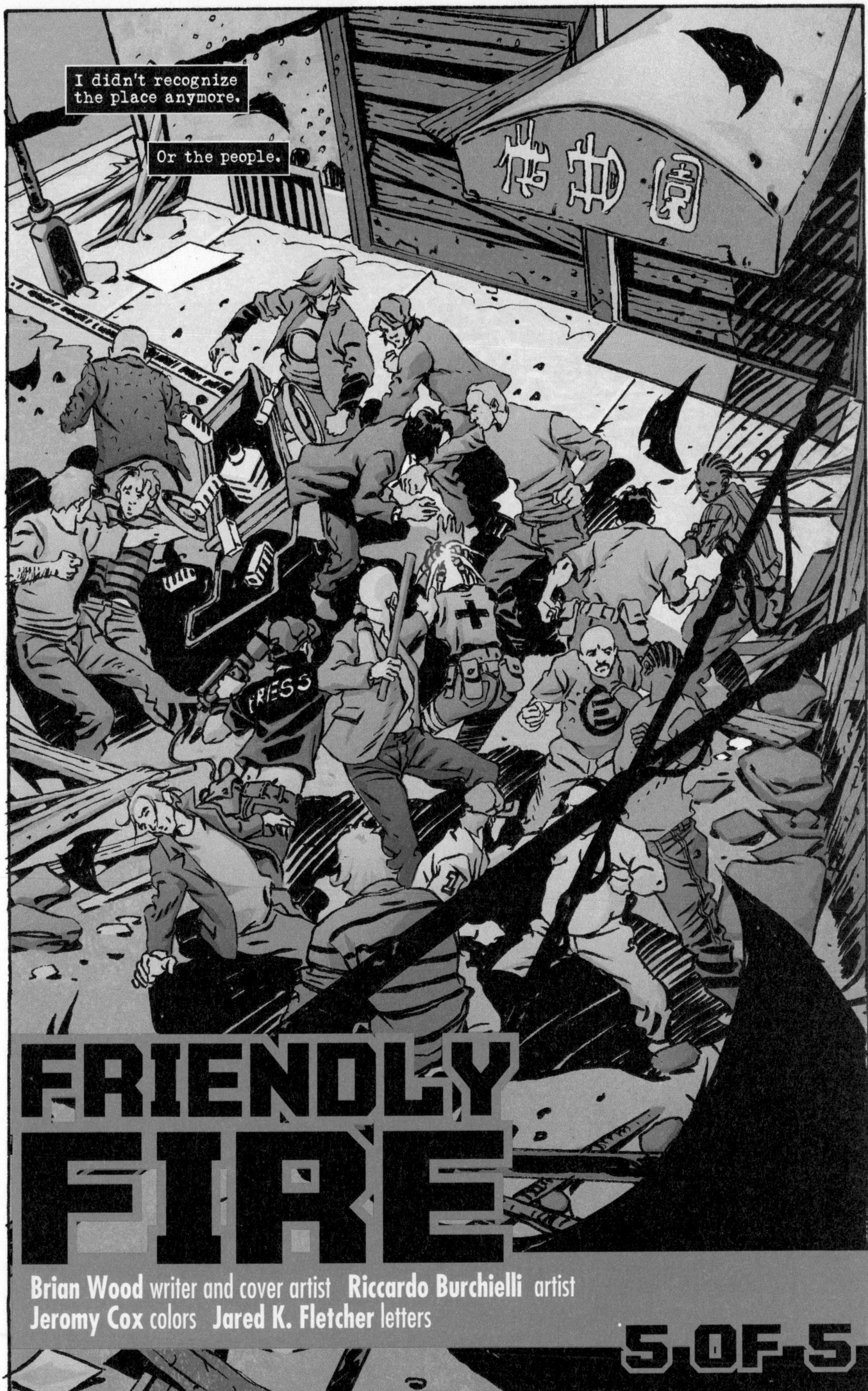
I didn't recognize the place anymore.
Or the people.
PRESS
FRIENDLY FIRE
Brian Wood writer and cover artist Riccardo Burchielli artist
Jeromy Cox colors Jared K. Fletcher letters
5 OF 5

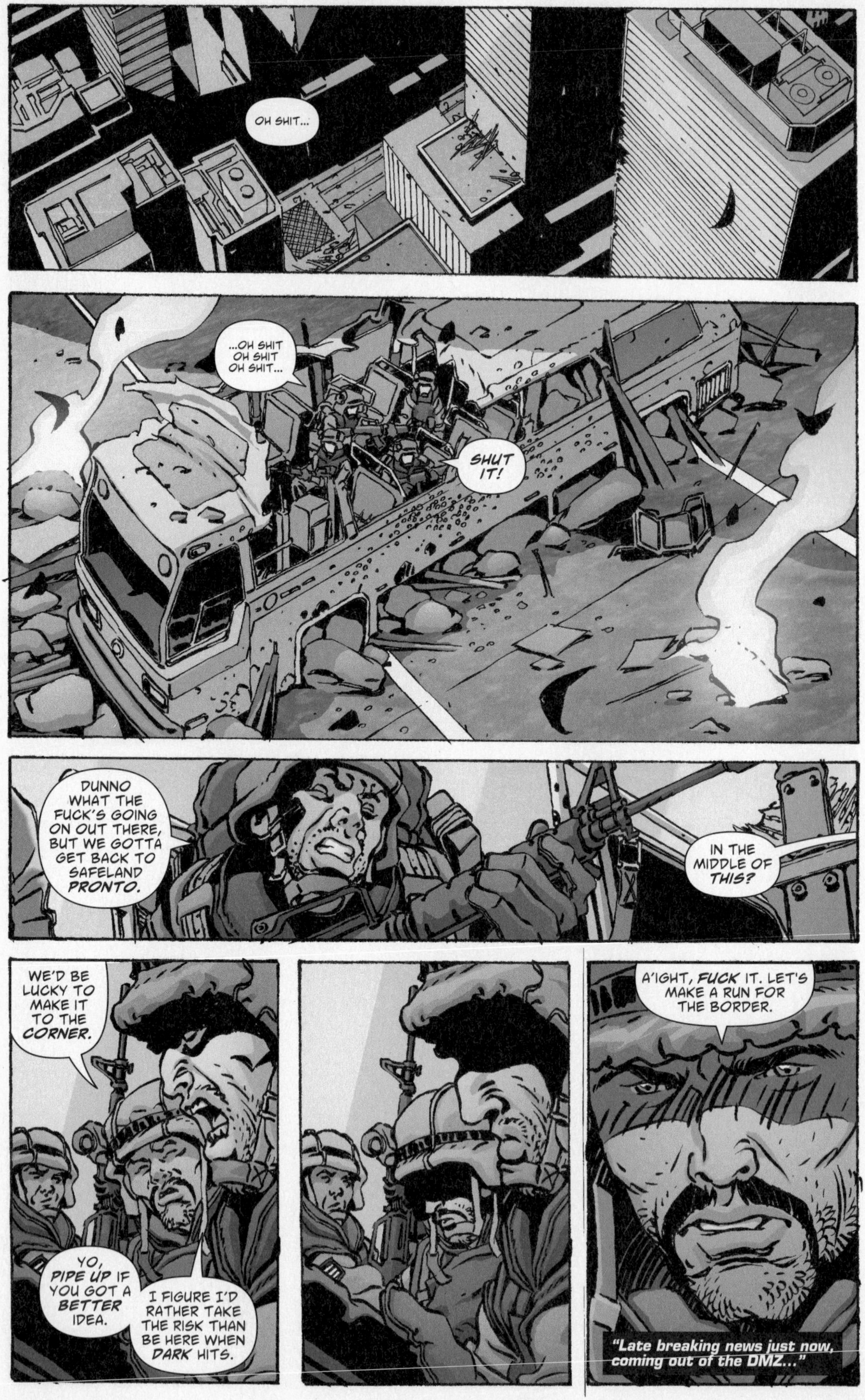
OH SHIT...
...OH SHIT OH SHIT OH SHIT...
SHUT IT!
DUNNO WHAT THE FUCK'S GOING ON OUT THERE, BUT WE GOTTA GET BACK TO SAFELAND PRONTO.
IN THE MIDDLE OF THIS?
WE'D BE LUCKY TO MAKE IT TO THE CORNER.
YO, PIPE UP IF YOU GOT A BETTER IDEA.
I FIGURE I'D RATHER TAKE THE RISK THAN BE HERE WHEN DARK HITS.
A'IGHT, FUCK IT. LET'S MAKE A RUN FOR THE BORDER.
"Late breaking news just now, coming out of the DMZ..."

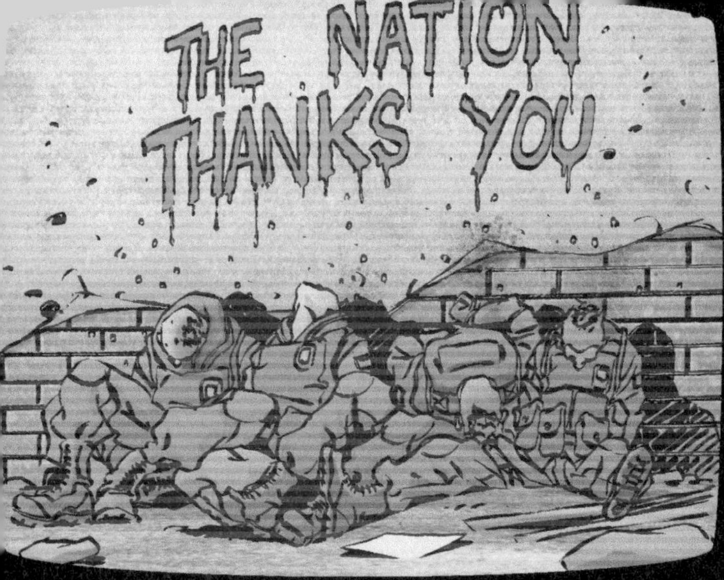
THE NATION THANKS YOU

"...five U.S.soldiers seen here, apparently the victims of torture and assassination at the hands of what experts claim is the 'Nation of Fearghus,' a violent hate-group known to operate within the city of Manhattan.

"These still images were emailed into Liberty News moments ago, and the identity of these heroic soldiers is being withheld pending identification.

"The riots following the 'Day 204' verdict enter their fifth hour, and with dusk approaching and nighttime to follow soon after, the death toll associated with this latest unrest threatens to skyrocket.

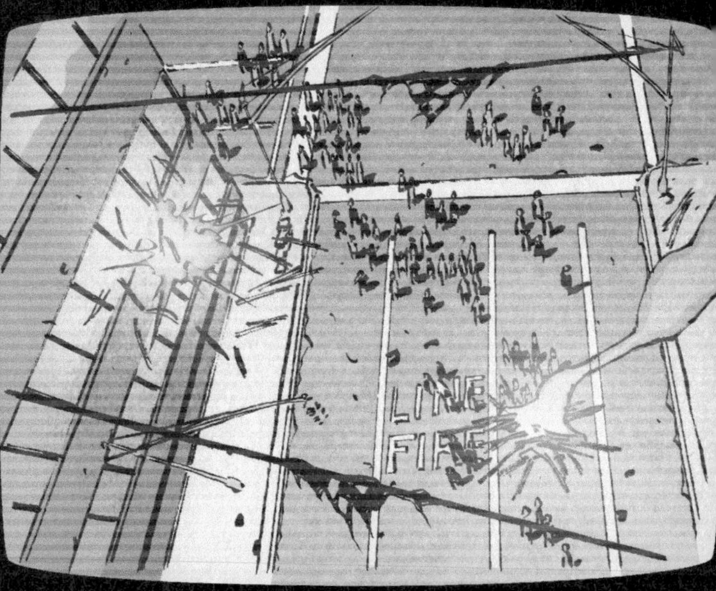

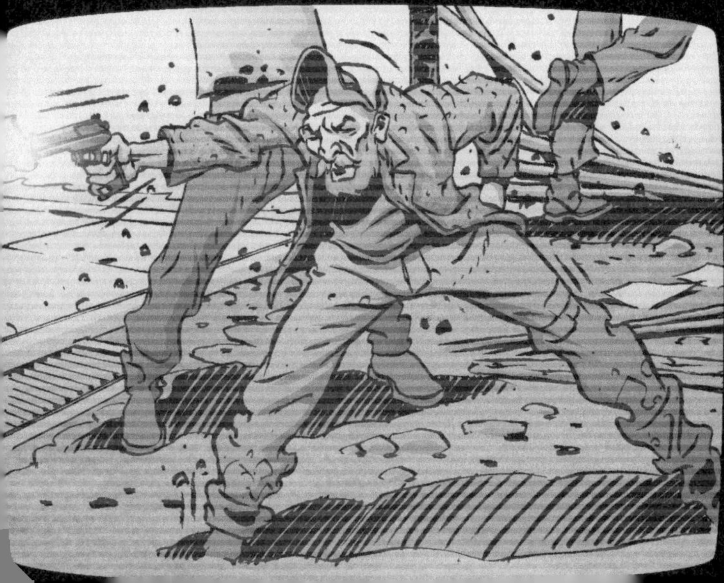

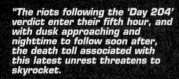

"The United States military remains helpless to intervene, and the various militant factions within the city show no desire to police themselves.

"A tragic ending to a tragic story."

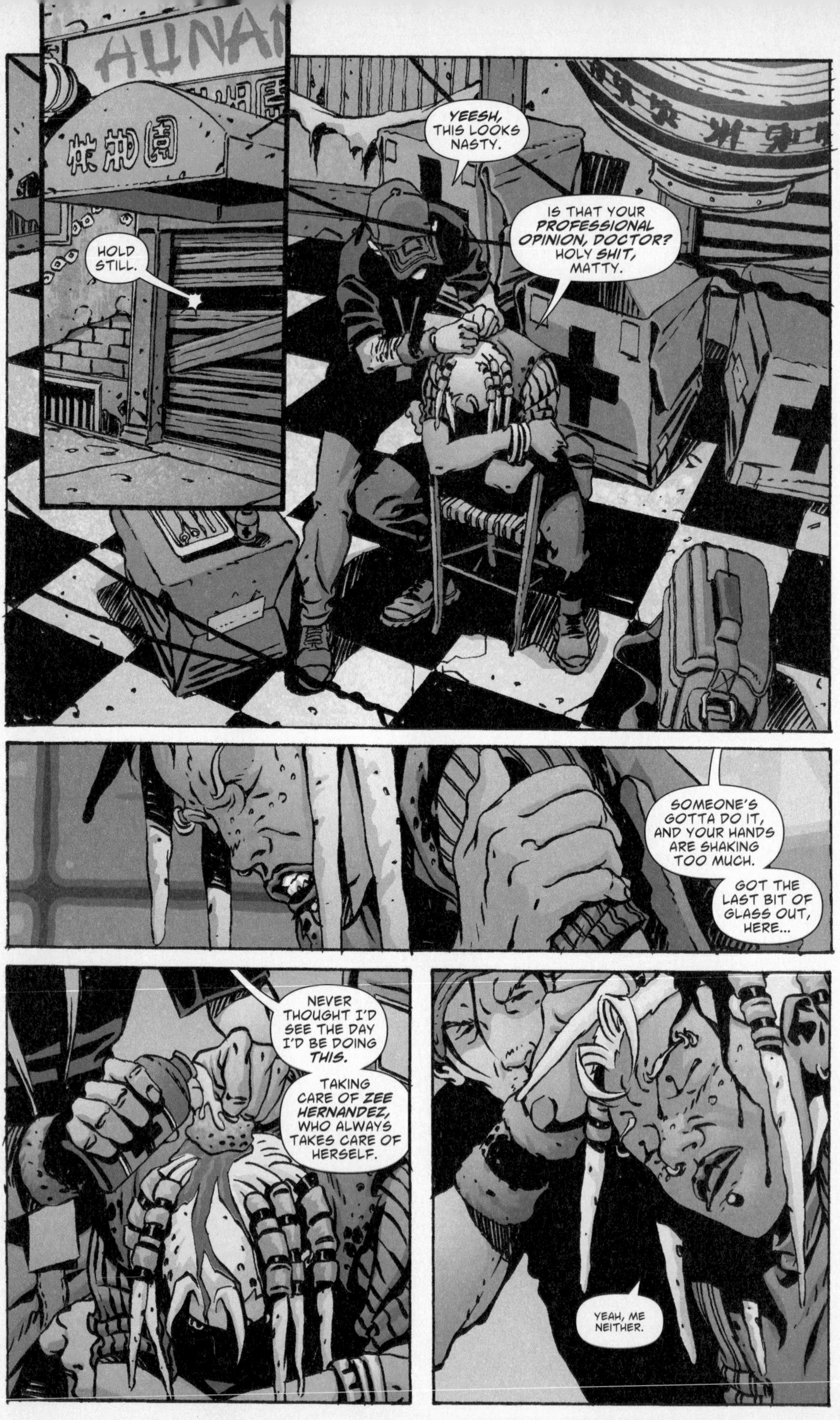
HOLD STILL.
YEESH, THIS LOOKS NASTY.
IS THAT YOUR PROFESSIONAL OPINION, DOCTOR? HOLY SHIT, MATTY.
SOMEONE'S GOTTA DO IT, AND YOUR HANDS ARE SHAKING TOO MUCH.
GOT THE LAST BIT OF GLASS OUT, HERE...
NEVER THOUGHT I'D SEE THE DAY I'D BE DOING THIS.
TAKING CARE OF ZEE HERNANDEZ, WHO ALWAYS TAKES CARE OF HERSELF.
YEAH, ME NEITHER.

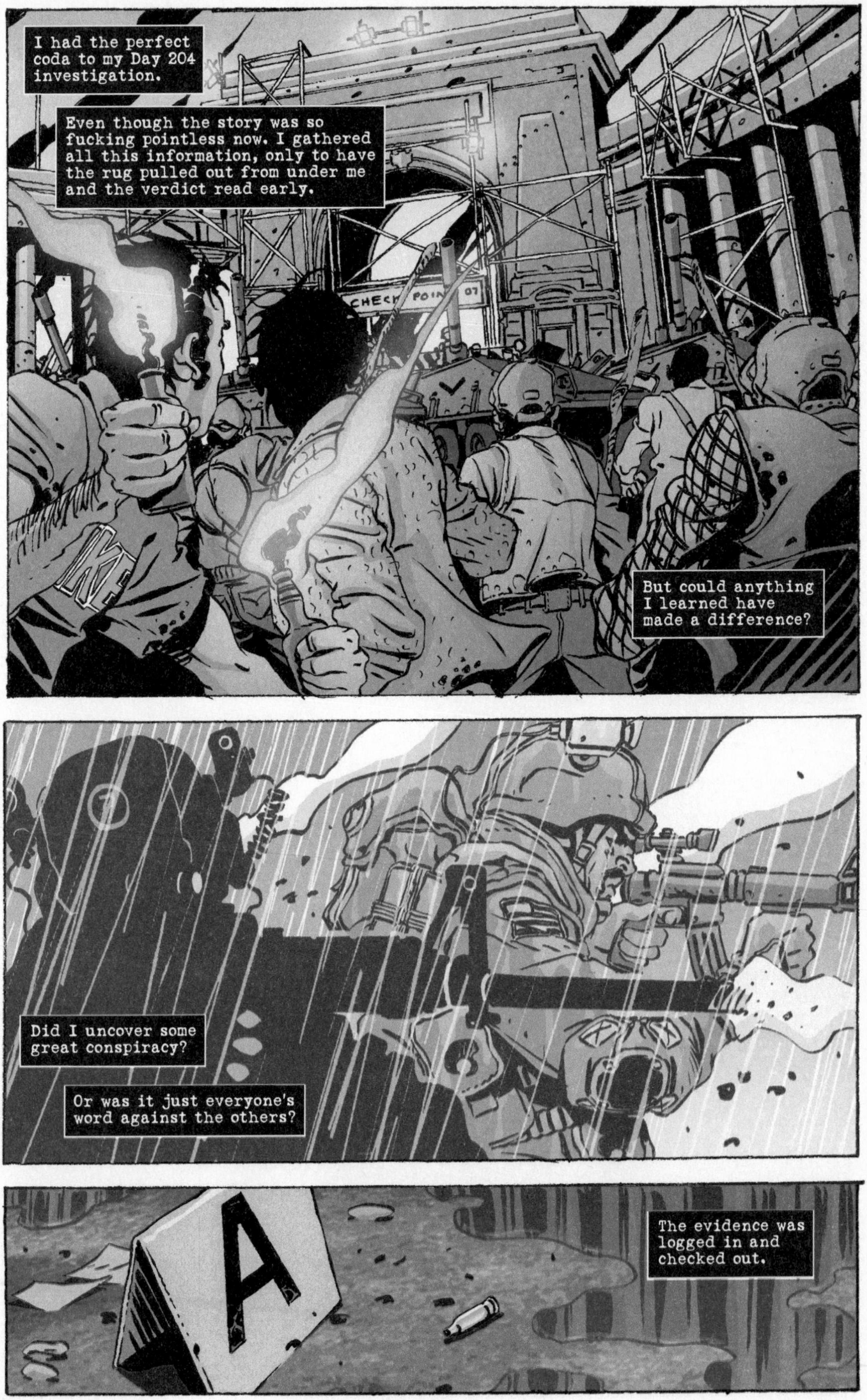
I had the perfect coda to my Day 204 investigation.
Even though the story was so fucking pointless now. I gathered all this information, only to have the rug pulled out from under me and the verdict read early.
But could anything I learned have made a difference?
Did I uncover some great conspiracy?
Or was it just everyone's word against the others?
The evidence was logged in and checked out.

Stevens gave compelling testimony, of Nunez's ordering his squad to fire too soon, of planting a weapon, and of minimizing the evidence by having him, Stevens, collect as many shell casings as he could before forensics arrived.

Sergeant Nunez's story is different, but also compelling, about being confronted and outnumbered by an unknown mob, a weapon being pulled on his team, and the righteous order to open fire.

Stevens, a private from the midwest with multiple convictions for possession, substance abuse, and theft on his record.

Nunez, a career soldier with more decorations and awards than I care to recall right now, who has risked his life hundreds of times in service of his country.

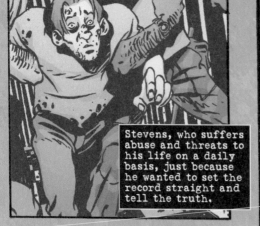

Stevens, who suffers abuse and threats to his life on a daily basis, just because he wanted to set the record straight and tell the truth.

Nunez, who's racked up an impressive body-count over the years.

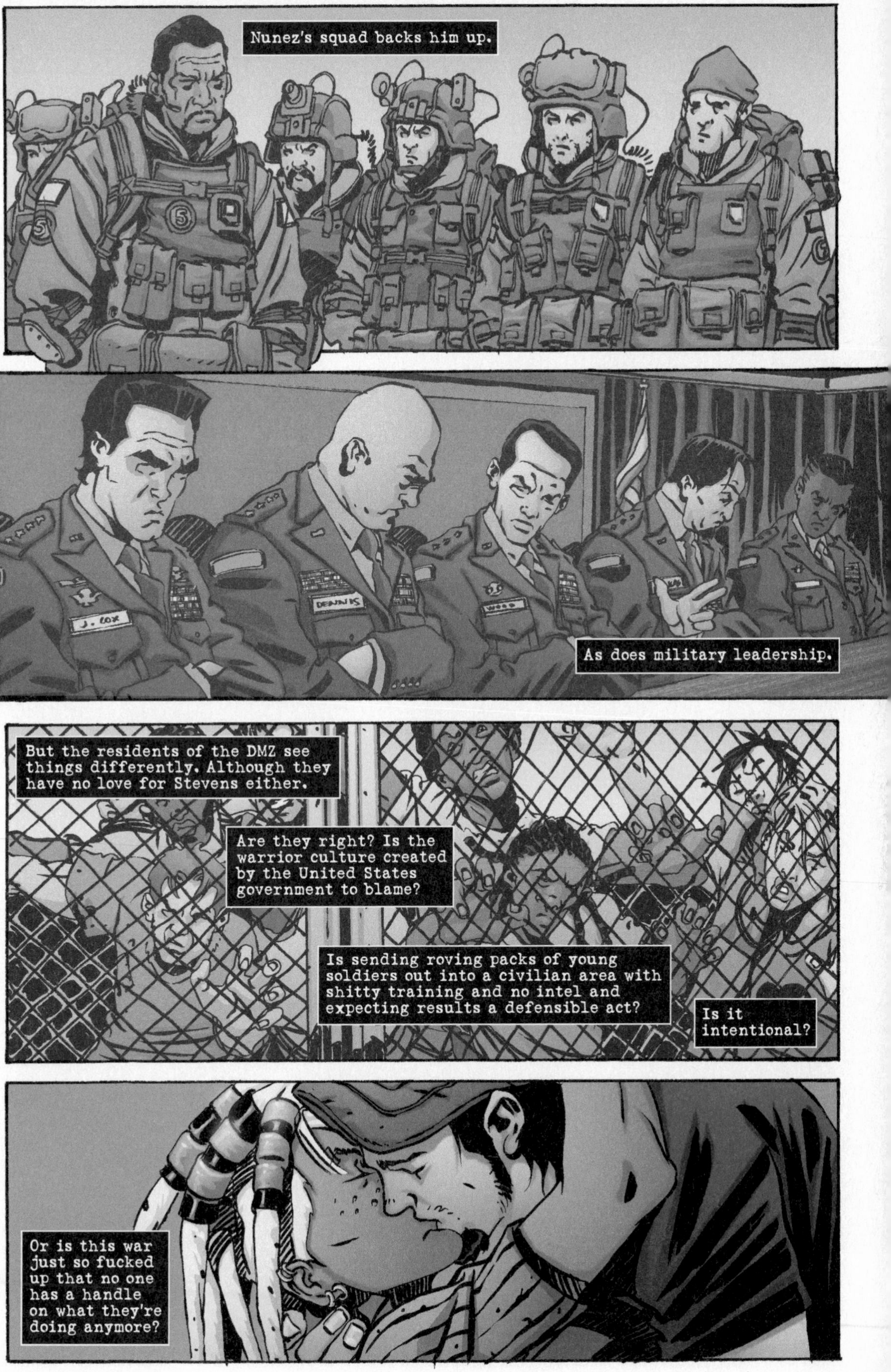
Nunez's squad backs him up.
J. COX
DENNIS
WOOD
As does military leadership.
But the residents of the DMZ see things differently. Although they have no love for Stevens either.
Are they right? Is the warrior culture created by the United States government to blame?
Is sending roving packs of young soldiers out into a civilian area with shitty training and no intel and expecting results a defensible act?
Is it intentional?
Or is this war just so fucked up that no one has a handle on what they're doing anymore?

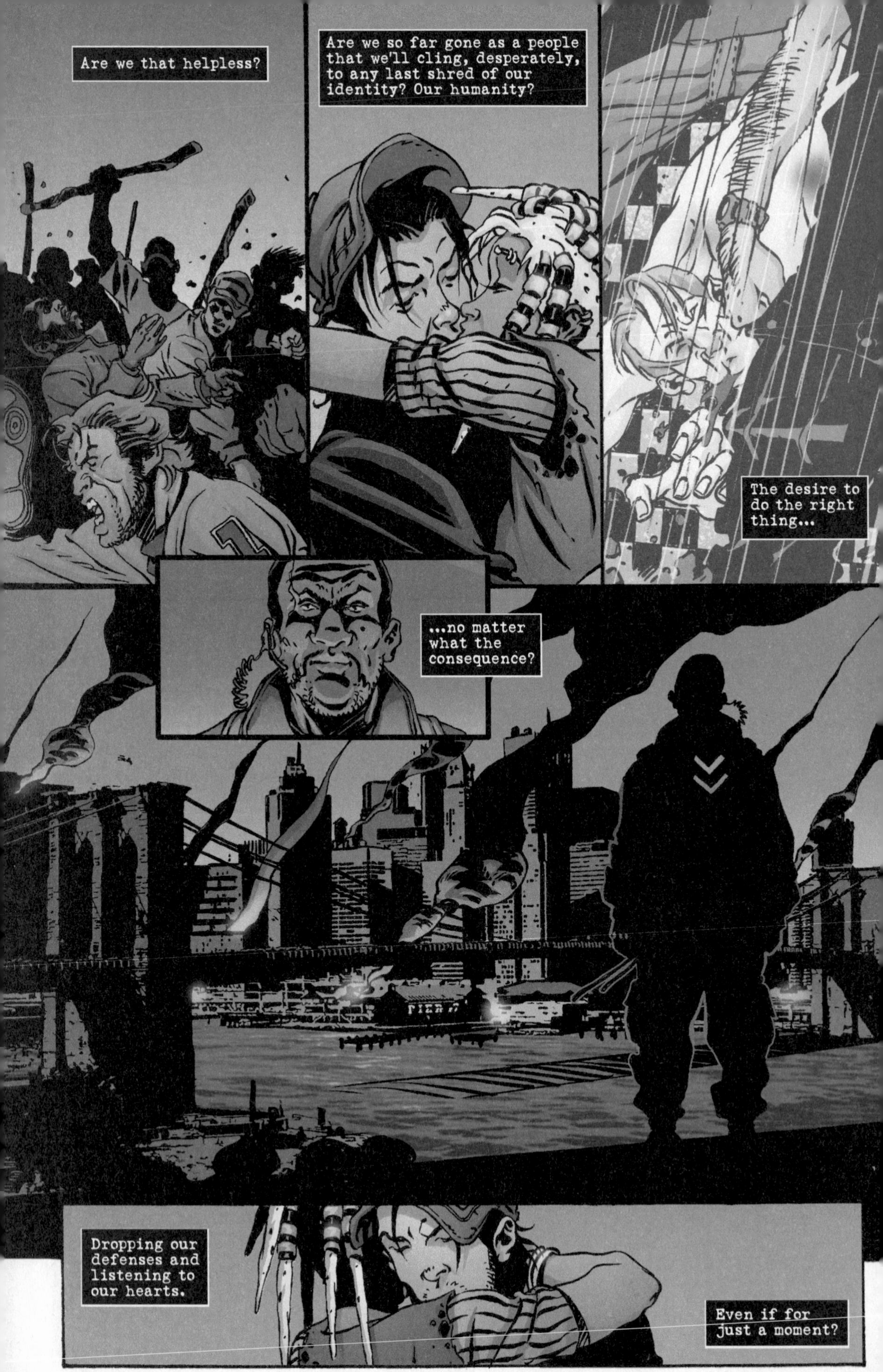
Are we that helpless?
Are we so far gone as a people that we'll cling, desperately, to any last shred of our identity? Our humanity?
The desire to do the right thing...
...no matter what the consequence?
Dropping our defenses and listening to our hearts.
Even if for just a moment?

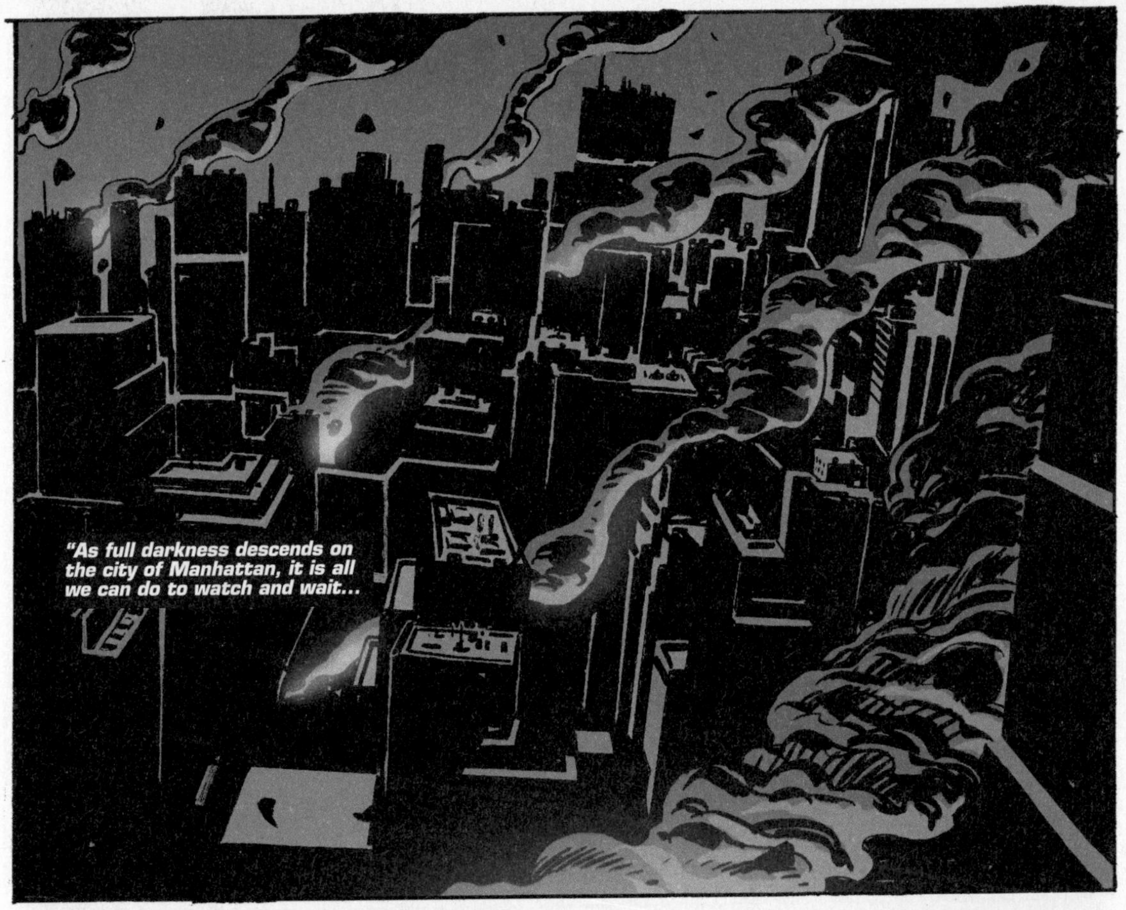
"As full darkness descends on the city of Manhattan, it is all we can do to watch and wait...

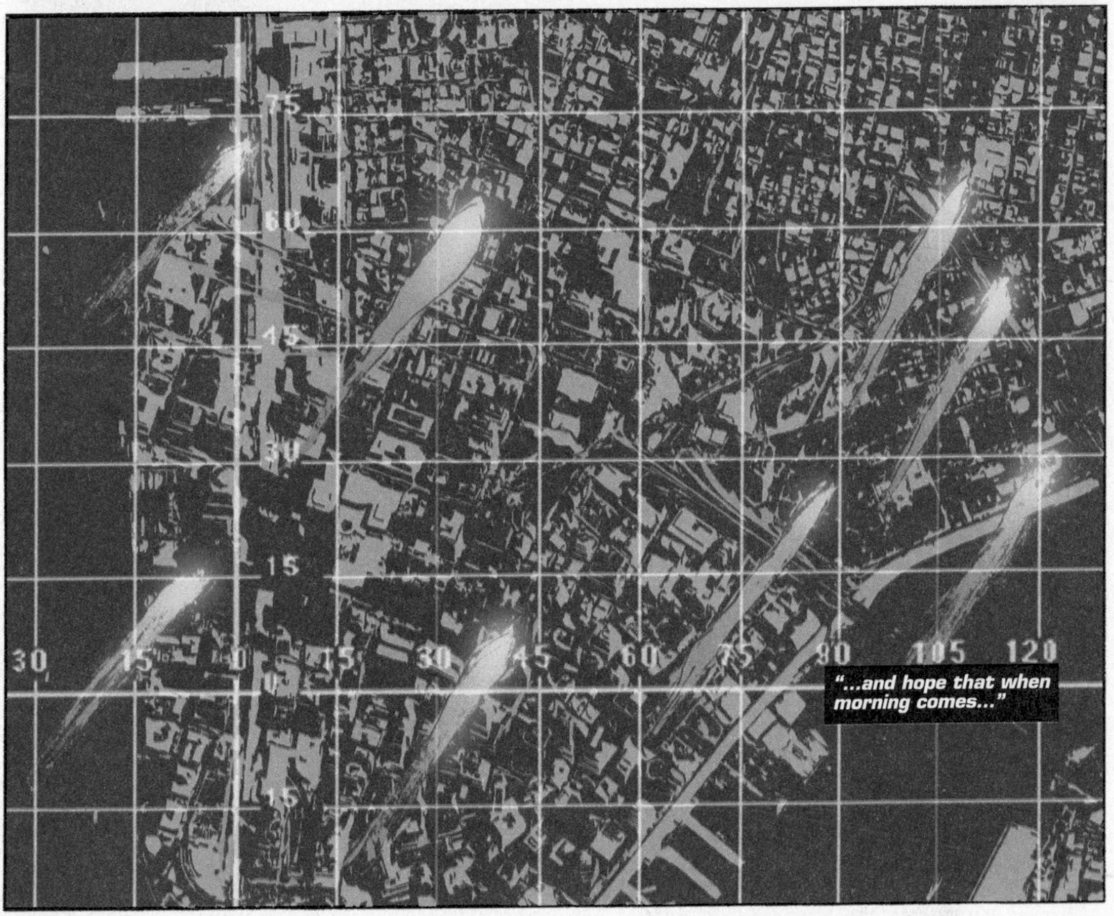
75
60
45
30
15
30 15 0 15 30 45 60 75 90 105 120
0
15
"...and hope that when morning comes..."

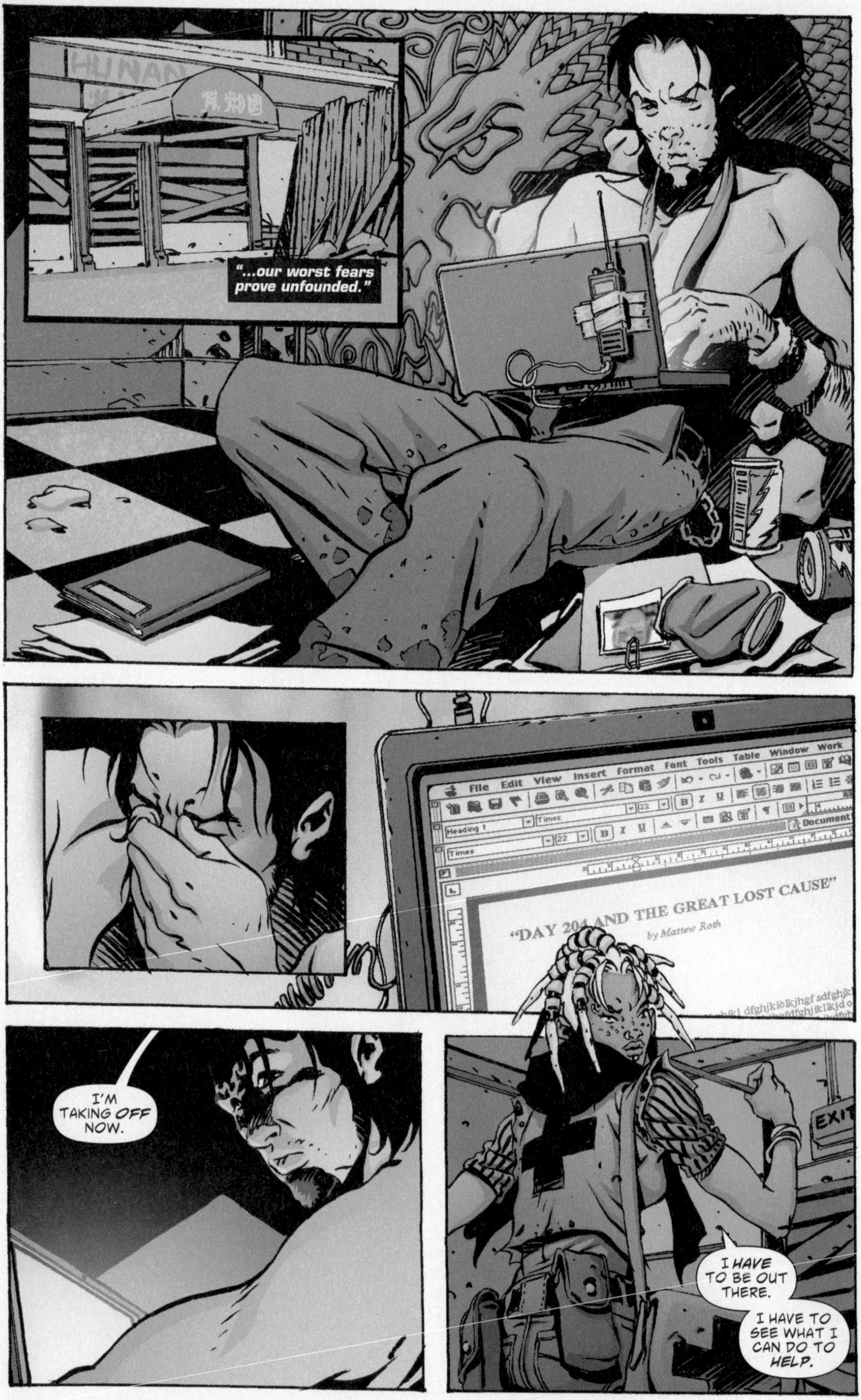
HUNAN
"...our worst fears prove unfounded."
File Edit View Insert Format Font Tools Table Window Work
"DAY 204 AND THE GREAT LOST CAUSE"
by Mattew Roth
I'M TAKING OFF NOW.
EXIT
I HAVE TO BE OUT THERE.
I HAVE TO SEE WHAT I CAN DO TO HELP.

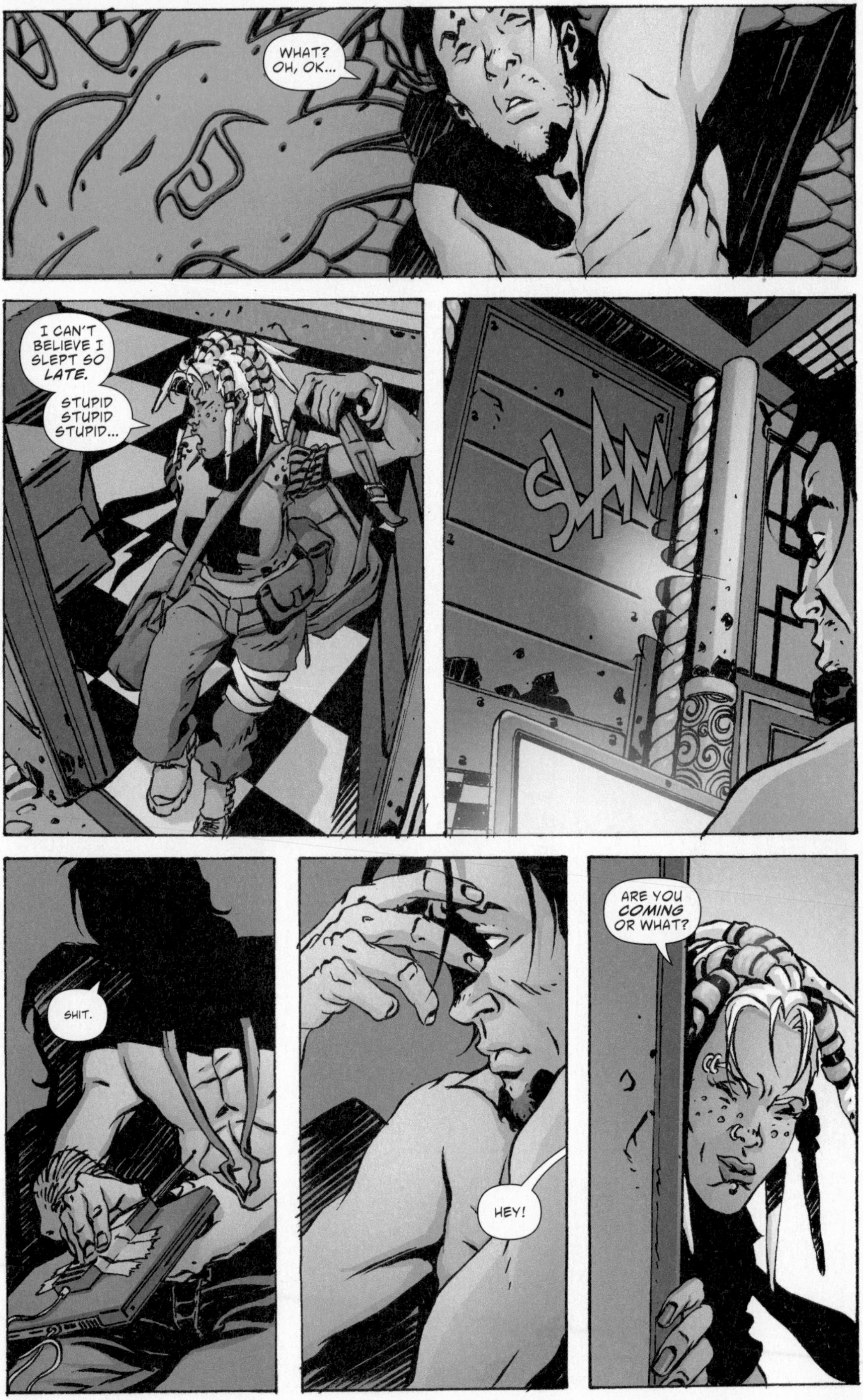
WHAT? OH, OK...
I CAN'T BELIEVE I SLEPT SO LATE.
STUPID STUPID STUPID...
SLAM
SHIT.
HEY!
ARE YOU COMING OR WHAT?

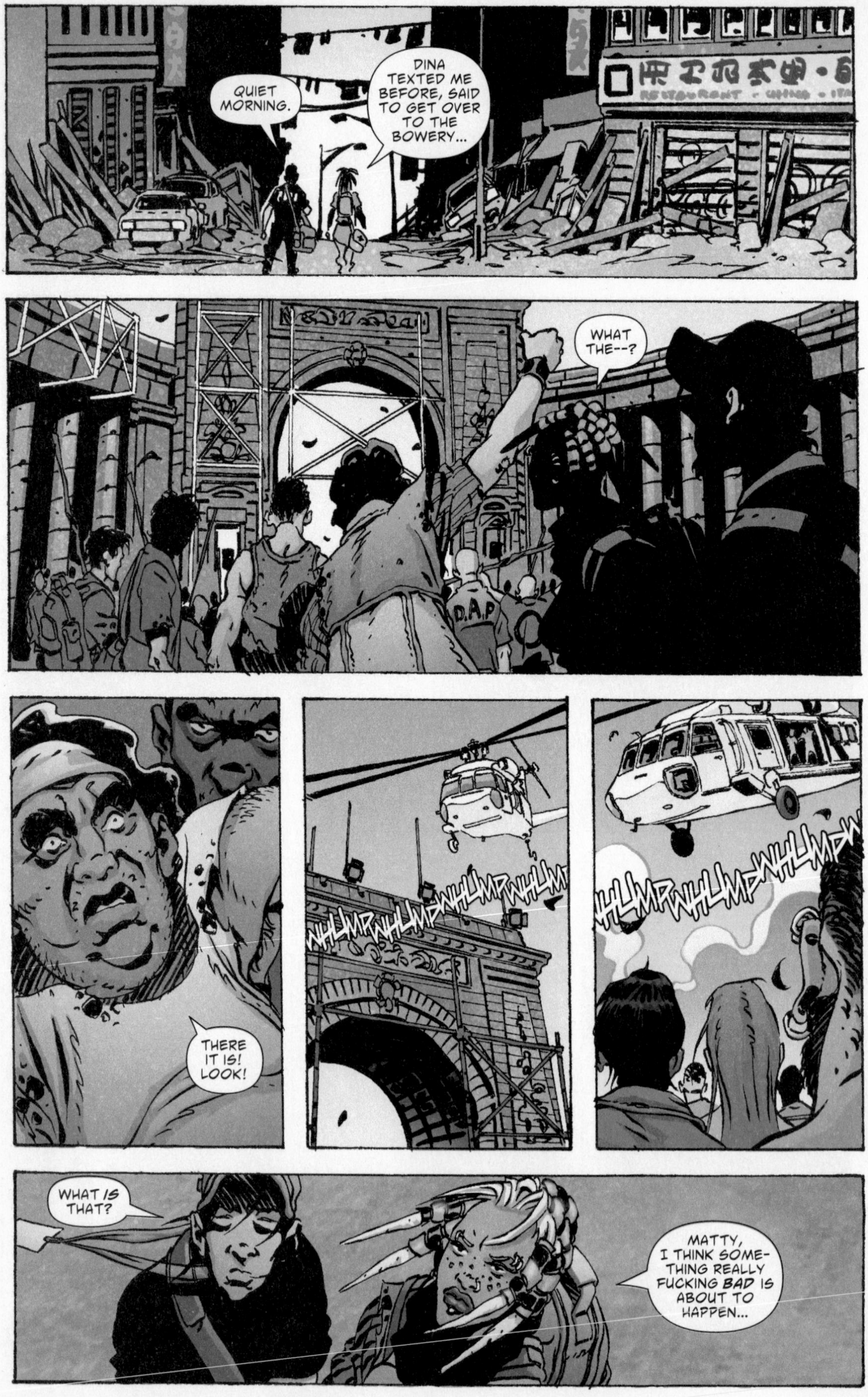
QUIET MORNING.
DINA TEXTED ME BEFORE, SAID TO GET OVER TO THE BOWERY...
WHAT THE--?
THERE IT IS! LOOK!
WHUMPWHUMPWHUMPWHUMPWHUM
WHUMPWHUMPWHUMPWHUMPWHUMPW
WHAT *IS* THAT?
MATTY, I THINK SOMETHING REALLY FUCKING *BAD* IS ABOUT TO HAPPEN...

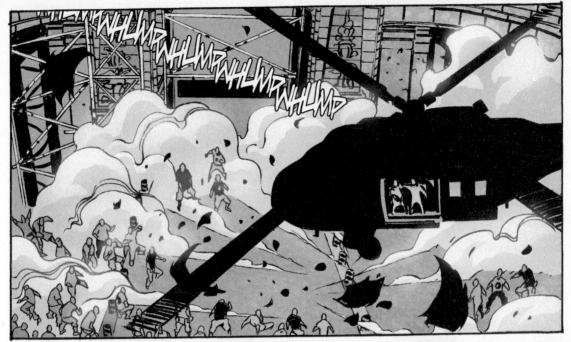

WHUMP WHUMP WHUMP WHUMP

I HAVE A PRESENT FOR YOU!

COURTESY OF THE UNITED STATES OF AMERICA!

OH, NO... ZEE... I KNOW WHO THAT IS...

YOU WANT HIM, YOU GOT HIM!

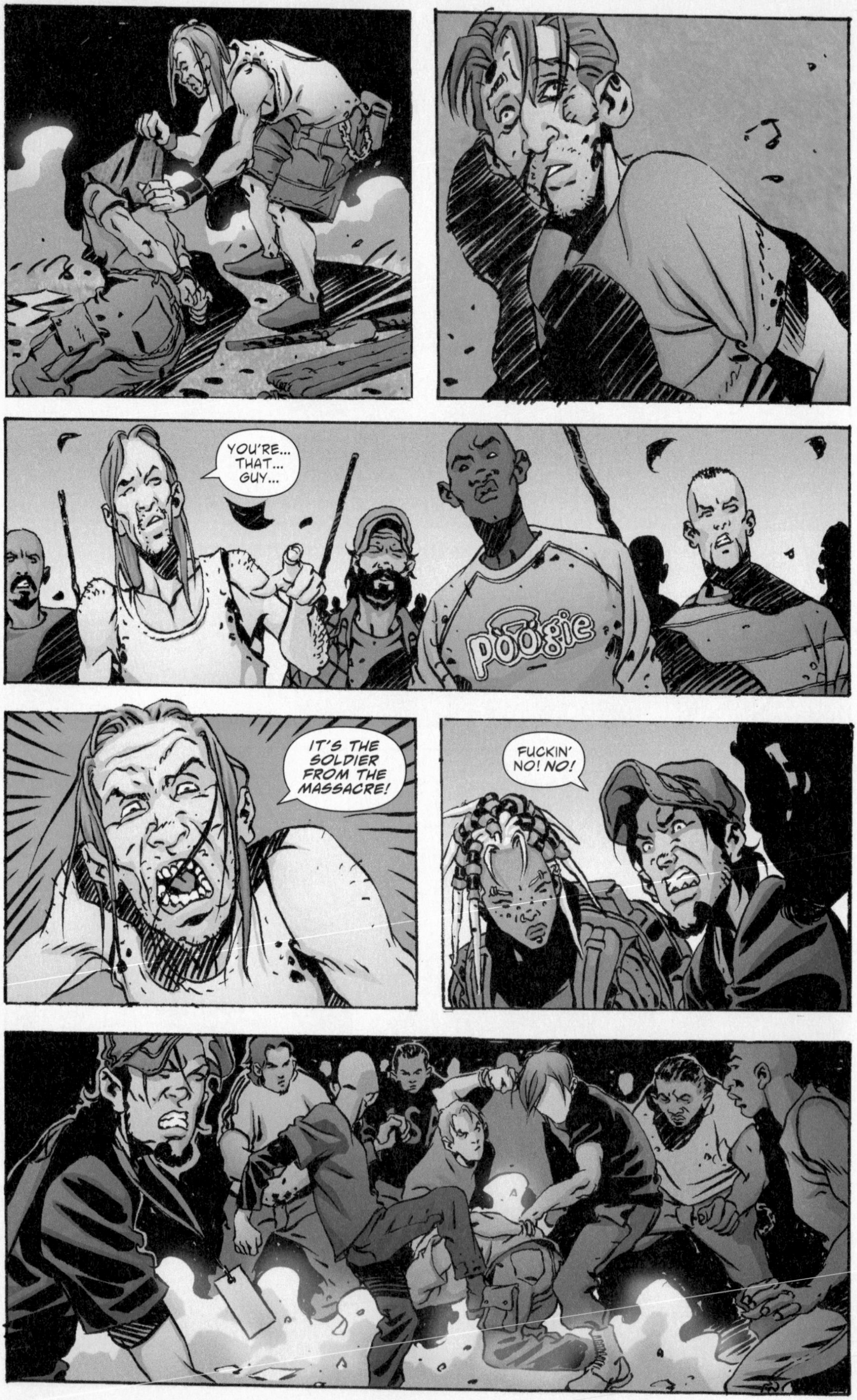
YOU'RE... THAT... GUY...
IT'S THE SOLDIER FROM THE MASSACRE!
FUCKIN' NO! NO!
poogie

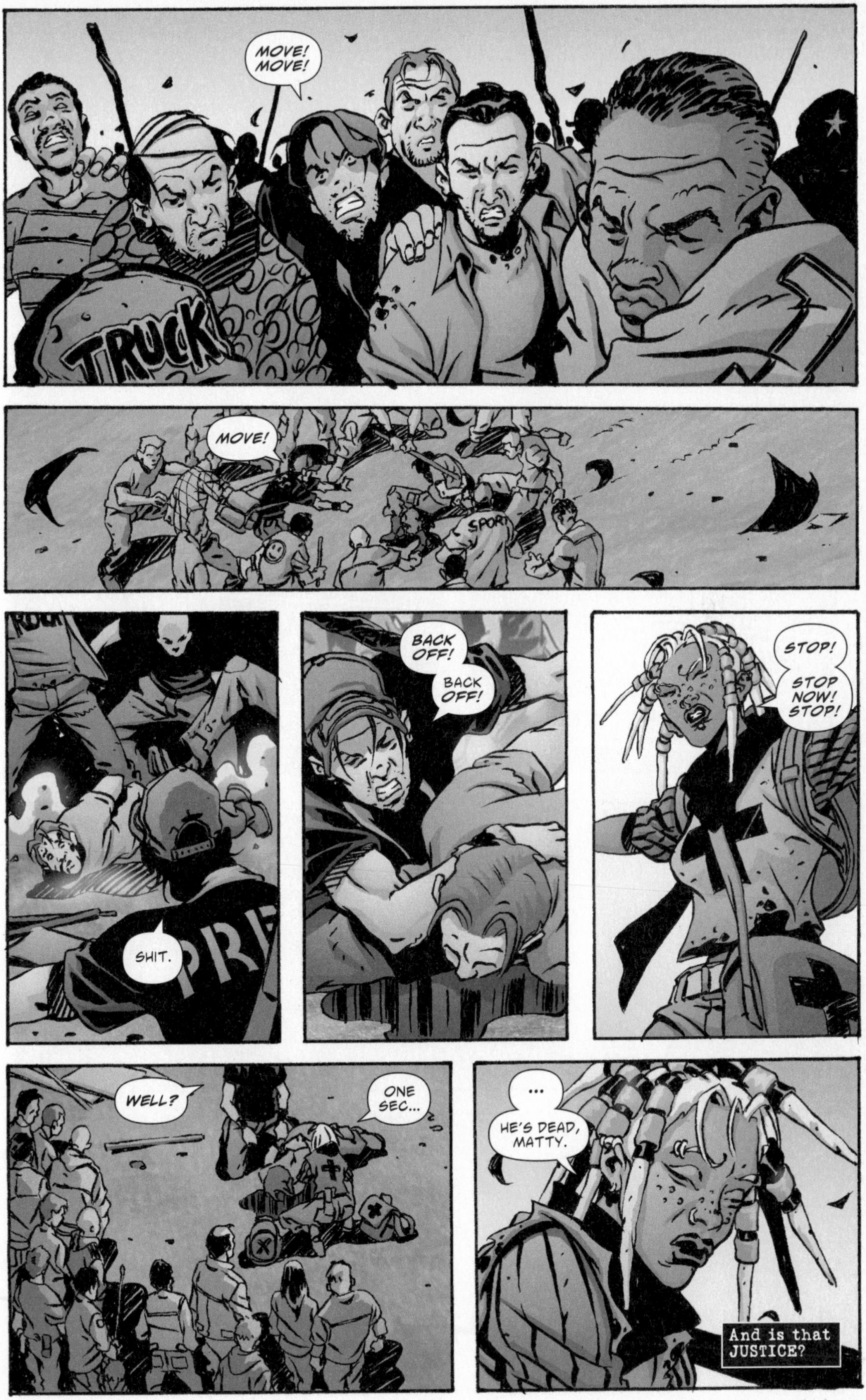
MOVE! MOVE!
TRUCK
MOVE!
SPORT
SHIT.
PRE
BACK OFF!
BACK OFF!
STOP!
STOP NOW! STOP!
WELL?
ONE SEC...
...
HE'S DEAD, MATTY.
And is that JUSTICE?

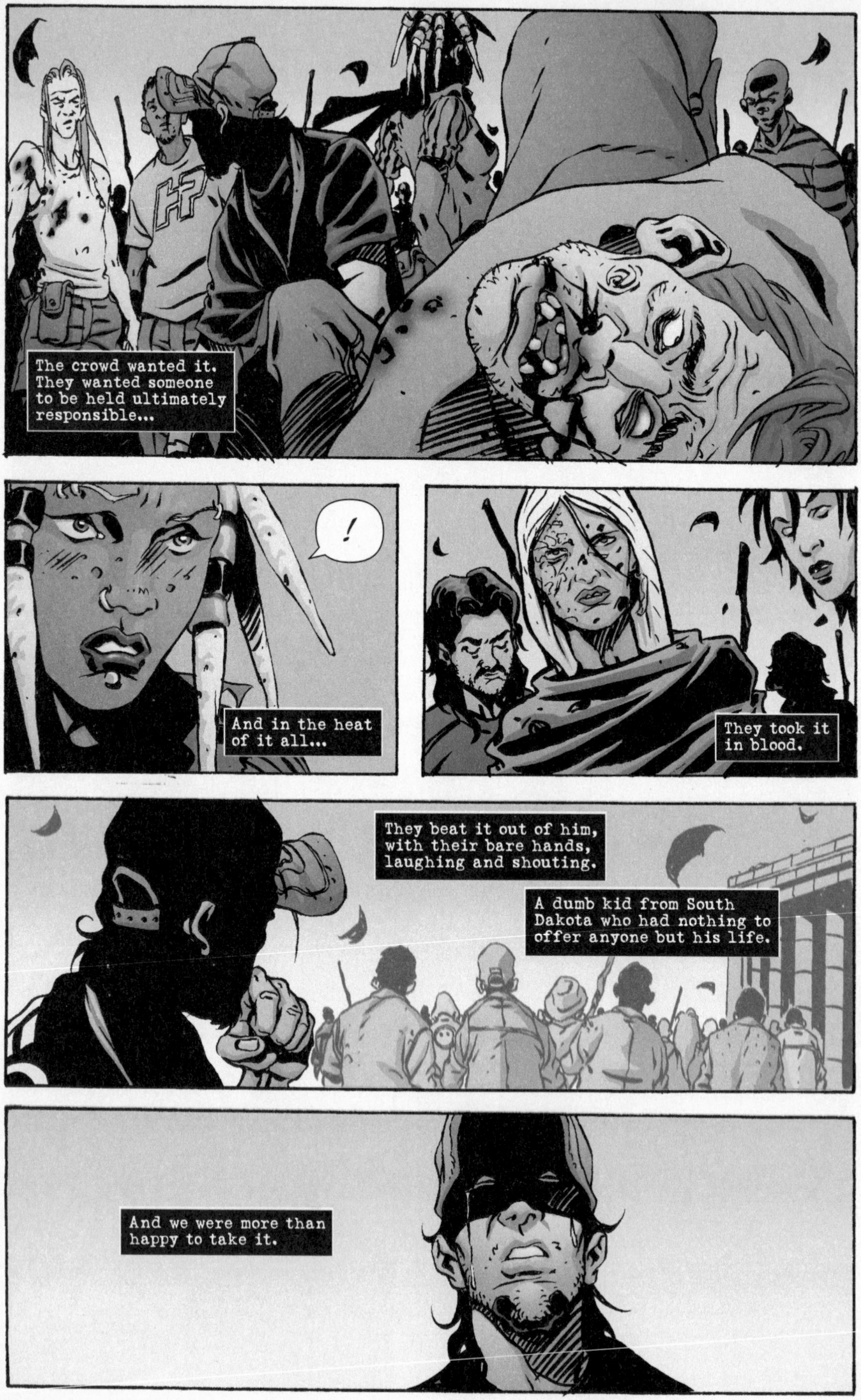

The crowd wanted it. They wanted someone to be held ultimately responsible...
!
And in the heat of it all...
They took it in blood.
They beat it out of him, with their bare hands, laughing and shouting.
A dumb kid from South Dakota who had nothing to offer anyone but his life.
And we were more than happy to take it.

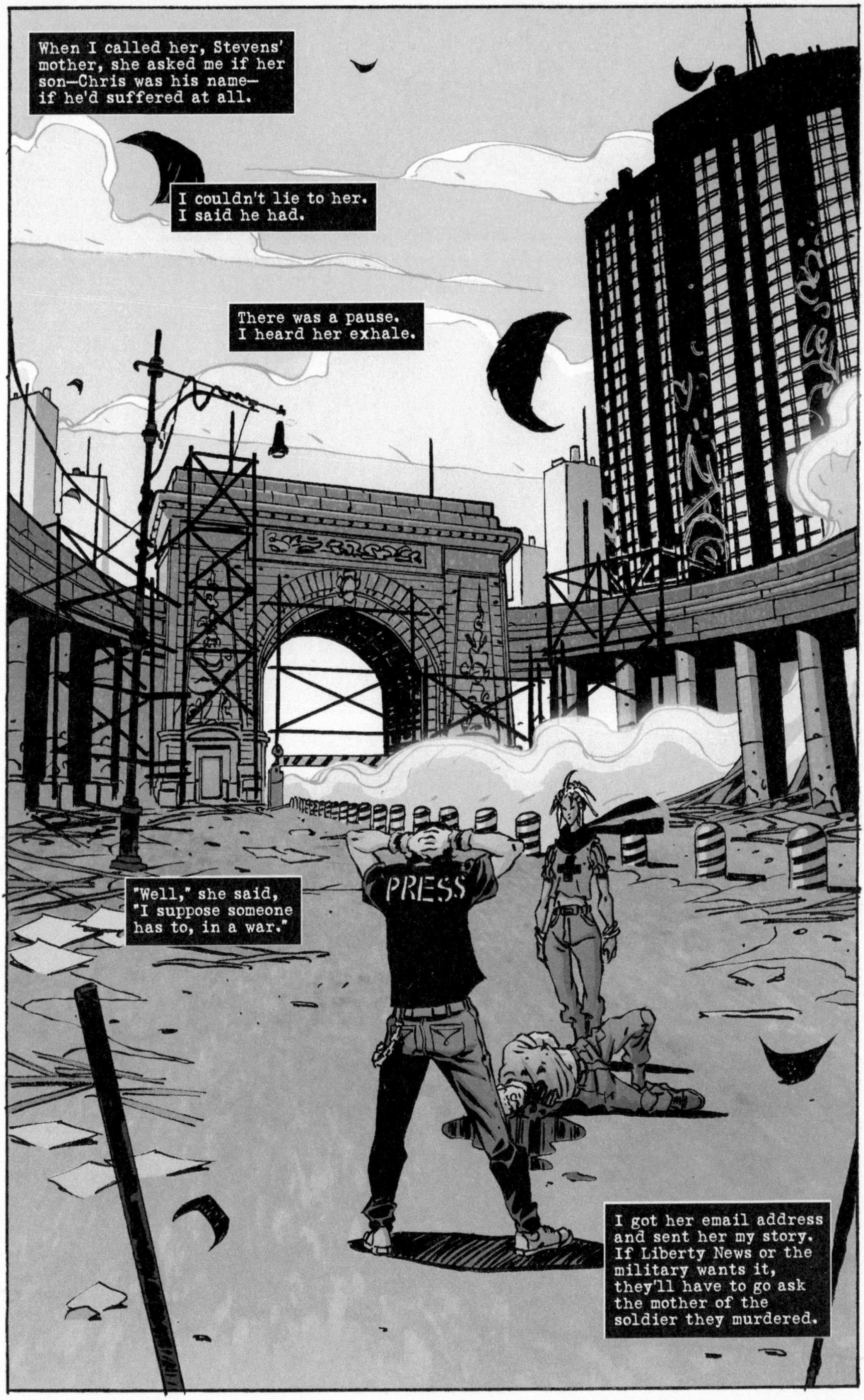

When I called her, Stevens' mother, she asked me if her son—Chris was his name—if he'd suffered at all.
I couldn't lie to her. I said he had.
There was a pause. I heard her exhale.
PRESS
"Well," she said, "I suppose someone has to, in a war."
I got her email address and sent her my story. If Liberty News or the military wants it, they'll have to go ask the mother of the soldier they murdered.

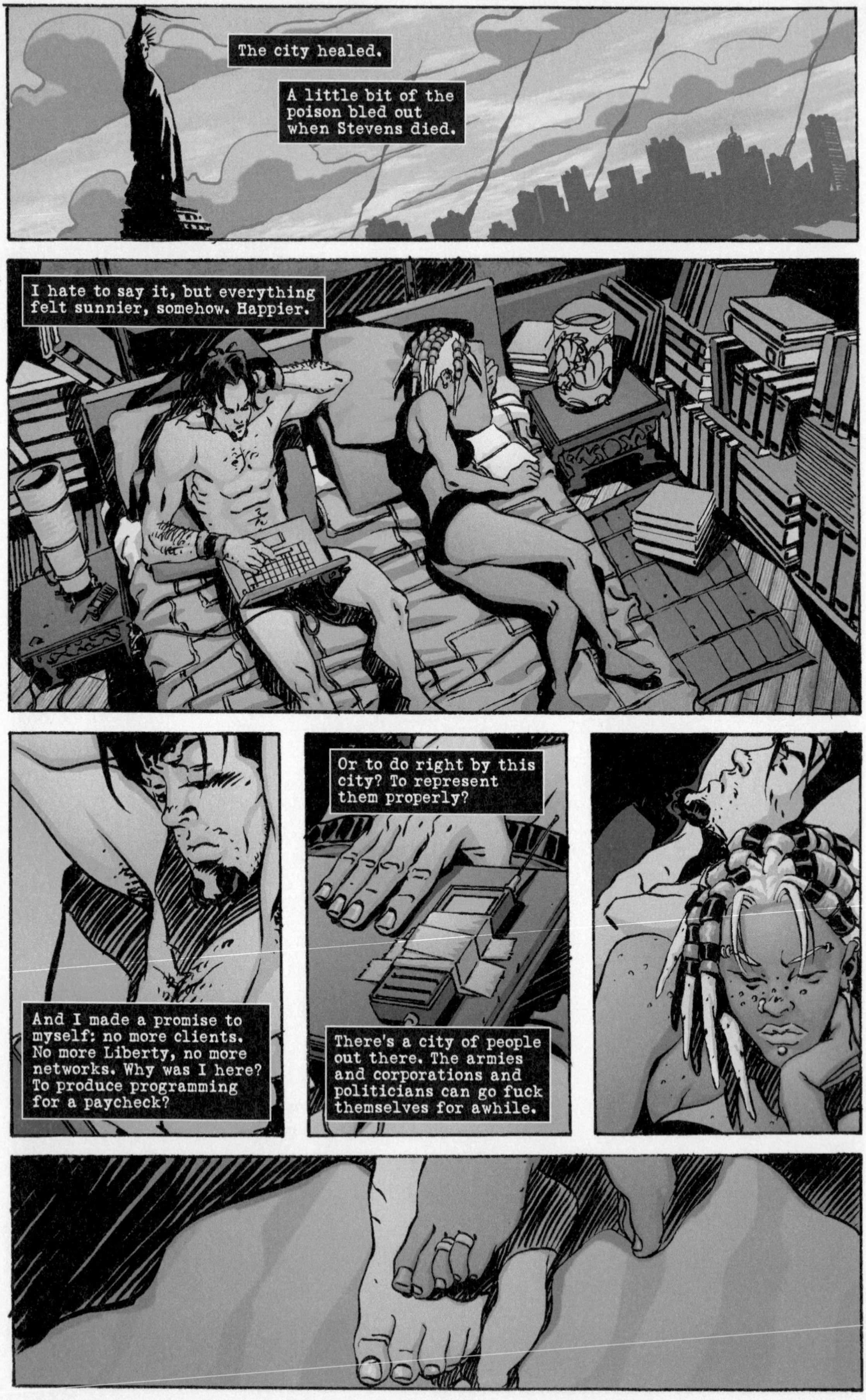
The city healed.
A little bit of the poison bled out when Stevens died.
I hate to say it, but everything felt sunnier, somehow. Happier.
And I made a promise to myself: no more clients. No more Liberty, no more networks. Why was I here? To produce programming for a paycheck?
Or to do right by this city? To represent them properly?
There's a city of people out there. The armies and corporations and politicians can go fuck themselves for awhile.

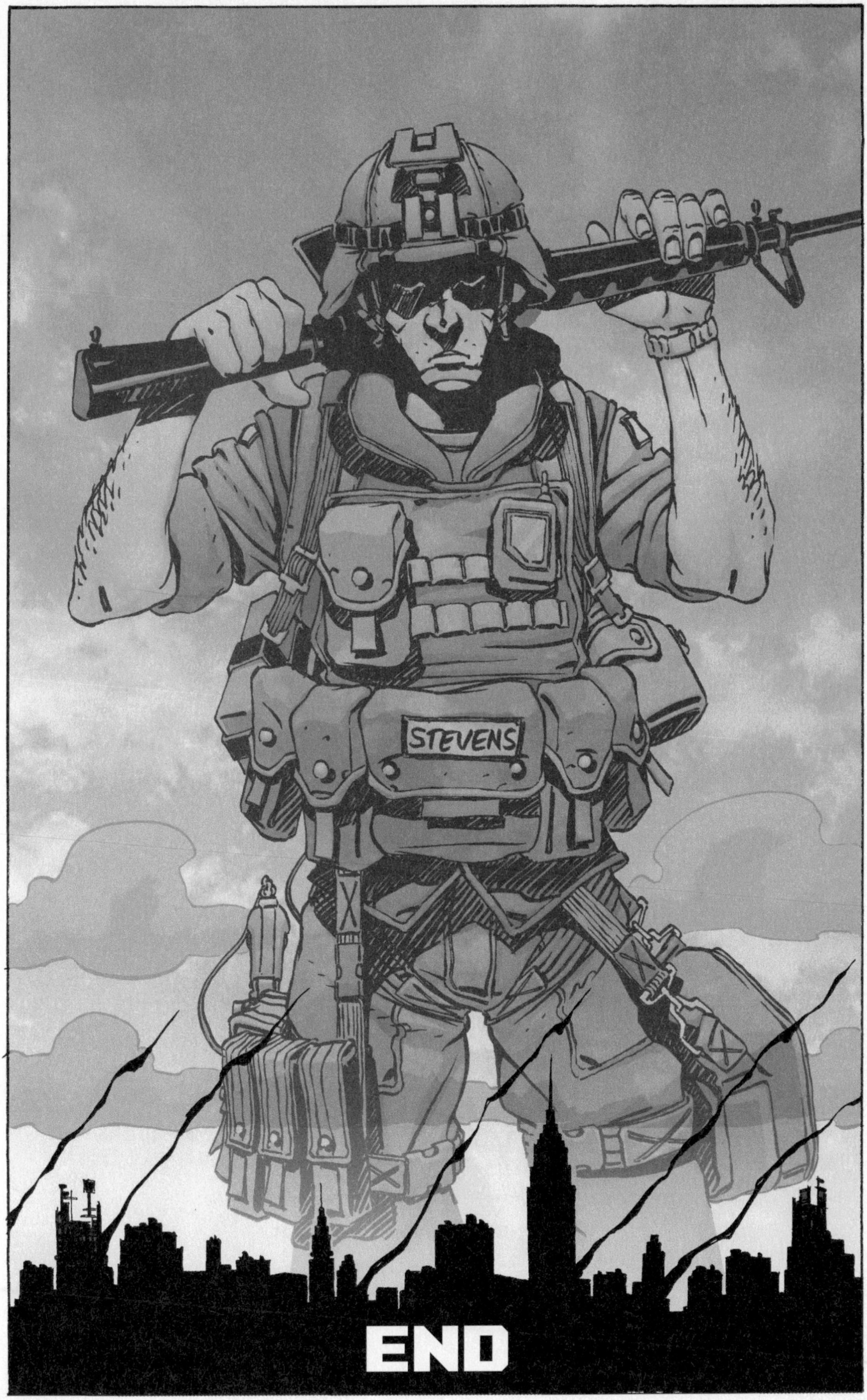
STEVENS
END

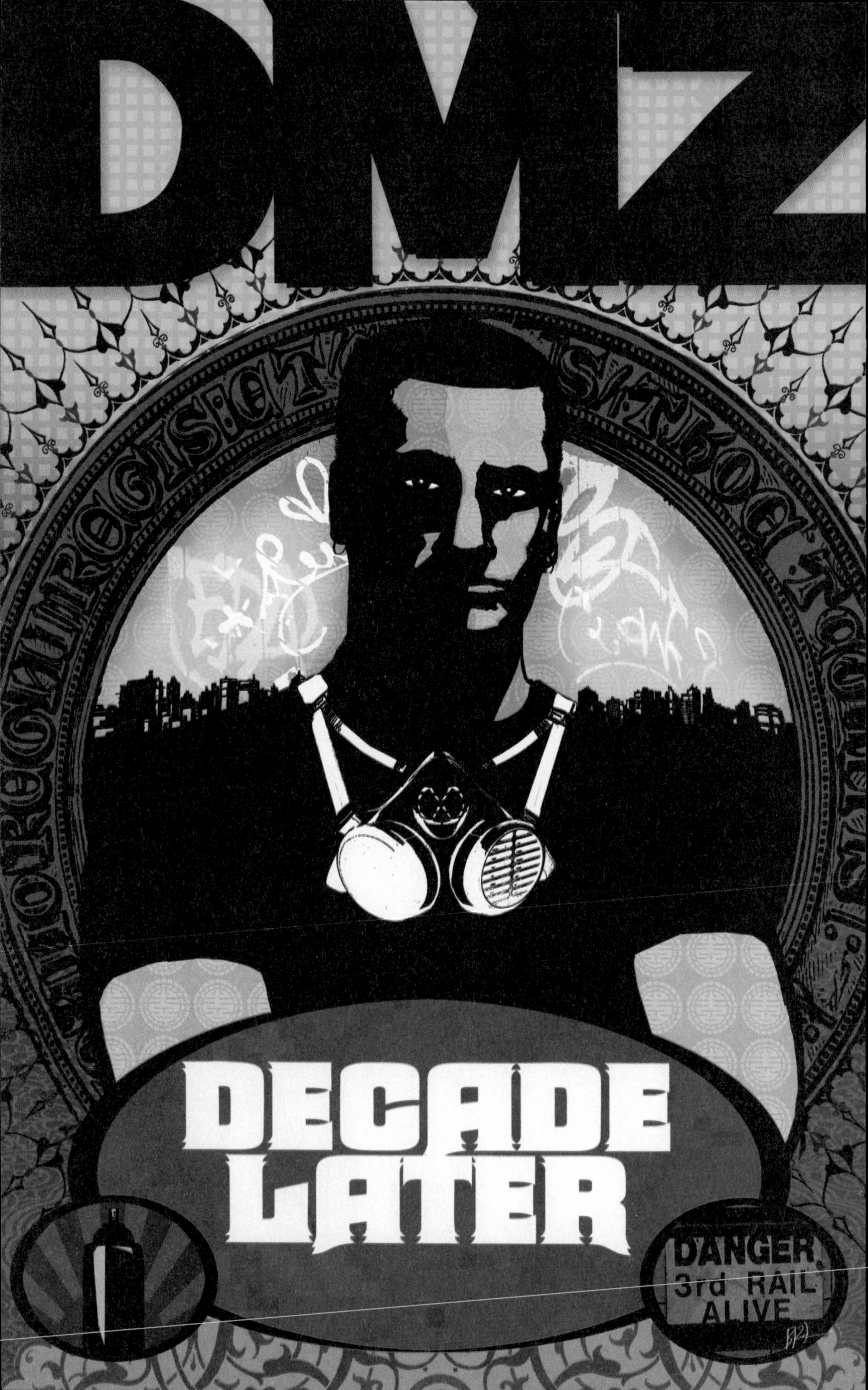
DMZ
DECADE LATER
DANGER
3rd RAIL
ALIVE

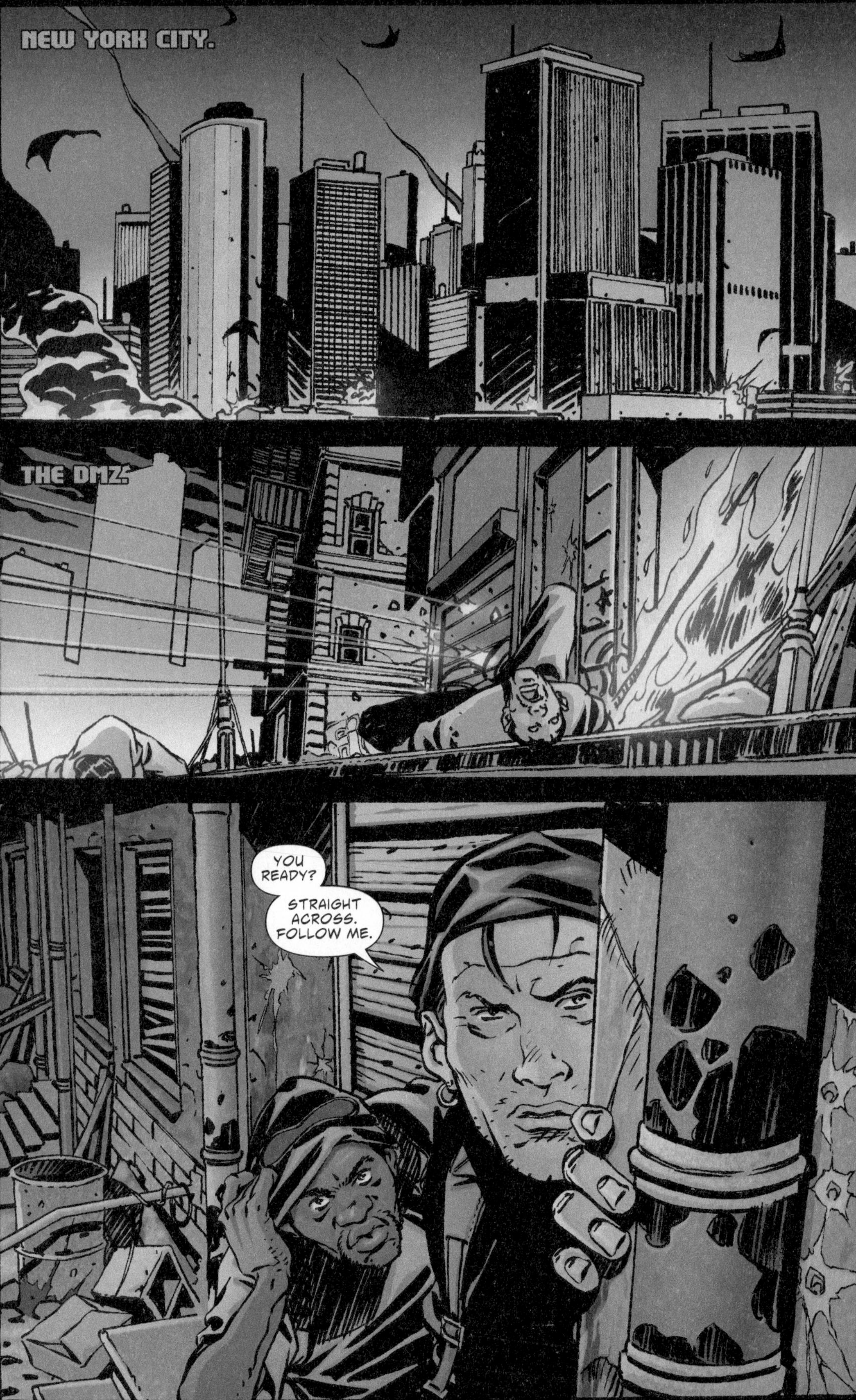
NEW YORK CITY.
THE DMZ.
YOU READY?
STRAIGHT ACROSS. FOLLOW ME.

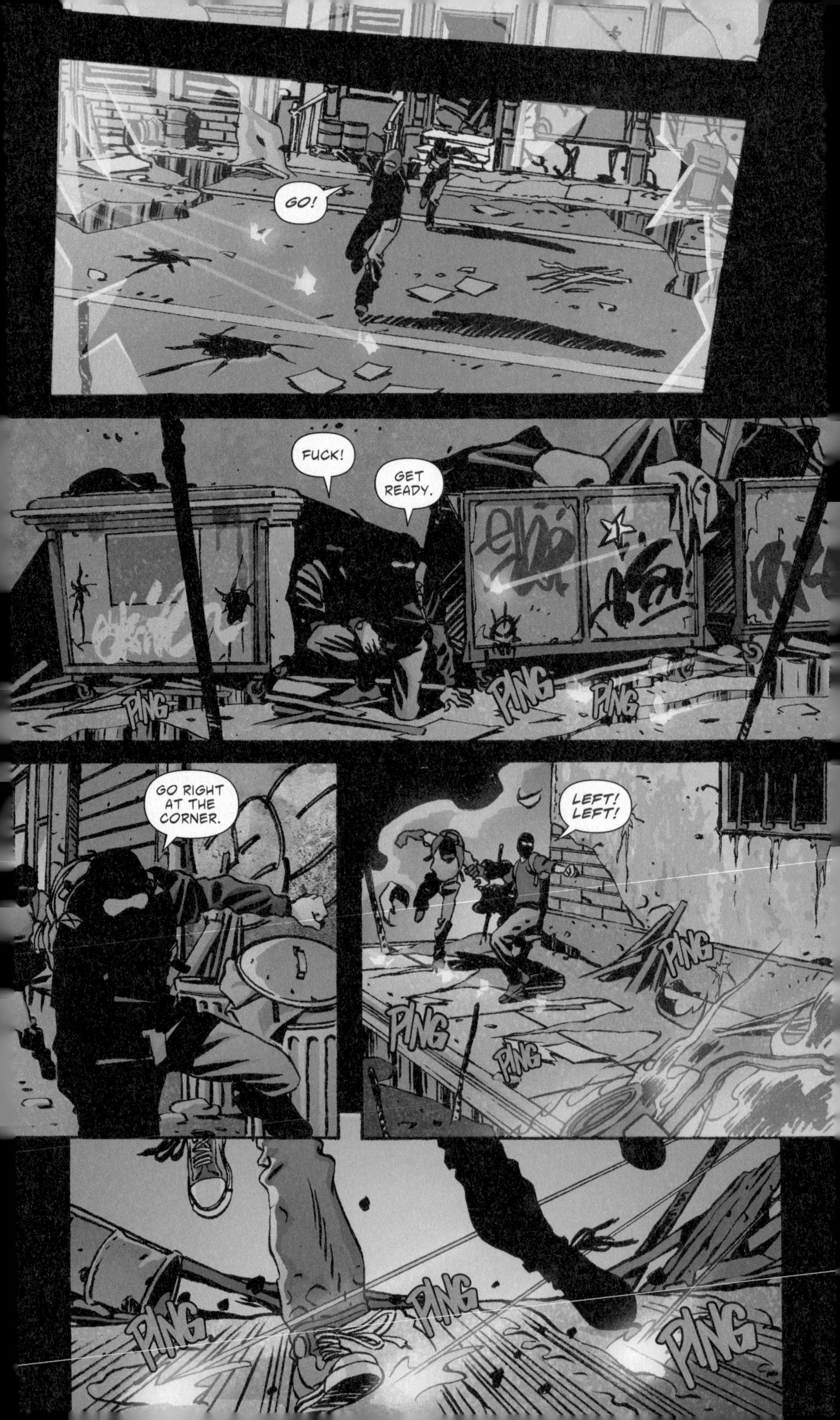
GO!
FUCK!
GET READY.
PING
PING
PING
GO RIGHT AT THE CORNER.
LEFT! LEFT!
PING
PING
PING
PING
PING
PING

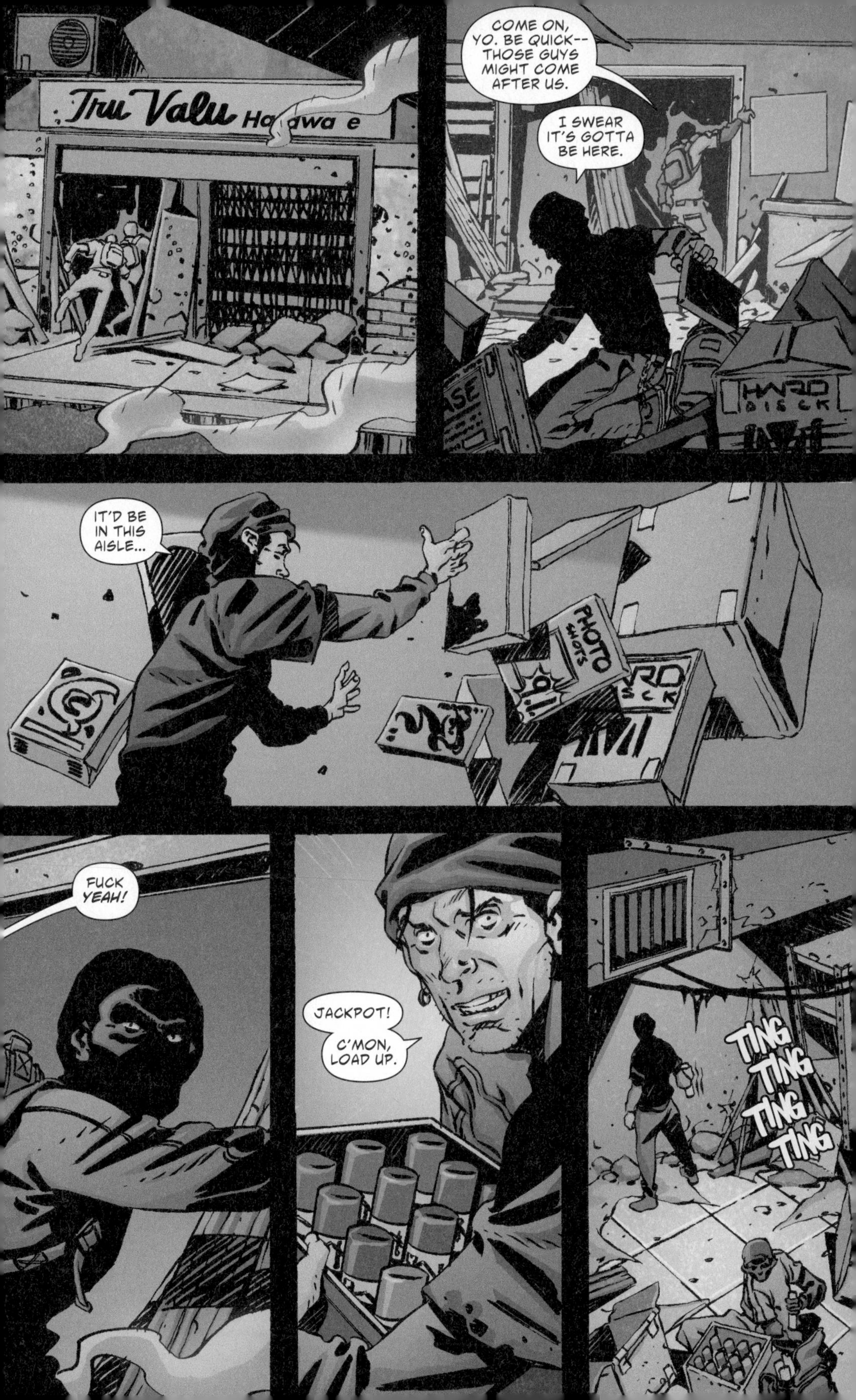
Tru Valu Hardwa e
COME ON, YO. BE QUICK-- THOSE GUYS MIGHT COME AFTER US.
I SWEAR IT'S GOTTA BE HERE.
HARD DISCK
IT'D BE IN THIS AISLE...
PHOTO SHOTS
FUCK YEAH!
JACKPOT!
C'MON, LOAD UP.
TING TING TING TING

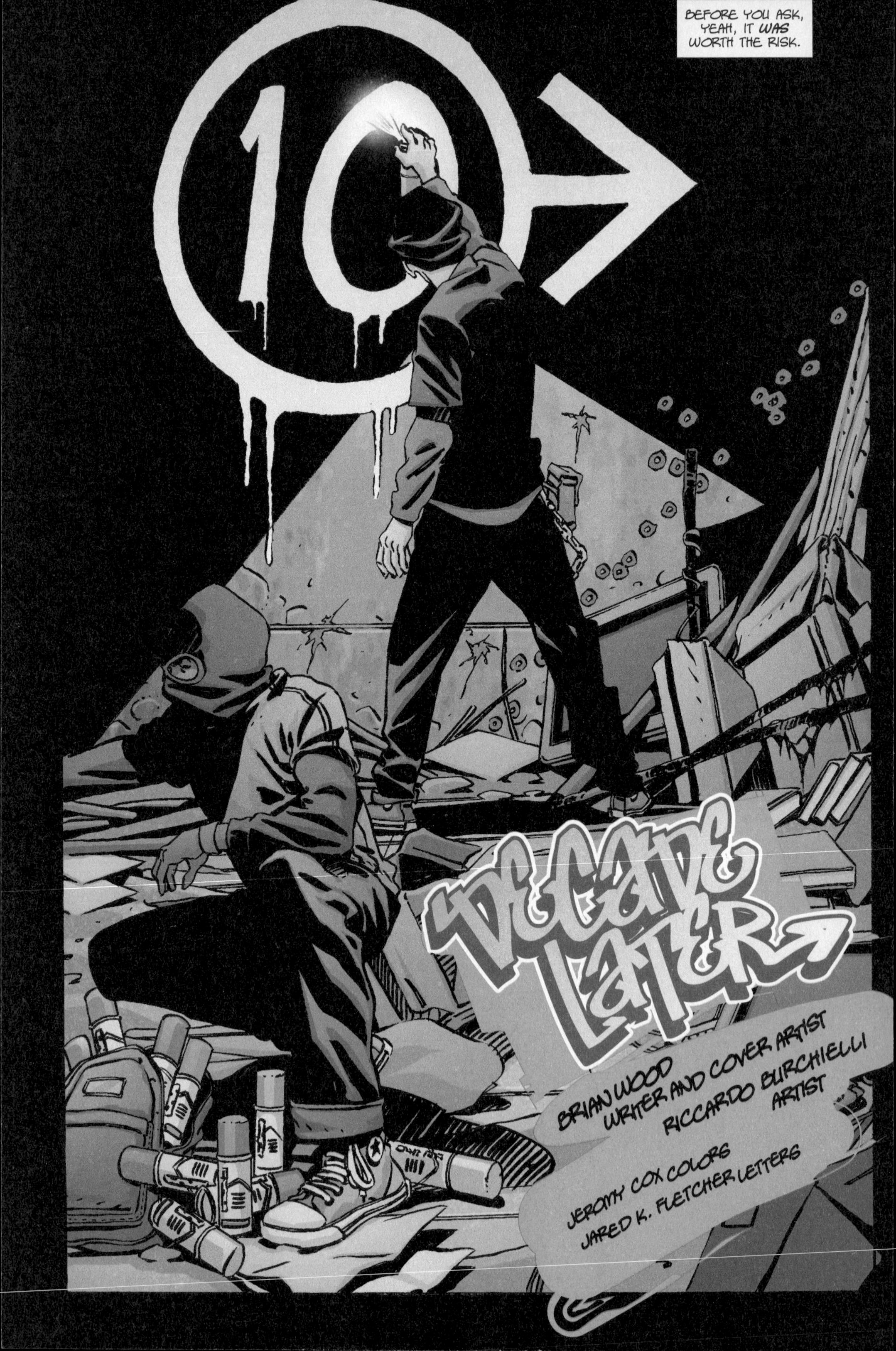
BEFORE YOU ASK, YEAH, IT WAS WORTH THE RISK.
DECADE LATER
BRIAN WOOD WRITER AND COVER ARTIST
RICCARDO BURCHIELLI ARTIST
JEROMY COX COLORS
JARED K. FLETCHER LETTERS

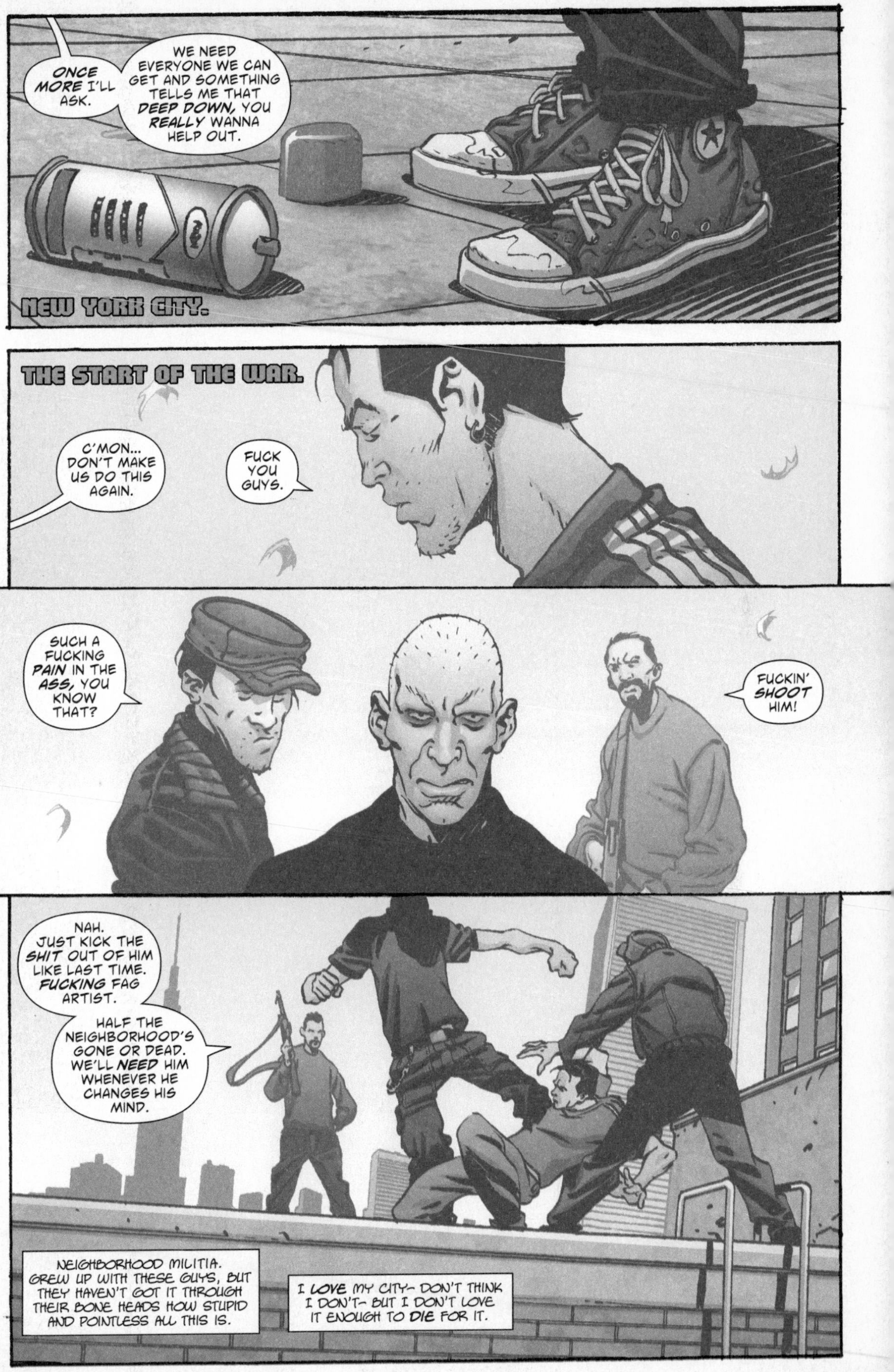
ONCE MORE I'LL ASK.
WE NEED EVERYONE WE CAN GET AND SOMETHING TELLS ME THAT DEEP DOWN, YOU REALLY WANNA HELP OUT.
NEW YORK CITY.
THE START OF THE WAR.
C'MON... DON'T MAKE US DO THIS AGAIN.
FUCK YOU GUYS.
SUCH A FUCKING PAIN IN THE ASS, YOU KNOW THAT?
FUCKIN' SHOOT HIM!
NAH. JUST KICK THE SHIT OUT OF HIM LIKE LAST TIME. FUCKING FAG ARTIST.
HALF THE NEIGHBORHOOD'S GONE OR DEAD. WE'LL NEED HIM WHENEVER HE CHANGES HIS MIND.
NEIGHBORHOOD MILITIA. GREW UP WITH THESE GUYS, BUT THEY HAVEN'T GOT IT THROUGH THEIR BONE HEADS HOW STUPID AND POINTLESS ALL THIS IS.
I LOVE MY CITY- DON'T THINK I DON'T- BUT I DON'T LOVE IT ENOUGH TO DIE FOR IT.

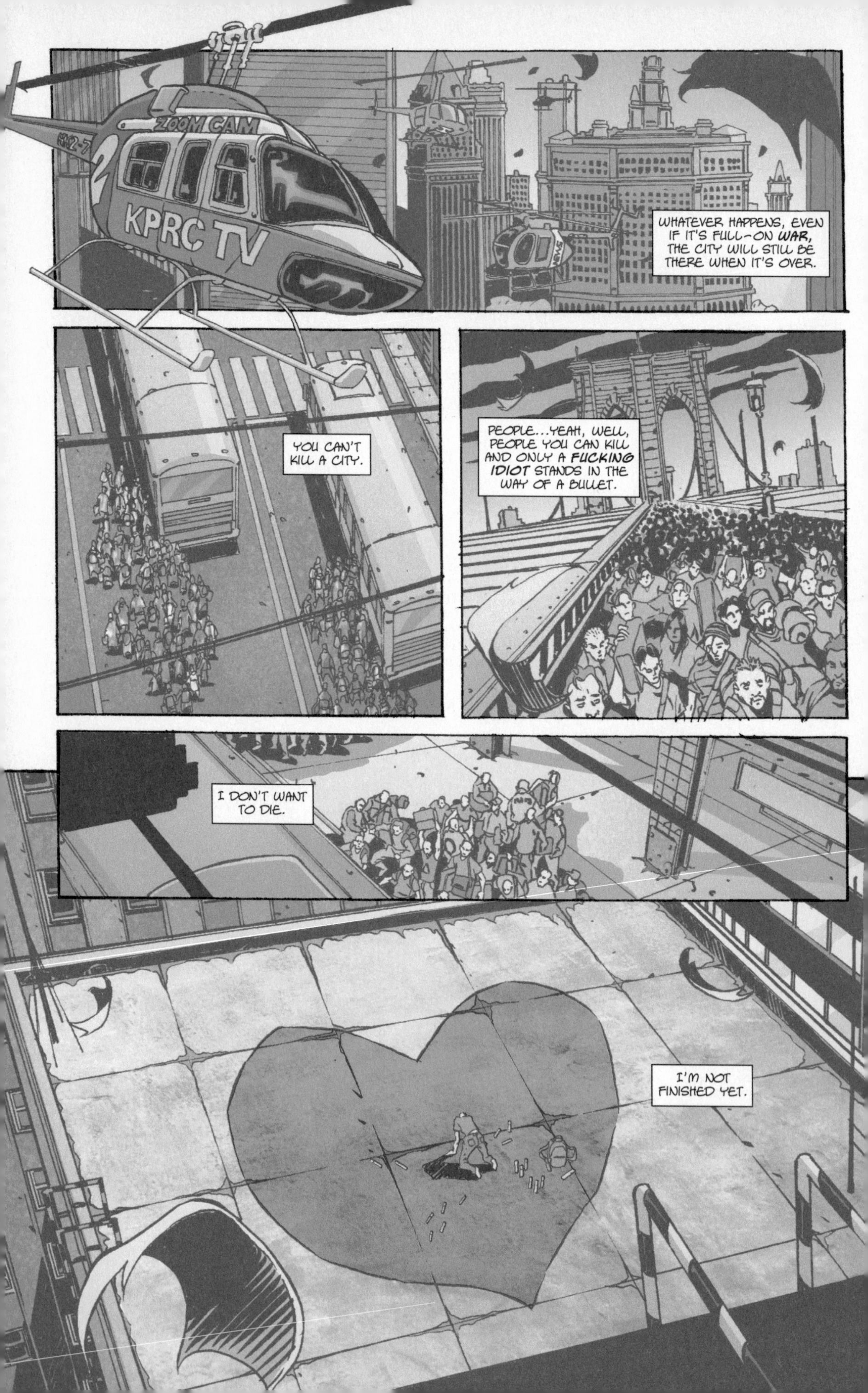
ZOOM CAM
KPRC TV
WHATEVER HAPPENS, EVEN IF IT'S FULL-ON WAR, THE CITY WILL STILL BE THERE WHEN IT'S OVER.
YOU CAN'T KILL A CITY.
PEOPLE...YEAH, WELL, PEOPLE YOU CAN KILL AND ONLY A FUCKING IDIOT STANDS IN THE WAY OF A BULLET.
I DON'T WANT TO DIE.
I'M NOT FINISHED YET.

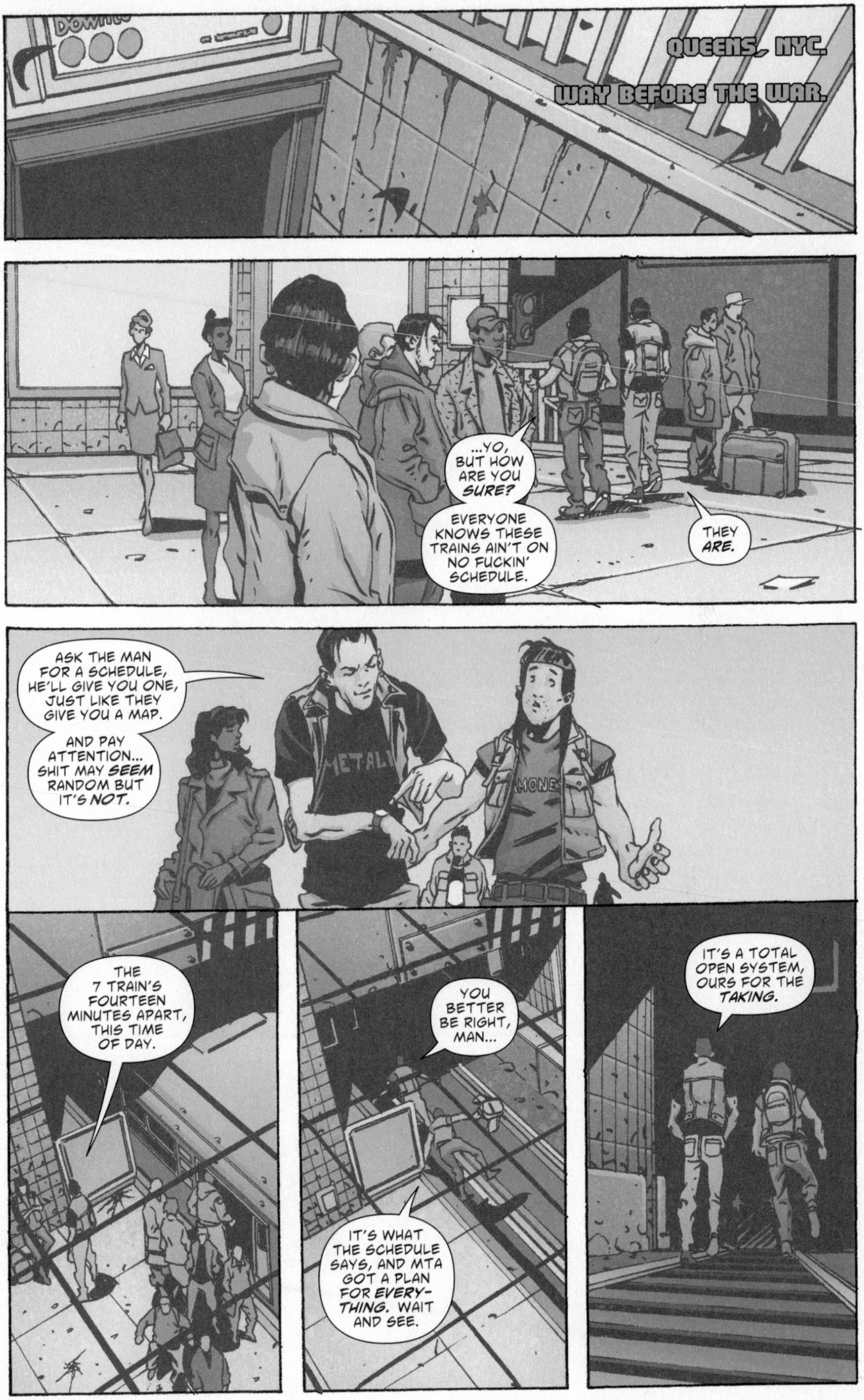
QUEENS, NYC.
WAY BEFORE THE WAR.
...YO, BUT HOW ARE YOU SURE?
EVERYONE KNOWS THESE TRAINS AIN'T ON NO FUCKIN' SCHEDULE.
THEY ARE.
ASK THE MAN FOR A SCHEDULE, HE'LL GIVE YOU ONE, JUST LIKE THEY GIVE YOU A MAP.
AND PAY ATTENTION... SHIT MAY SEEM RANDOM BUT IT'S NOT.
THE 7 TRAIN'S FOURTEEN MINUTES APART, THIS TIME OF DAY.
YOU BETTER BE RIGHT, MAN...
IT'S WHAT THE SCHEDULE SAYS, AND MTA GOT A PLAN FOR EVERY-THING. WAIT AND SEE.
IT'S A TOTAL OPEN SYSTEM, OURS FOR THE TAKING.

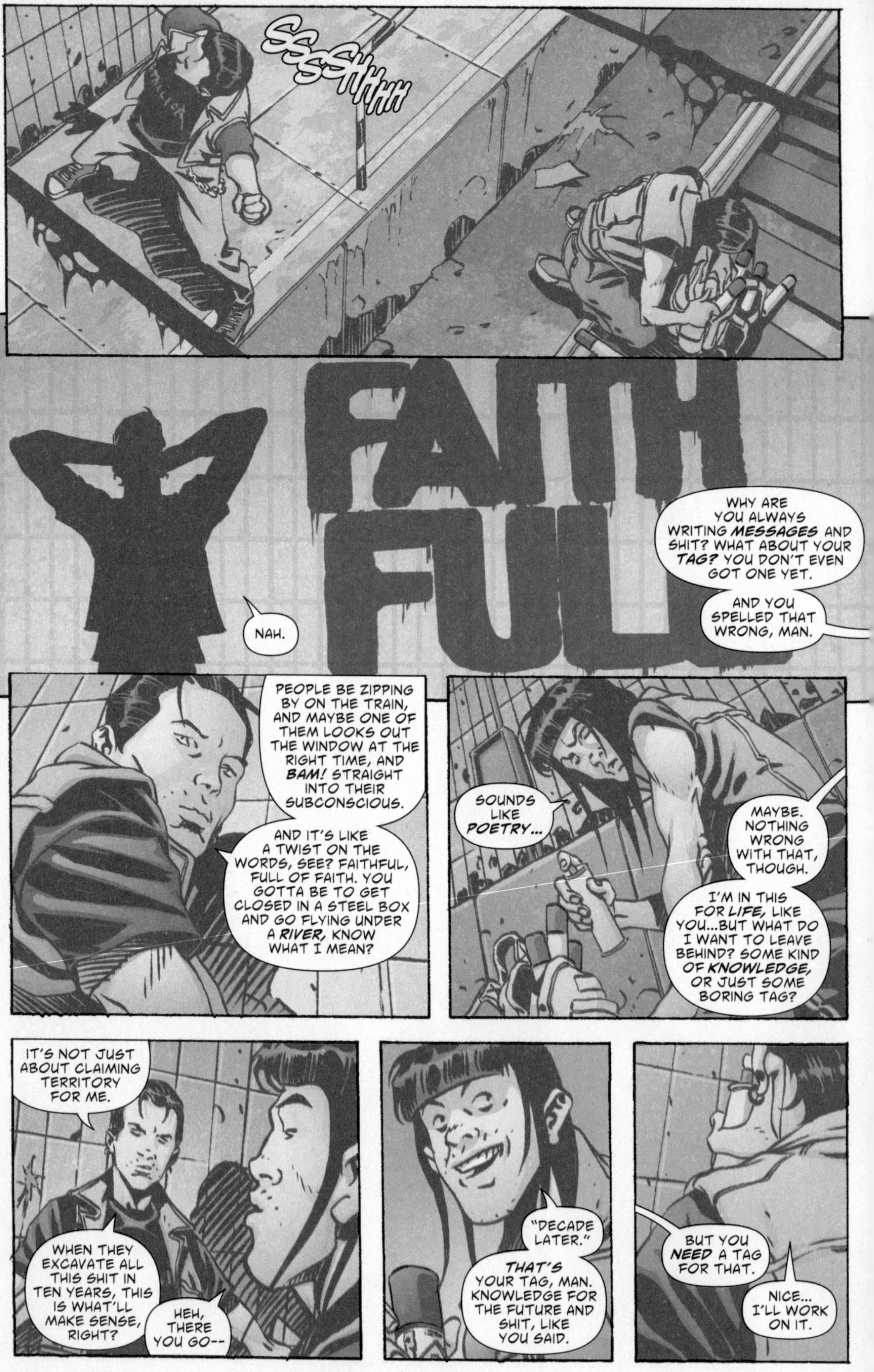
SSSSHHHHH
FAITH FULL
WHY ARE YOU ALWAYS WRITING MESSAGES AND SHIT? WHAT ABOUT YOUR TAG? YOU DON'T EVEN GOT ONE YET.
AND YOU SPELLED THAT WRONG, MAN.
NAH.
PEOPLE BE ZIPPING BY ON THE TRAIN, AND MAYBE ONE OF THEM LOOKS OUT THE WINDOW AT THE RIGHT TIME, AND BAM! STRAIGHT INTO THEIR SUBCONSCIOUS.
AND IT'S LIKE A TWIST ON THE WORDS, SEE? FAITHFUL, FULL OF FAITH. YOU GOTTA BE TO GET CLOSED IN A STEEL BOX AND GO FLYING UNDER A RIVER, KNOW WHAT I MEAN?
SOUNDS LIKE POETRY...
MAYBE. NOTHING WRONG WITH THAT, THOUGH.
I'M IN THIS FOR LIFE, LIKE YOU...BUT WHAT DO I WANT TO LEAVE BEHIND? SOME KIND OF KNOWLEDGE, OR JUST SOME BORING TAG?
IT'S NOT JUST ABOUT CLAIMING TERRITORY FOR ME.
WHEN THEY EXCAVATE ALL THIS SHIT IN TEN YEARS, THIS IS WHAT'LL MAKE SENSE, RIGHT?
HEH, THERE YOU GO--
"DECADE LATER."
THAT'S YOUR TAG, MAN. KNOWLEDGE FOR THE FUTURE AND SHIT, LIKE YOU SAID.
BUT YOU NEED A TAG FOR THAT.
NICE... I'LL WORK ON IT.

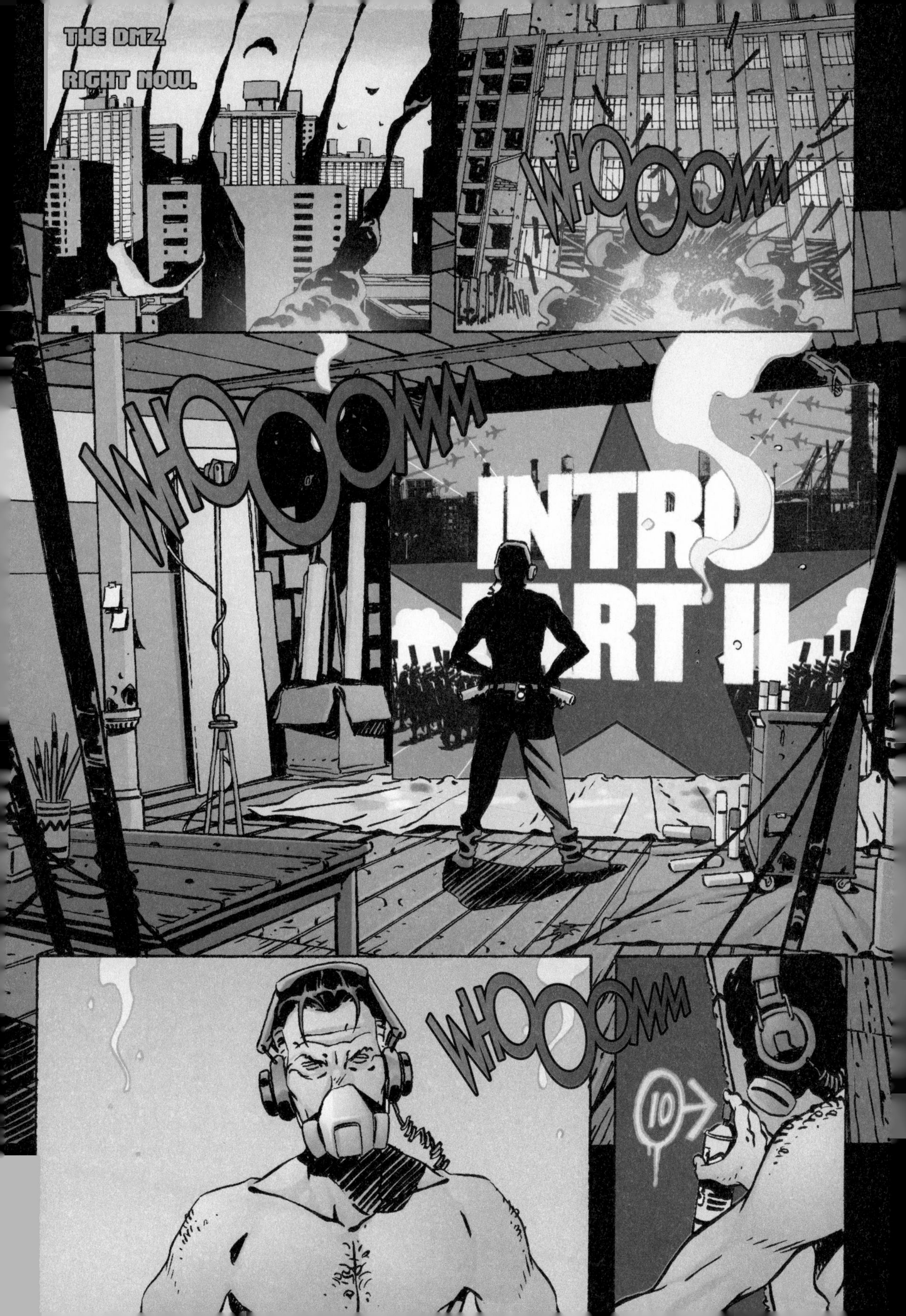
THE DMZ.
RIGHT NOW.
WHOOOMM
WHOOOMM
INTR
ART II
WHOOOMM
10

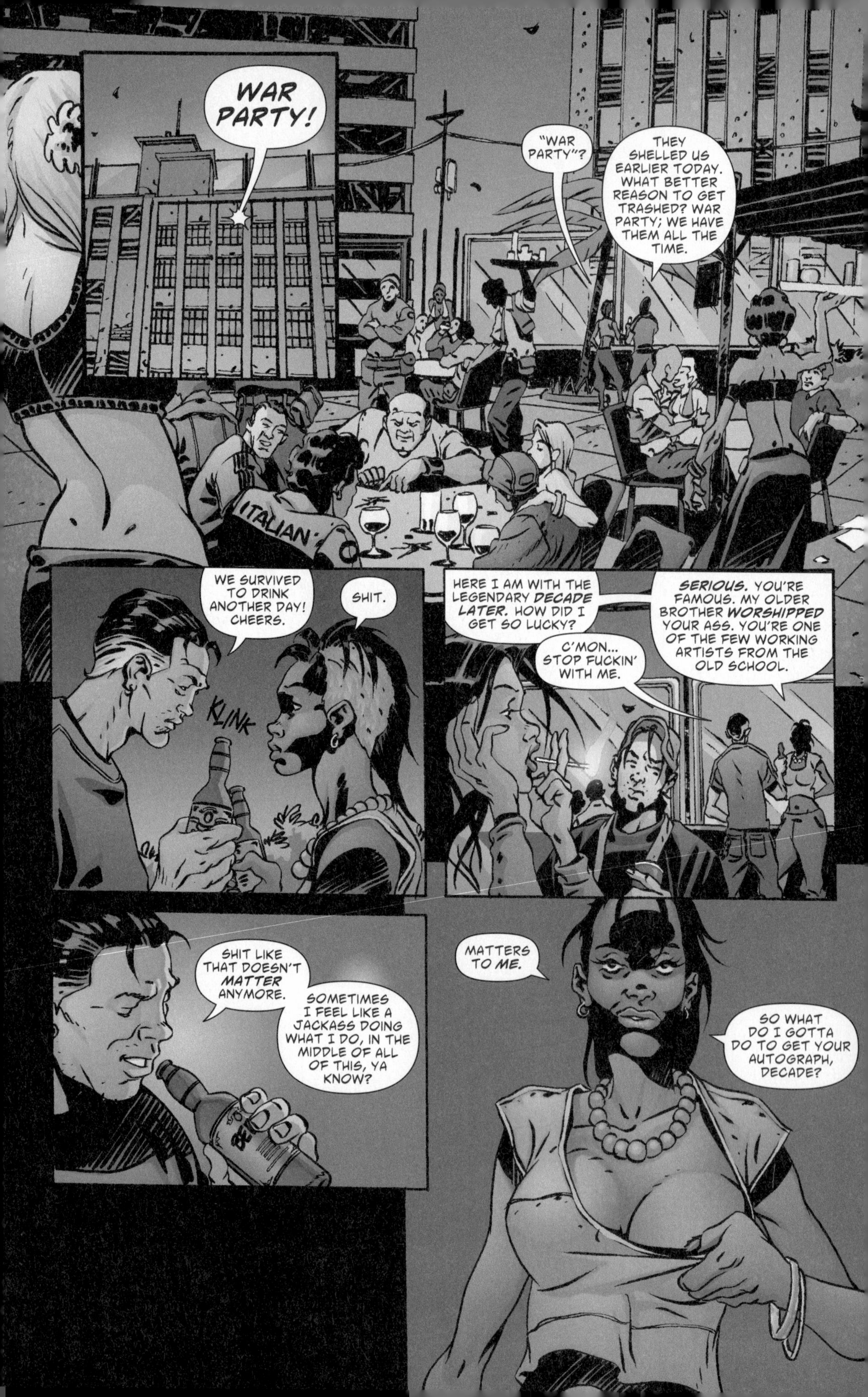
WAR PARTY!
"WAR PARTY"?
THEY SHELLED US EARLIER TODAY. WHAT BETTER REASON TO GET TRASHED? WAR PARTY; WE HAVE THEM ALL THE TIME.
ITALIAN
WE SURVIVED TO DRINK ANOTHER DAY! CHEERS.
SHIT.
KLINK
HERE I AM WITH THE LEGENDARY DECADE LATER. HOW DID I GET SO LUCKY?
C'MON... STOP FUCKIN' WITH ME.
SERIOUS. YOU'RE FAMOUS. MY OLDER BROTHER WORSHIPPED YOUR ASS. YOU'RE ONE OF THE FEW WORKING ARTISTS FROM THE OLD SCHOOL.
SHIT LIKE THAT DOESN'T MATTER ANYMORE.
SOMETIMES I FEEL LIKE A JACKASS DOING WHAT I DO, IN THE MIDDLE OF ALL OF THIS, YA KNOW?
MATTERS TO ME.
SO WHAT DO I GOTTA DO TO GET YOUR AUTOGRAPH, DECADE?

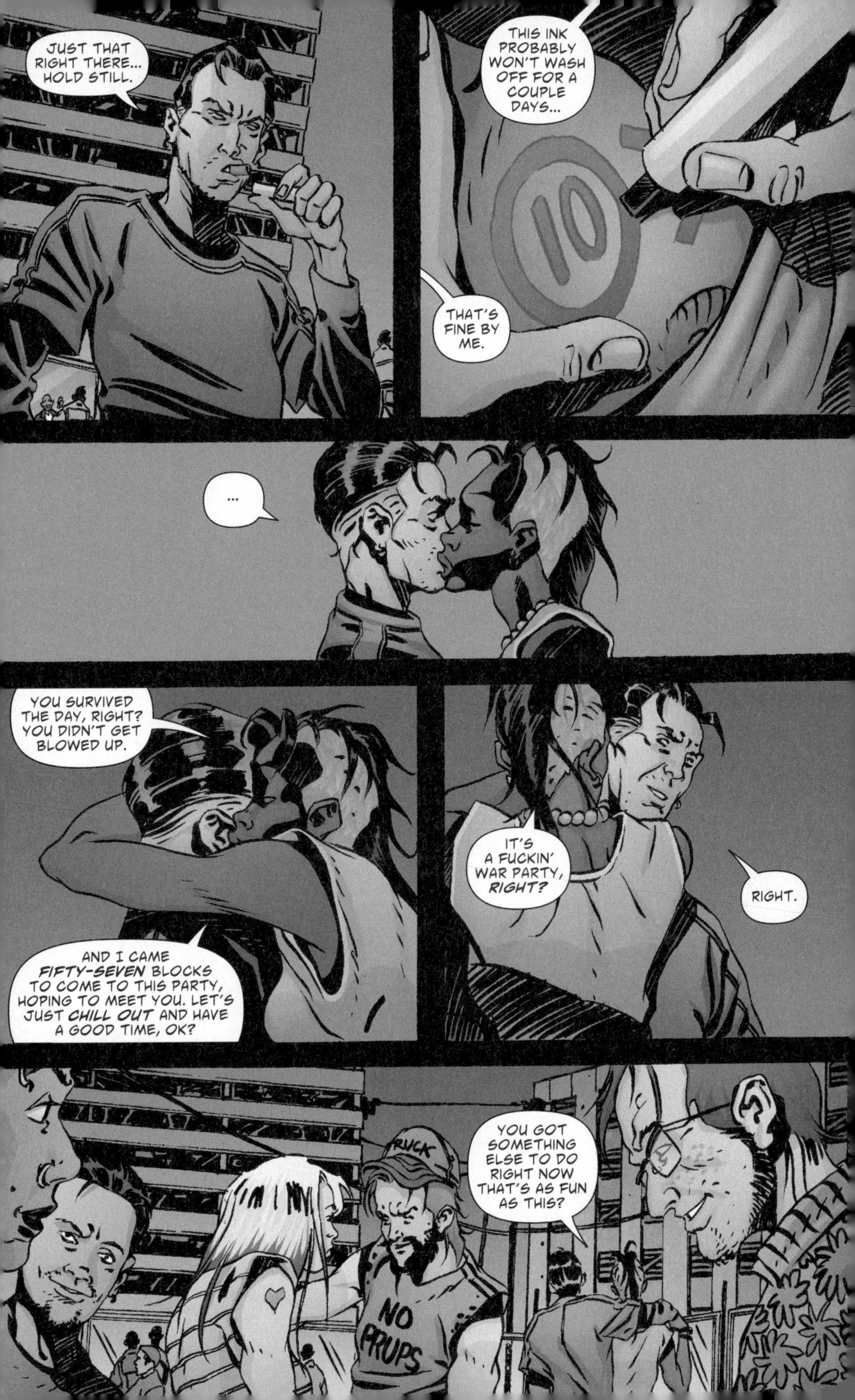
JUST THAT RIGHT THERE... HOLD STILL.
THIS INK PROBABLY WON'T WASH OFF FOR A COUPLE DAYS...
10
THAT'S FINE BY ME.
...
YOU SURVIVED THE DAY, RIGHT? YOU DIDN'T GET BLOWED UP.
AND I CAME FIFTY-SEVEN BLOCKS TO COME TO THIS PARTY, HOPING TO MEET YOU. LET'S JUST CHILL OUT AND HAVE A GOOD TIME, OK?
IT'S A FUCKIN' WAR PARTY, RIGHT?
RIGHT.
YOU GOT SOMETHING ELSE TO DO RIGHT NOW THAT'S AS FUN AS THIS?
NO PRUPS

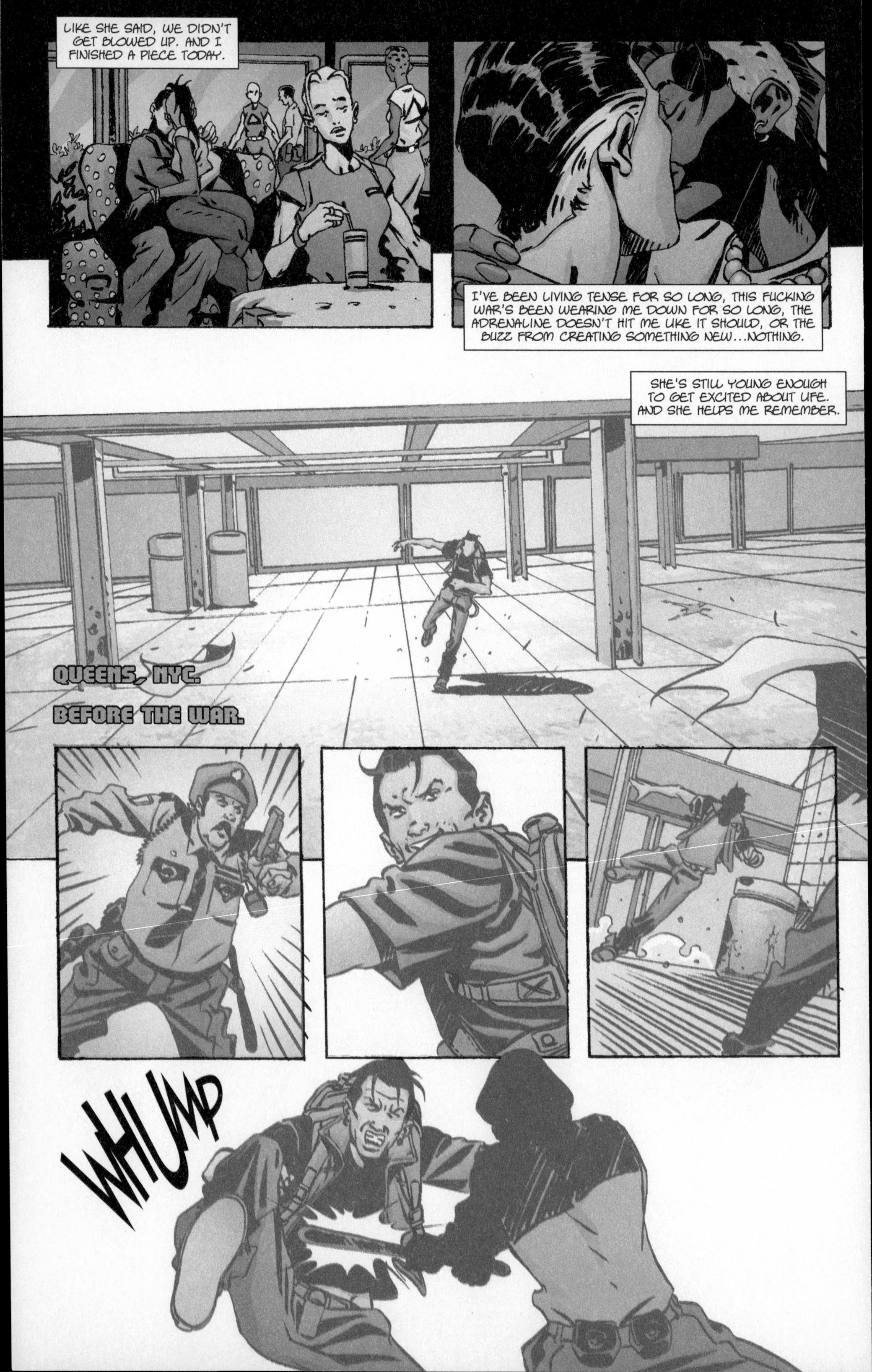
LIKE SHE SAID, WE DIDN'T GET BLOWED UP. AND I FINISHED A PIECE TODAY.
I'VE BEEN LIVING TENSE FOR SO LONG, THIS FUCKING WAR'S BEEN WEARING ME DOWN FOR SO LONG, THE ADRENALINE DOESN'T HIT ME LIKE IT SHOULD, OR THE BUZZ FROM CREATING SOMETHING NEW...NOTHING.
SHE'S STILL YOUNG ENOUGH TO GET EXCITED ABOUT LIFE. AND SHE HELPS ME REMEMBER.
QUEENS, NYC.
BEFORE THE WAR.
WHUMP

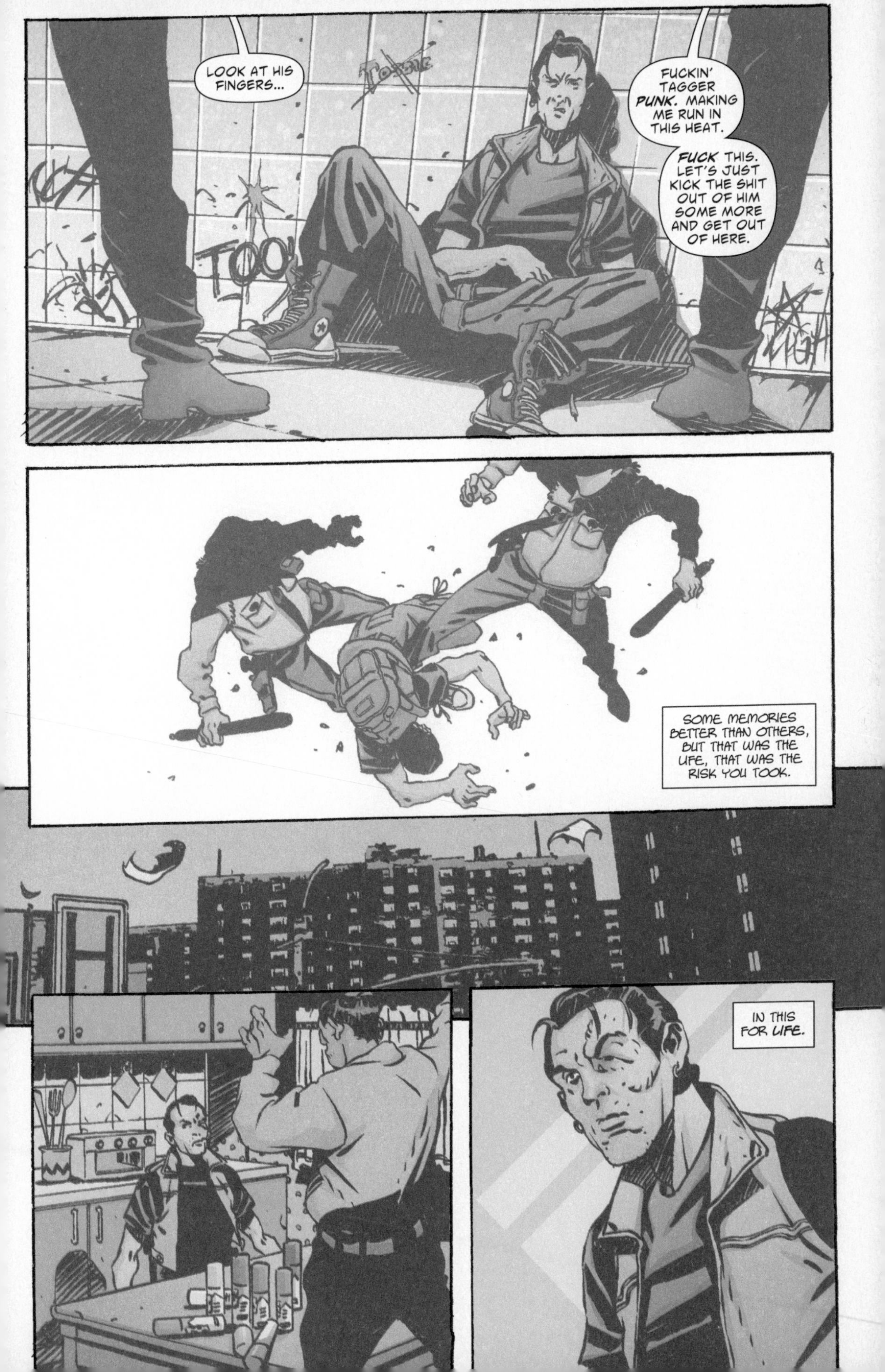
LOOK AT HIS FINGERS...
FUCKIN' TAGGER PUNK. MAKING ME RUN IN THIS HEAT.
FUCK THIS. LET'S JUST KICK THE SHIT OUT OF HIM SOME MORE AND GET OUT OF HERE.
SOME MEMORIES BETTER THAN OTHERS, BUT THAT WAS THE LIFE, THAT WAS THE RISK YOU TOOK.
IN THIS FOR LIFE.

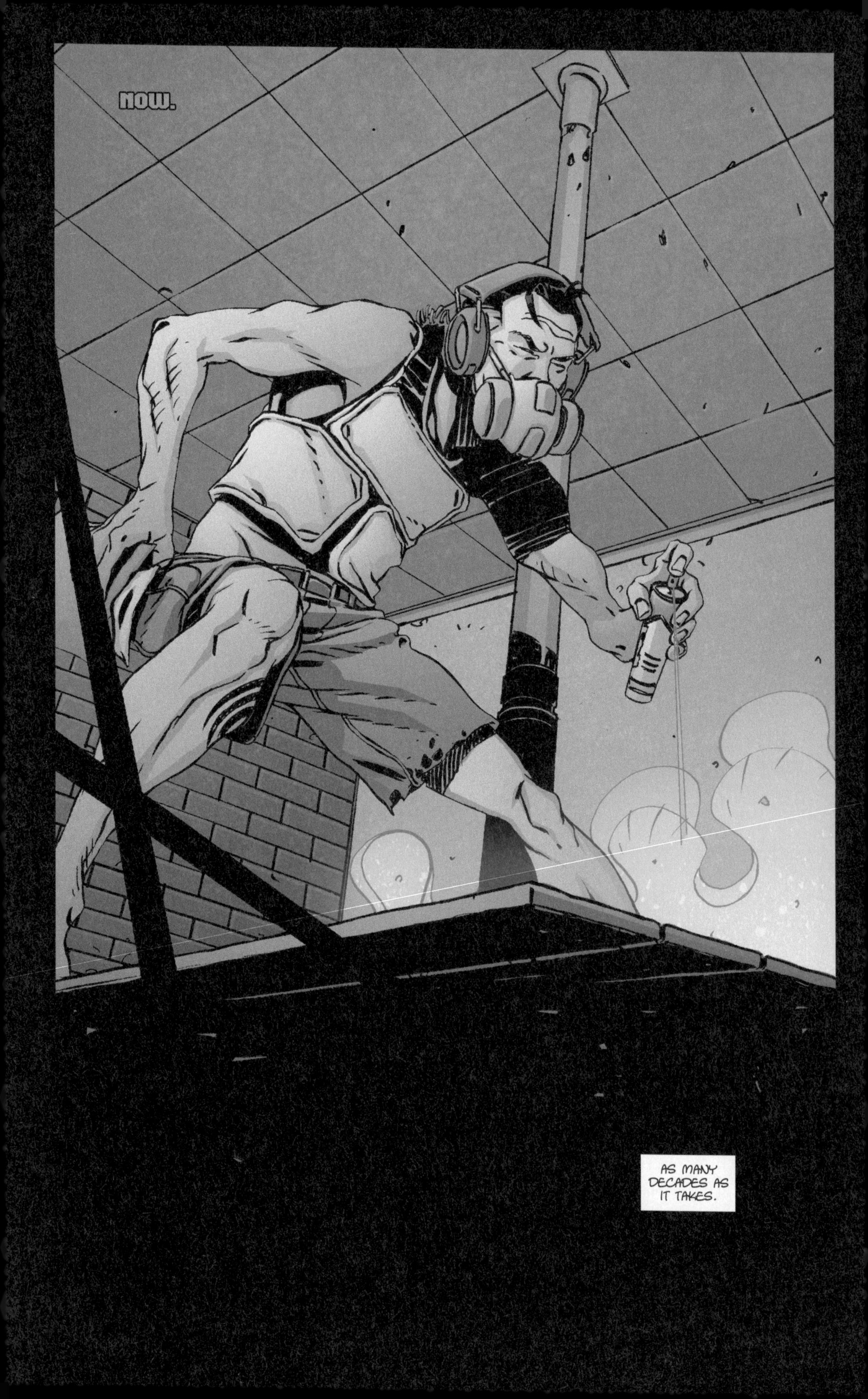
NOW.
AS MANY DECADES AS IT TAKES.

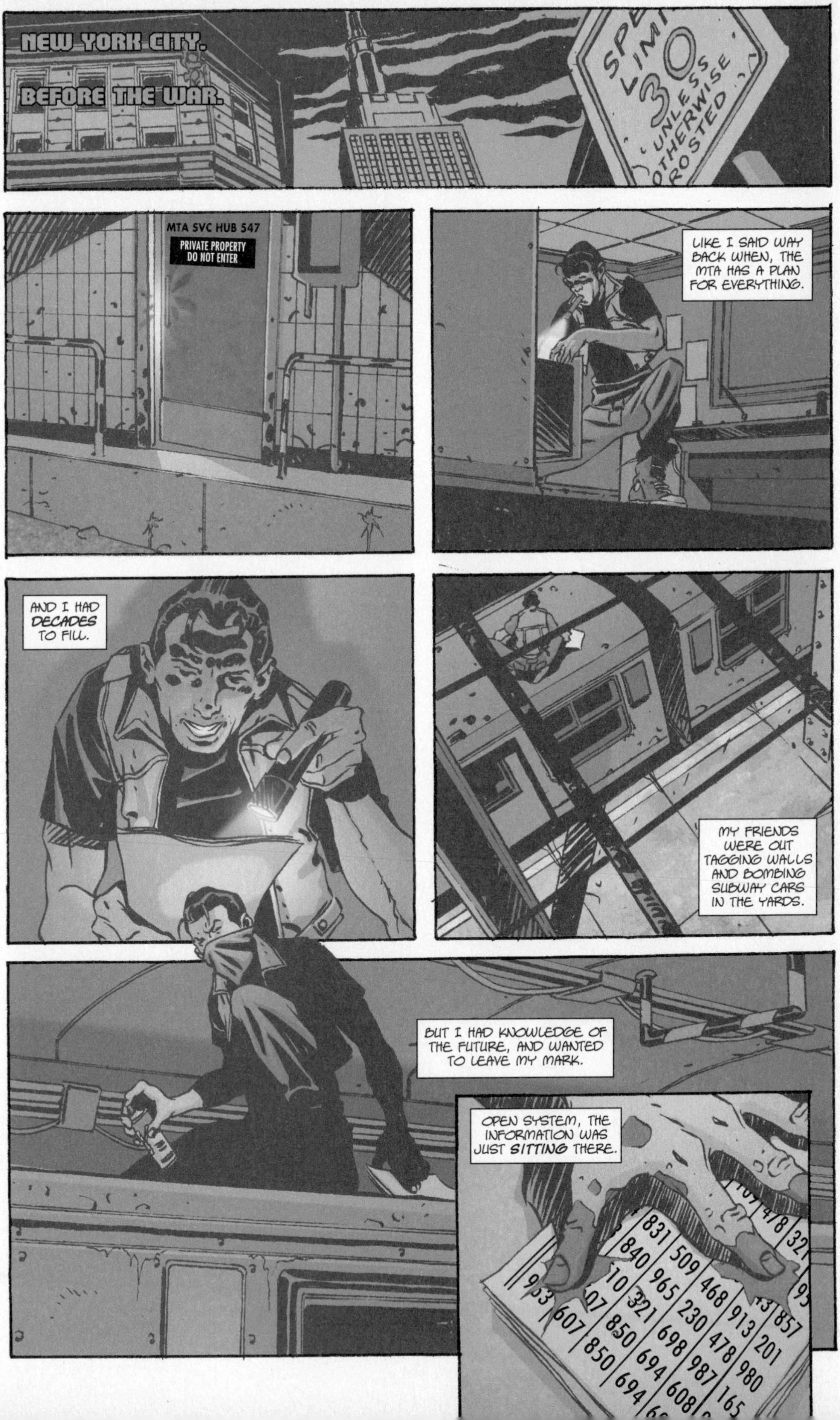
NEW YORK CITY.
BEFORE THE WAR.
MTA SVC HUB 547
PRIVATE PROPERTY DO NOT ENTER
LIKE I SAID WAY BACK WHEN, THE MTA HAS A PLAN FOR EVERYTHING.
AND I HAD *DECADES* TO FILL.
MY FRIENDS WERE OUT TAGGING WALLS AND BOMBING SUBWAY CARS IN THE YARDS.
BUT I HAD KNOWLEDGE OF THE FUTURE, AND WANTED TO LEAVE MY MARK.
OPEN SYSTEM, THE INFORMATION WAS JUST *SITTING* THERE.

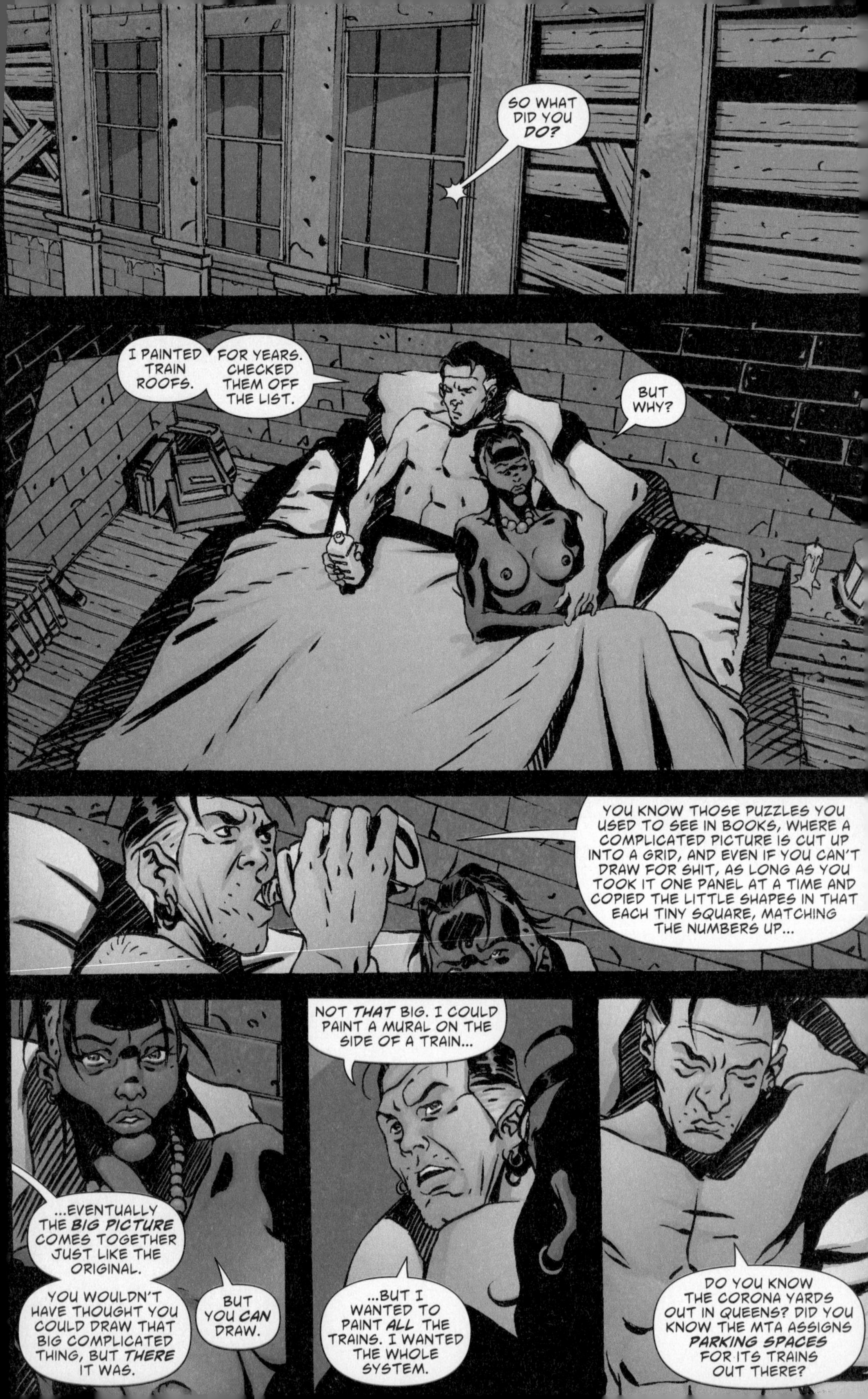
SO WHAT DID YOU *DO?*
I PAINTED TRAIN ROOFS.
FOR YEARS. CHECKED THEM OFF THE LIST.
BUT WHY?
YOU KNOW THOSE PUZZLES YOU USED TO SEE IN BOOKS, WHERE A COMPLICATED PICTURE IS CUT UP INTO A GRID, AND EVEN IF YOU CAN'T DRAW FOR SHIT, AS LONG AS YOU TOOK IT ONE PANEL AT A TIME AND COPIED THE LITTLE SHAPES IN THAT EACH TINY SQUARE, MATCHING THE NUMBERS UP...
...EVENTUALLY THE *BIG PICTURE* COMES TOGETHER JUST LIKE THE ORIGINAL.
YOU WOULDN'T HAVE THOUGHT YOU COULD DRAW THAT BIG COMPLICATED THING, BUT *THERE* IT WAS.
BUT YOU *CAN* DRAW.
NOT *THAT* BIG. I COULD PAINT A MURAL ON THE SIDE OF A TRAIN...
...BUT I WANTED TO PAINT *ALL* THE TRAINS. I WANTED THE WHOLE SYSTEM.
DO YOU KNOW THE CORONA YARDS OUT IN QUEENS? DID YOU KNOW THE MTA ASSIGNS *PARKING SPACES* FOR ITS TRAINS OUT THERE?

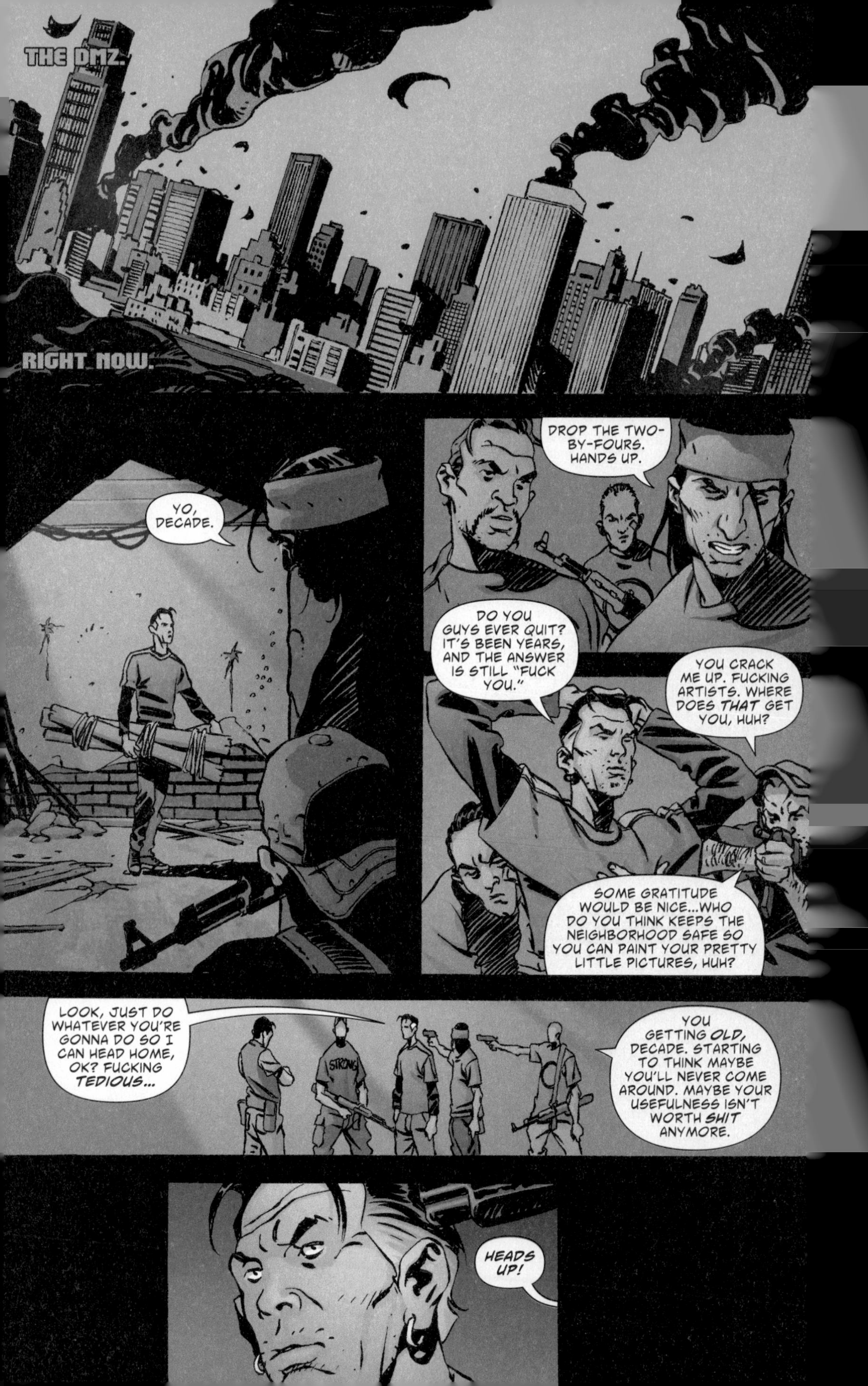
THE DMZ.
RIGHT NOW.
YO, DECADE.
DROP THE TWO-BY-FOURS. HANDS UP.
DO YOU GUYS EVER QUIT? IT'S BEEN YEARS, AND THE ANSWER IS STILL "FUCK YOU."
YOU CRACK ME UP. FUCKING ARTISTS. WHERE DOES *THAT* GET YOU, HUH?
SOME GRATITUDE WOULD BE NICE...WHO DO YOU THINK KEEPS THE NEIGHBORHOOD SAFE SO YOU CAN PAINT YOUR PRETTY LITTLE PICTURES, HUH?
LOOK, JUST DO WHATEVER YOU'RE GONNA DO SO I CAN HEAD HOME, OK? FUCKING *TEDIOUS*...
STRONG
YOU GETTING *OLD*, DECADE. STARTING TO THINK MAYBE YOU'LL NEVER COME AROUND. MAYBE YOUR USEFULNESS ISN'T WORTH *SHIT* ANYMORE.
HEADS UP!

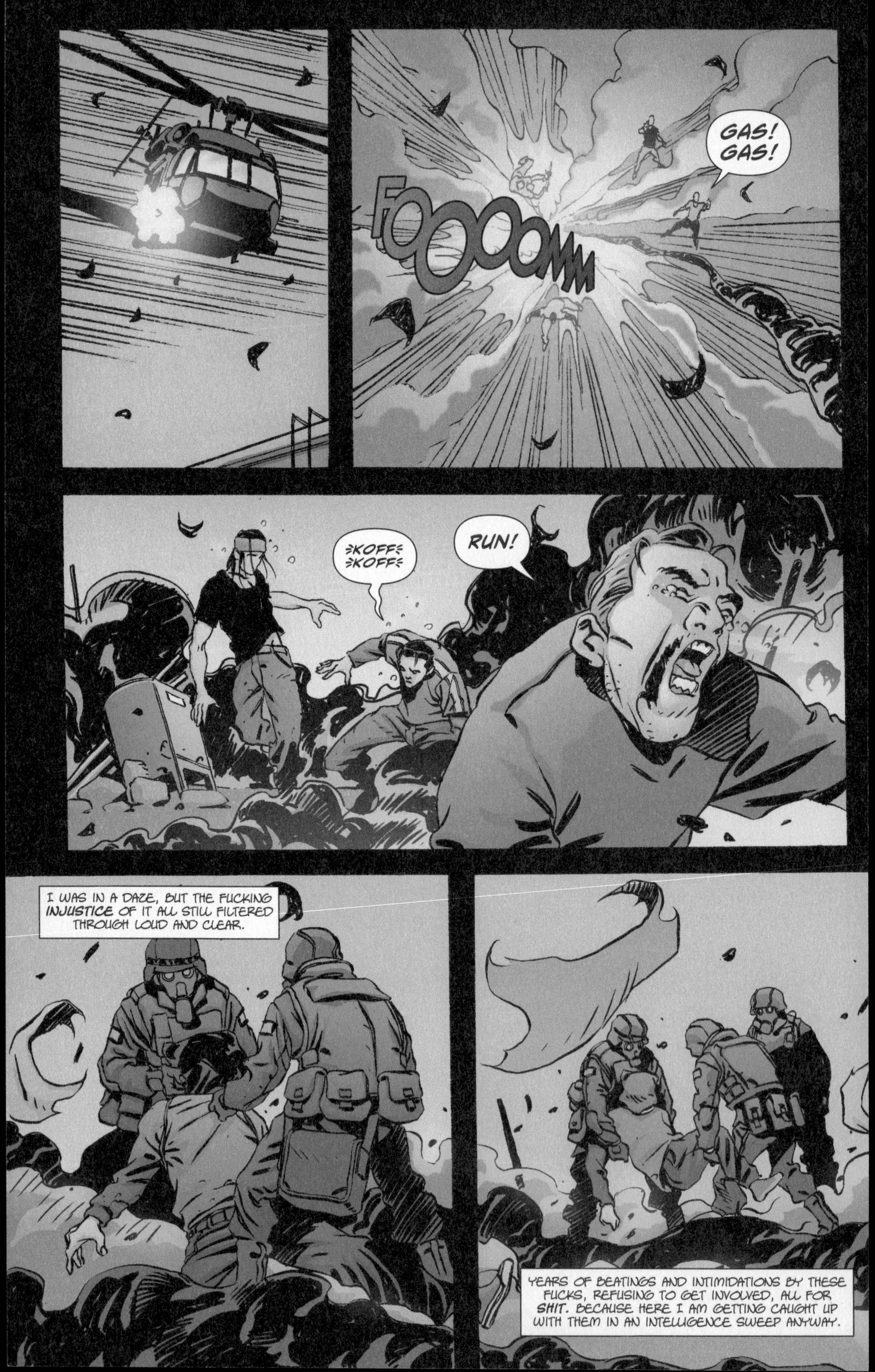
FOOOOOMM
GAS! GAS!
KOFF KOFF
RUN!
I WAS IN A DAZE, BUT THE FUCKING INJUSTICE OF IT ALL STILL FILTERED THROUGH LOUD AND CLEAR.
YEARS OF BEATINGS AND INTIMIDATIONS BY THESE FUCKS, REFUSING TO GET INVOLVED, ALL FOR SHIT. BECAUSE HERE I AM GETTING CAUGHT UP WITH THEM IN AN INTELLIGENCE SWEEP ANYWAY.

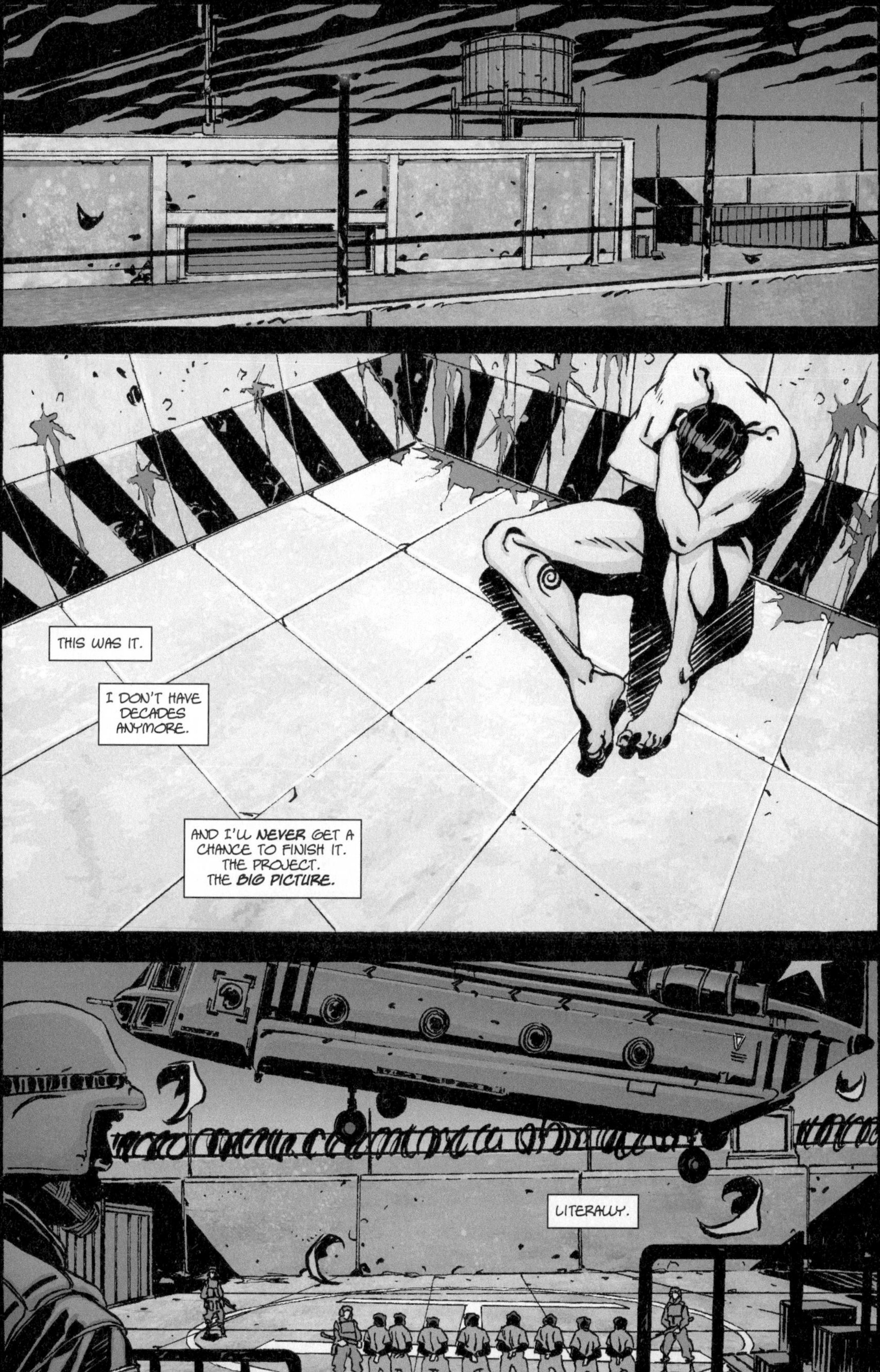
THIS WAS IT.
I DON'T HAVE DECADES ANYMORE.
AND I'LL NEVER GET A CHANCE TO FINISH IT. THE PROJECT. THE BIG PICTURE.
LITERALLY.

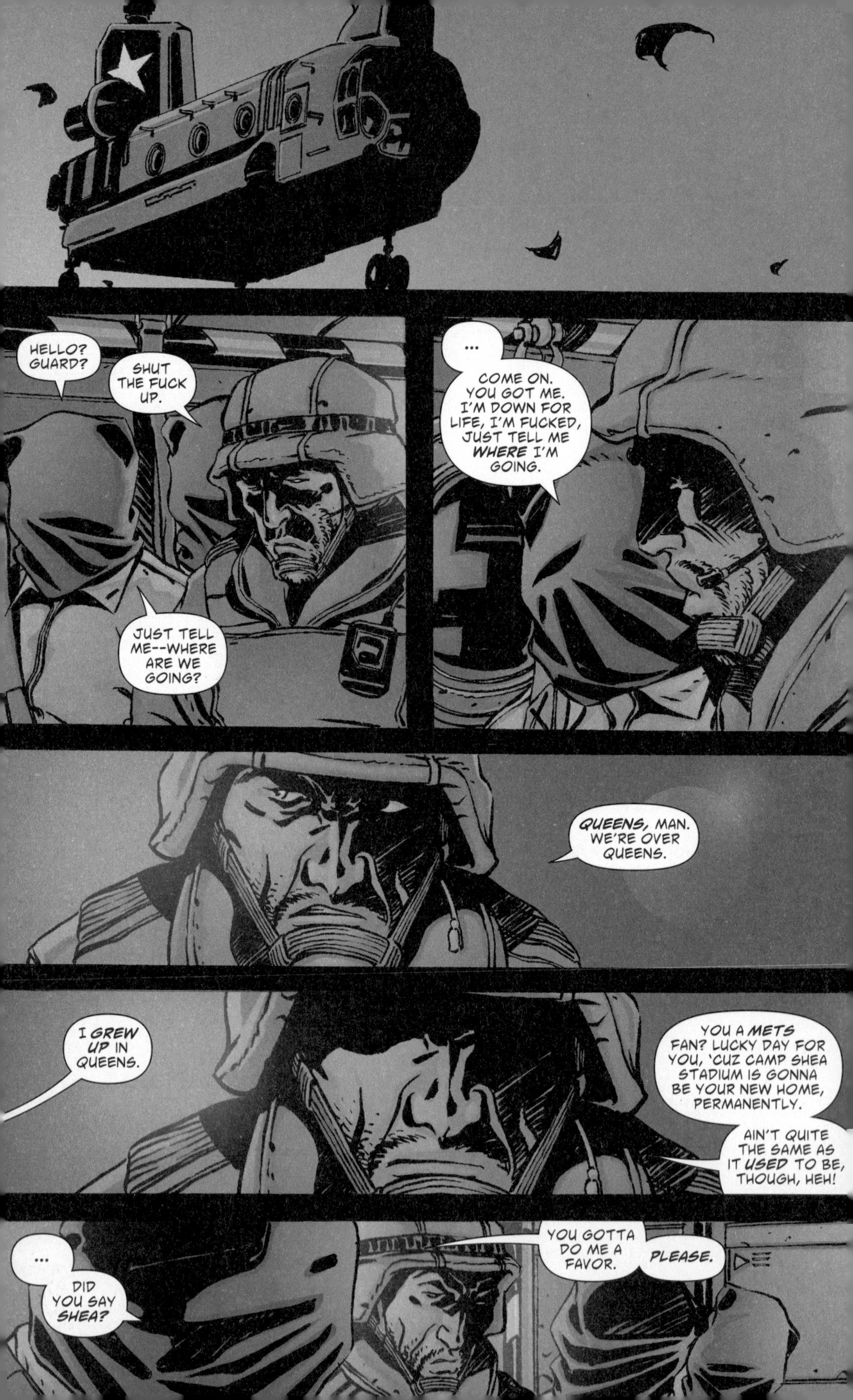
HELLO? GUARD?
SHUT THE FUCK UP.
JUST TELL ME--WHERE ARE WE GOING?
...
COME ON. YOU GOT ME. I'M DOWN FOR LIFE, I'M FUCKED, JUST TELL ME WHERE I'M GOING.
QUEENS, MAN. WE'RE OVER QUEENS.
I GREW UP IN QUEENS.
YOU A METS FAN? LUCKY DAY FOR YOU, 'CUZ CAMP SHEA STADIUM IS GONNA BE YOUR NEW HOME, PERMANENTLY.
AIN'T QUITE THE SAME AS IT USED TO BE, THOUGH, HEH!
...
DID YOU SAY SHEA?
YOU GOTTA DO ME A FAVOR.
PLEASE.

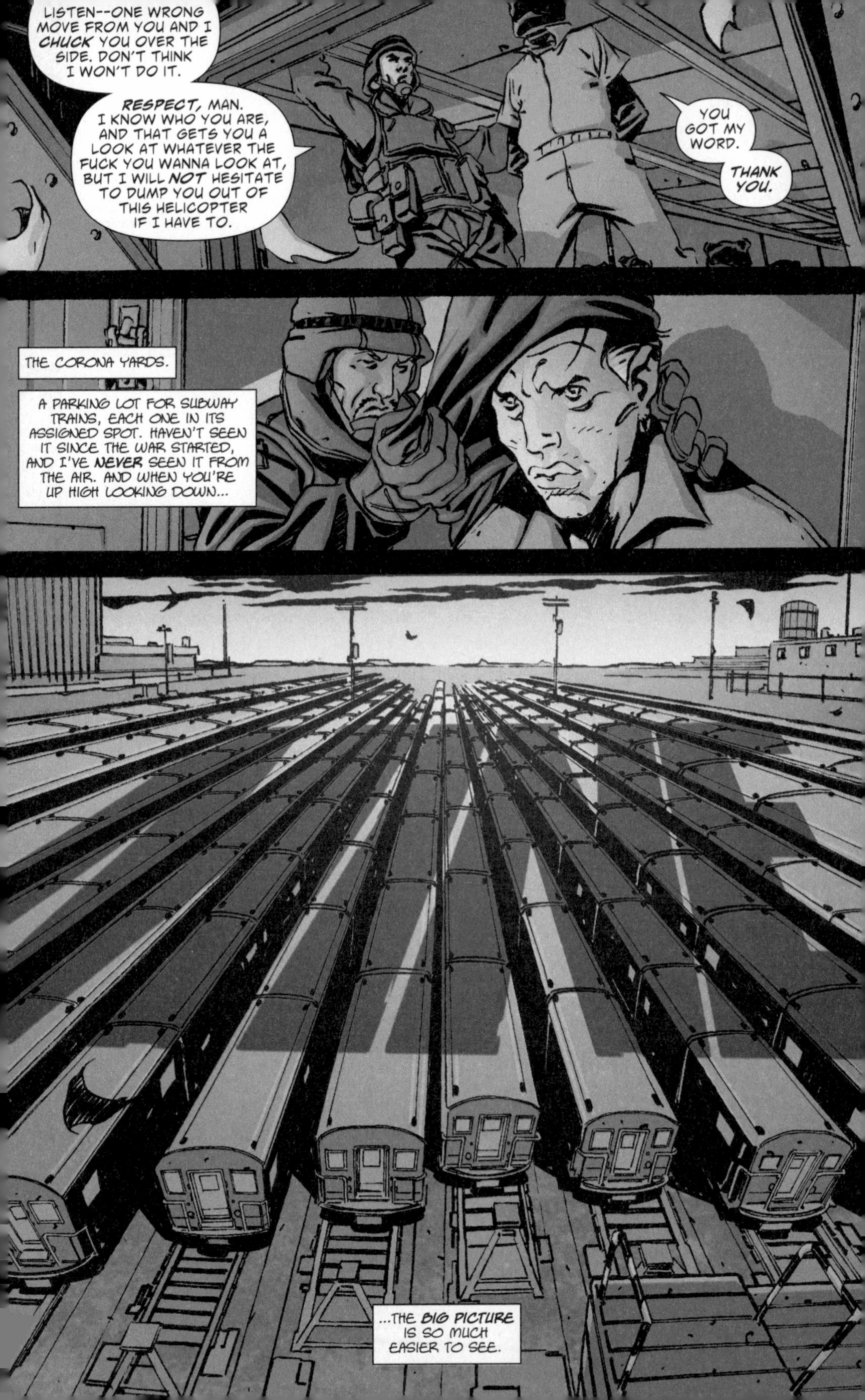
LISTEN--ONE WRONG MOVE FROM YOU AND I CHUCK YOU OVER THE SIDE. DON'T THINK I WON'T DO IT.
RESPECT, MAN. I KNOW WHO YOU ARE, AND THAT GETS YOU A LOOK AT WHATEVER THE FUCK YOU WANNA LOOK AT, BUT I WILL NOT HESITATE TO DUMP YOU OUT OF THIS HELICOPTER IF I HAVE TO.
YOU GOT MY WORD.
THANK YOU.
THE CORONA YARDS.
A PARKING LOT FOR SUBWAY TRAINS, EACH ONE IN ITS ASSIGNED SPOT. HAVEN'T SEEN IT SINCE THE WAR STARTED, AND I'VE NEVER SEEN IT FROM THE AIR. AND WHEN YOU'RE UP HIGH LOOKING DOWN...
...THE BIG PICTURE IS SO MUCH EASIER TO SEE.

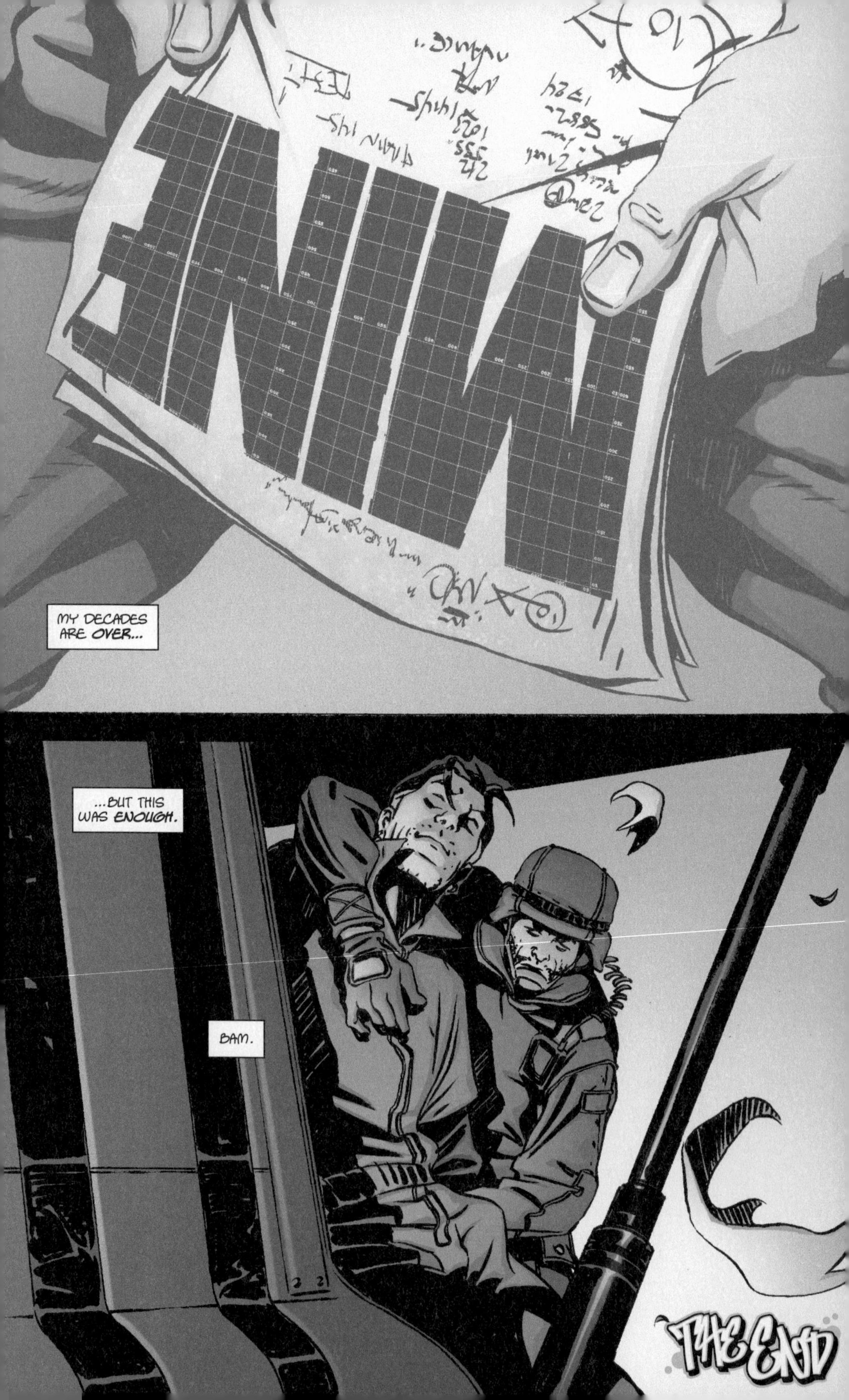
MY DECADES ARE OVER...
...BUT THIS WAS ENOUGH.
BAM.
THE END

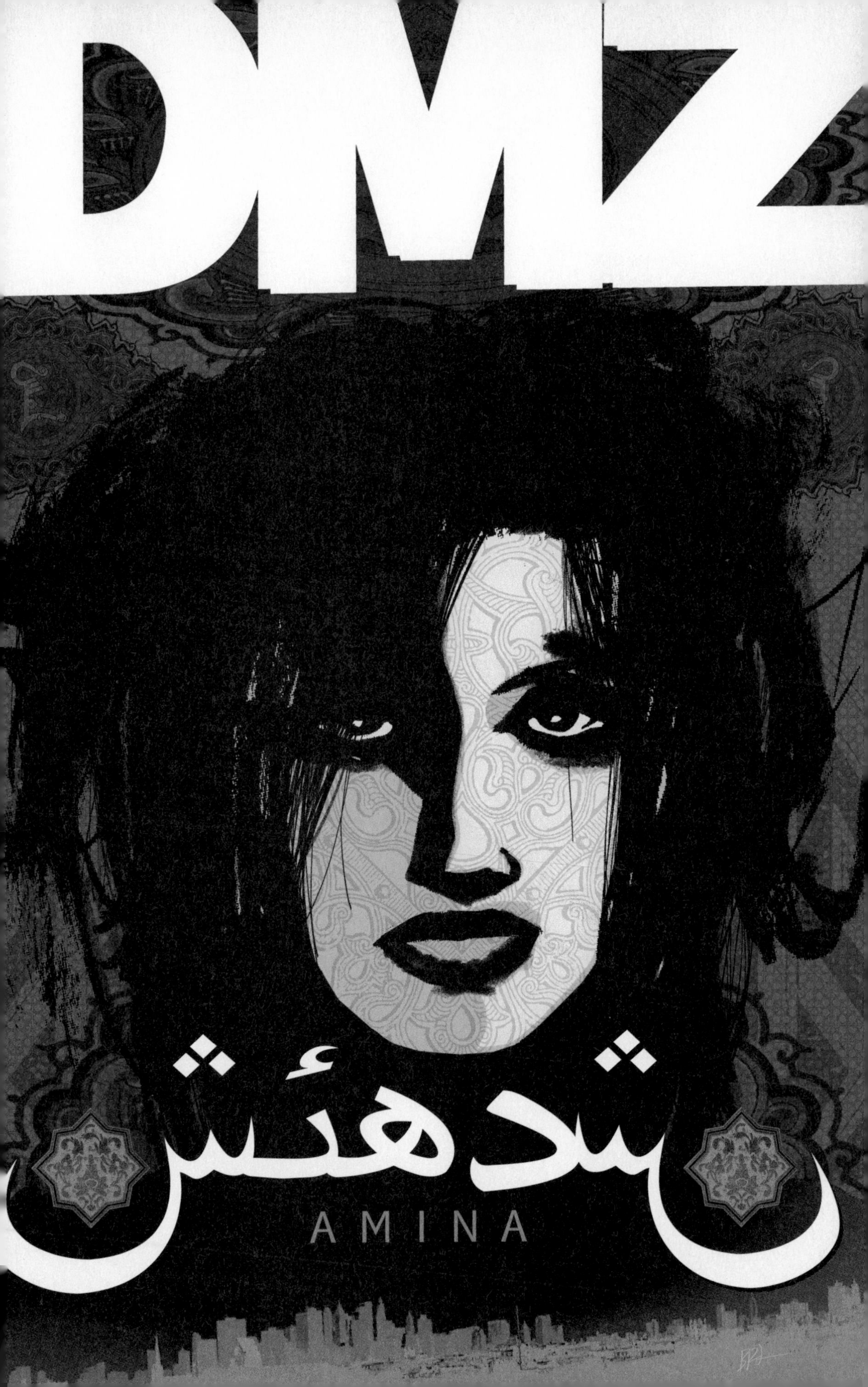
DMZ
AMINA

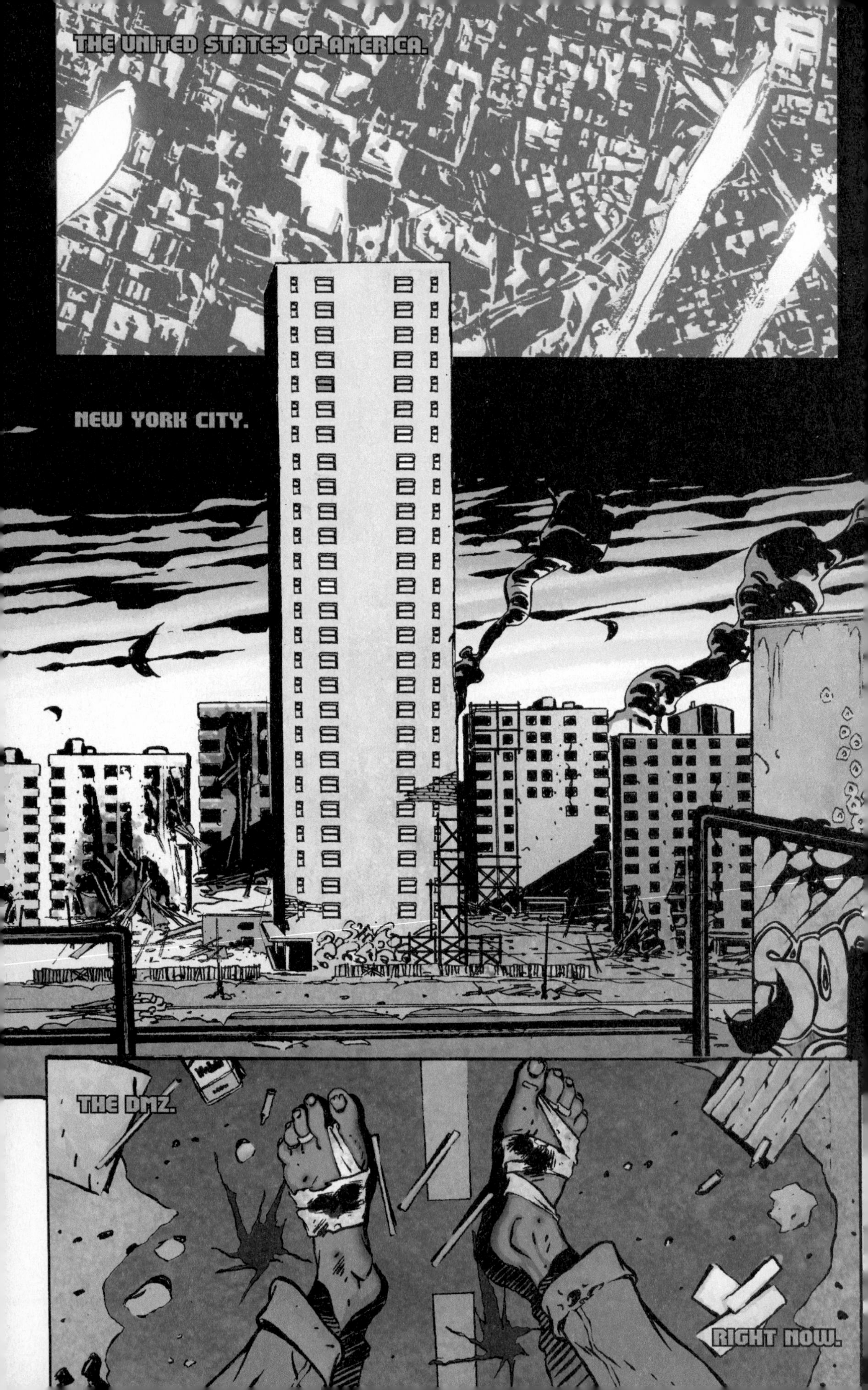
THE UNITED STATES OF AMERICA.
NEW YORK CITY.
THE DMZ.
RIGHT NOW.

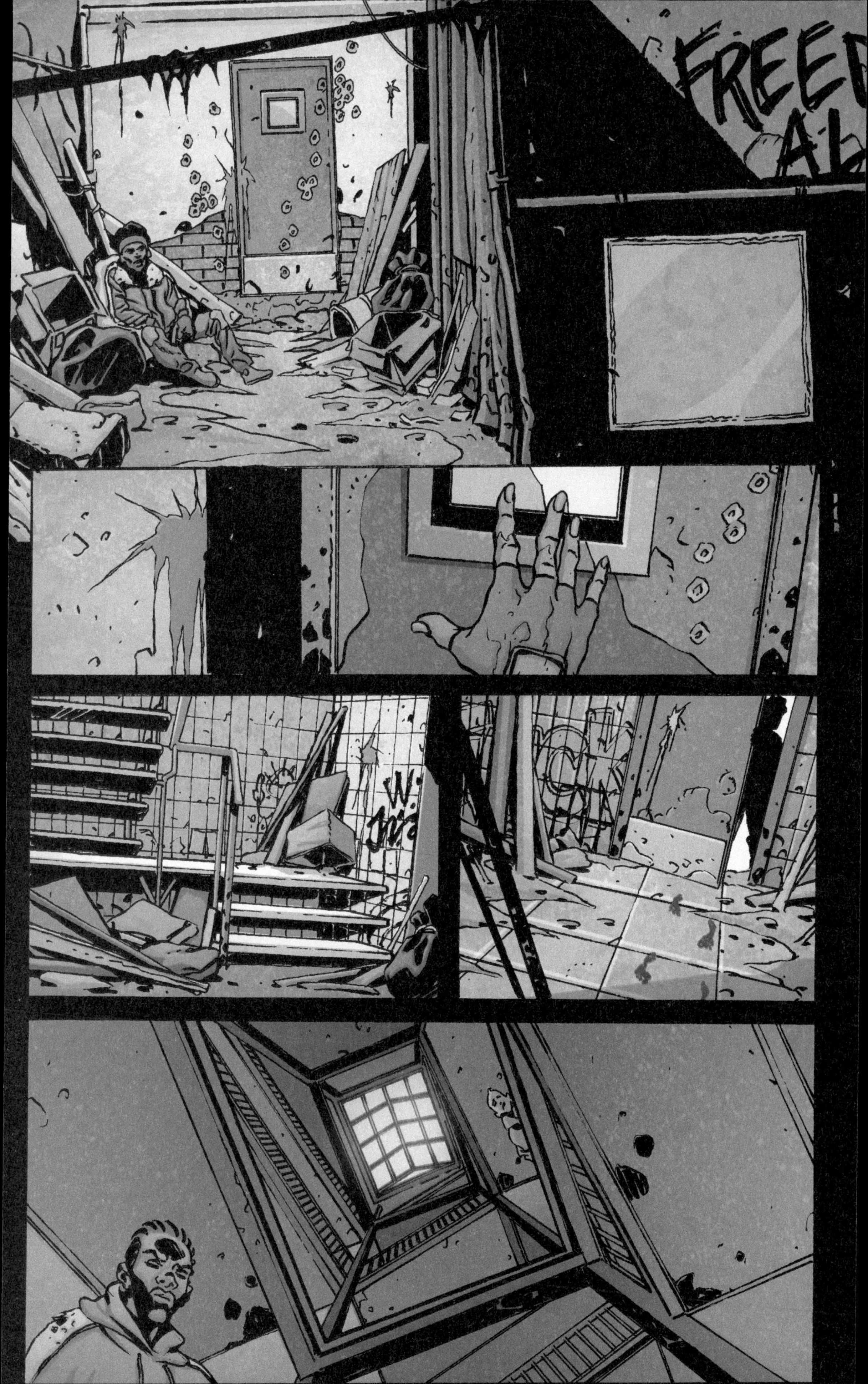
FREED
AL

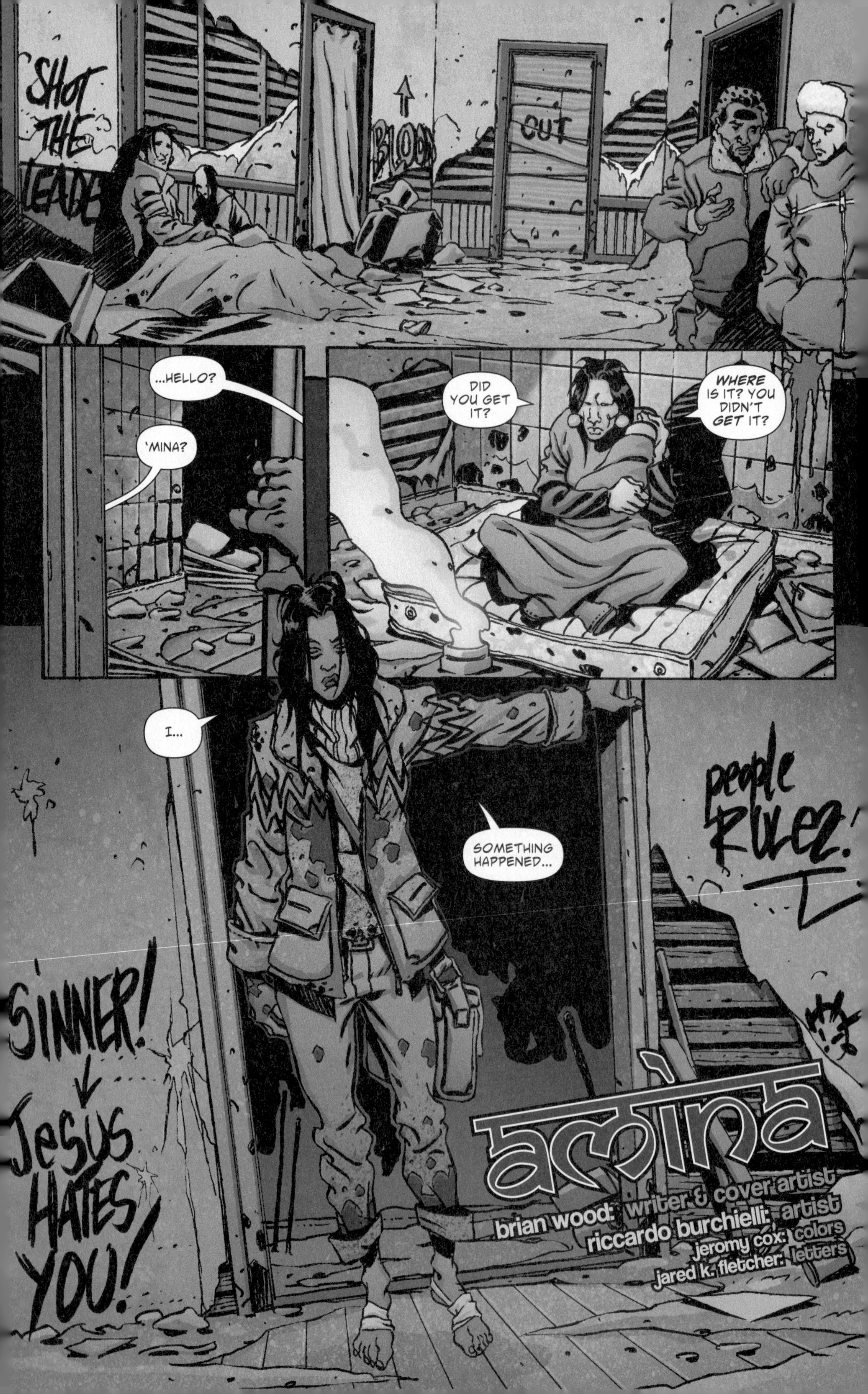
SHOT THE LEADE
BLOO
OUT
...HELLO?
'MINA?
DID YOU GET IT?
WHERE IS IT? YOU DIDN'T GET IT?
I...
SOMETHING HAPPENED...
people RULEZ!
SINNER!
JESUS HATES YOU!
amina
brian wood: writer & cover artist
riccardo burchielli: artist
jeromy cox: colors
jared k. fletcher: letters

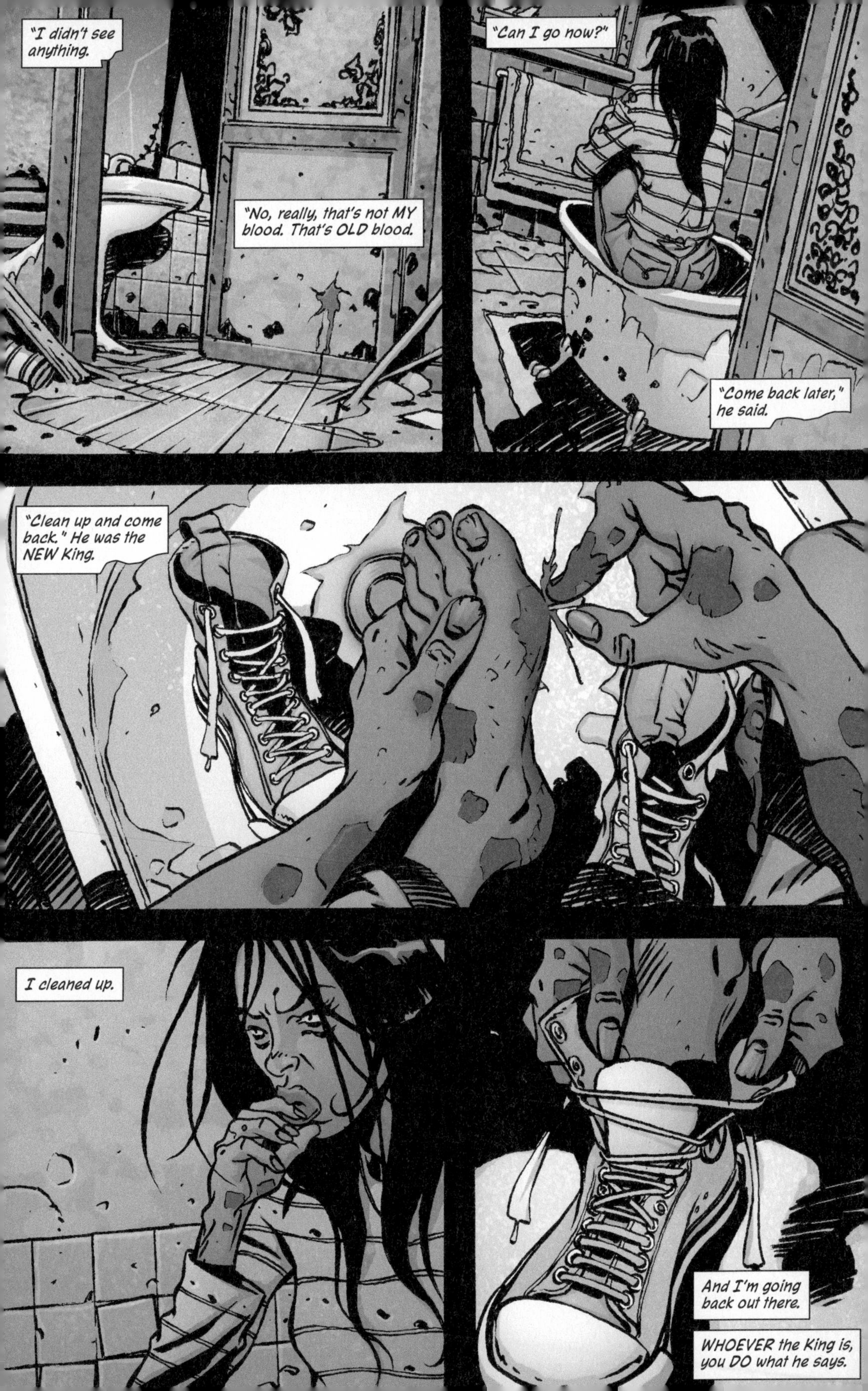
"I didn't see anything.
"No, really, that's not MY blood. That's OLD blood.
"Can I go now?"
"Come back later," he said.
"Clean up and come back." He was the NEW King.
I cleaned up.
And I'm going back out there.
WHOEVER the King is, you DO what he says.

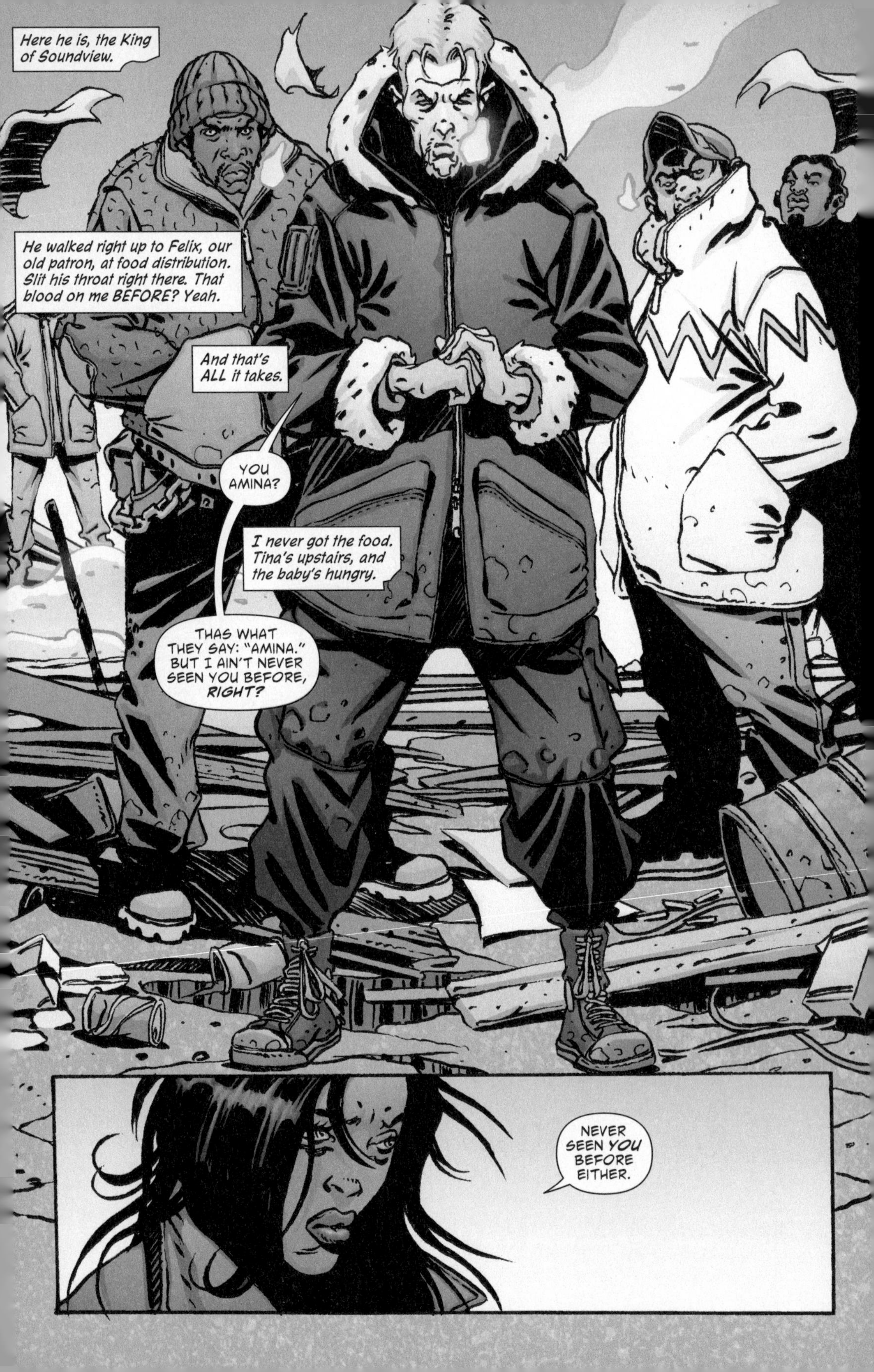
Here he is, the King of Soundview.
He walked right up to Felix, our old patron, at food distribution. Slit his throat right there. That blood on me BEFORE? Yeah.
And that's ALL it takes.
YOU AMINA?
I never got the food. Tina's upstairs, and the baby's hungry.
THAS WHAT THEY SAY: "AMINA." BUT I AIN'T NEVER SEEN YOU BEFORE, RIGHT?
NEVER SEEN YOU BEFORE EITHER.

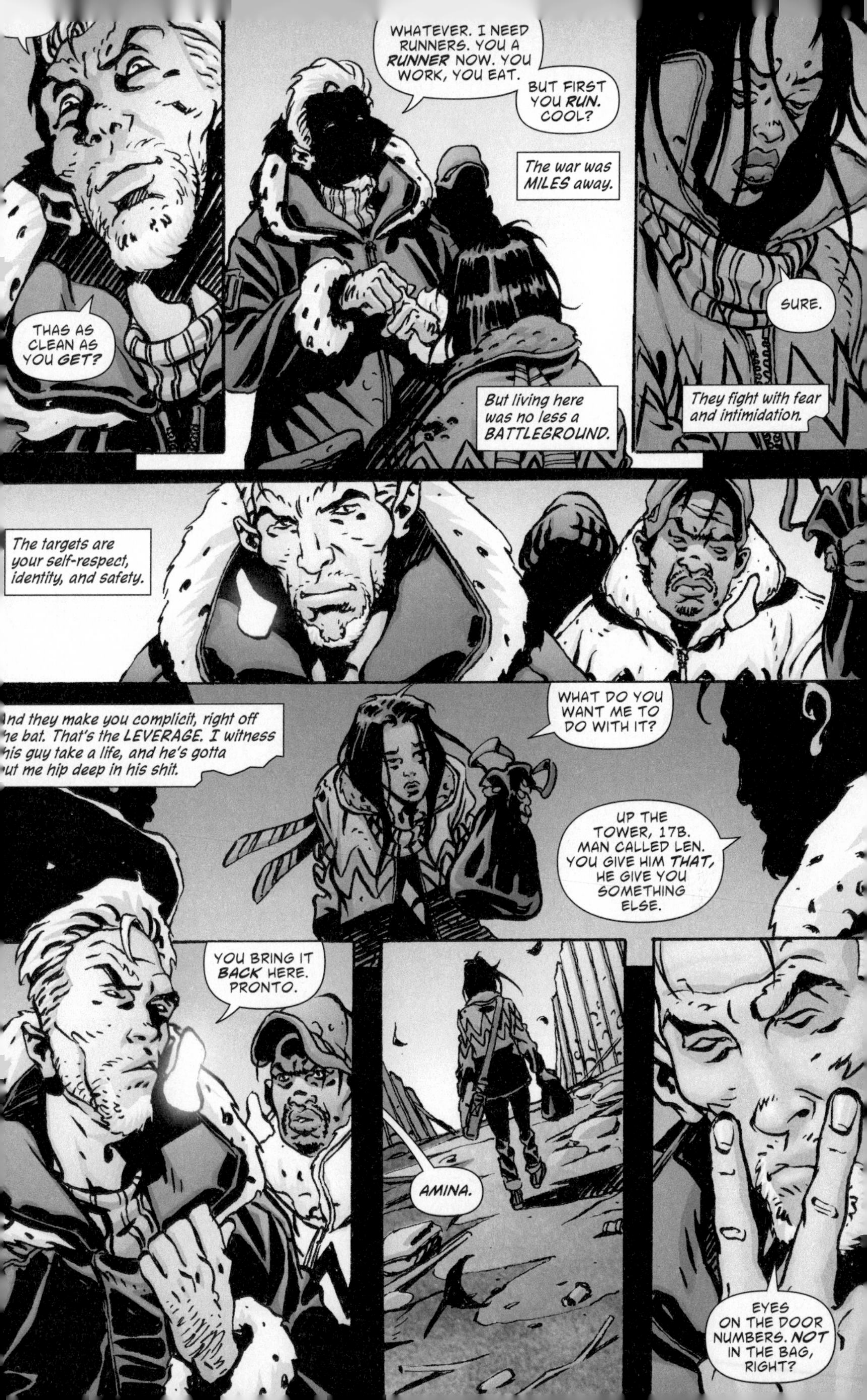
THAS AS CLEAN AS YOU GET?
WHATEVER. I NEED RUNNERS. YOU A RUNNER NOW. YOU WORK, YOU EAT.
BUT FIRST YOU RUN. COOL?
The war was MILES away.
But living here was no less a BATTLEGROUND.
SURE.
They fight with fear and intimidation.
The targets are your self-respect, identity, and safety.
nd they make you complicit, right off e bat. That's the LEVERAGE. I witness his guy take a life, and he's gotta ut me hip deep in his shit.
WHAT DO YOU WANT ME TO DO WITH IT?
UP THE TOWER, 17B. MAN CALLED LEN. YOU GIVE HIM THAT, HE GIVE YOU SOMETHING ELSE.
YOU BRING IT BACK HERE. PRONTO.
AMINA.
EYES ON THE DOOR NUMBERS. NOT IN THE BAG, RIGHT?

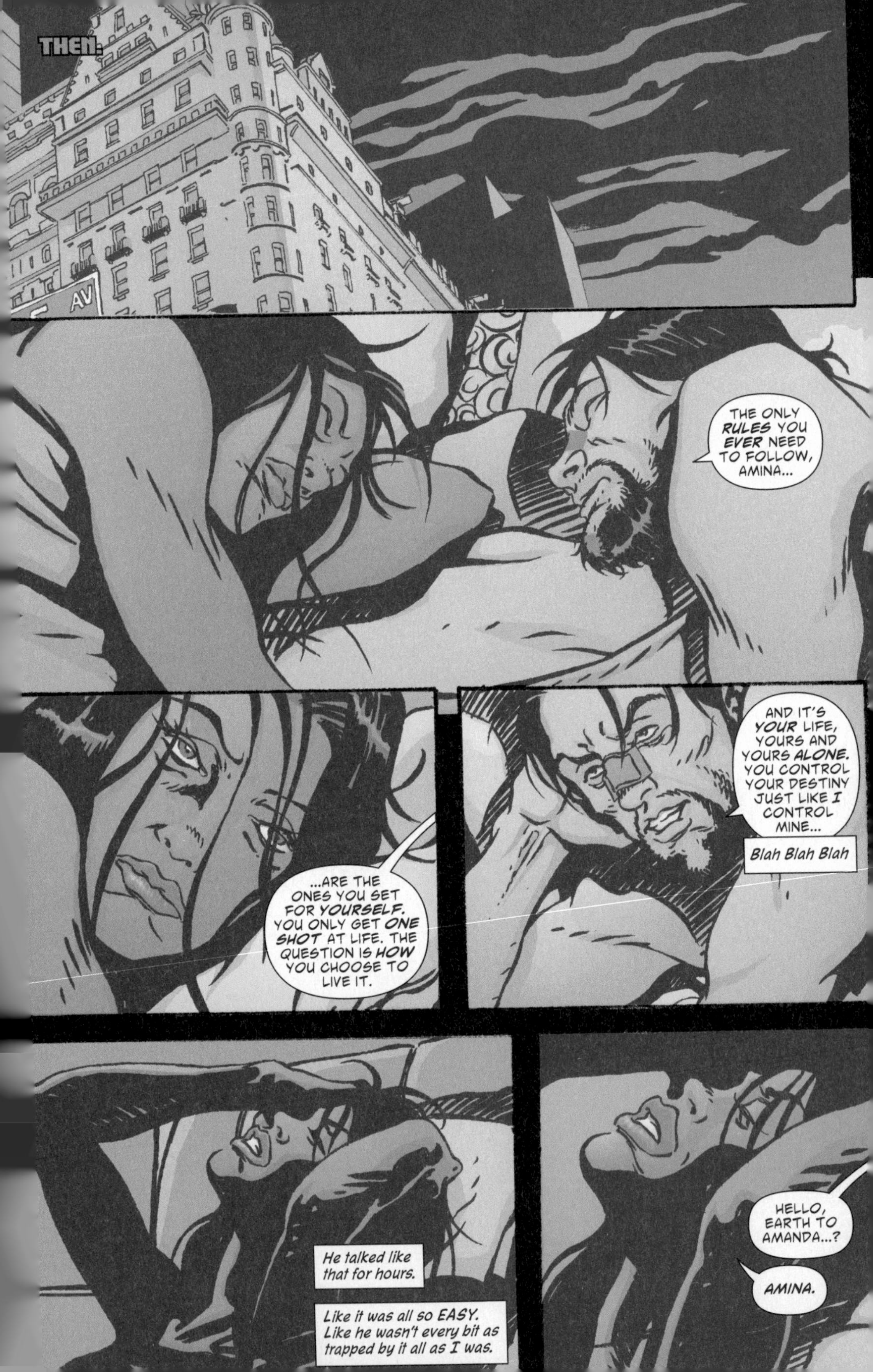
THEN.
THE ONLY RULES YOU EVER NEED TO FOLLOW, AMINA...
...ARE THE ONES YOU SET FOR YOURSELF. YOU ONLY GET ONE SHOT AT LIFE. THE QUESTION IS HOW YOU CHOOSE TO LIVE IT.
AND IT'S YOUR LIFE, YOURS AND YOURS ALONE. YOU CONTROL YOUR DESTINY JUST LIKE I CONTROL MINE...
Blah Blah Blah
He talked like that for hours.
Like it was all so EASY. Like he wasn't every bit as trapped by it all as I was.
HELLO, EARTH TO AMANDA...?
AMINA.

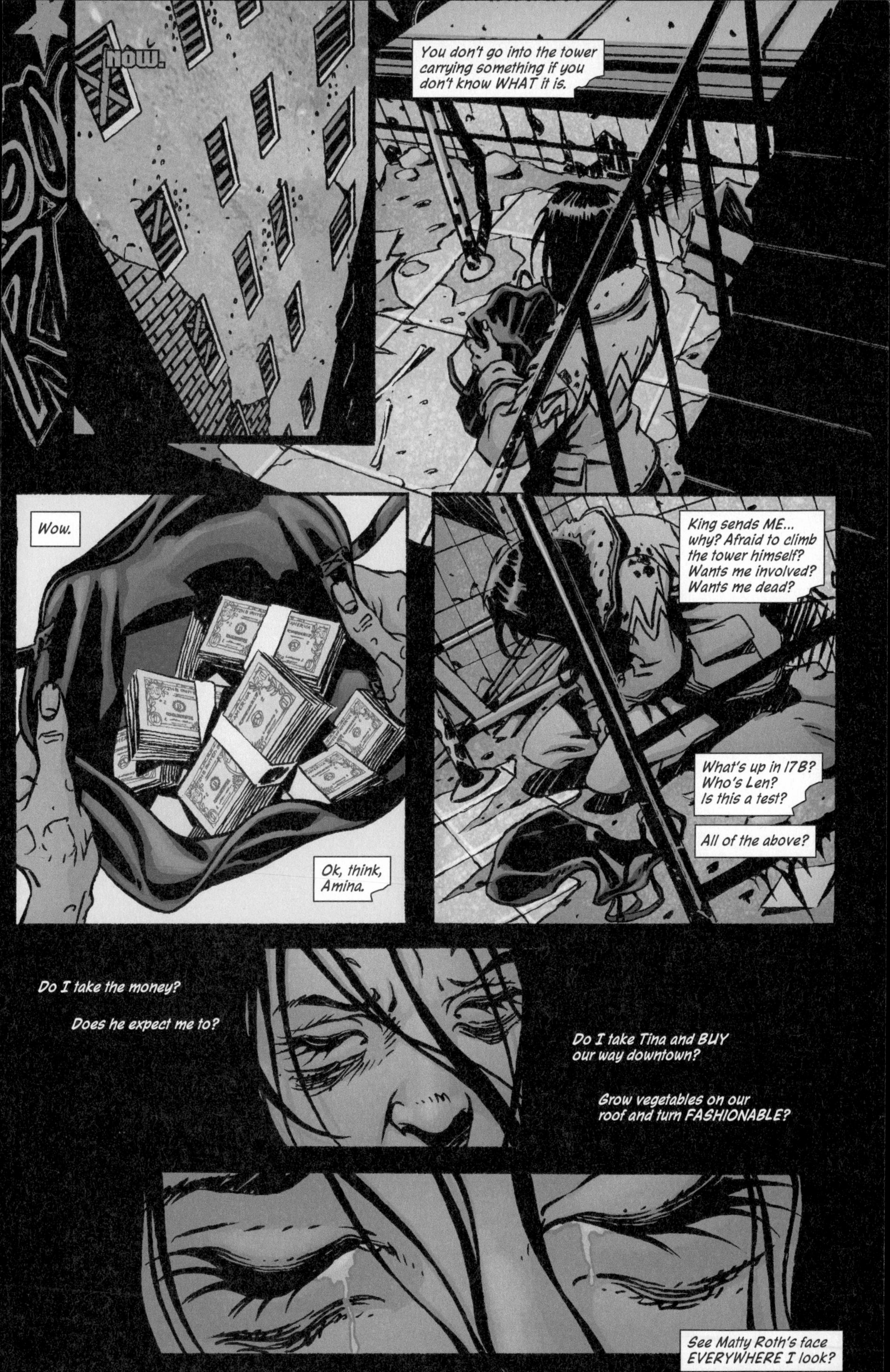
NOW.
You don't go into the tower carrying something if you don't know WHAT it is.
Wow.
Ok, think, Amina.
King sends ME... why? Afraid to climb the tower himself? Wants me involved? Wants me dead?
What's up in 17B? Who's Len? Is this a test?
All of the above?
Do I take the money?
Does he expect me to?
Do I take Tina and BUY our way downtown?
Grow vegetables on our roof and turn FASHIONABLE?
See Matty Roth's face EVERYWHERE I look?

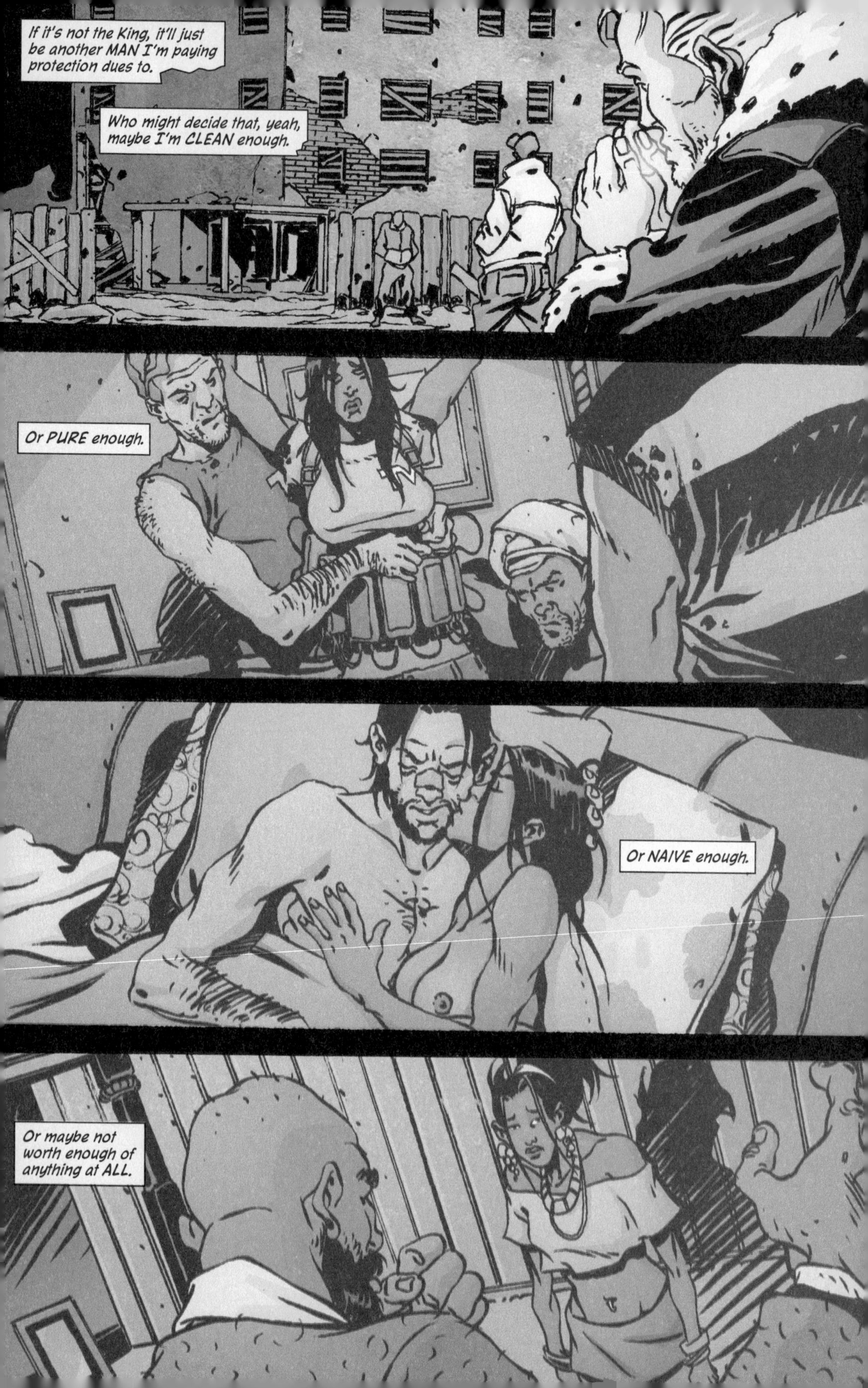
If it's not the King, it'll just be another MAN I'm paying protection dues to.
Who might decide that, yeah, maybe I'm CLEAN enough.
Or PURE enough.
Or NAIVE enough.
Or maybe not worth enough of anything at ALL.

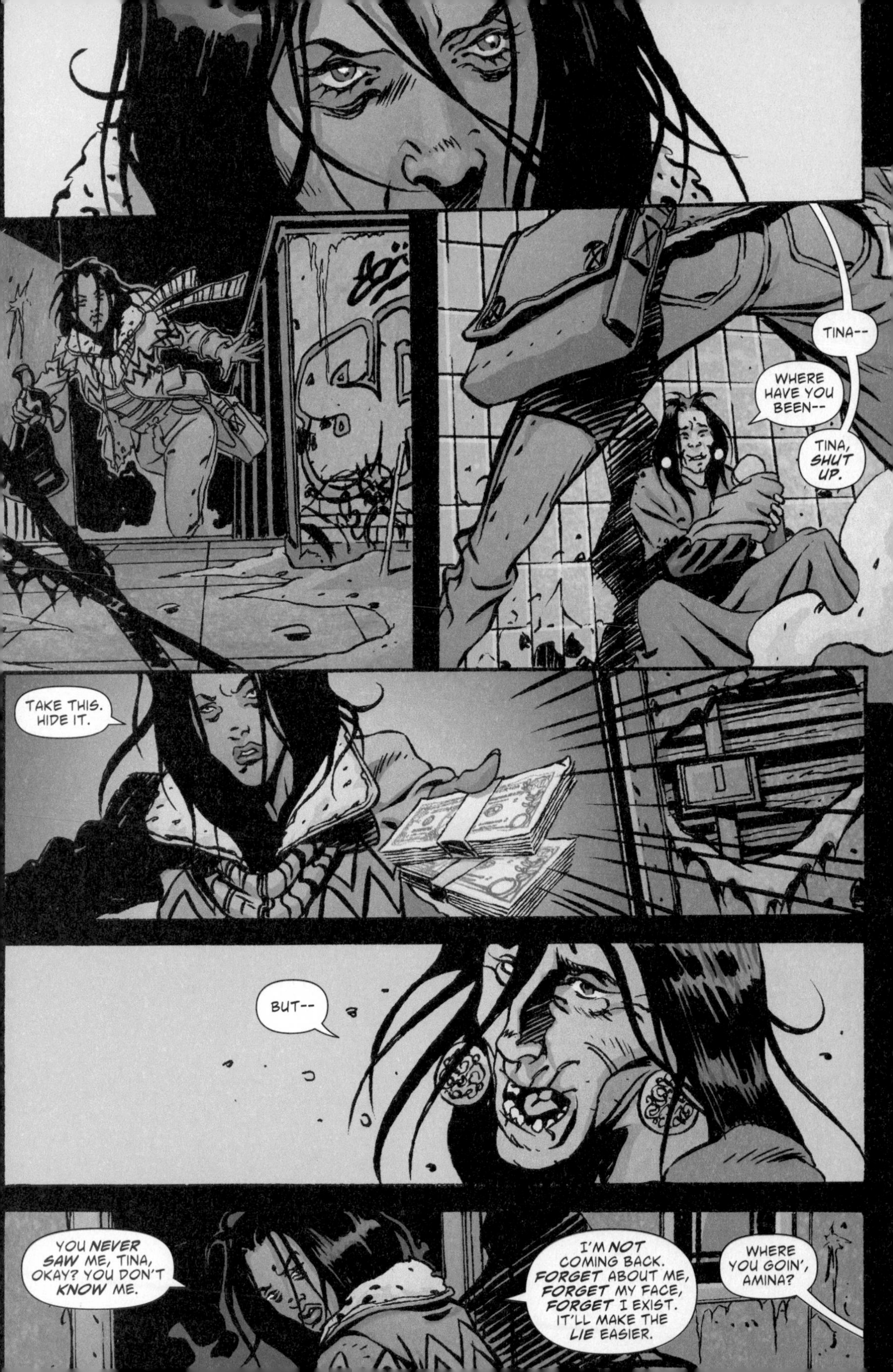
TINA--
WHERE HAVE YOU BEEN--
TINA, SHUT UP.
TAKE THIS. HIDE IT.
BUT--
YOU NEVER SAW ME, TINA, OKAY? YOU DON'T KNOW ME.
I'M NOT COMING BACK. FORGET ABOUT ME, FORGET MY FACE, FORGET I EXIST. IT'LL MAKE THE LIE EASIER.
WHERE YOU GOIN', AMINA?

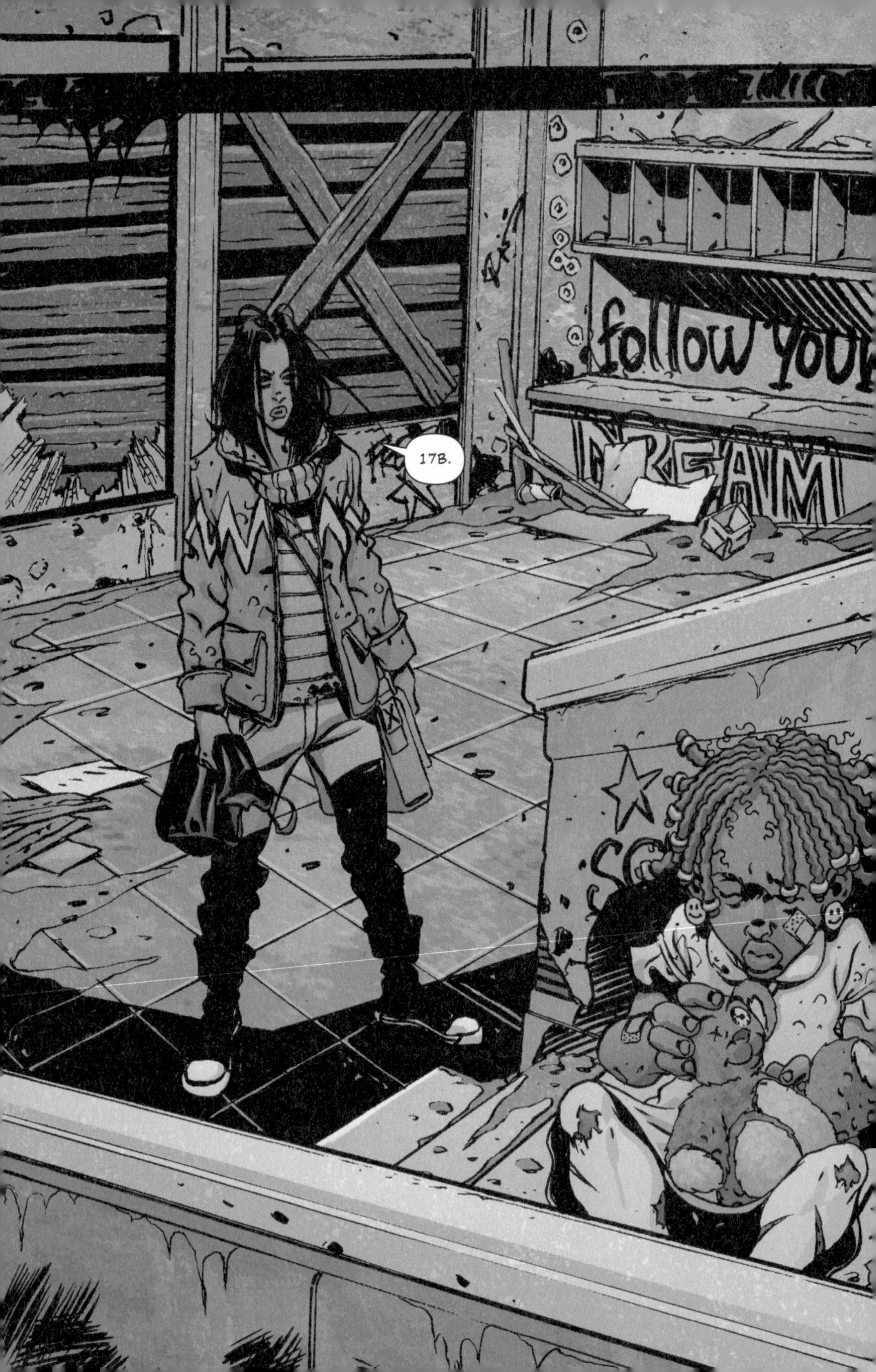
17B.
follow your
DREAM

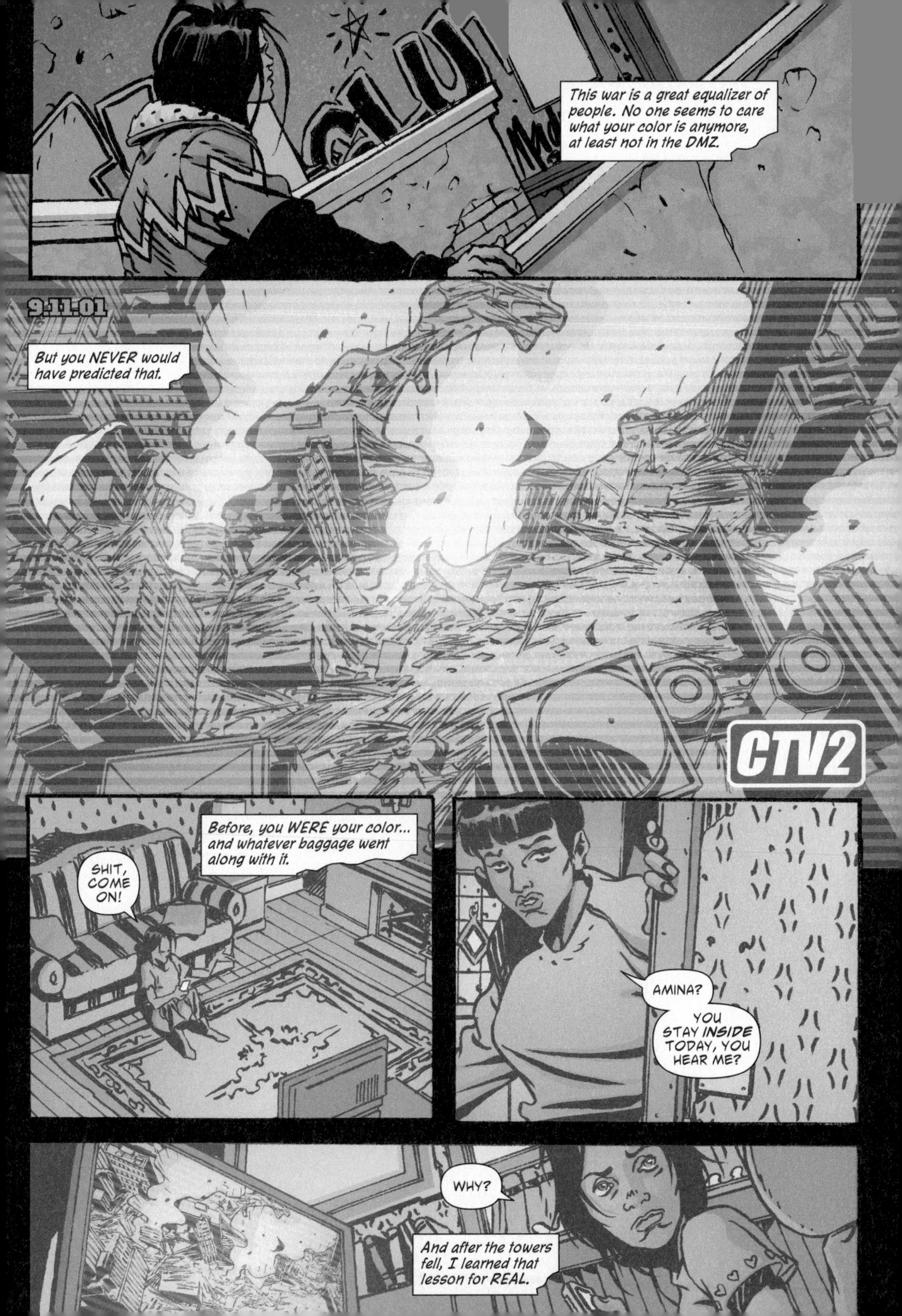
This war is a great equalizer of people. No one seems to care what your color is anymore, at least not in the DMZ.
9.11.01
But you NEVER would have predicted that.
CTV2
Before, you WERE your color... and whatever baggage went along with it.
SHIT, COME ON!
AMINA?
YOU STAY INSIDE TODAY, YOU HEAR ME?
WHY?
And after the towers fell, I learned that lesson for REAL.

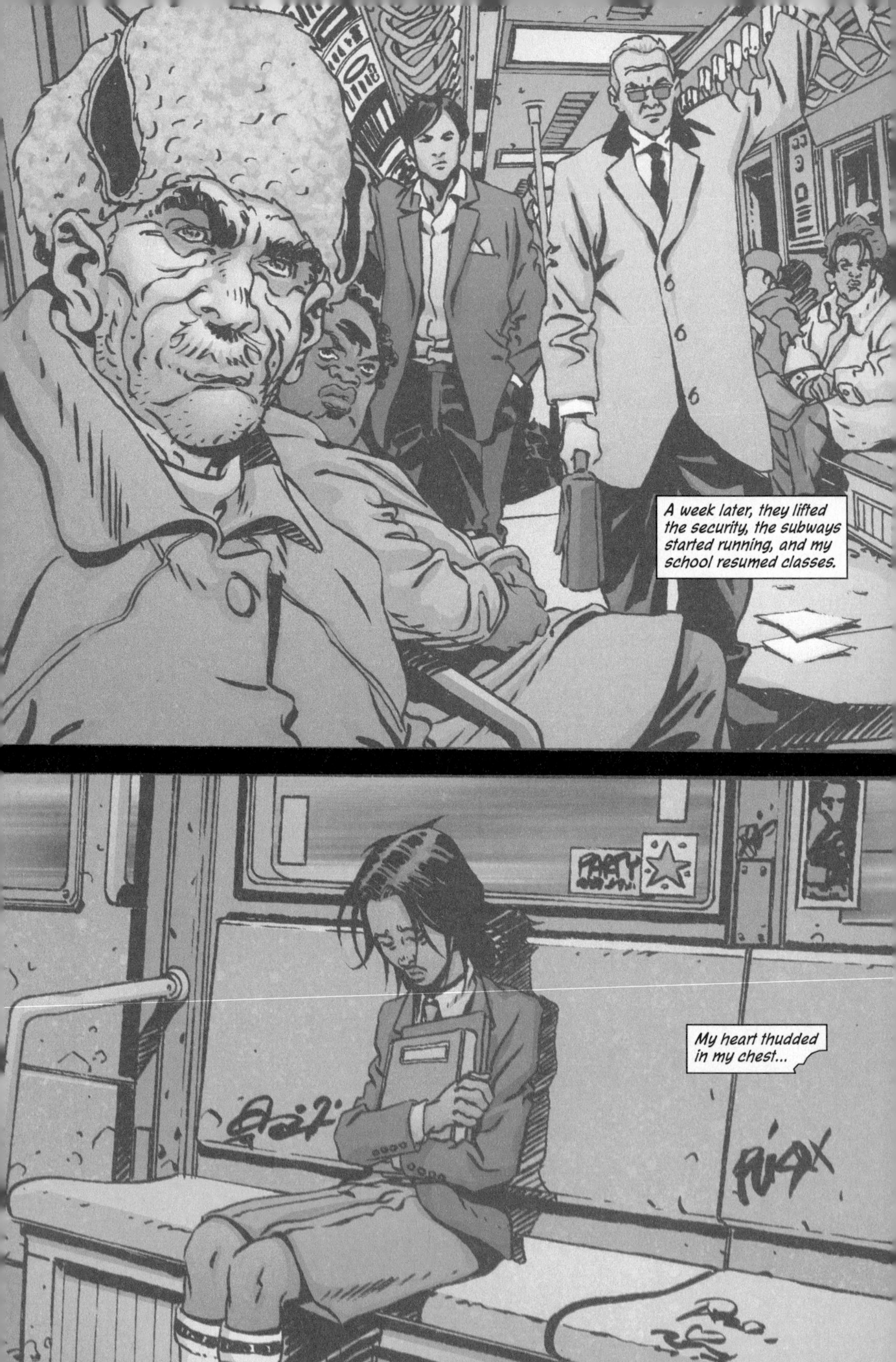
A week later, they lifted the security, the subways started running, and my school resumed classes.
My heart thudded in my chest...

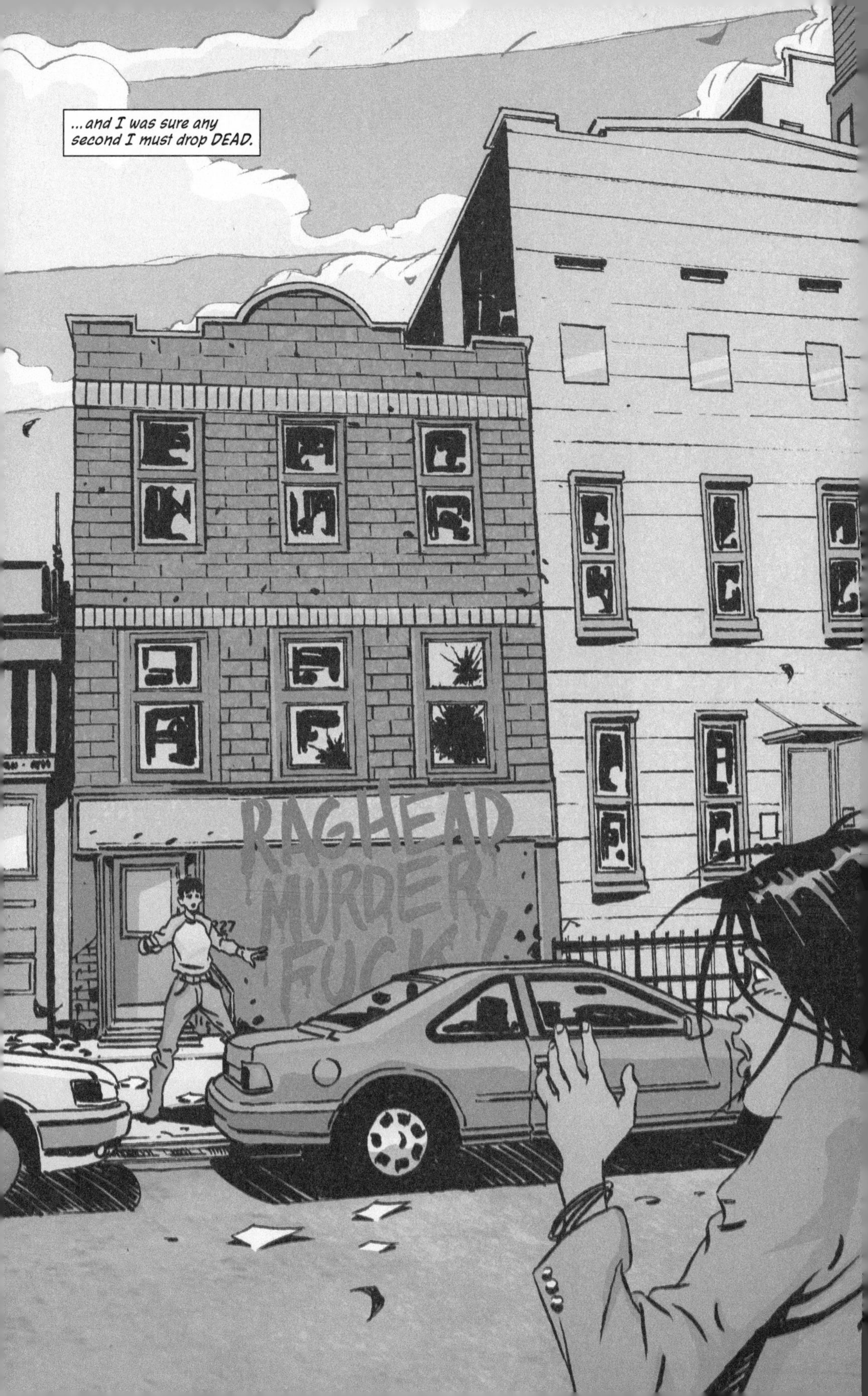
...and I was sure any second I must drop DEAD.
RAGHEAD MURDER FUCK!
227

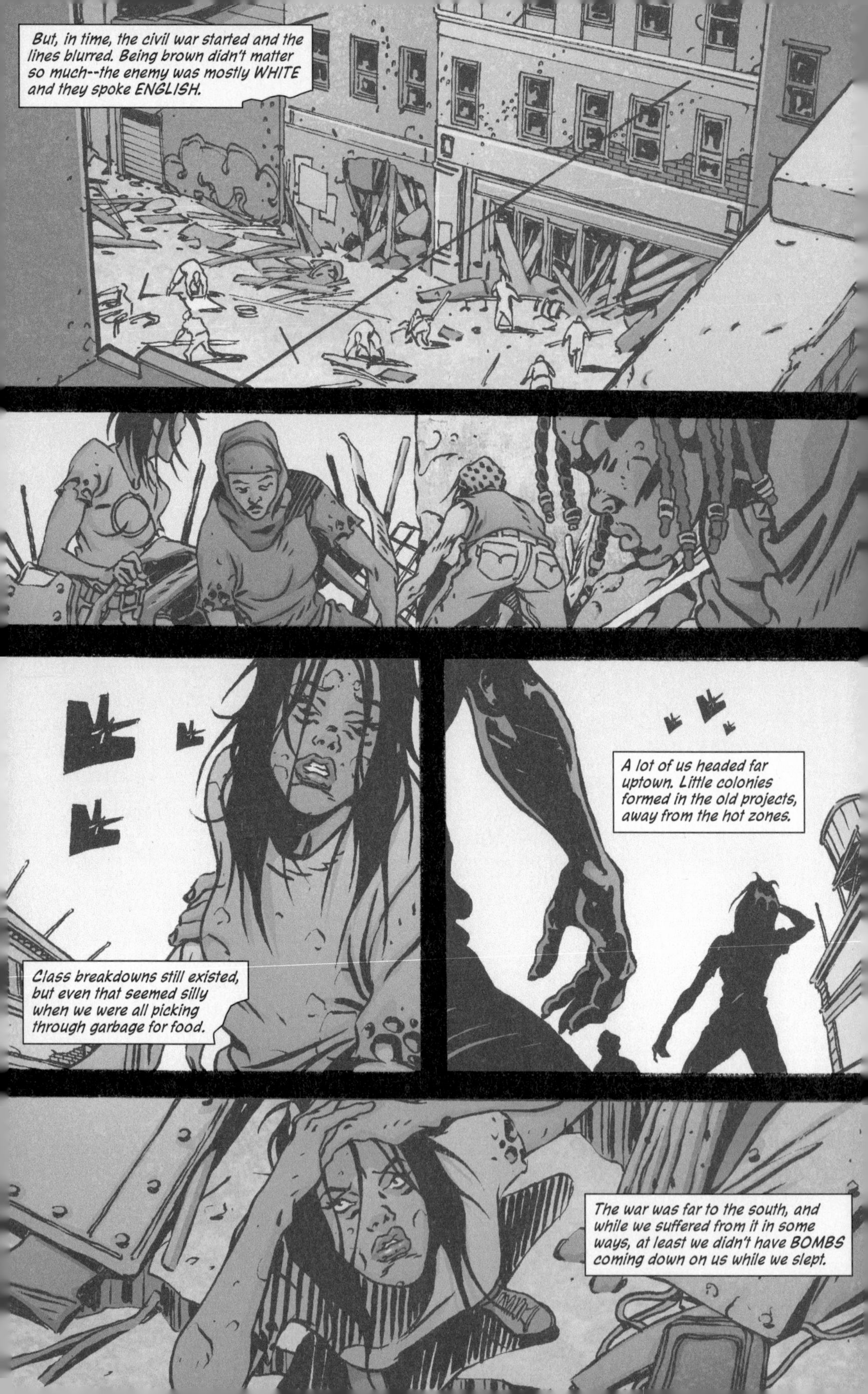

But, in time, the civil war started and the lines blurred. Being brown didn't matter so much--the enemy was mostly WHITE and they spoke ENGLISH.
Class breakdowns still existed, but even that seemed silly when we were all picking through garbage for food.
A lot of us headed far uptown. Little colonies formed in the old projects, away from the hot zones.
The war was far to the south, and while we suffered from it in some ways, at least we didn't have BOMBS coming down on us while we slept.

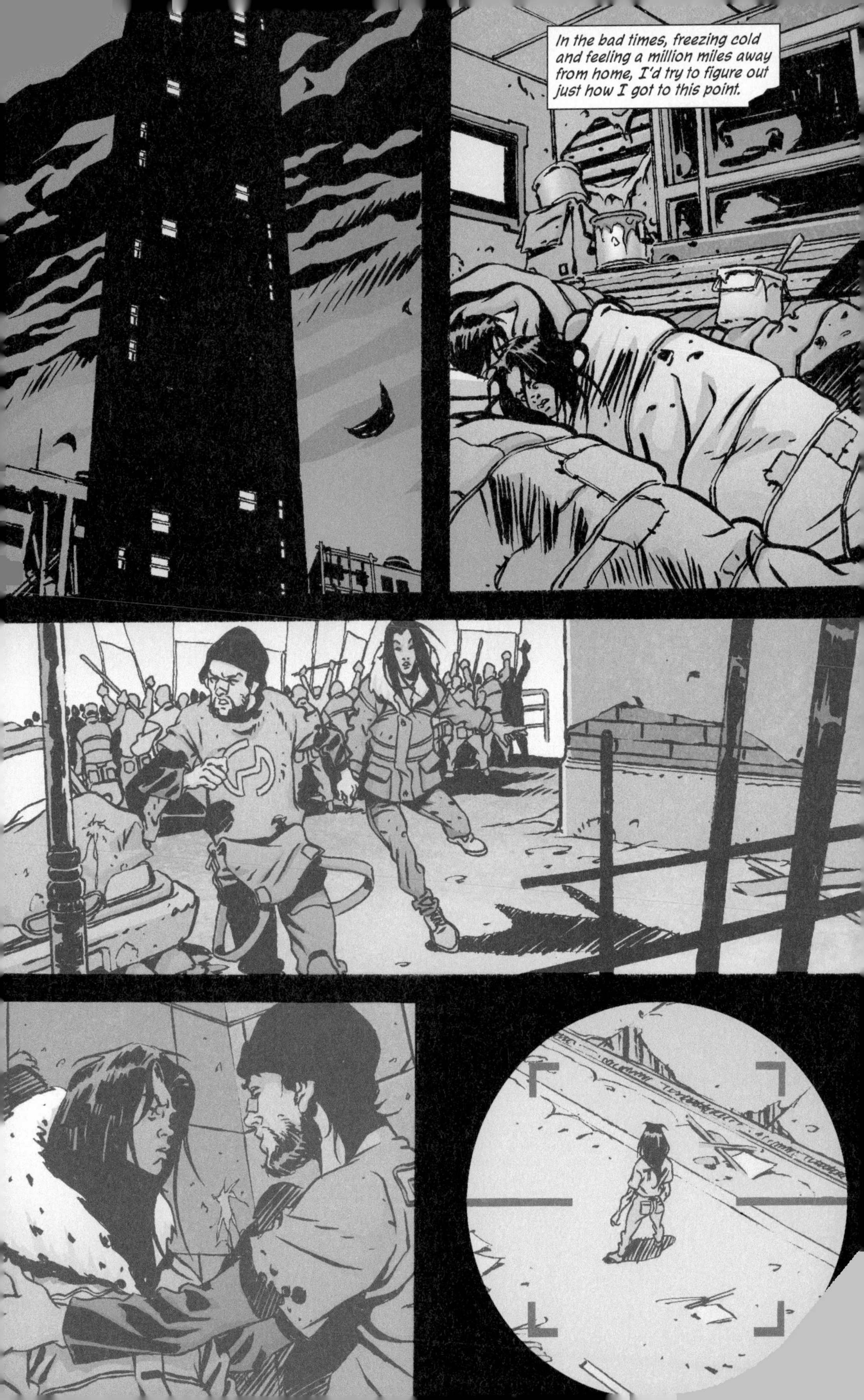
In the bad times, freezing cold and feeling a million miles away from home, I'd try to figure out just how I got to this point.

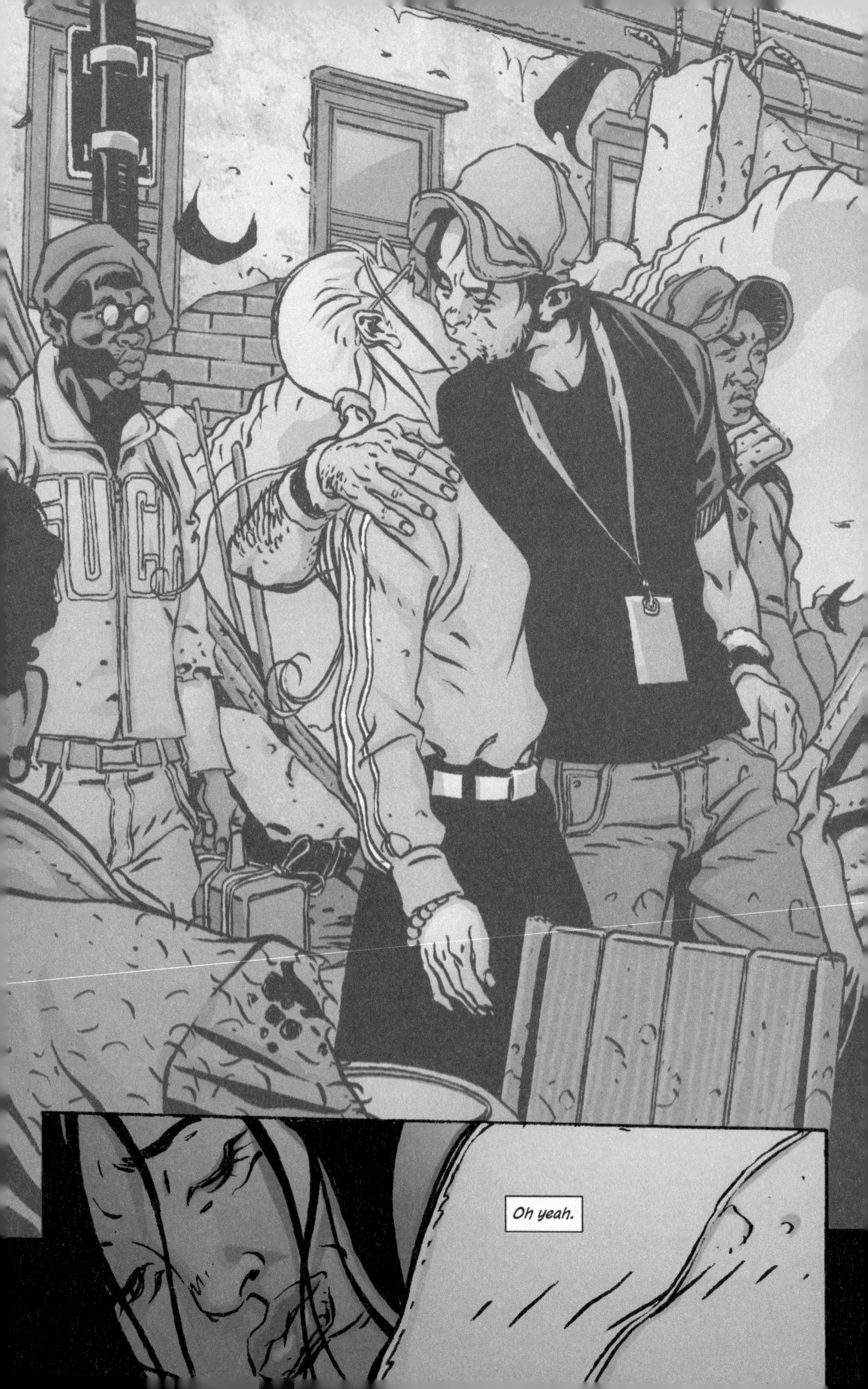
Oh yeah.

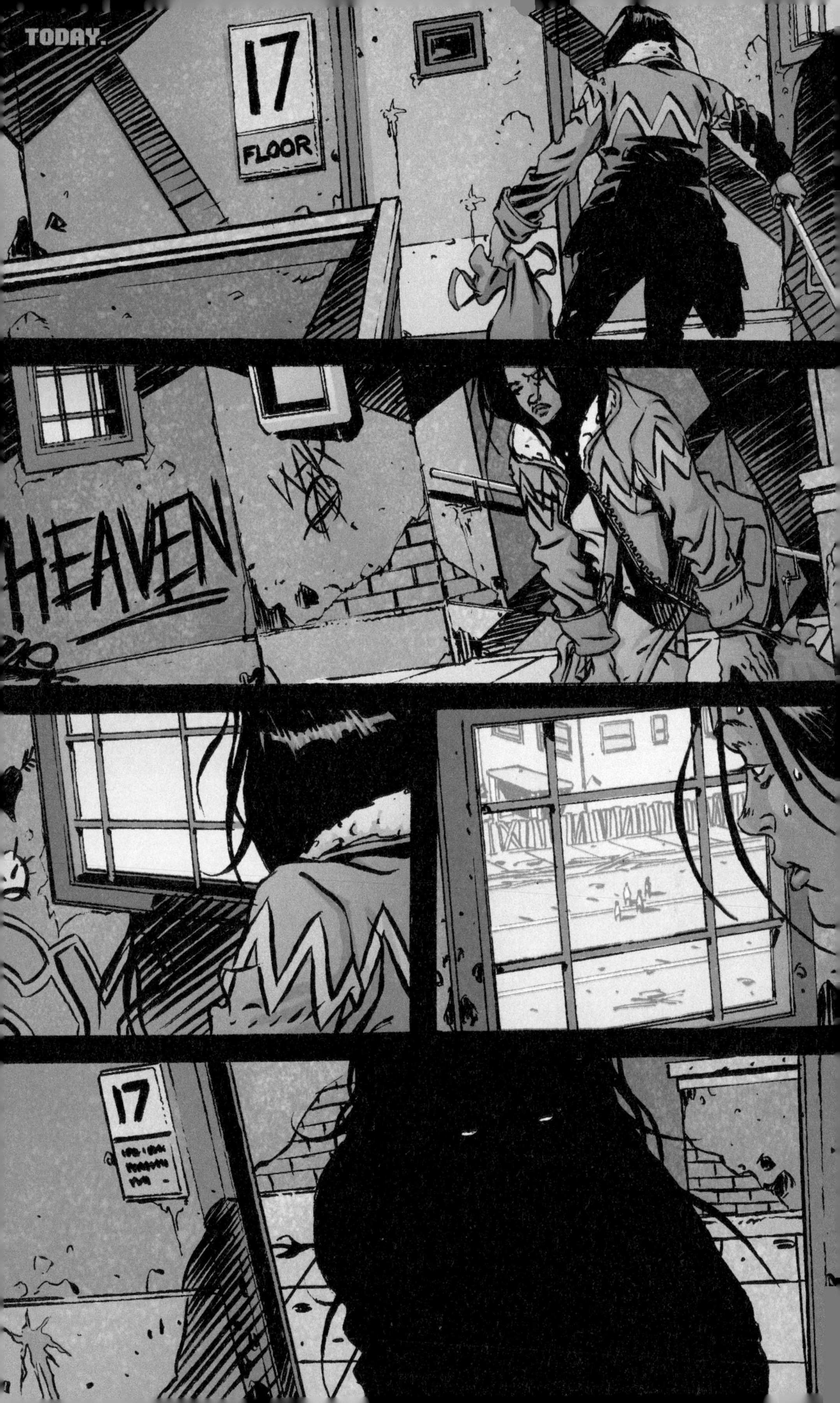
TODAY.
17
FLOOR
HEAVEN
17

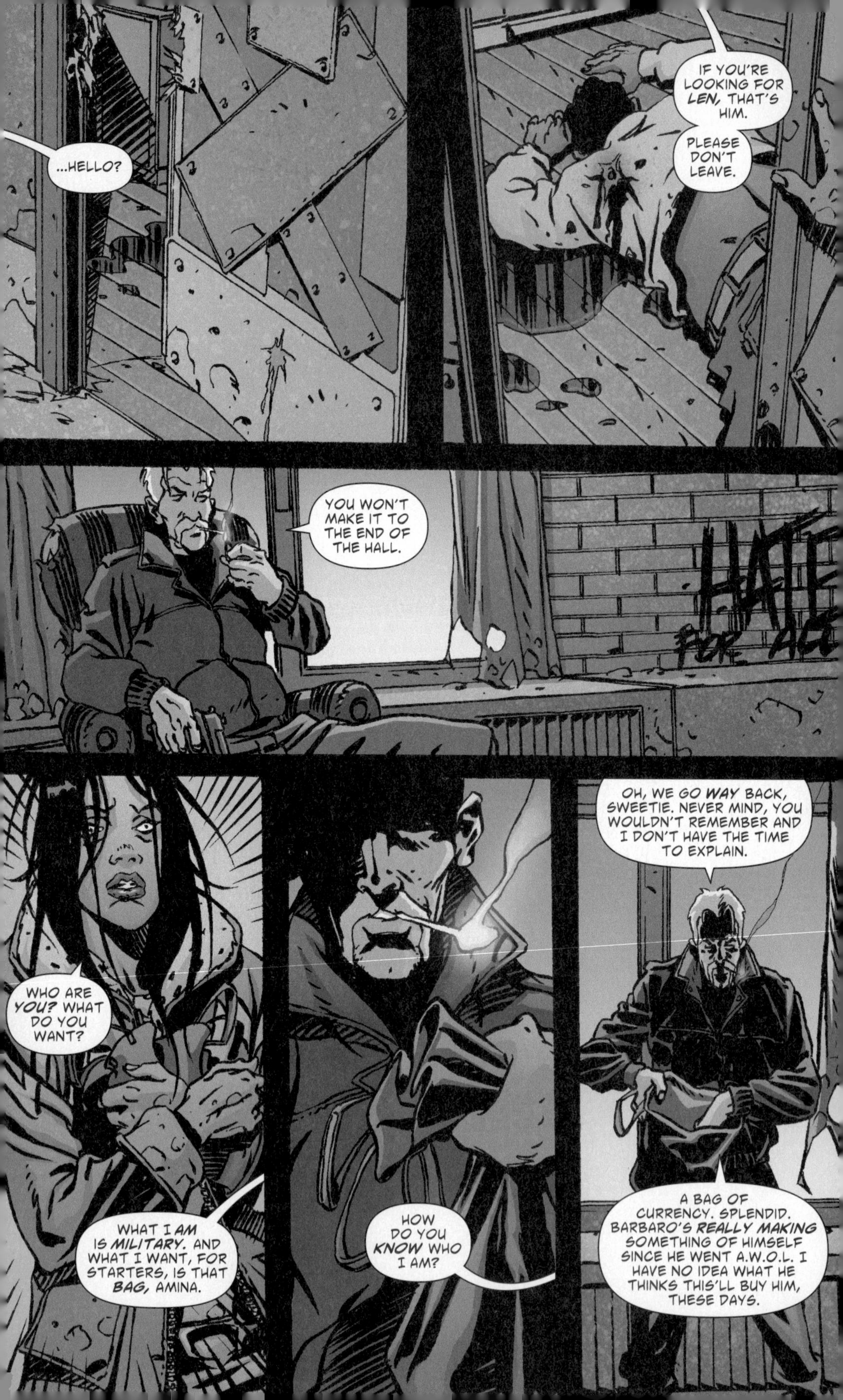
...HELLO?
IF YOU'RE LOOKING FOR LEN, THAT'S HIM.
PLEASE DON'T LEAVE.
YOU WON'T MAKE IT TO THE END OF THE HALL.
HATE
FOR
WHO ARE YOU? WHAT DO YOU WANT?
WHAT I AM IS MILITARY. AND WHAT I WANT, FOR STARTERS, IS THAT BAG, AMINA.
HOW DO YOU KNOW WHO I AM?
OH, WE GO WAY BACK, SWEETIE. NEVER MIND, YOU WOULDN'T REMEMBER AND I DON'T HAVE THE TIME TO EXPLAIN.
A BAG OF CURRENCY. SPLENDID. BARBARO'S REALLY MAKING SOMETHING OF HIMSELF SINCE HE WENT A.W.O.L. I HAVE NO IDEA WHAT HE THINKS THIS'LL BUY HIM, THESE DAYS.

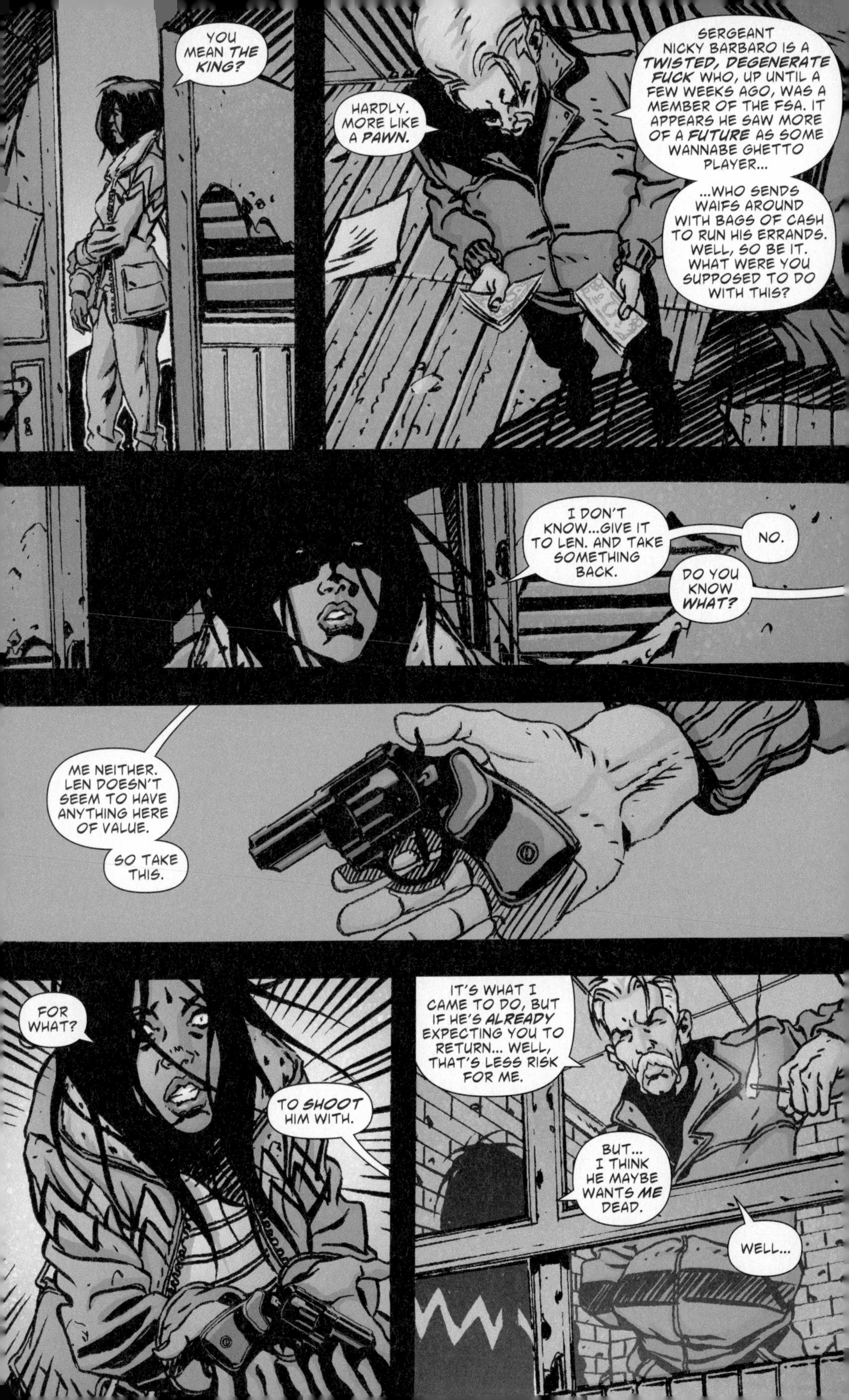
YOU MEAN THE KING?
HARDLY. MORE LIKE A PAWN.
SERGEANT NICKY BARBARO IS A TWISTED, DEGENERATE FUCK WHO, UP UNTIL A FEW WEEKS AGO, WAS A MEMBER OF THE FSA. IT APPEARS HE SAW MORE OF A FUTURE AS SOME WANNABE GHETTO PLAYER...
...WHO SENDS WAIFS AROUND WITH BAGS OF CASH TO RUN HIS ERRANDS. WELL, SO BE IT. WHAT WERE YOU SUPPOSED TO DO WITH THIS?
I DON'T KNOW...GIVE IT TO LEN. AND TAKE SOMETHING BACK.
NO.
DO YOU KNOW WHAT?
ME NEITHER. LEN DOESN'T SEEM TO HAVE ANYTHING HERE OF VALUE.
SO TAKE THIS.
FOR WHAT?
TO SHOOT HIM WITH.
IT'S WHAT I CAME TO DO, BUT IF HE'S ALREADY EXPECTING YOU TO RETURN... WELL, THAT'S LESS RISK FOR ME.
BUT... I THINK HE MAYBE WANTS ME DEAD.
WELL...

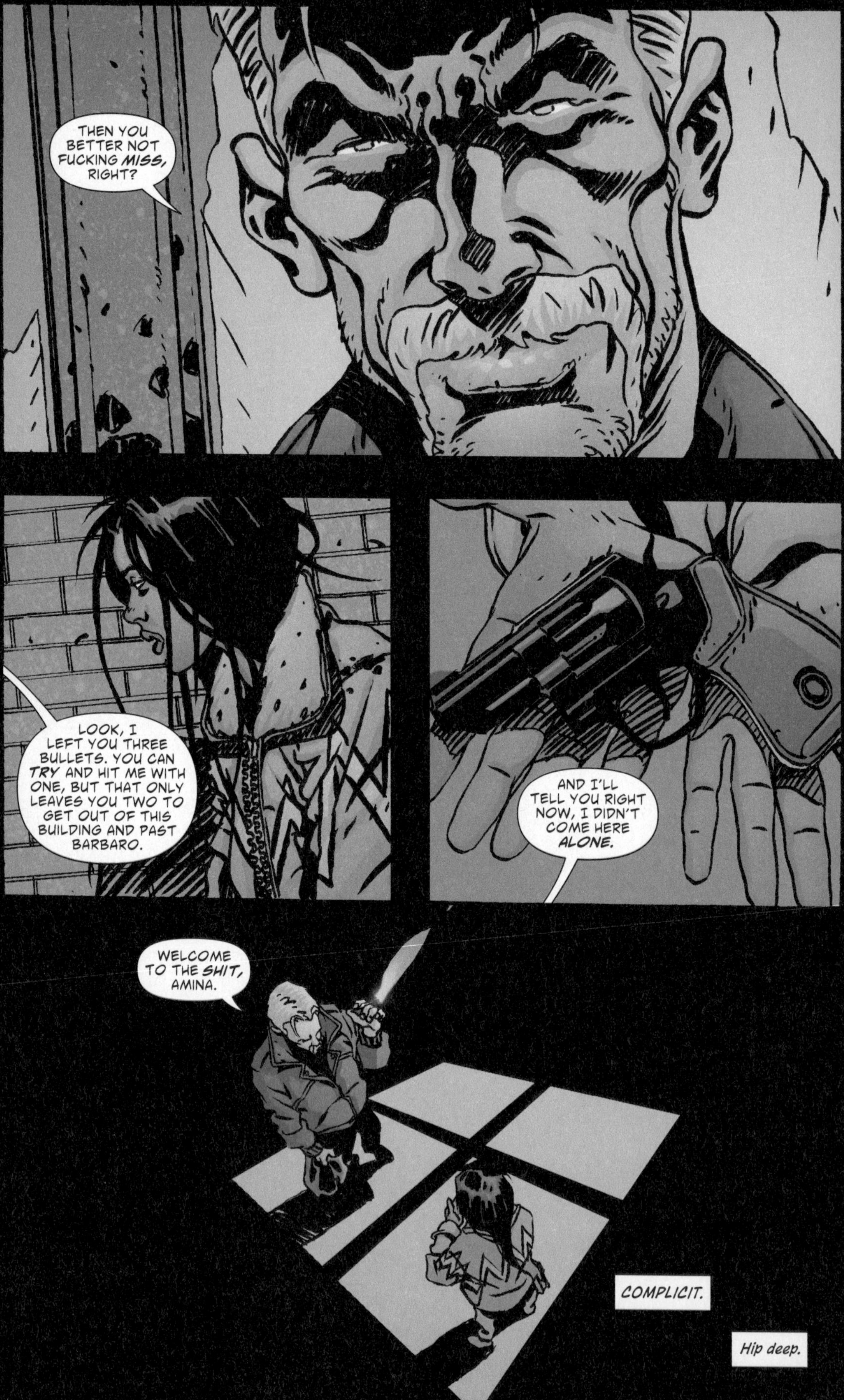
THEN YOU BETTER NOT FUCKING *MISS,* RIGHT?
LOOK, I LEFT YOU THREE BULLETS. YOU CAN *TRY* AND HIT ME WITH ONE, BUT THAT ONLY LEAVES YOU TWO TO GET OUT OF THIS BUILDING AND PAST BARBARO.
AND I'LL TELL YOU RIGHT NOW, I DIDN'T COME HERE *ALONE.*
WELCOME TO THE *SHIT,* AMINA.
COMPLICIT.
Hip deep.

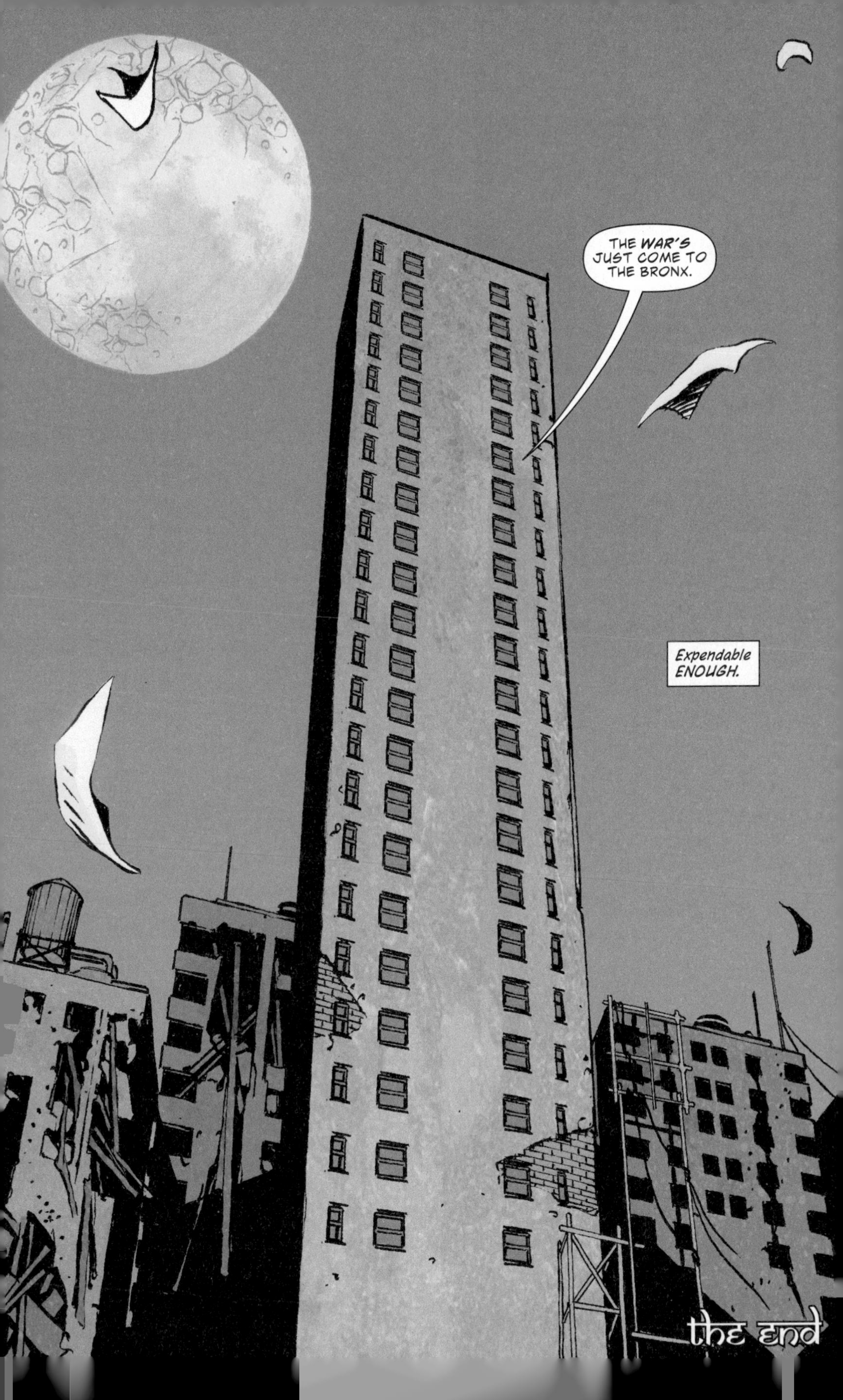
THE WAR'S JUST COME TO THE BRONX.
Expendable ENOUGH.
the end

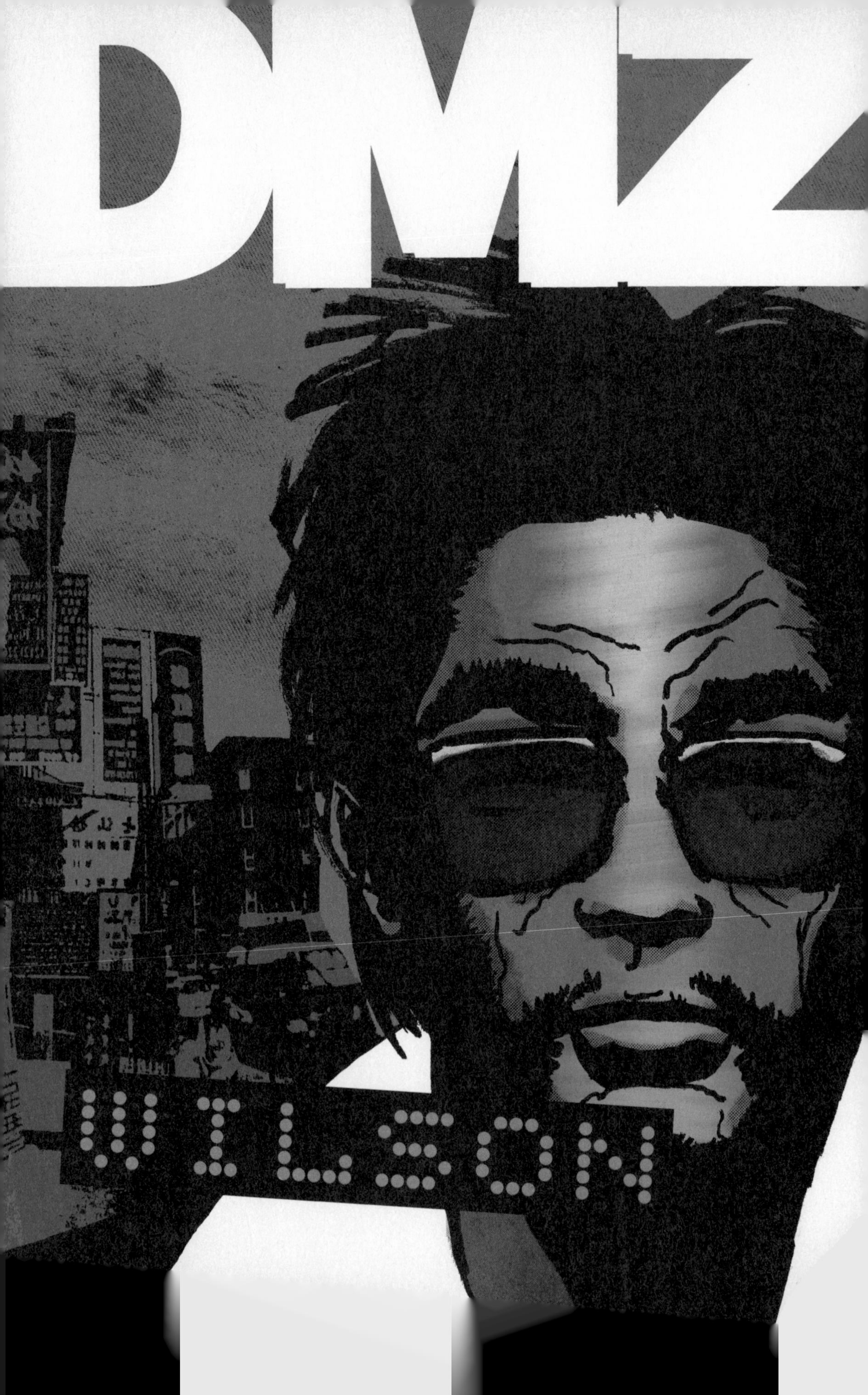
DMZ
WILSON

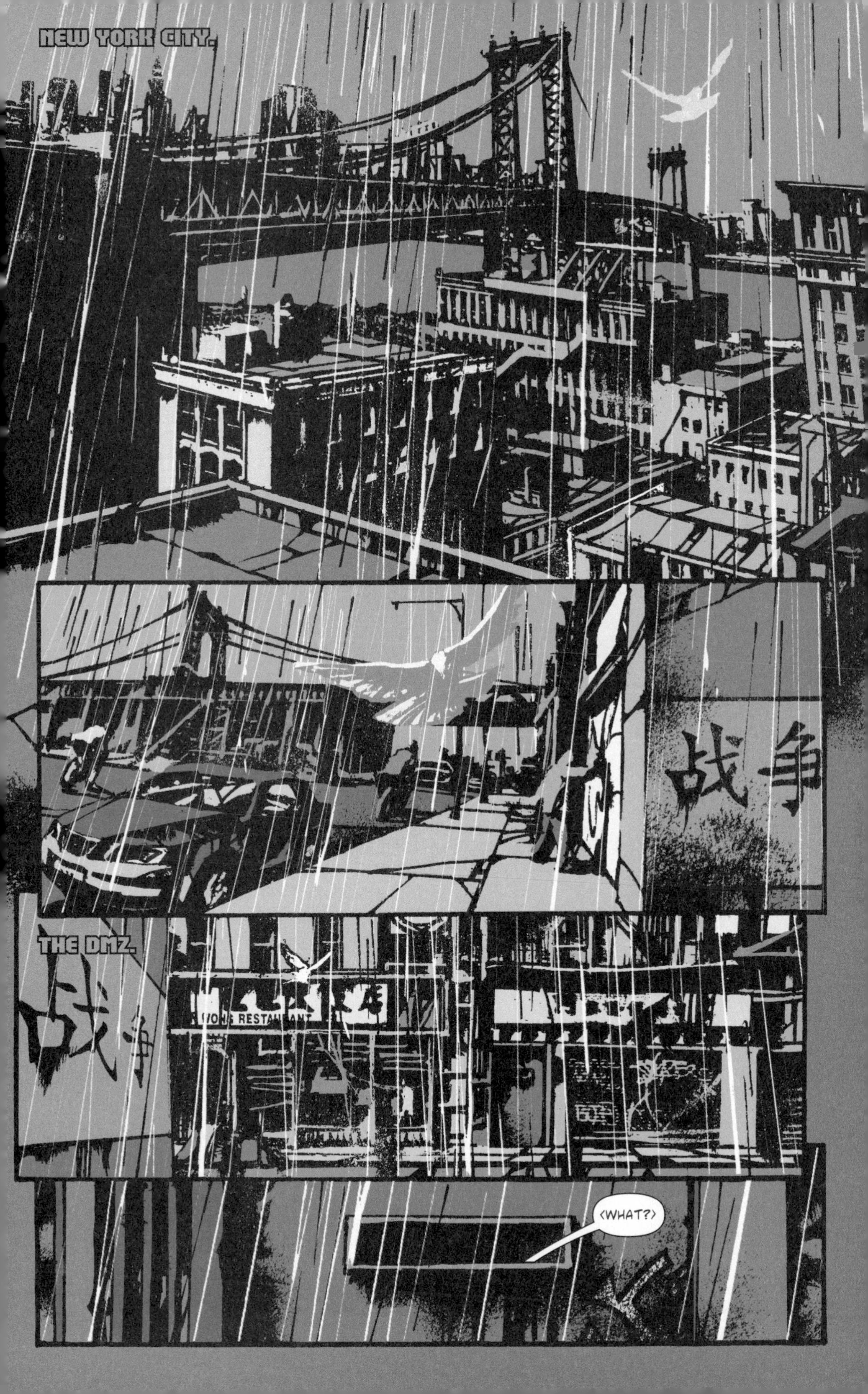
NEW YORK CITY.
战争
THE DMZ.
战争
WONG RESTAURANT
<WHAT?>

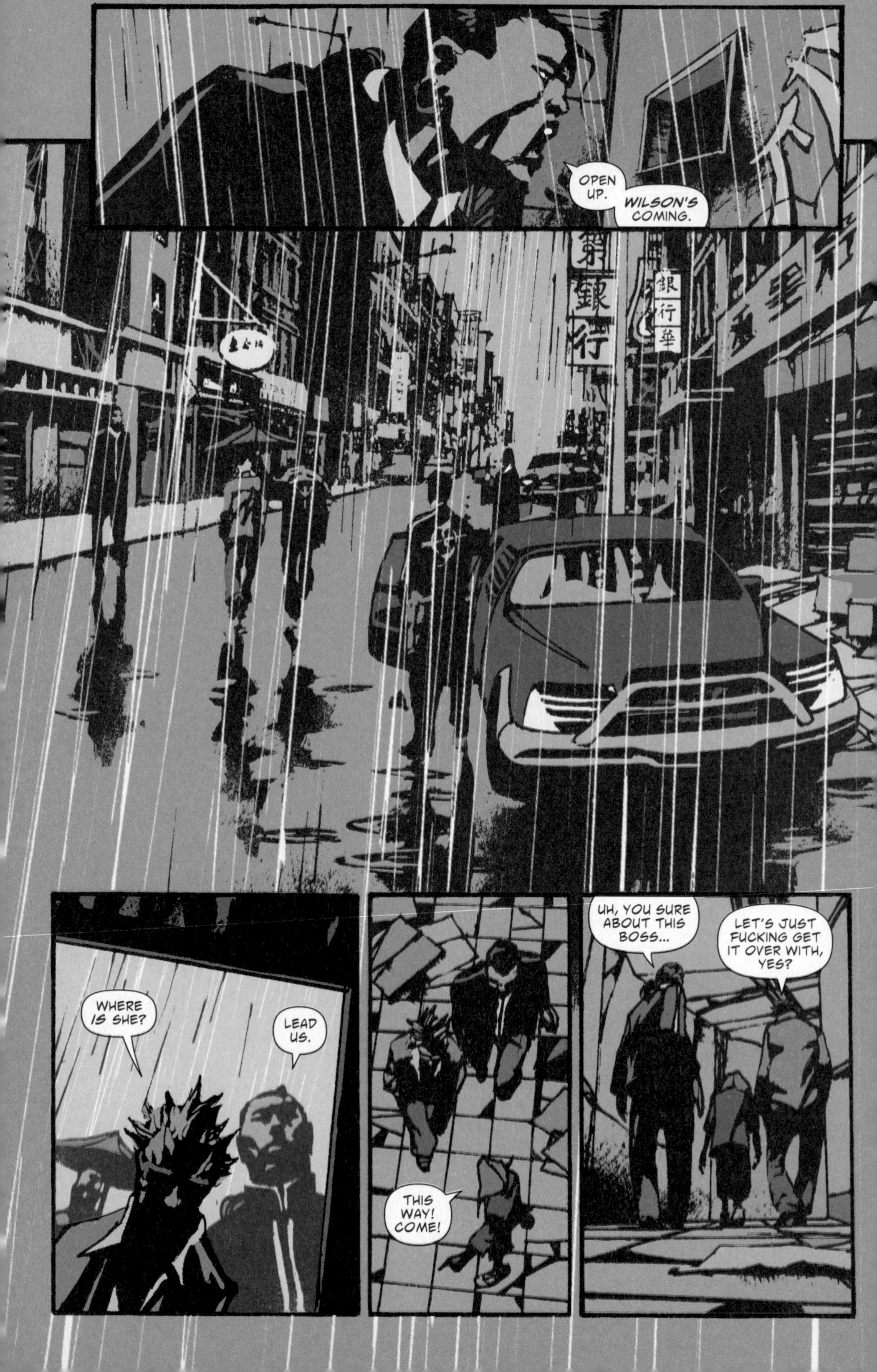
OPEN UP.
WILSON'S COMING.
WHERE IS SHE?
LEAD US.
THIS WAY! COME!
UH, YOU SURE ABOUT THIS BOSS...
LET'S JUST FUCKING GET IT OVER WITH, YES?

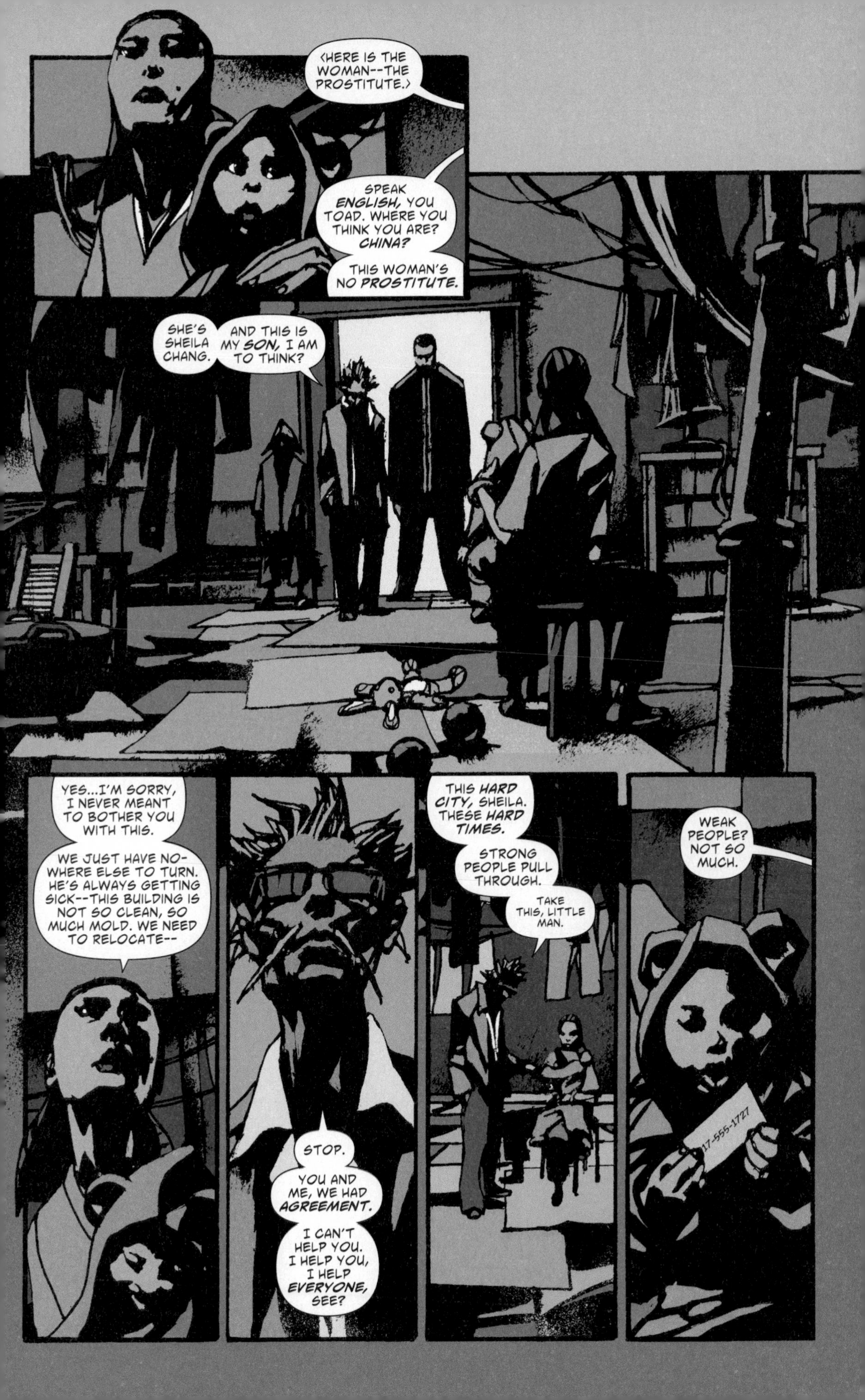

<HERE IS THE WOMAN--THE PROSTITUTE.>
SPEAK ENGLISH, YOU TOAD. WHERE YOU THINK YOU ARE? CHINA?
THIS WOMAN'S NO PROSTITUTE.
SHE'S SHEILA CHANG.
AND THIS IS MY SON, I AM TO THINK?
YES...I'M SORRY, I NEVER MEANT TO BOTHER YOU WITH THIS.
WE JUST HAVE NOWHERE ELSE TO TURN. HE'S ALWAYS GETTING SICK--THIS BUILDING IS NOT SO CLEAN, SO MUCH MOLD. WE NEED TO RELOCATE--
STOP.
YOU AND ME, WE HAD AGREEMENT.
I CAN'T HELP YOU. I HELP YOU, I HELP EVERYONE, SEE?
THIS HARD CITY, SHEILA. THESE HARD TIMES.
STRONG PEOPLE PULL THROUGH.
TAKE THIS, LITTLE MAN.
WEAK PEOPLE? NOT SO MUCH.
17-555-1727

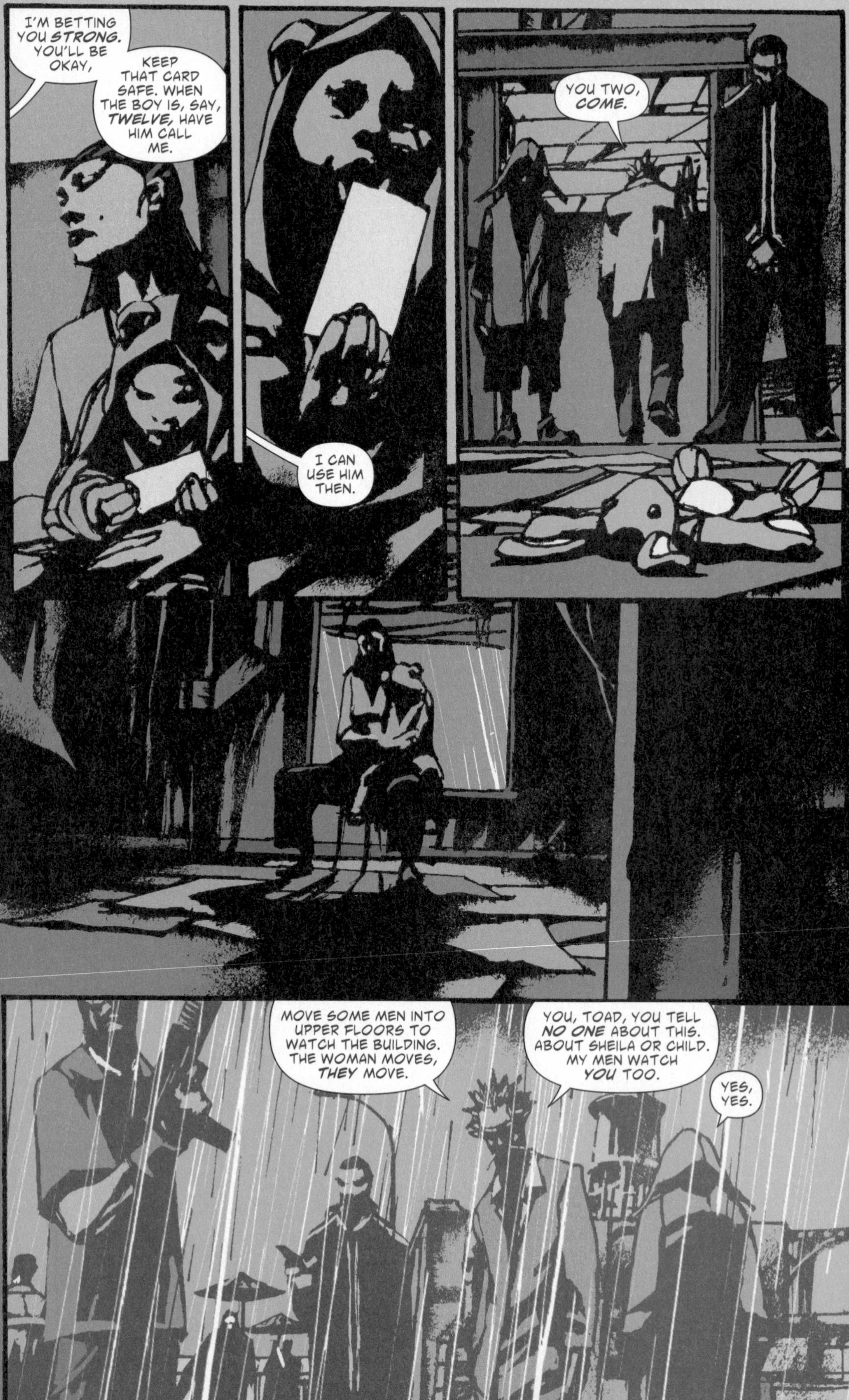
I'M BETTING YOU STRONG. YOU'LL BE OKAY,
KEEP THAT CARD SAFE. WHEN THE BOY IS, SAY, TWELVE, HAVE HIM CALL ME.
I CAN USE HIM THEN.
YOU TWO, COME.
MOVE SOME MEN INTO UPPER FLOORS TO WATCH THE BUILDING. THE WOMAN MOVES, THEY MOVE.
YOU, TOAD, YOU TELL NO ONE ABOUT THIS. ABOUT SHEILA OR CHILD. MY MEN WATCH YOU TOO.
YES, YES.

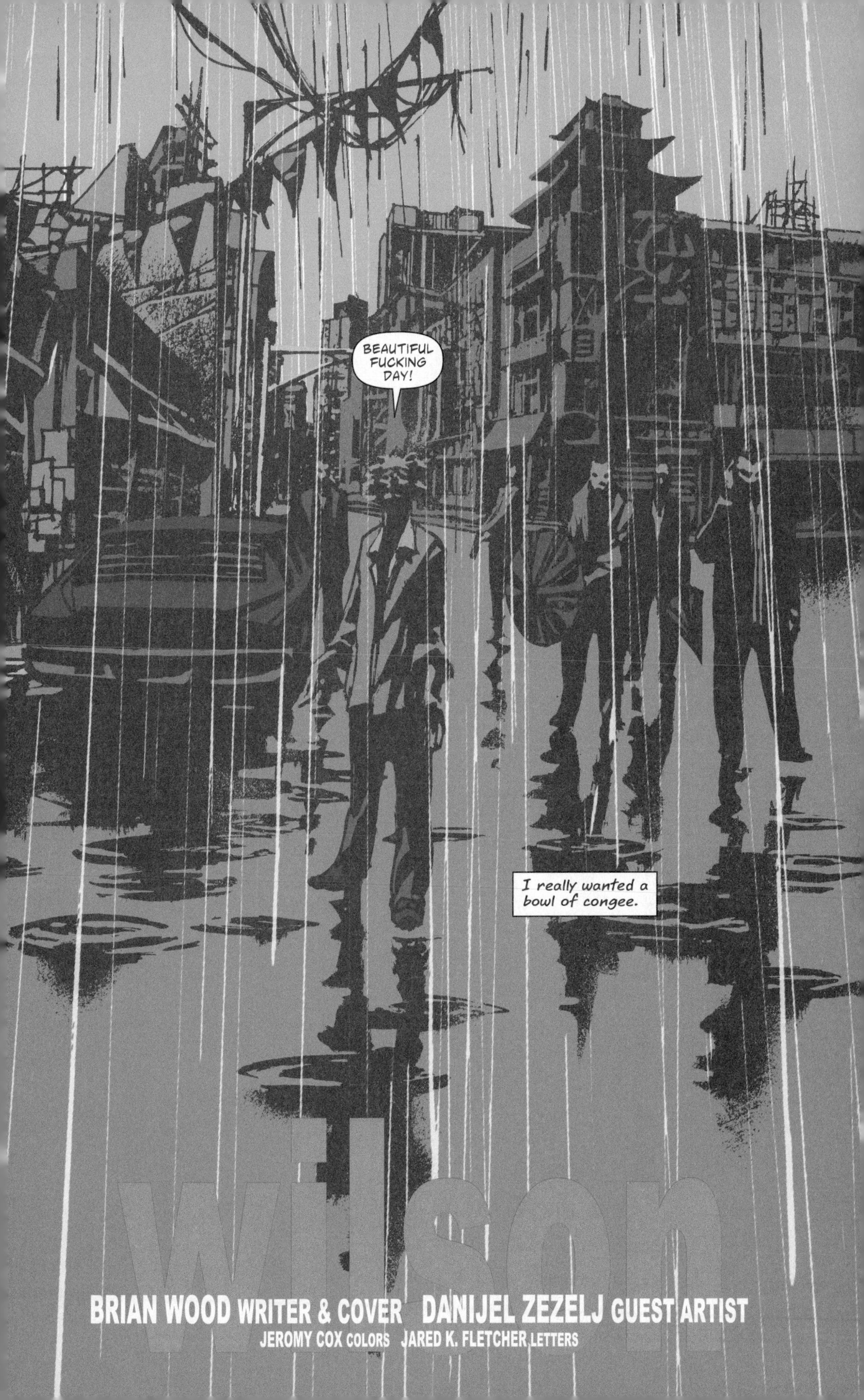
BEAUTIFUL FUCKING DAY!
I really wanted a bowl of congee.
wilson
BRIAN WOOD WRITER & COVER DANIJEL ZEZELJ GUEST ARTIST
JEROMY COX COLORS JARED K. FLETCHER LETTERS

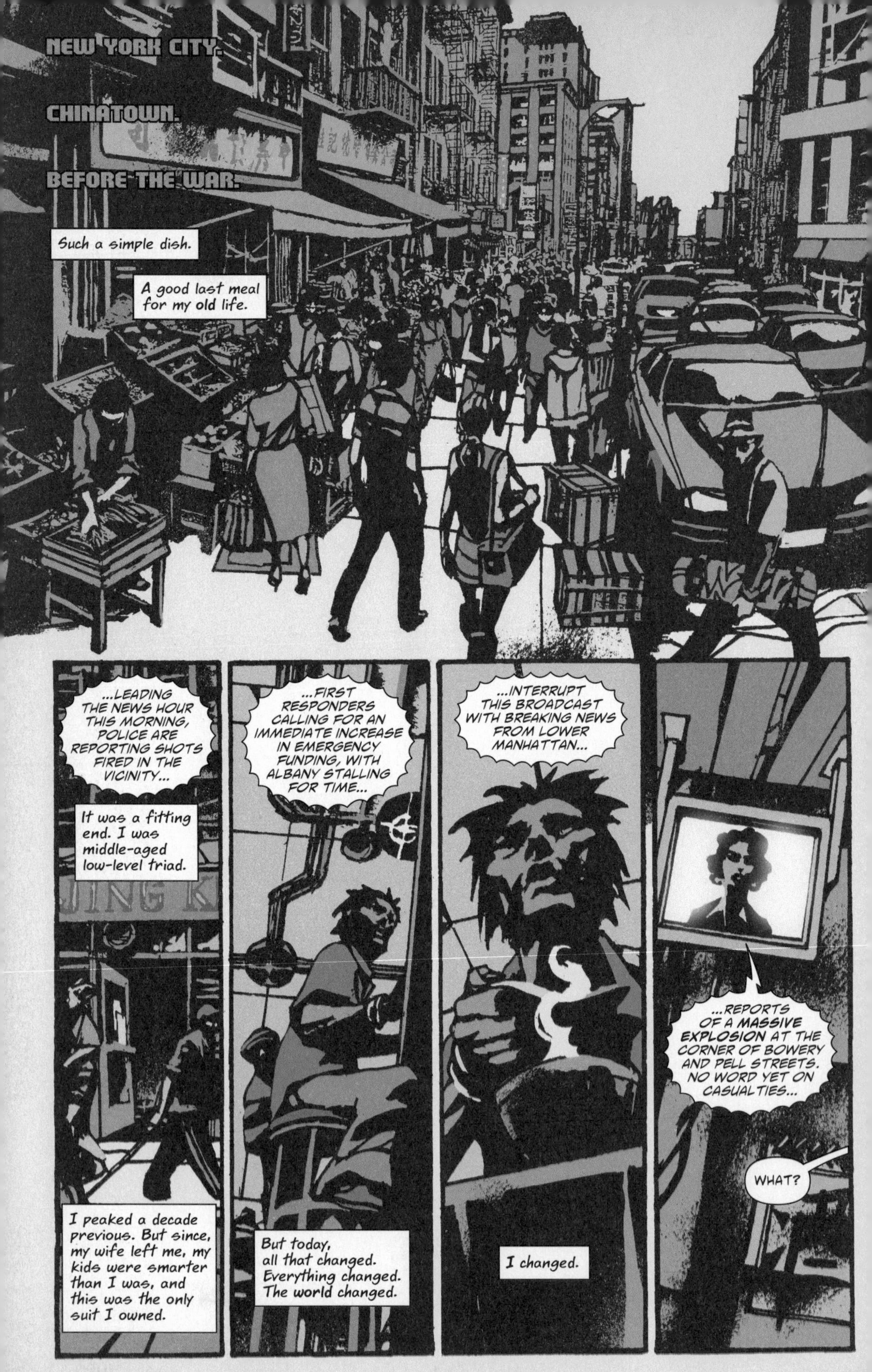
NEW YORK CITY.
CHINATOWN.
BEFORE THE WAR.
Such a simple dish.
A good last meal for my old life.
...LEADING THE NEWS HOUR THIS MORNING, POLICE ARE REPORTING SHOTS FIRED IN THE VICINITY...
It was a fitting end. I was middle-aged low-level triad.
I peaked a decade previous. But since, my wife left me, my kids were smarter than I was, and this was the only suit I owned.
...FIRST RESPONDERS CALLING FOR AN IMMEDIATE INCREASE IN EMERGENCY FUNDING, WITH ALBANY STALLING FOR TIME...
But today, all that changed. Everything changed. The world changed.
...INTERRUPT THIS BROADCAST WITH BREAKING NEWS FROM LOWER MANHATTAN...
I changed.
...REPORTS OF A MASSIVE EXPLOSION AT THE CORNER OF BOWERY AND PELL STREETS. NO WORD YET ON CASUALTIES...
WHAT?

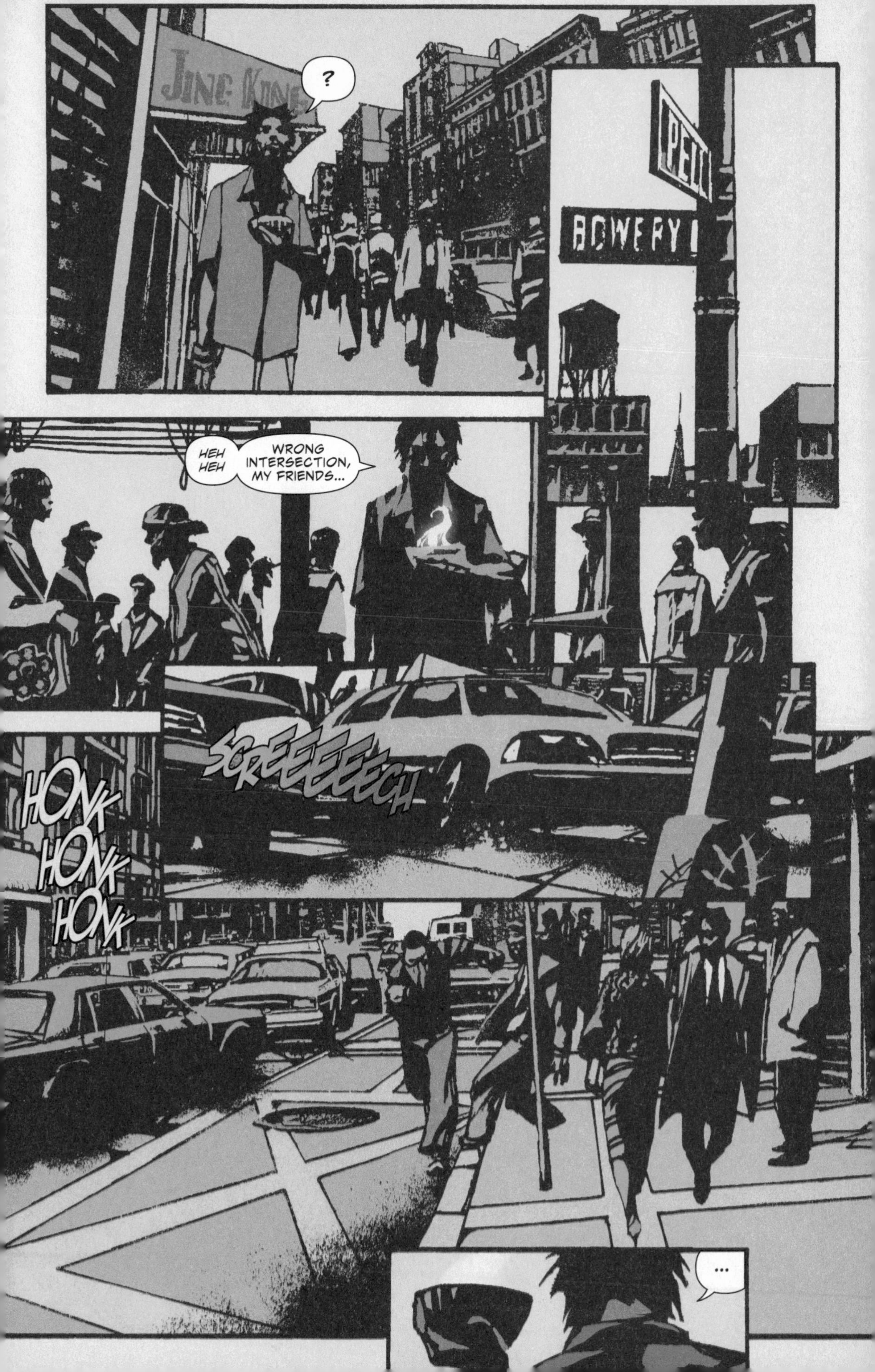
JING KING
?
BOWERY
HEH HEH
WRONG INTERSECTION, MY FRIENDS...
SCREEEEEECH
HONK HONK HONK
...

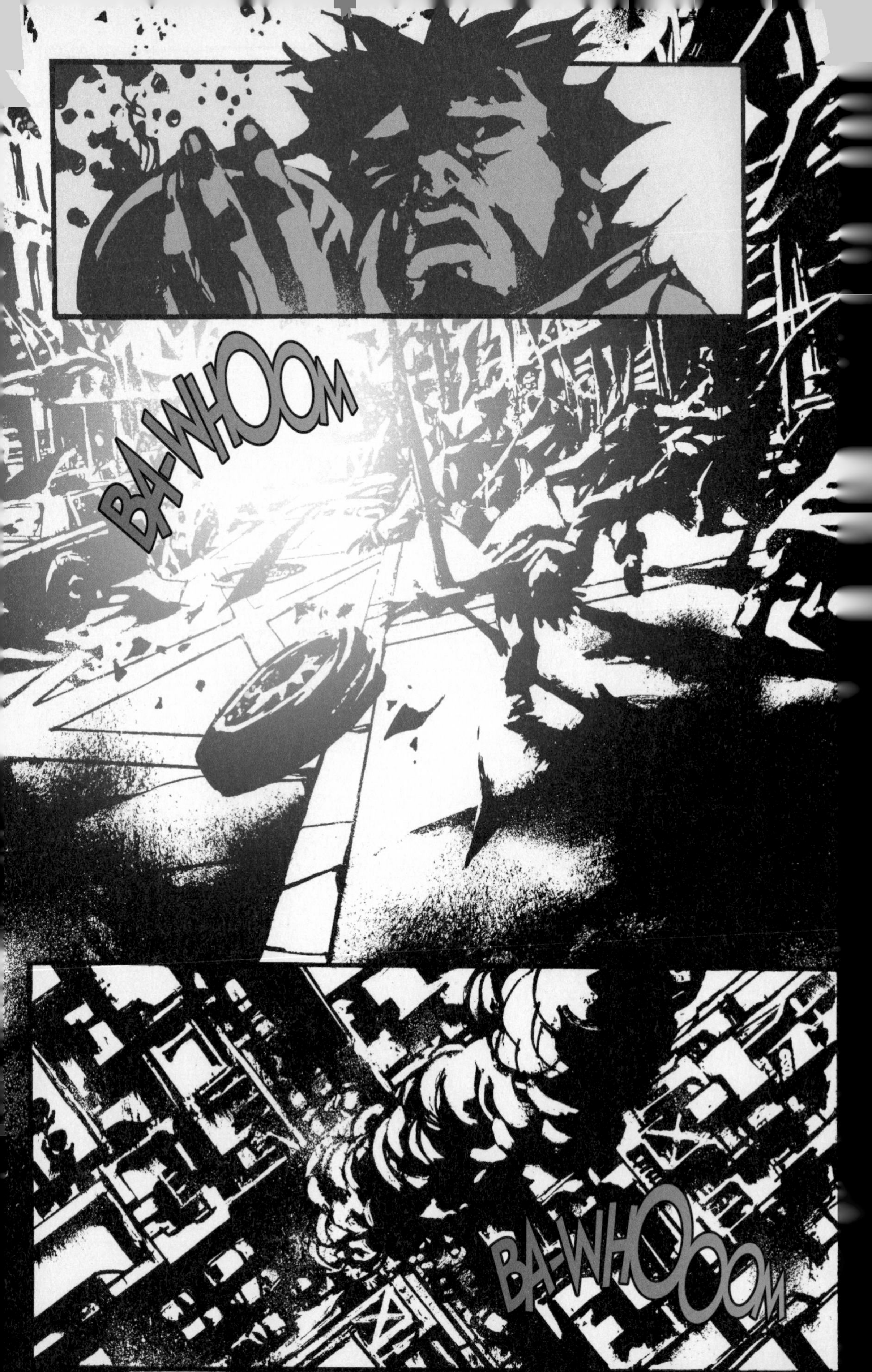
BA-WHOOM
BA-WHOOOOM

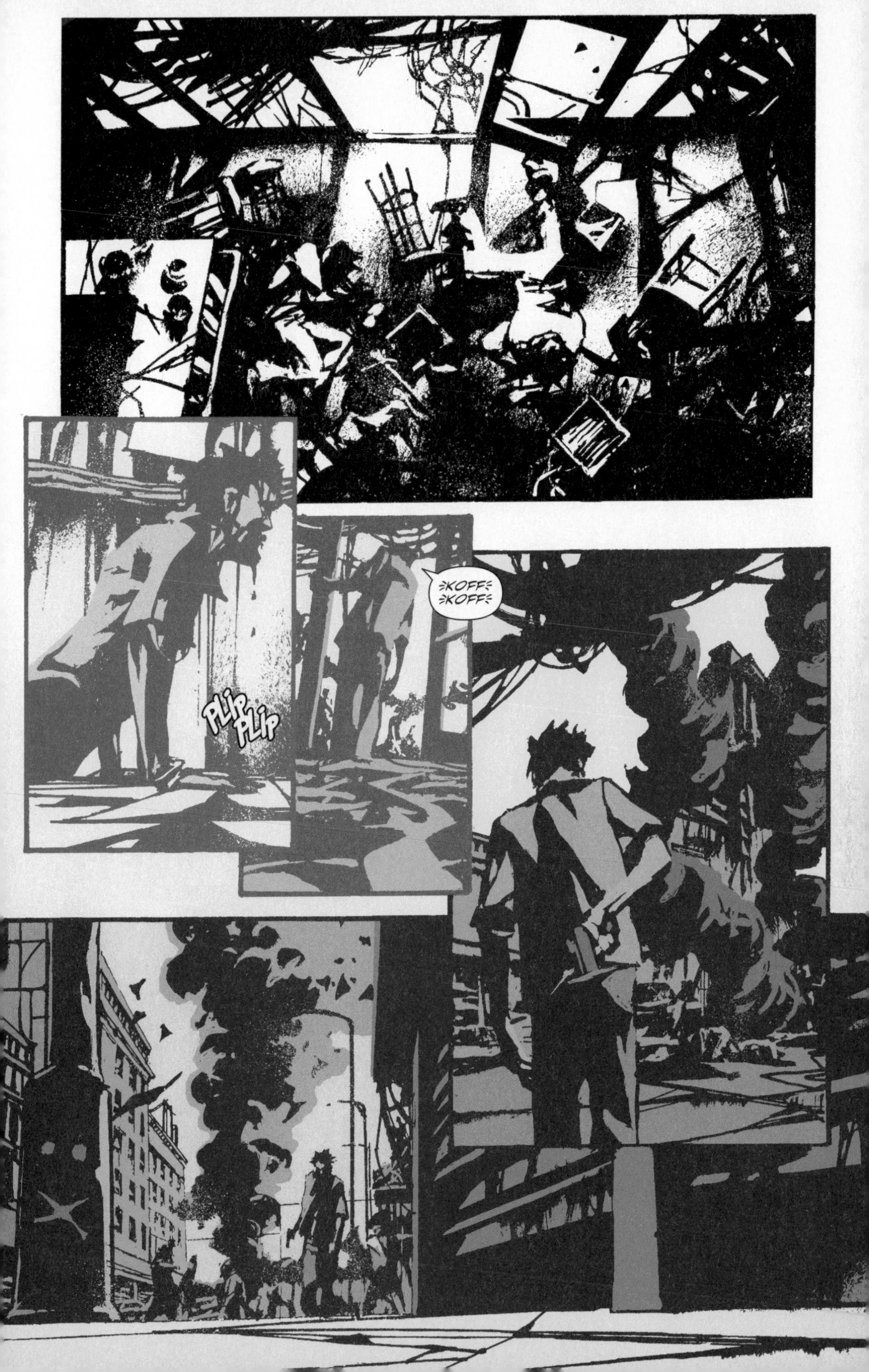
PLIP PLIP
KOFF KOFF

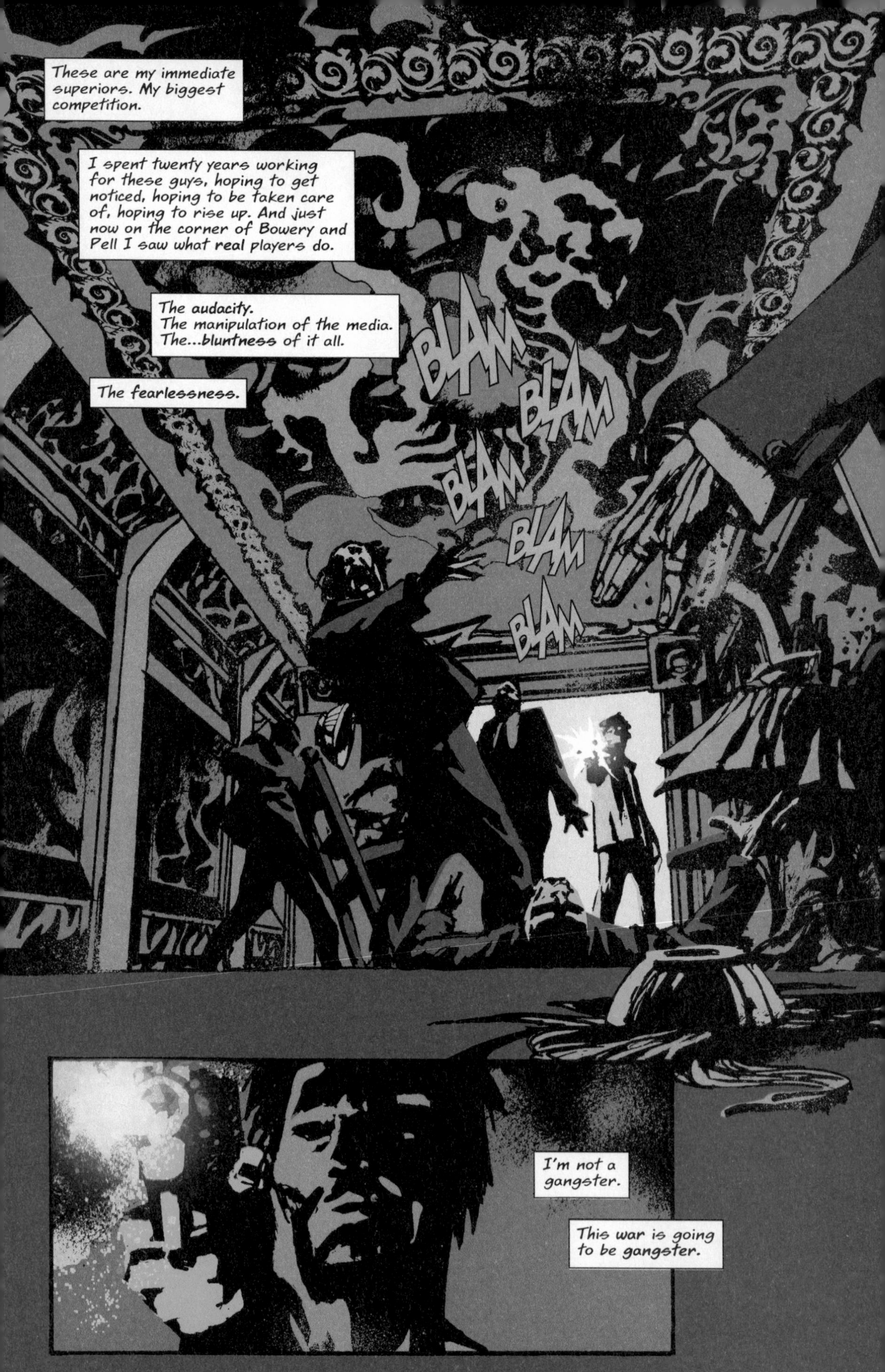
These are my immediate superiors. My biggest competition.
I spent twenty years working for these guys, hoping to get noticed, hoping to be taken care of, hoping to rise up. And just now on the corner of Bowery and Pell I saw what real players do.
The audacity.
The manipulation of the media.
The...bluntness of it all.
The fearlessness.
BLAM
BLAM
BLAM
BLAM
BLAM
I'm not a gangster.
This war is going to be gangster.

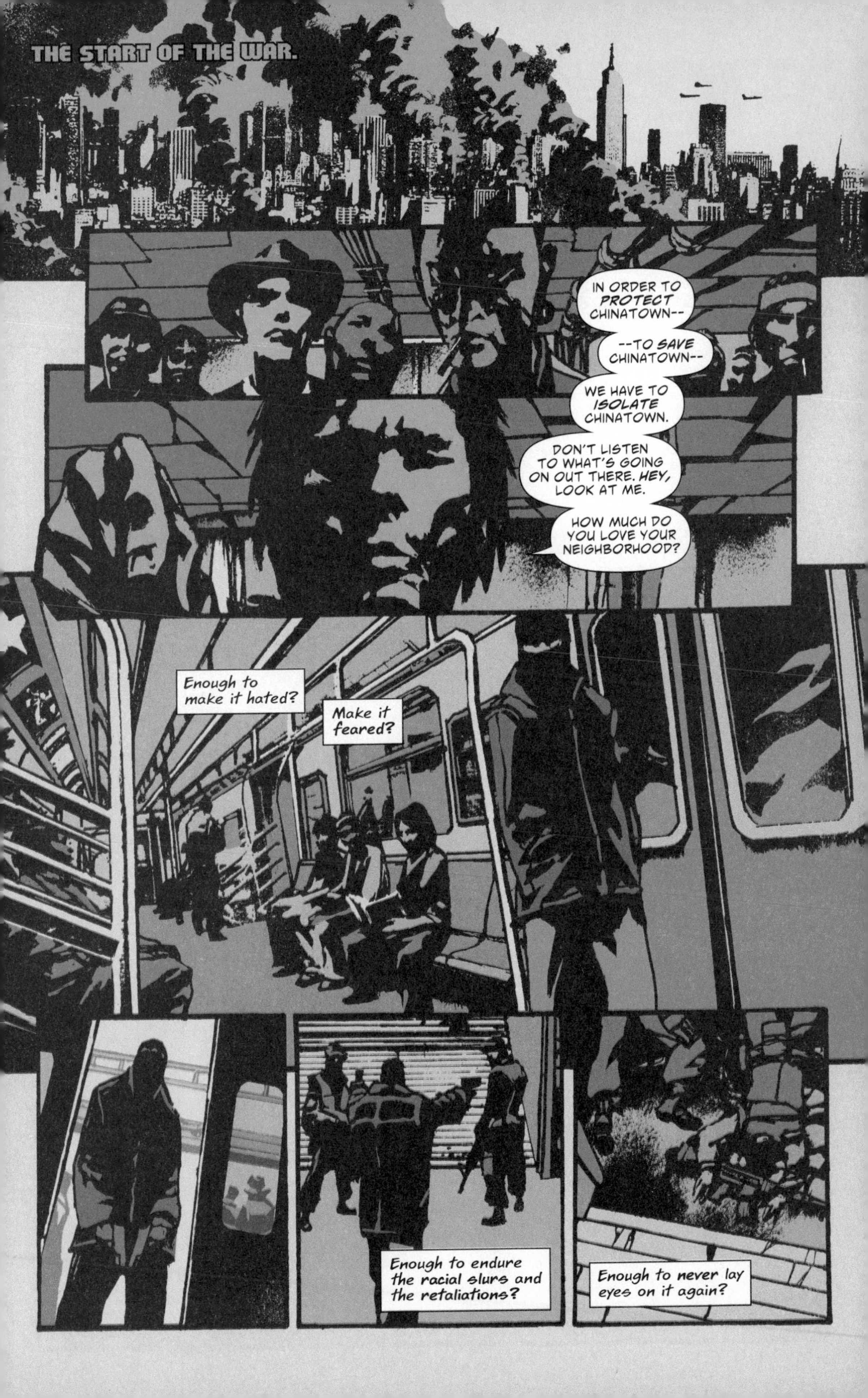
THE START OF THE WAR.
IN ORDER TO PROTECT CHINATOWN--
--TO SAVE CHINATOWN--
WE HAVE TO ISOLATE CHINATOWN.
DON'T LISTEN TO WHAT'S GOING ON OUT THERE. HEY, LOOK AT ME.
HOW MUCH DO YOU LOVE YOUR NEIGHBORHOOD?
Enough to make it hated?
Make it feared?
Enough to endure the racial slurs and the retaliations?
Enough to never lay eyes on it again?

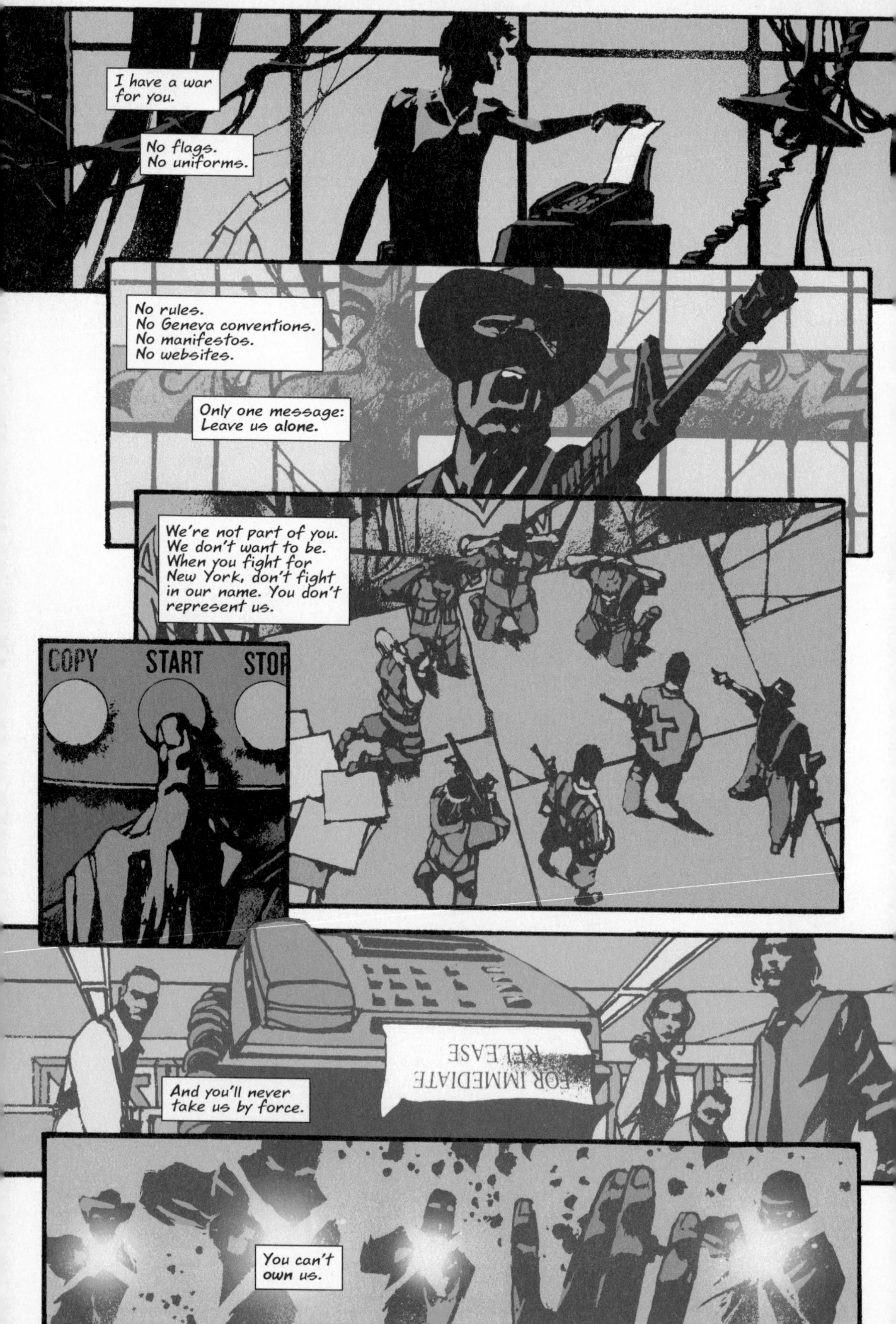
I have a war for you.
No flags. No uniforms.
No rules. No Geneva conventions. No manifestos. No websites.
Only one message: Leave us alone.
We're not part of you. We don't want to be. When you fight for New York, don't fight in our name. You don't represent us.
COPY
START
FOR IMMEDIATE RELEASE
And you'll never take us by force.
You can't own us.

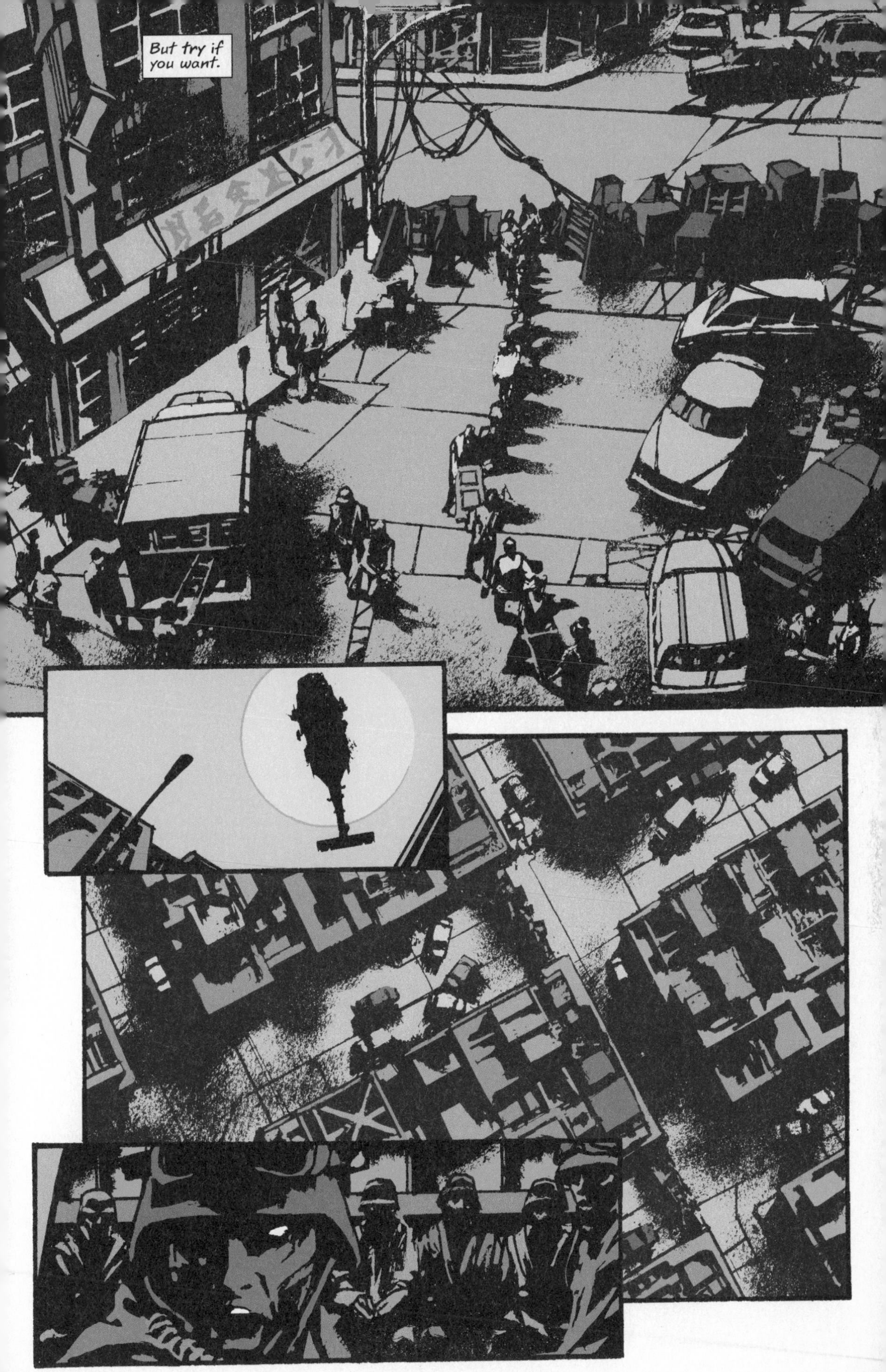
But try if you want.

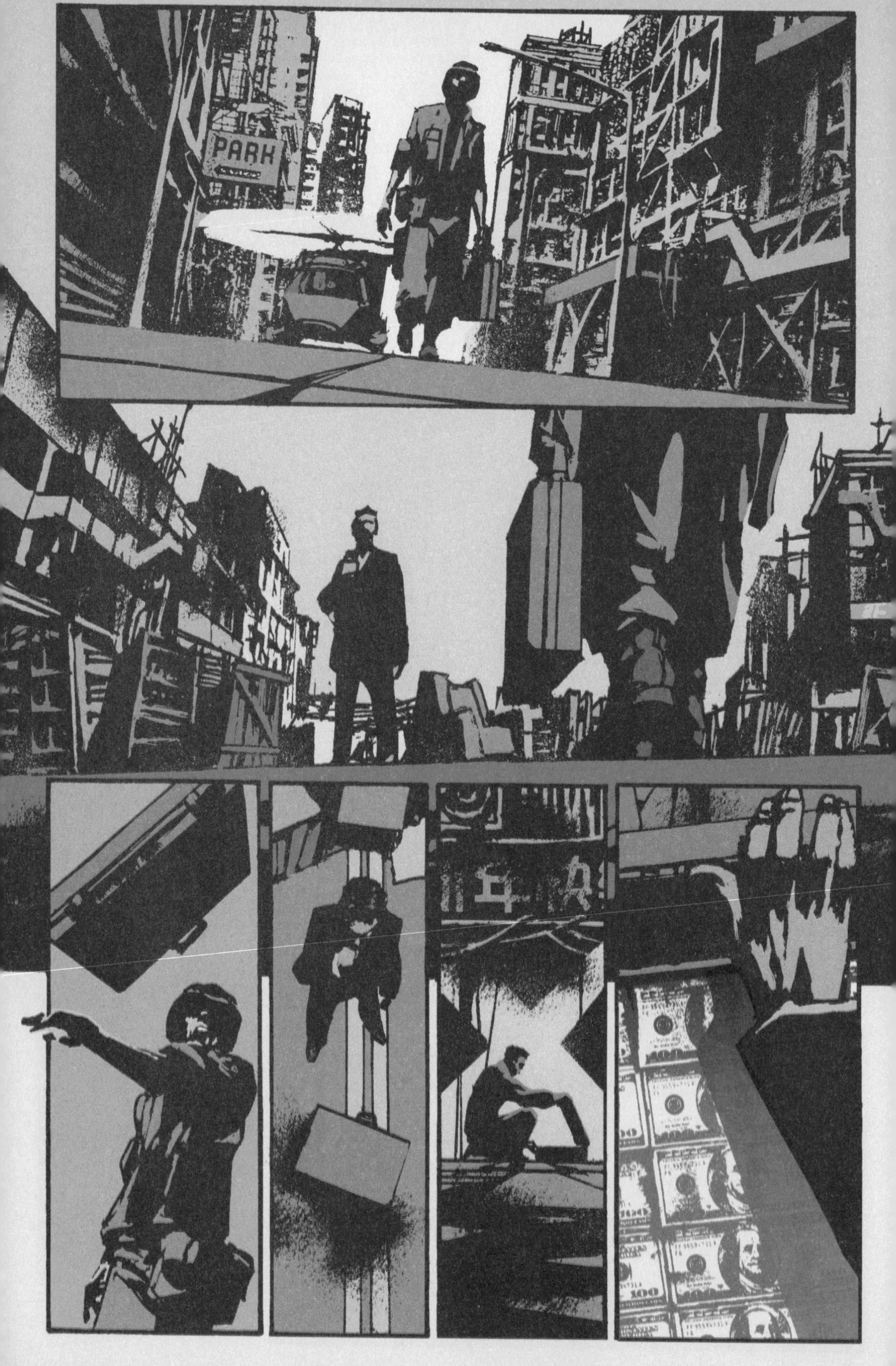
PARK

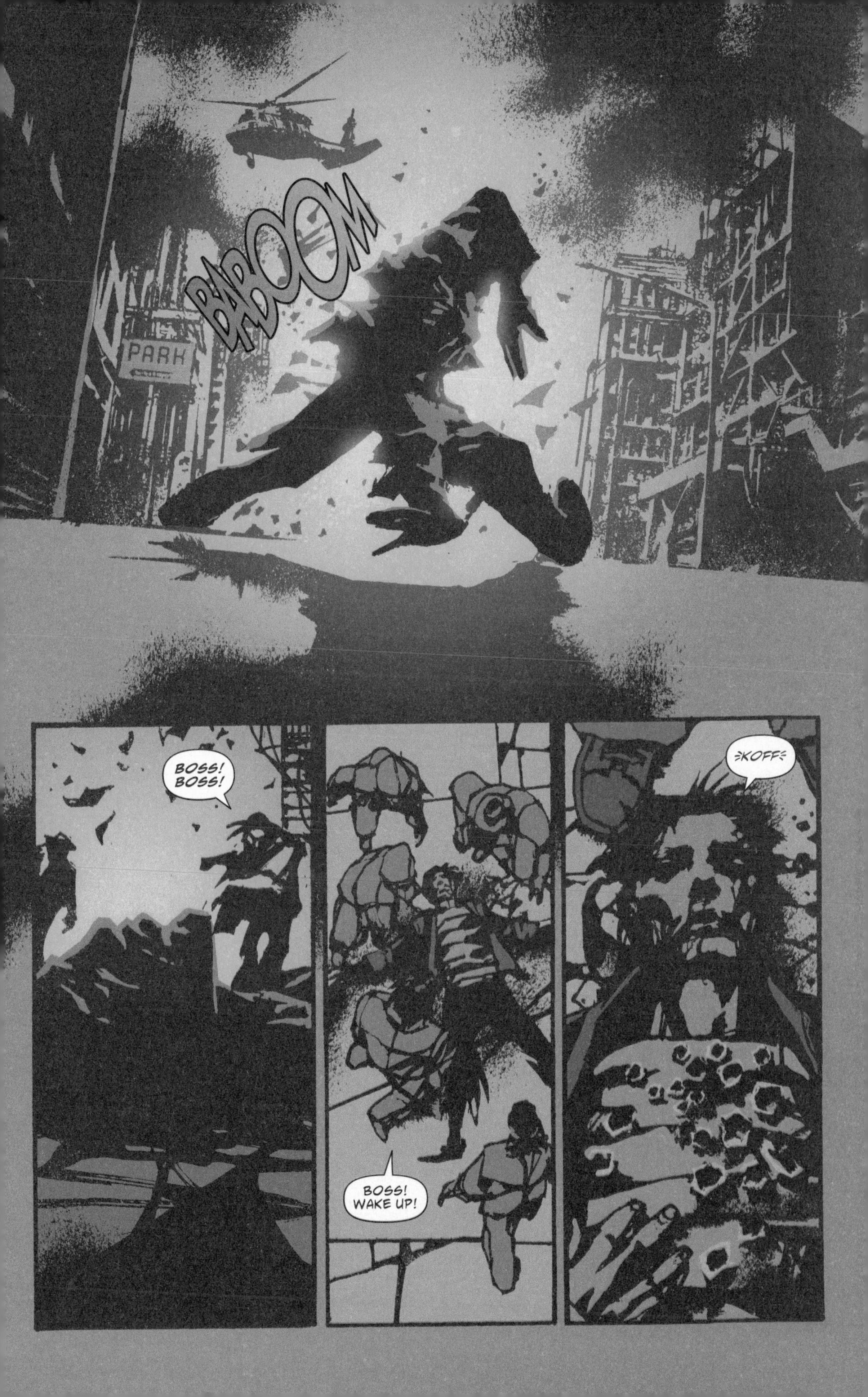
BABOOM
PARK
BOSS! BOSS!
BOSS! WAKE UP!
KOFF

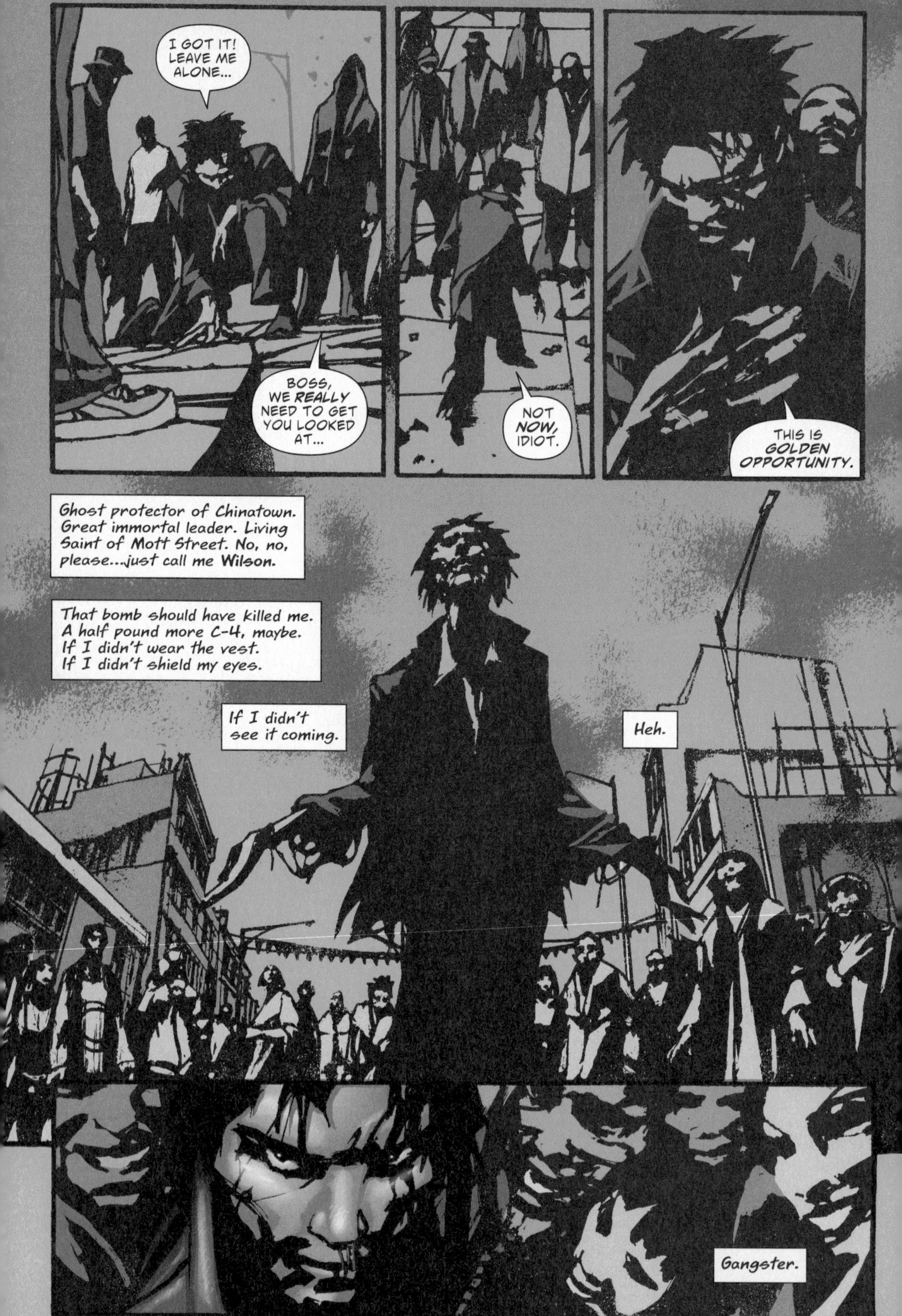
I GOT IT! LEAVE ME ALONE...
BOSS, WE REALLY NEED TO GET YOU LOOKED AT...
NOT NOW, IDIOT.
THIS IS GOLDEN OPPORTUNITY.
Ghost protector of Chinatown. Great immortal leader. Living Saint of Mott Street. No, no, please...just call me Wilson.
That bomb should have killed me. A half pound more C-4, maybe. If I didn't wear the vest. If I didn't shield my eyes.
If I didn't see it coming.
Heh.
Gangster.

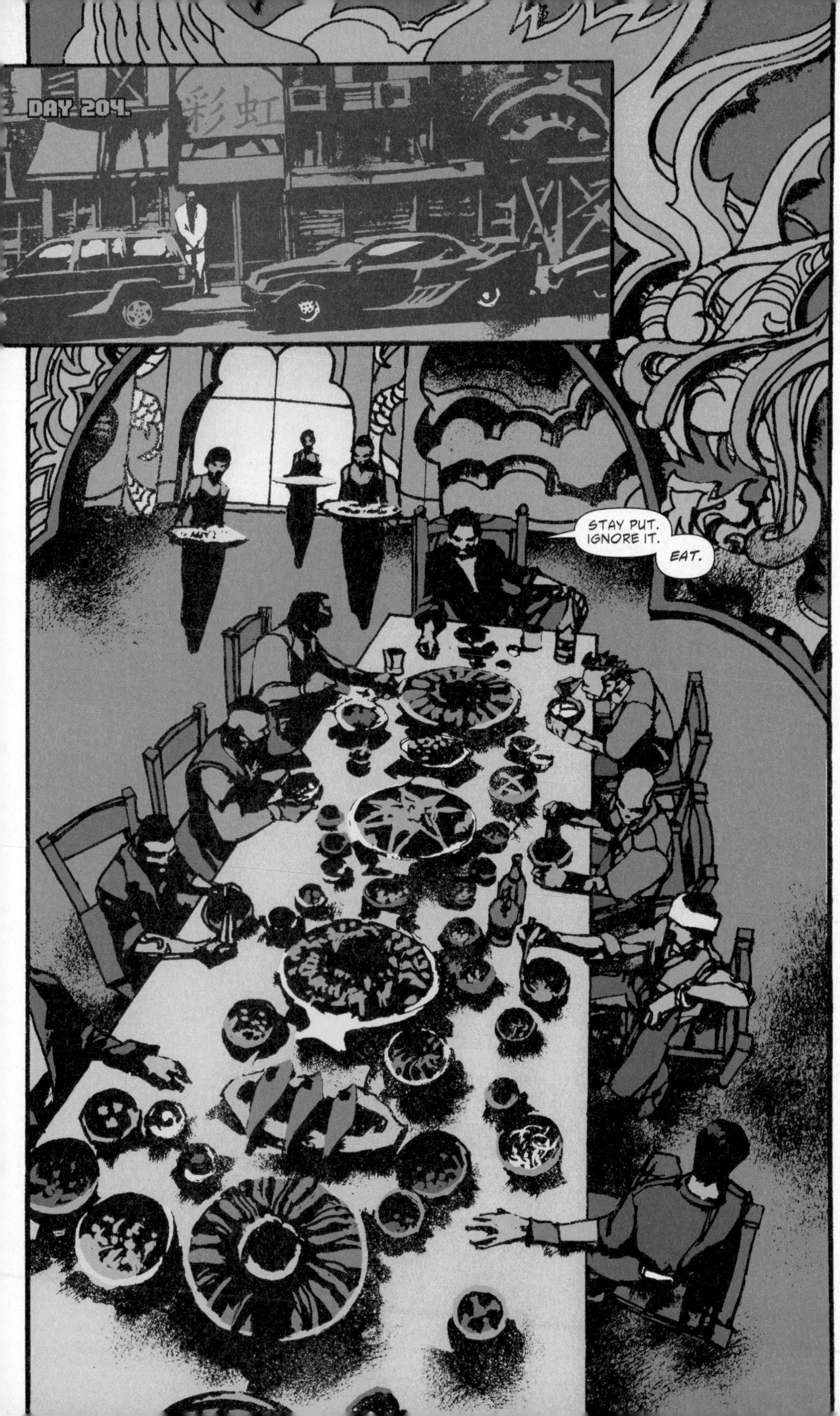
DAY 204.
彩虹
STAY PUT. IGNORE IT.
EAT.

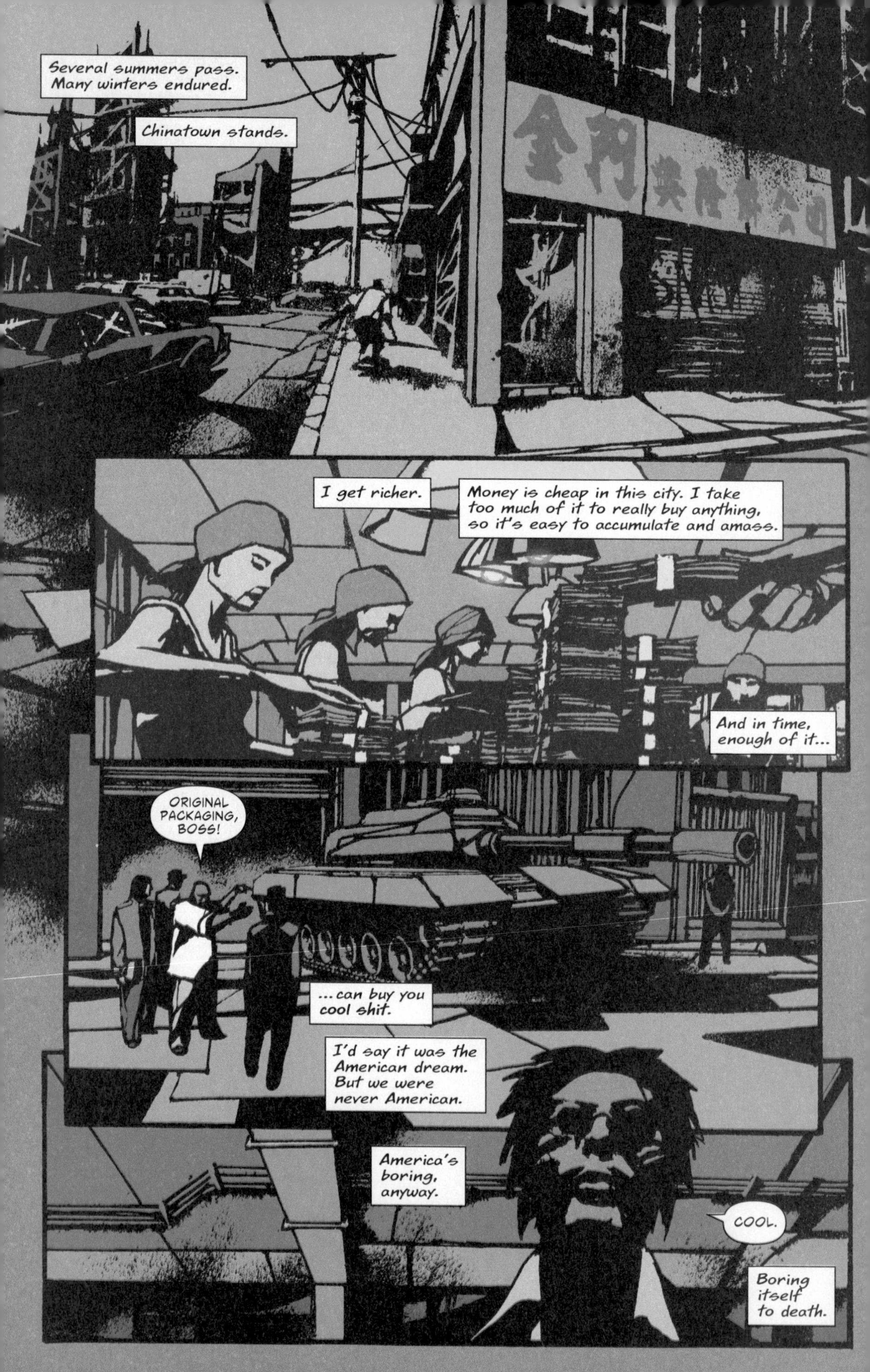
Several summers pass. Many winters endured.
Chinatown stands.
I get richer.
Money is cheap in this city. I take too much of it to really buy anything, so it's easy to accumulate and amass.
And in time, enough of it...
ORIGINAL PACKAGING, BOSS!
...can buy you cool shit.
I'd say it was the American dream. But we were never American.
America's boring, anyway.
COOL.
Boring itself to death.

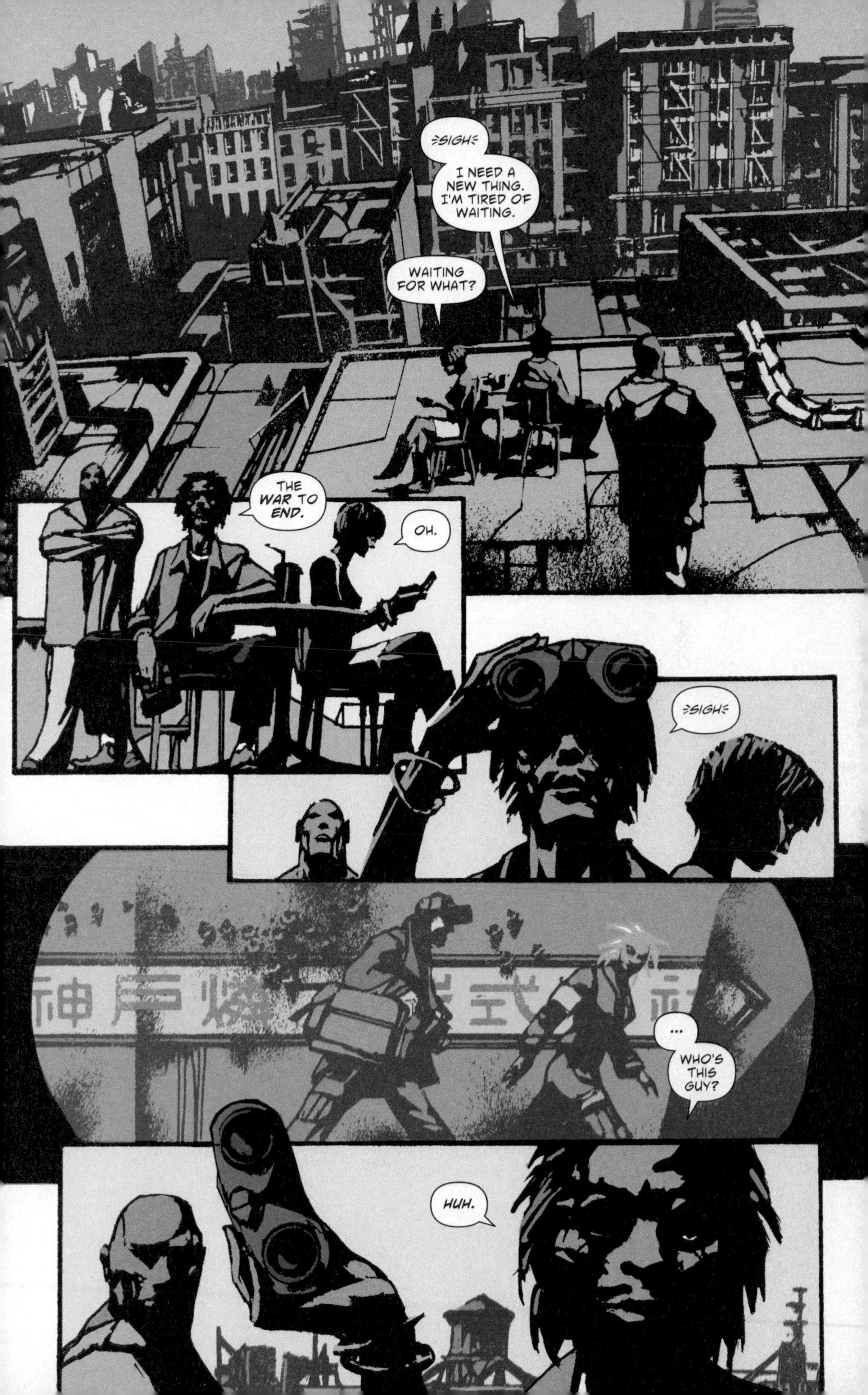

≶SIGH≶
I NEED A NEW THING. I'M TIRED OF WAITING.
WAITING FOR WHAT?
THE WAR TO END.
OH.
≶SIGH≶
...
WHO'S THIS GUY?
HUH.

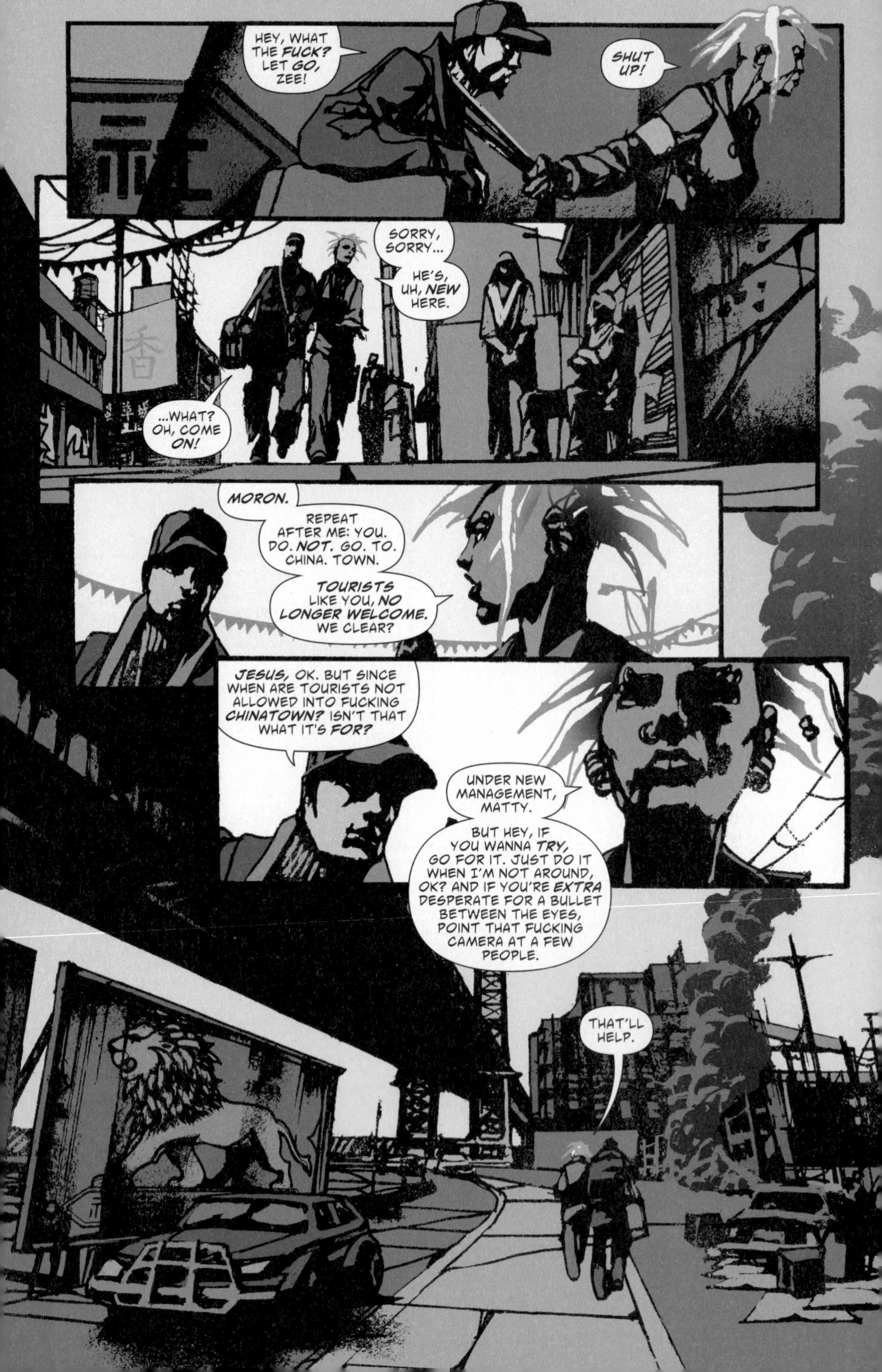
HEY, WHAT THE FUCK? LET GO, ZEE!
SHUT UP!
SORRY, SORRY...
HE'S, UH, NEW HERE.
...WHAT? OH, COME ON!
MORON.
REPEAT AFTER ME: YOU. DO. NOT. GO. TO. CHINA. TOWN.
TOURISTS LIKE YOU, NO LONGER WELCOME. WE CLEAR?
JESUS, OK. BUT SINCE WHEN ARE TOURISTS NOT ALLOWED INTO FUCKING CHINATOWN? ISN'T THAT WHAT IT'S FOR?
UNDER NEW MANAGEMENT, MATTY.
BUT HEY, IF YOU WANNA TRY, GO FOR IT. JUST DO IT WHEN I'M NOT AROUND, OK? AND IF YOU'RE EXTRA DESPERATE FOR A BULLET BETWEEN THE EYES, POINT THAT FUCKING CAMERA AT A FEW PEOPLE.
THAT'LL HELP.

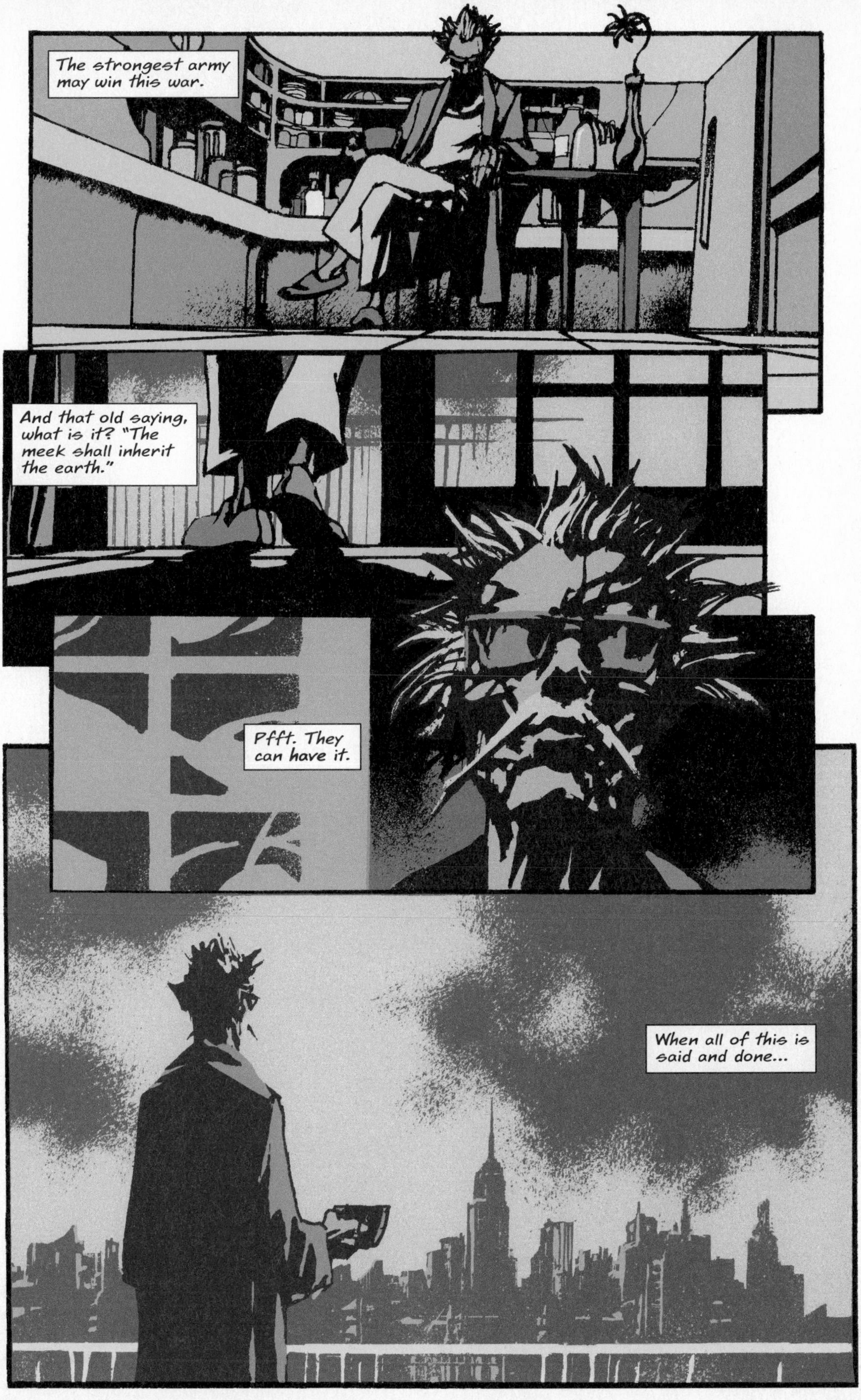

The strongest army may win this war.
And that old saying, what is it? "The meek shall inherit the earth."
Pfft. They can have it.
When all of this is said and done...

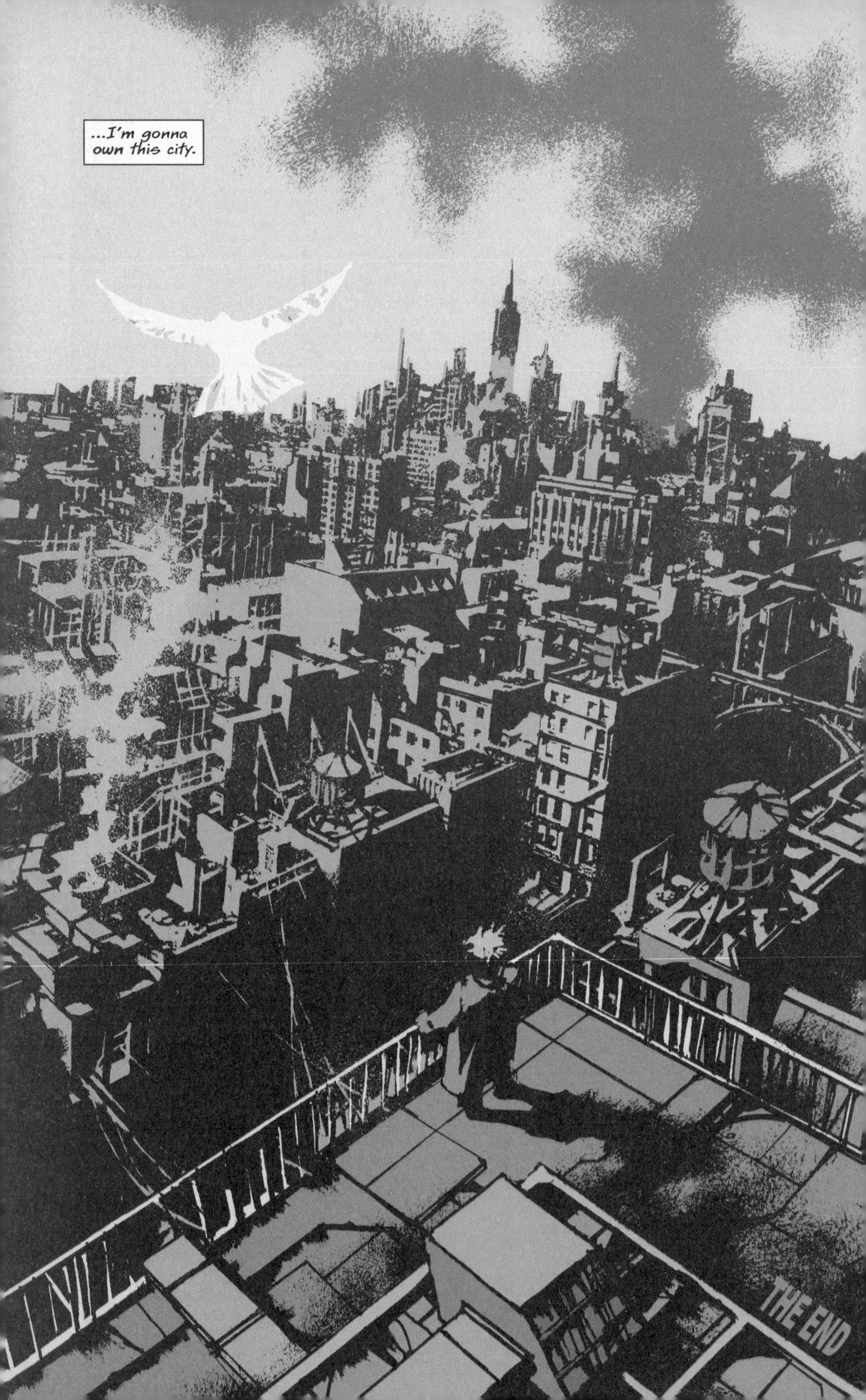
...I'm gonna own this city.
THE END

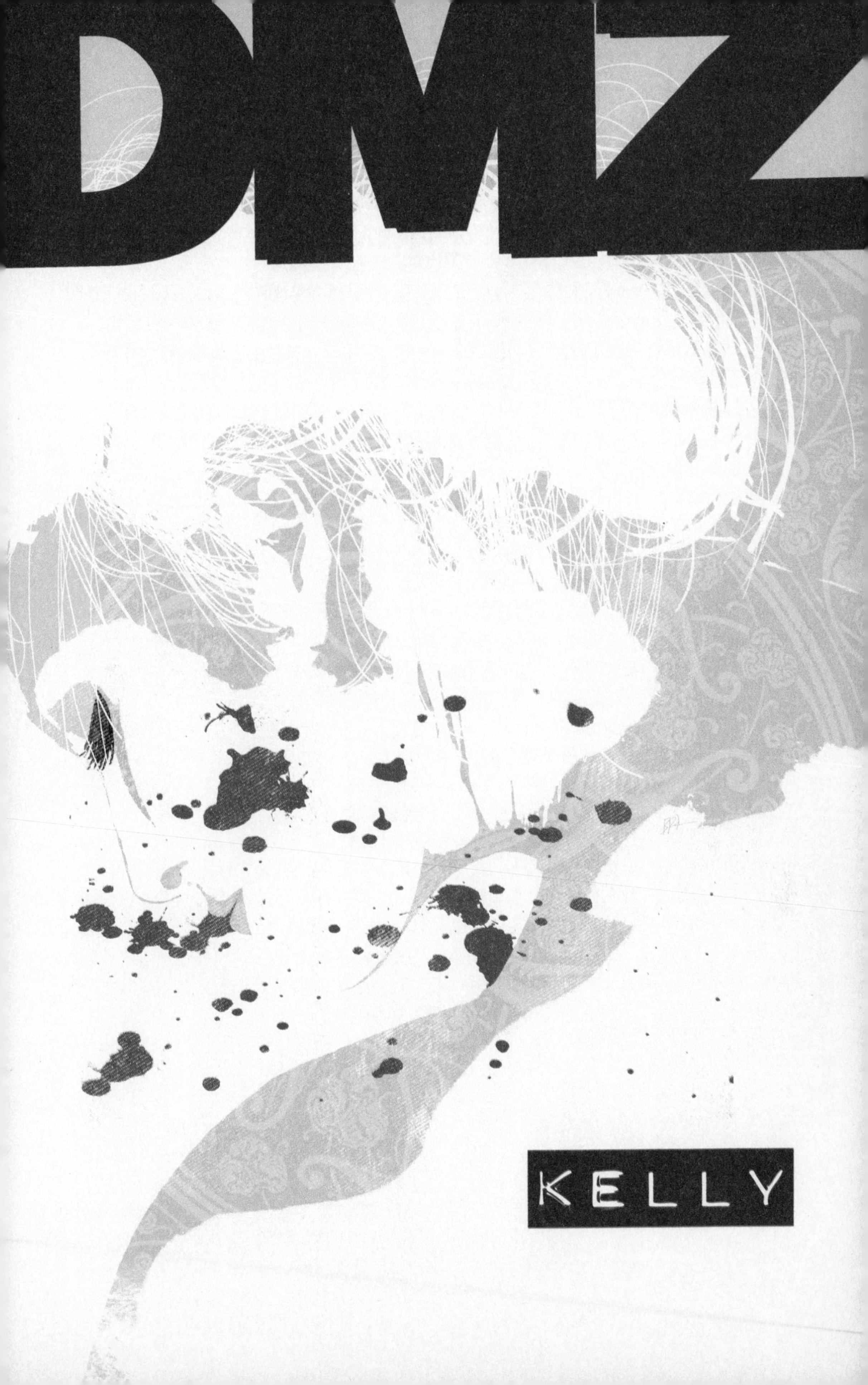
DMZ
KELLY

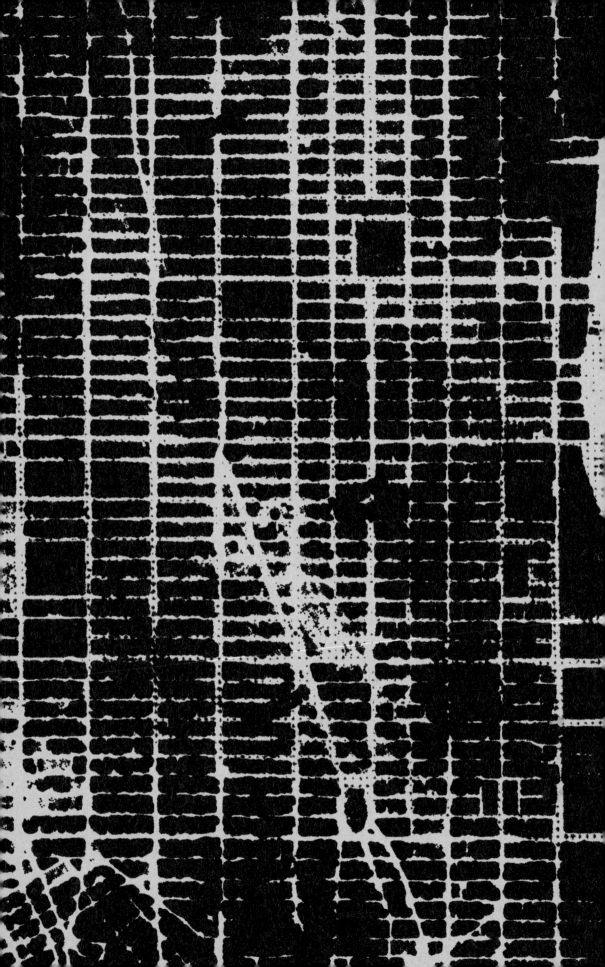

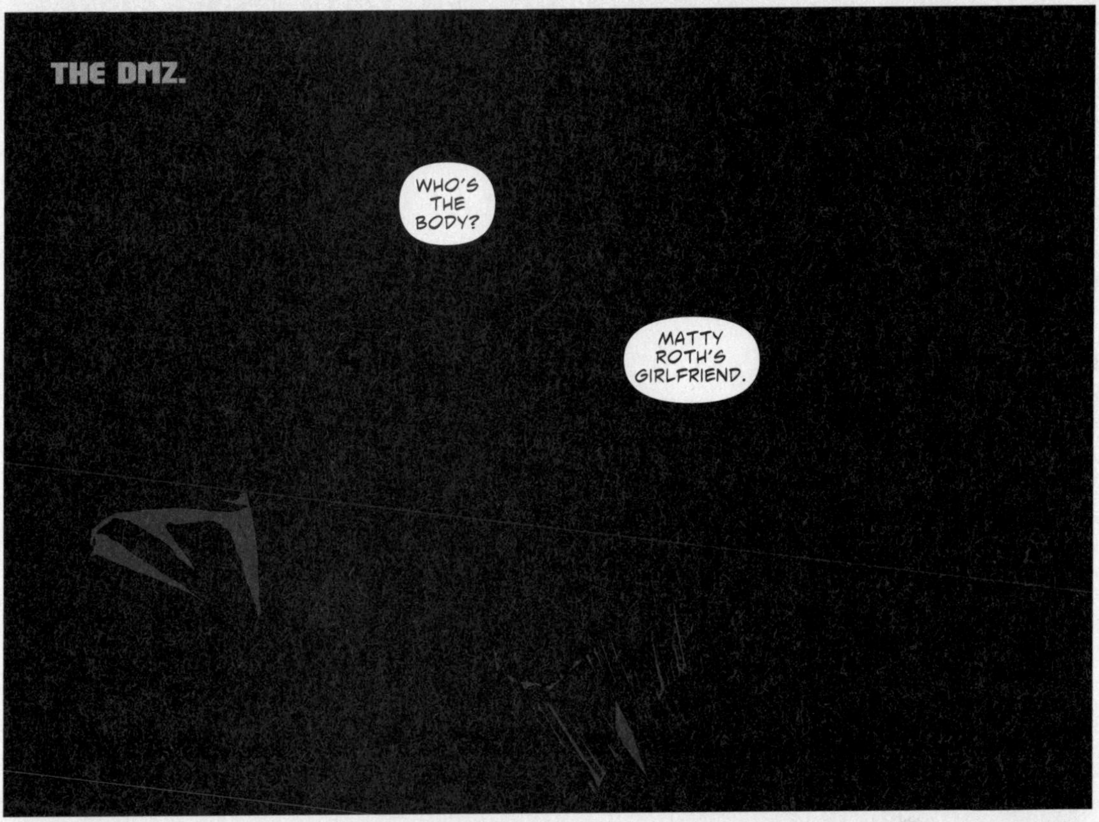
THE DMZ.
WHO'S THE BODY?
MATTY ROTH'S GIRLFRIEND.

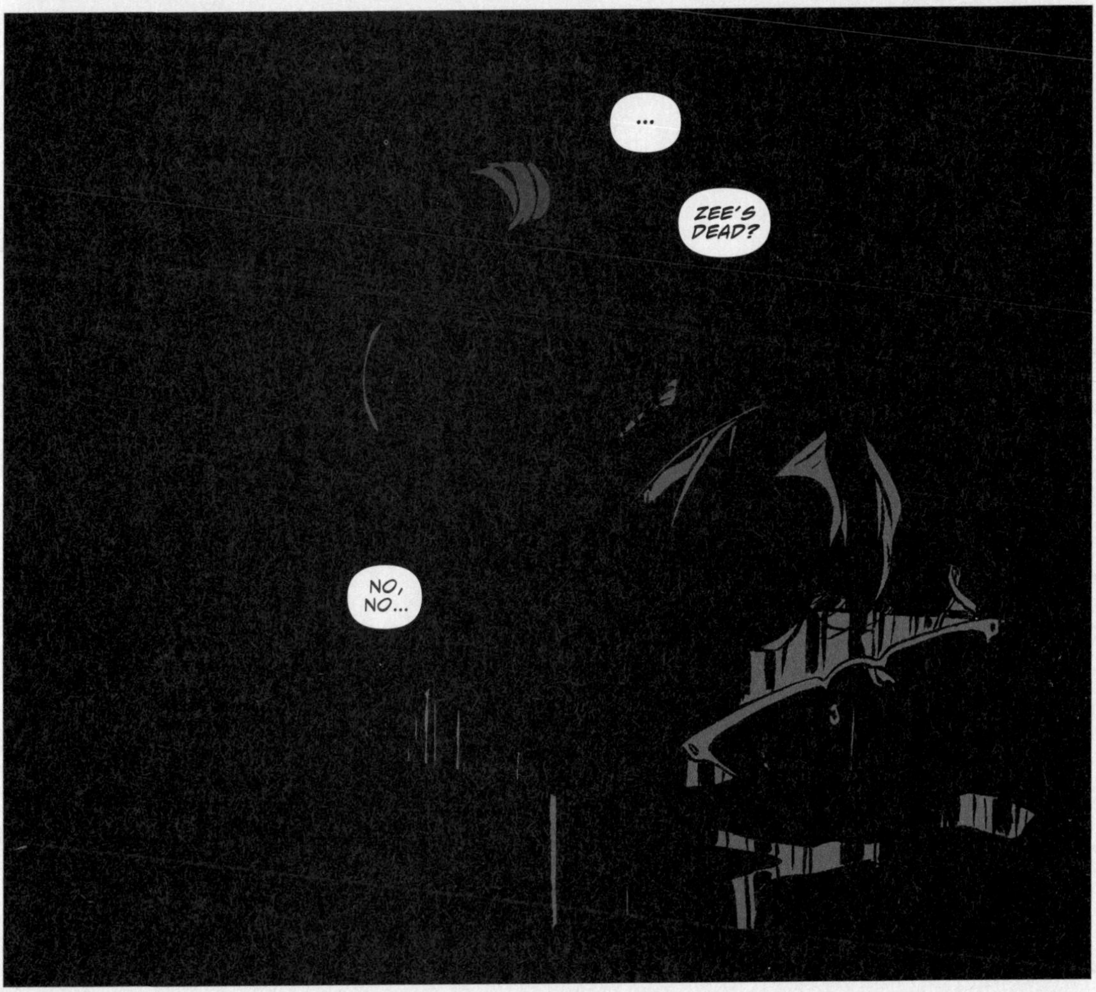
...
ZEE'S DEAD?
NO, NO...

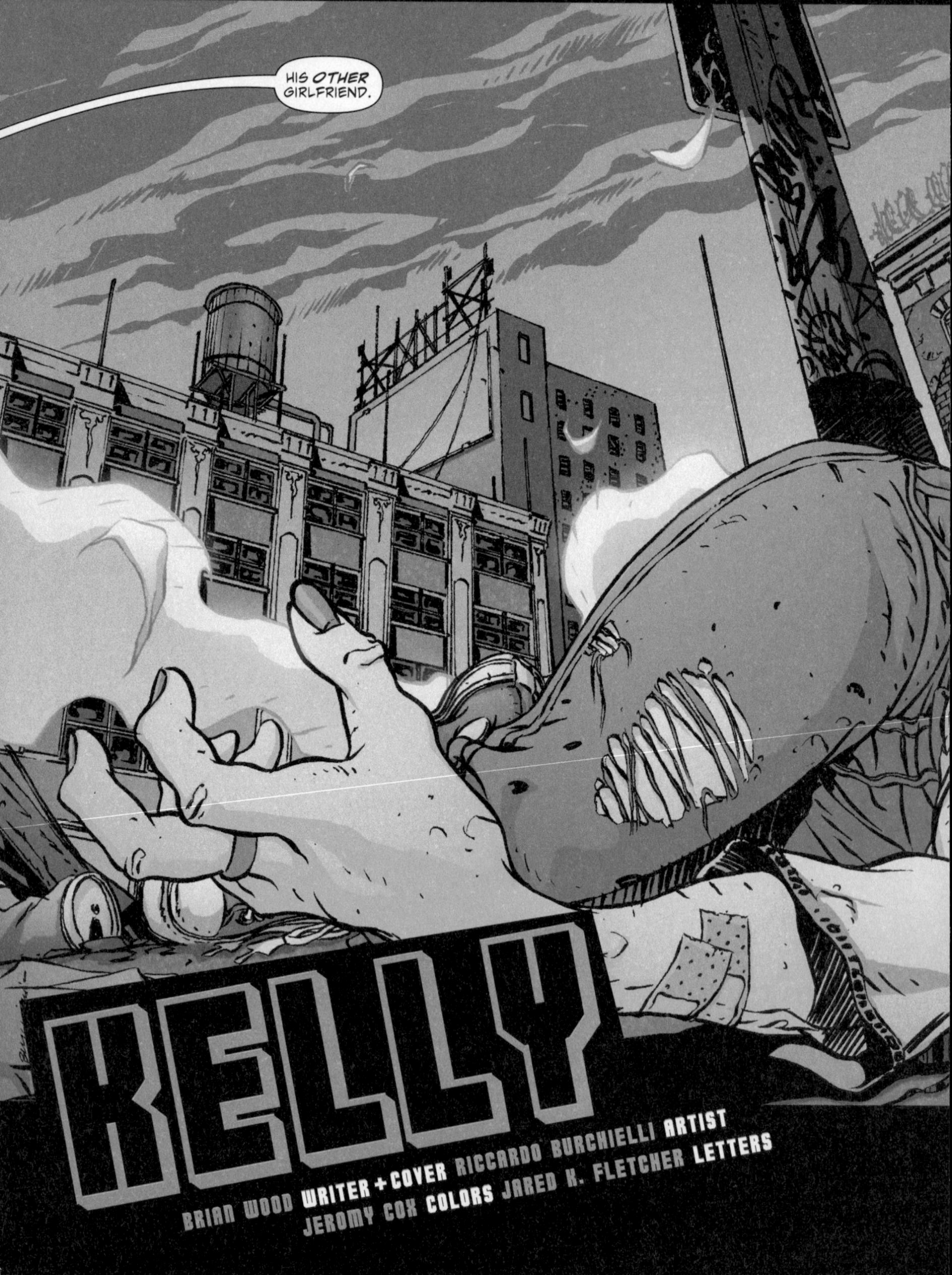
HIS OTHER GIRLFRIEND.
KELLY
BRIAN WOOD WRITER + COVER RICCARDO BURCHIELLI ARTIST
JEROMY COX COLORS JARED K. FLETCHER LETTERS

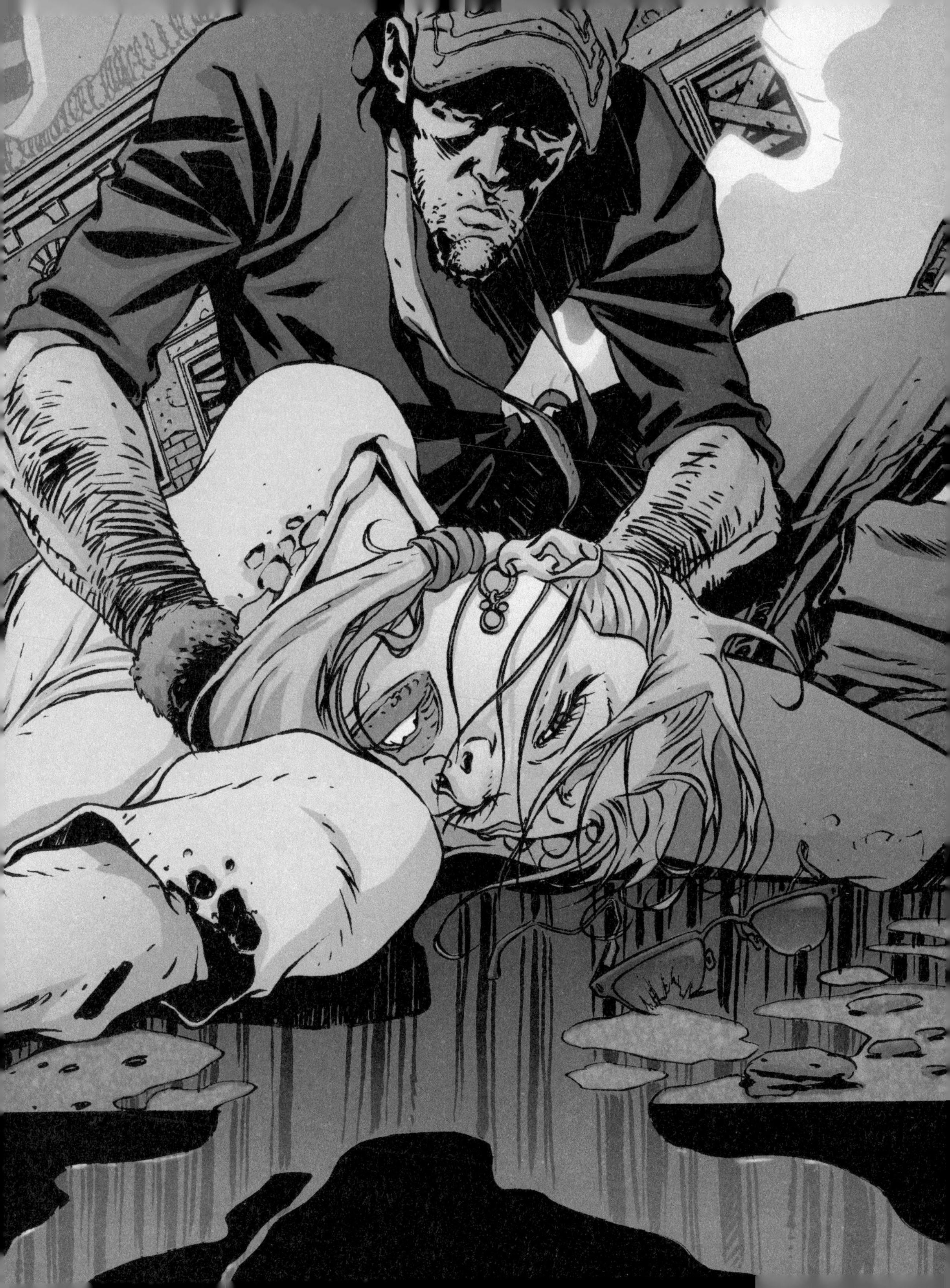

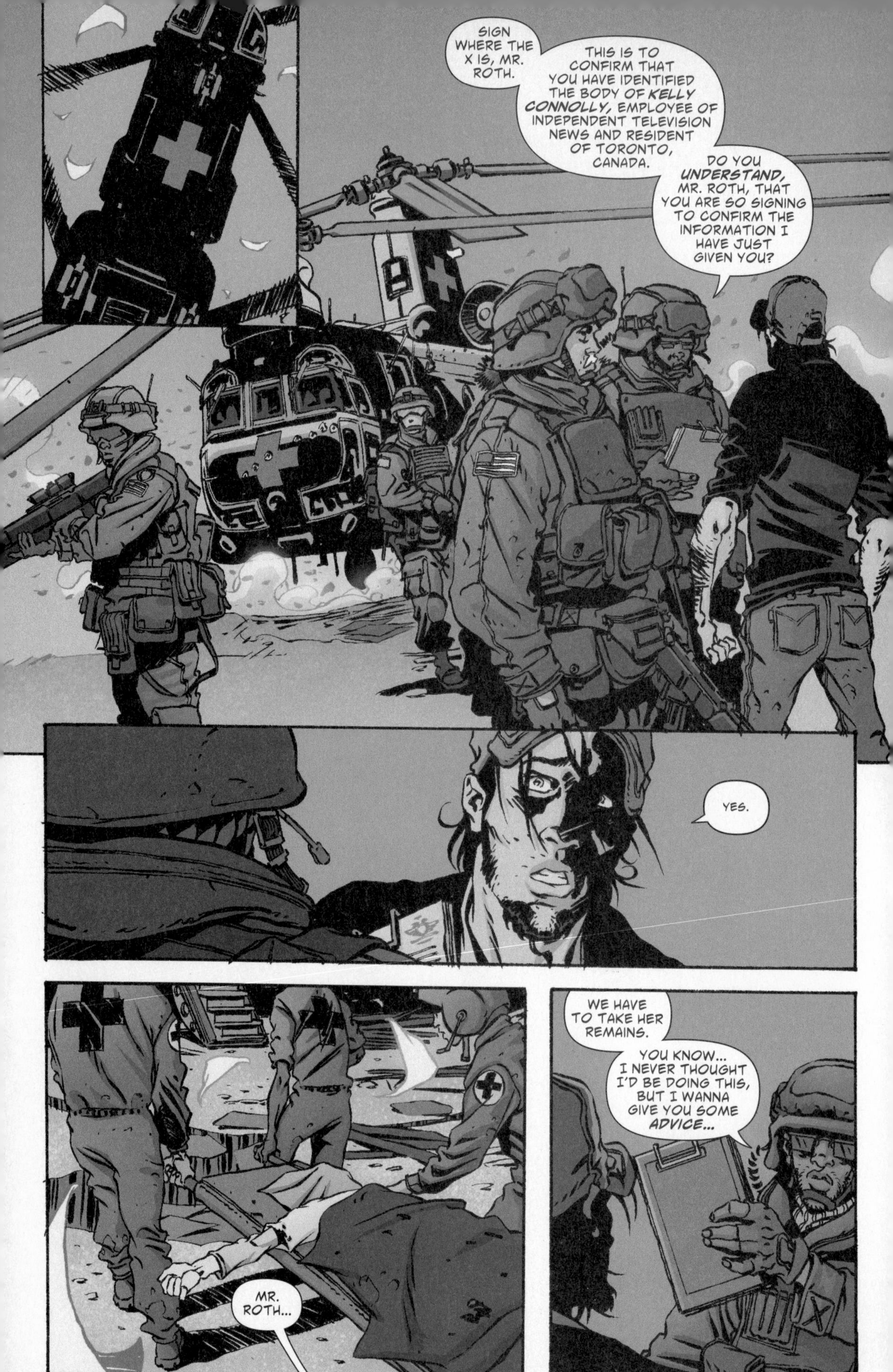
SIGN WHERE THE X IS, MR. ROTH.
THIS IS TO CONFIRM THAT YOU HAVE IDENTIFIED THE BODY OF KELLY CONNOLLY, EMPLOYEE OF INDEPENDENT TELEVISION NEWS AND RESIDENT OF TORONTO, CANADA.
DO YOU UNDERSTAND, MR. ROTH, THAT YOU ARE SO SIGNING TO CONFIRM THE INFORMATION I HAVE JUST GIVEN YOU?
YES.
MR. ROTH...
WE HAVE TO TAKE HER REMAINS.
YOU KNOW... I NEVER THOUGHT I'D BE DOING THIS, BUT I WANNA GIVE YOU SOME ADVICE...

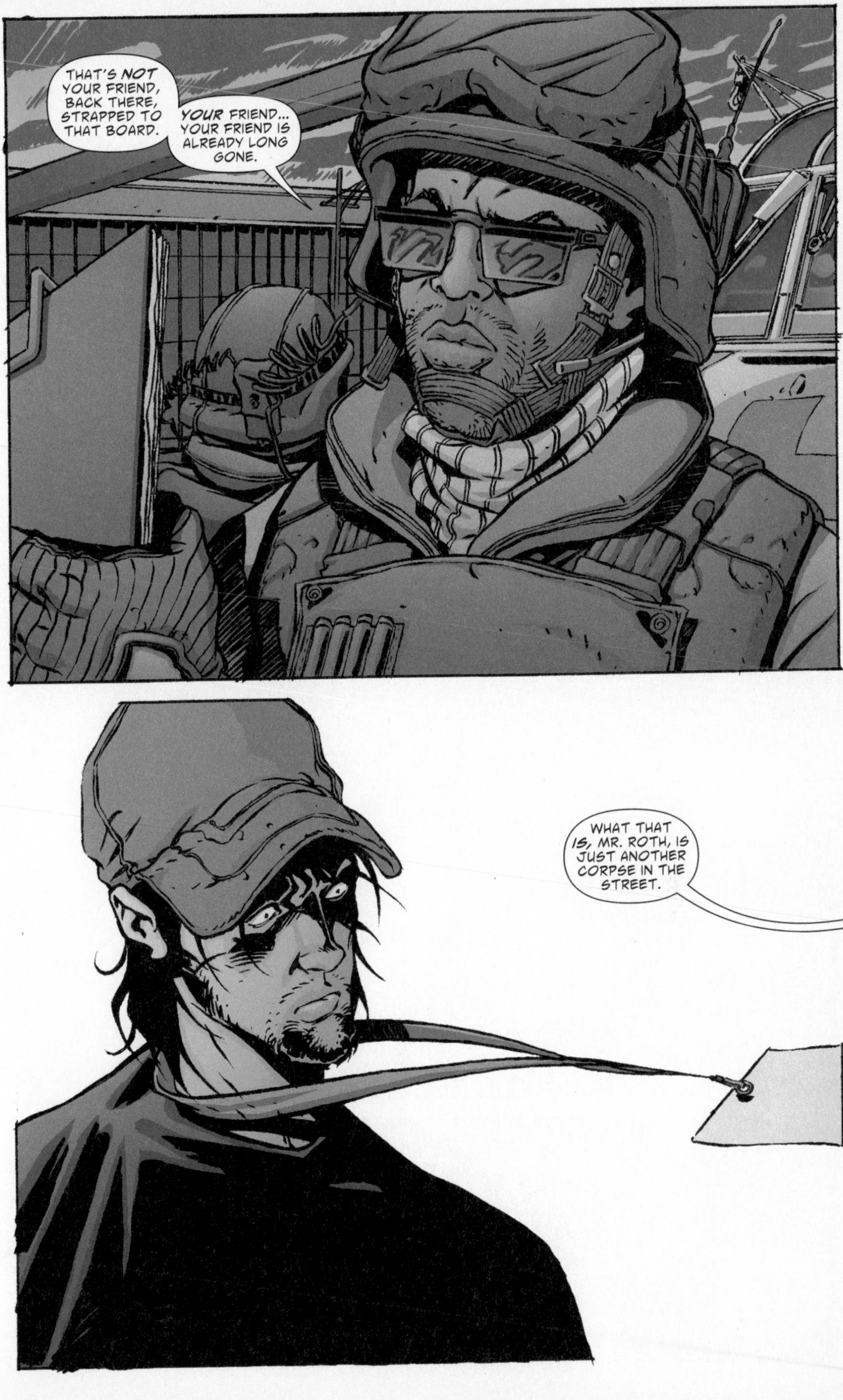
THAT'S NOT YOUR FRIEND, BACK THERE, STRAPPED TO THAT BOARD.
YOUR FRIEND... YOUR FRIEND IS ALREADY LONG GONE.
WHAT THAT IS, MR. ROTH, IS JUST ANOTHER CORPSE IN THE STREET.

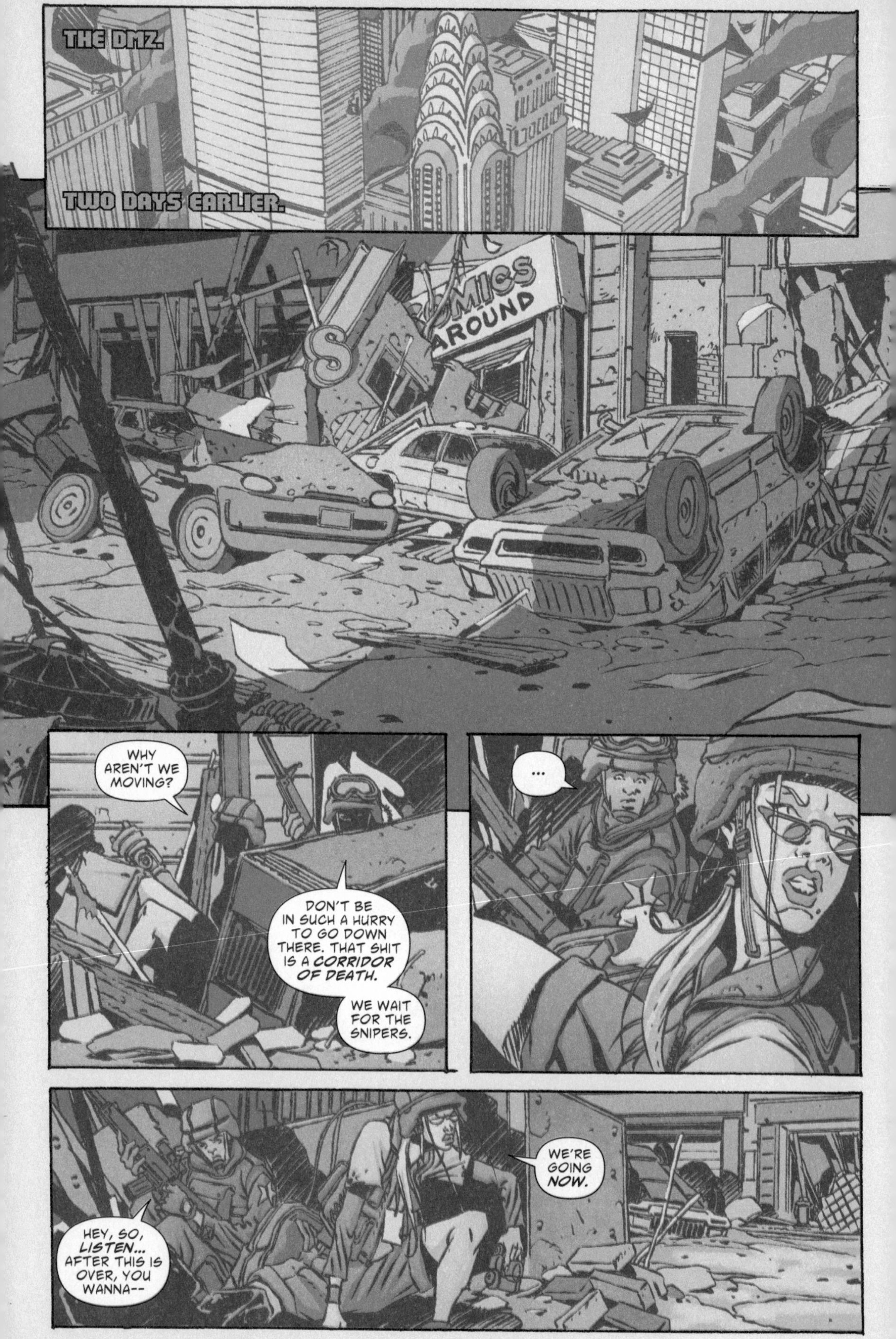
THE DMZ.
TWO DAYS EARLIER.
COMICS
AROUND
WHY AREN'T WE MOVING?
DON'T BE IN SUCH A HURRY TO GO DOWN THERE. THAT SHIT IS A CORRIDOR OF DEATH.
WE WAIT FOR THE SNIPERS.
...
WE'RE GOING NOW.
HEY, SO, LISTEN... AFTER THIS IS OVER, YOU WANNA--

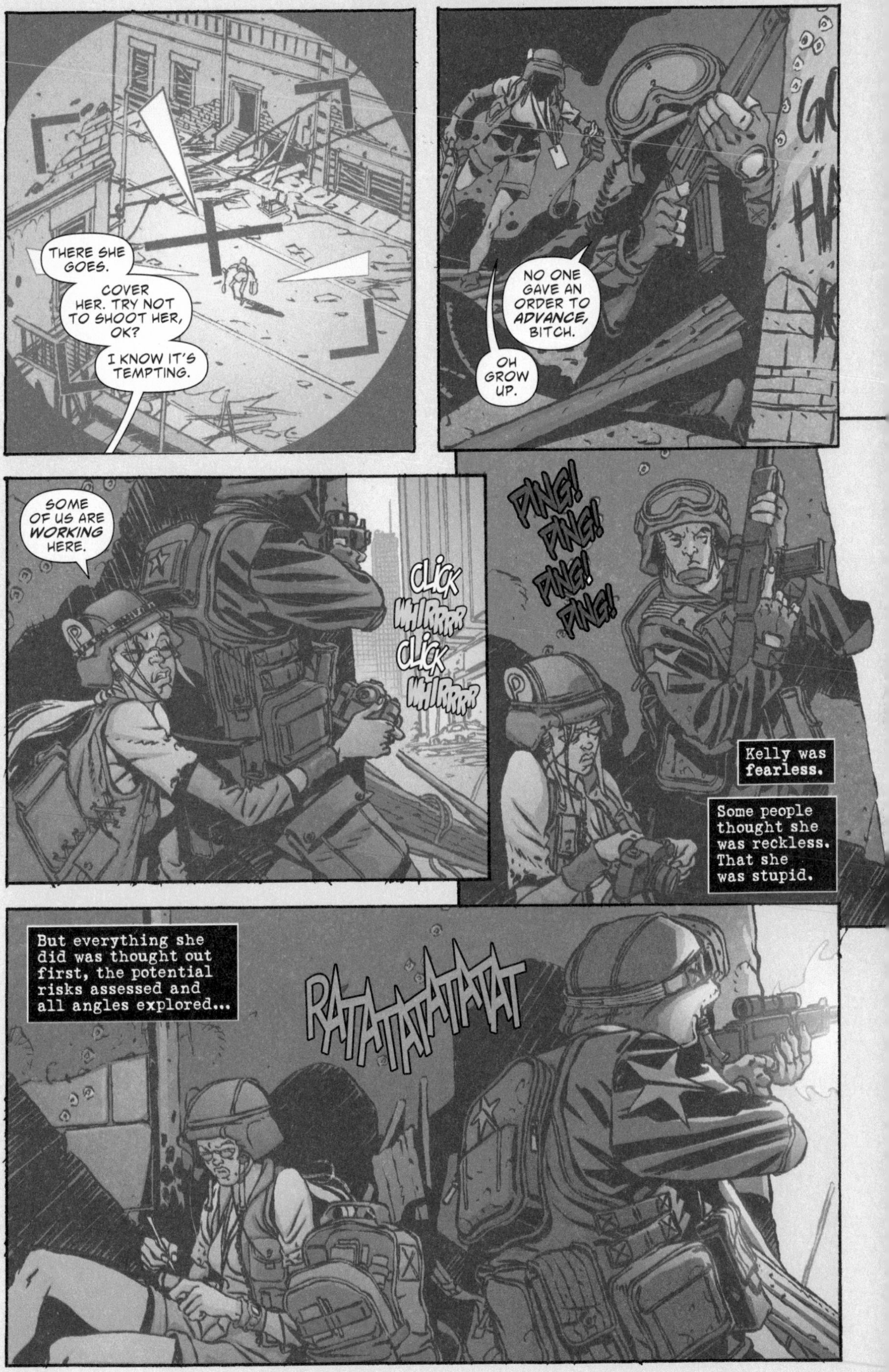
THERE SHE GOES.
COVER HER. TRY NOT TO SHOOT HER, OK?
I KNOW IT'S TEMPTING.
NO ONE GAVE AN ORDER TO ADVANCE, BITCH.
OH GROW UP.
SOME OF US ARE WORKING HERE.
CLICK
WHIRRRR
CLICK
WHIRRRR
PING! PING! PING! PING!
Kelly was fearless.
Some people thought she was reckless. That she was stupid.
But everything she did was thought out first, the potential risks assessed and all angles explored...
RATATATATATATAT

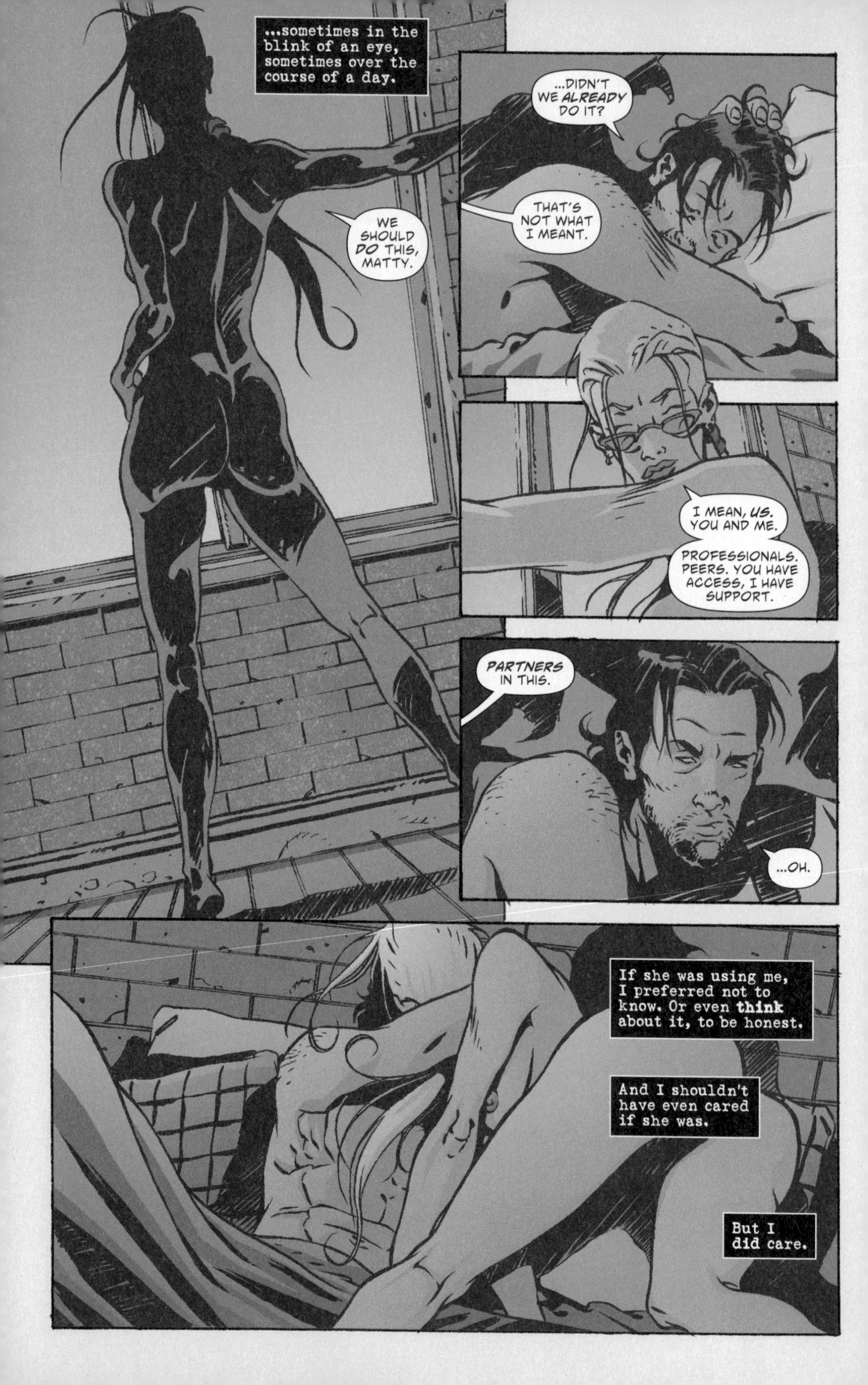
...sometimes in the blink of an eye, sometimes over the course of a day.
WE SHOULD DO THIS, MATTY.
...DIDN'T WE ALREADY DO IT?
THAT'S NOT WHAT I MEANT.
I MEAN, US. YOU AND ME.
PROFESSIONALS. PEERS. YOU HAVE ACCESS, I HAVE SUPPORT.
PARTNERS IN THIS.
...OH.
If she was using me, I preferred not to know. Or even think about it, to be honest.
And I shouldn't have even cared if she was.
But I did care.

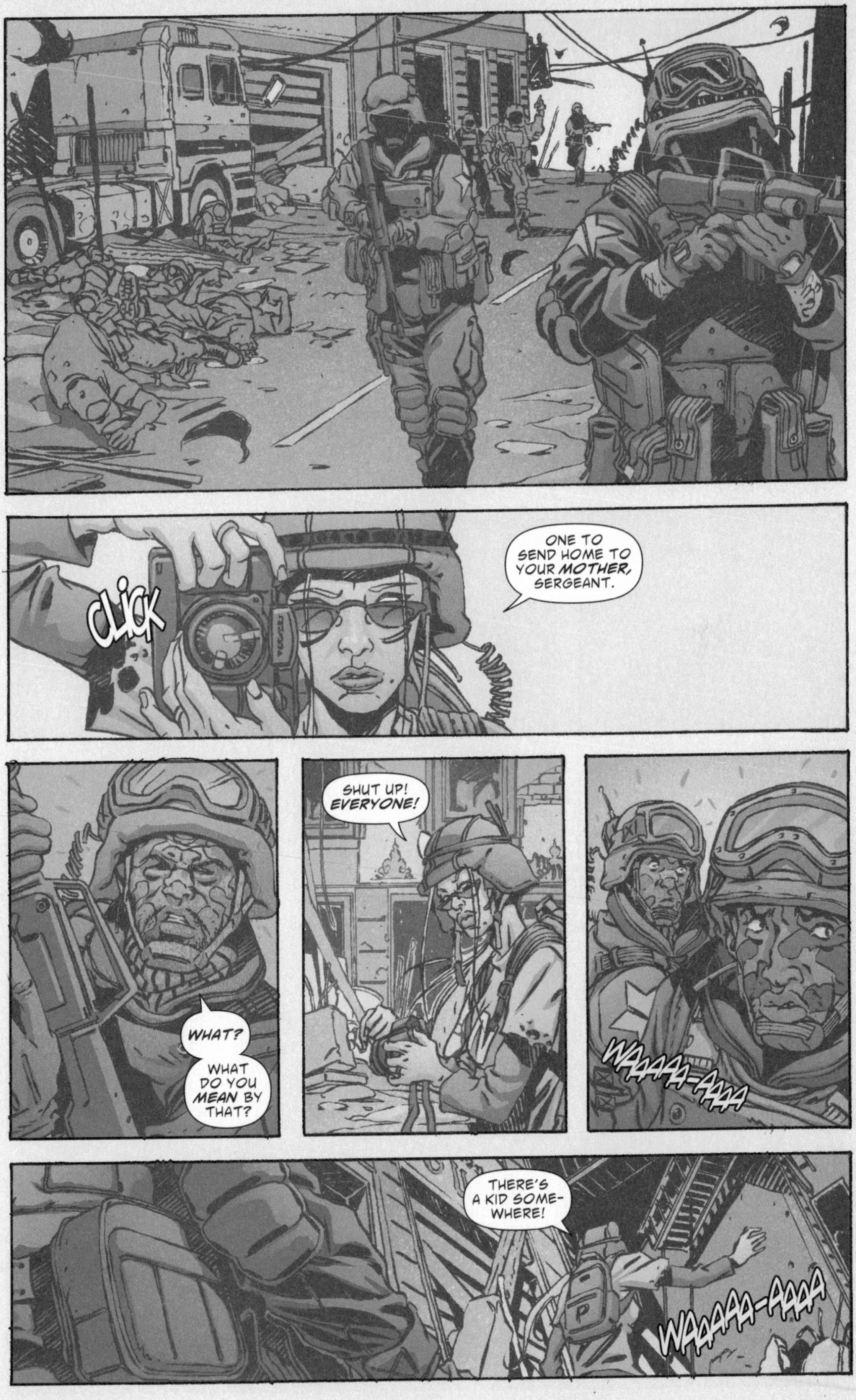
CLICK
ONE TO SEND HOME TO YOUR MOTHER, SERGEANT.
WHAT?
WHAT DO YOU MEAN BY THAT?
SHUT UP! EVERYONE!
WAAAAA-AAAA
THERE'S A KID SOME-WHERE!
WAAAAA-AAAA

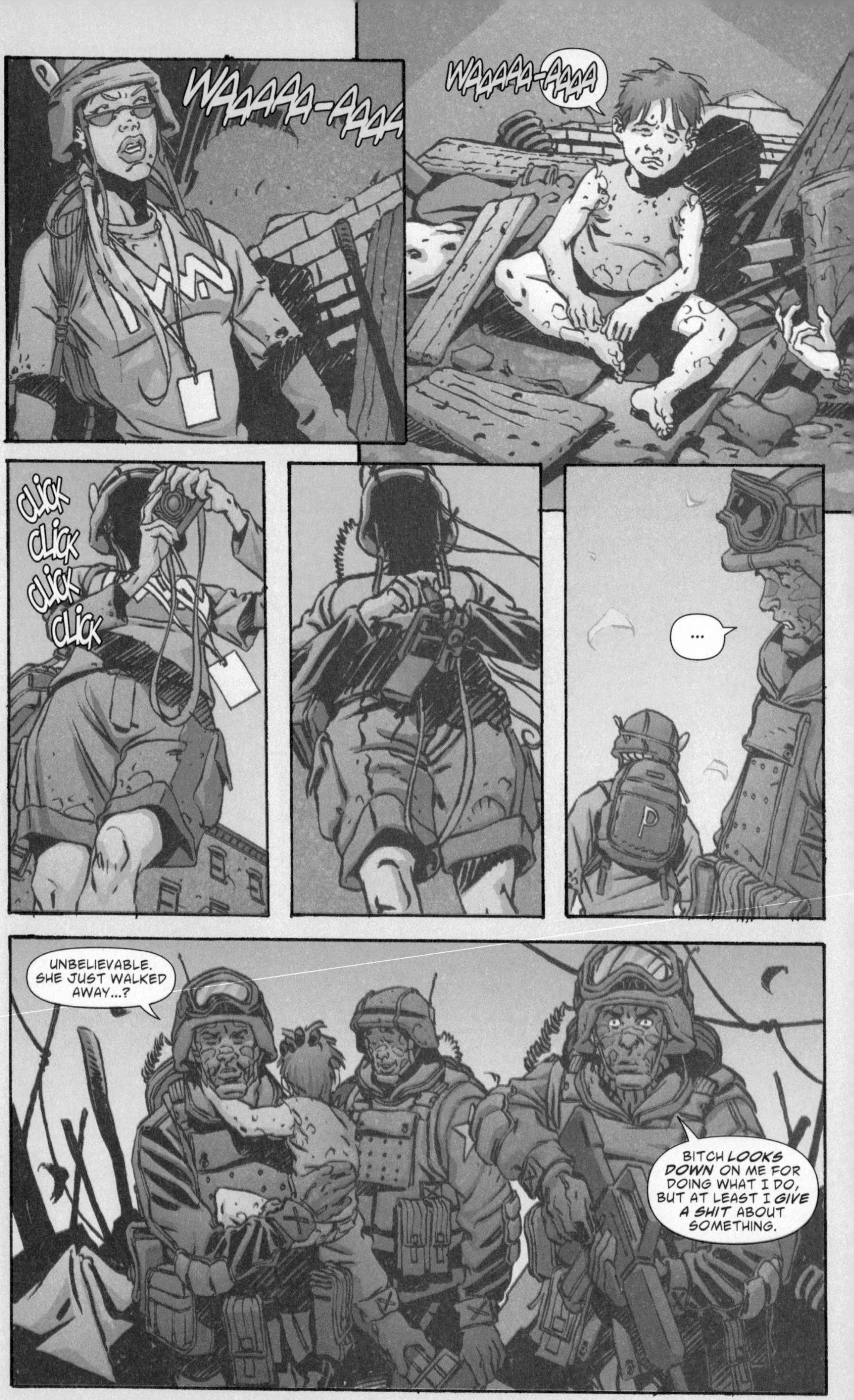
WAAAAA-AAAA
WAAAAA-AAAA
CLICK
CLICK
CLICK
CLICK
...
UNBELIEVABLE. SHE JUST WALKED AWAY...?
BITCH LOOKS DOWN ON ME FOR DOING WHAT I DO, BUT AT LEAST I GIVE A SHIT ABOUT SOMETHING.

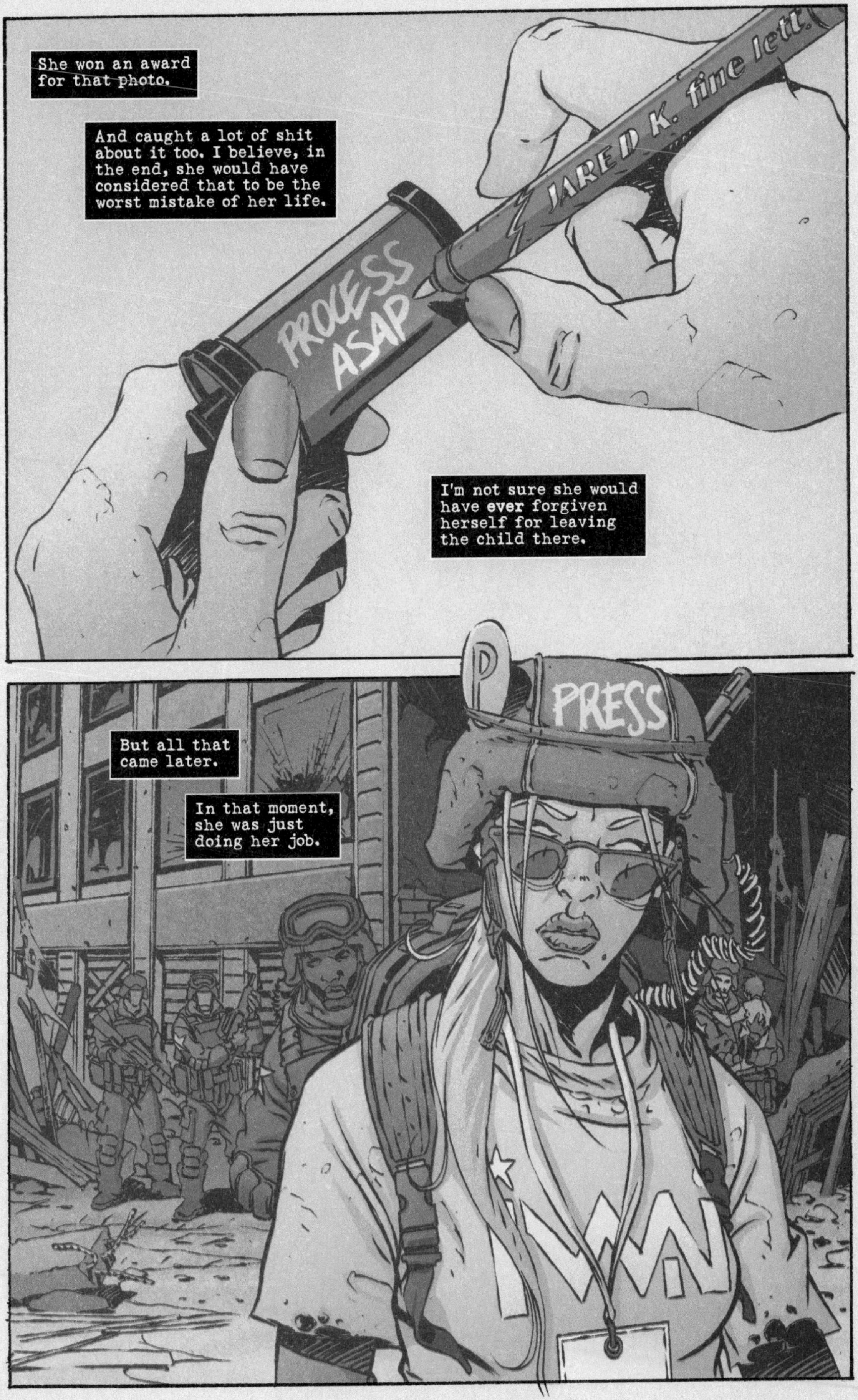

She won an award for that photo.
And caught a lot of shit about it too. I believe, in the end, she would have considered that to be the worst mistake of her life.
JARED K. fine lett
PROCESS ASAP
I'm not sure she would have **ever** forgiven herself for leaving the child there.
PRESS
But all that came later.
In that moment, she was just doing her job.

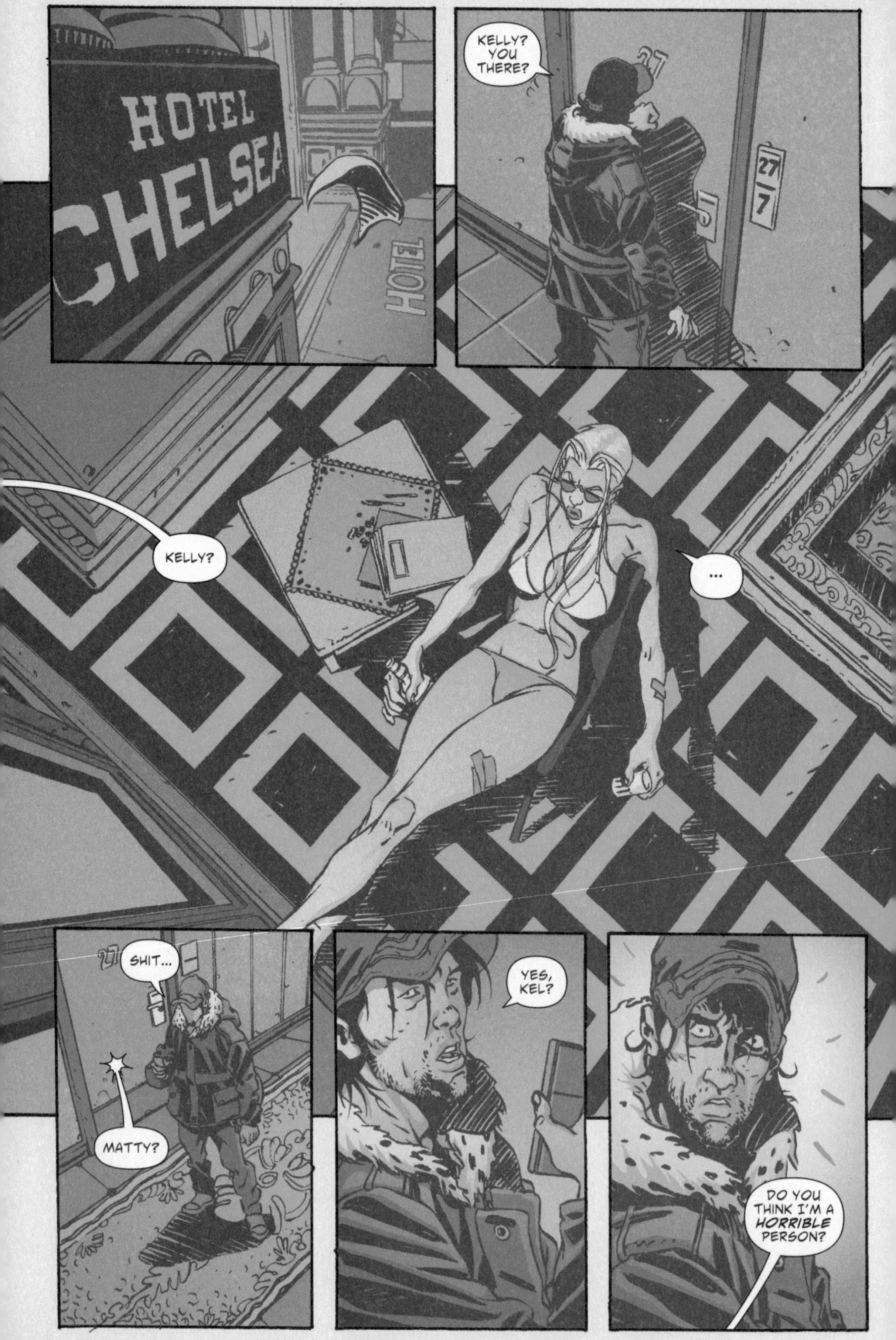
HOTEL
CHELSEA
HOTEL
KELLY? YOU THERE?
27
27
7
KELLY?
...
SHIT...
MATTY?
YES, KEL?
DO YOU THINK I'M A *HORRIBLE* PERSON?

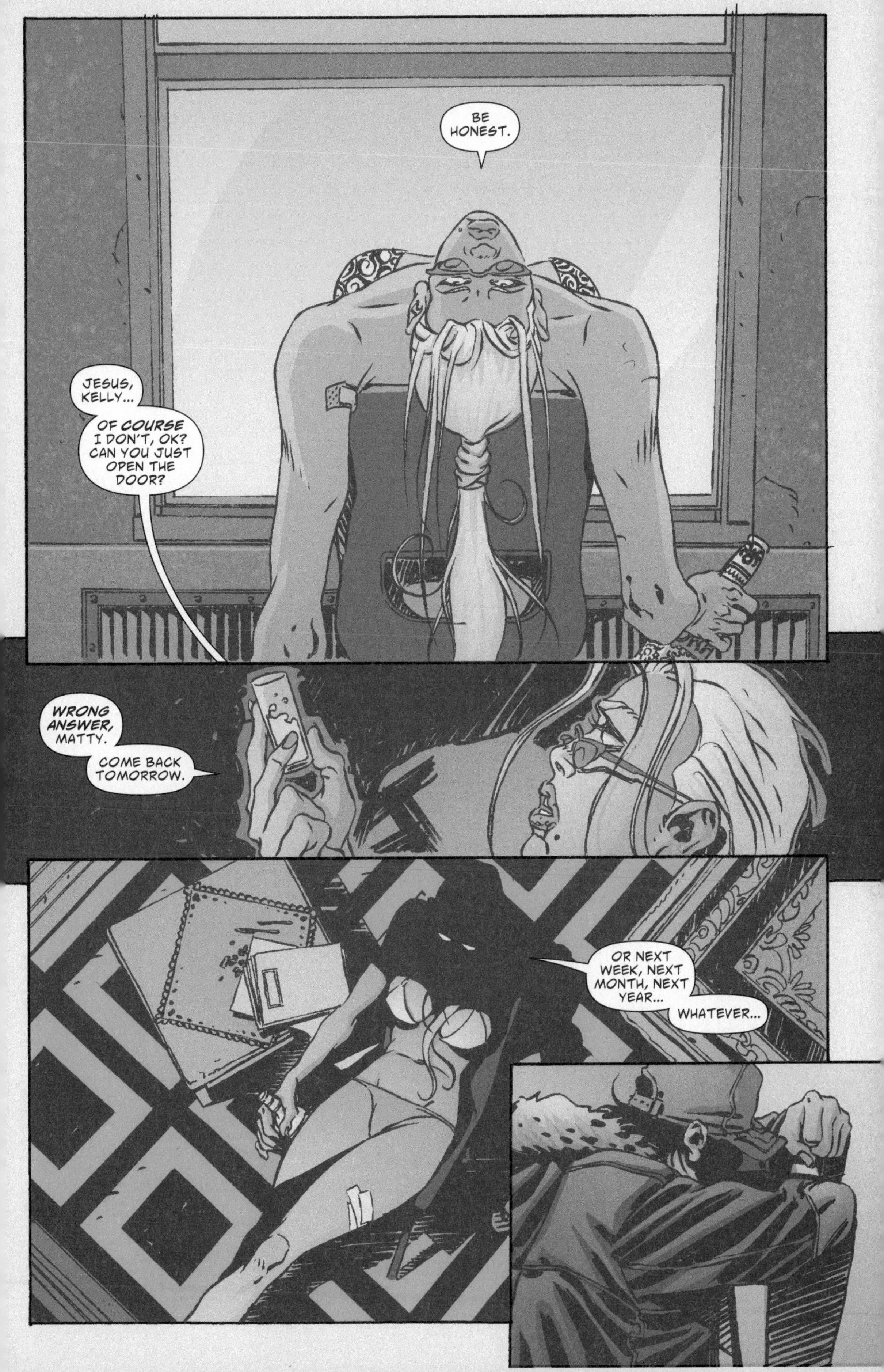
BE HONEST.
JESUS, KELLY...
OF COURSE I DON'T, OK? CAN YOU JUST OPEN THE DOOR?
WRONG ANSWER, MATTY.
COME BACK TOMORROW.
OR NEXT WEEK, NEXT MONTH, NEXT YEAR...
WHATEVER...

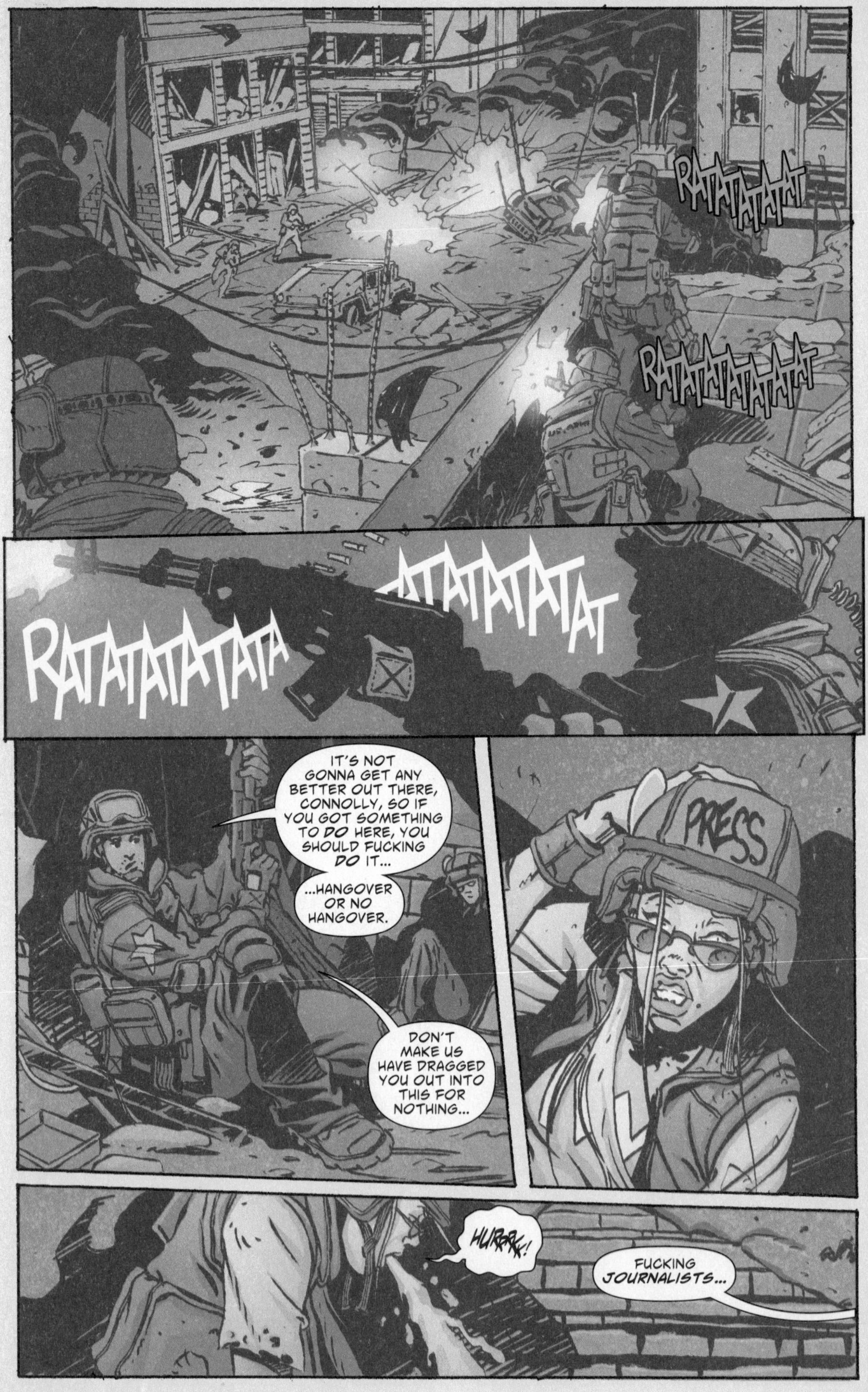
RATATATATAT
RATATATATATATAT
RATATATATATA
RATATATATAT
IT'S NOT GONNA GET ANY BETTER OUT THERE, CONNOLLY, SO IF YOU GOT SOMETHING TO DO HERE, YOU SHOULD FUCKING DO IT...
...HANGOVER OR NO HANGOVER.
DON'T MAKE US HAVE DRAGGED YOU OUT INTO THIS FOR NOTHING...
PRESS
HURRKK!
FUCKING JOURNALISTS...

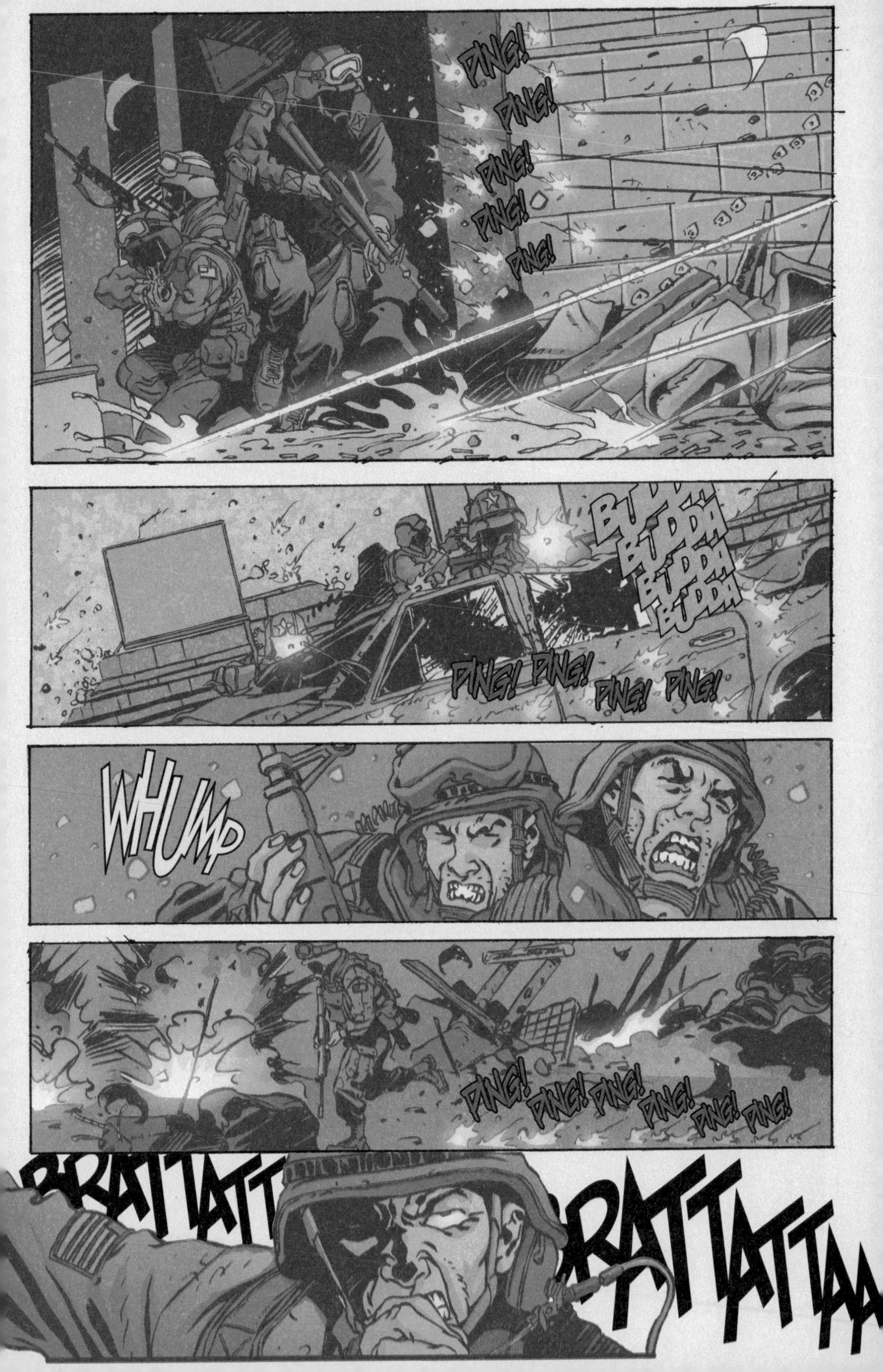
PING!
PING!
PING!
PING!
PING!
BUDDA
BUDDA
BUDDA
BUDDA
PING! PING!
PING! PING!
WHUMP
PING!
PING! PING!
PING!
PING! PING!
BRATTATT
BRATTATTAA

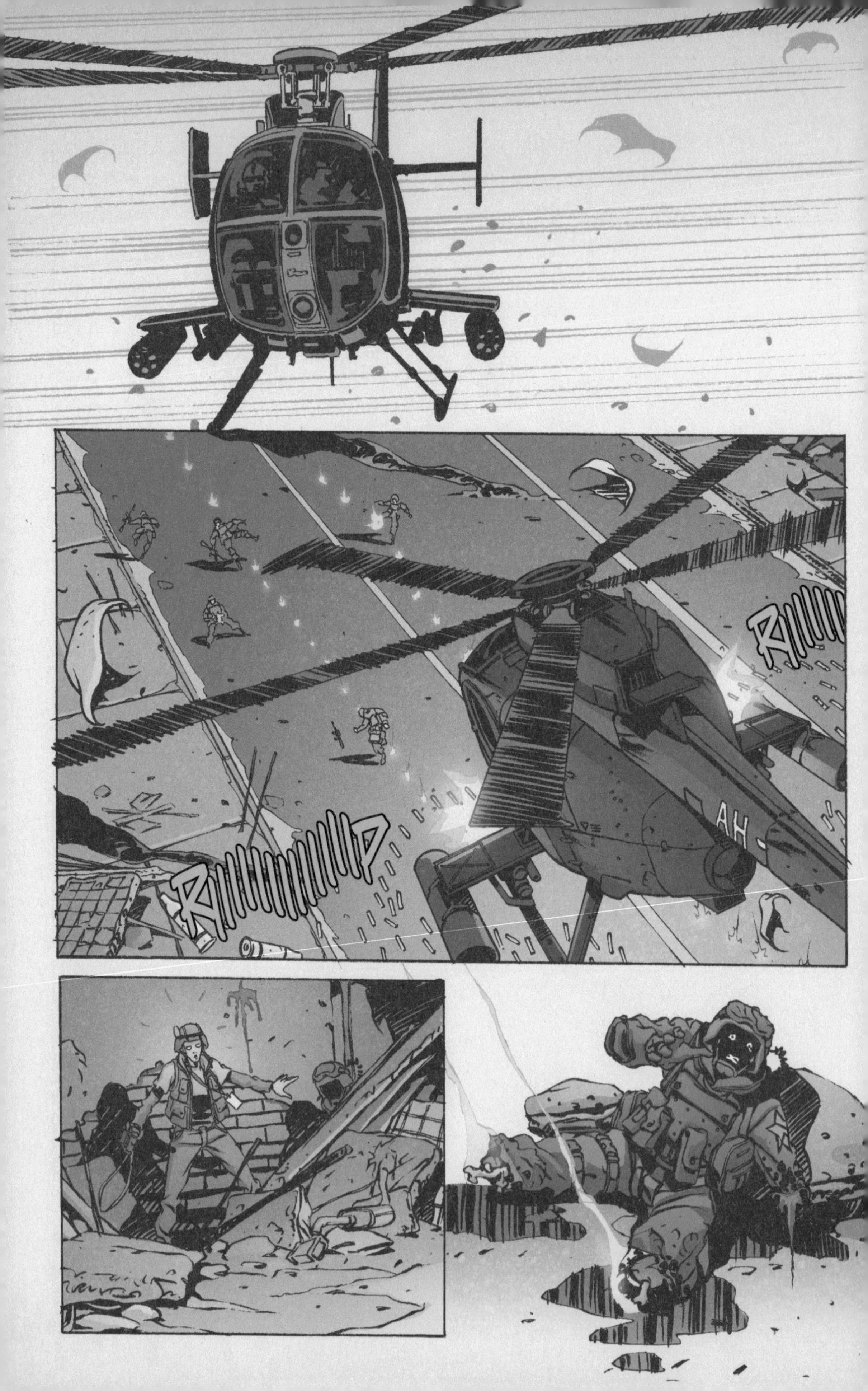
AH-

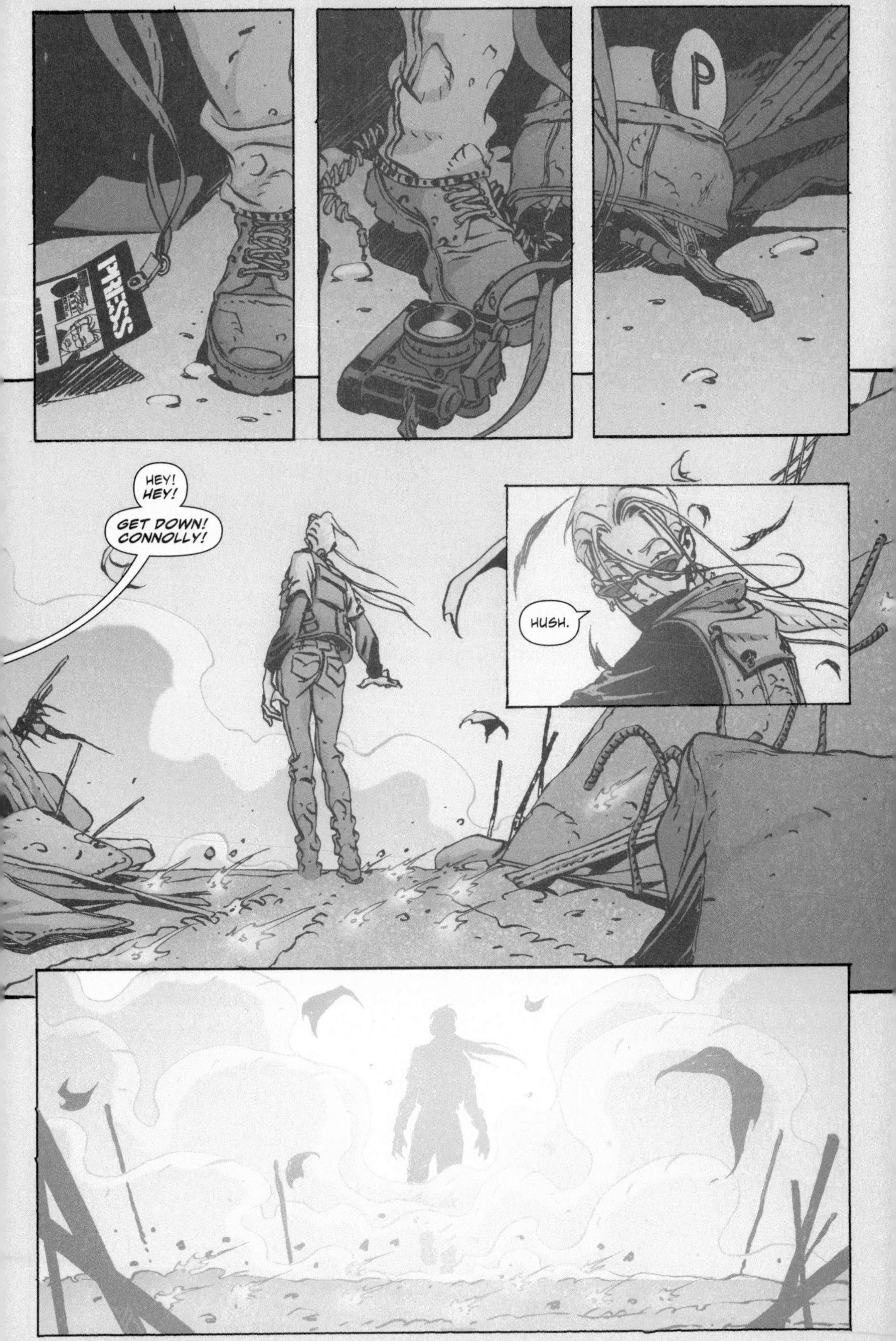
PRESS
P
HEY! HEY!
GET DOWN! CONNOLLY!
HUSH.

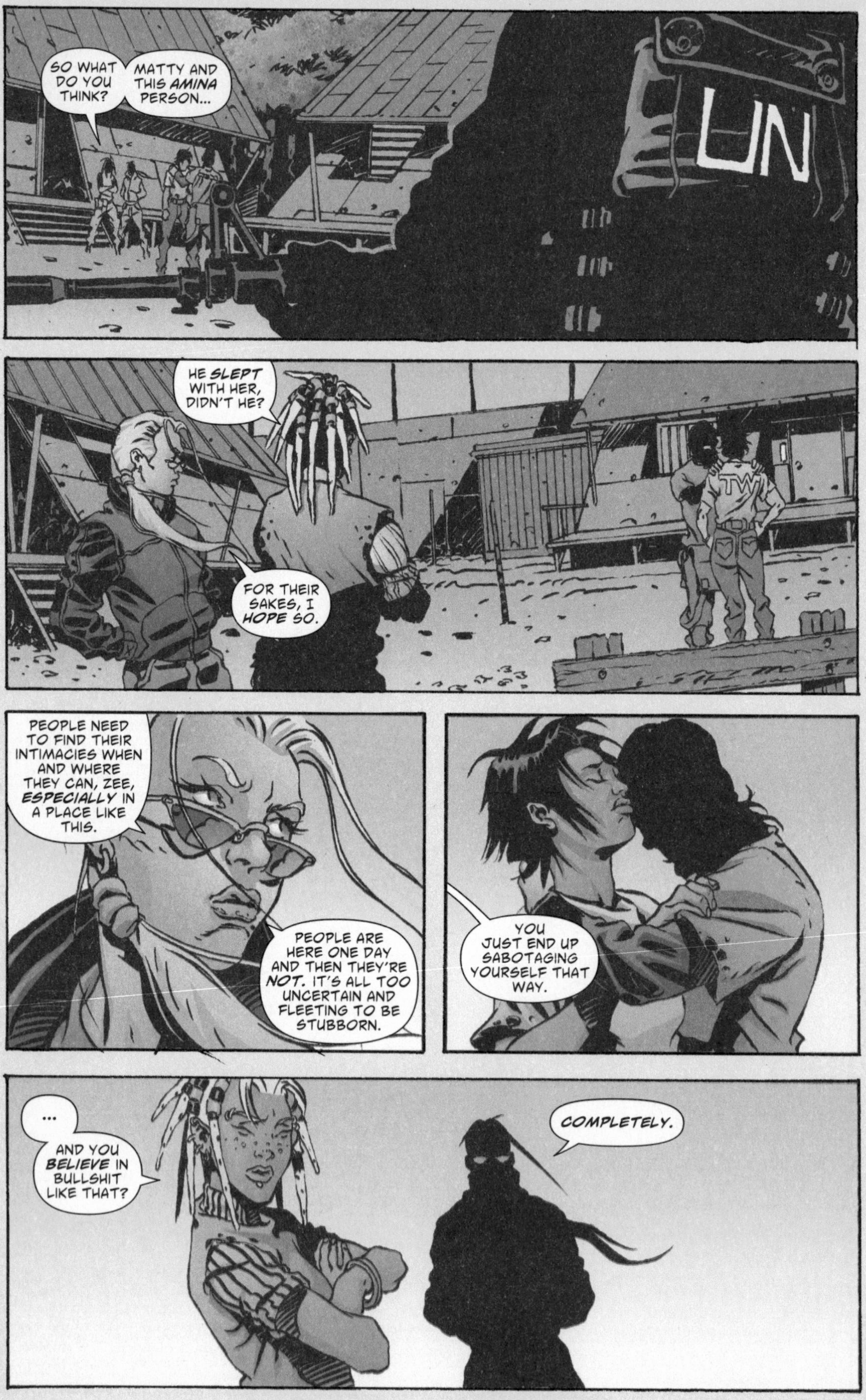
SO WHAT DO YOU THINK?
MATTY AND THIS AMINA PERSON...
HE SLEPT WITH HER, DIDN'T HE?
FOR THEIR SAKES, I HOPE SO.
PEOPLE NEED TO FIND THEIR INTIMACIES WHEN AND WHERE THEY CAN, ZEE, ESPECIALLY IN A PLACE LIKE THIS.
PEOPLE ARE HERE ONE DAY AND THEN THEY'RE NOT. IT'S ALL TOO UNCERTAIN AND FLEETING TO BE STUBBORN.
YOU JUST END UP SABOTAGING YOURSELF THAT WAY.
...
AND YOU BELIEVE IN BULLSHIT LIKE THAT?
COMPLETELY.

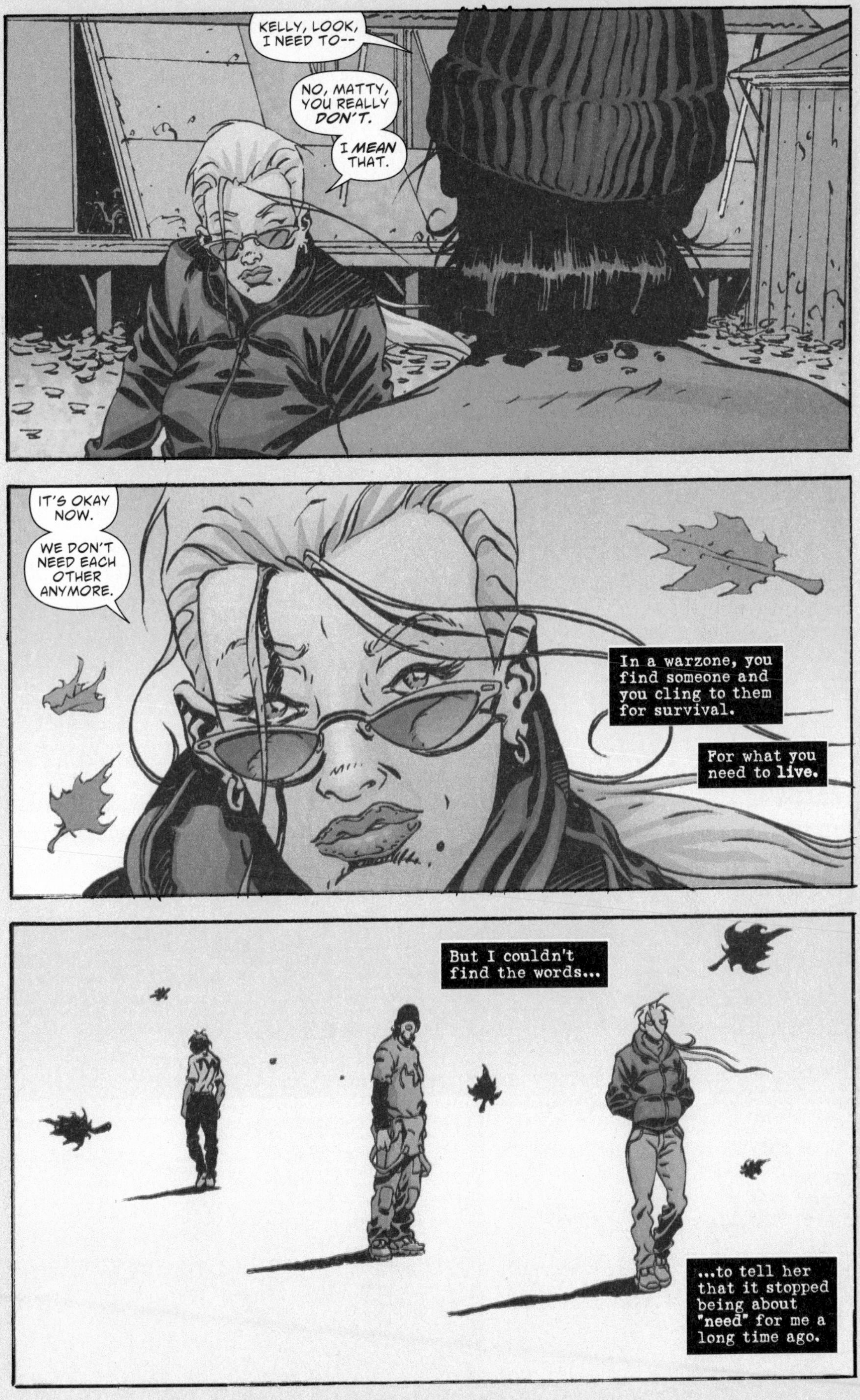
KELLY, LOOK, I NEED TO--
NO, MATTY, YOU REALLY DON'T.
I MEAN THAT.
IT'S OKAY NOW.
WE DON'T NEED EACH OTHER ANYMORE.
In a warzone, you find someone and you cling to them for survival.
For what you need to live.
But I couldn't find the words...
...to tell her that it stopped being about "need" for me a long time ago.

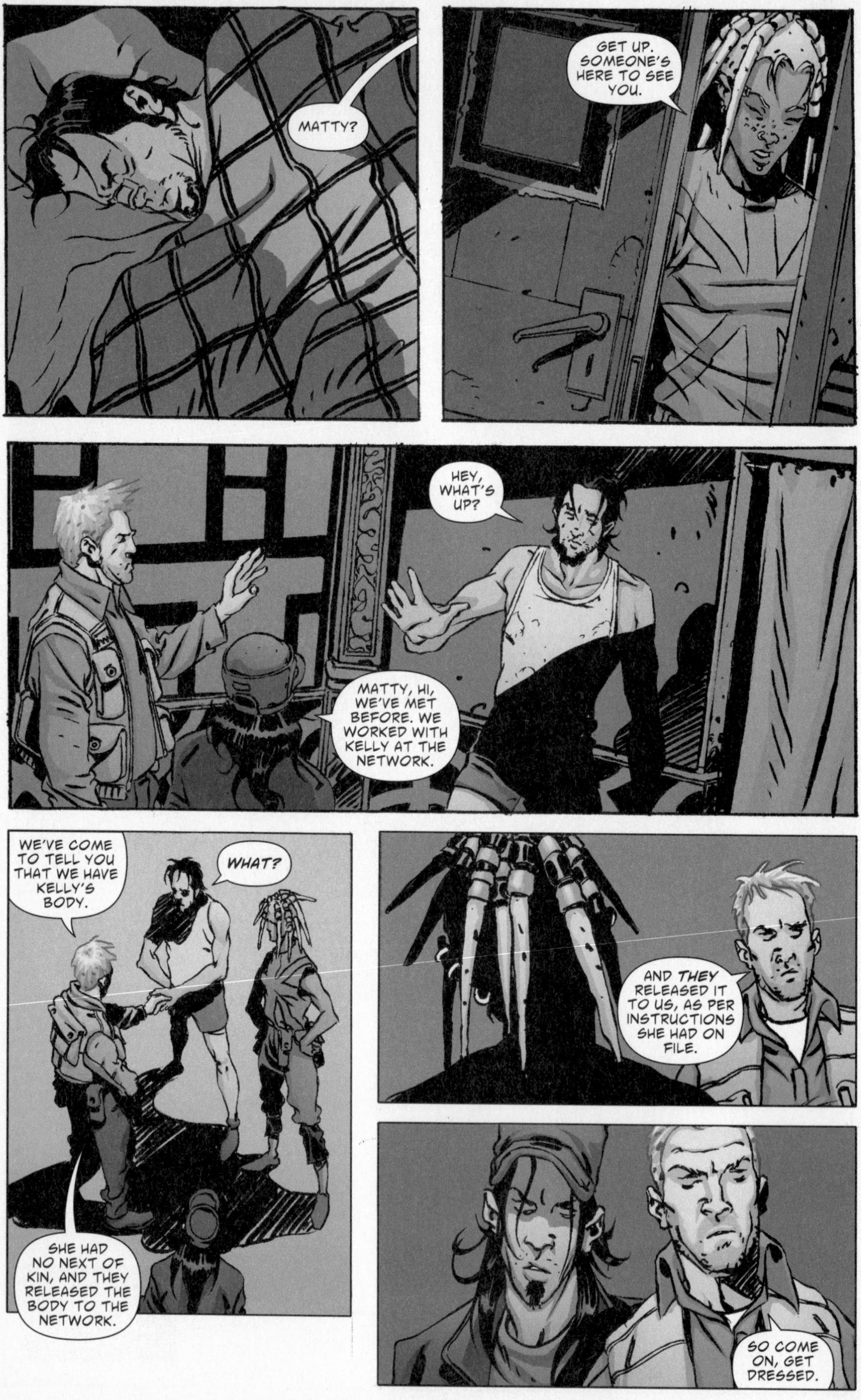
MATTY?
GET UP. SOMEONE'S HERE TO SEE YOU.
HEY, WHAT'S UP?
MATTY, HI, WE'VE MET BEFORE. WE WORKED WITH KELLY AT THE NETWORK.
WE'VE COME TO TELL YOU THAT WE HAVE KELLY'S BODY.
WHAT?
SHE HAD NO NEXT OF KIN, AND THEY RELEASED THE BODY TO THE NETWORK.
AND THEY RELEASED IT TO US, AS PER INSTRUCTIONS SHE HAD ON FILE.
SO COME ON, GET DRESSED.

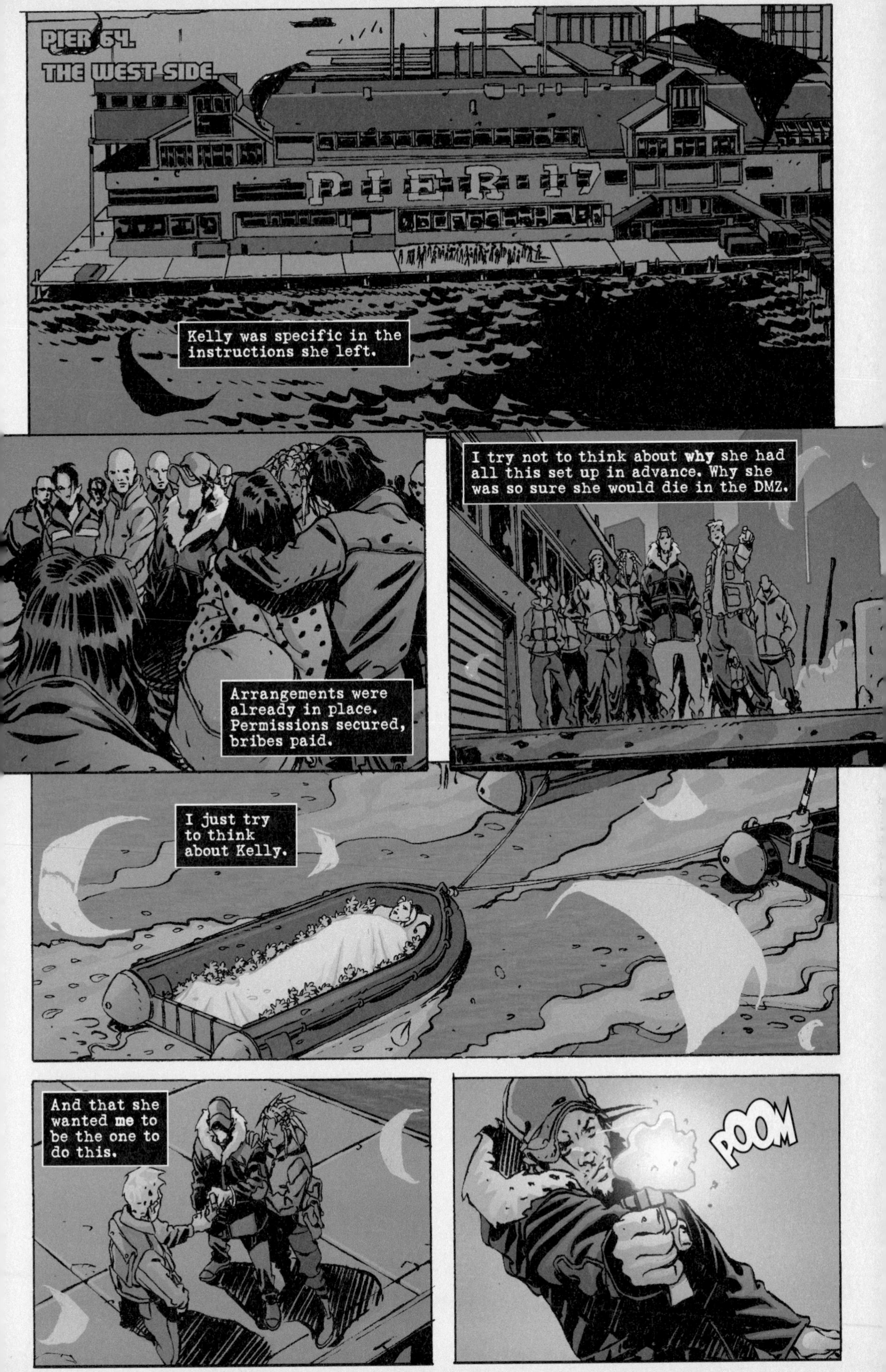
PIER 64.
THE WEST SIDE.
PIER 17
Kelly was specific in the instructions she left.
Arrangements were already in place. Permissions secured, bribes paid.
I try not to think about why she had all this set up in advance. Why she was so sure she would die in the DMZ.
I just try to think about Kelly.
And that she wanted me to be the one to do this.
POOM

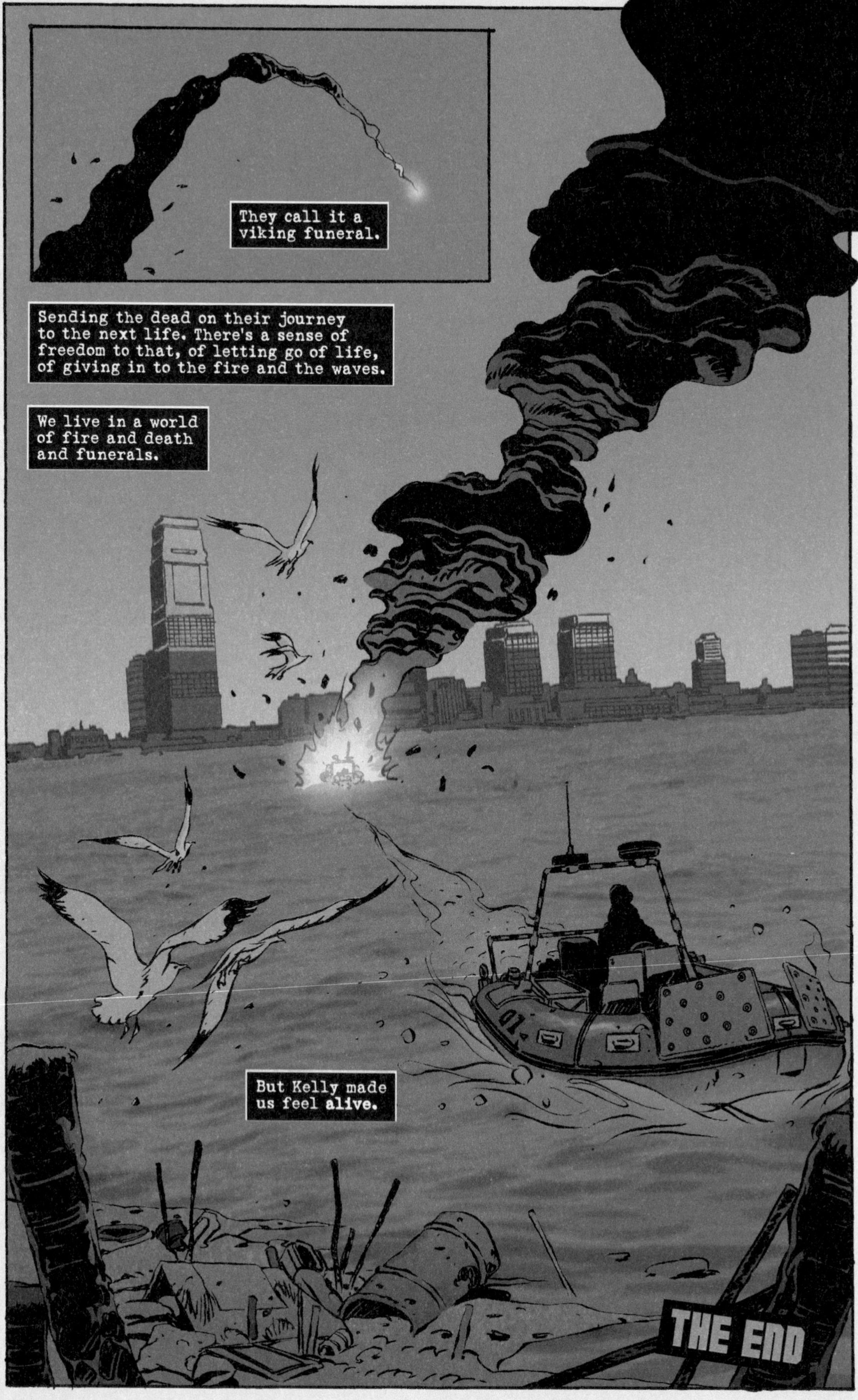

They call it a viking funeral.
Sending the dead on their journey to the next life. There's a sense of freedom to that, of letting go of life, of giving in to the fire and the waves.
We live in a world of fire and death and funerals.
But Kelly made us feel **alive.**
THE END

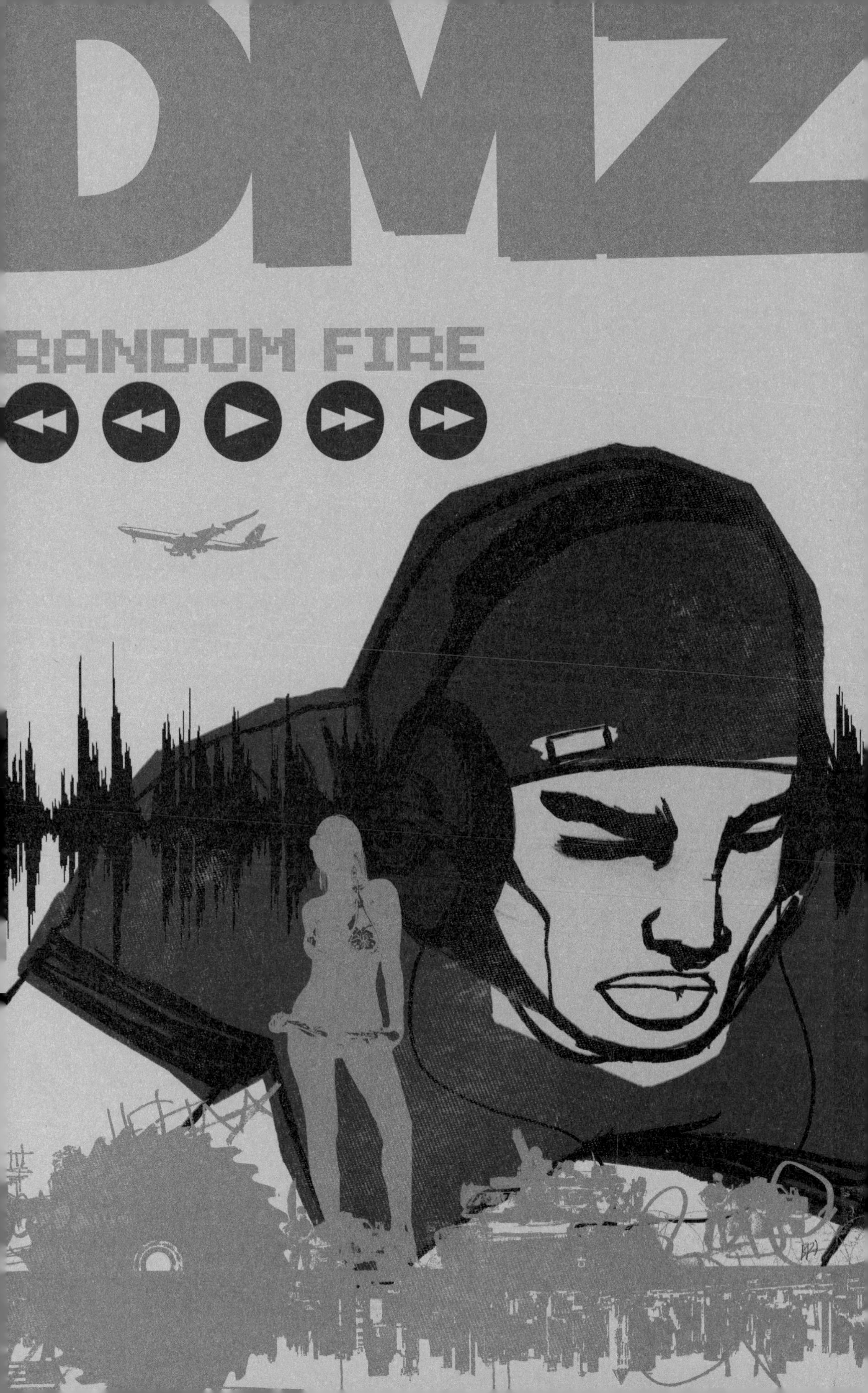
DMZ
RANDOM FIRE

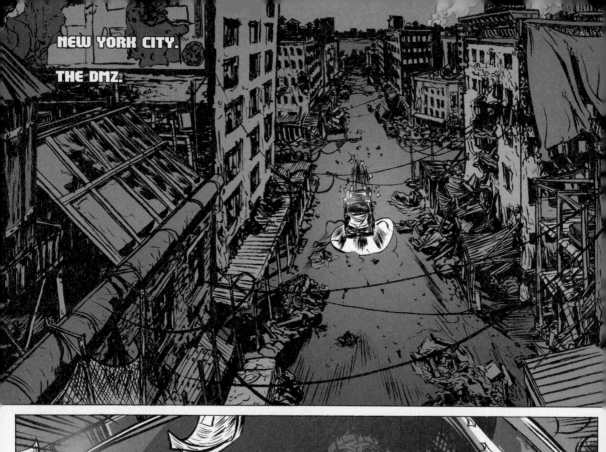

NEW YORK CITY.

THE DMZ:

BOOM!

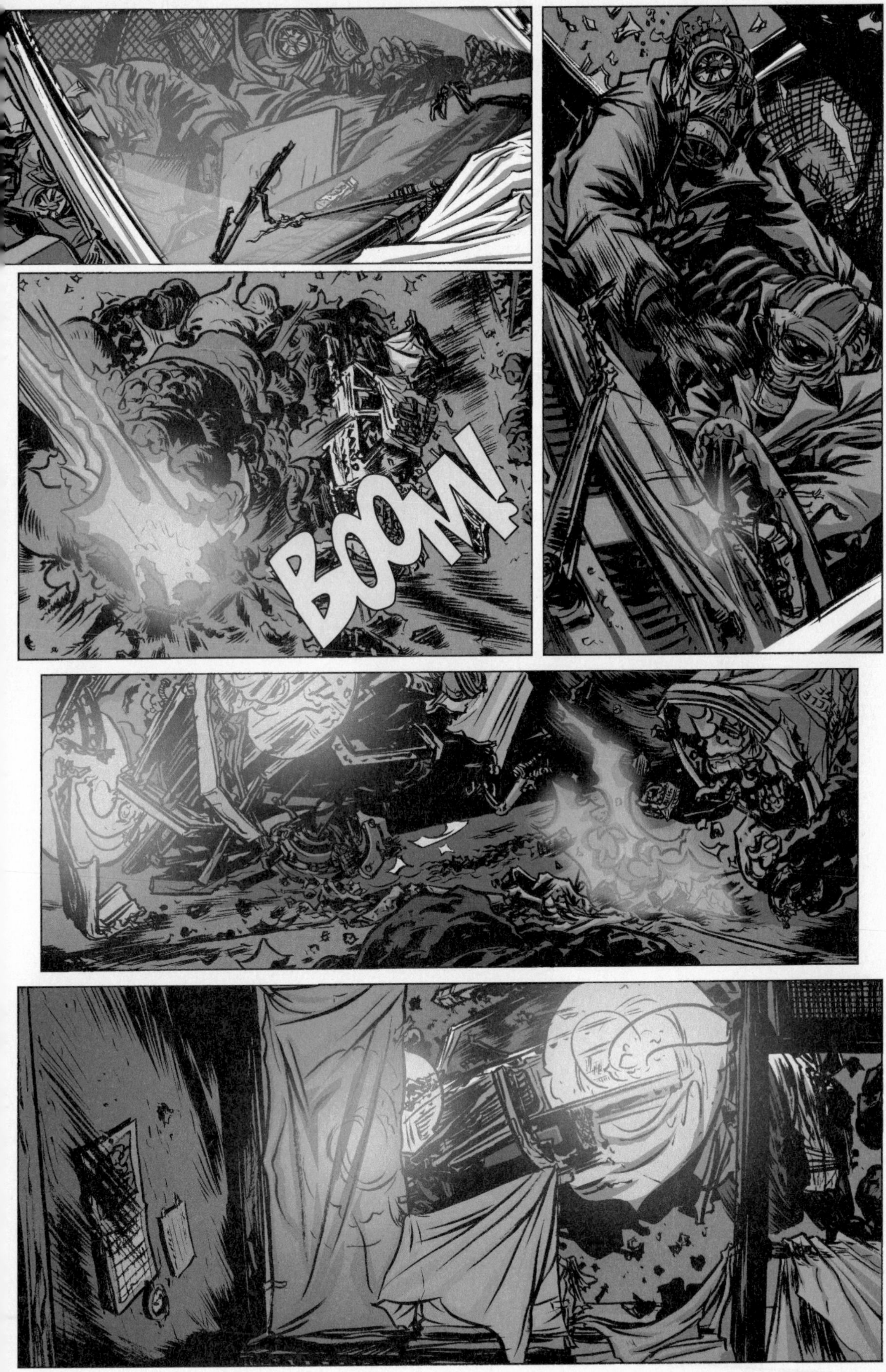
BOOM!

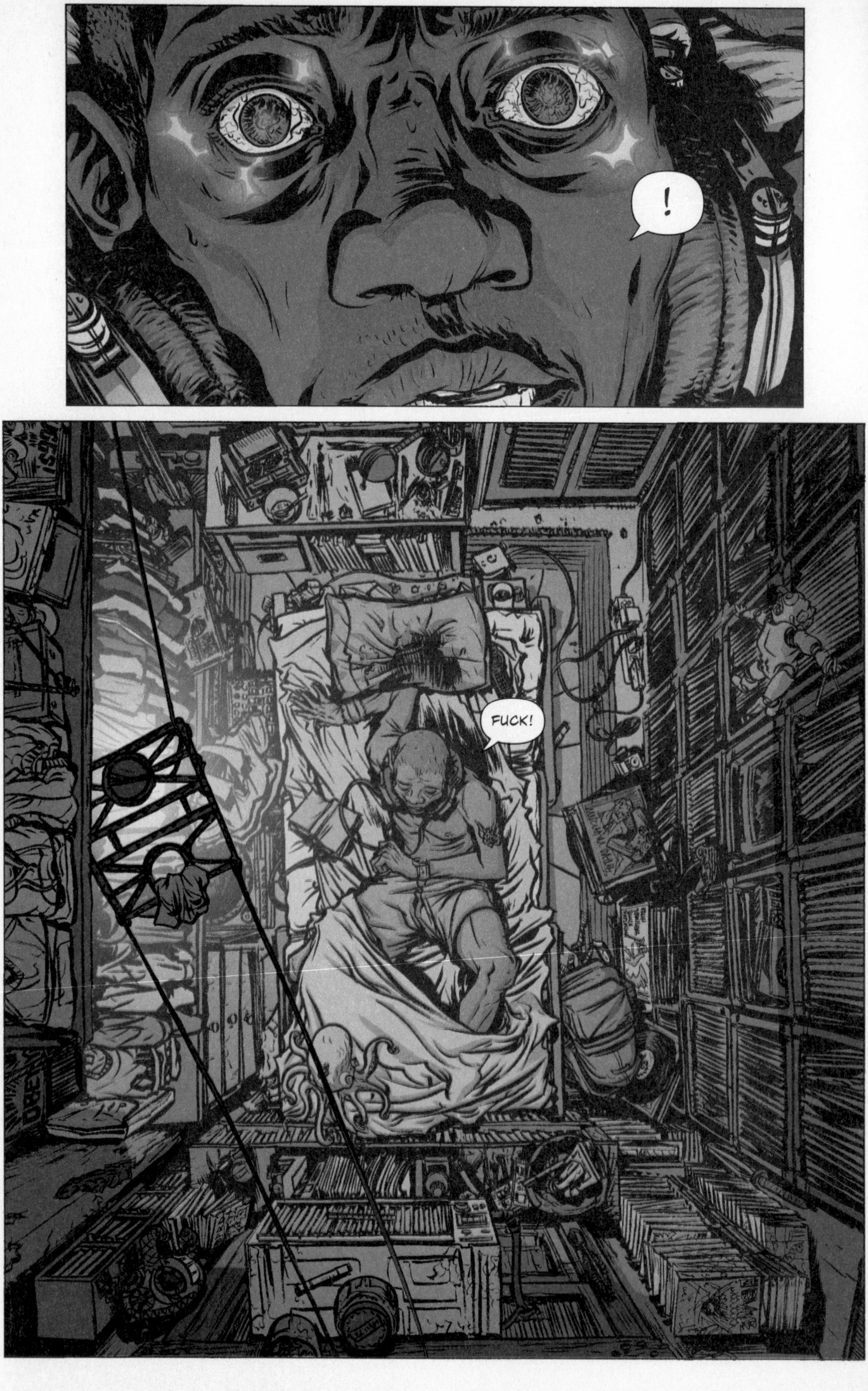
!
FUCK!

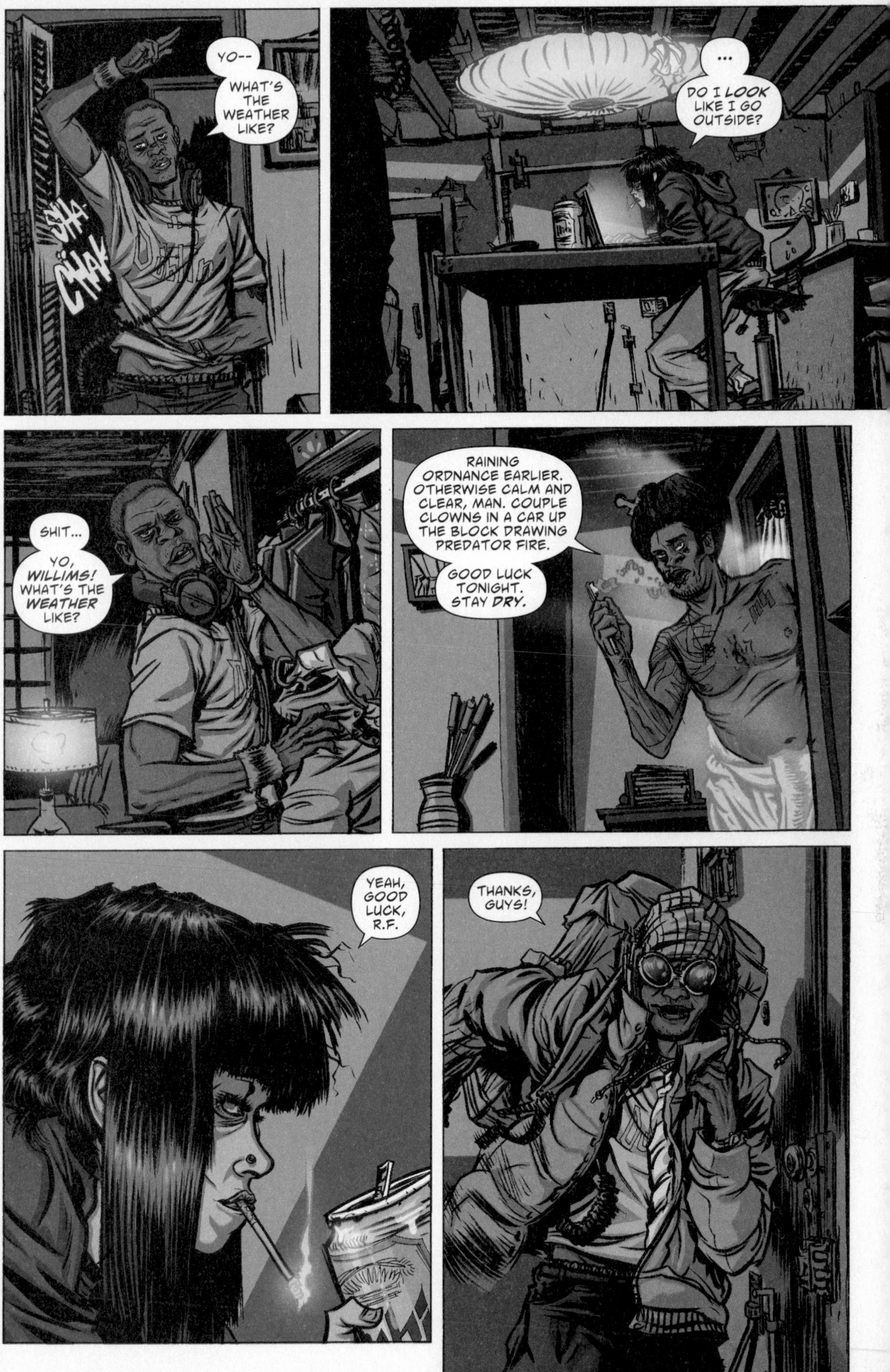
YO--
WHAT'S THE WEATHER LIKE?
SHA-CHAK
...
DO I LOOK LIKE I GO OUTSIDE?
SHIT...
YO, WILLIMS! WHAT'S THE WEATHER LIKE?
RAINING ORDNANCE EARLIER. OTHERWISE CALM AND CLEAR, MAN. COUPLE CLOWNS IN A CAR UP THE BLOCK DRAWING PREDATOR FIRE.
GOOD LUCK TONIGHT. STAY DRY.
YEAH, GOOD LUCK, R.F.
THANKS, GUYS!

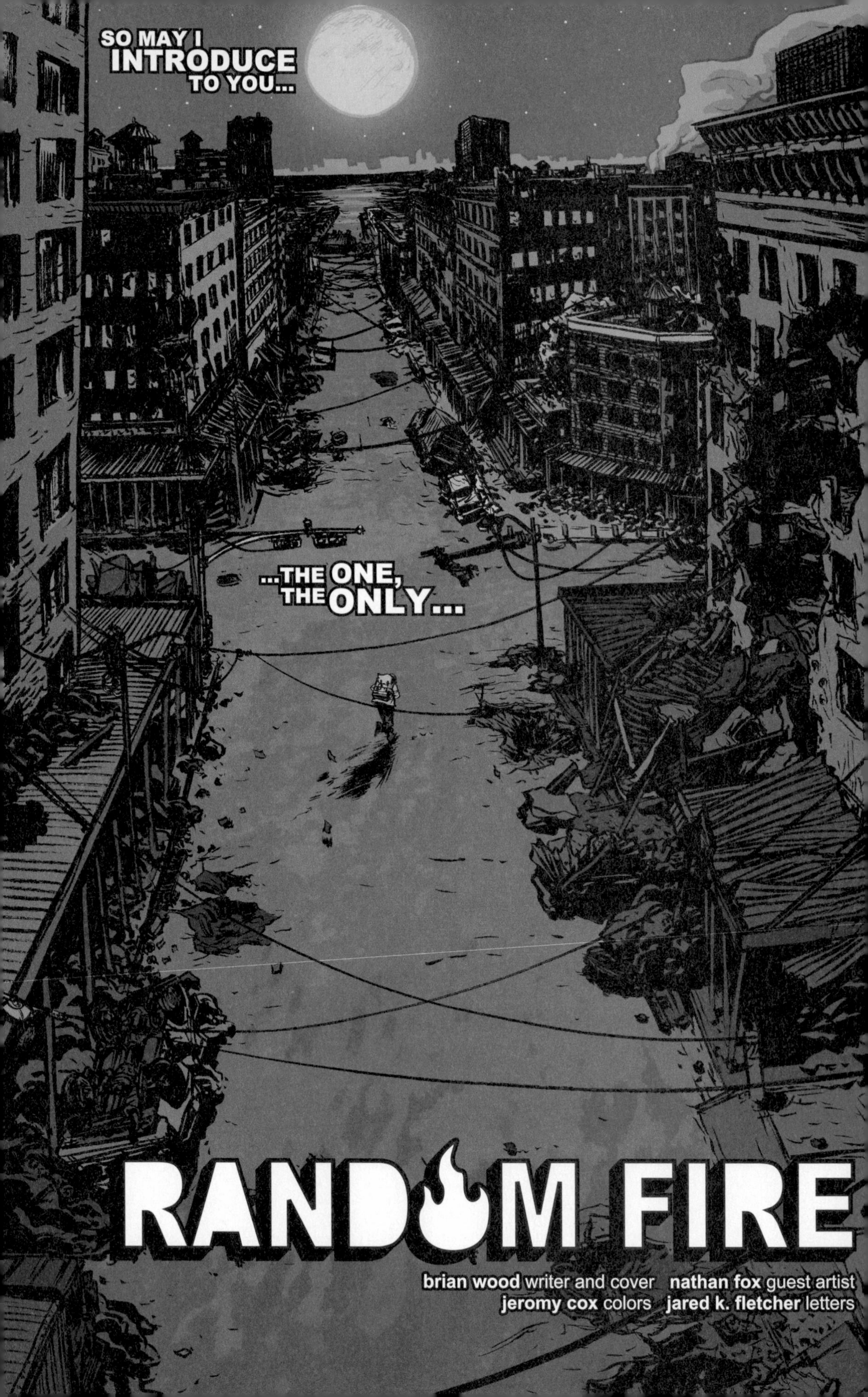
SO MAY I INTRODUCE TO YOU...
...THE ONE, THE ONLY...
RANDOM FIRE
brian wood writer and cover nathan fox guest artist
jeromy cox colors jared k. fletcher letters

...THE **TALK** OF THE **TOWN**...

...**LOCALLY** ACCEPTED, WORLDWIDE **RESPECTED**...

...DROP DEAD **BEATS** FOR THESE SAVAGE **STREETS**...

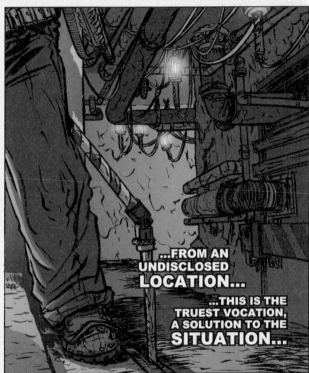

...**FROM AN UNDISCLOSED LOCATION**...

...THIS IS THE TRUEST VOCATION, A SOLUTION TO THE **SITUATION**...

...JUST THIS **ONE NIGHT** TO GET IT **ALL RIGHT**...

...WE IN THIS **TOGETHER** WHATEVER THE **WEATHER**, SO MAKE SOME **NOISE FOR**...

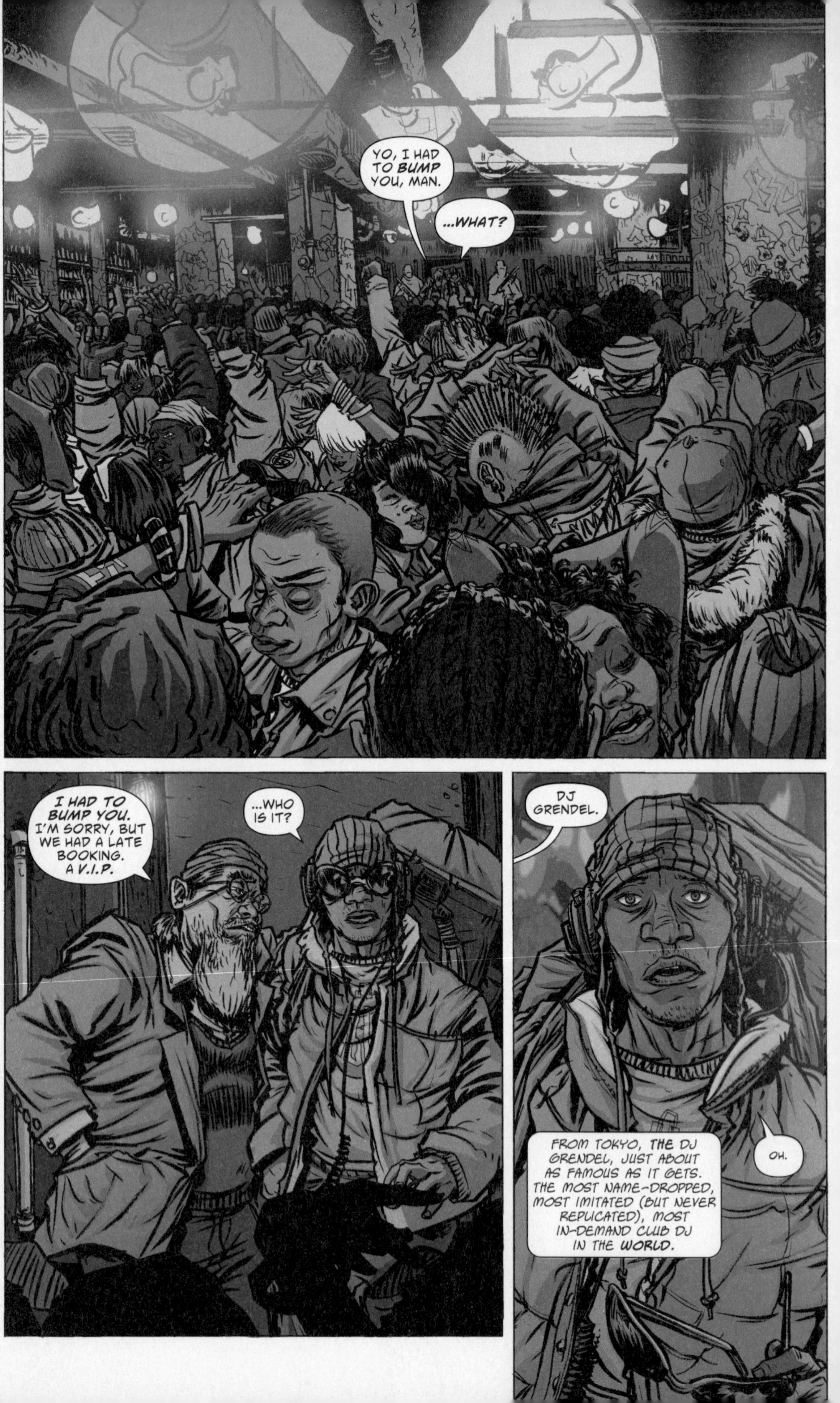
YO, I HAD TO BUMP YOU, MAN.
...WHAT?
I HAD TO BUMP YOU. I'M SORRY, BUT WE HAD A LATE BOOKING. A V.I.P.
...WHO IS IT?
DJ GRENDEL.
FROM TOKYO, THE DJ GRENDEL, JUST ABOUT AS FAMOUS AS IT GETS. THE MOST NAME-DROPPED, MOST IMITATED (BUT NEVER REPLICATED), MOST IN-DEMAND CLUB DJ IN THE WORLD.
OH.

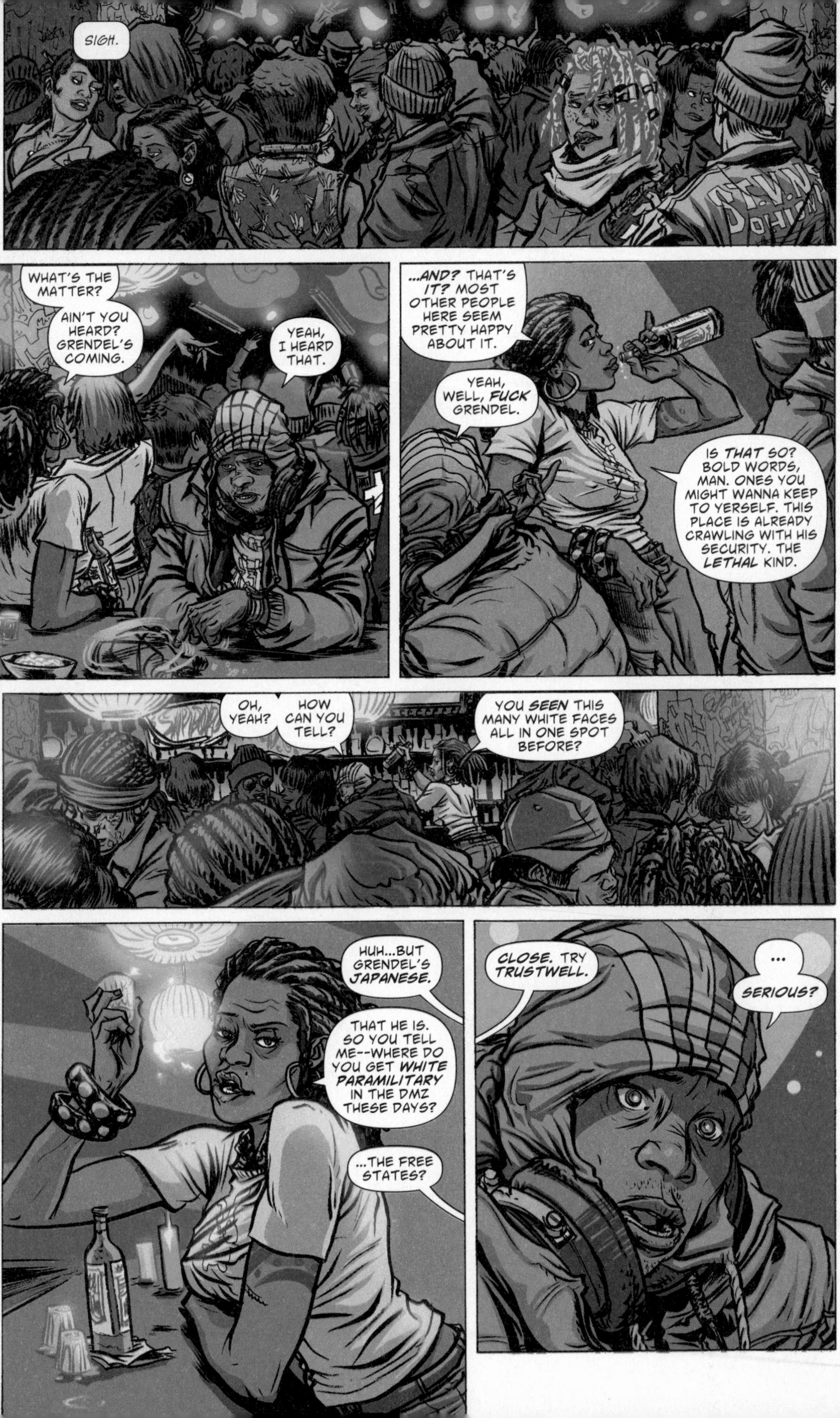
SIGH.
WHAT'S THE MATTER?
AIN'T YOU HEARD? GRENDEL'S COMING.
YEAH, I HEARD THAT.
...AND? THAT'S IT? MOST OTHER PEOPLE HERE SEEM PRETTY HAPPY ABOUT IT.
YEAH, WELL, FUCK GRENDEL.
IS THAT SO? BOLD WORDS, MAN. ONES YOU MIGHT WANNA KEEP TO YERSELF. THIS PLACE IS ALREADY CRAWLING WITH HIS SECURITY. THE LETHAL KIND.
OH, YEAH?
HOW CAN YOU TELL?
YOU SEEN THIS MANY WHITE FACES ALL IN ONE SPOT BEFORE?
HUH...BUT GRENDEL'S JAPANESE.
THAT HE IS. SO YOU TELL ME--WHERE DO YOU GET WHITE PARAMILITARY IN THE DMZ THESE DAYS?
...THE FREE STATES?
CLOSE. TRY TRUSTWELL.
...
SERIOUS?

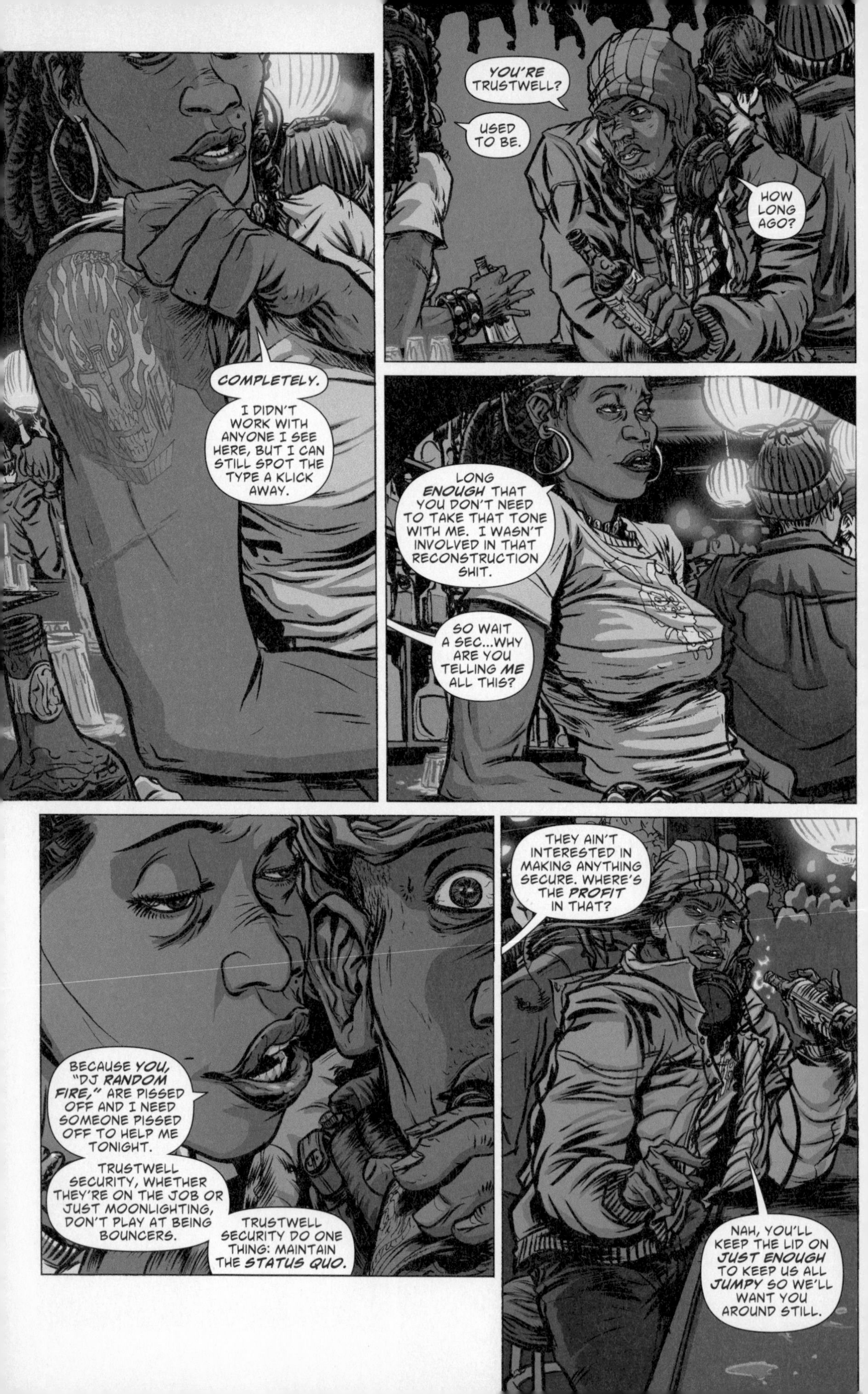
YOU'RE TRUSTWELL?
USED TO BE.
HOW LONG AGO?
COMPLETELY.
I DIDN'T WORK WITH ANYONE I SEE HERE, BUT I CAN STILL SPOT THE TYPE A KLICK AWAY.
LONG ENOUGH THAT YOU DON'T NEED TO TAKE THAT TONE WITH ME. I WASN'T INVOLVED IN THAT RECONSTRUCTION SHIT.
SO WAIT A SEC...WHY ARE YOU TELLING ME ALL THIS?
BECAUSE YOU, "DJ RANDOM FIRE," ARE PISSED OFF AND I NEED SOMEONE PISSED OFF TO HELP ME TONIGHT.
TRUSTWELL SECURITY, WHETHER THEY'RE ON THE JOB OR JUST MOONLIGHTING, DON'T PLAY AT BEING BOUNCERS.
TRUSTWELL SECURITY DO ONE THING: MAINTAIN THE STATUS QUO.
THEY AIN'T INTERESTED IN MAKING ANYTHING SECURE. WHERE'S THE PROFIT IN THAT?
NAH, YOU'LL KEEP THE LID ON JUST ENOUGH TO KEEP US ALL JUMPY SO WE'LL WANT YOU AROUND STILL.

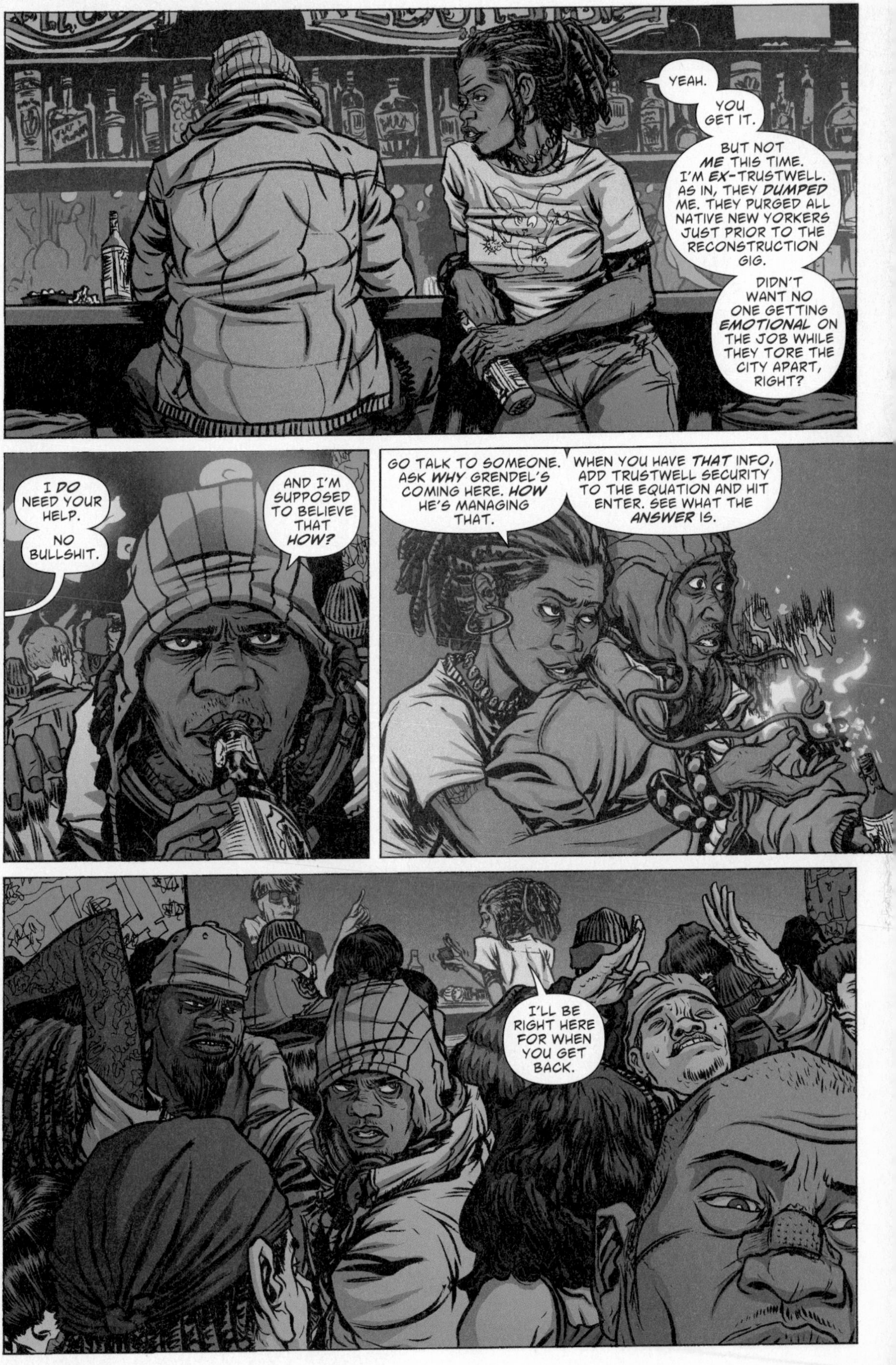
YEAH.
YOU GET IT.
BUT NOT ME THIS TIME. I'M EX-TRUSTWELL. AS IN, THEY DUMPED ME. THEY PURGED ALL NATIVE NEW YORKERS JUST PRIOR TO THE RECONSTRUCTION GIG.
DIDN'T WANT NO ONE GETTING EMOTIONAL ON THE JOB WHILE THEY TORE THE CITY APART, RIGHT?
I DO NEED YOUR HELP.
NO BULLSHIT.
AND I'M SUPPOSED TO BELIEVE THAT HOW?
GO TALK TO SOMEONE. ASK WHY GRENDEL'S COMING HERE. HOW HE'S MANAGING THAT.
WHEN YOU HAVE THAT INFO, ADD TRUSTWELL SECURITY TO THE EQUATION AND HIT ENTER. SEE WHAT THE ANSWER IS.
I'LL BE RIGHT HERE FOR WHEN YOU GET BACK.

I HAD SOME QUESTIONS FOR THAT CRAZY CHICK-- WHO IS SHE EXACTLY? HOW DOES SHE KNOW MY NAME? WHAT'S *HER* ANGLE ON ALL OF THIS?

I SET THEM ASIDE FOR THE TIME BEING BECAUSE, YEAH, I WAS PISSED OFF AND I WANTED SOMEONE TO GIVE ME ANSWERS. ANY ANSWERS.

THIS WAS *MY* BIG NIGHT... I WAS HEADLINING. BUT INSTEAD I'M STUCK AT THE BAR WITH TWO COMPLIMENTARY DRINK TICKETS.

RANDOM!

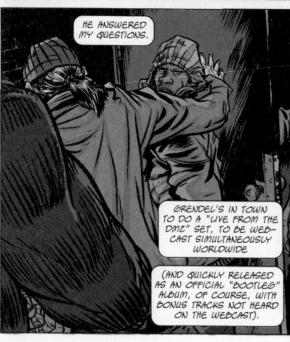

HE ANSWERED MY QUESTIONS.

GRENDEL'S IN TOWN TO DO A "LIVE FROM THE DMZ" SET, TO BE WEBCAST SIMULTANEOUSLY WORLDWIDE

(AND QUICKLY RELEASED AS AN OFFICIAL "BOOTLEG" ALBUM, OF COURSE, WITH BONUS TRACKS NOT HEARD ON THE WEBCAST).

"LIVE FROM THE DMZ." WEBCAST. PROMOTIONS. ALBUM RELEASE. BONUS TRACKS.

DOES HE NOT GET THAT PEOPLE DIE HERE?

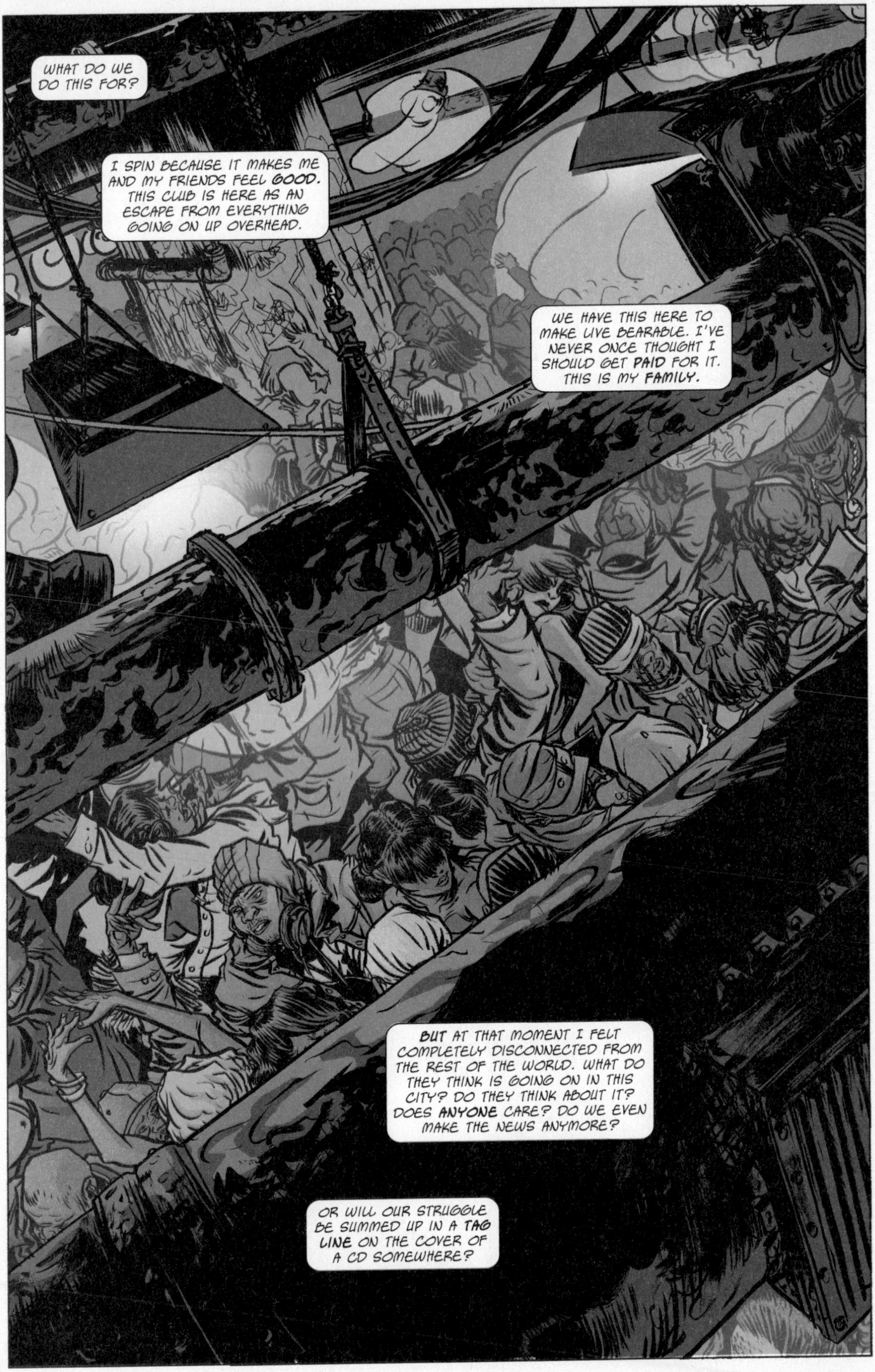
WHAT DO WE DO THIS FOR?
I SPIN BECAUSE IT MAKES ME AND MY FRIENDS FEEL GOOD. THIS CLUB IS HERE AS AN ESCAPE FROM EVERYTHING GOING ON UP OVERHEAD.
WE HAVE THIS HERE TO MAKE LIVE BEARABLE. I'VE NEVER ONCE THOUGHT I SHOULD GET PAID FOR IT. THIS IS MY FAMILY.
BUT AT THAT MOMENT I FELT COMPLETELY DISCONNECTED FROM THE REST OF THE WORLD. WHAT DO THEY THINK IS GOING ON IN THIS CITY? DO THEY THINK ABOUT IT? DOES ANYONE CARE? DO WE EVEN MAKE THE NEWS ANYMORE?
OR WILL OUR STRUGGLE BE SUMMED UP IN A TAG LINE ON THE COVER OF A CD SOMEWHERE?

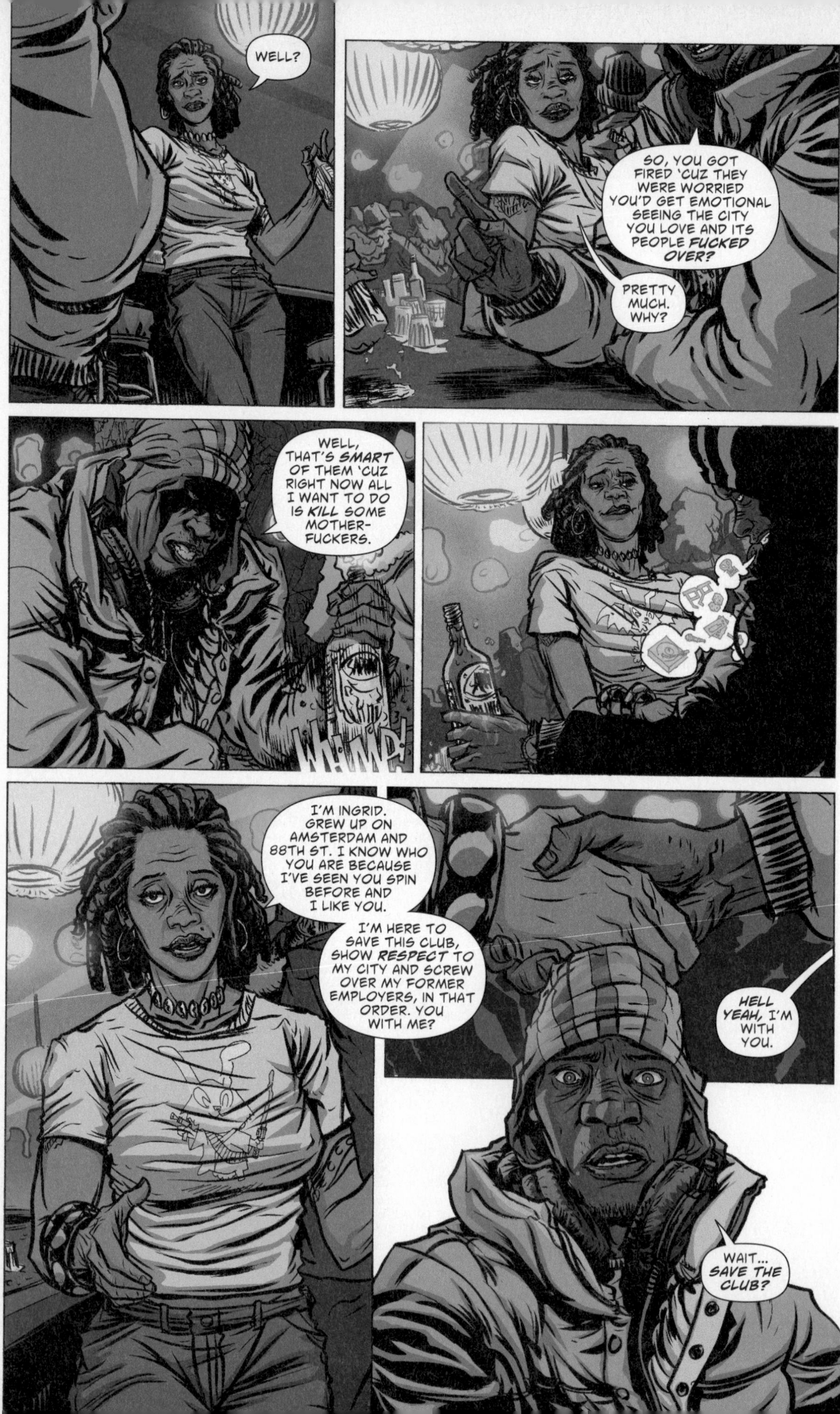
WELL?
SO, YOU GOT FIRED 'CUZ THEY WERE WORRIED YOU'D GET EMOTIONAL SEEING THE CITY YOU LOVE AND ITS PEOPLE FUCKED OVER?
PRETTY MUCH. WHY?
WELL, THAT'S SMART OF THEM 'CUZ RIGHT NOW ALL I WANT TO DO IS KILL SOME MOTHER-FUCKERS.
WHMP!
I'M INGRID. GREW UP ON AMSTERDAM AND 88TH ST. I KNOW WHO YOU ARE BECAUSE I'VE SEEN YOU SPIN BEFORE AND I LIKE YOU.
I'M HERE TO SAVE THIS CLUB, SHOW RESPECT TO MY CITY AND SCREW OVER MY FORMER EMPLOYERS, IN THAT ORDER. YOU WITH ME?
HELL YEAH, I'M WITH YOU.
WAIT... SAVE THE CLUB?

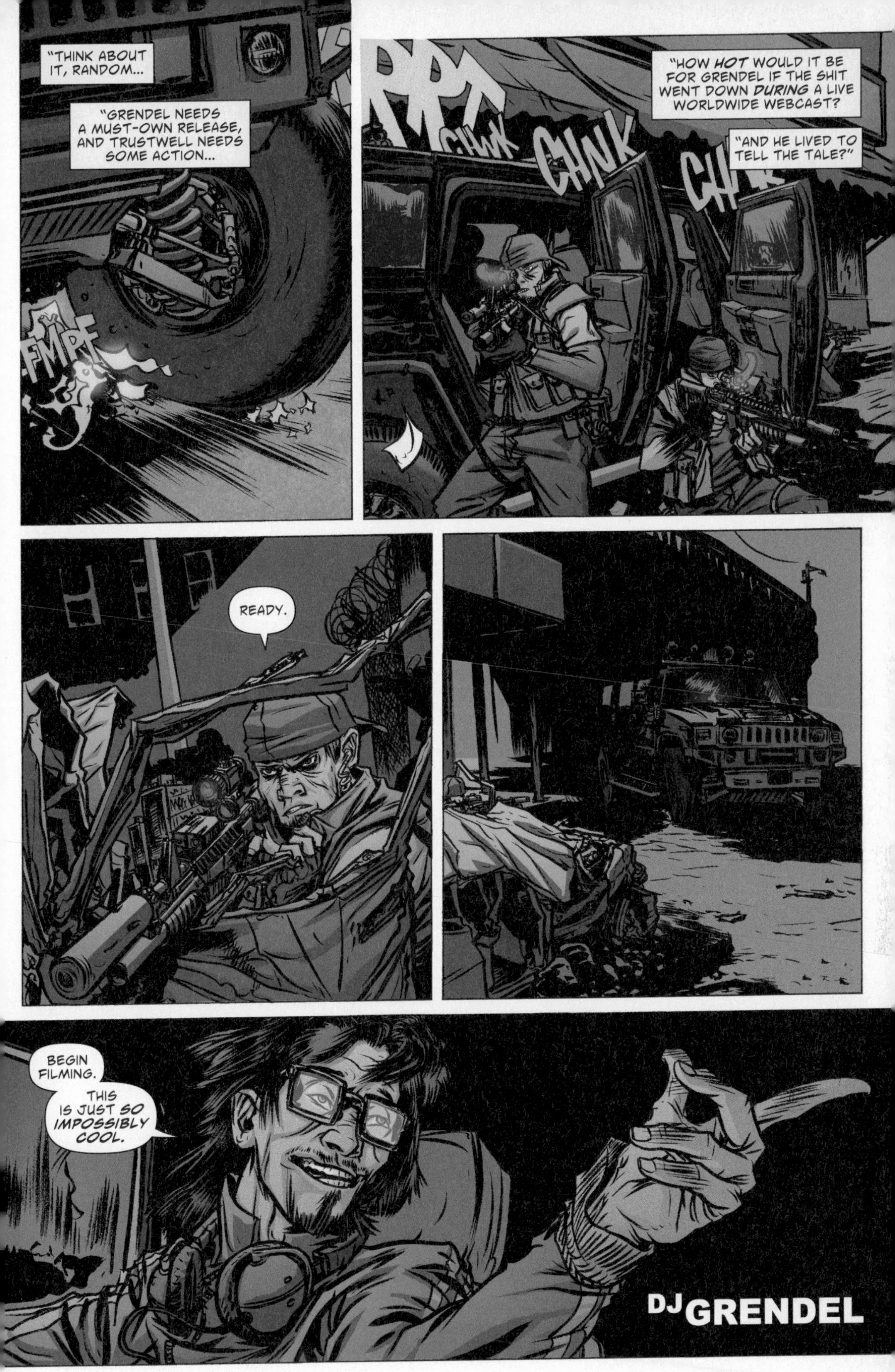
"THINK ABOUT IT, RANDOM...
"GRENDEL NEEDS A MUST-OWN RELEASE, AND TRUSTWELL NEEDS SOME ACTION...
FMPF
"HOW HOT WOULD IT BE FOR GRENDEL IF THE SHIT WENT DOWN DURING A LIVE WORLDWIDE WEBCAST?
"AND HE LIVED TO TELL THE TALE?"
CHNK
READY.
BEGIN FILMING.
THIS IS JUST SO IMPOSSIBLY COOL.
DJ GRENDEL

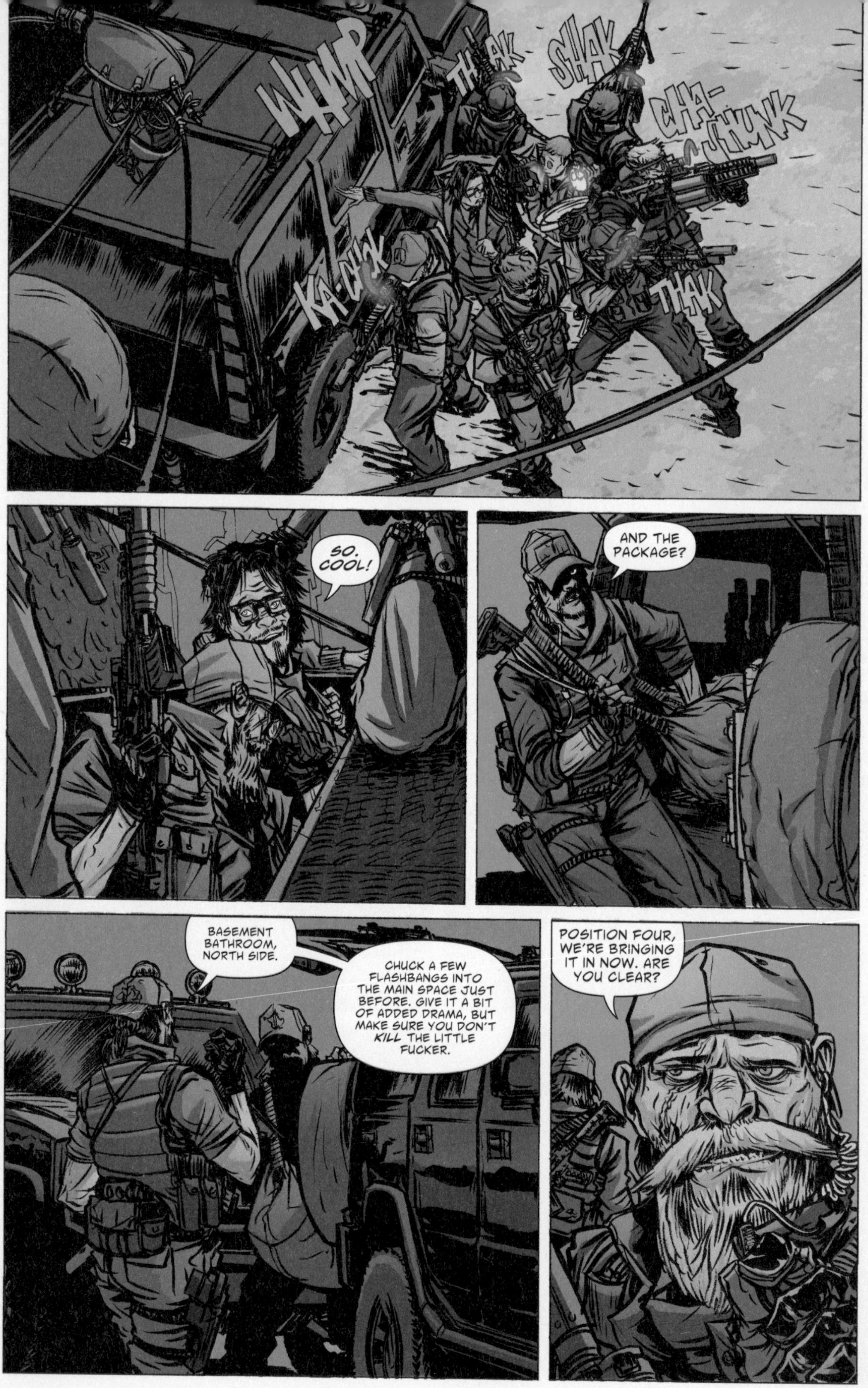
WHAP
THAK
SHAK
CHA-SHUNK
KA-CHCK
THAK
SO. COOL!
AND THE PACKAGE?
BASEMENT BATHROOM, NORTH SIDE.
CHUCK A FEW FLASHBANGS INTO THE MAIN SPACE JUST BEFORE. GIVE IT A BIT OF ADDED DRAMA, BUT MAKE SURE YOU DON'T *KILL* THE LITTLE FUCKER.
POSITION FOUR, WE'RE BRINGING IT IN NOW. ARE YOU CLEAR?

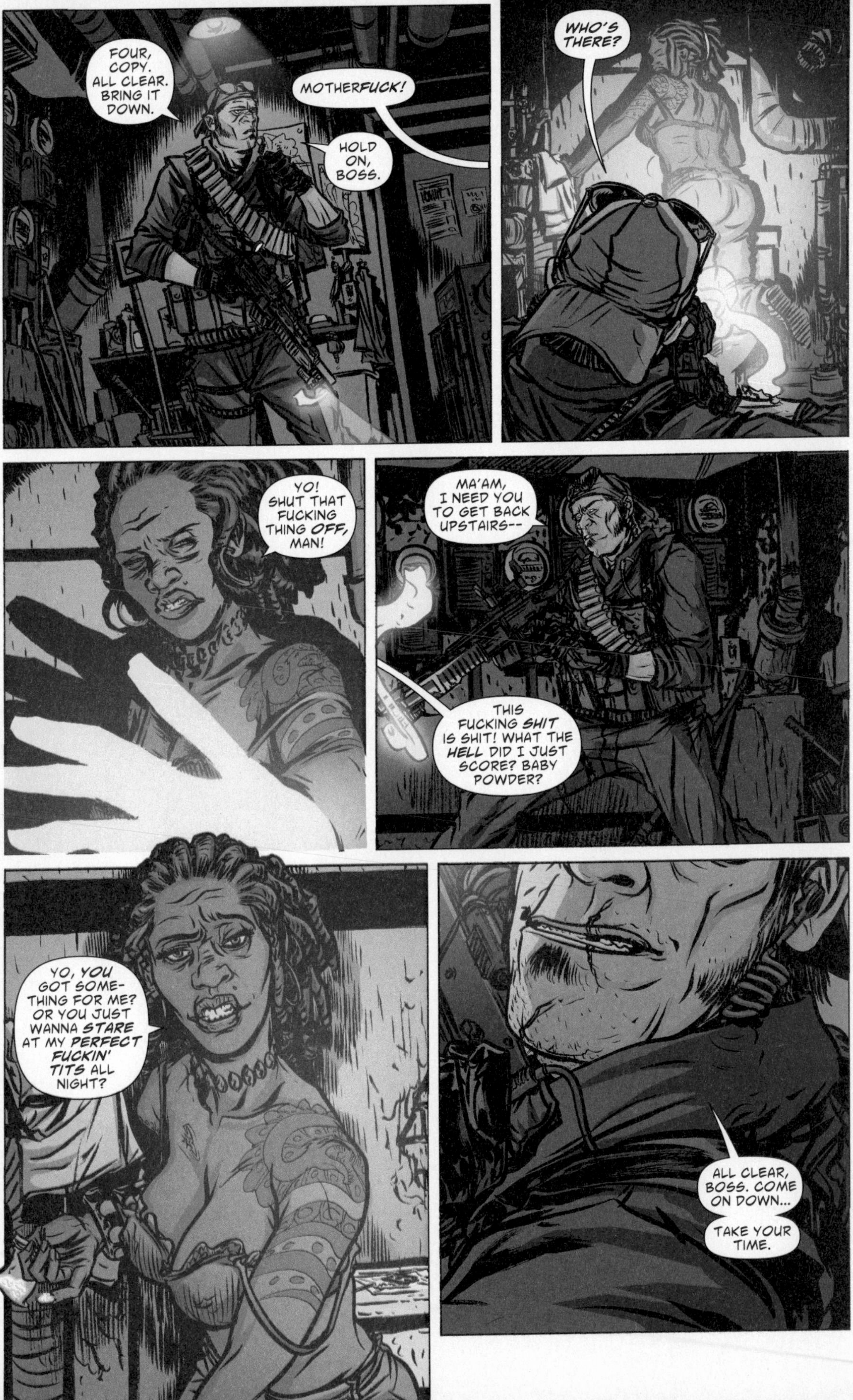
FOUR, COPY. ALL CLEAR. BRING IT DOWN.
HOLD ON, BOSS.
MOTHERFUCK!
WHO'S THERE?
YO! SHUT THAT FUCKING THING OFF, MAN!
MA'AM, I NEED YOU TO GET BACK UPSTAIRS--
THIS FUCKING SHIT IS SHIT! WHAT THE HELL DID I JUST SCORE? BABY POWDER?
YO, YOU GOT SOME-THING FOR ME? OR YOU JUST WANNA STARE AT MY PERFECT FUCKIN' TITS ALL NIGHT?
ALL CLEAR, BOSS. COME ON DOWN...
TAKE YOUR TIME.

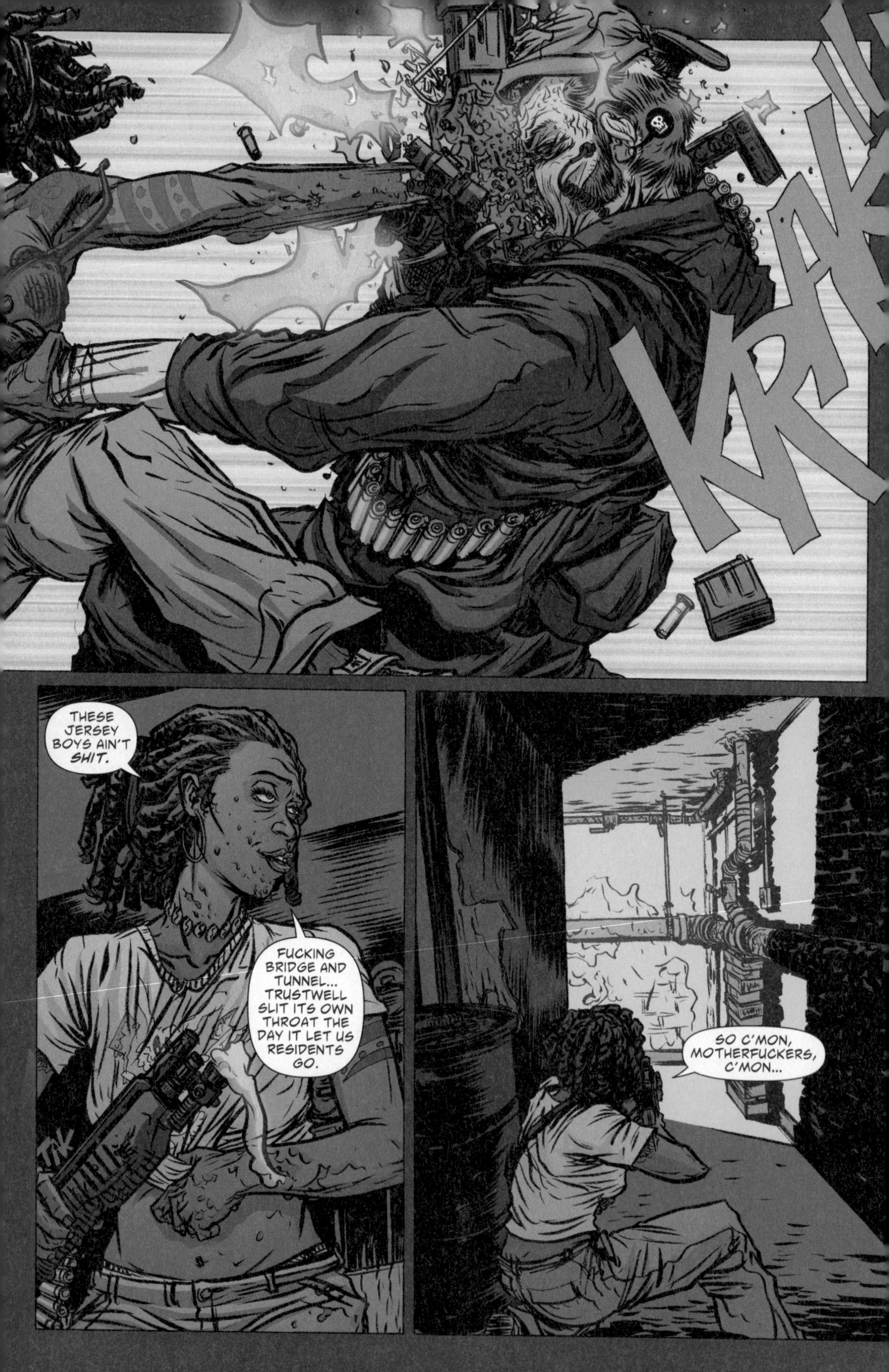
KRAK
THESE JERSEY BOYS AIN'T SHIT.
FUCKING BRIDGE AND TUNNEL... TRUSTWELL SLIT ITS OWN THROAT THE DAY IT LET US RESIDENTS GO.
SO C'MON, MOTHERFUCKERS, C'MON...

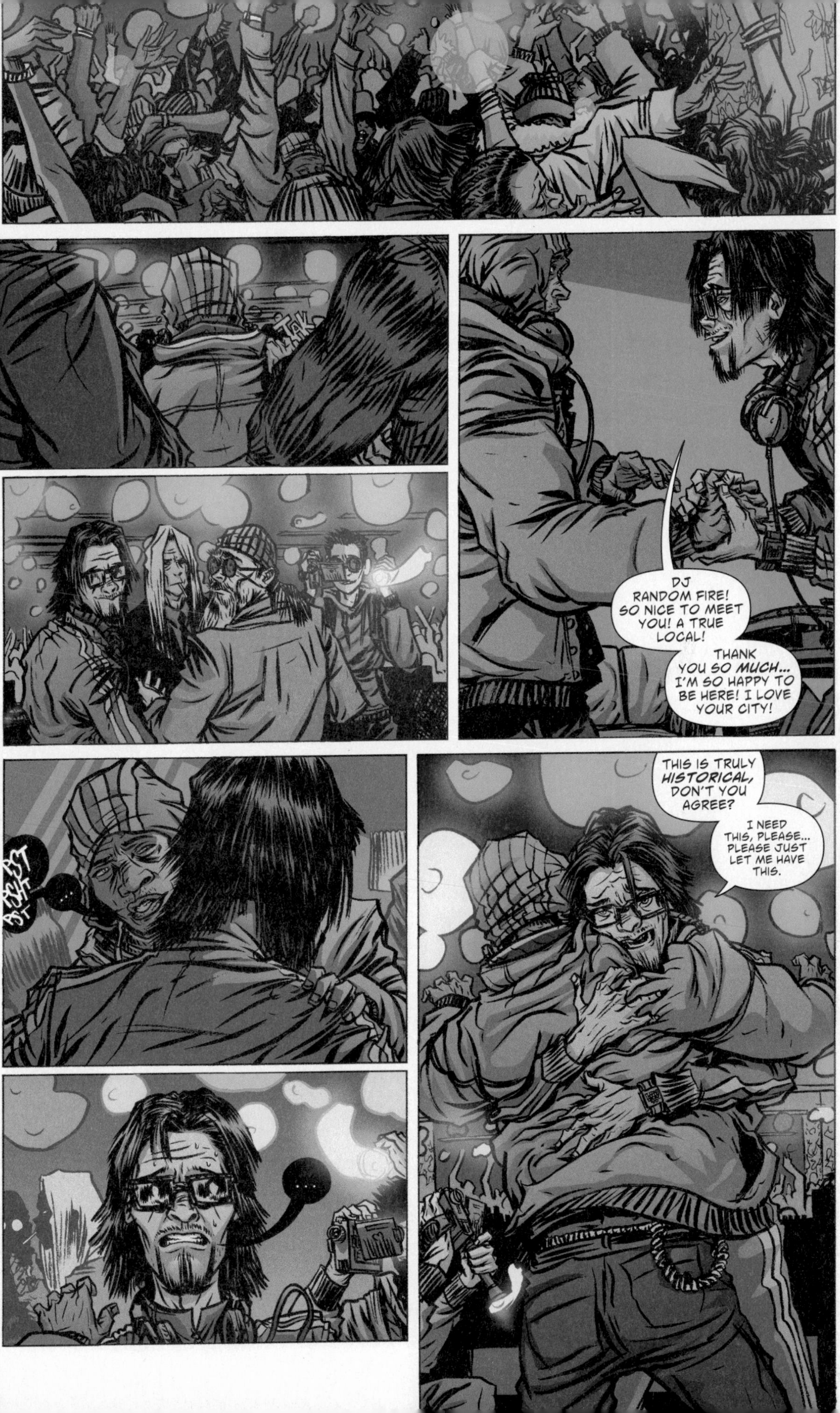
DJ RANDOM FIRE! SO NICE TO MEET YOU! A TRUE LOCAL!
THANK YOU SO *MUCH*... I'M SO HAPPY TO BE HERE! I LOVE YOUR CITY!
THIS IS TRULY *HISTORICAL*, DON'T YOU AGREE?
I NEED THIS, PLEASE... PLEASE JUST LET ME HAVE THIS.

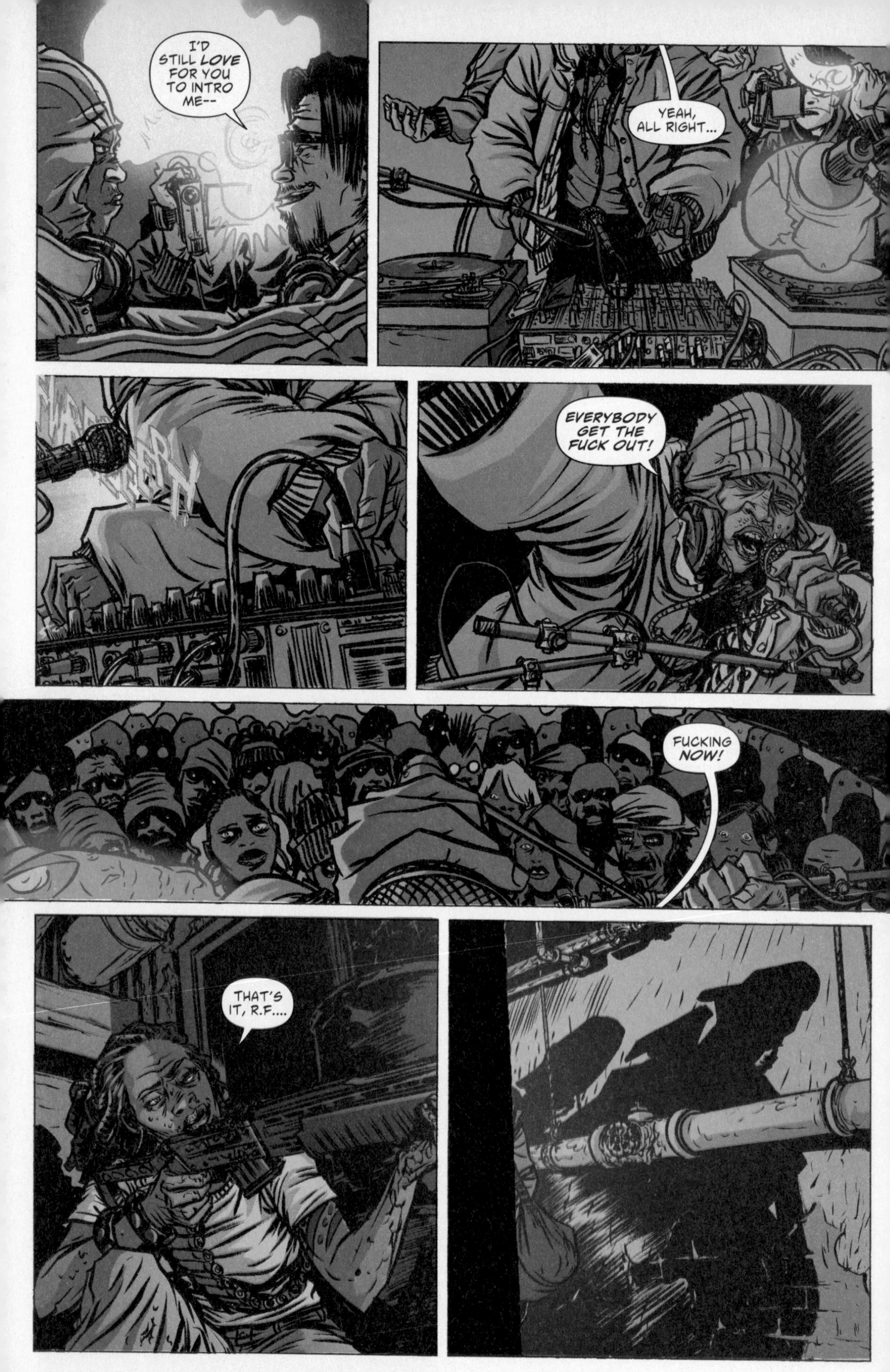
I'D STILL LOVE FOR YOU TO INTRO ME--
YEAH, ALL RIGHT...
EVERYBODY GET THE FUCK OUT!
FUCKING NOW!
THAT'S IT, R.F....

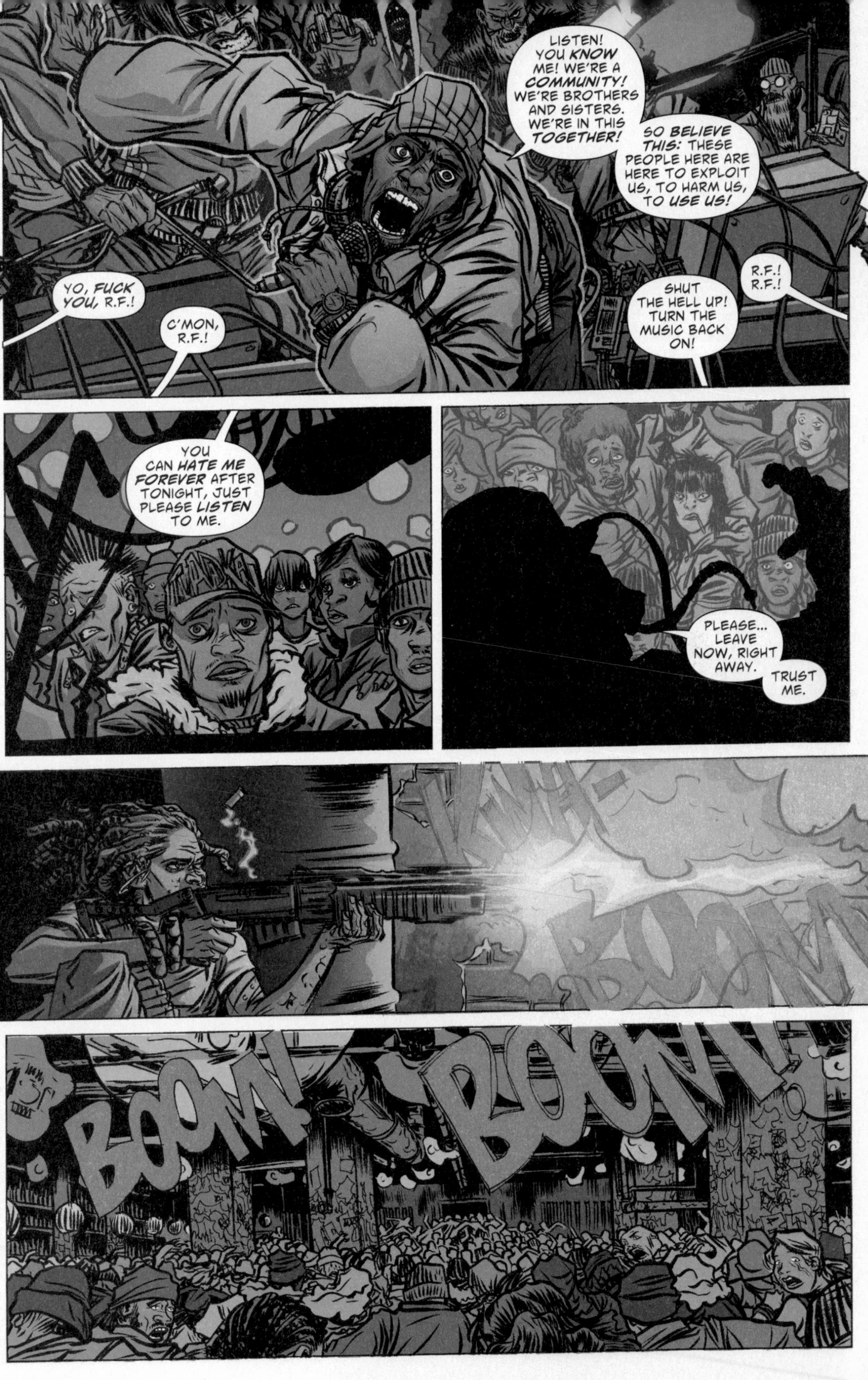

LISTEN! YOU KNOW ME! WE'RE A COMMUNITY! WE'RE BROTHERS AND SISTERS. WE'RE IN THIS TOGETHER!
SO BELIEVE THIS: THESE PEOPLE HERE ARE HERE TO EXPLOIT US, TO HARM US, TO USE US!
YO, FUCK YOU, R.F.!
C'MON, R.F.!
SHUT THE HELL UP! TURN THE MUSIC BACK ON!
R.F.! R.F.!
YOU CAN HATE ME FOREVER AFTER TONIGHT, JUST PLEASE LISTEN TO ME.
PLEASE... LEAVE NOW, RIGHT AWAY.
TRUST ME.
BOOM
BOOM
BOOM!

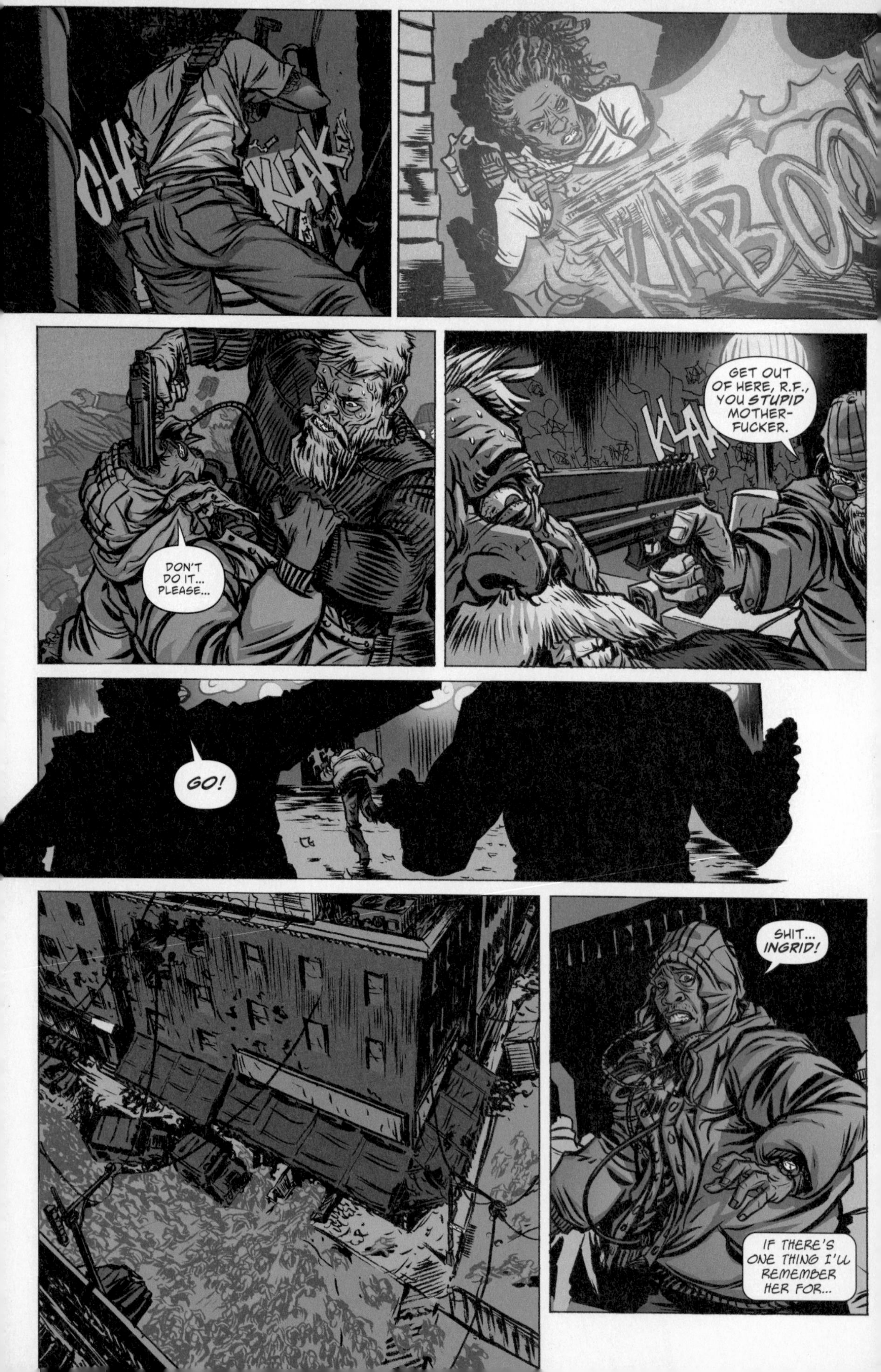
CHK
KLAK
KABOOM
DON'T DO IT... PLEASE...
KLAK
GET OUT OF HERE, R.F., YOU STUPID MOTHER-FUCKER.
GO!
SHIT... INGRID!
IF THERE'S ONE THING I'LL REMEMBER HER FOR...

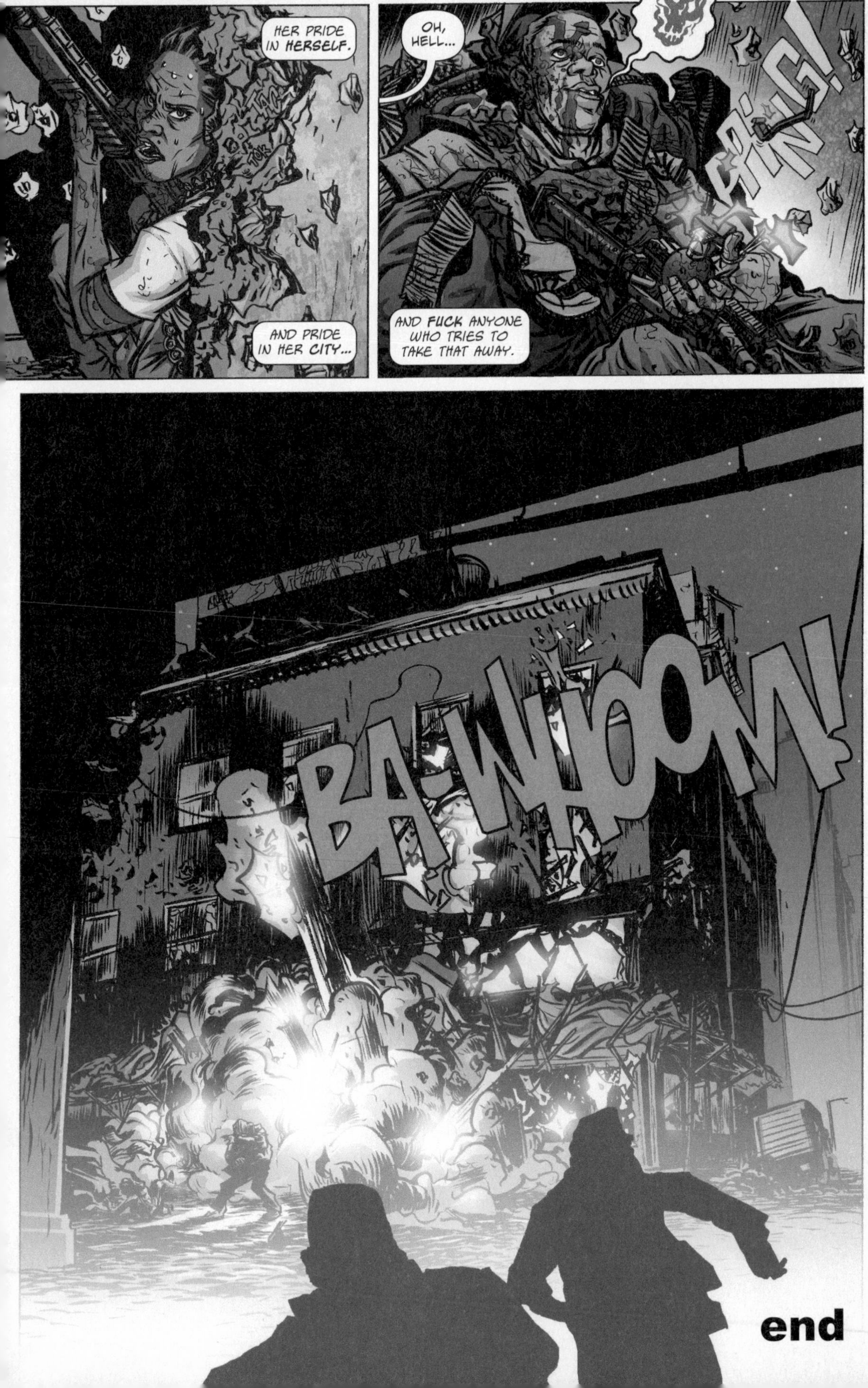
HER PRIDE IN HERSELF.
AND PRIDE IN HER CITY...
OH, HELL...
AND FUCK ANYONE WHO TRIES TO TAKE THAT AWAY.
BA-WHOOM!
end

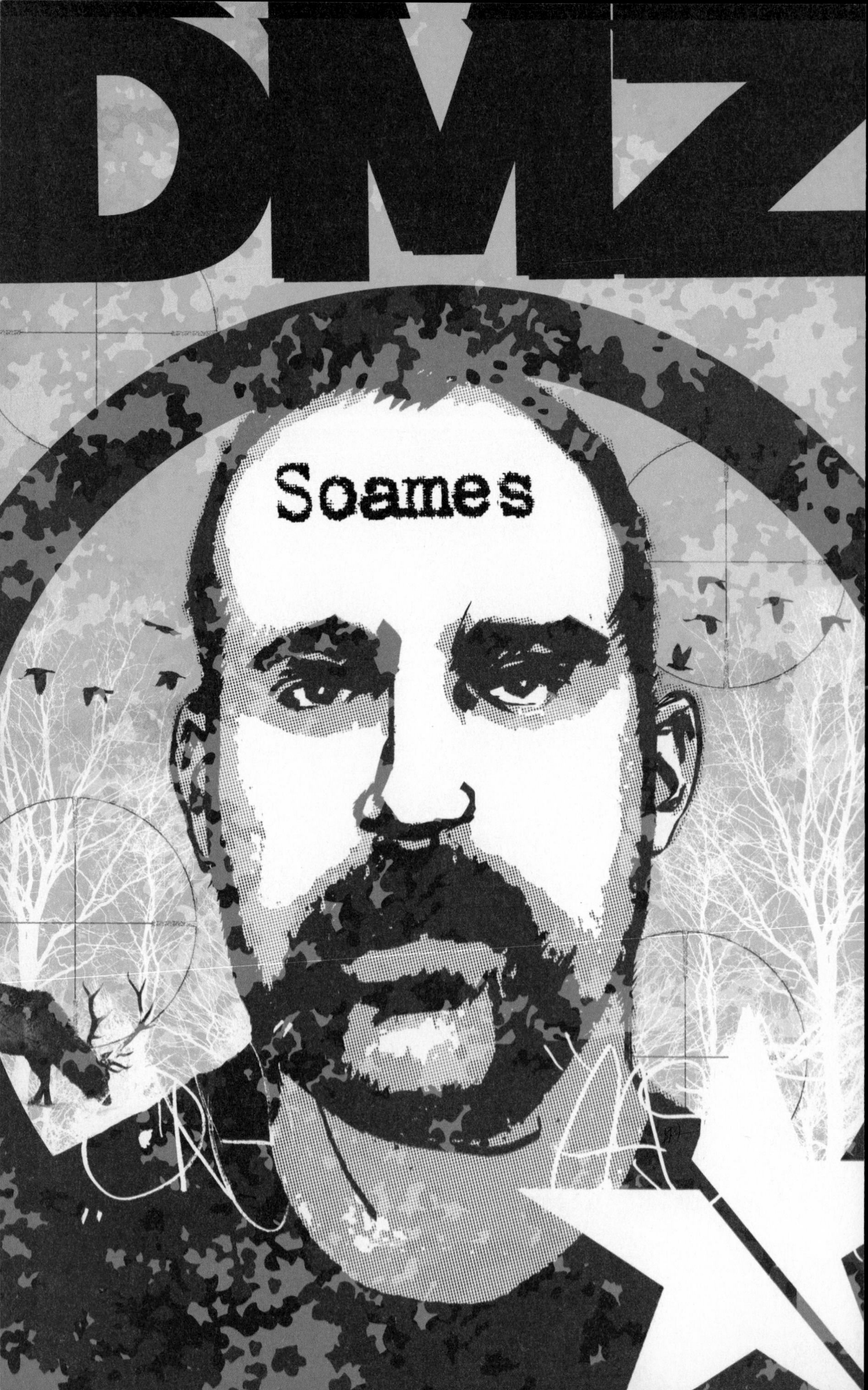
DMZ
Soames

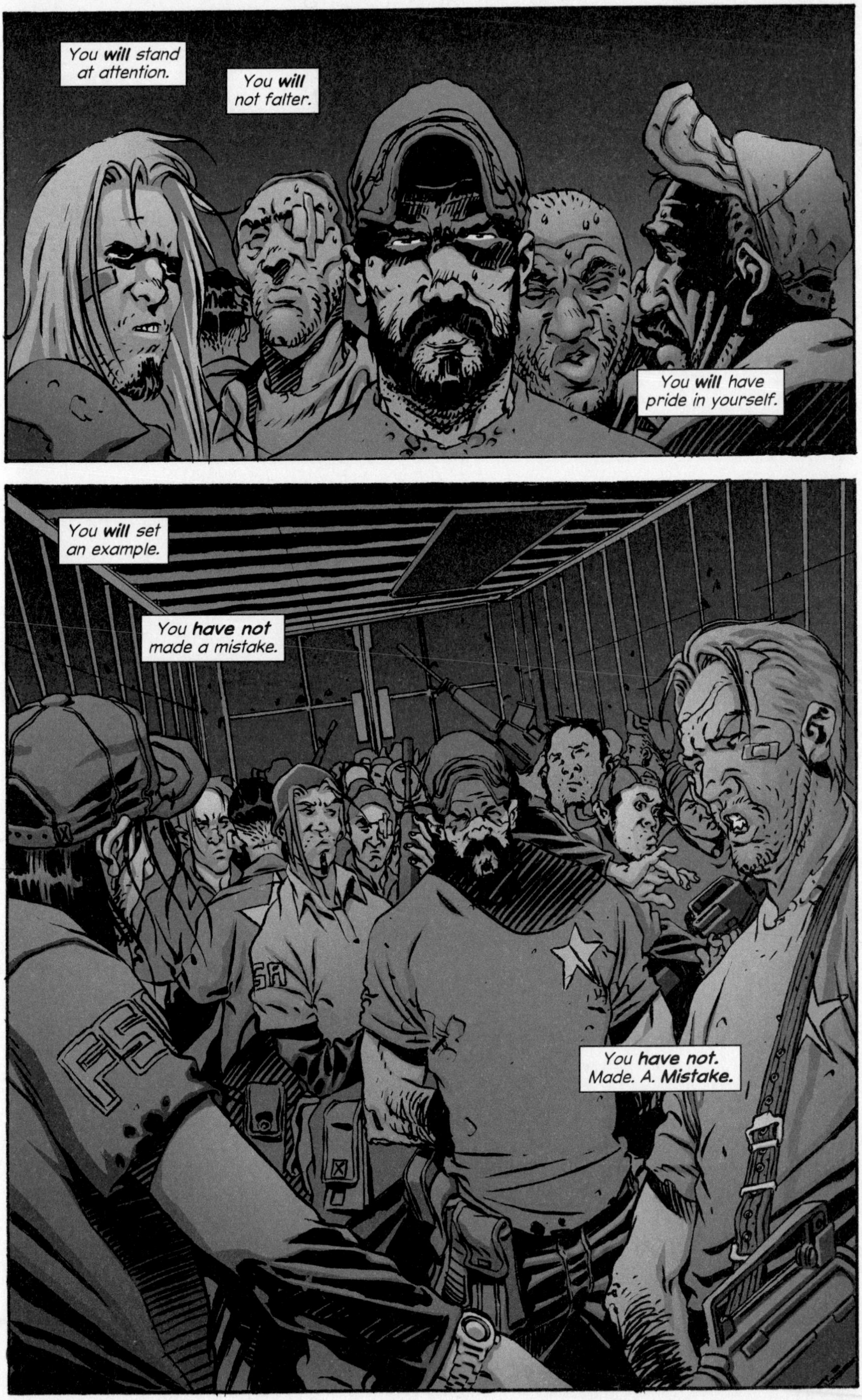
You **will** stand at attention.
You **will** not falter.
You **will** have pride in yourself.
You **will** set an example.
You **have not** made a mistake.
You **have not.** Made. A. **Mistake.**

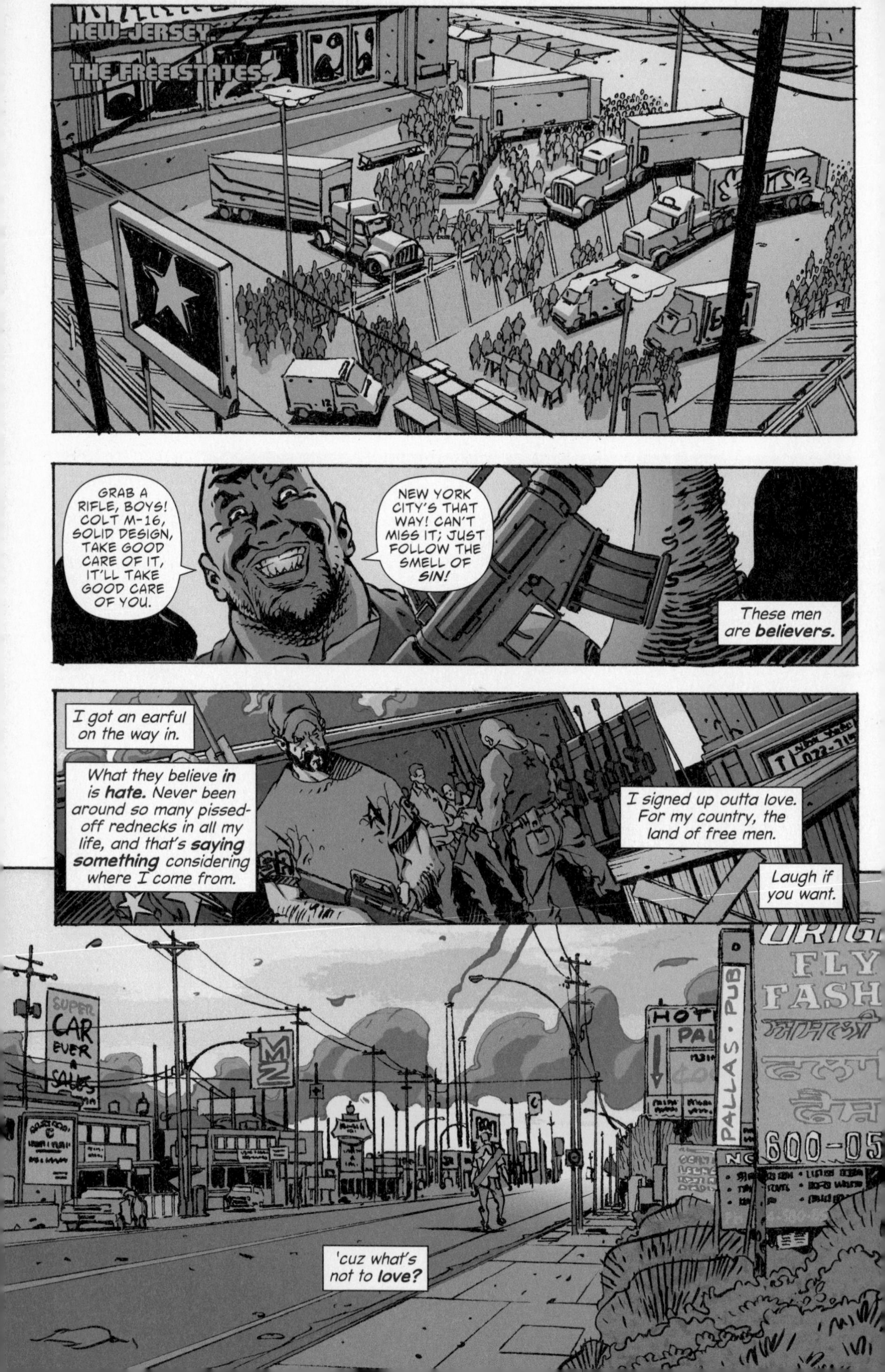
NEW JERSEY.
THE FREE STATES.
GRAB A RIFLE, BOYS! COLT M-16, SOLID DESIGN, TAKE GOOD CARE OF IT, IT'LL TAKE GOOD CARE OF YOU.
NEW YORK CITY'S THAT WAY! CAN'T MISS IT; JUST FOLLOW THE SMELL OF SIN!
These men are believers.
I got an earful on the way in.
What they believe in is hate. Never been around so many pissed-off rednecks in all my life, and that's saying something considering where I come from.
I signed up outta love. For my country, the land of free men.
Laugh if you want.
SUPER CAR EVER A SALES
HOTEL
PALLAS · PUB
FLY FASH
600-05
'cuz what's not to love?

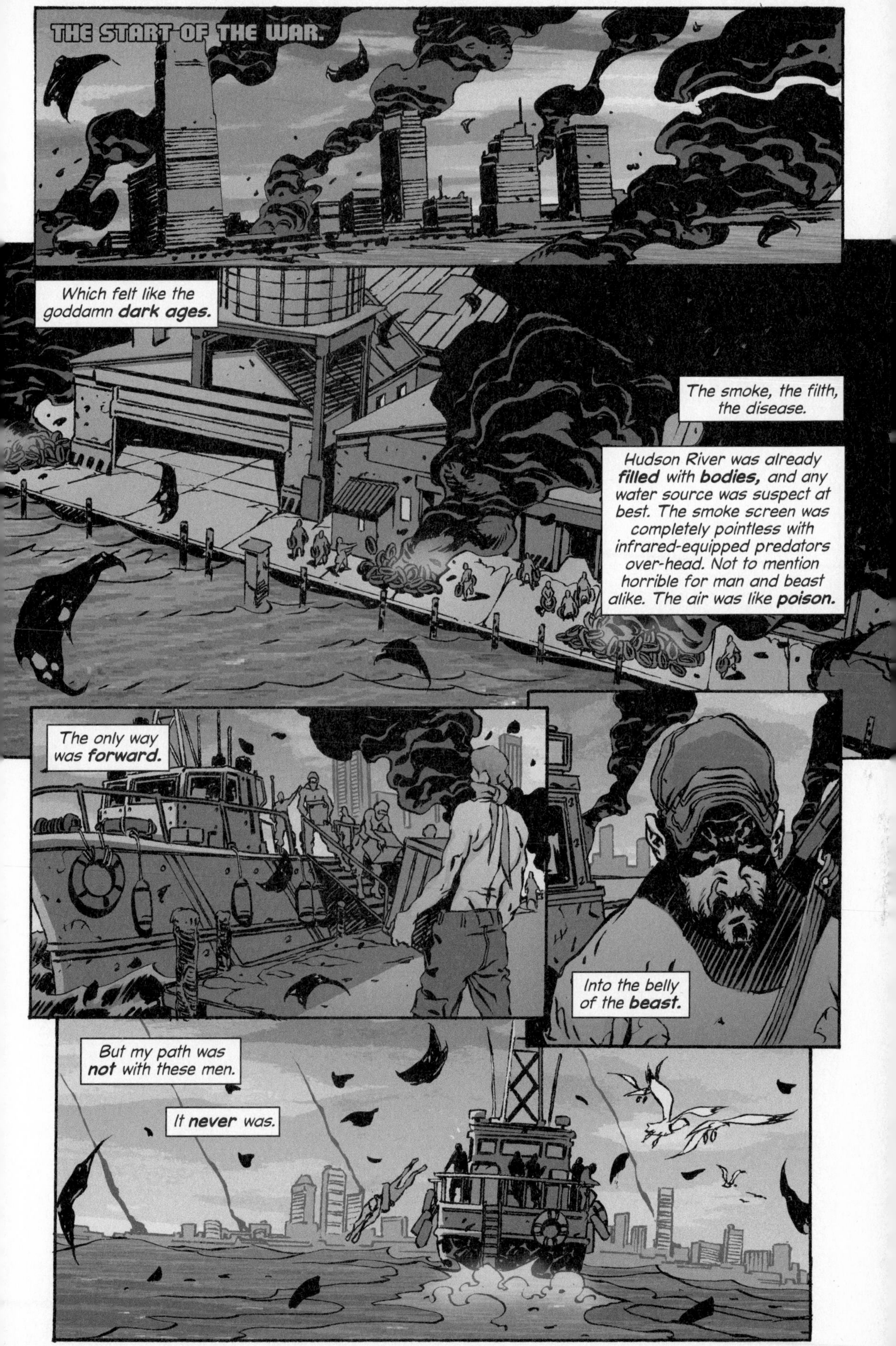
THE START OF THE WAR.
Which felt like the goddamn dark ages.
The smoke, the filth, the disease.
Hudson River was already filled with bodies, and any water source was suspect at best. The smoke screen was completely pointless with infrared-equipped predators over-head. Not to mention horrible for man and beast alike. The air was like poison.
The only way was forward.
Into the belly of the beast.
But my path was not with these men.
It never was.

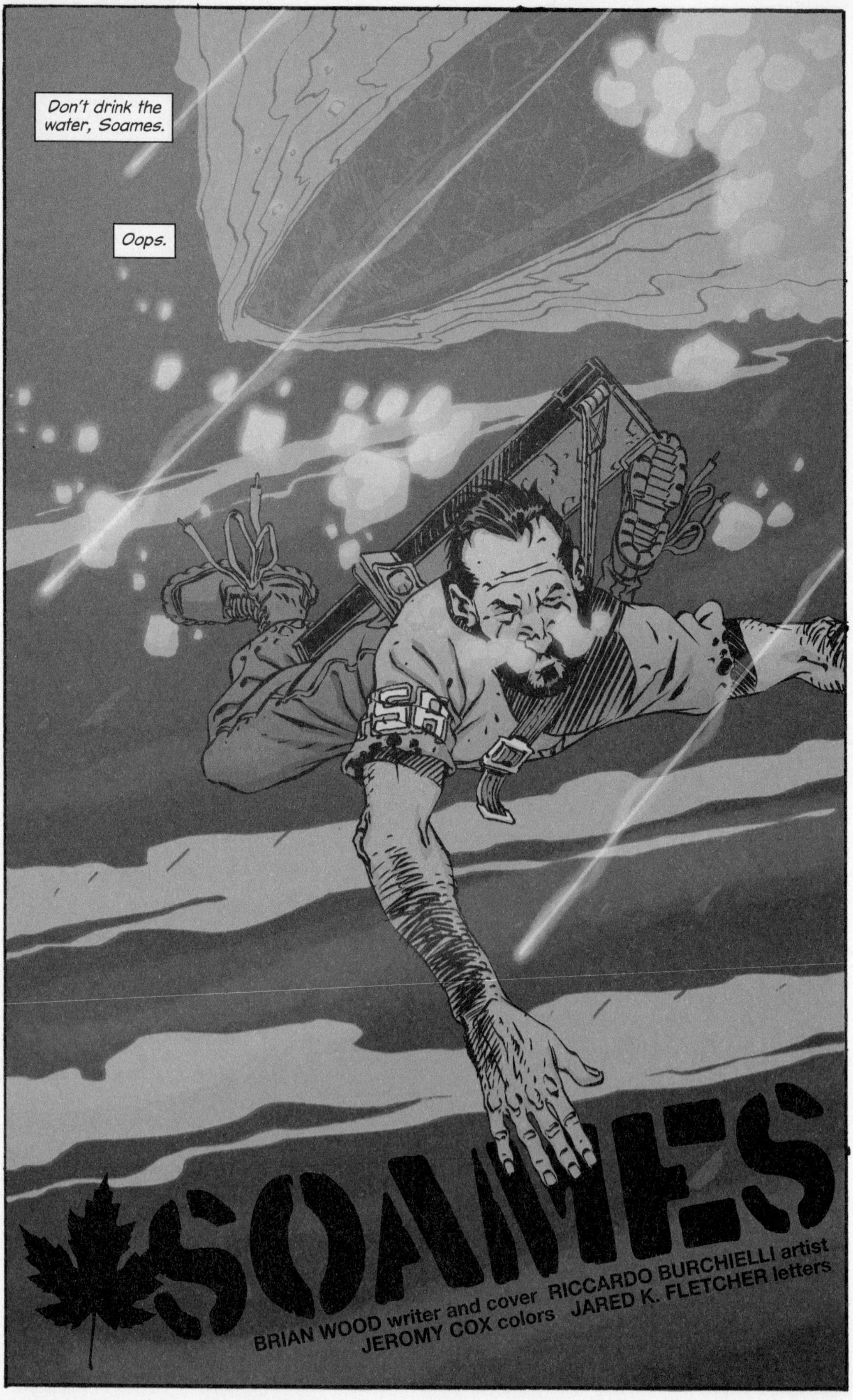

Don't drink the water, Soames.
Oops.
SOAMES
BRIAN WOOD writer and cover RICCARDO BURCHIELLI artist
JEROMY COX colors JARED K. FLETCHER letters

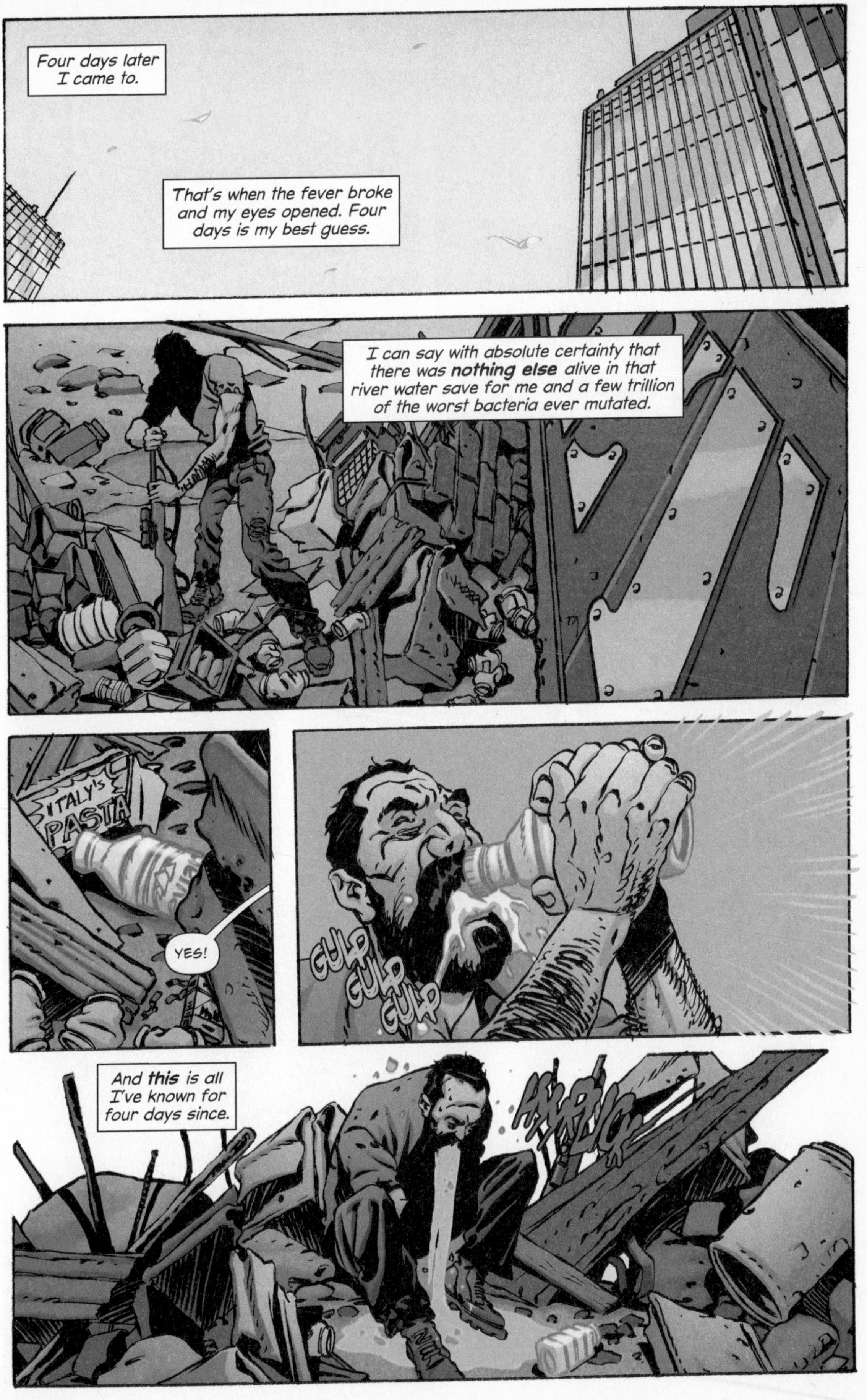

Four days later I came to.
That's when the fever broke and my eyes opened. Four days is my best guess.
I can say with absolute certainty that there was **nothing else** alive in that river water save for me and a few trillion of the worst bacteria ever mutated.
ITALY'S PASTA
YES!
GULP GULP GULP
And **this** is all I've known for four days since.

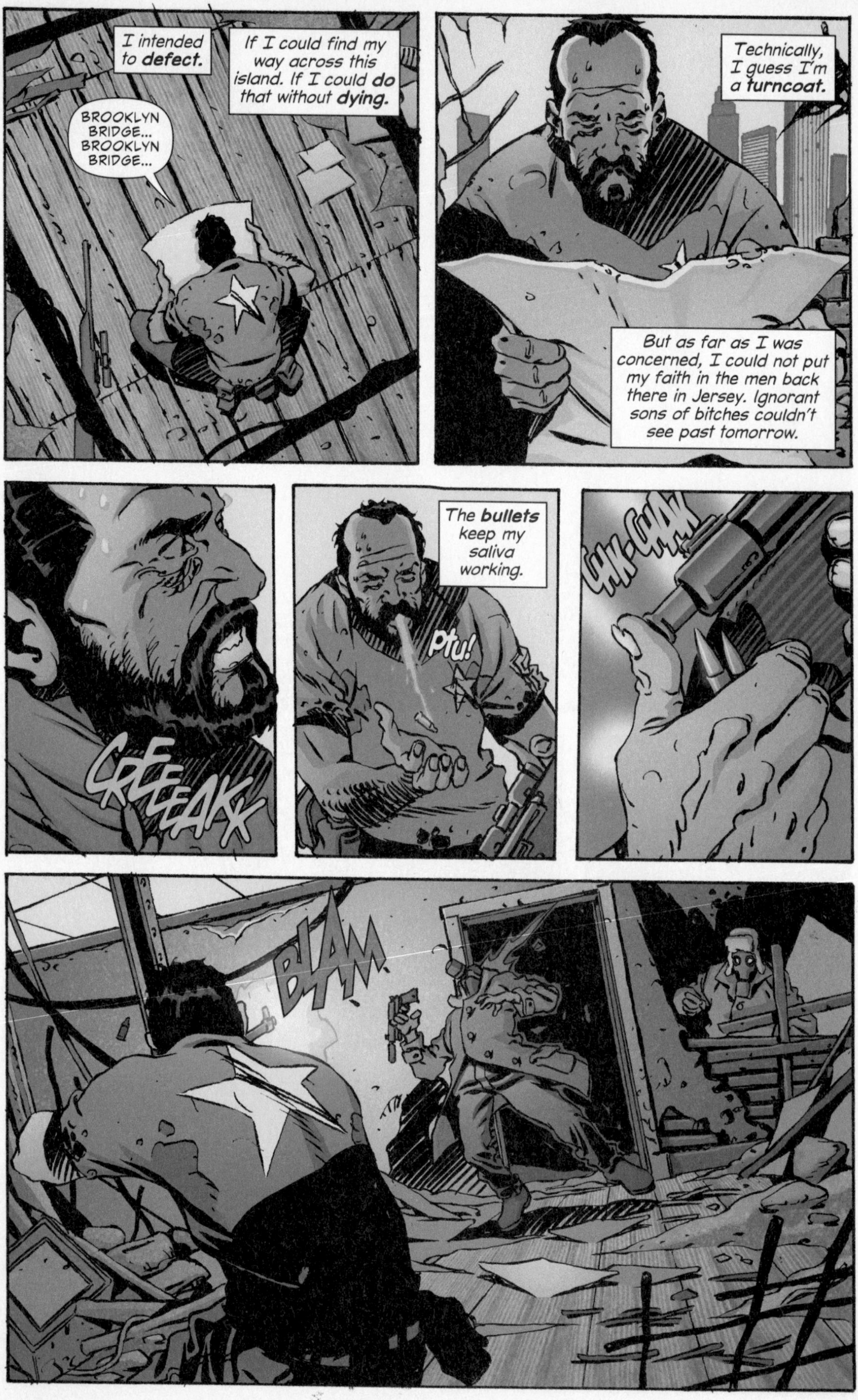
I intended to defect.
If I could find my way across this island. If I could do that without dying.
BROOKLYN BRIDGE... BROOKLYN BRIDGE...
Technically, I guess I'm a turncoat.
But as far as I was concerned, I could not put my faith in the men back there in Jersey. Ignorant sons of bitches couldn't see past tomorrow.
CREEEAKK
The bullets keep my saliva working.
Ptu!
CHK-CHAK
BLAM

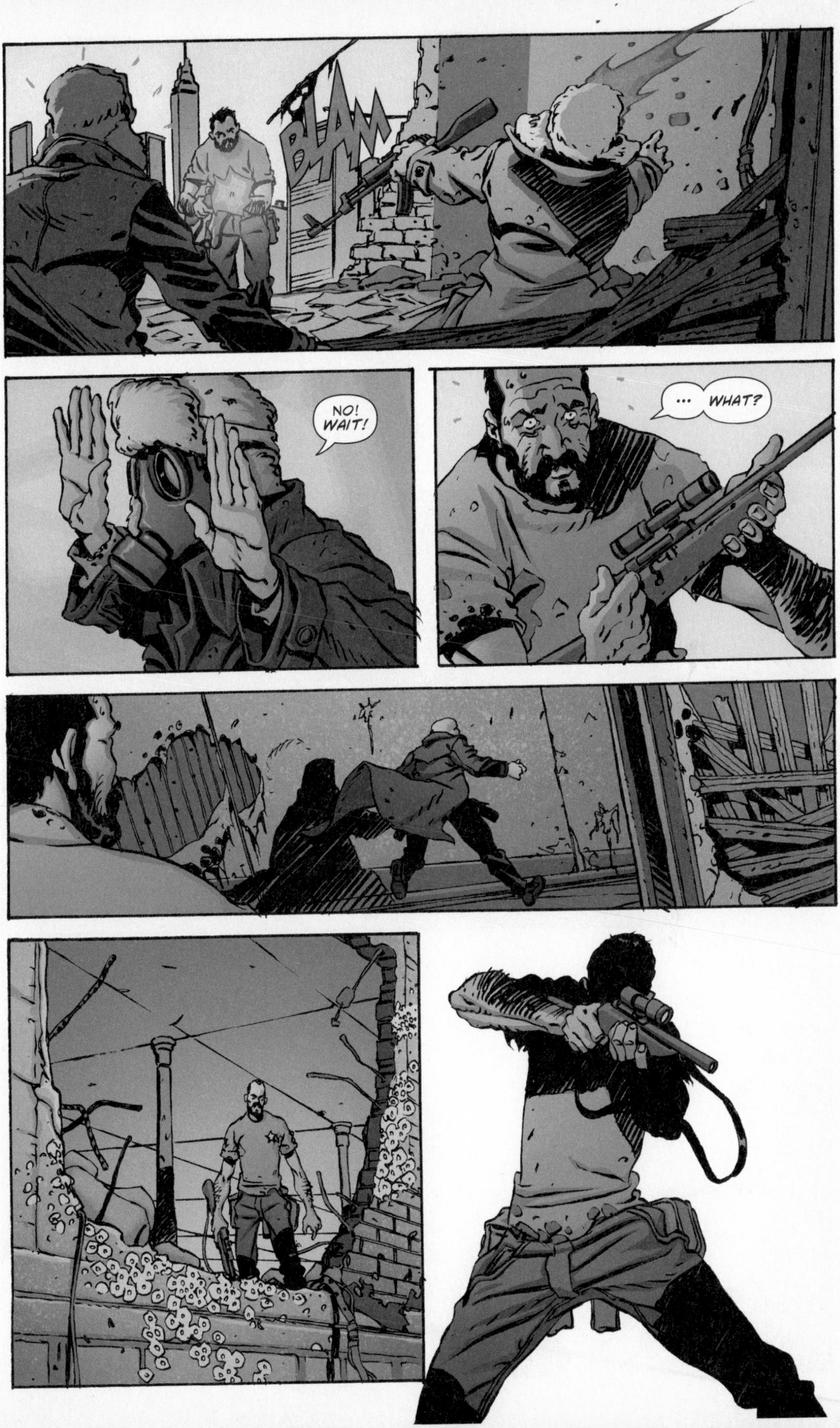
BLAM
NO! WAIT!
... WHAT?

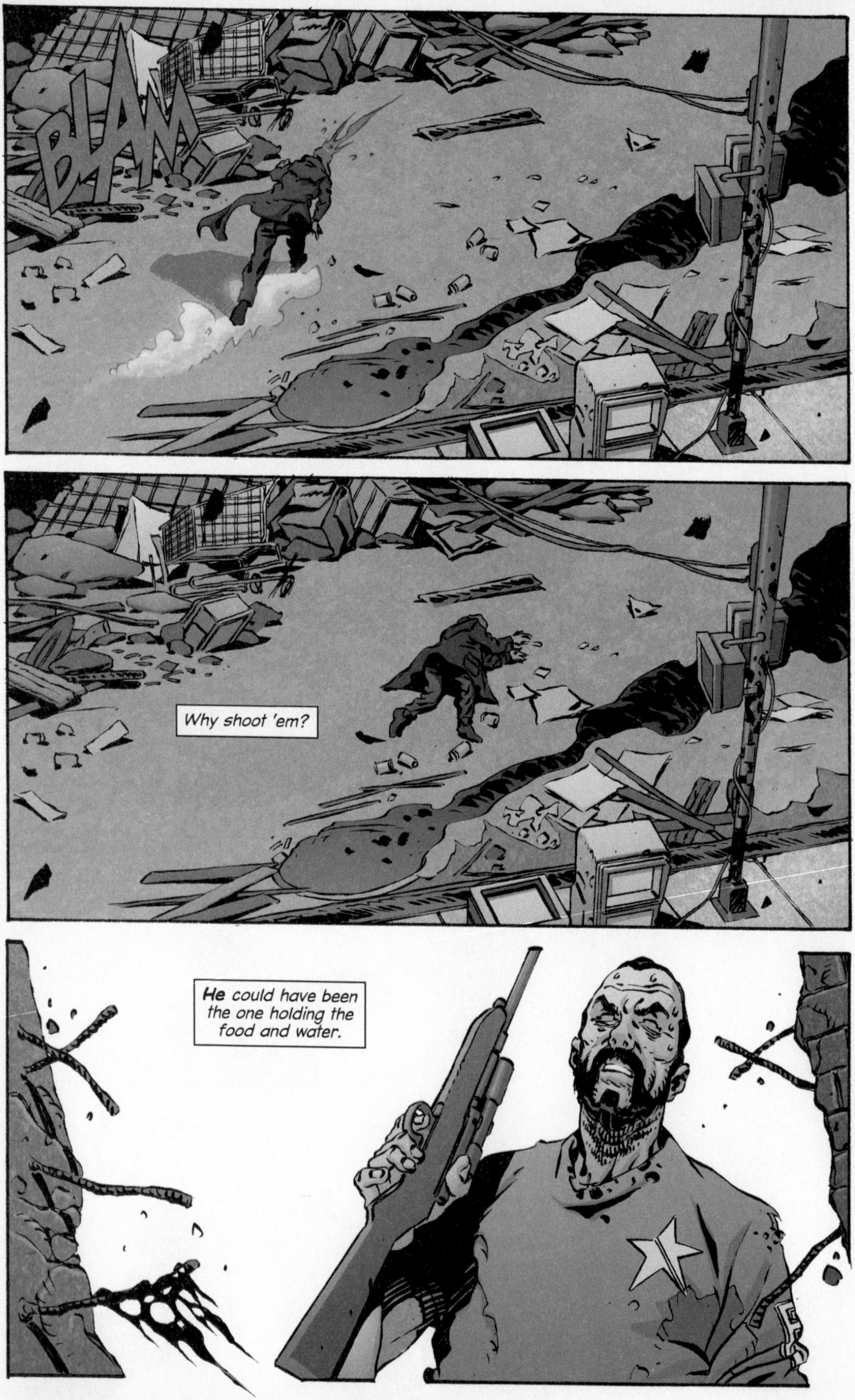
BLAM
Why shoot 'em?
He could have been the one holding the food and water.

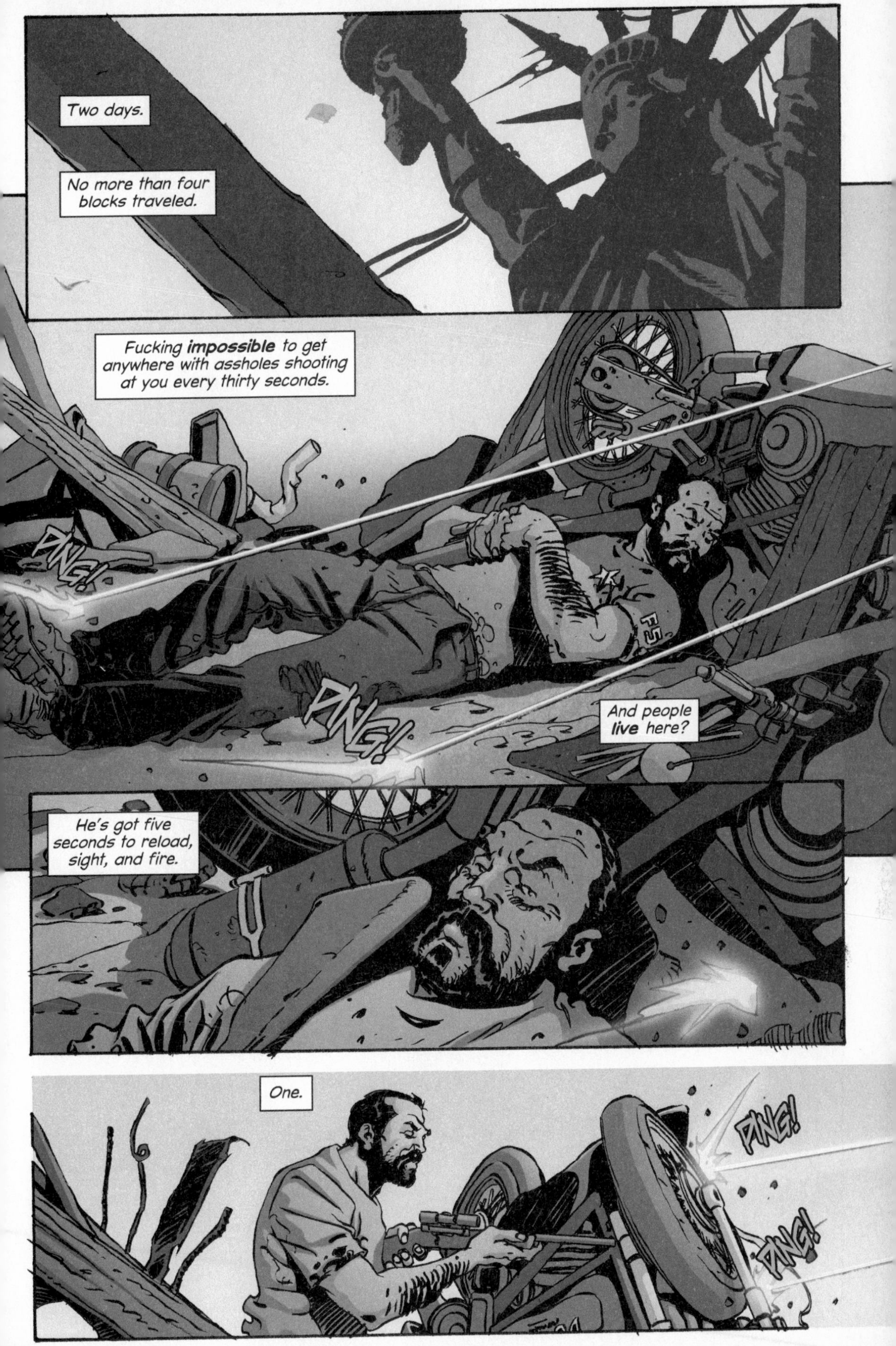
Two days.
No more than four blocks traveled.
Fucking impossible to get anywhere with assholes shooting at you every thirty seconds.
PING!
PING!
And people live here?
He's got five seconds to reload, sight, and fire.
One.
PING!
PING!

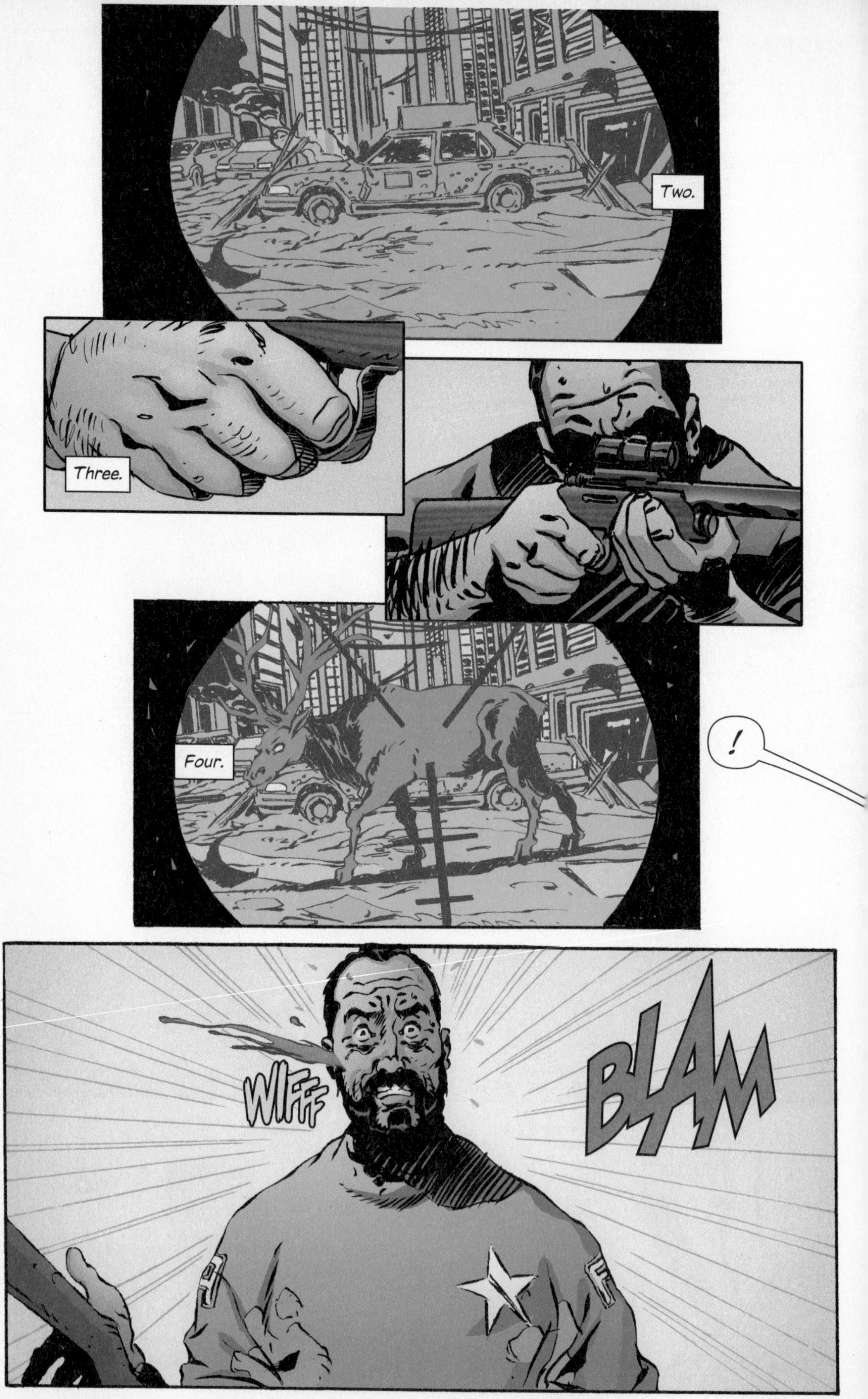
Two.
Three.
Four.
!
WIFFF
BLAM

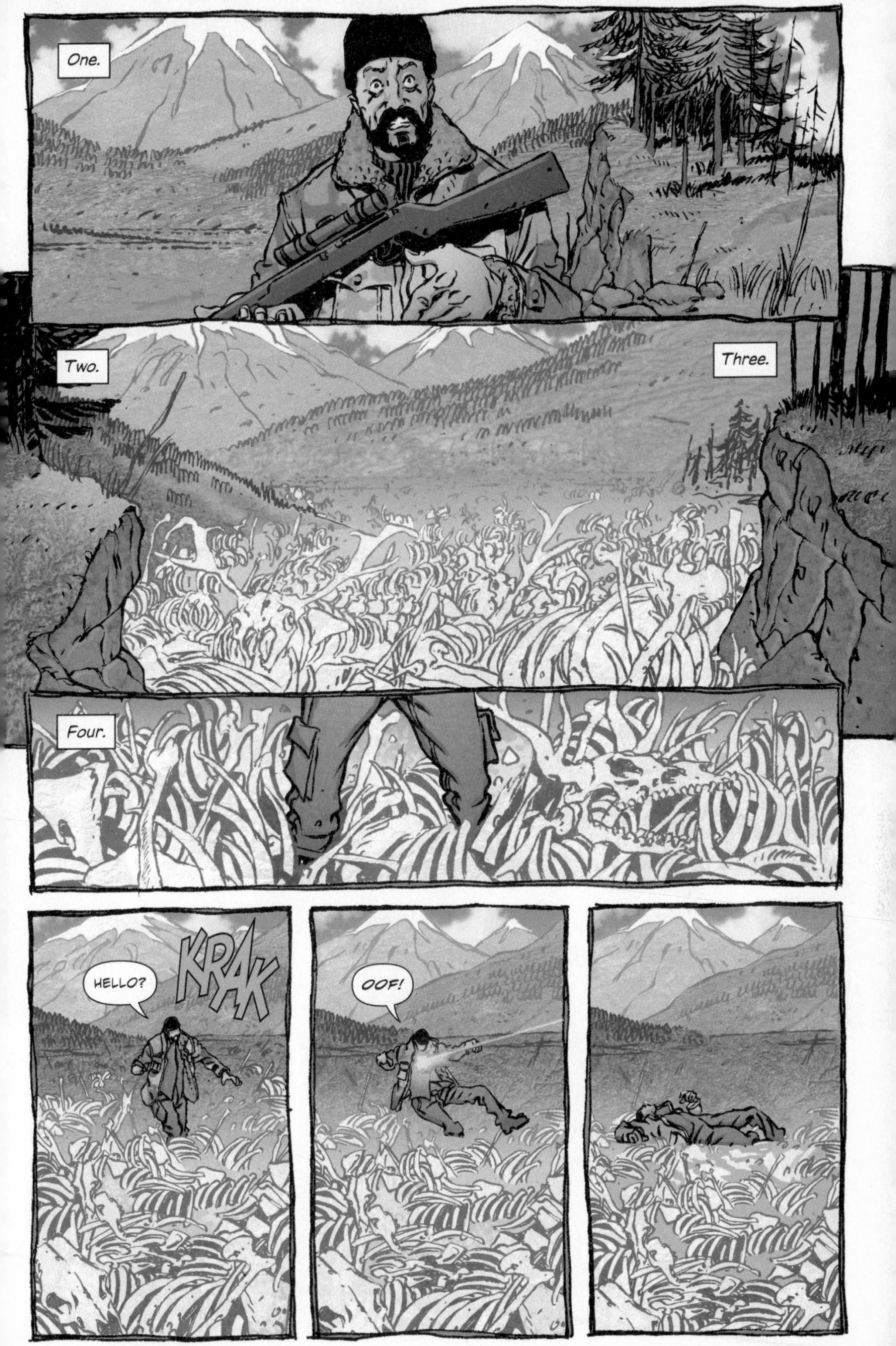
One.
Two.
Three.
Four.
HELLO?
KRAK
OOF!

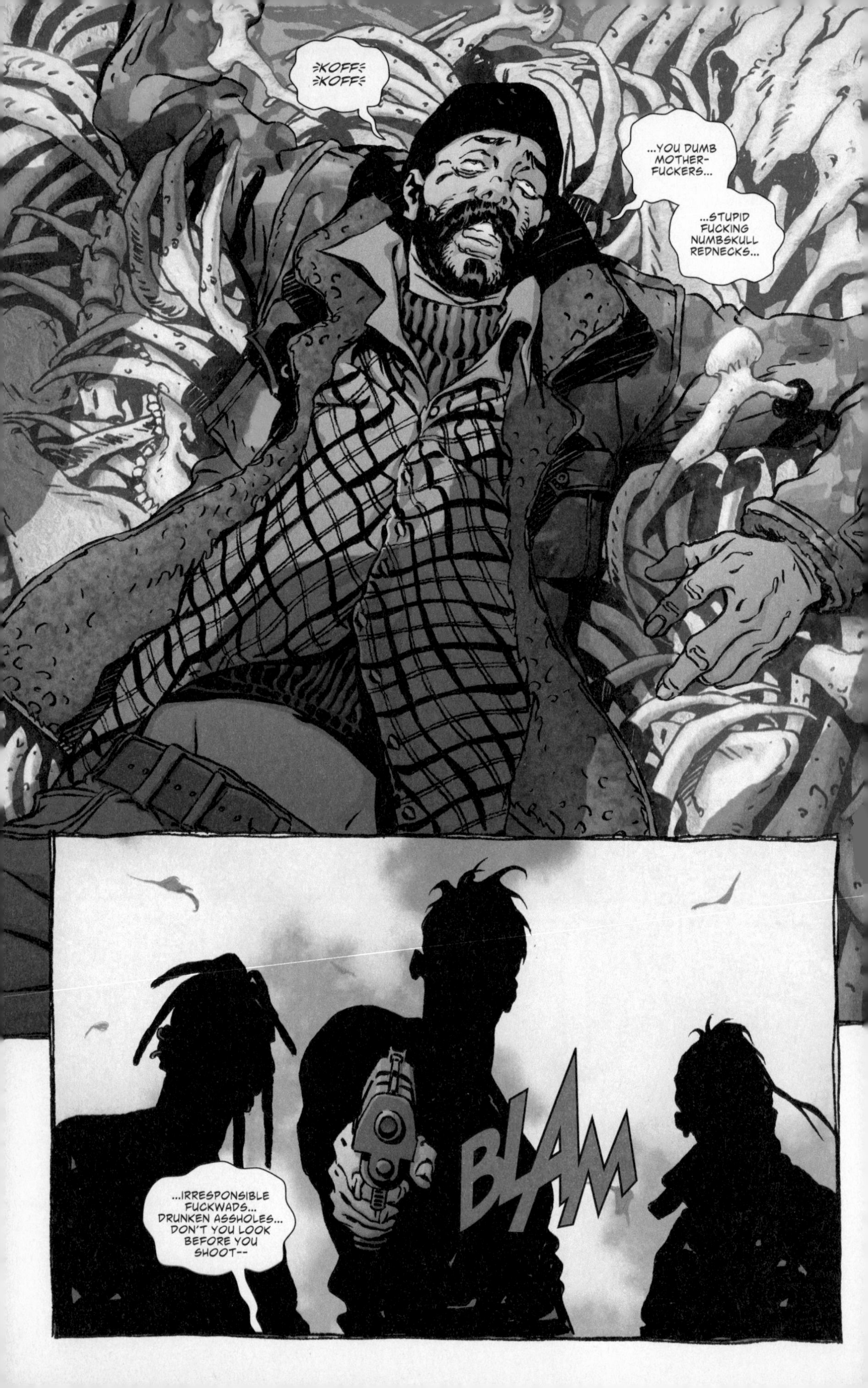

KOFF KOFF
...YOU DUMB MOTHER-FUCKERS...
...STUPID FUCKING NUMBSKULL REDNECKS...
...IRRESPONSIBLE FUCKWADS... DRUNKEN ASSHOLES... DON'T YOU LOOK BEFORE YOU SHOOT--
BLAM

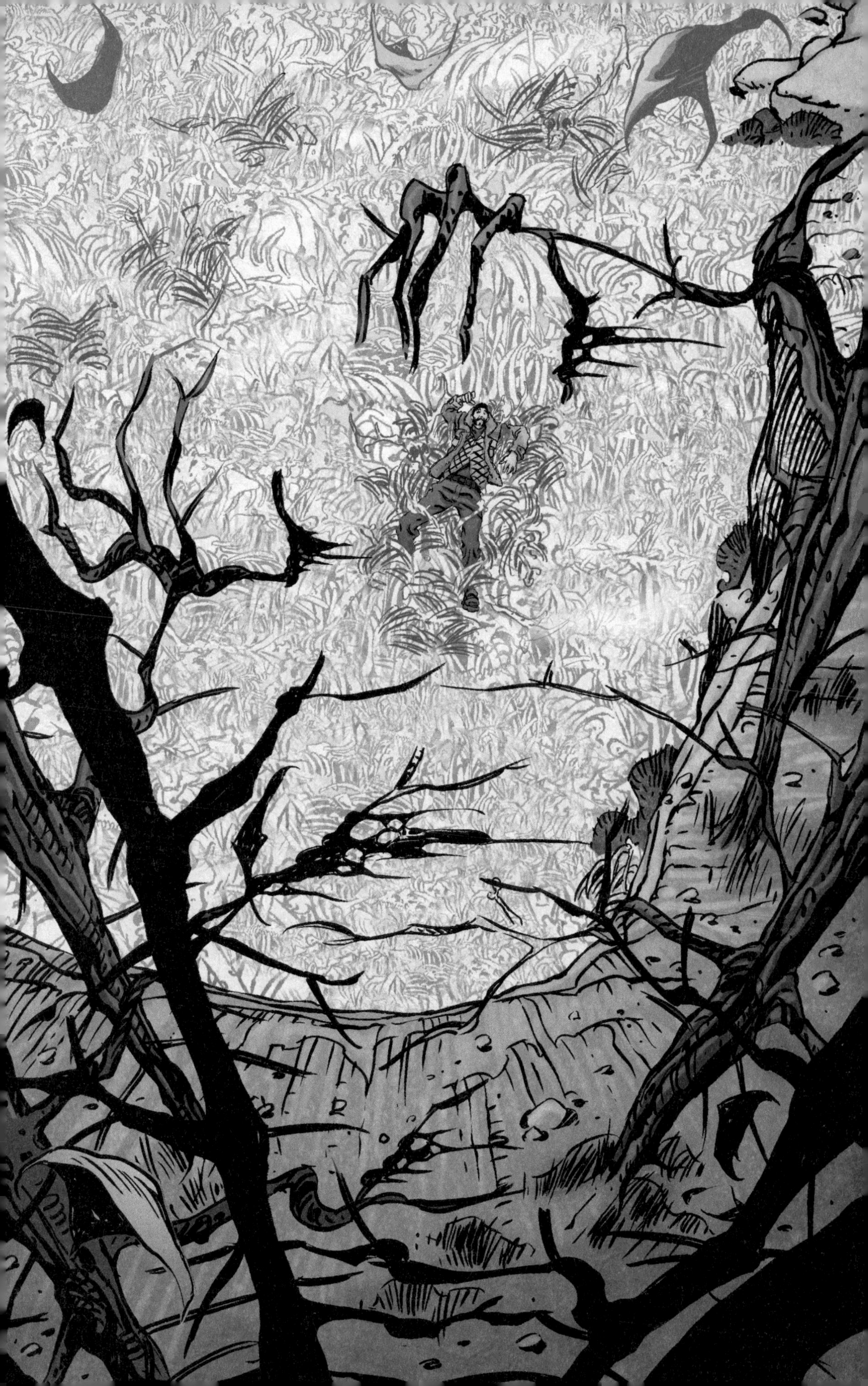

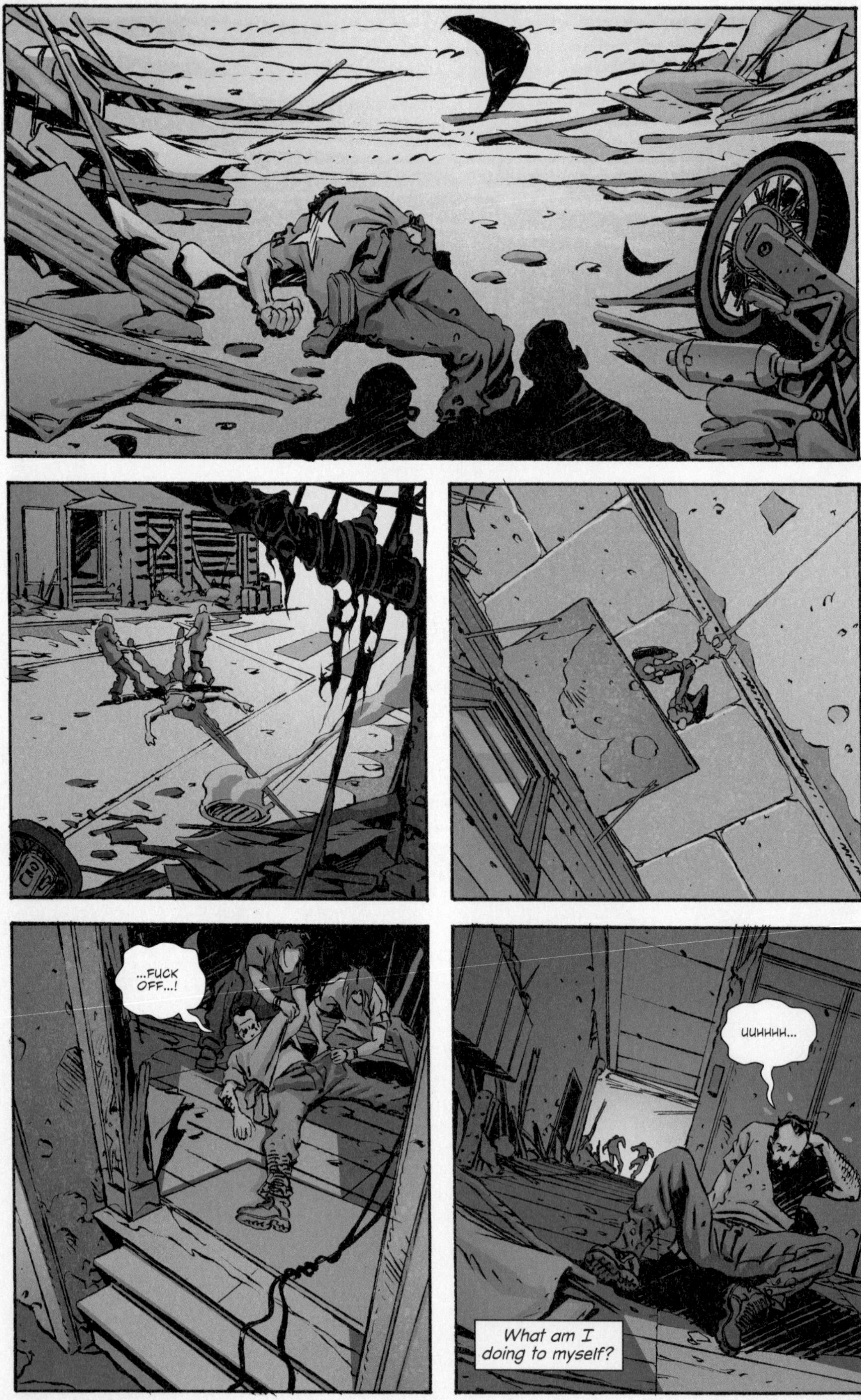
...FUCK OFF...!
UUHHHH...
What am I doing to myself?

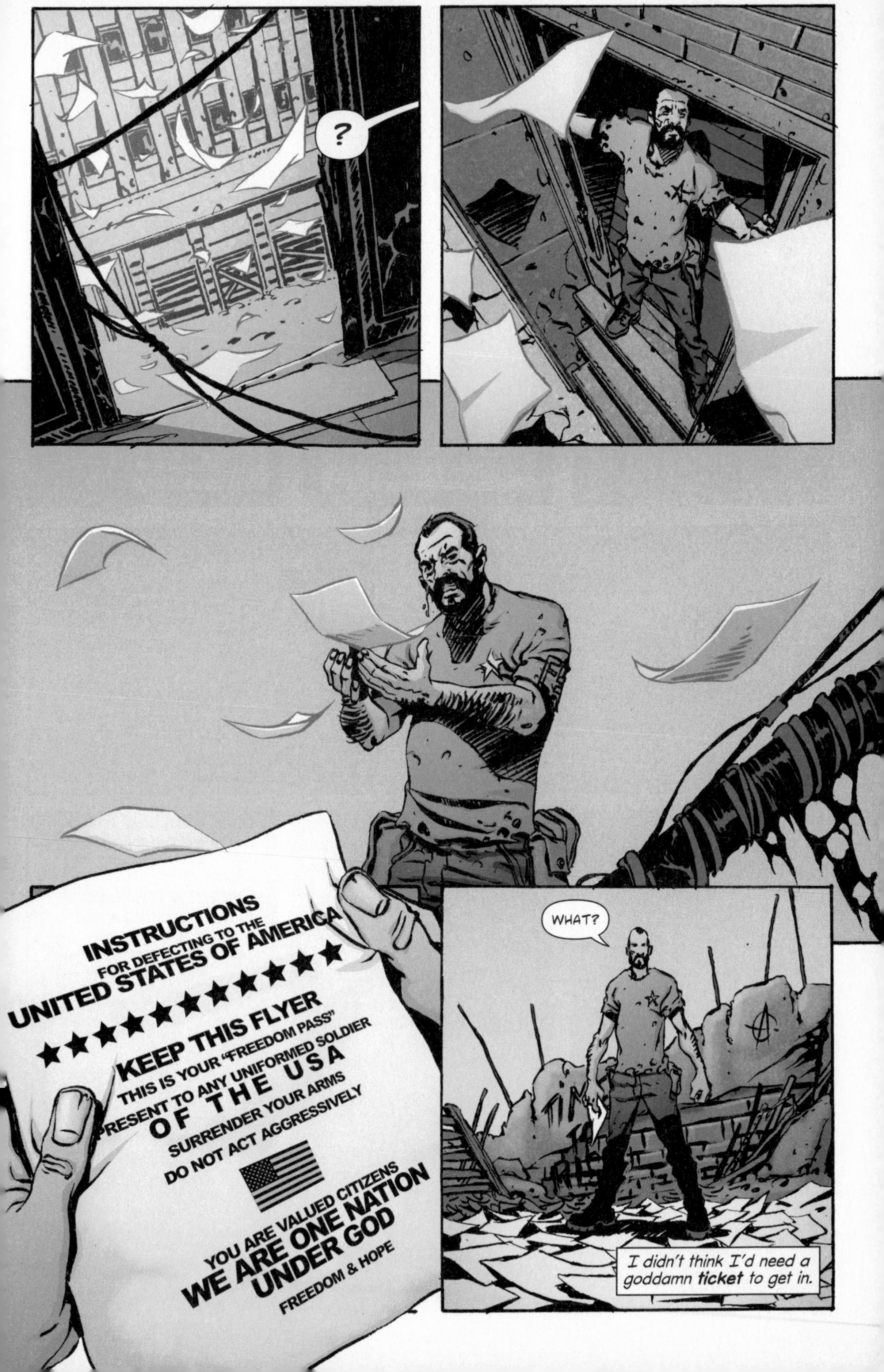
?
INSTRUCTIONS
FOR DEFECTING TO THE
UNITED STATES OF AMERICA
KEEP THIS FLYER
THIS IS YOUR "FREEDOM PASS"
PRESENT TO ANY UNIFORMED SOLDIER
OF THE USA
SURRENDER YOUR ARMS
DO NOT ACT AGGRESSIVELY
YOU ARE VALUED CITIZENS
WE ARE ONE NATION
UNDER GOD
FREEDOM & HOPE
WHAT?
I didn't think I'd need a goddamn **ticket** to get in.

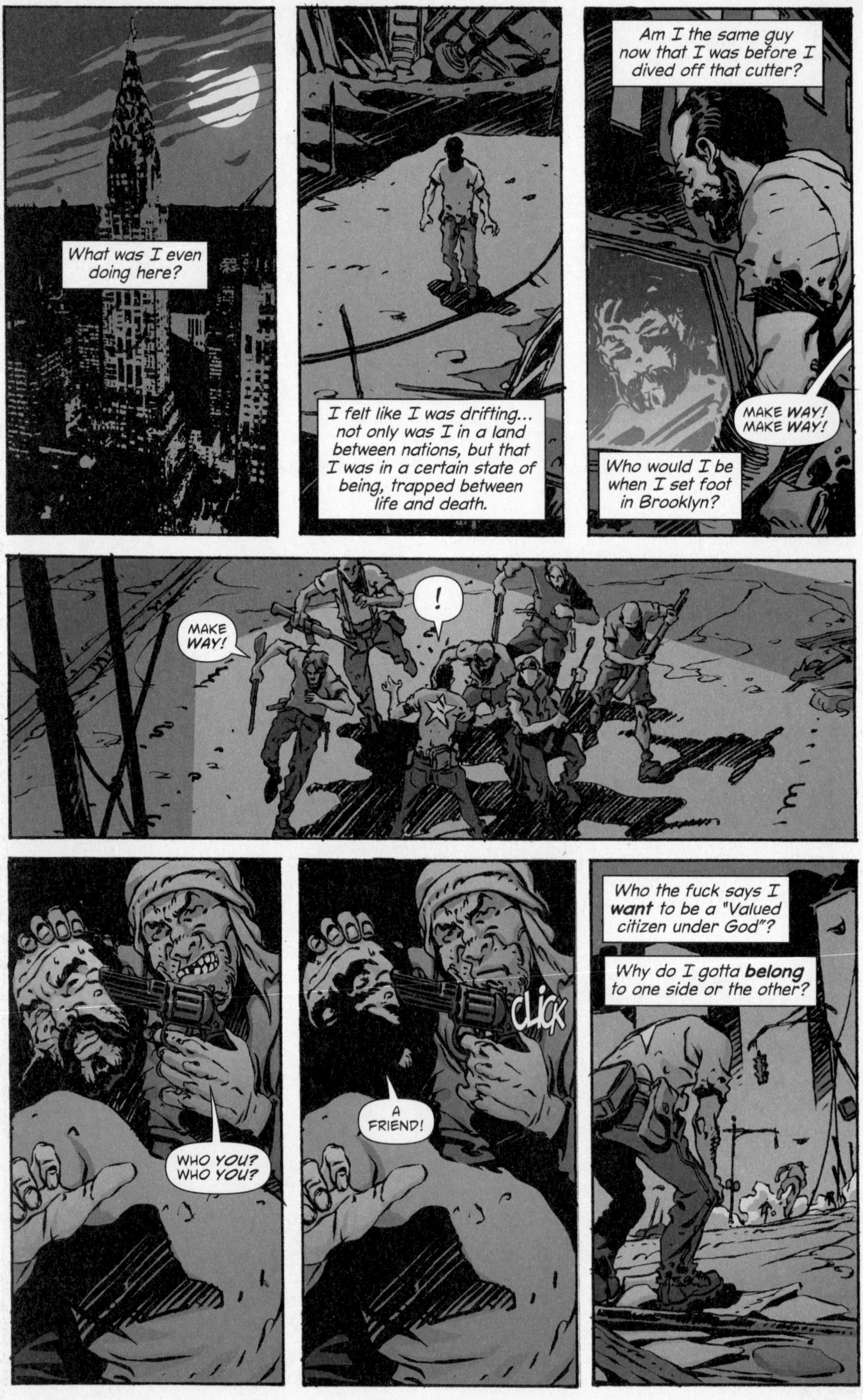
What was I even doing here?
I felt like I was drifting... not only was I in a land between nations, but that I was in a certain state of being, trapped between life and death.
Am I the same guy now that I was before I dived off that cutter?
MAKE WAY! MAKE WAY!
Who would I be when I set foot in Brooklyn?
MAKE WAY!
!
WHO YOU? WHO YOU?
CLICK
A FRIEND!
Who the fuck says I **want** to be a "Valued citizen under God"?
Why do I gotta **belong** to one side or the other?

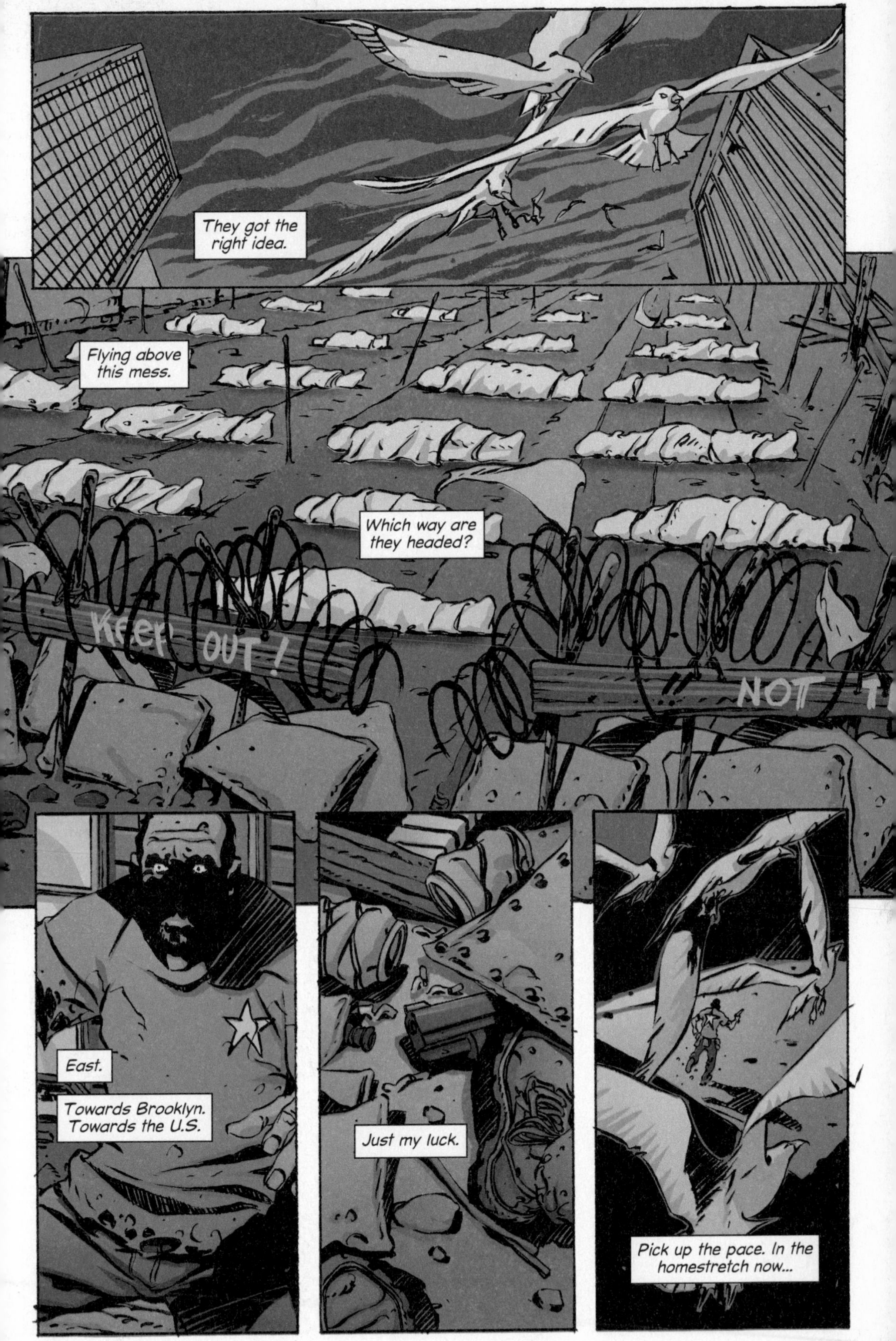
They got the right idea.
Flying above this mess.
Which way are they headed?
KEEP OUT!
NOT
East.
Towards Brooklyn. Towards the U.S.
Just my luck.
Pick up the pace. In the homestretch now...

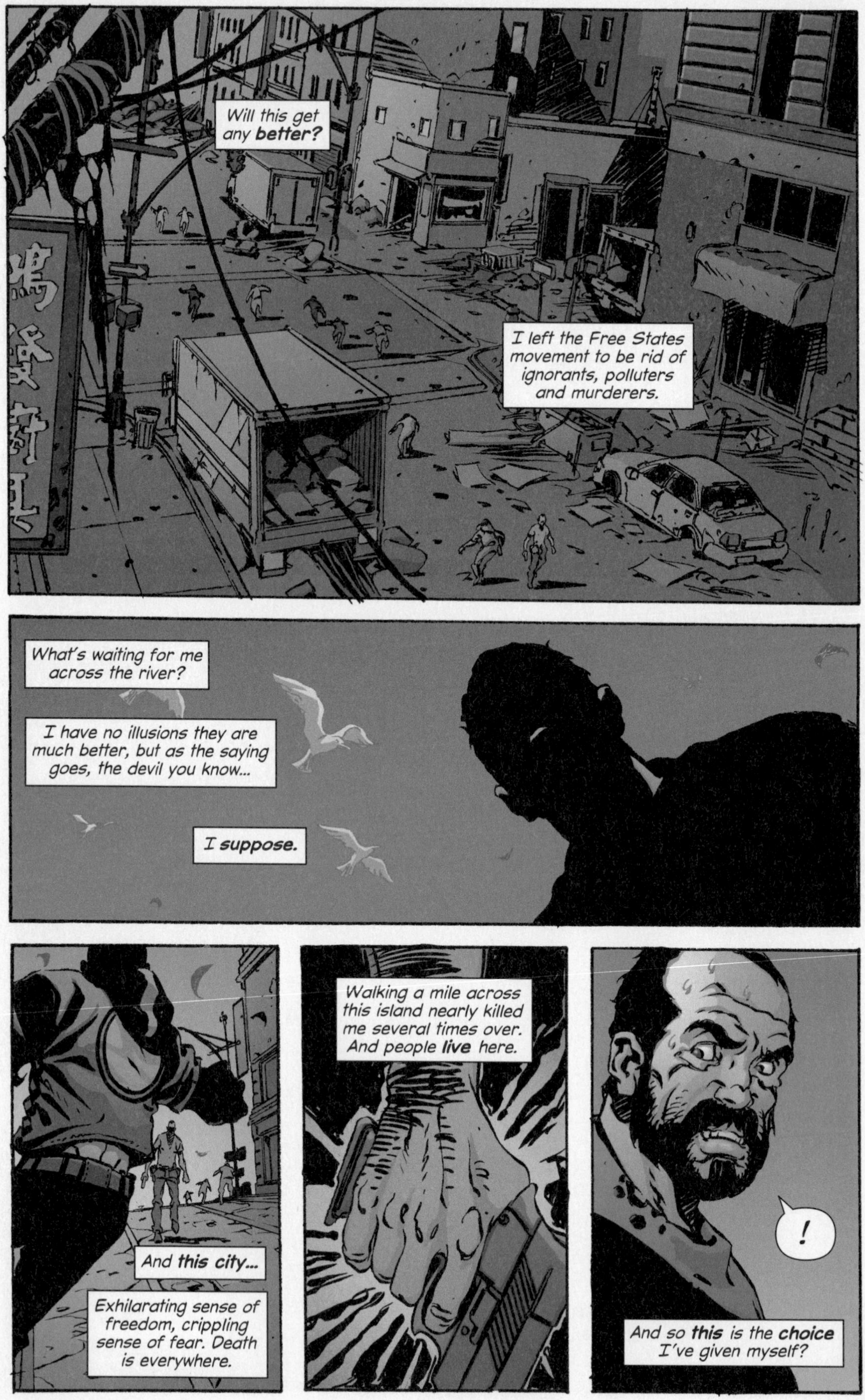
Will this get any **better?**
I left the Free States movement to be rid of ignorants, polluters and murderers.
What's waiting for me across the river?
I have no illusions they are much better, but as the saying goes, the devil you know...
I **suppose.**
And **this city...**
Exhilarating sense of freedom, crippling sense of fear. Death is everywhere.
Walking a mile across this island nearly killed me several times over. And people **live** here.
!
And so **this** is the **choice** I've given myself?

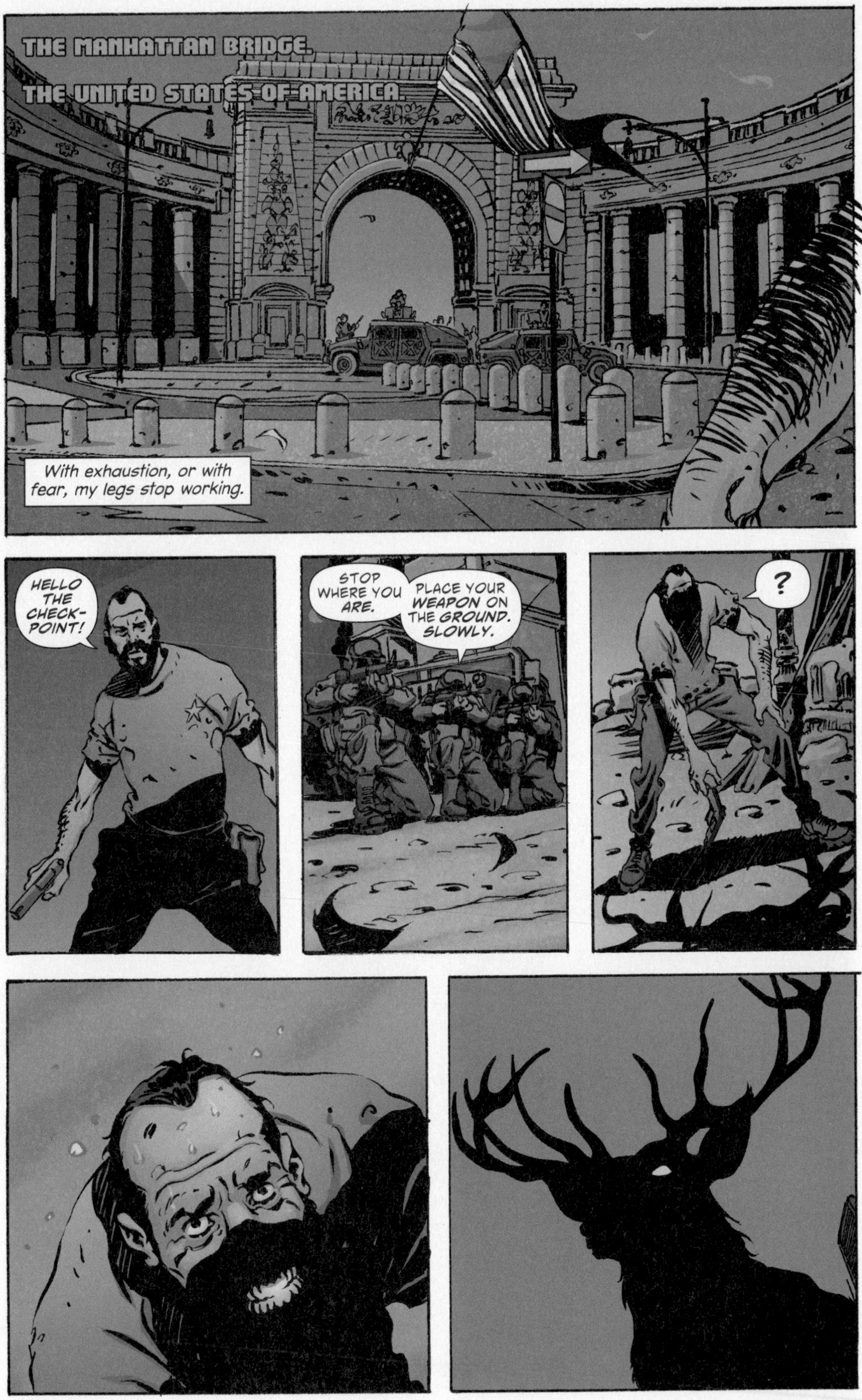
THE MANHATTAN BRIDGE.
THE UNITED STATES OF AMERICA.
With exhaustion, or with fear, my legs stop working.
HELLO THE CHECK-POINT!
STOP WHERE YOU ARE.
PLACE YOUR WEAPON ON THE GROUND. SLOWLY.
?

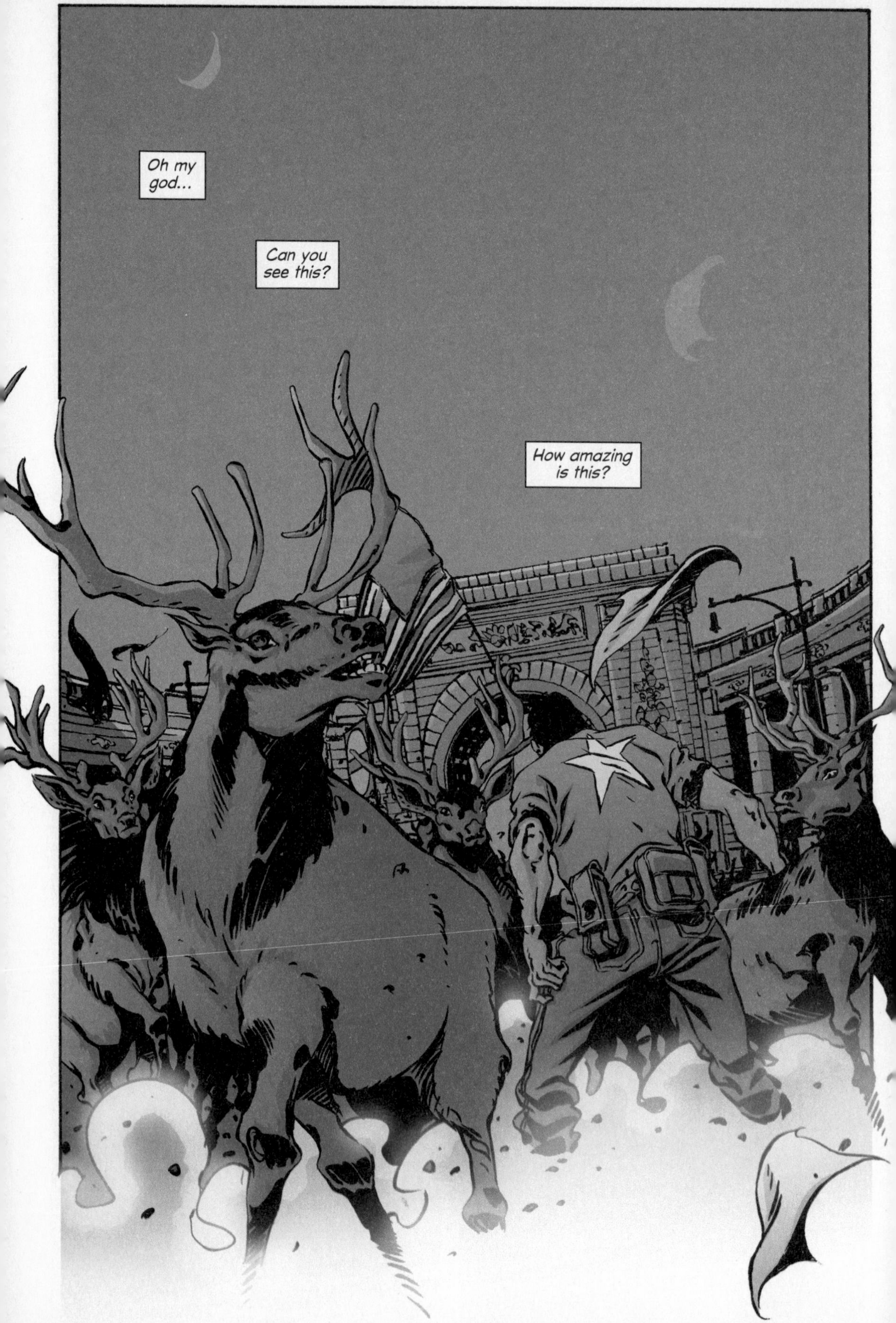
Oh my god...
Can you see this?
How amazing is this?

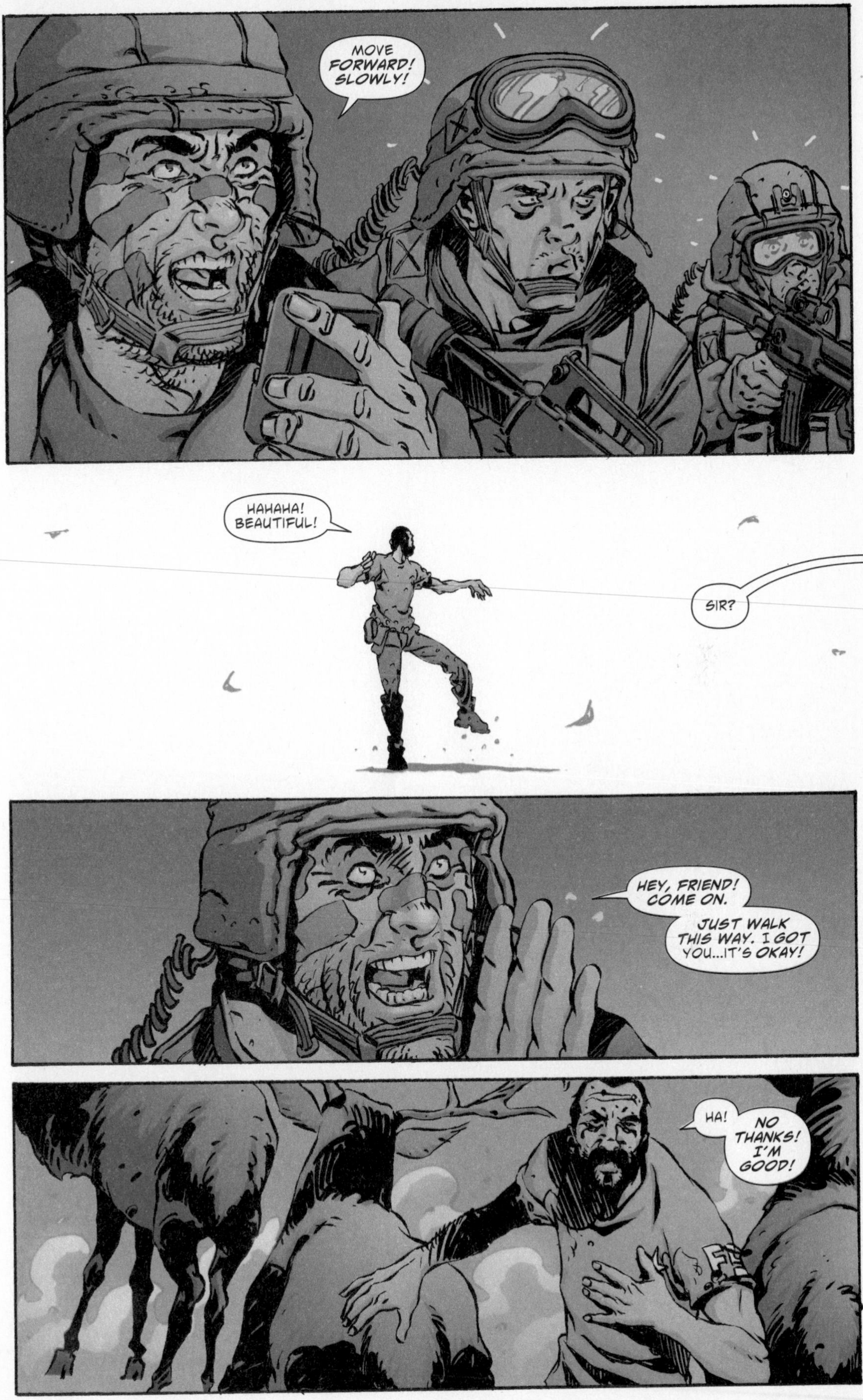
MOVE FORWARD! SLOWLY!
HAHAHA! BEAUTIFUL!
SIR?
HEY, FRIEND! COME ON.
JUST WALK THIS WAY. I GOT YOU...IT'S OKAY!
HA!
NO THANKS! I'M GOOD!

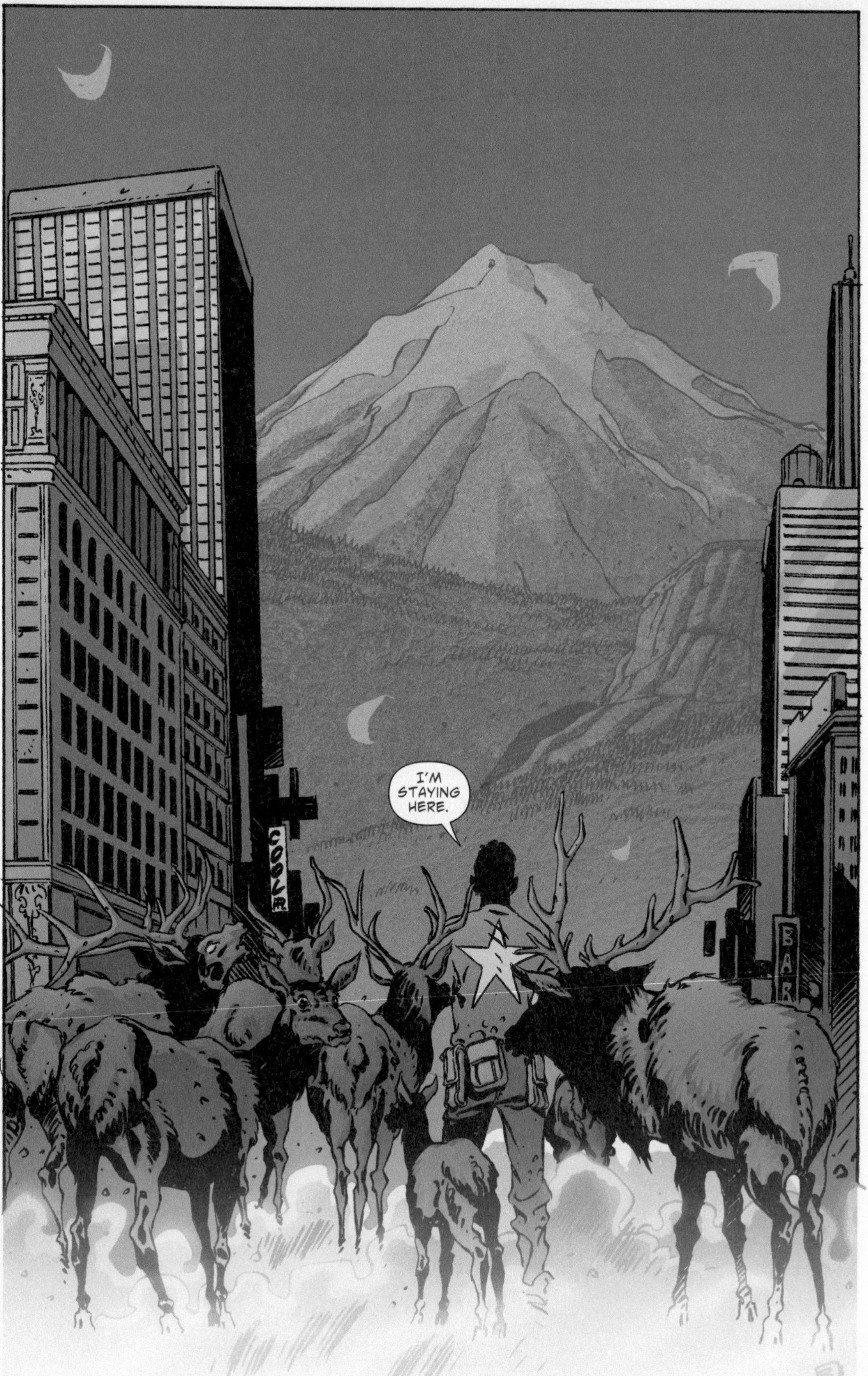
I'M STAYING HERE.
COOLER
BAR

END

FRIENDLY FIRE is an oxymoron. Trust me, there is no such thing.

This is a cute little term that can be used in polite company. Ask any soldier what it means and they'll tell you it means "fucked up." Man, let me tell you, that is EXACTLY what it means. When someone higher than you in the food chain screws the pooch and you get placed in a bad situation with no support, you won't be thinking in polite terms. After serving a tour in Afghanistan and another tour in Iraq I've seen first hand what happens when something goes horribly wrong and the policy makers start thinking "exit strategy."

When I first picked up an issue of DMZ I was mesmerized. I was thinking "FINALLY, someone out there gets it. At last, someone had the stones to put something on the market that resonated with me and the other grunts, something real and hard and ugly." DMZ is Black Hawk Down meets Black Flag, and nothing is sugar-coated. This is WAR and all bets are off.

Some friends of mine sent me a few early issues of DMZ while I was in Northern Iraq and Kurdistan but I'd missed a lot of the series. First thing I did when I got back stateside was get caught up—and low and behold I picked up with the Friendly Fire storyline. Man...breathtaking. Here we have a PFC Nobody from the Midwest whose options are revolution or jail and not much else. But hey, if—he joins up maybe he'll get to make something of himself, maybe learn a trade, and if he's really lucky—money for college.

Now put him in a bad situation, scratch that, a NIGHTMARE situation, with minimum support, poor leadership, and the ever-present reality of punishment for any and every action. Shit goes down and he's the one left holding the blame, "Game over, man." Set up for failure from Day One.

You don't think this goes down? Go to war and then disagree with me.

Now comes damage control. Those in charge have "careers" to think about, promotions to deserve, asses to cover. Coming forward and admitting the system is broken or that the military is hurting is not an option. There's too much at stake for those in charge. This is timeless, this is historic, and it could happen to anybody, military or not.

Declaring war will not be a declining trend. Defense spending is one of the only things keeping our economy alive. When DMZ happens I just hope I get to choose sides. And trust me ain't nothing going to be "friendly" about that.

SGT. JOHN G. FORD
U.S. ARMY

John G. Ford is a veteran of the Navy and the Army, having been to Afghanistan, South America and Iraq.

BOOK TWO

Justin Giampaoli is an award-winning writer at *Thirteen Minutes*, a contributing writer at *Comics Bulletin*, and created *Live From The DMZ*, the only site featuring extensive interviews and bonus content dedicated to Brian Wood's contemporary classic.

Brian, you play with allegory in the political discourse of DMZ. Trustwell is not entirely dissimilar to, say, Blackwater or Halliburton. How much of the story is inspired by the real world?

I think this one is rather "ripped from the headlines," which is saying something in a series that's ripped from the headlines. I'm trying to think back to when I was writing these issues and what was going on in the world. I know there was dirty stuff being done by Blackwater for sure, and that's absolutely where Trustwell came from. I'm fascinated by Blackwater...although now they rebranded as "Xe." You know how that's pronounced? "Zee." Love it. [Note: They've since rebranded yet again as "Academi," the largest of the U.S. State Department's three private security contractors.]

At the time, I remember getting some of the first negative feedback on some of the choices I made, specifically making the terrorist cell Muslim. This decision came out of a back-and-forth with Will [Dennis] because I'd originally made them white guys. He called me on it, essentially for making all bad guys in the book up to that point white, and perhaps I was playing it safe, or avoiding potentially tricky decisions. I agreed with his logic, that all the various ethnic groups who live in NYC didn't just vanish once the war started. They're still there, and just as apt to be up to no good as anyone else, and Trustwell was using them as a front. They're obvious scapegoats because of their religion and skin color. At the time, a lot of lefty types were loath to let this sort of depiction go by unremarked, and I got a lot of emails from a lot of people.

Trustwell is basically a front company for war profiteering. Is that your most politically perverse creation?

I don't know. Maybe Liberty News is? I always regret not doing more with Trustwell, but like so many things in DMZ, there was too much to say and too little space and time. I'm clearly not done with the subject though, since following DMZ, over in *The Missive* at Dark Horse, I created a similar company called "Blackbell." It's still on the brain.

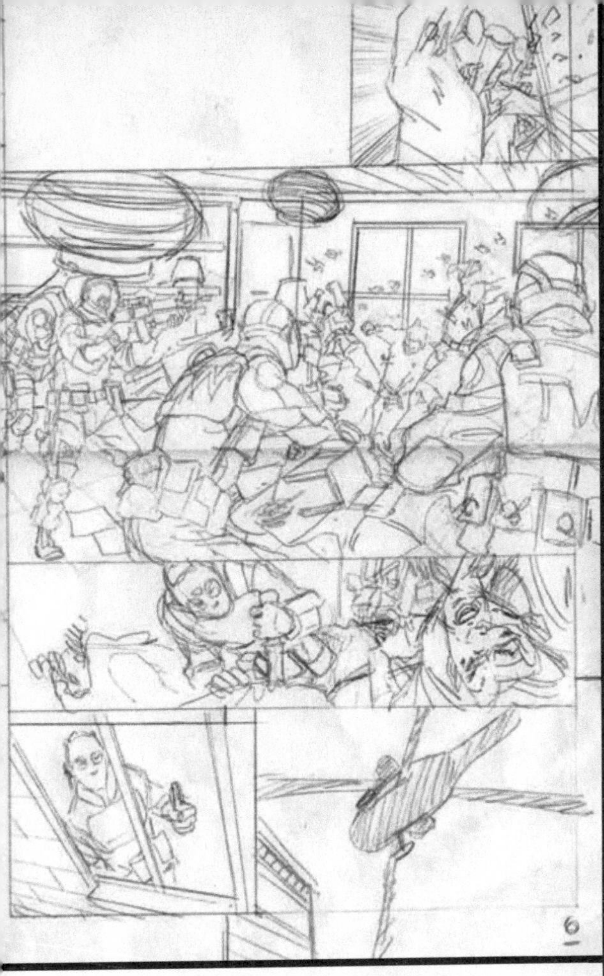
6

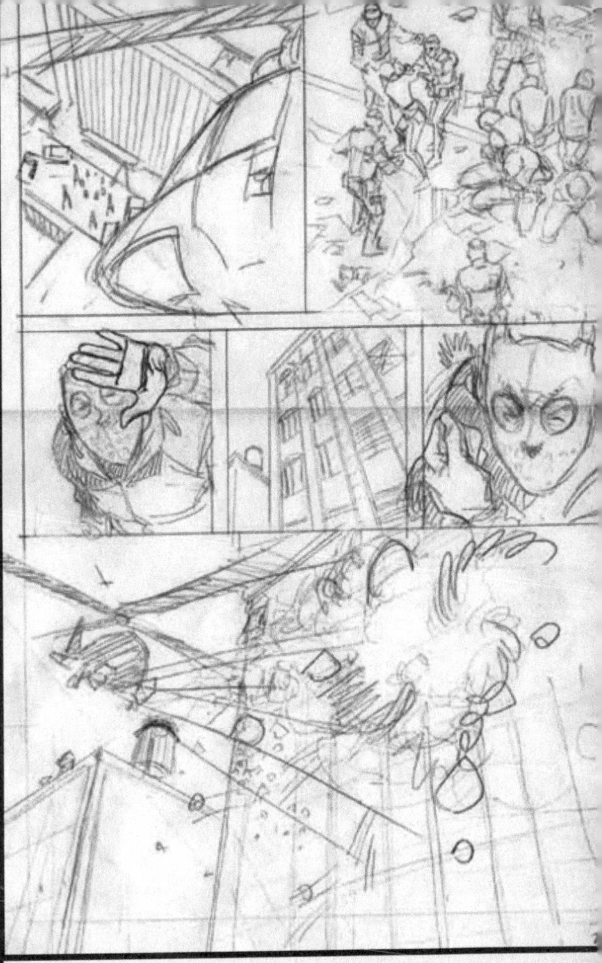

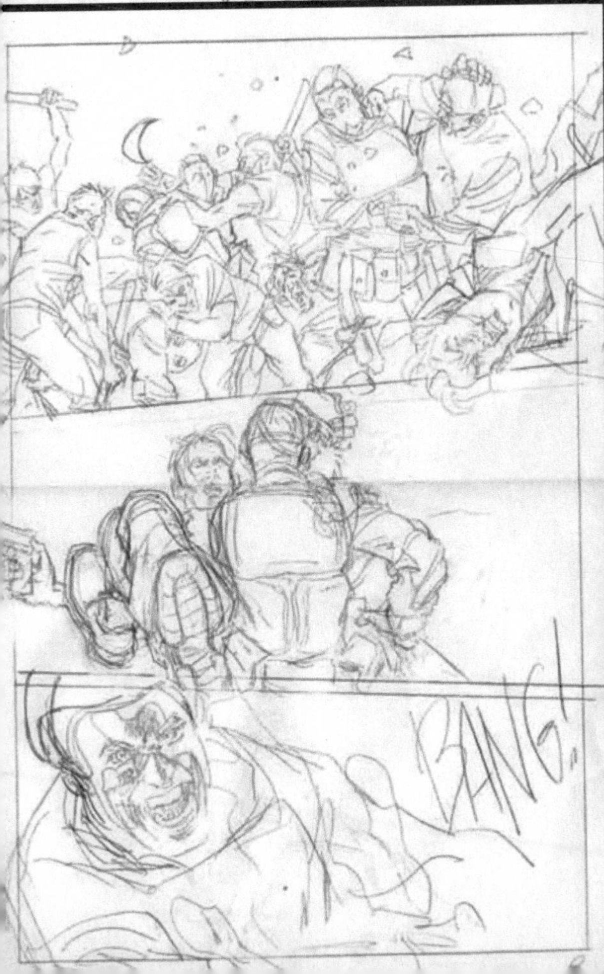
BANG!

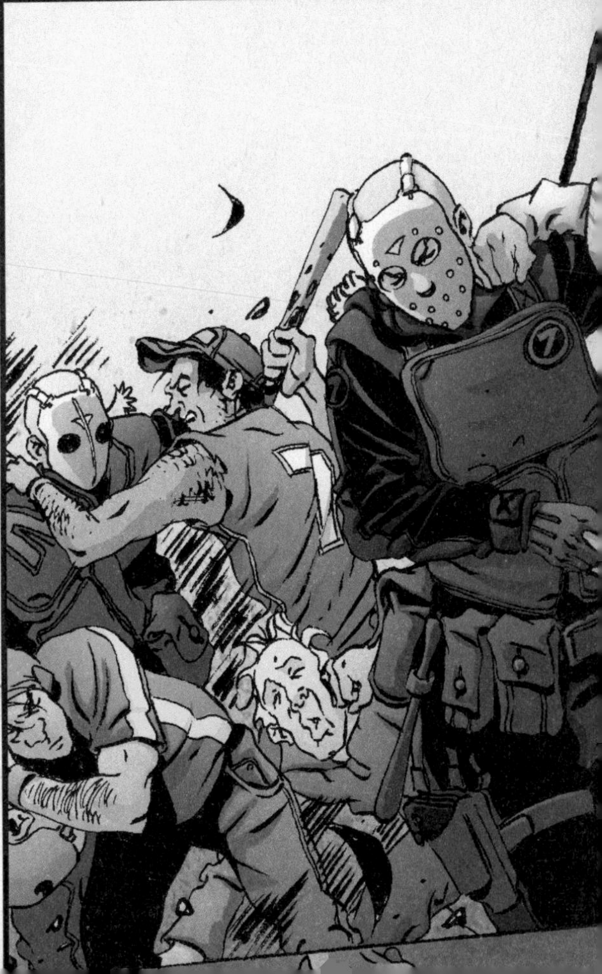

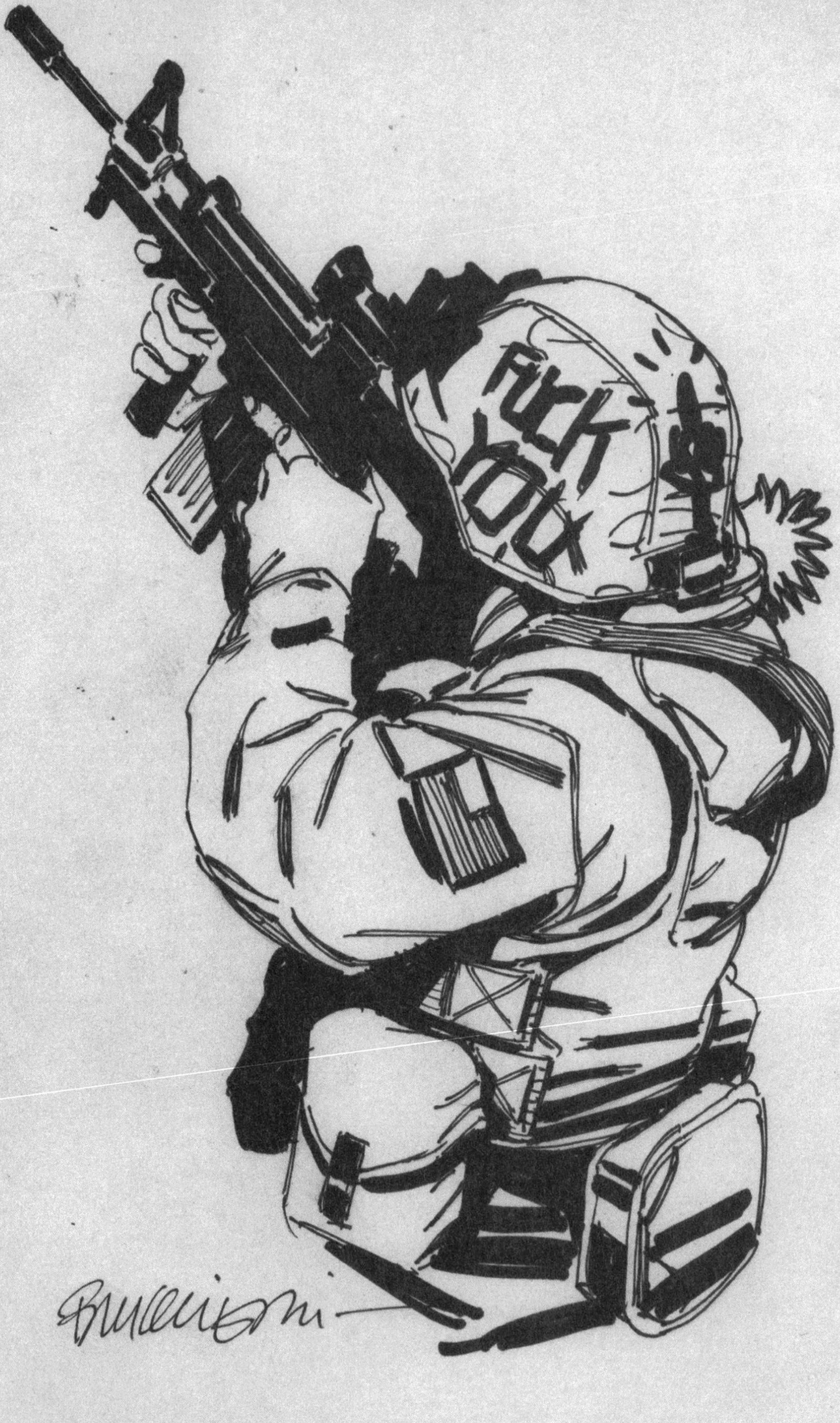
FUCK YOU

Matty witnesses a suicide bombing on his first day at Trustwell. I kept hearing that adage about putting your protagonists where they'd least like to be for the most dramatic tension. Are you conscious of these writing tools or is it truly an organic process?

Most things I do are gut actions. That one in particular was rather bluntly done, since, if I recall (I never have copies of the books handy!), the bombing took place at Ground Zero. It's easy to do what you describe in DMZ because the whole environment is a place most characters don't really want to be. I try not to follow those writer's rules, at least not consciously. A lot of those rules are just common sense and happen organically whether or not the writer even knows they exist.

The structure of a monthly comic is also not a natural one in the world of storytelling. DMZ is essentially a 1,550-page story and, on the face of it, that's fine. But it's serialized, and designed to accommodate a huge second act, a potentially infinite and flexible second act that needs to work for 72 issues, or 36 issues, or 24 issues, had we gotten cancelled. It's also a six-year ongoing and, as such, impossible to map out in detail and stick to religiously (for all but the most pious of writers). So, a lot of the rules or standards for writing don't always apply in comics. I try to think about that as I go.

That's interesting from a craft standpoint. At any given moment, you could run two or three more years or be cancelled. Are you always aware of that, creating parallel back-up plans for various scenarios?

I'm actually going through this right now, setting up a new creator-owned book. It's designed to be a 30-issue series, but the publisher, like all publishers (including DC), only commits to a certain amount of issues at first. Meaning, DC would not put it in writing that they'll publish 72 issues of this weird book called DMZ in case, by issue nine, it was really tanking. They cover their bets and do it a year at a time.

So, when you start, the prudent thing to do is not get your hopes up too high, but at the same time, it's not like I can structure my new book so it can end neatly at 12 or 24 issues. Not without screwing everything up. All you can really do is wrap it up the best you can in the time you have left, should the worst come to pass.

How does Matty lose himself and his identity while he's undercover at Trustwell?

The thing I keep reminding people, and reminded myself when writing, is that Matty is not a journalist. He never was. He signed up to be an intern in a cubicle somewhere. He was dropped into the DMZ with zero experience and zero training. He PLAYS at being a journalist, and perhaps he is one at times, for some fleeting moments. Maybe at the end of the series he can look back and say, yeah, that was the point where I became one for real. But, at the time of "Public Works"? Not even close. He's in way over his head, and probably lost himself right away.

The water torture scene is particularly disturbing. Did you research any of the Guantanamo Bay incidents, or is this all intuitive?

It was steeped in the culture of the time, in the news, and on people's lips. No research was really required for that, sadly. It was pointed out to me, well after the fact, that what I did was essentially recreate a similar scene from V FOR VENDETTA, which I can see, but it certainly wasn't deliberate.

Why is Amina an important character to the DMZ narrative?

Amina is a total tragedy. She's a living, breathing example of Matty fucking up. Not that she wouldn't have come to a tragic end if Matty hadn't decided to intervene, but whatever good came out of the "Public Works" story—and Matty did do some good in terms of exposing Trustwell, earning back some good will from Liberty News, paving the way for his extraordinary access in "Friendly Fire"—will forever be tainted by the fact that he messed up with Amina. I check back in with her a few times, and not until her final chapter does she get back on track with her life. What's all the more tragic is that Matty has no idea how he screwed her life up.

The FSA is ubiquitous. They pop up everywhere at the most interesting moments, even undercover at Trustwell. Is everyone underestimating the FSA and their reach?

The FSA was always more of a concept than a formal army, and while they did accomplish a lot as an army, they never had much of a leadership or stated goals. So, they're able to be everywhere...the FSA can exist in the individual, and that's a scary concept. At the start of the series, a lot of readers were eager to draw the lines and find comparisons, and the FSA were tagged as the "good guys," the ones that I, the writer, was politically in line with, the lefties, the justice-seekers. But, from the get-go, I never put them in that position. They're horrible, just like the US shock troops are horrible, just like Liberty News and Trustwell are horrible, just like Parco and Matty did all these horrible things. There's no good guy/bad guy divide to be found here. Not a simple one, anyway.

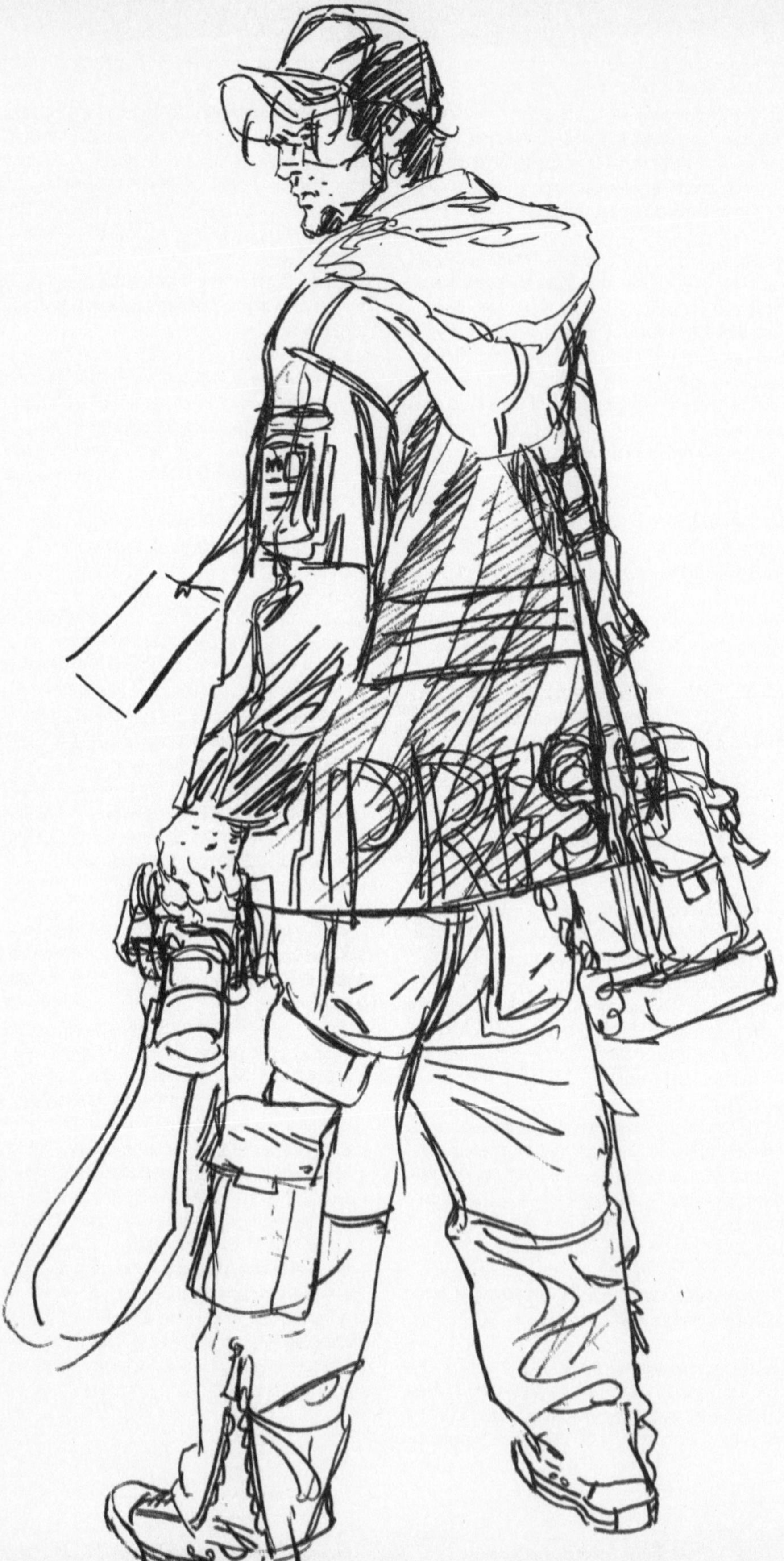

Sure, everyone has the capacity to do "bad" under the right set of stressors. The FSA is scary because of the idea of asymmetrical warfare you play with. How do you fight the enemy if they can't be identified, if they're among you? Point of view is also a factor. We used very similar hit-and-run guerrilla tactics to win the Revolutionary War. It might have been Howard Zinn who made the point that from the perspective of the British, an event like the Boston Tea Party wasn't some birth-of-a-nation incident, but a terrorist act by a local insurgent cell.

I'm sure it's beyond scary and frustrating for the people who try to fight asymmetry with conventional tactics. I remember a really awkward phase of the Iraq invasion where Donald Rumsfeld was complaining about how all these insurgents do unfair things, like not wearing uniforms, or identifying themselves, and hiding. The implication being that he wished they would wear bright colors and line up in the street so they could be shot more easily.

Is DMZ a title like NORTHLANDERS that required large amounts of research?

I'd say it was DMZ that started me on my research kick, my desire to write books that require that level of work on my part to get the details right. I read a ton of books for DMZ, a good chunk of the plethora that sprang up dealing with both Iraq wars, as well as some earlier ones on Bosnia and the Soviets in Afghanistan. With DMZ and NORTHLANDERS, I front-loaded my brain to the point where I literally could not bear to read another word, and that research has carried me through.

I might be at the end of that, though. I might have reached my limit. I wrote this crime thriller pitch that's set in Italy during the time of Leonardo da Vinci, and I knew I couldn't handle it. The Church, the Medici, the Masons...all in one story, all requiring more research than I could bear to take on right now. It's not just a lot of work, but it's a lot of pressure to anticipate, since people will actively look for mistakes.

Nathan Fox is an artist I was immediately impressed by. He captures the danger and unpredictability of the environment, but also the warmth of the people. How did this collaboration happen?

Nathan and I started talking a long time ago, but I honestly can't remember how it started. I know for a brief moment I talked to him about drawing *Local* (how's that for a "what if"?!), and like a lot of artists I work with, we spent years talking until the right thing came up. I love his art, and I really enjoy working with him. It depresses me every time I offer him a book and he's busy doing something else.

How did you arrive at the plan to have different artists depict differing accounts of the Day 204 Massacre? Was this purely artistic or a more functional conceit?

We, meaning me and Vertigo editorial, are always looking for opportunities to be creative within the pretty uncreative world of the DC Comics monthly grind. There's such a system in place, a deeply entrenched way of doing things, and breaking away from that is pretty difficult. But we always try, and this was a really successful example. Riccardo was originally contracted to do 10 issues a year, that's what he wanted, what he was comfortable with, which is why DMZ has a lot of guest artists. At the time "Friendly Fire" started, he was due to take that short break, so I decided to find a way we could use that to the advantage of the story, to not just have fill-in artists in the middle of an arc. This way, Riccardo could have a hand in each issue, even if only for a couple pages, and the *Rashomon*-style narrative could be reinforced by the guests.

It's all part of the arrangement. I'm sure Riccardo wishes he could have drawn every page of DMZ, but I know he also wants to be a human being with a life and see his girlfriend and his friends. DMZ is not an easy book to draw, and I think the fact that he takes two issues off out of every 12 is pretty sane. But, there are also times when he doesn't take that break. As the series rolled to an end, he drew #62 to #72, which is 11 in a row, and there was another time, around "Hearts & Minds" to "MIA," where he worked straight through for more than a year. So, it's a little flexible. There were other times when the reason was different, like with "Collective Punishment," which was designed to allow Riccardo to take a much needed break from DMZ and draw some NORTHLANDERS.

In 72 issues and six years, the book never shipped late that I recall. That's gotta be some kind of record.

I'm sure there were times it missed by a week, but most people don't consider it "late" unless it skips a whole month. We've been pretty consistent.

One of my favorite bits of imagery is the U.S. Army general that looks suspiciously like Abraham Lincoln, overtly emphasizing the Civil War motif.

See, Justin, this is one of those times you have me running to look at a copy of the trade, because what you just described I have zero recollection of, and didn't notice the first time around! I'll have to hand that one to Riccardo...I never give him much direction for these sorts of nameless "suit" characters. Generally, I say something like "Army officer, white guy, pretty typical," and then Riccardo just turns it on. Only in civil wars, I guess, do military commanders have chin beards.

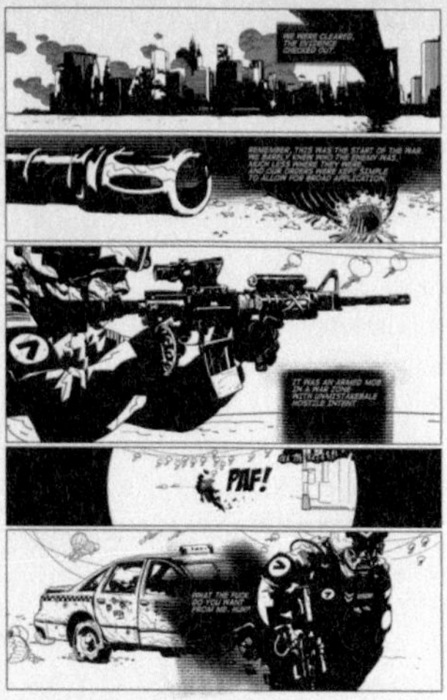
WE WERE CLEARED. THE EVIDENCE CHECKED OUT.
REMEMBER, THIS WAS THE START OF THE WAR. WE BARELY KNEW WHO THE ENEMY WAS. MUCH LESS WHERE THEY WERE. AND OUR ORDERS WERE KEPT SIMPLE TO ALLOW FOR BROAD APPLICATION.
IT WAS AN ARMED MOB IN A WAR ZONE WITH UNMISTAKEABLE HOSTILE INTENT.
PAF!
WHAT THE FUCK DO YOU WANT FROM ME, HUH?

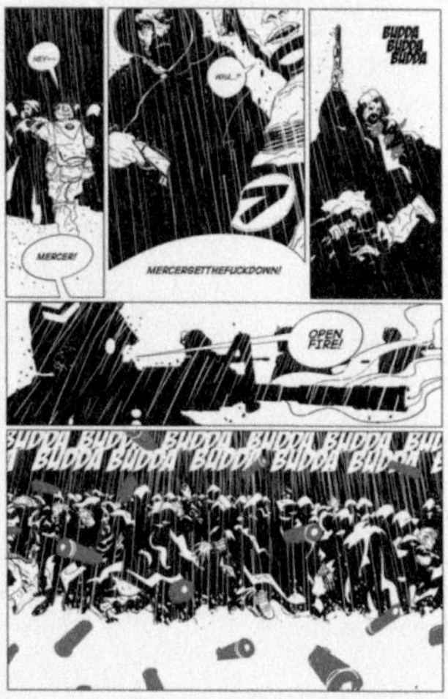
HEY—
MERCER!
MERCERSETTHEFUCKDOWN!
BUDDA BUDDA BUDDA
OPEN FIRE!
BUDDA BUDDA BUDDA BUDDA BUDDA BUDDA BUDDA BUDDA

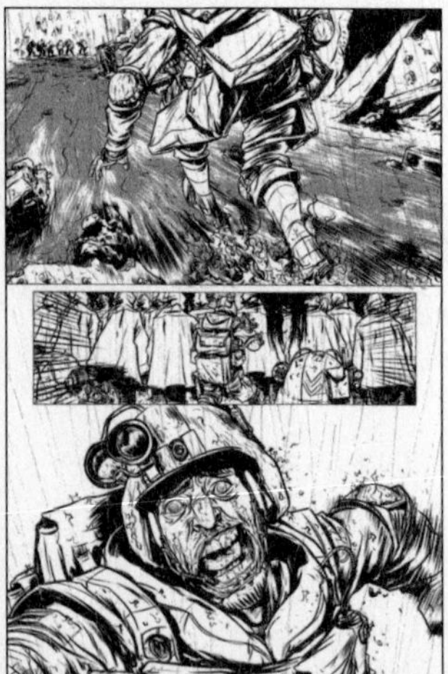

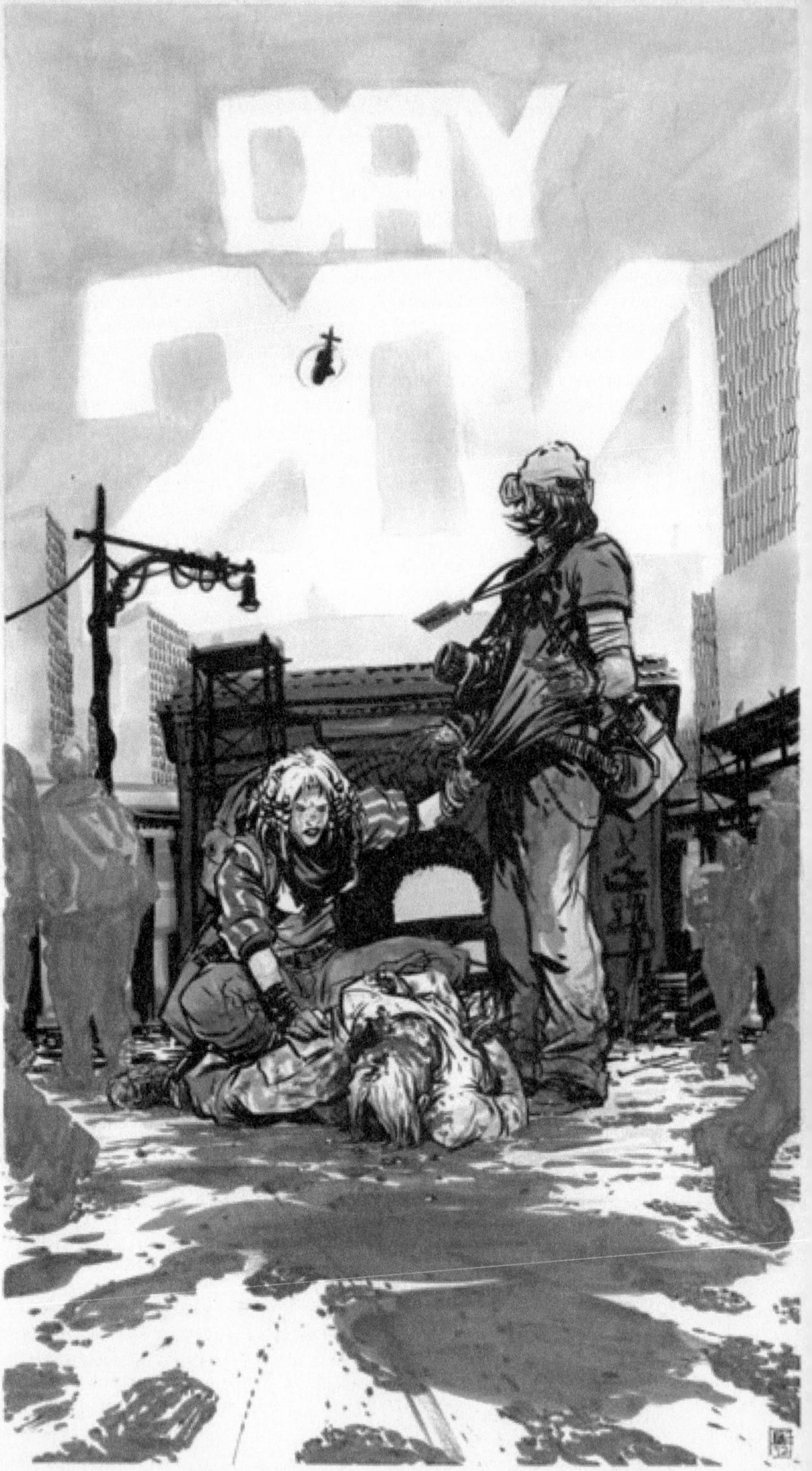
DAY

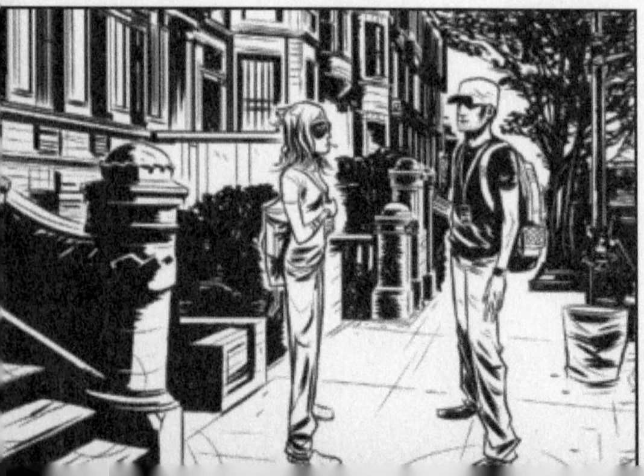

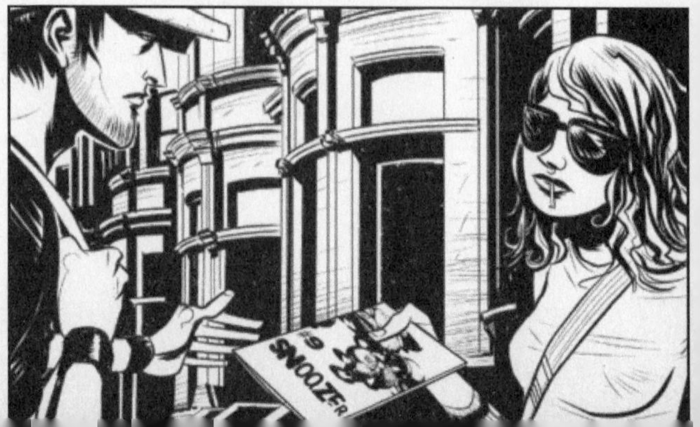

Kristian Donaldson provides Zee's account of Day 204. Kristian drew Zee a lot during the course of the series. Was that pairing intentional?

I'm sure it was in my subconscious. Kristian is actually our #1 guest artist, in terms of sheer number of pages drawn. I love the way he draws the city. I mean, I love the way he draws everything, but he never shies away from the backgrounds.

Jeromy Cox's palette runs these huge color swings, from dark greens and dull earth tones, to vibrant reds and oranges. What's your interaction with Jeromy like?

It's pretty non-existent, and I don't mean that in a bad way. I consider Jeromy to be like Riccardo, in that he's an original member of the band who's stuck with this book of mine since day one, turning in the work like a pro for six straight years. But the nature of the monthly comics system means that he and I don't really interact—I don't get to proof colors at DC (I wish I did!), or really give him notes other than what I write into the script. Every so often he does email me for clarification on something, so that's our chance to talk. I consider it a sign of things humming along nicely when I DON'T have to be in constant contact with a collaborator. I like to place all my trust in them, and vice versa, and then we stay out of each other's way and get the job done.

You never say what job Matty's dad holds, but he works for Liberty News, right? He's an executive there, or some liaison with the military? He's clearly complicit in the whole relationship.

Yeah, that's been fuzzy. Early on, I had his dad as an executive at Liberty, but it didn't matter what it was specifically. All that mattered was that he'd be in a position to secure a job for his son. As the series grew over time, I evolved him into less of a binary guy with much more nuance, like perhaps he was starting to see both sides just like Matty was. At some point, he's stripped of his job, and then is able to use whatever leverage he still possesses to smooth a path for his son. It's a little tragic, I suppose, but speaking as the writer, he only ever existed to do those things for Matty.

Who is the zinester girl who publishes Snoozer #9? She seems too specific to be purely fictional.

Snoozer is one of the characters I wish I had the space to develop more. Snoozer is pure fiction, and she first appeared in #12. She surfaces much later, incognito, as the voice of Radio Free DMZ, but that's a little detail that's more for my own personal entertainment than anything else, in that it was never revealed. Snoozer and Radio Free DMZ were both ideas that came along too late in the

series to be properly utilized. She's yet another regret. It was too big an idea too late in the game.

It seems like you enjoy taking familiar NYC landmarks and turning them on their head. Is that a fair statement?

Well, it's a couple things. First, it's just fun to do that. Second, it's an expectation of the series. Third, these landmarks are what people who don't live here, or haven't spent much time in the city, know of NYC. For most of the audience, a generic street means nothing to someone halfway around the world, but the Empire State Building or the Flatiron does. They're visual elements that ground the story in real life, and making that emotional connection is important.

I was thinking of the shots of JFK being used as an entry point to war, or the jarring panels with the Statue of Liberty riddled with bullet holes and missing part of the torch. Did you ever incorporate horror elements into DMZ?

I wouldn't say so. Horror is a genre I don't feel I have a good grip on. I'd say the same thing about comedy. I remember a few years back, Brian Azzarello was really pushing me to do a run on HELLBLAZER, he really thought that was a good career move for me to make. I spent weeks trying to wrap my mind around it, to figure out what I would do with that book, and in the end, I just drew a blank. Not my thing. Since NORTHLANDERS, I feel like I have a slightly better capacity for it. There were a few NORTHLANDERS stories that grazed the edges of the horror genre, and I went on to do something pretty overtly horror in SUPERNATURAL.

What's the ultimate message of "Friendly Fire"?

This arc had a very specific genesis. I think I was gearing up to start the election story and, one Monday morning, my editor Will Dennis and I were swapping emails about a *60 Minutes* episode we'd seen the previous night on the Haditha killings in Iraq. The soldiers who were involved were being interviewed by one of the anchors, and it was appalling how they were being treated. The hatred was plainly visible on the anchor's face...it was clear he found these soldiers to be the lowest of the low, and his questions were skewed that way. It made me really uncomfortable to watch, and Will agreed.

That was the basic idea, the notion that a low-level soldier is given some impossible set of instructions—impossible in the sense that the conditions on the ground are something that no soldier could predict or be trained for—and once they screw up, all the blame is loaded onto this one person, while no one up the chain of command takes any responsibility. We changed the DMZ story on the fly, at the last minute, one of very few times in the series we let something happening in the real world direct us. "Friendly Fire" is a high point for me, and is the volume I've found most often cited as a reader favorite.

I've been dying to discuss the DJ Random Fire issue with Nathan Fox. This was a quintessential moment in DMZ that shows how somewhere in the middle of this conflict, there's a vibrant underground culture happening, even as war attempts to derail society and crumble the city. It's like a B-side deep cut about a new culture being forged in fire. It opens with that Jared K. Fletcher free-floating rhyme that pounds like bass against your chest. I'm losing it here. I can't even come up with a question.

Well, I should start by talking about the arc as a whole, or rather, this run of single-issue stories. It's not really an arc at all—it only got "The Hidden War" tag when we needed a title to put on the trade. As I recall, Riccardo was running a little behind schedule and, like I said, he was only contracted for something like 10 issues out of every 12. So, he was due his break and this gave us a chance to have a little fun with some guest artists and some one-shots.

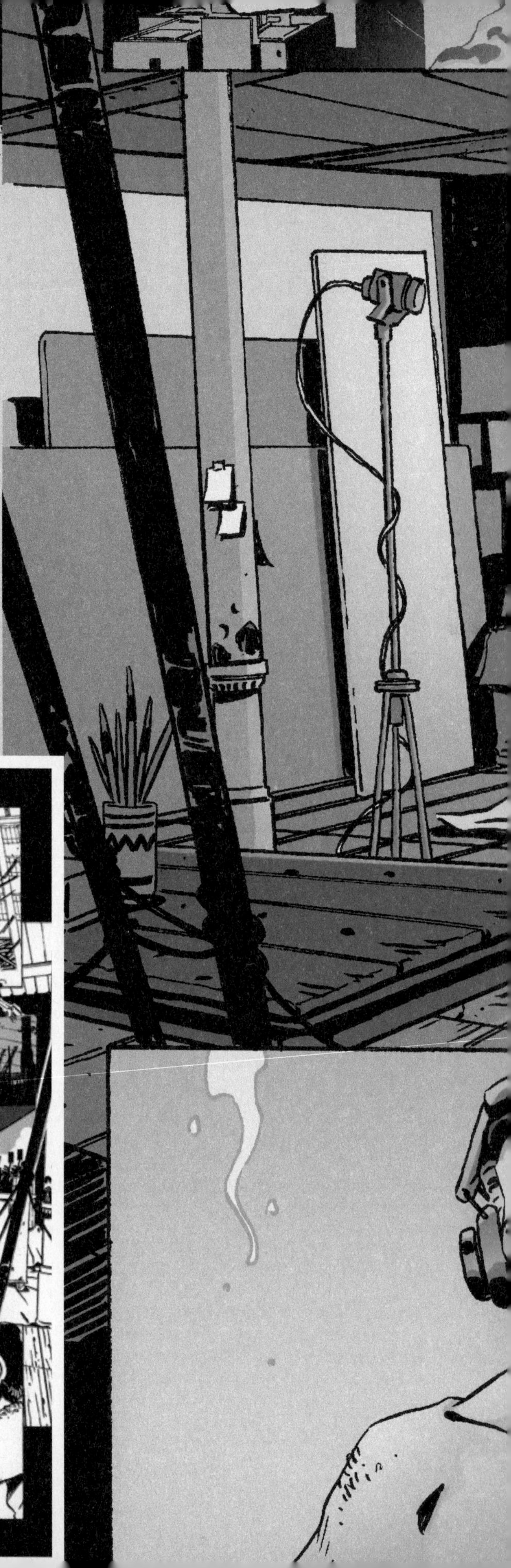

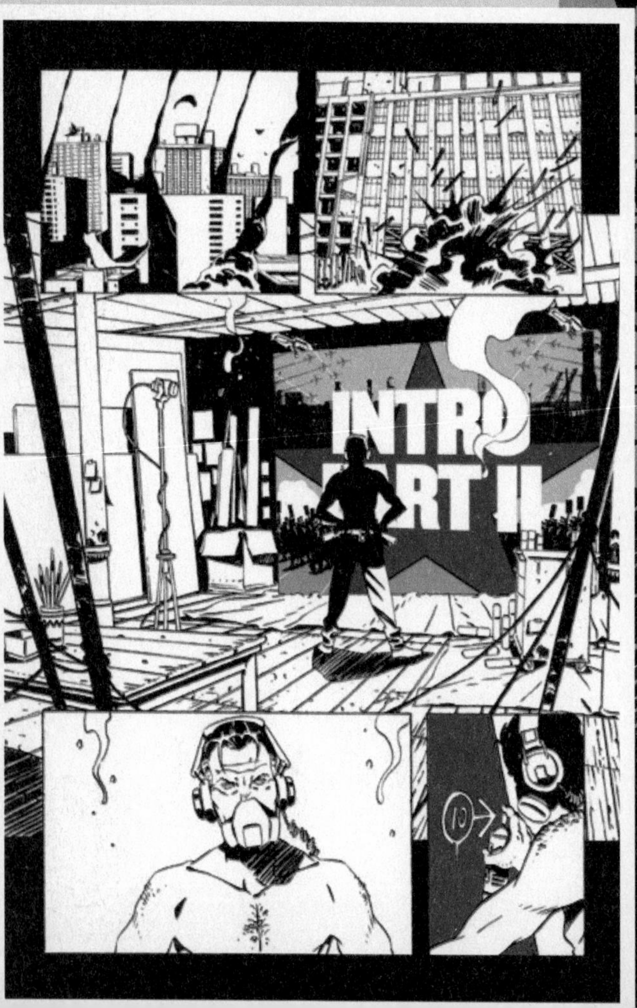
INTRO

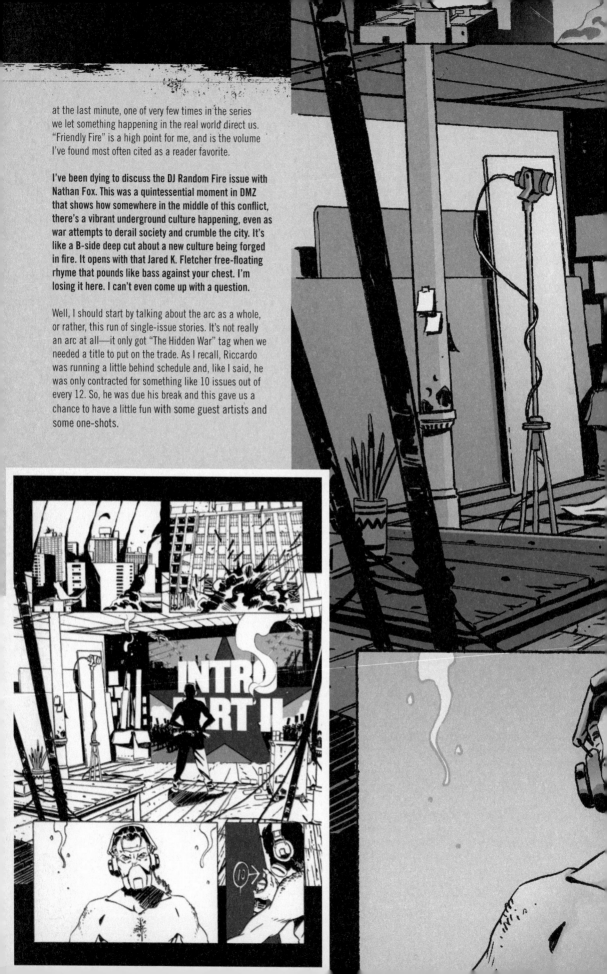

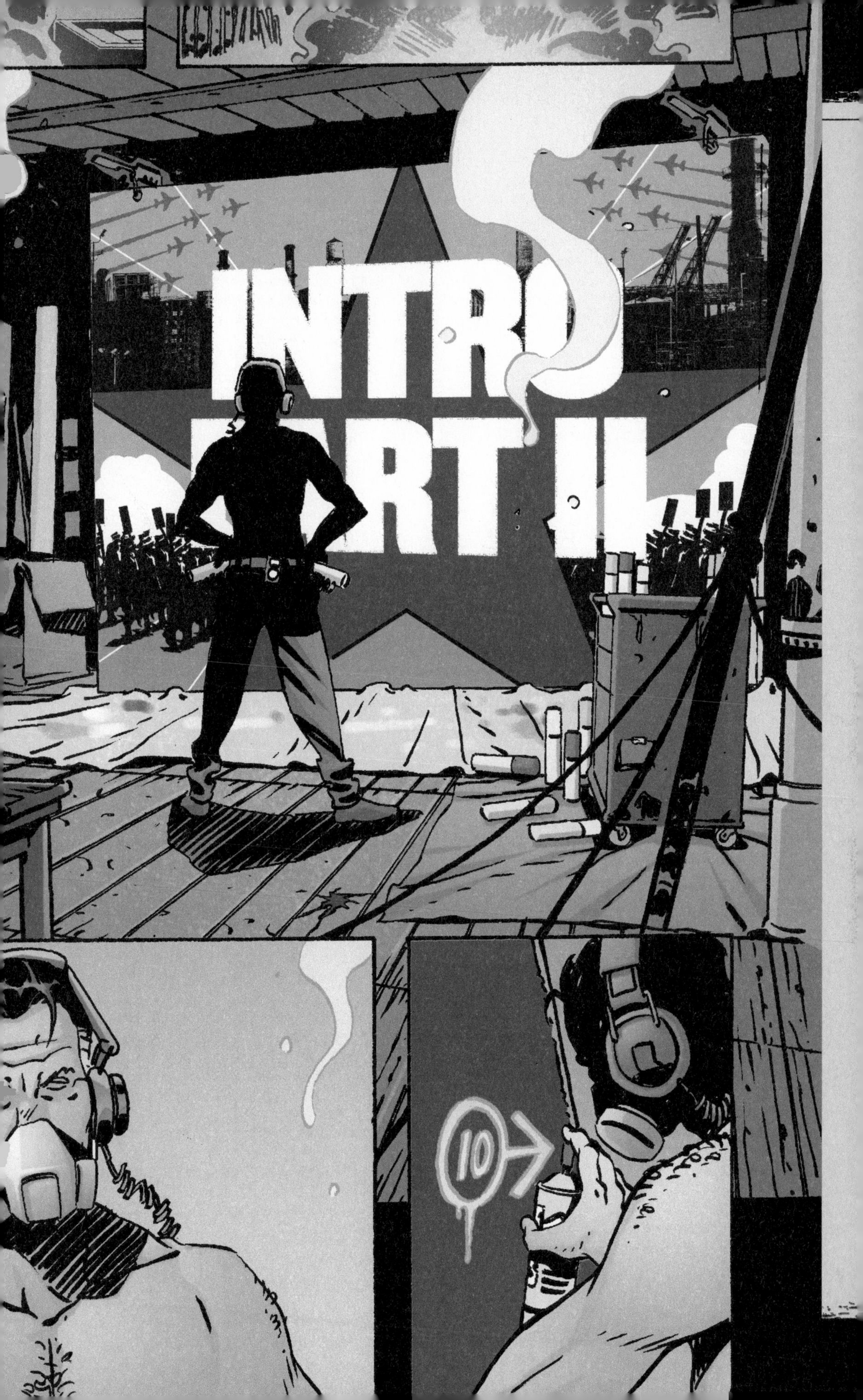

INTRO
ART II
10

One of the constant struggles I had with DMZ was how to fit all of the story elements into the container. In the end, it proved impossible, but the function of these periodic one-shots was to give Matty a break and explore what else is happening in the DMZ. Typically, to a hell of a lot of angry and frustrated comments from readers who don't see these one-shots as integral stories, or as part of DMZ, but as obstacles in the way of them knowing what's going on with Matty. But, now I'm really getting away from the issue.

The DJ Random Fire story came out of a single image in #12, the guide to the city, something I've tapped a few times for characters I made and sorta forgot about. The whole city in the DMZ is the underground, but I wanted to do something with a more traditional, cultural underground, the classic underground club, and a kid who just wants to rock out. I also like hitting that note of exploitation, the outsider DJ who wants to capitalize on the "realness" of the war zone to hype his record. I wish I had done more with that, actually.

Music is one of your deep interests, so it's interesting that it found its way into DMZ. Is *Anthem* with Ryan Kelly going to scratch the itch to do more with the intersection of music and comics?

Anthem will allow me to talk about music with comics, yeah. To what extent the form of music and the form of comics will intersect, I don't really know. I've seen skeptics suggest that music can't work in comics, and while I don't agree with such a blanket statement, I can see what they're saying...which is that music SO RARELY works in comics, but I think I'm taking the right approach. It's not about a change in form per se, it's just about writing a terrific story, a comic about music as opposed to a "music comic," if that makes any sense. I think that DMZ story was some kind of subconscious dry run at the idea.

The Decade Later tag is really iconic, was that your design or one of the artists?

It's mine. I consciously wanted something that wasn't so "graffiti" in style, since I don't feel I can claim enough authenticity to pull that off, it's just not me. Poor Jared Fletcher mistook something in the script and created a really complex bit of graffiti lettering and dropped it into the art, and then I had to ask him to take it out. I felt horrible. So, Decade's art looks like my art, which may sound egotistical, but it was really the only thing I felt I could pull off authentically and "own."

What part of the city or culture does Decade Later represent?

He's old-school '70's, basically. He's a mixture of the old class of NYC street artists and Ramones-era rockers from the outer boroughs. It's me kind of making something up by combining two things I think are cool, from an era I wish I lived in. I remember catching hell from my editor for making him look too much like Henry Rollins on the cover, so I had to change that.

What I like about Decade Later is that he's the one guy *creating*, on a mass scale at times, while all of this destruction is happening around him. His very existence seems anathema to the war.

He's not a protest artist, though. It's very personal for him and he's never seeking an audience (the gallery scene in #12 doesn't count). I've been labeled, or have had DMZ labeled, as a piece of anti-war "protest," and while that's flattering on one level, I've also found that categorization is always more about the person using the label than the work itself. Which is fine, but the artist—me, in the case of DMZ—can hold a different viewpoint.

Does the FSA Commander have a name? I'm jumping ahead, but is this the same guy we meet later in "Free States Rising"?

Yeah. I never gave him a name, even in the scripts, other than "Commander." He's in a lot of arcs, from #5, to "Body of a Journalist," and all the way up to "Free States," which is an origin of sorts.

Obviously DMZ (the book) is a post-9/11 piece of art, but you start to suggest that DMZ (the place) is also post-racial. What do you mean by that?

I mean that, in a place that's shot to shit, race is probably the last thing on people's minds. Regardless of past events, or dark times in New York's history, we (residents) have been known to pull it together in moments of crisis... like 9/11, like the most recent blackout, etc. Perhaps that would be amplified in the DMZ. It's "us against the world," that sort of thing. We gotta stick together as New Yorkers.

Danijel Žeželj is a remarkable talent. What did he bring to this rendition of Wilson?

I think he defined Wilson as more than the kooky neighbor I had written him as up until this point. Once I decided I wanted to write his origin, I needed to get serious and detailed about just who and what he was. Danijel really brought what I wrote to life, to use a corny phrase. But it's true—he took the more "out there" look that Riccardo gave him and scaled it back in time to when Wilson was "normal" and made it make sense. His heavy art was perfect for the mood, and he can draw the hell out of the city. I've been a huge fan of his for forever. It's an honor any time I get to write something for him.

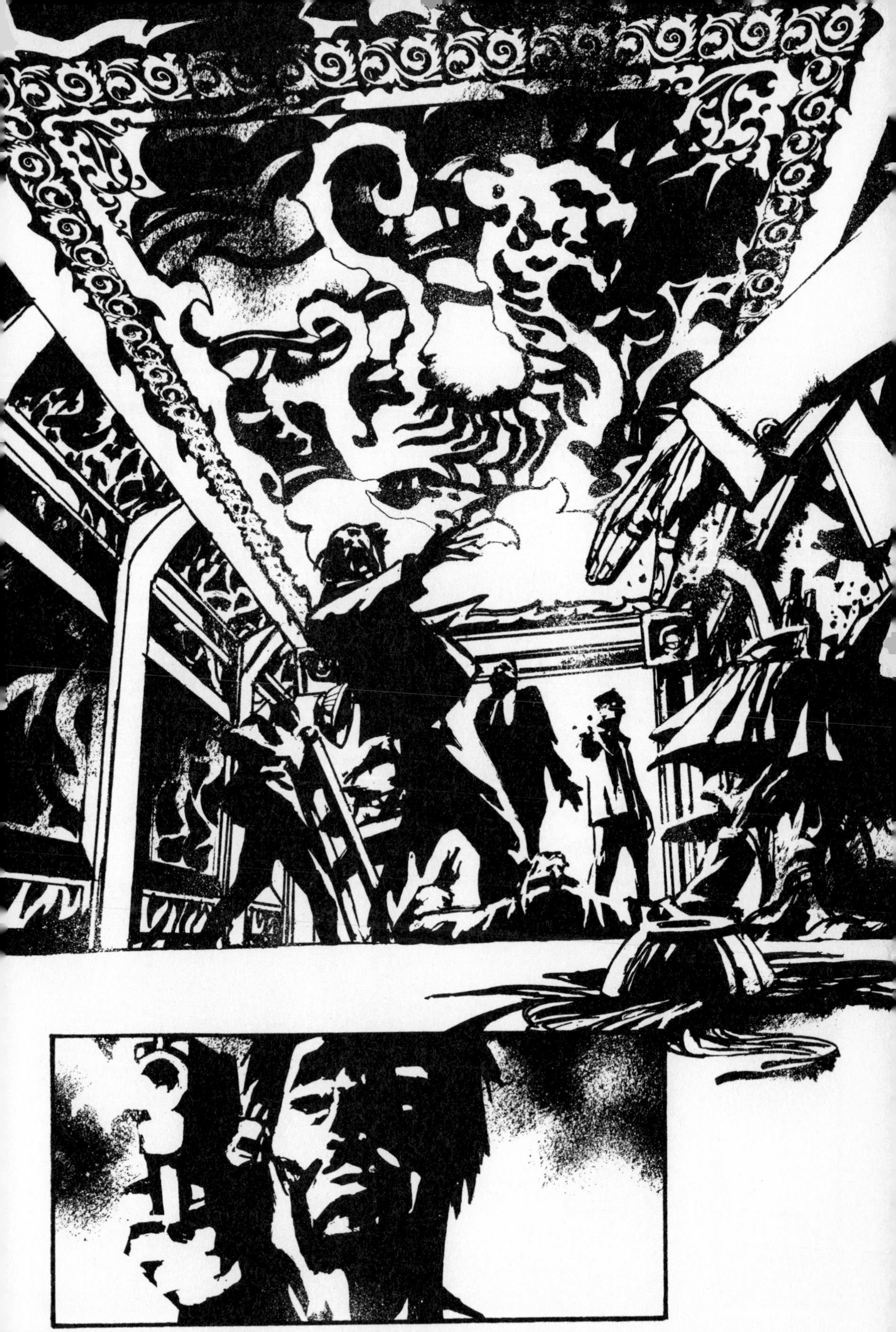

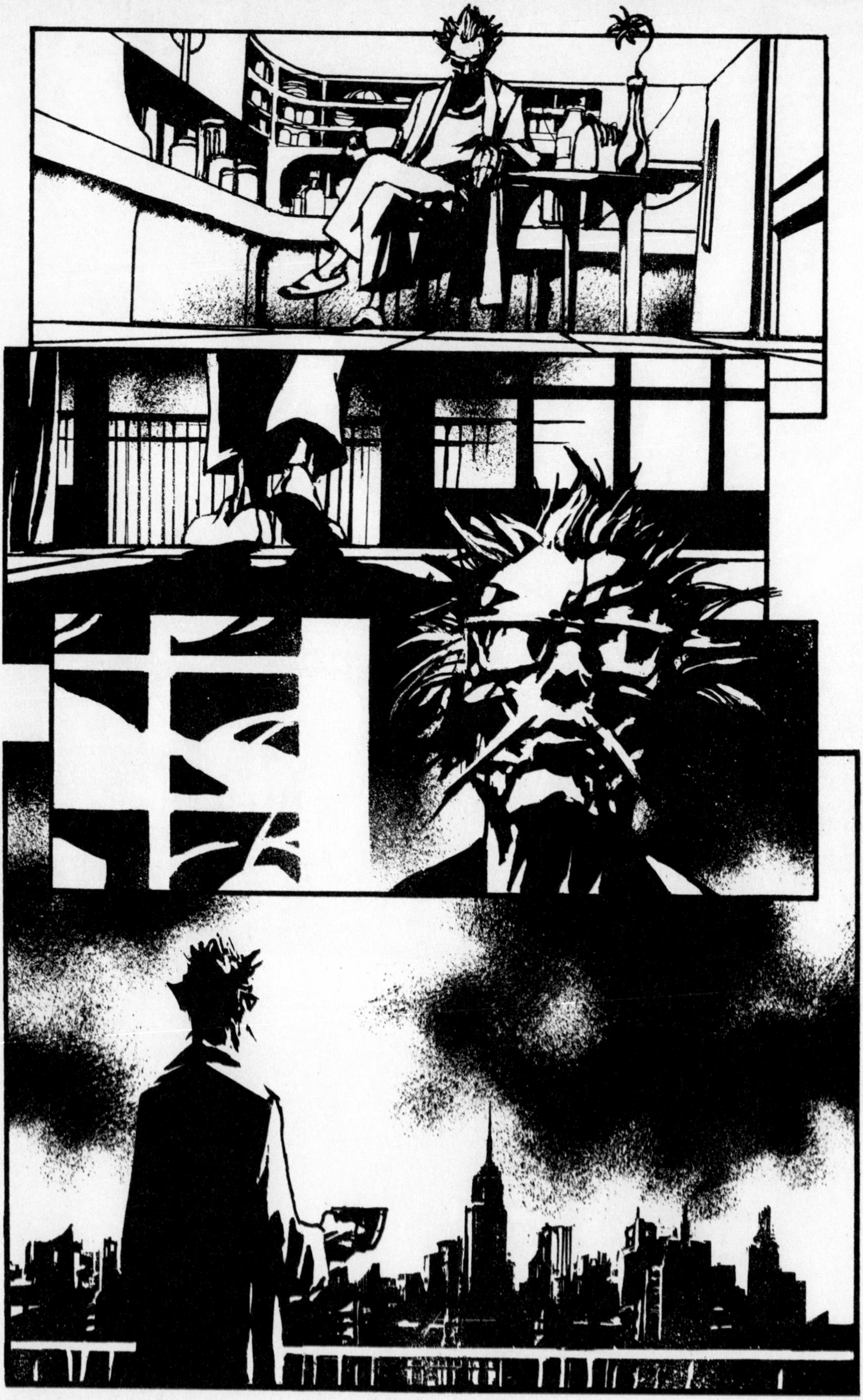

There's something really charming about how Wilson tries to keep Chinatown so insular. What drives that approach?

I think it's just as simple a thing as identity, as "home." It's where he lives, so he wants to protect it. Locking the doors seems like the most logical way to go about that, and for almost the entire war it works really well. It's a bit racist, and a bit xenophobic, but as you say, it's also charming.

The FSA is essentially seceding from the Union, but it's like Wilson wants to temporarily secede Chinatown from New York, and just hope the war will pass him by. The tragedy of Wilson is that he mistakes his ability to do just that.

He wants to secede for the purposes of protection, yeah. I remember writing a line of dialogue for Wilson that I kinda had to live down, something about how when the war was over he would own the city. That was a line I couldn't really ignore, so I had to reconcile that somehow.

Is Kelly Connolly the female Matthew Roth?

I think Kelly is the female Matty Roth that Matty Roth wishes he could be. Perhaps to others, she's the Matty Roth that doesn't fuck up.

Kelly's "Viking Funeral" was a huge wake-up call. It had a real sense of consequence about it, signaling that you were willing to kill off characters.

I think Viktor was the first, but yeah, no one's really safe in the series. Many people I know are expecting to see Matty die.

The imagery toward the end of the Soames issue is more symbolic than a typical Brian Wood script. It almost plays like "Mon Dernier Jour Avec Toi," a very ethereal issue of *Demo: Volume 01* you did with Becky [Cloonan]. How did this issue come about?

I realize in retrospect that I was pushing it with that issue, writing something that would've been more appropriate in a NORTHLANDERS one-shot (like "The Hunt"), and I think that most readers didn't care for it. I wanted to explain Soames' motivation, but in a really roundabout and subtle way, to suggest that perhaps he isn't so clear on his own motivations, that maybe it's partially in his head. The visions—the deer, the field of bones, etc.—definitely suggest an outdoorsman troubled by the destruction happening around him, but also calls into question how sound he is mentally. It's a story idea I wanted to try again, and to a degree I did with parts of "M.I.A."—one man navigating the city. Soames remains one of the characters I wish I had more time with.

End Transmission

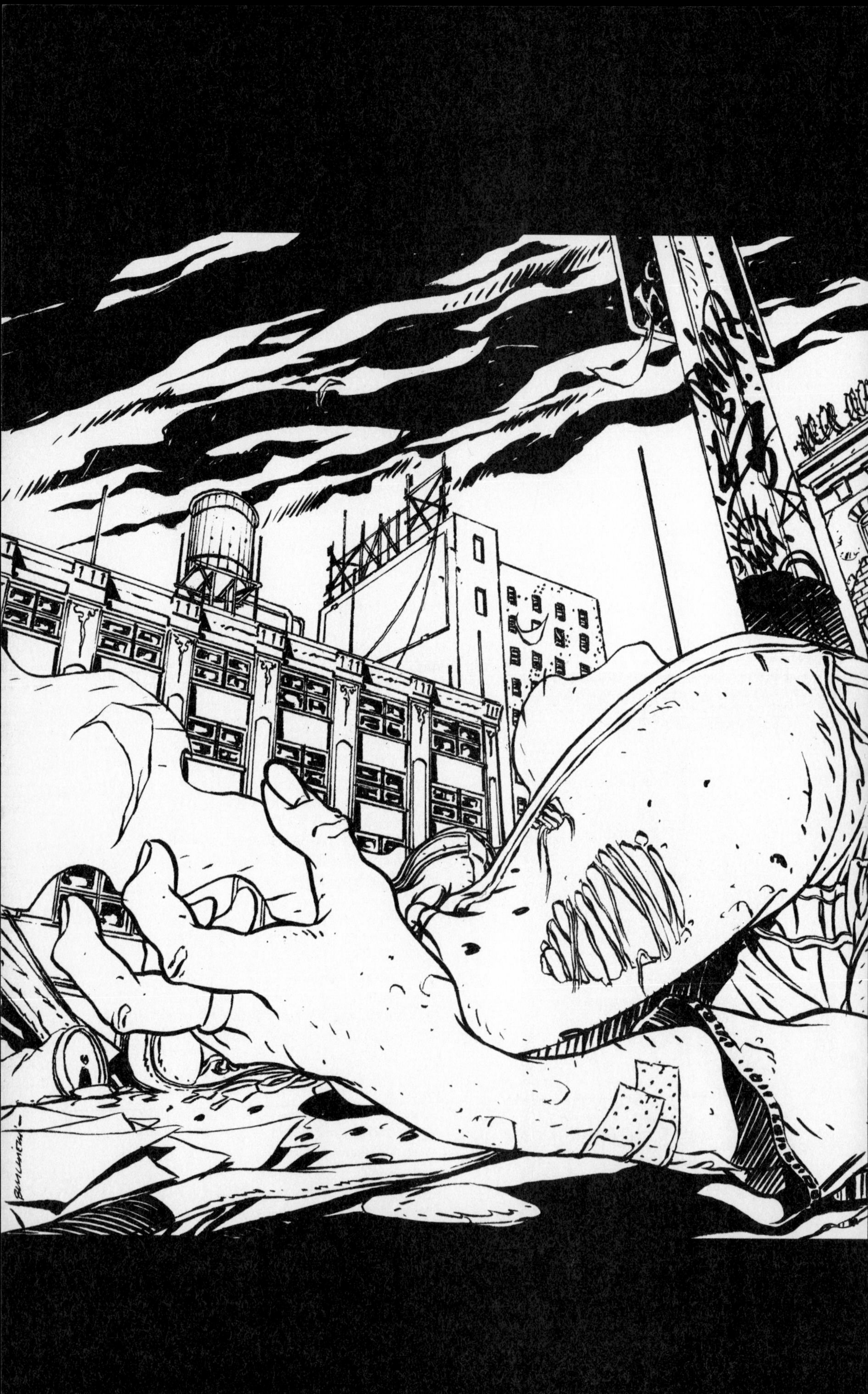

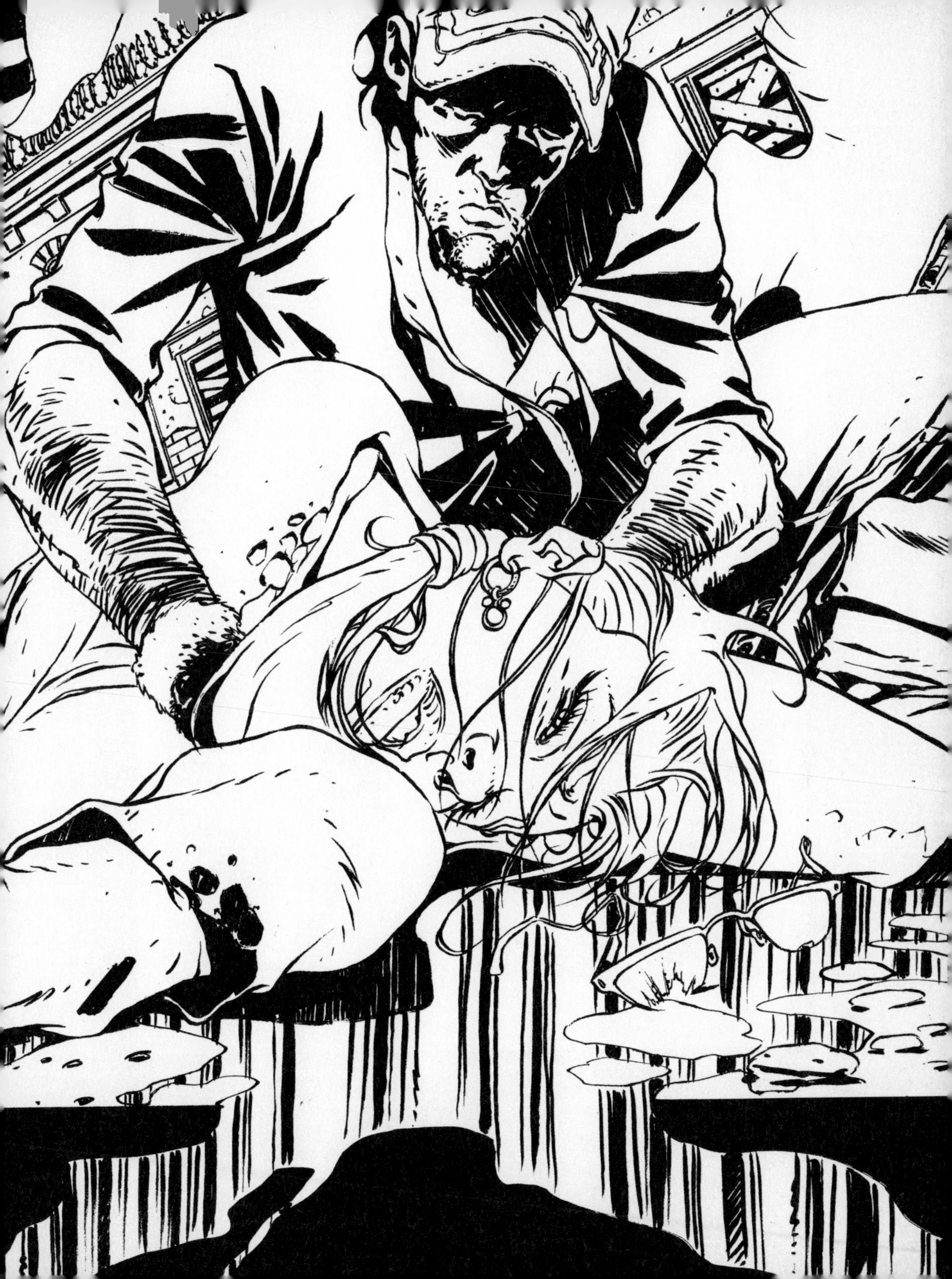

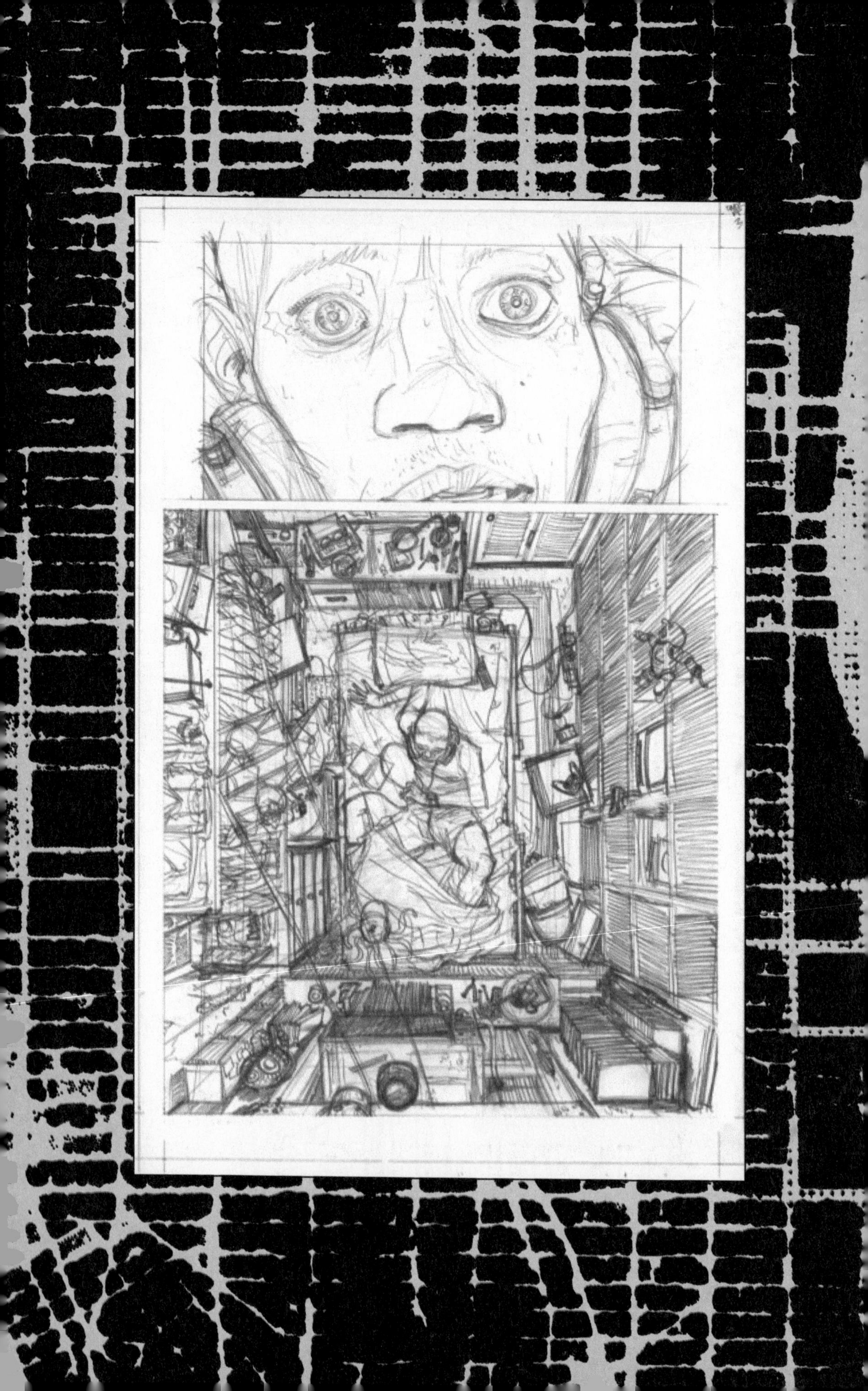

NATHAN FOX INTERVIEW

Justin Giampaoli is an award-winning writer at *Thirteen Minutes*, a contributing writer at *Comics Bulletin*, and created *Live From The DMZ*, the only site featuring extensive interviews and bonus content dedicated to Brian Wood's contemporary classic.

~~~~~~
~~~~~~~~~~~~~~~~~~~~~~~~~~~~~~~~~~~~~

Nathan, the first time I saw your work was in *Pigeons from Hell*. I've been a fan ever since. I loved the subversive nature of *Dark Reign: Zodiac*, and *Flourescent Black* was great dystopian fiction. What's it like jumping in and out of a series like DMZ where you're not the exclusive artist?

Thanks, man. Really kind words. Flattered and glad you dug it all. Getting a chance to be a part of DMZ repeatedly was an honor. I was a fan of the series from issue one and was inspired by Brian and Riccardo's work. So, to get more than one chance to collaborate and contribute was an amazing opportunity. I'm sad to see it end, but excited for what's to come, and whatever Brian has up his sleeve next.

How did your collaboration with Brian come about, and what's he like to work with?

I don't recall if it was Brian or Will that called about the "Friendly Fire" arc, but when I found out what the project was, I was beyond excited. Before DMZ, I did cover #4 for Brian's FIGHT FOR TOMORROW series. I hoped it might be a strong portfolio piece for more work in the future. I was a fan of DMZ, had my fanboy moment getting to work with Brian, but once we got started, I took it pretty seriously. Working with Brian was smooth and painless. He's a pretty quiet, passionate guy, and a pleasure to work with. He gave me great notes and direction and then just backed off and let me run with it. We went through one or two versions of PFC Stevens, but by the time I nailed it down we were pretty confident on where it was headed.

Why does your particular style of art work well in the DMZ?

I think I was aware of wanting to comment on what was going on in the world at the time. I was trying to put some of that into the series, and I felt confident it could be done working with Brian's characters and his scripts. I'm not from New York originally, but lived there from 2000 to 2005, so I also felt that I had enough of a connection with the city that I could pay due respect to its inhabitants, to the characters, and the story we were telling. Living in NYC wasn't the smoothest of existences—I was happily struggling and paying some heavy dues along the way. It was rough, but worth every minute. No regrets, I'm looking forward to moving back someday...

Your first work on DMZ was the flashback scenes for PFC Stevens during "Friendly Fire." What can you tell us about that?

Creatively, it was a chance to comment on a lot of things, especially the Haditha Massacre in Iraq. I usually end up acting most characters out or trying to get into character somehow. I had my own feelings about the war in Iraq and tried to imagine what it would be like if I joined the military knowing I had no place soldiering in war. Stevens was a shell of a man, only beginning to grow into, and fill the shoes of, what a man like that should be. You could just see it in his eyes from reading the script. He didn't even know who HE was, let alone have any place being in the military fighting for someone else's ideas. It was a poor decision that could have the potential to do real harm, to himself and others, if he wasn't careful.

In Brian's script, Stevens tried to be careful and responsible, to do the things he was supposed to do—the "right" things, but in the end his caution and the collective delirium of his unit's actions would inevitably decide his fate. He didn't join in the massacre—and because of that he became the weakest link, then an outspoken threat—so in the end, he'd be forced to take the fall. I enjoyed destroying him from the inside out. I hated doing it because I got pretty attached to him, but in the end I learned a lot from the challenge of my first real character design. Brian's writing set it all up. I just got the opportunity to bring it to life. I've been fortunate to work with great writers, starting with him.

Issue #27 with DJ Random Fire is absolutely one of my favorite singles. Walk us through your memories of this one.

Thanks. Random Fire was a trip. I remember reading the script and turning to the intro page, almost a full splash of Random Fire in his room. Looking down at him from above, waking up after a nightmare or something. The book opened with a stolen cop car chase, two guys in gas masks. It ends badly and SNAP!—we're thrust into a-day-in-the-life of Random Fire for the rest of the book. There's a rival DJ with an armed security detail, a club full of people trying to forget the war that's literally raging outside the front door (and eventually inside), and a sexy saboteur who uses DJ Random Fire as a pawn. As soon as I got the script, I was on the edge of my seat to work on the next page, then the next, and the next. The pace of that script was really challenging and the process was a great learning experience.

You have the distinction of illustrating the final issue with Wilson, a fan-favorite character. Were you cognizant of that task. Did you alter your approach considering it was the last Wilson story?

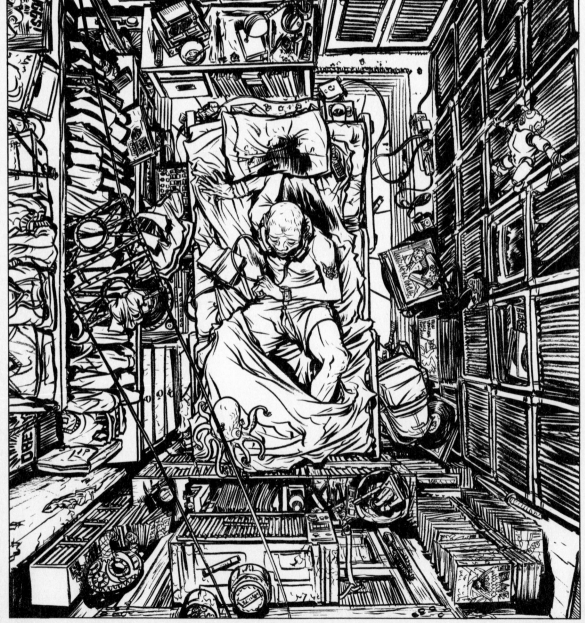

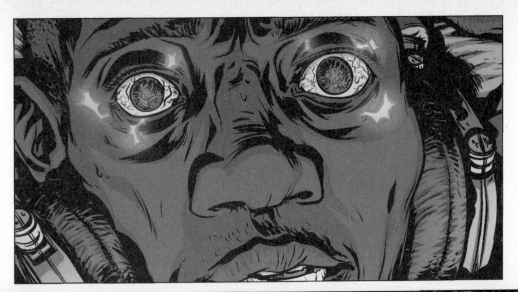

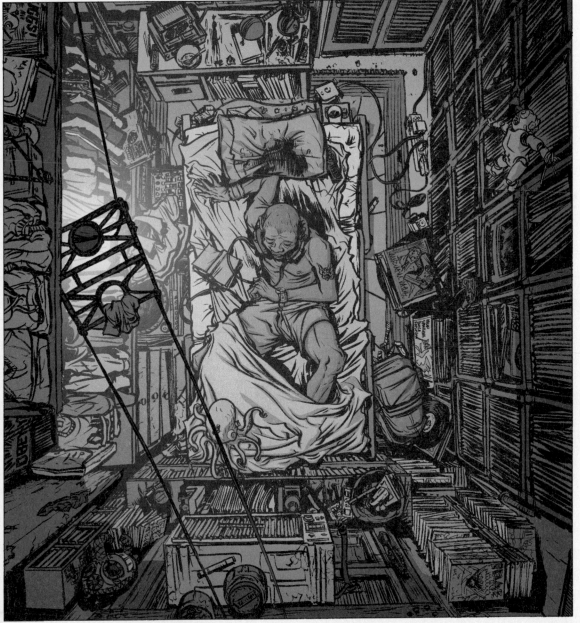

Definitely. Wilson was easily one of my own "fan favorites" too, and I really wanted to up my game on this issue. Before I started working on it, I got a chance to shoot reference for the issue on a visit back to N.Y.C. I walked Chinatown, found the streets and restaurants I wanted to shoot for the issue, and started to plot it all out in my head. It was hard, as sappy as it may sound, to close the curtain on Wilson, and something I'm still not used to—killing off or leaving characters, especially the ones you get attached to. As a reader, it's hard enough to see a favorite go, but illustrating it was a weird and funky honor, a blast to work on, but a bummer nonetheless.

I have to admit that it took a bit longer to finish the book because of it. Knowing that the end was coming, I wanted to send him off in style. I was hoping to amp up the flashbacks and nostalgia, and was working on some ink washes at the time, and that style fit Wilson's younger, freer days like a glove. That shot of him on the roof with the automatic rifle and cigarette did it for me. Reading the script for the first time, that scene really struck a chord, along with the bowing scene on the street toward the end— it hooked me immediately. Hopefully, I did him justice and am looking forward to revisiting the series in these new editions.

That image of young Wilson sitting in his Eames chair stuck with me. The end result was this washed out water-color effect that lent some aesthetic nostalgia. How did you and colorist Jeromy Cox create that sequence?

Brian laid out the scene and flashbacks script-wise, but Jeromy and I were left to tackle its execution. We'd talked about what I was thinking, how to approach it in ink wash, and he was totally up for it, so we just ran with it. It felt not so much like "life flashing before your eyes" before you think you're going to die, but more like an epic "looking back on better days." With Wilson, being the anchor and supporting cast member that he was, it felt like it really needed some power, some silkiness and flow as he looked back. I wanted to portray it in a way that would harken back to that sense of nostalgia.

Brian knew what he was doing, and in the DMZ, Wilson made no illusions that the end would always come. He couldn't run from it, and in the end Wilson chose to be, and was written to be, The Ghost Protector of Chinatown. His hands were far from clean, but Wilson chose to go out in style. Having sampled everything on the menu, inevitably, someone's got to pay the bill.

Was the possibility of you providing art for an entire arc ever discussed?

It was a few times, for an arc of two or three issues. I so very much wanted to take it on. But previous obligations just didn't allow for it. One missed arc in particular was a really heavy and gut-wrenching narrative. Our second daughter had just been born and I knew what kind of sleepless nights were ahead of me on top of the free-lance schedule I had at the time. Knowing the amount of research and time commitment it would require—to give it my all and not just phone it in—I chose to pass. In the end, the arc came out stellar and much better than I would have been able to do. It all worked out in the end, but that dash to my ego and ambition will always make me wish I could have contributed again. I can't complain, I got to work on some amazing issues. Hopefully it won't be the last time I get to collaborate with Brian.

Do you have a favorite panel, moment, or issue you're particularly proud of?

I do. That Wilson panel I mentioned above is one. But in all honesty, my favorite moments belong to the other contributors on the series. I can not tell you how rad it was to be a part of this series. So far, there are only a few books I've been a fan of before I worked on them. Working on DMZ was like dropping a hungry chubby kid into a specialty candy store. It was a blast, as a fanboy, and as an artist.

What do you attribute the success of DMZ to?

Originality. The characters, the art, and the relevance to current events. The last 10 years have been pretty heavy. I think DMZ started out as a side view commentary, satire in fiction, on what it might be like if the US suffered through a lot of what the real world was going through at the time— in real time—in one of the most populated, popular cities in the world. "Never here in the US" was a phrase I heard a lot when the series first came out. It was too close to home and unapologetic in every way, so people's reaction was in awe of something so unimaginable. I think Brian and Riccardo tapped into that vibe and were able to address a lot of real world issues, and their readers identified with that.

There's no happy ending and there are no real answers. I'd say that the unveiled parallel of the series and real world events gave us a direction to aim those issues, and page by page, a reflection of current events with very little censorship or disguise. It's still a work of fiction and we read it for the characters, writing, and art. But, historically, I think the commentary on humanity, government, and the legacy of established order will remain an important original work, and mean a great deal more to people who read it than just an entertaining story about war and New York City under siege. As time ticks on, I'm sure it will lose some of that weight and relevance, as the Iraq war gets further back in time, for future generations and readers, but its importance in the history of original comics will stand the test of time.

End Transmission

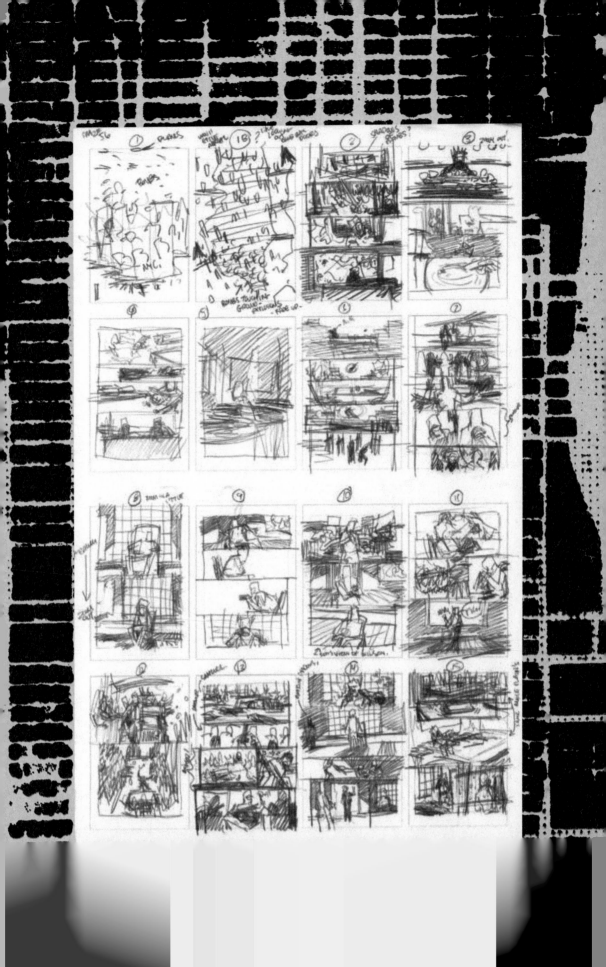

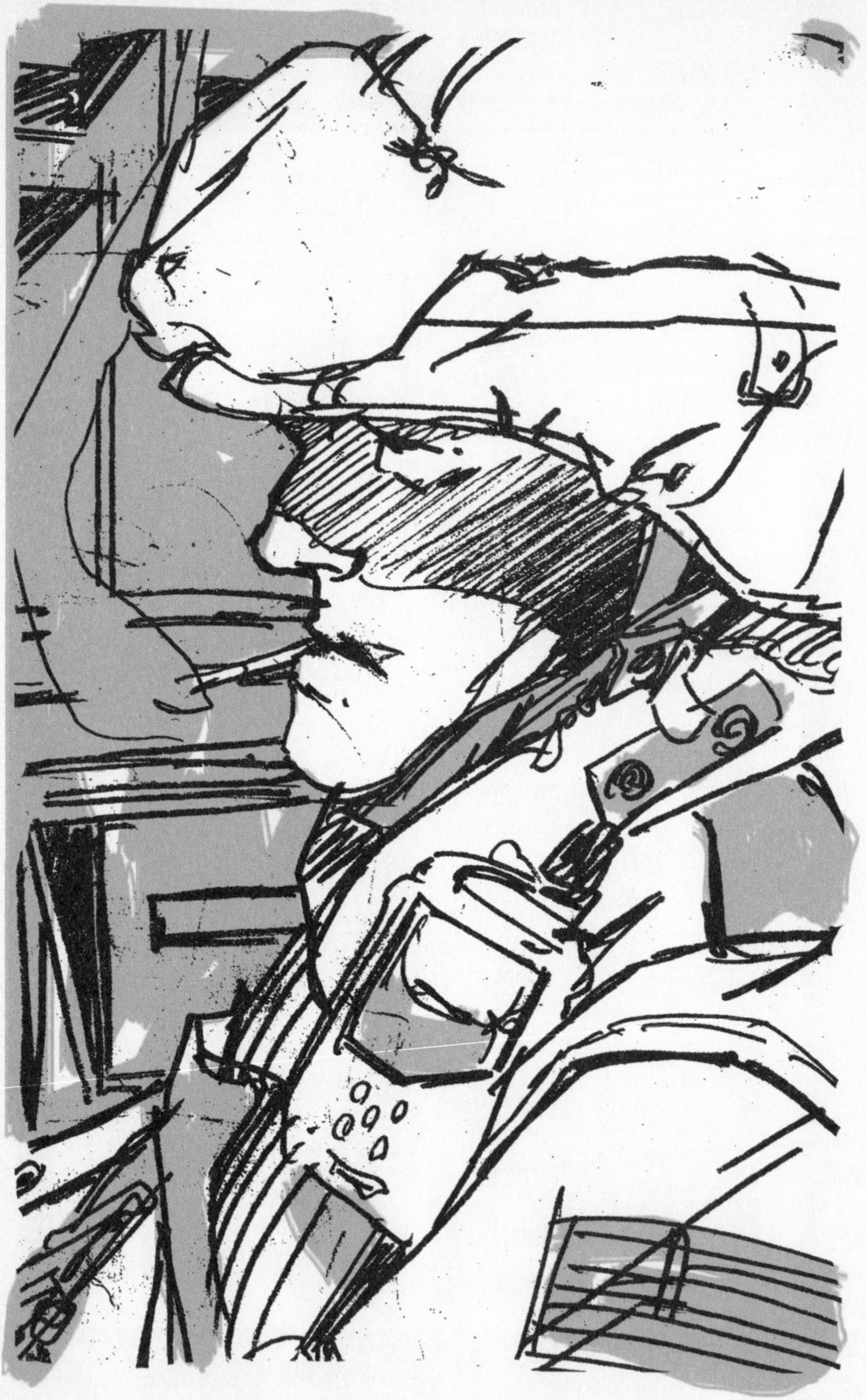

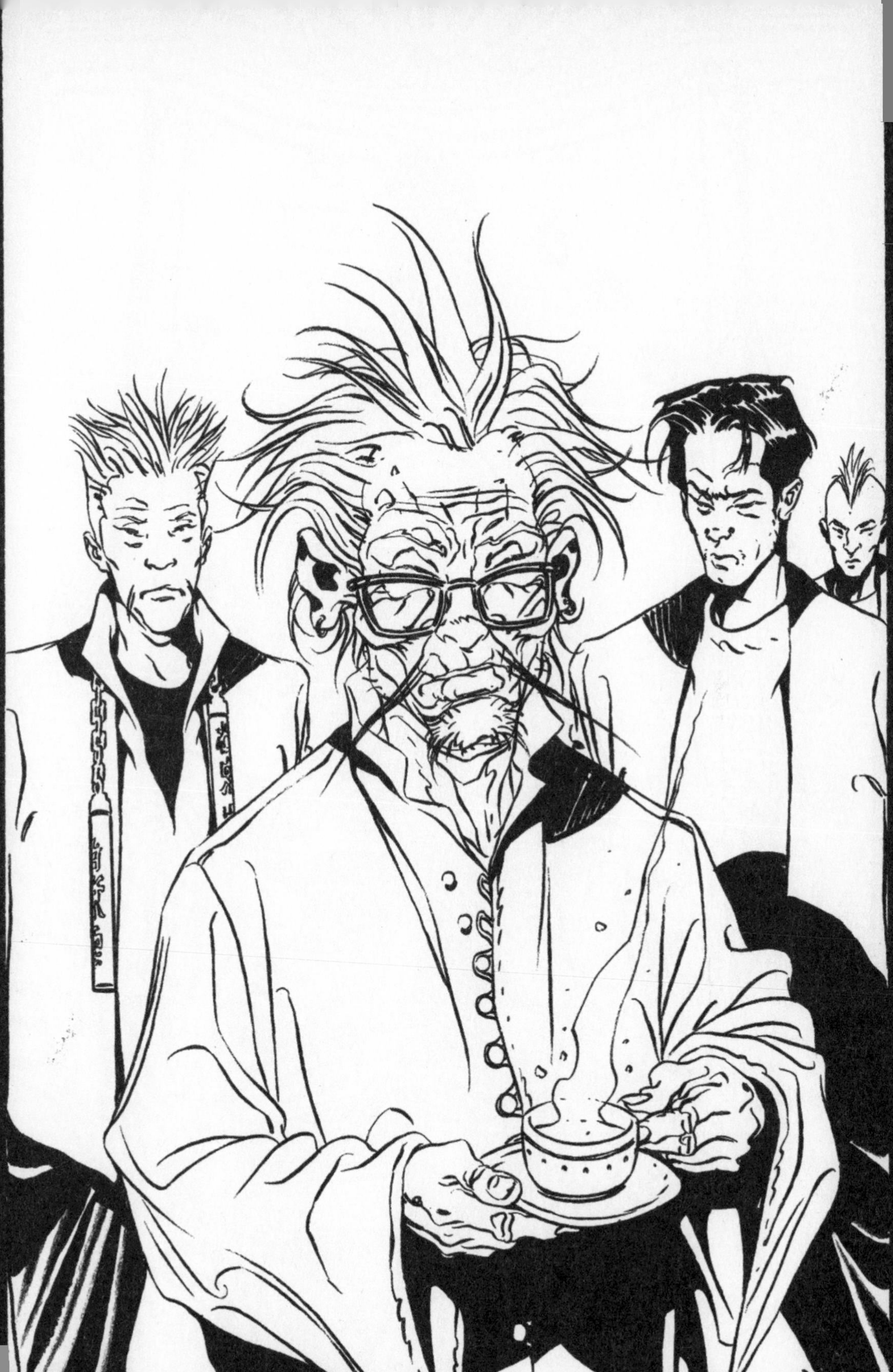

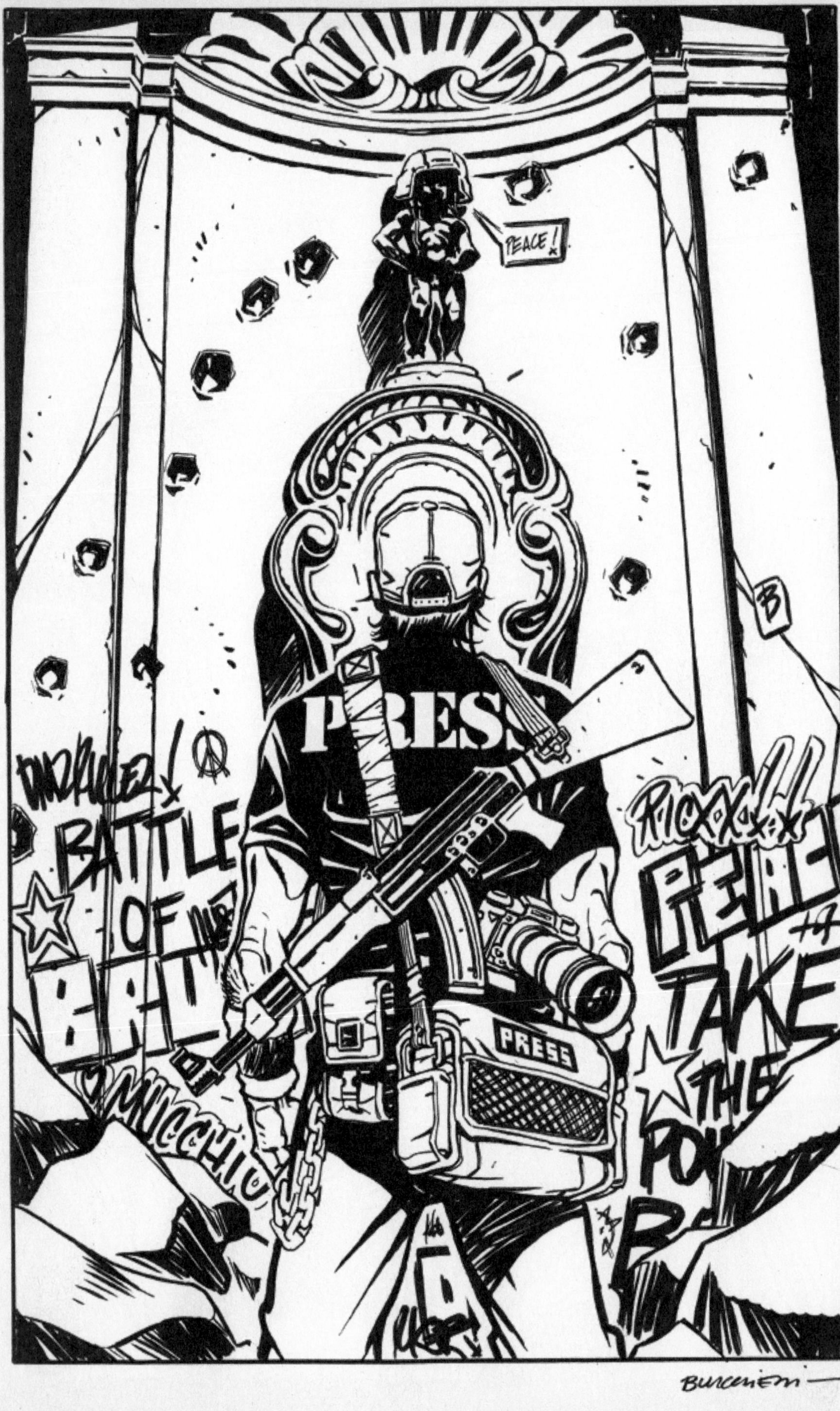
PEACE!
PRESS
BATTLE
OF
TAKE
THE
PRESS

BUCCHIERI

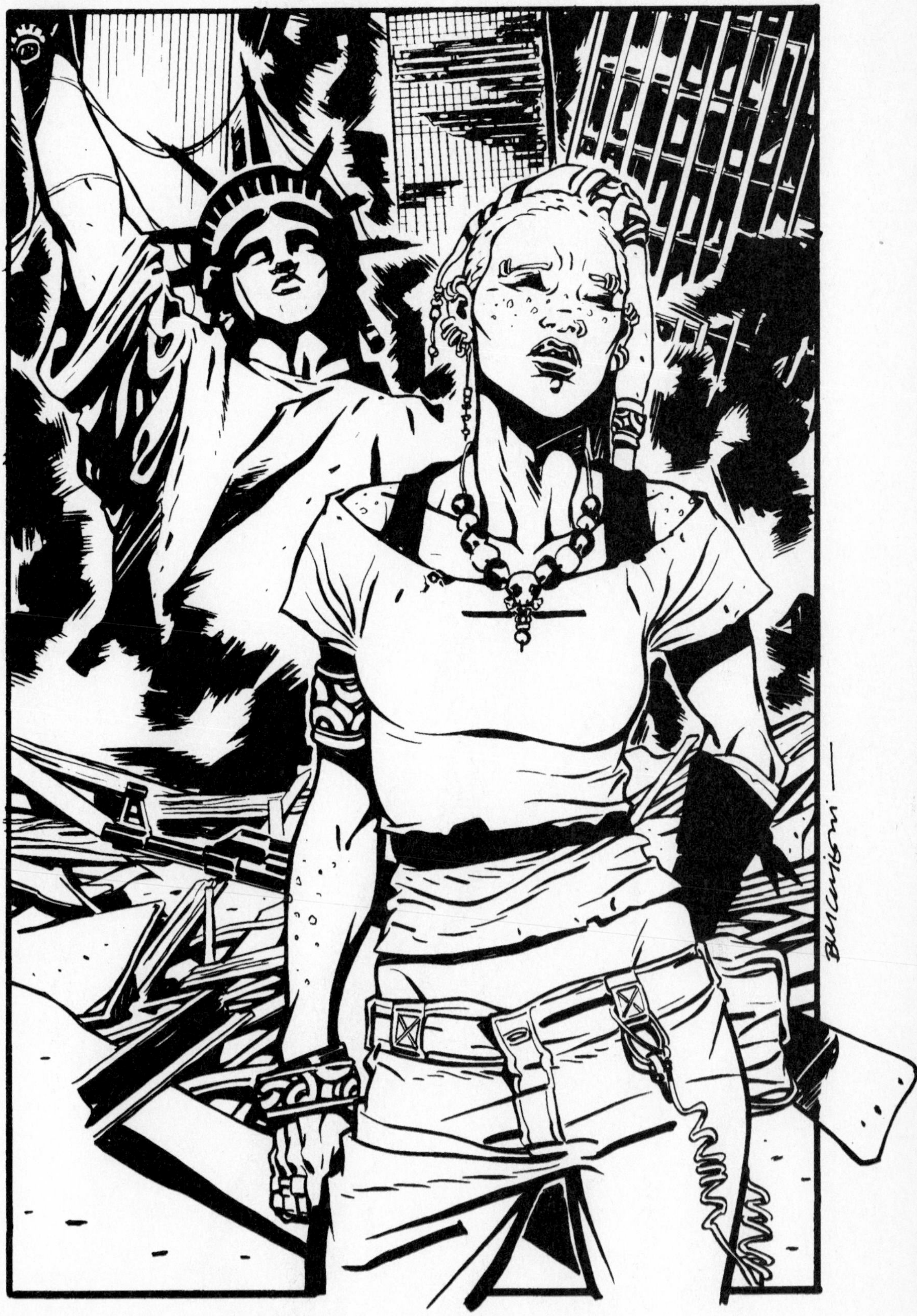

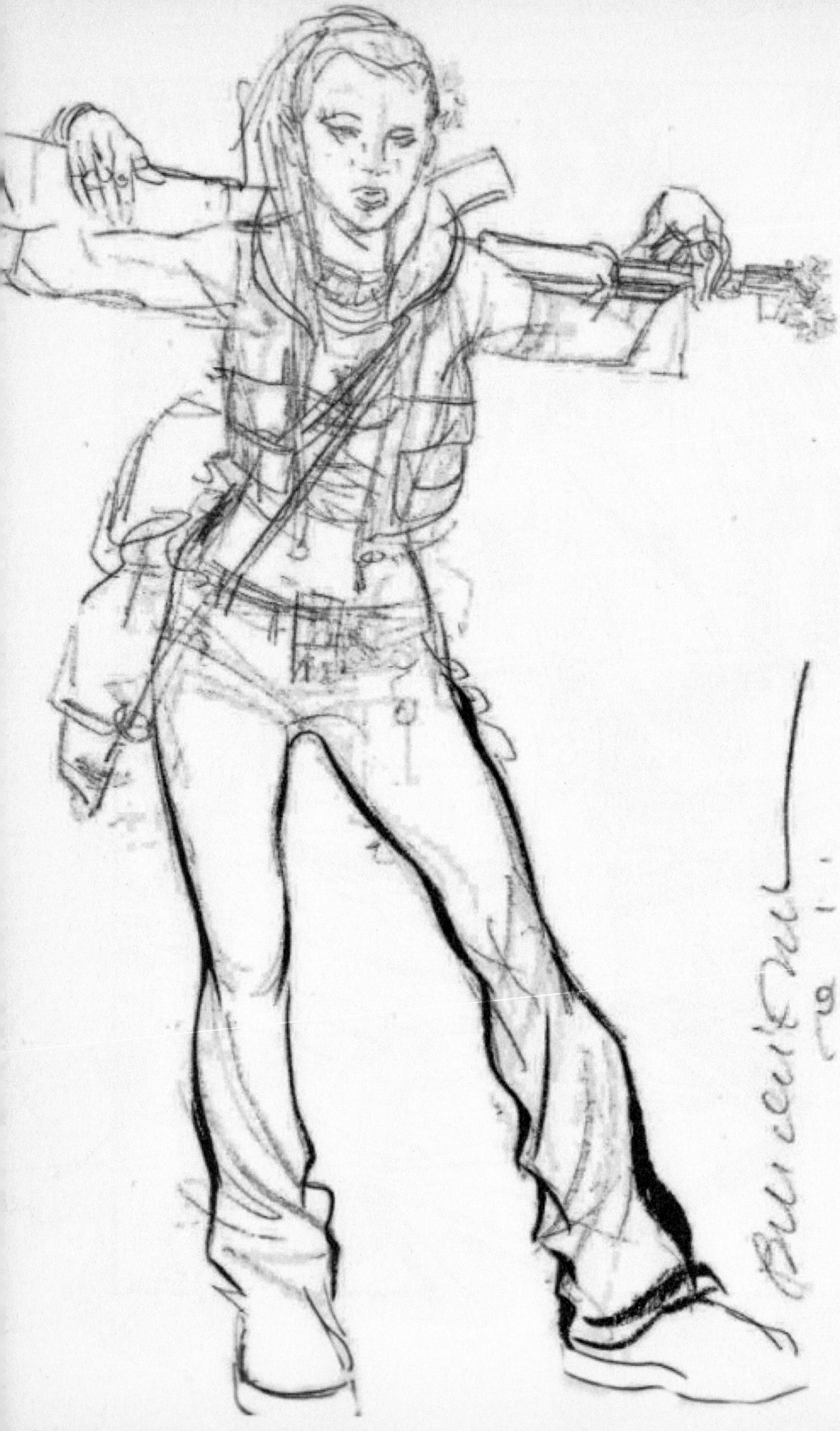

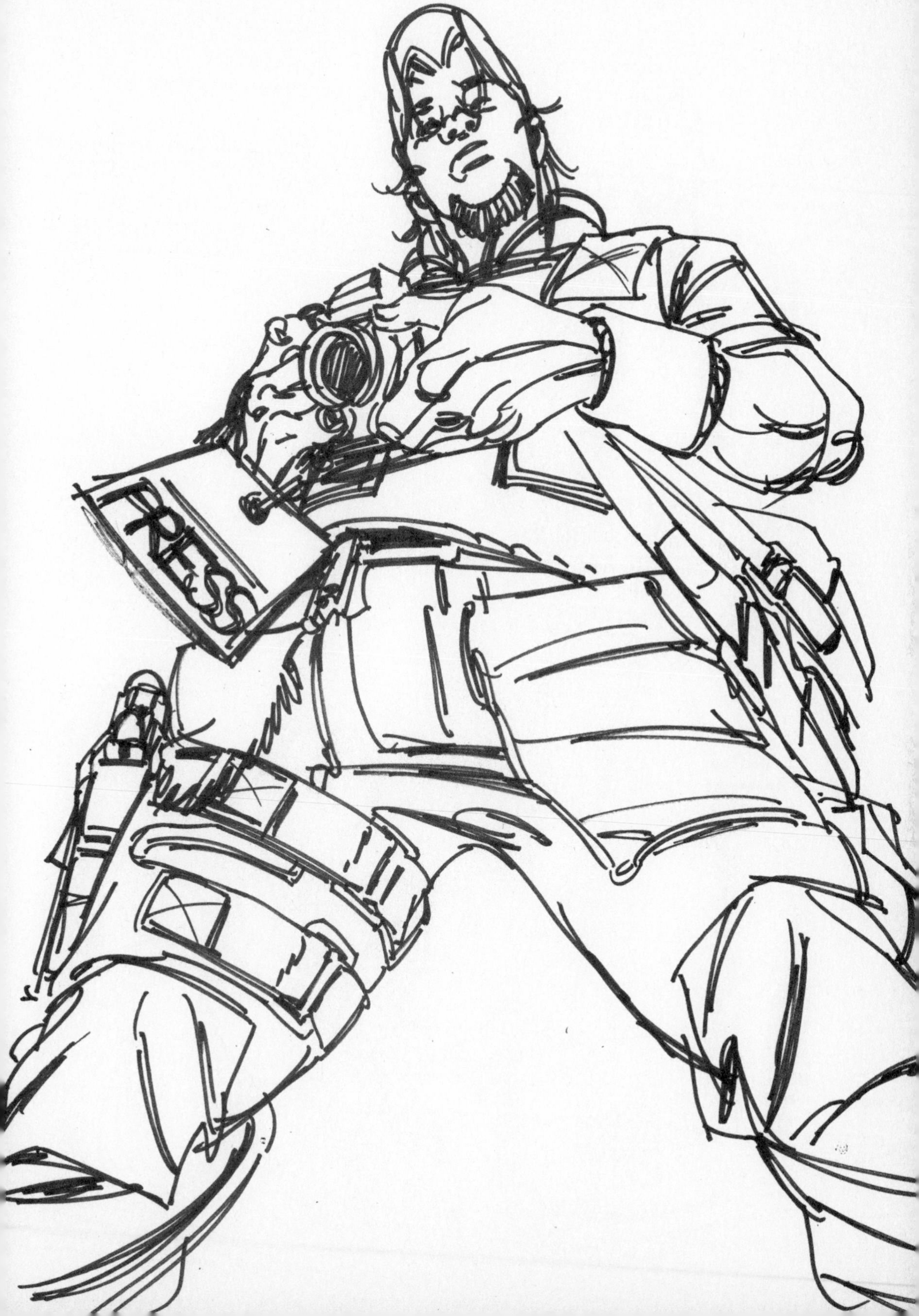
PRESS

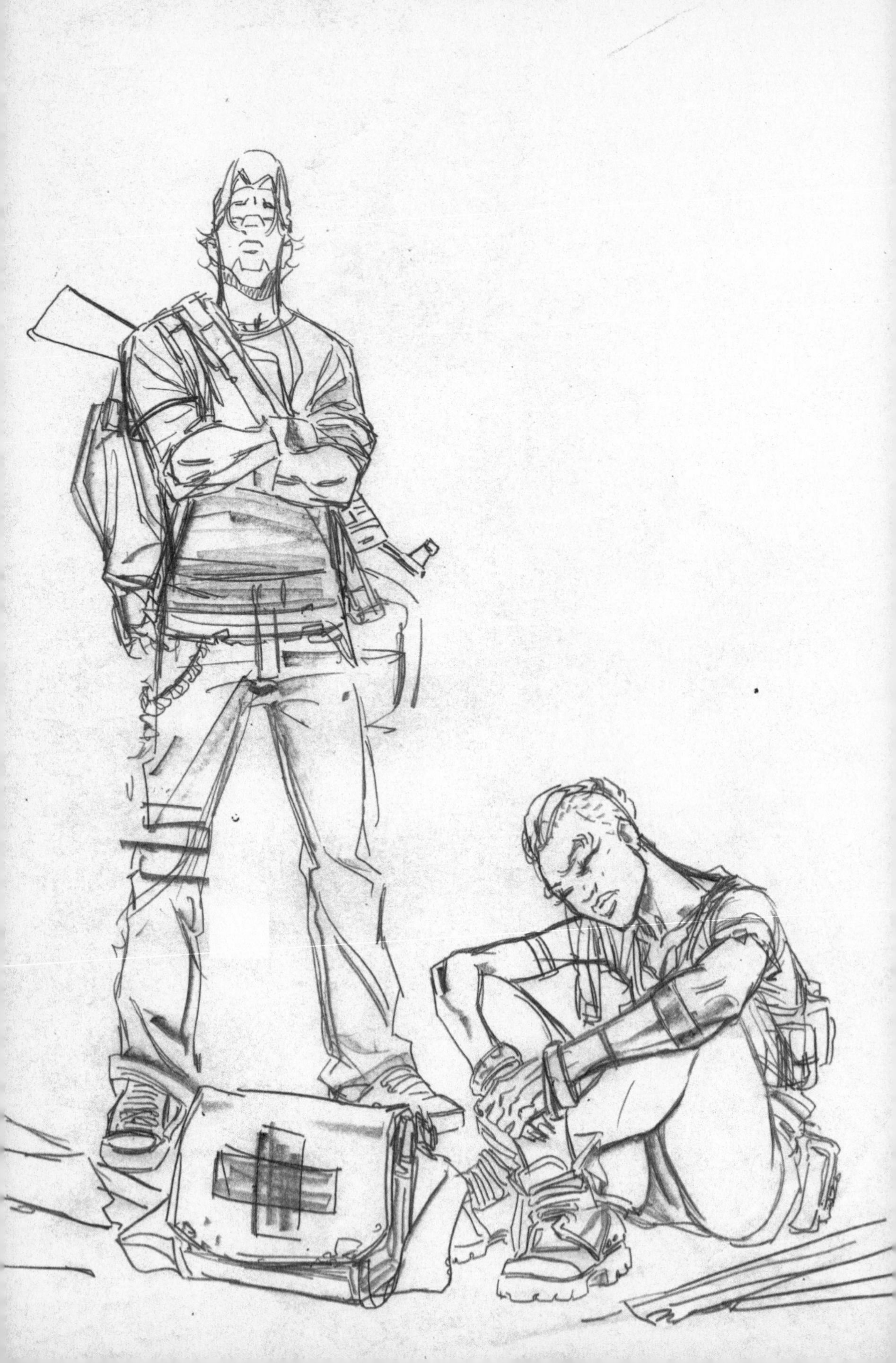

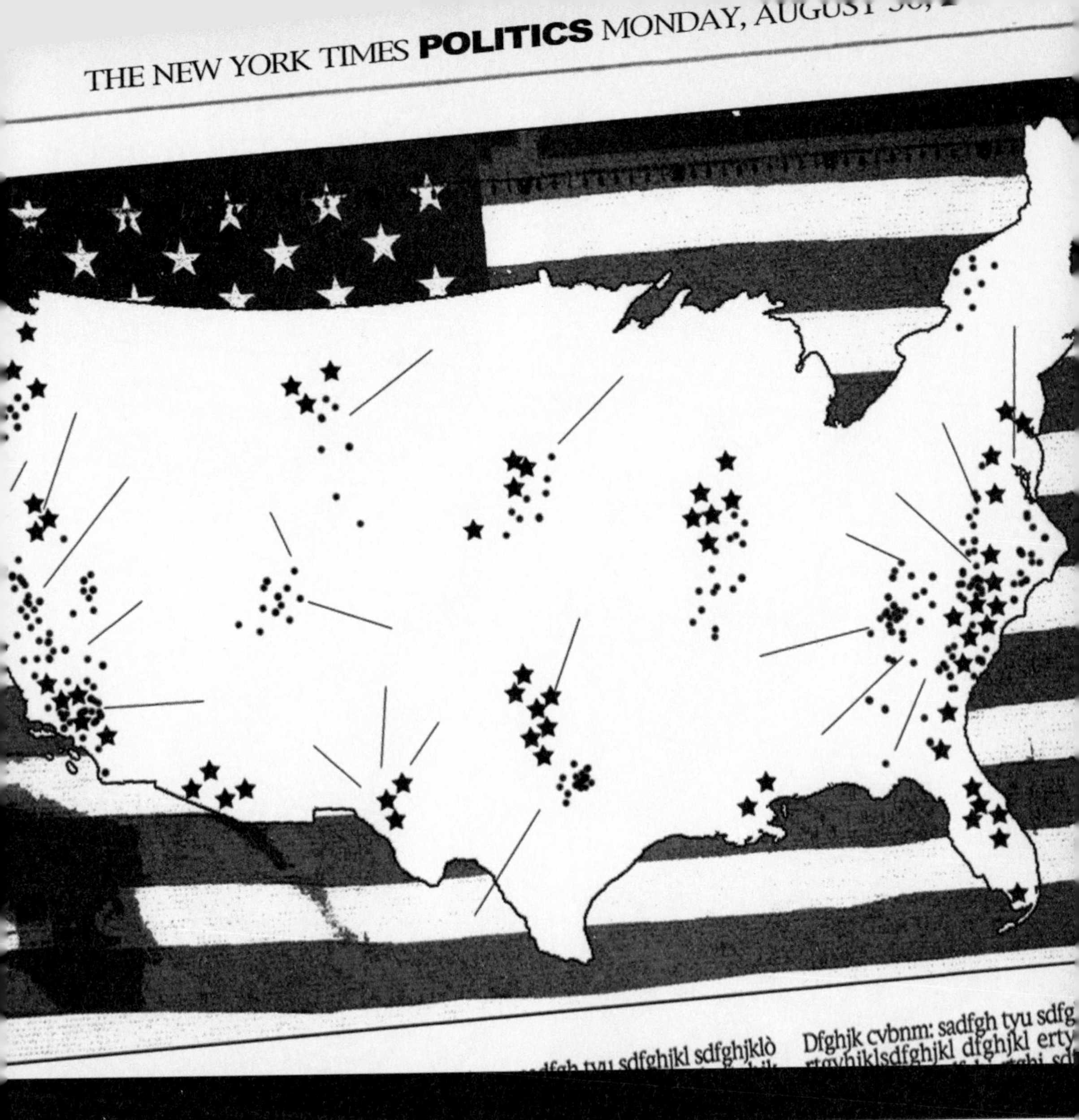

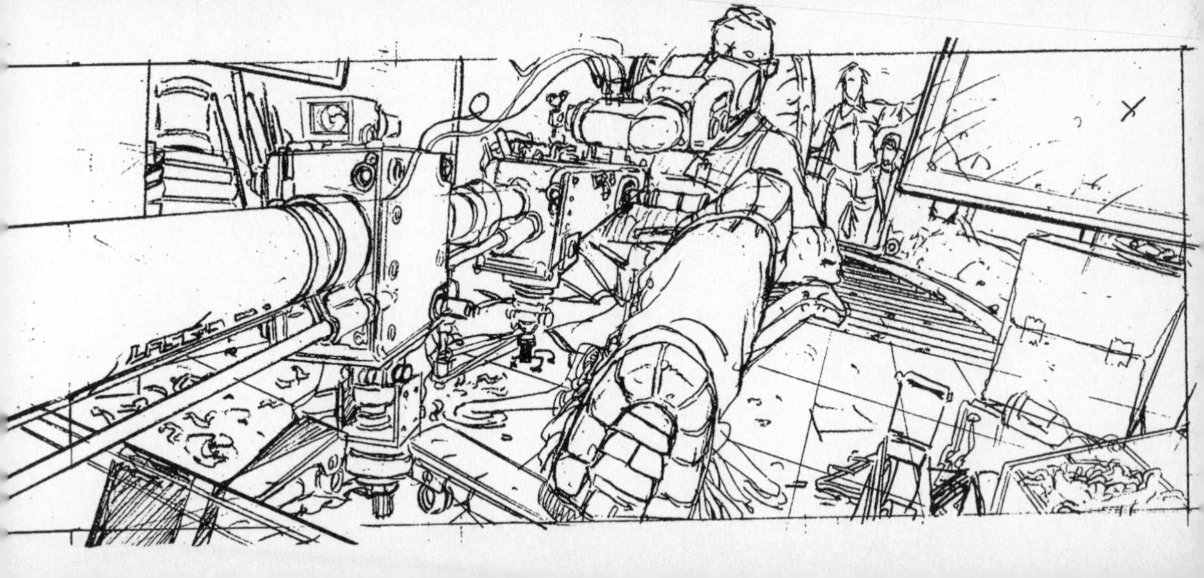

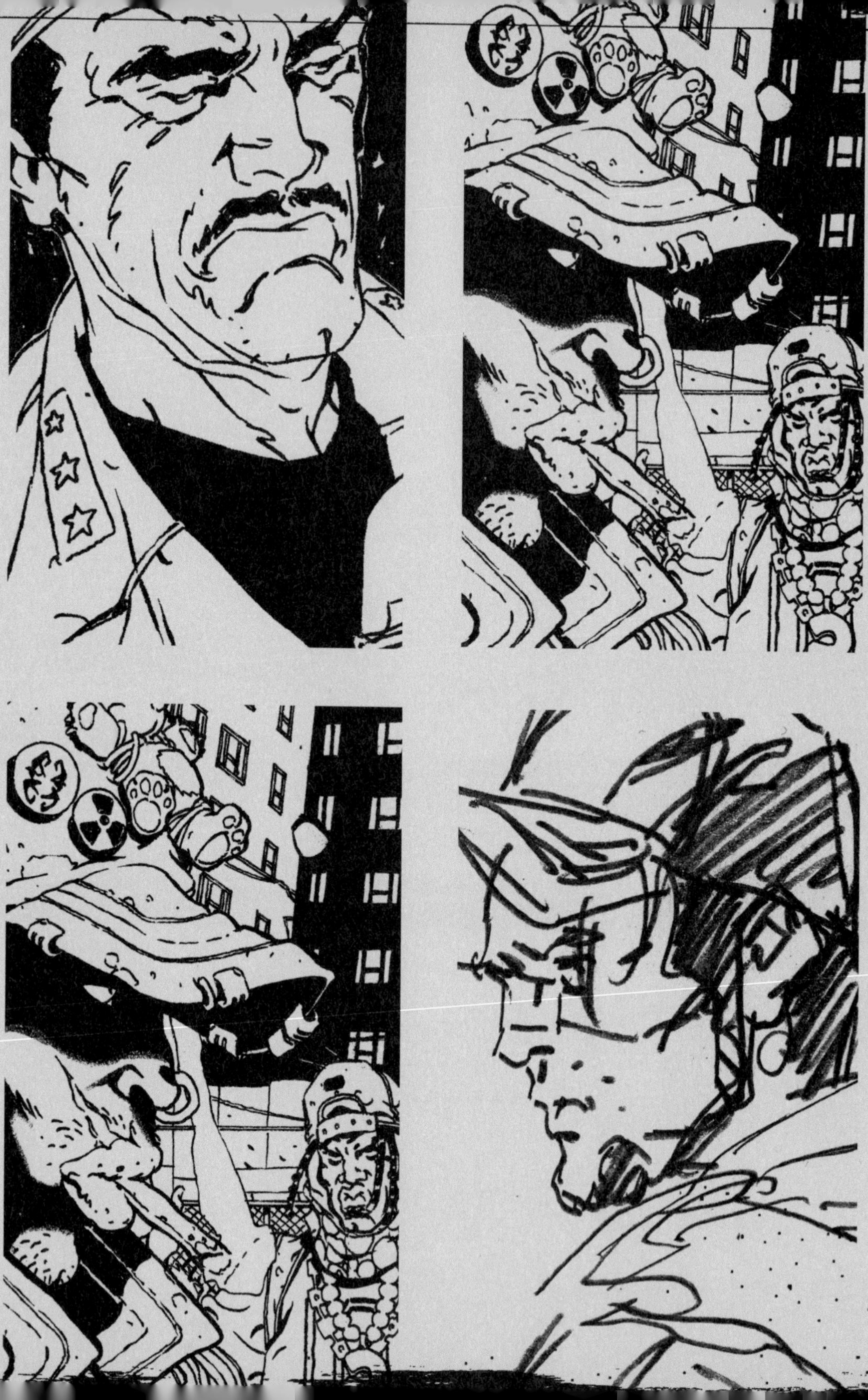

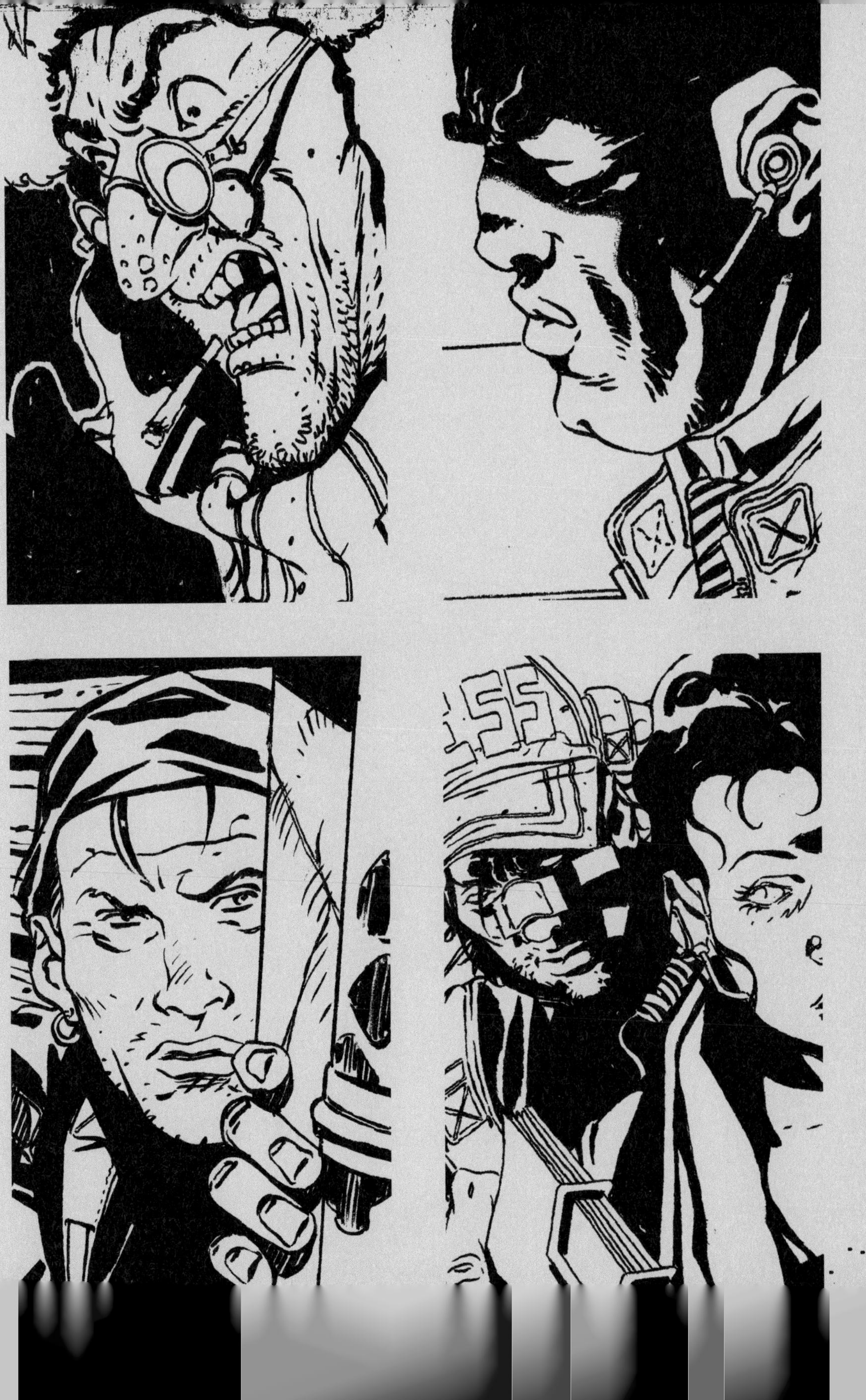

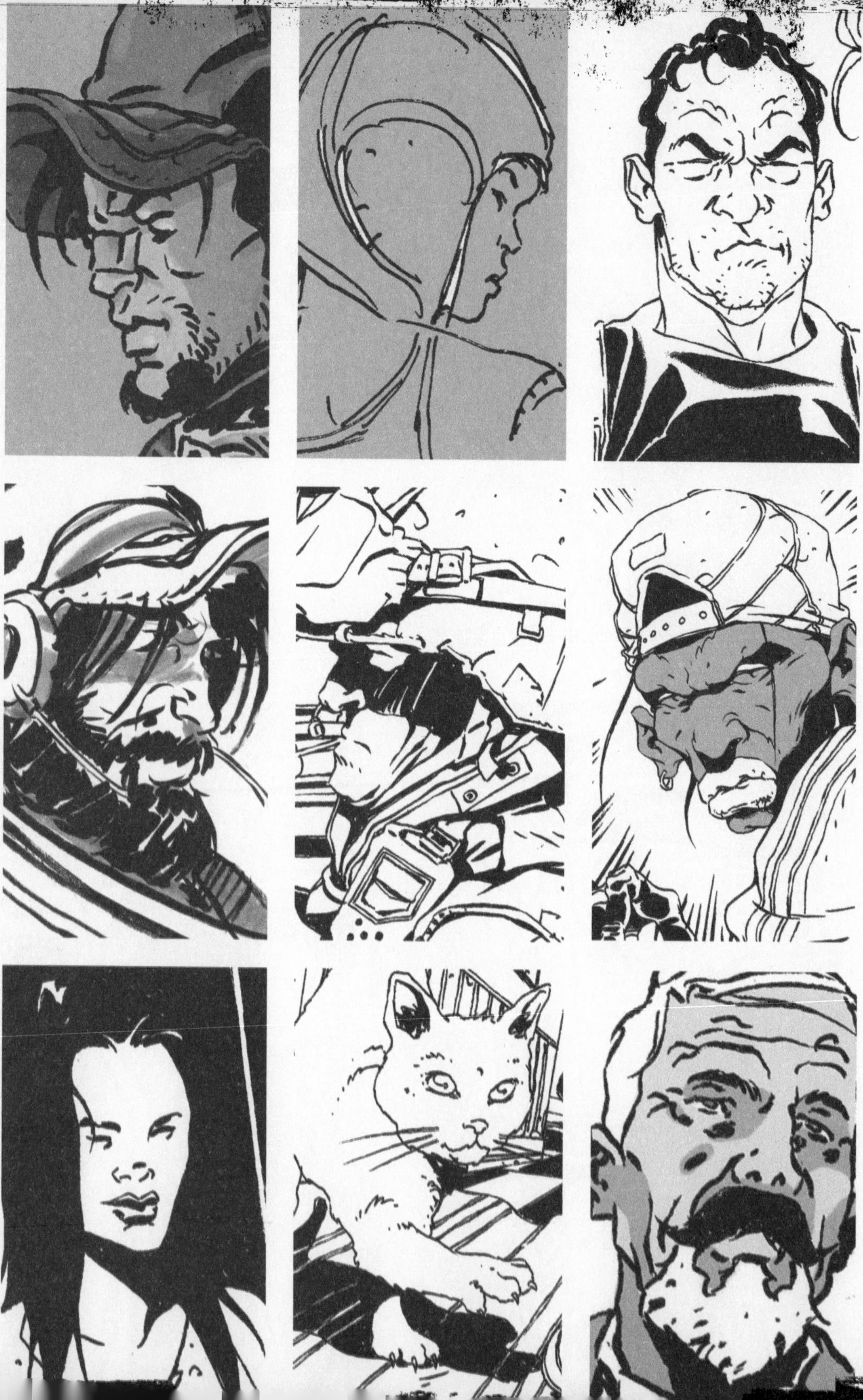

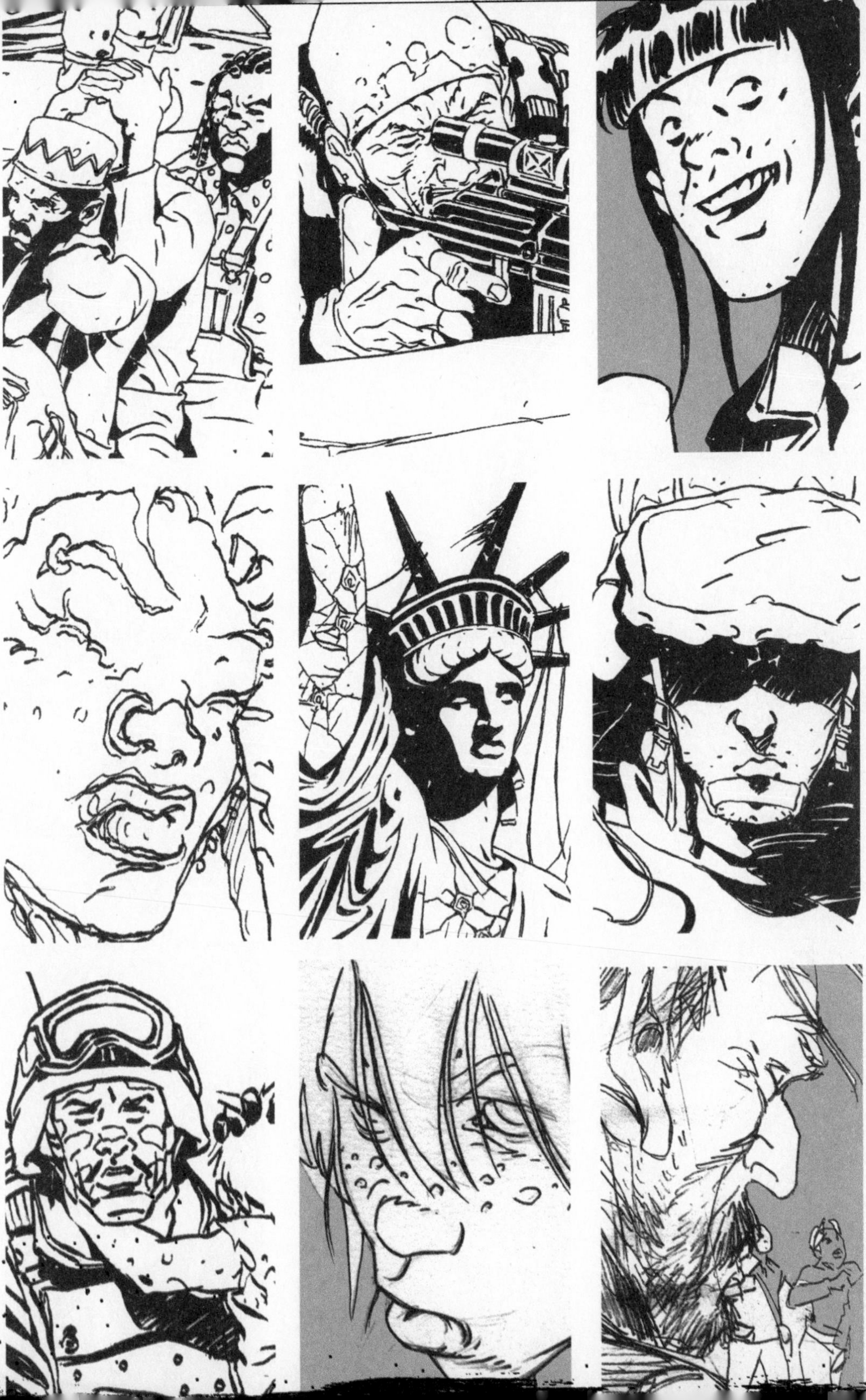

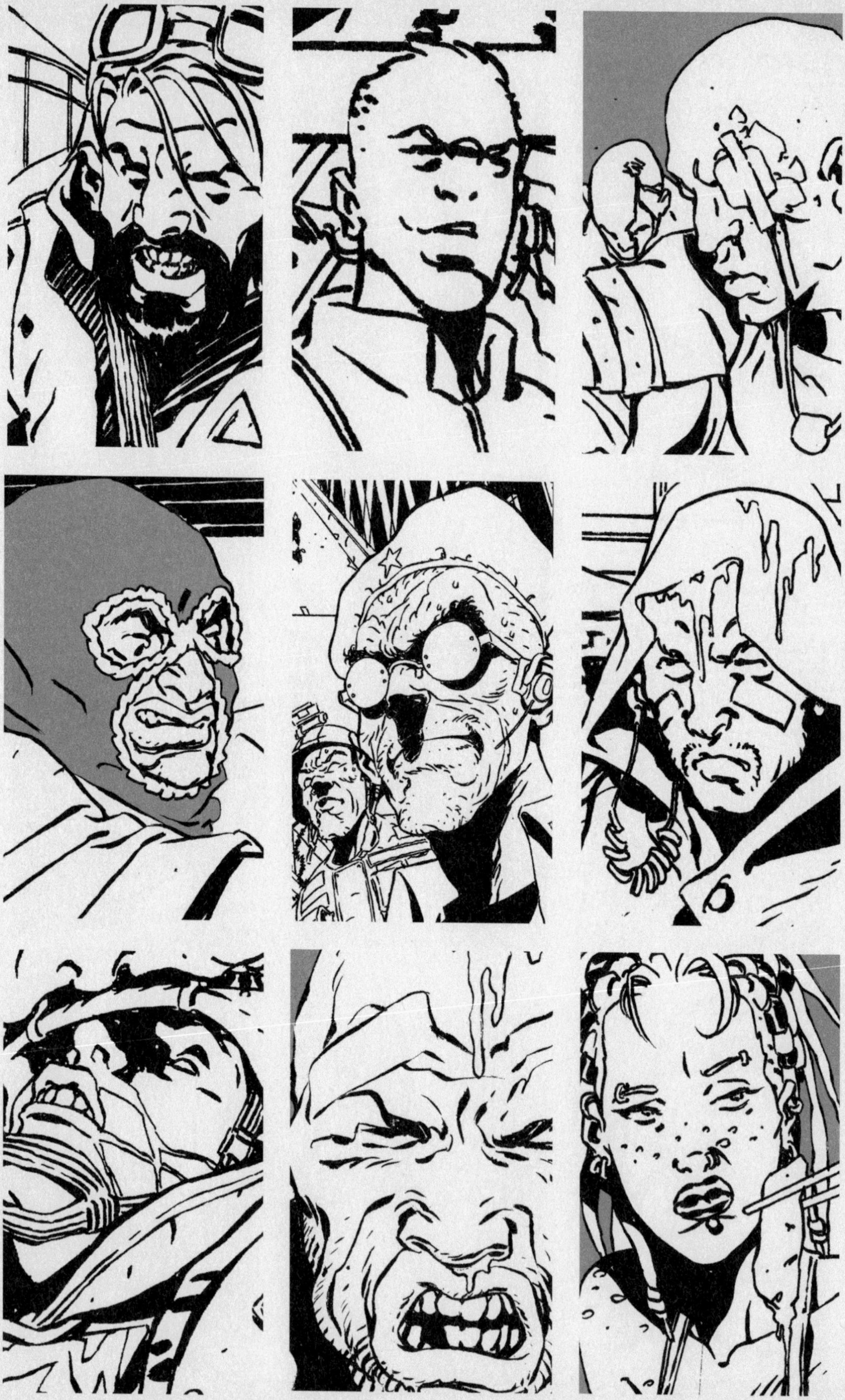

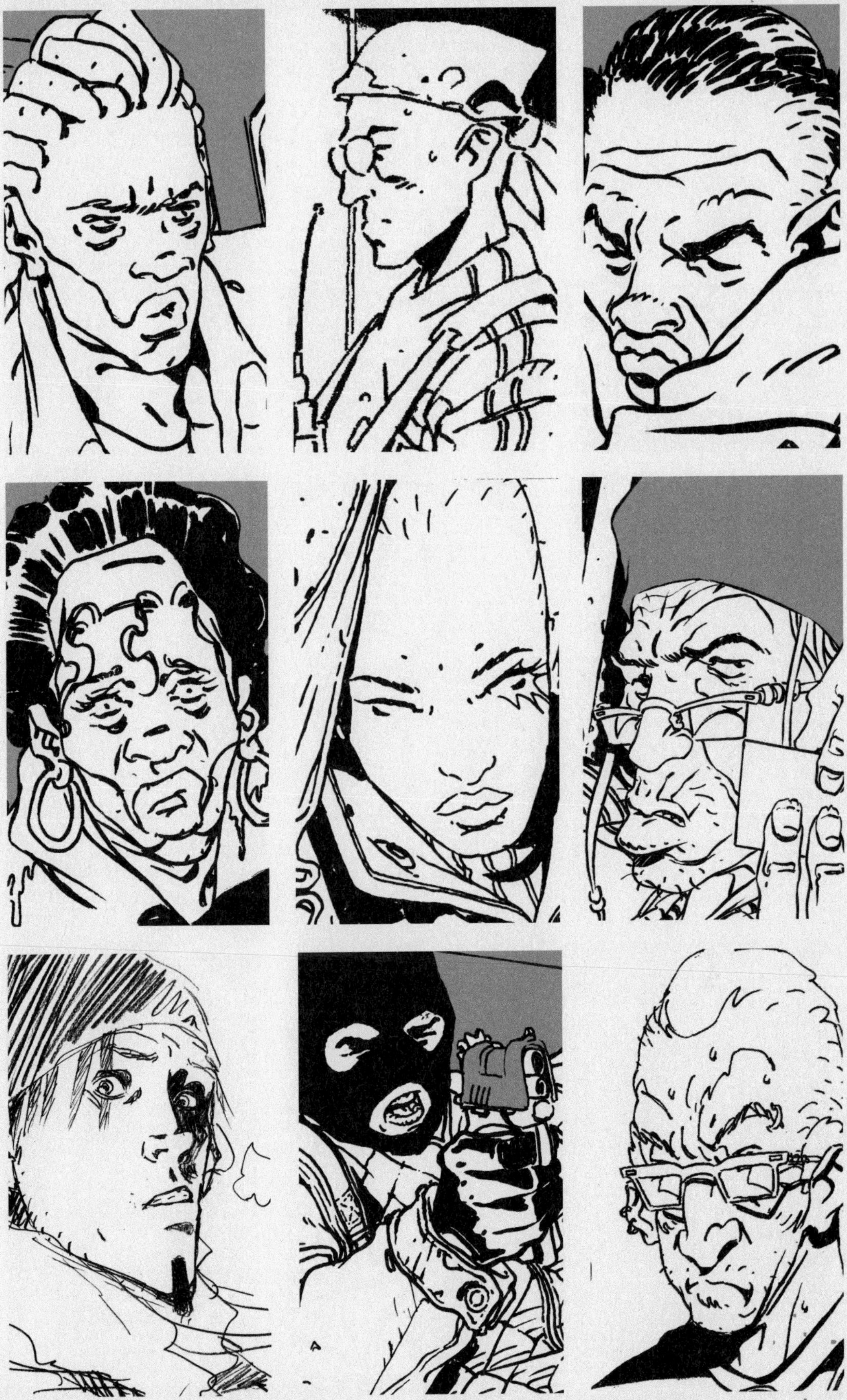

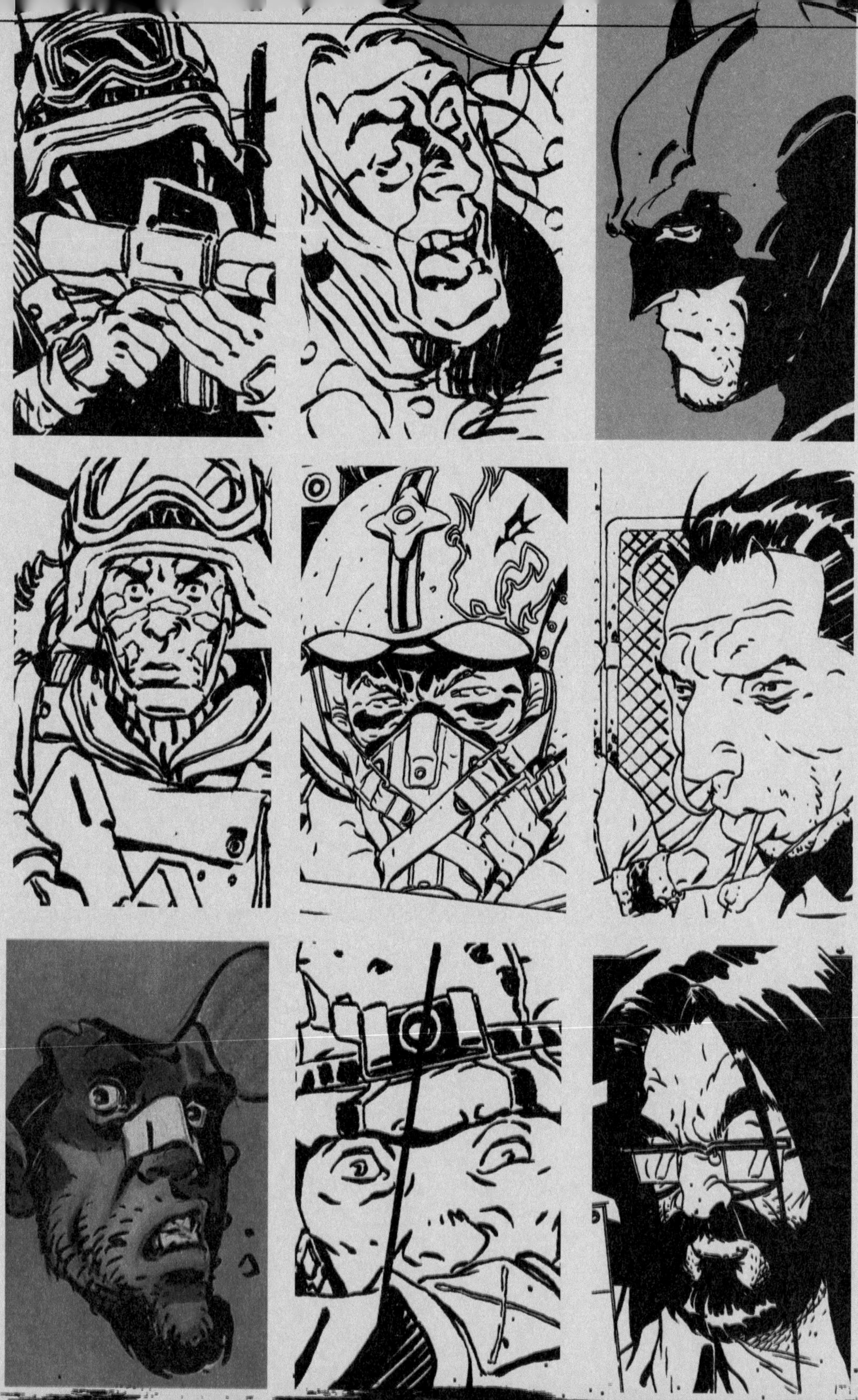

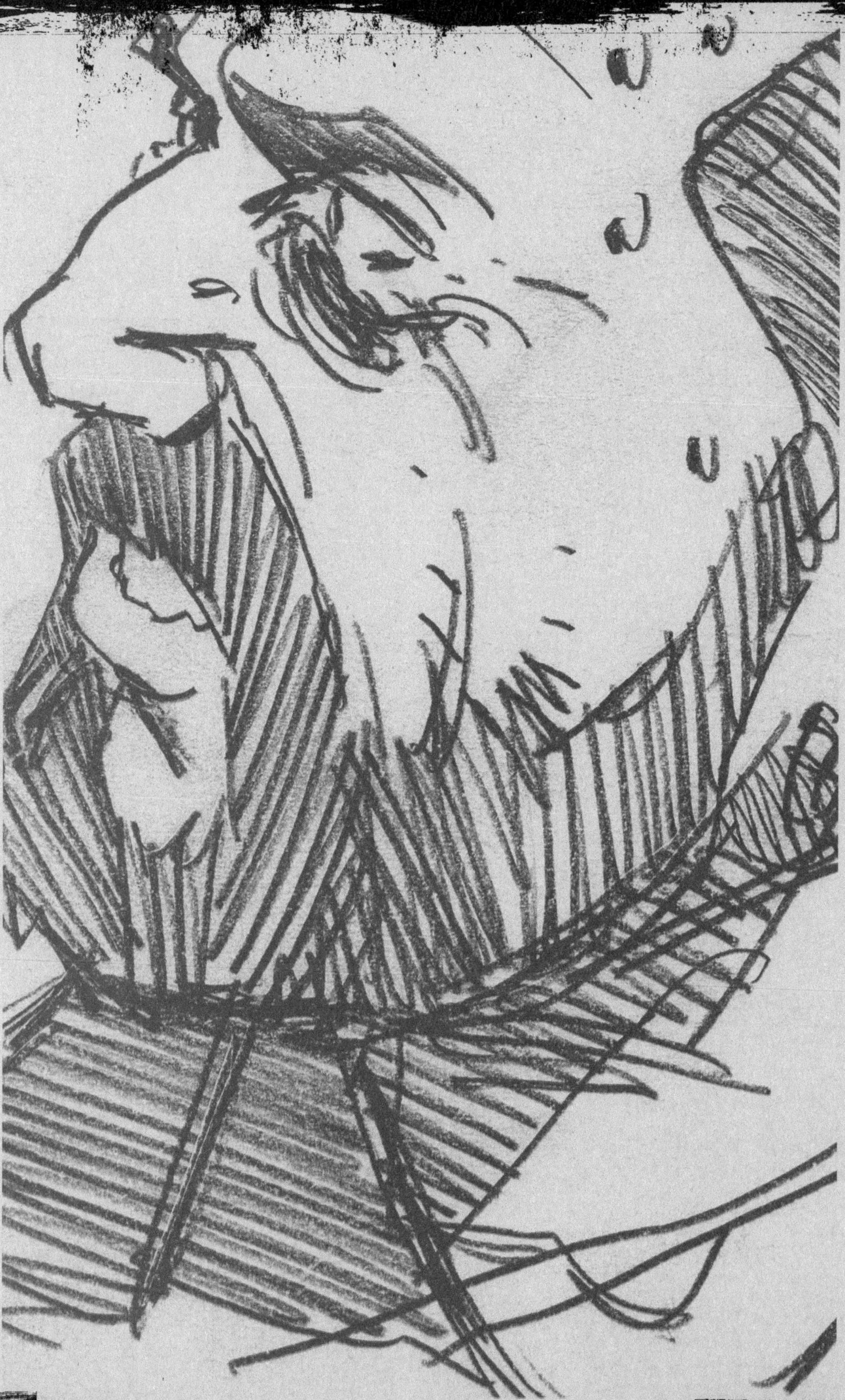

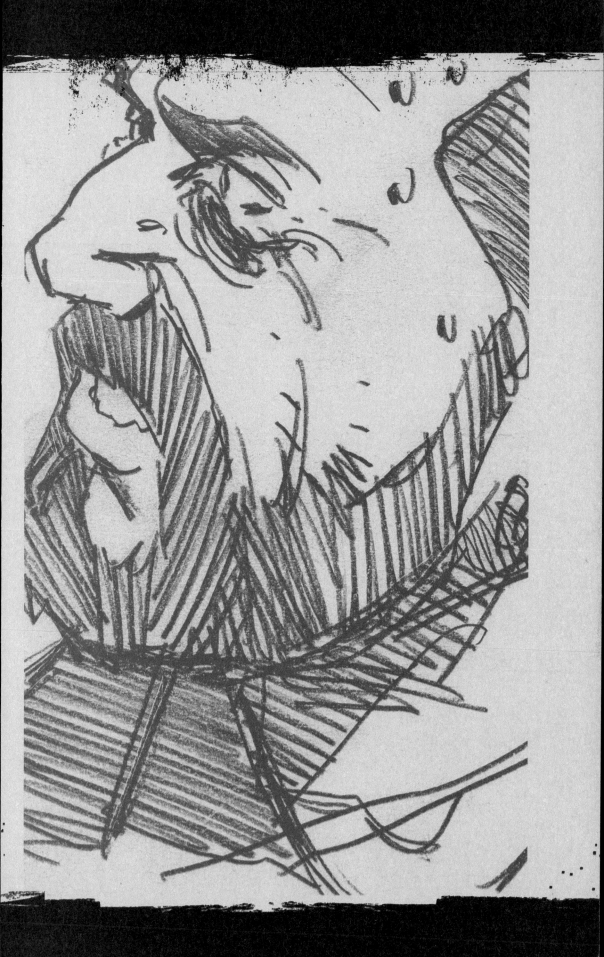

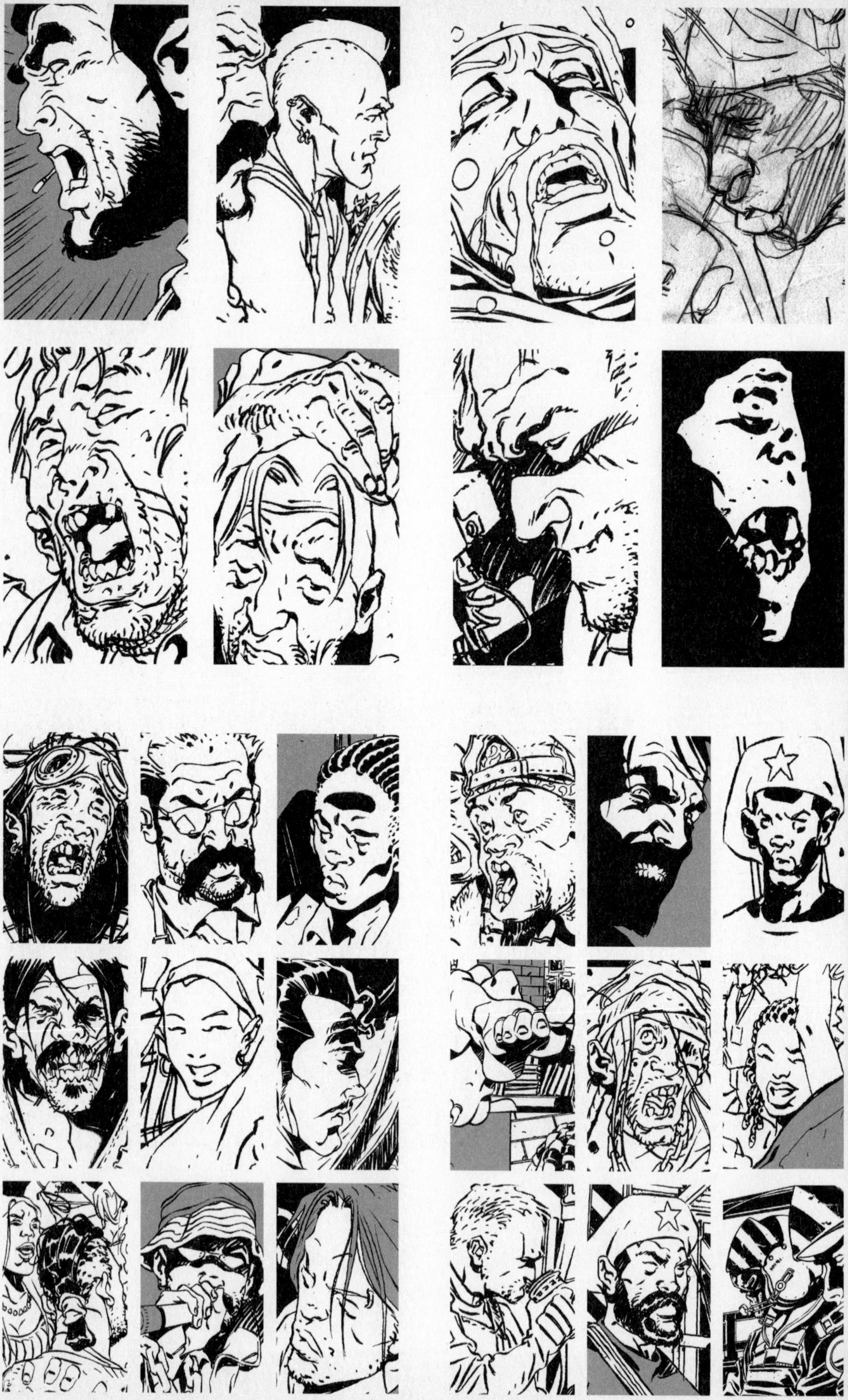

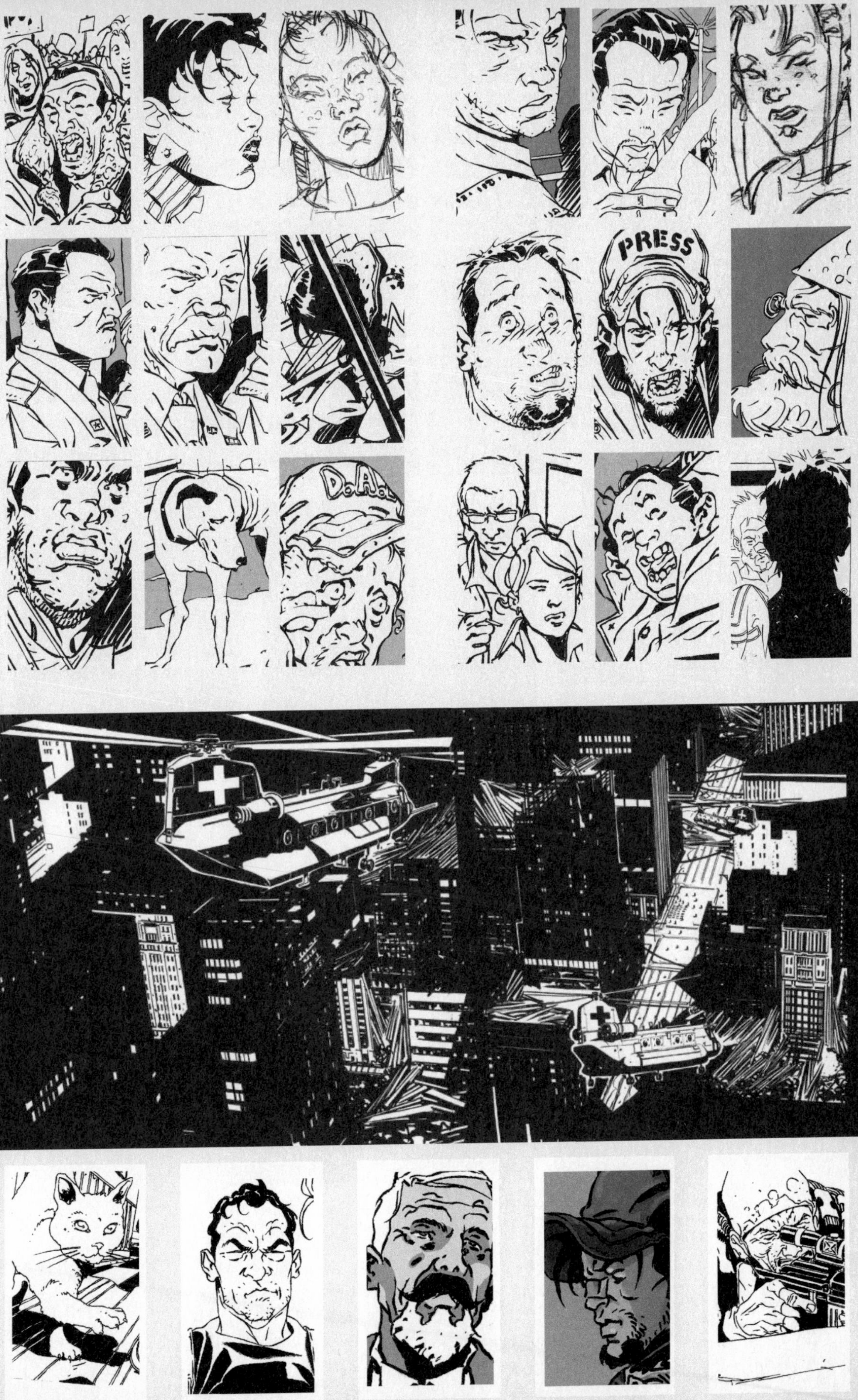
PRESS

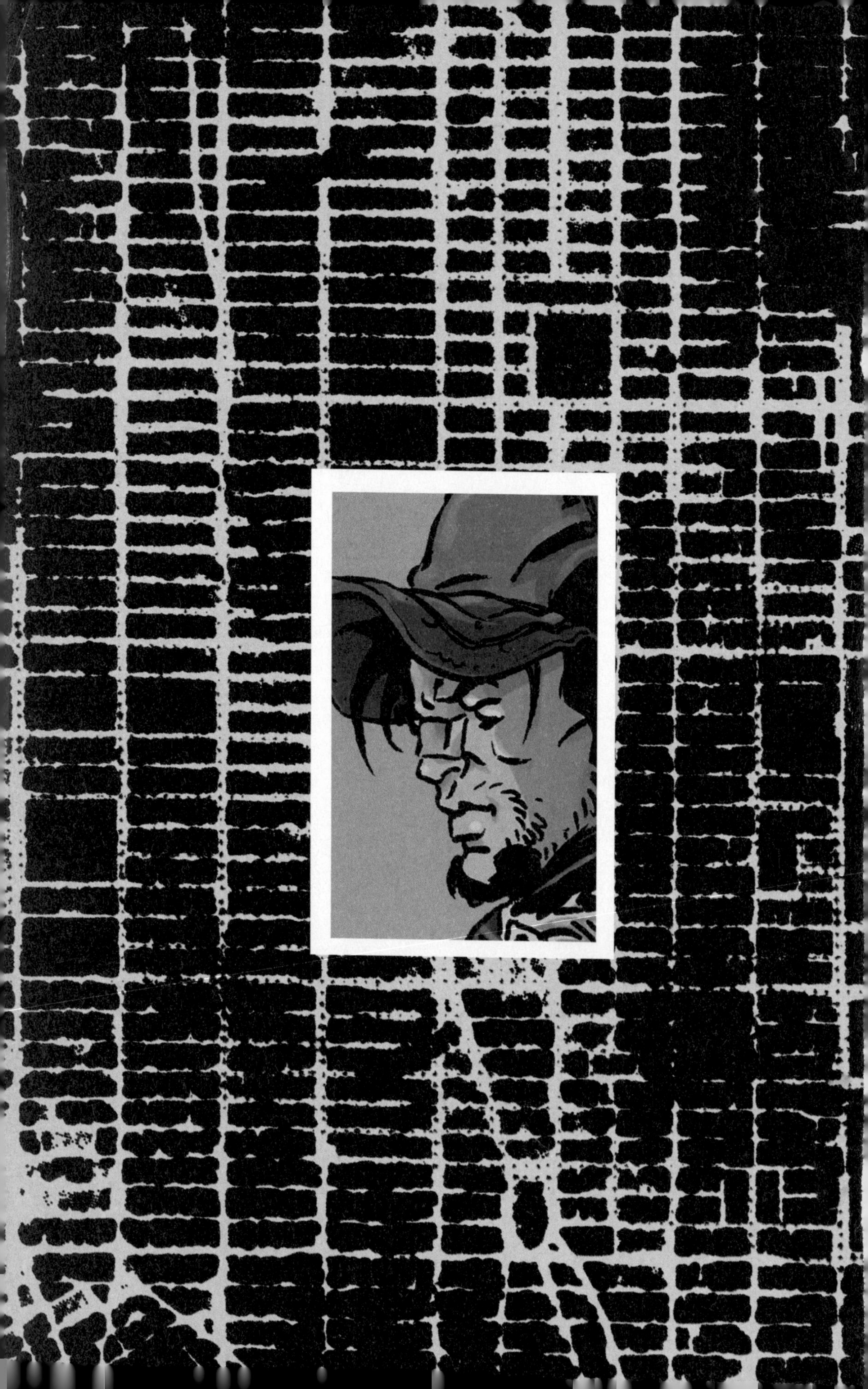